T0184332

Lecture Notes in Computer Science 11244

Commenced Publication in 1973
Founding and Former Series Editors:
Gerhard Goos, Juris Hartmanis, and Jan van Leeuwen

More information about this series at http://www.springer.com/series/7407

Tiziana Margaria · Bernhard Steffen (Eds.)

Leveraging Applications of Formal Methods, Verification and Validation

Modeling

8th International Symposium, ISoLA 2018
Limassol, Cyprus, November 5–9, 2018
Proceedings, Part I

 Springer

Editors
Tiziana Margaria
University of Limerick
Limerick, Ireland

Bernhard Steffen
TU Dortmund
Dortmund, Germany

ISSN 0302-9743   ISSN 1611-3349   (electronic)
Lecture Notes in Computer Science
ISBN 978-3-030-03417-7   ISBN 978-3-030-03418-4   (eBook)
https://doi.org/10.1007/978-3-030-03418-4

Library of Congress Control Number: 2018960390

LNCS Sublibrary: SL1 – Theoretical Computer Science and General Issues

This Springer imprint is published by the registered company Springer Nature Switzerland AG
The registered company address is: Gewerbestrasse 11, 6330 Cham, Switzerland

Preface

Welcome to ISoLA 2018, the *8th International Symposium on Leveraging Applications of Formal Methods, Verification and Validation*, that was held in Limassol (Cyprus) during November 5–9, 2018, endorsed by EASST, the European Association of Software Science and Technology.

This year's event followed the tradition of its symposia forerunners held 2004 and 2006 in Cyprus, 2008 in Chalkidiki, 2010 and 2012 in Crete, 2014 and 2016 in Corfu, and the series of ISoLA Workshops in Greenbelt (USA) in 2005, Poitiers (France) in 2007, Potsdam (Germany) in 2009, in Vienna (Austria) in 2011, and 2013 in Palo Alto (USA).

As in the previous editions, ISoLA 2018 provided a forum for developers, users, and researchers to discuss issues related to the **adoption and use of rigorous tools and methods** for the specification, analysis, verification, certification, construction, test, and maintenance of systems from the point of view of their different application domains. Thus, since 2004 the ISoLA series of events has served the purpose of bridging the gap between designers and developers of rigorous tools on one hand, and users in engineering and in other disciplines on the other hand. It fosters and exploits synergetic relationships among scientists, engineers, software developers, decision makers, and other critical thinkers in companies and organizations. By providing a specific, dialogue-oriented venue for the discussion of common problems, requirements, algorithms, methodologies, and practices, ISoLA aims in particular at supporting researchers in their quest to improve the usefulness, reliability, flexibility, and efficiency of tools for building systems, and users in their search for adequate solutions to their problems.

The program of the symposium consisted of a collection of *special tracks* devoted to the following hot and emerging topics:

- A Broader View on Verification: From Static to Runtime and Back
  (Organizers: Wolfgang Ahrendt, Marieke Huisman, Giles Reger, Kristin Yvonne Rozier)
- Evaluating Tools for Software Verification
  (Organizers: Markus Schordan, Dirk Beyer, Stephen F. Siegel)
- Towards a Unified View of Modeling and Programming
  (Organizers: Manfred Broy, Klaus Havelund, Rahul Kumar, Bernhard Steffen)
- RV-TheToP: Runtime Verification from Theory to Industry Practice
  (Organizers: Ezio Bartocci and Ylies Falcone)
- Rigorous Engineering of Collective Adaptive Systems
  (Organizers: Rocco De Nicola, Stefan Jähnichen, Martin Wirsing)
- Reliable Smart Contracts: State of the Art, Applications, Challenges, and Future Directions
  (Organizers: Gerardo Schneider, Martin Leucker, César Sánchez)

- Formal Methods in Industrial Practice—Bridging the Gap
  (Organizers: Michael Felderer, Dilian Gurov, Marieke Huisman, Björn Lisper, Rupert Schlick)
- X-by-Construction
  (Organizers: Maurice H. ter Beek, Loek Cleophas, Ina Schaefer, and Bruce W. Watson)
- Statistical Model Checking
  (Organizers: Axel Legay and Kim Larsen)
- Verification and Validation of Distributed Systems
  (Organizer: Cristina Seceleanu)
- Cyber-Physical Systems Engineering
  (Organizers: J Paul Gibson, Marc Pantel, Peter Gorm Larsen, Jim Woodcock, John Fitzgerald)

The following events were also held:

- RERS: Challenge on Rigorous Examination of Reactive Systems (Bernhard Steffen)
- Doctoral Symposium and Poster Session (Anna-Lena Lamprecht)
- Industrial Day (Axel Hessenkämper, Falk Howar, Andreas Rausch)

Co-located with the ISoLA Symposium were:

- RV 2018: 18th International Conference on Runtime Verification (Saddek Bensalem, Christian Colombo, and Martin Leucker)
- STRESS 2018: 5th International School on Tool-based Rigorous Engineering of Software Systems (John Hatcliff, Tiziana Margaria, Robby, Bernhard Steffen)

Owing to the growth of ISoLA 2018, the proceedings of this edition are published in four volumes of LNCS: Part 1: Modeling, Part 2: Verification, Part 3: Distributed Systems, and Part 4: Industrial Practice. In addition to the contributions of the main conference, the proceedings also include contributions of the four embedded events and tutorial papers for STRESS.

We thank the track organizers, the members of the Program Committee and their referees for their effort in selecting the papers to be presented, the local Organization Chair, Petros Stratis, the EasyConferences team for their continuous precious support during the week as well as during the entire two-year period preceding the events, and Springer for being, as usual, a very reliable partner in the proceedings production. Finally, we are grateful to Kyriakos Georgiades for his continuous support for the website and the program, and to Markus Frohme and Julia Rehder for their help with the online conference service (EquinOCS).

Special thanks are due to the following organization for their endorsement: EASST (European Association of Software Science and Technology) and Lero – The Irish Software Research Centre, and our own institutions: TU Dortmund and the University of Limerick.

November 2018   Tiziana Margaria
                                                                Bernhard Steffen

Organization

Symposium Chair

Bernhard Steffen   TU Dortmund, Germany

Program Chair

Tiziana Margaria   University of Limerick, Ireland

Program Committee

Wolfgang Ahrendt	Chalmers University of Technology, Sweden
Jesper Andersen	Deon Digital AG
Ezio Bartocci	TU Wien, Austria
Dirk Beyer	LMU Munich, Germany
Manfred Broy	Technische Universität München
Loek Cleophas	TU Eindhoven, The Netherlands
Rocco De Nicola	IMT School for Advanced Studies, Italy
Boris Düdder	University of Copenhagen, Denmark
Ylies Falcone	University of Grenoble, France
Michael Felderer	University of Innsbruck, Austria
John Fitzgerald	Newcastle University, UK
Paul Gibson	Telecom Sud Paris, France
Kim Guldstrand Larsen	Aalborg University, Denmark
Dilian Gurov	KTH Royal Institute of Technology, Sweden
John Hatcliff	Kansas State University, USA
Klaus Havelund	Jet Propulsion Laboratory, USA
Fritz Henglein	University of Copenhagen, Denmark
Axel Hessenkämper	Hottinger Baldwin Messtechnik GmbH
Falk Howar	Dortmund University of Technology and Fraunhofer ISST, Germany
Marieke Huisman	University of Twente, The Netherlands
Michael Huth	Imperial College London, UK
Stefan Jaehnichen	TU Berlin, Germany
Rahul Kumar	Microsoft Research
Anna-Lena Lamprecht	Utrecht University, The Netherlands
Peter Gorm Larsen	Aarhus University, Denmark
Axel Legay	Inria, France
Martin Leucker	University of Lübeck, Germany

Björn Lisper	Mälardalen University, Sweden
Leif-Nissen Lundæk	XAIN AG
Tiziana Margaria	Lero, Ireland
Marc Pantel	Université de Toulouse, France
Andreas Rausch	TU Clausthal, Germany
Giles Reger	University of Manchester, UK
Robby	Kansas State University, USA
Kristin Yvonne Rozier	Iowa State University, USA
Ina Schaefer	TU Braunschweig, Germany
Rupert Schlick	AIT Austrian Institute of Technology, Austria
Gerardo Schneider	University of Gothenburg, Sweden
Markus Schordan	Lawrence Livermore National Laboratory, USA
Cristina Seceleanu	Mälardalen University, Sweden
Stephen F. Siegel	University of Delaware, USA
César Sánchez	IMDEA Software Institute, Spain
Bruce W. Watson	Stellenbosch University, South Africa
Martin Wirsing	LMU München, Germany
James Woodcock	University of York, UK
Maurice ter Beek	ISTI-CNR, Italy
Jaco van de Pol	University of Twente, The Netherlands

Additional Reviewers

Yehia Abd Alrahman
Dhaminda Abeywickrama
Lenz Belzner
Saddek Bensalem
Egon Boerger
Marius Bozga
Tomas Bures
Rance Cleaveland
Giovanna Di Marzo Serugendo
Matthew Dwyer
Benedikt Eberhardinger
Rim El Ballouli
Thomas Gabor
Stephen Gilmore
Emma Hart
Arnd Hartmanns
Rolf Hennicker
Petr Hnetynka
Reiner Hähnle
Patrik Jansson
Einar Broch Johnsen

Neil Jones
Sebastiaan Joosten
Gabor Karsai
Alexander Knapp
Timothy Lethbridge
Chunhua Liao
Alberto Lluch-Lafuente
Alessandro Maggi
Dominique Méry
Birger Møller-Pedersen
Stefan Naujokat
Ayoub Nouri
Liam O'Connor
Doron Peled
Thomy Phan
Jeremy Pitt
Hella Ponsar
Andre Reichstaller
Jeff Sanders
Sean Sedwards
Christoph Seidl

Bran Selic
Steven Smyth
Josef Strnadel
Jan Sürmeli
Louis-Marie Traonouez

Mirco Tribastone
Andrea Vandin
Markus Voelter
Franco Zambonelli
Natalia Zon

(Some) Security by Construction Through a LangSec Approach (X-by-Construction)

Erik Poll

Digital Security Group, Radboud University Nijmegen, The Netherlands
erikpoll@cs.ru.nl

This talk discusses some good and bad experiences in applying formal methods to security and sketches directions for using formal methods to improve security using insights from the LangSec (language-based security) paradigm.

On the face of it, security looks like a promising application area for formal methods. Cyber security is a huge and still growing concern. It is widely recognized that security should be addressed *throughout* the software development life cycle, ideally by practising so-called Security-by-Design, and not bolted on later as an afterthought; this means that formal methods for security could be applied at any stage of the software development life cycle, from the earliest stages of requirements engineering to the final stages such as pen-testing or patching.

Still, all this is easier said than done. Security requirements can be tricky to formalise – or even to spot at all – and it can be difficult to say what it means for an application to be secure. It is often easier to say what may make an application insecure, as is done by lists of standard security flaws such as the OWASP Top Ten[1] or the CWE/SANS Top 25[2]. Such lists are very useful, but always incomplete, and lend themselves more naturally to testing for certain types of security flaws post-hoc than to guaranteeing their absence by construction.

A more constructive approach to security can be taken by realising that security problems typically arise in interactions and exploit the *languages* used in these interactions. The most obvious example is the interaction between an attacker and a system, where the attacker tries to abuse the interface the system exposes. This interface can be a network protocol, but it may also involve a file format, say JPEG, or a language such as HTML. Security problems can also arise in the interaction between two applications (or an application and an external service) even if neither of them is malicious. Classic examples here are the interaction between a web application and its back-end database, where SQL injection becomes a worry, or the interaction between a web application and the browser, where XSS becomes a worry.

The LangSec paradigm[3] highlights the central role played by the languages used for these interactions – e.g. file formats, protocols, or query languages – in causing security problems. Root causes of security problems identified are: the large number of these

---

[1] https://www.owasp.org/index.php/Category:OWASP_Top_Ten_Project.

[2] https://cwe.mitre.org/top25/.

[3] See http://langsec.org, esp. http://langsec.org/bof-handout.pdf, or [5].

languages, their complexity, their expressivity, the lack of clear specifications, and finally the fact that parsers to process these languages are hand-written, and often mix parsing and processing of inputs.

This also provides a clear way forward in using formal methods to improve security, namely by providing formal descriptions of the input languages involved and using these descriptions to generate parser code, thus getting at least some security by construction. Ironically, formalisms for describing languages are some of the best-known and most basic formal methods around, and parsing is one of the oldest and best understood parts of computer science, with plenty of tools for generating code. So it is a bit of an embarrassment to the computer science community that this is where modern IT screws up so badly, with so many security flaws. In addition to parsers, one would also like to generate unparsers (aka pretty-printers or serialisers), as interactions between systems typically involve an unparser at one end and a parser at the other end. Recent initiatives here include Hammer [2] and Nail [1]. Formal descriptions of input languages can also be used for testing, in test generation or as test oracles.

Even if we get rid of all (un)parser bugs, there remains the risk of *unintentionally* parsing some inputs [7], especially inputs coming from sources that an attacker can control. Here formal methods can also help, with data flow analysis to trace where data comes from and/or where it might end up. Ideally, such data flows can then be controlled by a type system, where different types explicitly distinguish the various languages that the application handles (e.g. to avoid the chance of accidentally processing a user name or a fragment of HTML as an SQL statement), the various trust levels associated with different input channels (e.g. to distinguish tainted inputs from untainted data), or both. As these types can be application-specific, it is natural to use extensible type systems for this, e.g. using type qualifiers [4] or type annotations [3], or to turn to domain-specific languages [6].

References

1. Bangert, J., Zeldovich, N.: Nail: a practical interface generator for data formats. In: Security and Privacy Workshops (SPW), 2014, pp. 158–166. IEEE (2014)
2. Bratus, S., Crain, A.J., Hallberg, S.M., Hirsch, D.P., Patterson, M.L., Koo, M., Smith, S.W.: Implementing a vertically hardened DNP3 control stack for power applications. In: Industrial Control System Security Workshop (ICSS'16), pp. 45–53. ACM (2016)
3. Dietl, W., Dietzel, S., Ernst, M.D., Muşlu, K., Schiller, T.W.: Building and using pluggable type-checkers. In: ICSE'11, pp. 681–690. ACM (2011)
4. Foster, J.S., Terauchi, T., Aiken, A.: Flow-sensitive type qualifiers. In: PLDI'02, SIGPLAN Notices, vol. 37, pp. 1–12. ACM (2002)
5. Momot, F., Bratus, S., Hallberg, S.M., Patterson, M.L.: The seven turrets of Babel: a taxonomy of LangSec errors and how to expunge them. In: Cybersecurity Development (SecDev), pp. 45–52. IEEE (2016)
6. Omar, C., Kurilova, D., Nistor, L., Chung, B., Potanin, A., Aldrich, J.: Safely composable type-specific languages. In: Jones, R. (ed.) ECOOP 2014 – Object-Oriented Programming, ECOOP 2014. LNCS, vol, 8586, pp. 105–130. Springer, Heidelber (2014)
7. Poll, E.: LangSec revisited: input security flaws of the second kind. In: Symposium on Security and Privacy Workshops (SPW). IEEE (2018)

Contents – Part I

X-by-Construction

STRESS 2018

Towards a Unified View of Modeling and Programming

Towards a Unified View of Modeling and Programming (ISoLA 2018 Track Introduction)

Manfred Broy[1], Klaus Havelund[2(✉)], Rahul Kumar[3], and Bernhard Steffen[4]

[1] Technische Universität München, Munich, Germany
[2] Jet Propulsion Laboratory, California Institute of Technology, Pasadena, USA
klaus.havelund@jpl.nasa.gov
[3] Microsoft Research, Redmond, USA
[4] TU Dortmund University, Dortmund, Germany

Abstract. The article provides an introduction to the track: *Towards a Unified View of Modeling and Programming*, organized by the authors of this paper as part of ISoLA 2018: the 8th International Symposium On Leveraging Applications of Formal Methods, Verification and Validation. A total of 19 researchers presented their views on the two questions: what are the commonalities between modeling and programming languages?, and should we strive towards a unified view of modeling and programming? The idea behind the track, which is a continuation of a similar track at ISoLA 2016, emerged as a result of experiences gathered in the three fields: formal methods, model-based software engineering, and programming languages, and from the observation that these technologies share a large common part, to the extent where one may ask, does the following equation hold:

$$modeling = programming$$

Keywords: Modeling · Programming · Domain-specific languages
Similarities · Differences · Unification

1 Introduction

Since the 1960s we have seen a tremendous amount of scientific and methodological work in the fields of program modeling and specification, as well as the creation of numerous programming languages. In spite of the very high value of this work, however, this effort has found its limitation by the fact that we do not have a sufficient integration of these languages, as well as of methods and tools that support the development engineer in applying the corresponding techniques

The research performed by this author was carried out at Jet Propulsion Laboratory, California Institute of Technology, under a contract with the National Aeronautics and Space Administration.

© Springer Nature Switzerland AG 2018
T. Margaria and B. Steffen (Eds.): ISoLA 2018, LNCS 11244, pp. 3–21, 2018.
https://doi.org/10.1007/978-3-030-03418-4_1

and languages. A tighter integration between specification and verification logics, graphical modeling notations, and programming languages could have many benefits.

In a (possibly over) simplified view, as an attempt to impose some structure on this work, we will distinguish between three lines of work: formal methods, model-based software engineering, and programming. The first formal methods appeared in the 1970ties, and subsequently have included formalisms such as VDM [8,9,22], CIP [6], Z [59], Event-B [2], ASM [25], TLA+ [41], Alloy [34], and RAISE [24], as well as theorem proving systems such as Coq [5], Isabelle [49], and PVS [54]. These formalisms, usually referred to as specification languages, are based on mathematical concepts, such as functions, relations, set theory, logics etc. A specification typically consists of a signature, which is a collection of names and their types, and axioms over the signature, constraining the values that the names can denote. A specification as such denotes a set of models, each providing a binding of values to the names, satisfying the axioms. Such formal methods usually come equipped with proof systems, such that one can prove properties of the specifications, for example consistency of axioms, or that certain theorems are consequences of the axioms. A common characteristic of these formalisms is their representation as text, defined by context-free grammars, and their formalization in terms of semantics and/or logical proof systems. In parallel, we have seen several model checkers appearing, such as SPIN [30] and UPPAAL [61]. These usually prioritize automated and efficient verification algorithms over expressive specification languages. Exceptions are more recent model checkers for programming languages, including for example Java PathFinder (JPF) [29].

Starting in the 1980s, the model-based software engineering community developed graphical formalisms, most prominently represented by UML [53] and later SysML [52]. These formalisms, usually referred to as modeling languages, offer graphical notation for defining data structures as 'nodes and edge' diagrams, and behavioral descriptions by diagrams such as state machines and message sequence diagrams. These formalisms specifically address the ease of adoption and understanding amongst engineers. It is clear that these techniques have become more popular in industry than formal methods, in part likely due to their graphical and seemingly more light-weight nature. However, these formalisms are complex (the standard defining UML is much larger than the definition of any formal method or programming language), are incomplete (the UML standard for example has no expression-language, although OCL [1] is a recommended add-on), and they lack commonly agreed upon standardized semantics. This is not too surprising as UML has been designed on the basis of an intuitive informal understanding of the semantics of its individual parts and concepts, and not under the perspective of a potential formal semantics ideally covering the entire UML. This leaves users some freedom of interpretation, in particular concerning the conceptual interplay of individual model types, but often leads to misunderstandings. Nevertheless, it has been perceived to be sufficient in practice in order to support tool-based system development, such as, e.g., (partial) code generation.

Historically, programming languages have evolved over time, starting with numerical machine code, then assembly languages, and transitioning to higher-level languages with Cobol and Fortran in the late 1950s. Numerous programming languages have been developed since. The C programming language has since its creation in the early 1970s conquered the embedded software world in an impressive manner. Later efforts, however, have attempted to create even higher-level languages. These include languages such as Java and Python, in which collections such as sets, lists, and maps are built-in, either as constructs or as systems libraries. Especially the academic community has experimented with functional programming languages, such as ML [46], OCaml [50], and Haskell [37], and more recently with the integration of object-oriented programming and functional programming, as for example in Scala [55].

If we view each formalism in the above mentioned formalism classes as a set of abstract language constructs, it is likely that different formalisms will have elements (language constructs) that are not in common. Each formalism has advantageous features not owned by other formalisms. However, what is perhaps more important is that these formalisms for specification and modeling, from now on for simplicity referred to with the common term: modeling languages, and programming seem to have many language constructs in common, and to such an extent that one can ask the controversial two questions: *what are the commonalities between modeling and programming languages?*, and *should we strive towards a unified view of modeling and programming?* It is the goal of the track to discuss the relationship between modeling and programming, with the possible objective of achieving an agreement of what a unification of these concepts would mean at an abstract level, and what it would bring as benefits on the practical level. Note that this discussion is not meant to favor one view (that modeling = programming) over the other (that modeling ≠ programming). The track is a continuation of a first track on the same topic, held at ISoLA 2016 [15].

The paper is organized as follows. Section 2 presents arguments for the view that modeling fundamentally differs from programming. Section 3 presents arguments for the opposite view that modeling strongly overlaps with programming. Section 4 discusses the role of domain-specific languages. Section 5 provides an overview of the papers submitted to, and presented at, the track. Finally, Sect. 6 concludes the paper.

2 Differences Between Modeling and Programming

There is clearly a close relationship between formal modeling and programming. Every program can be seen as a formal model, and we can furthermore derive a number of limited perspective models (abstractions) from it, such as data flow descriptions, control flow models, and architecture models [13]. It can be argued, however, that there are a number of very elementary differences between modeling and programming. It is e.g. generally considered a good principle to separate the formalization of problems (what) and their solutions (how), as later expressed in an implementation, analogous to e.g. what happens in the engineering field. There are indeed some arguments for this separation.

Programming is traditionally algorithm oriented, relying on an operational semantics of the programming language. This means that when programming one has to bring what one wants to express into such an operational form (this is of course to a lesser extent the case for logic programming languages such as Prolog). Modeling can involve looseness, in the form of non-determinism and underspecification. Programming languages usually only support non-determinism indirectly, through concurrency or calls of random-functions. Modeling languages often support some form of first-order (or higher-order) logic, permitting quantification over infinite sets, which of course is not possible in a programming language. Finally, when writing programs, in some cases one has to deal with particularities of the execution platform. A clear example is assembler programs.

Related to this observation is the fact that algorithmic languages need some concept of iteration or recursion, which has to be captured by a fixpoint theoretic semantics. For models we usually do not need fixpoint theory, in general, although there are exceptions. In programming, one cannot avoid to deal with issues of termination, and even worse, of nontermination. This marks the borderline between universal programming languages and pure modeling languages for which execution is not considered.

A particular aspect of the algorithmic focus is that of efficiency and computational complexity. These are usually purely algorithmic notions in relation to programs. When modeling, we can use constructs which are not executable, and even if they are, we might not care very much about the question. It is an accepted view point that one should usually not consider the efficiency of a model. We can only talk about the efficiency of an algorithm.

The essential idea behind programming languages is that they are traditionally meant for communication between humans and the machine. In contrast, most modeling languages are for the communication between humans for the clarification of ideas, to understand a problem and its solution. This is of course a truth with modifications. New programming languages attempt to make programs yet easier to write and read by humans, and some modeling languages focus on efficiency calculations.

In the programming world there are very few accepted programming paradigms. These include procedural programming, object-oriented programming, functional programming, and logic programming. In modeling there seems to be a much larger variety of paradigms. These include e.g. ontologies, class diagrams, state charts, activity diagrams, sequence diagrams, timed automata, model-based formal specification languages (where one uses collection types such as sets, lists, and maps to build other types), algebraic specification (using equations between terms for specifying semantics), differential equations, etc. The playing field seems much larger. An important distinction here is between discrete systems (e.g. state machines) and continuous systems (e.g. speed and acceleration), e.g. modeled with differential equations, as encountered in cyber physical systems.

An interesting observation is that in the model-based engineering community, where formalisms are mostly graphical, there is less emphasis on concrete syntax, and more emphasis on abstract syntax. However, since abstract syntax is often itself represented as diagrams, it becomes somewhat of a challenge to precisely define what the 'modeling language' is. Although we do see this as an issue, we also recognize that the focus on abstract syntax rather than concrete syntax, as is done in the programming language community, may have advantages.

3   Similarities Between Modeling and Programming

Programming languages are indeed meant for description of data and algorithms in a way that machines can execute. However, programming languages have evolved over six decades since the conception of Fortran in the mid 1950ties, and today's high-level programming languages provide language constructs that can be used for modeling and not just implementation. Let's take a simple example. When Algol 60 was defined as the first committee programming language, the members of the committee decided not to standardize input and output. At that time, input and output was considered as an unimportant technical detail. Today, however, many applications are interactive. Therefore, the flow of input and output between different distributed programs is of a completely different and of a much more important nature. What was considered as unimportant in Algol during its initial design, is important today. Support for interactive programming is today supported in most newer programming languages, e.g. through the notion of actors, and is important for modeling as well. Other evolving programming concepts include object-oriented programming, functional programming, and advanced type systems, and specifically the combination of these concepts.

This point can in particular be illustrated by the large similarity between the modern programming language Scala [55], first appearing in 2004, and the long standing tried and proved VDM specification language [8,9,22], developed three decades earlier in the mid 1970ties, and in particular its subsequent object-oriented version VDM^{++} [22]. There are in fact very few language constructs in VDM^{++}, which one will not find in Scala, largely concerned with infinite structures, namely existential and universal quantification over infinite sets (e.g. $\forall x : \mathbb{Z} . P(x)$), and set comprehensions over infinite (e.g. $\{f(x) \mid x : \mathbb{Z} . P(x)\}$). In our experience, however, practical applications of VDM existential/universal quantifications are usually over finite sets (e.g. $\forall x \in S . P(x)$ for some finite set S), and similarly for set comprehension (e.g. $\{f(x) \mid x \in S . P(x)\}$). Such finite quantifications and comprehensions over collections exist also in a language such as Scala (e.g. S. forall (x $\Rightarrow$ P(x)) and for (x $\leftarrow$ S) yield f(x)). VDM also supports *design by contract*, meaning pre/post conditions on functions and class invariants. However, such concepts have found their way into programming languages, e.g. in Eiffel [19]. VDM finally supports predicate subtypes (e.g. type $\mathbb{N} = \{x : \mathbb{Z} \mid x \geq 0\}$). This kind of construct is now seen in programming languages supporting dependent types, such as Agda [3] and Idris [32].

If we consider UML/SysML, we can notice that an important part of UML/SysML is class diagrams, which essentially are class definitions with declarations of variables and methods specified with pre/post conditions, and occasionally code, plus constraints, typically written in OCL, which is a functional programming equivalent. These concepts can easily be represented in a programming language. Similar observations can be made about state charts, which fundamentally is a programming concept. It is not clear why we call the description of an algorithm by a state machine modeling and the description of the same algorithm by a program not necessarily modeling. Sequence diagrams are not directly representable as an executable programs. However, a sequence diagram can be considered as a property that a program execution has to obey. In that sense such a sequence diagram can be turned into a monitor of the executing system once built (a temporal assertion).

We have above argued that programming languages can handle finite data structures, and that these are useful and very common in modeling. However, so-called wide spectrum languages have been developed supporting a continuum, from models independent from any computational or algorithmic nature, to programs. In such systems one can establish and prove a refinement relation between a description at a higher level and a description at a lower level. We already mentioned VDM, which is an example of such a wide-spectrum language. Another example is the CIP-L language of the CIP system [6], where a full fledged programming language, comprising different programming styles such as functional as well as procedural programming, is integrated with non-executable constructs from set theory and predicate logic.

In summary, it seems worthwhile for the modeling community to benefit from the long chain of developments in programming languages, most of which have been tried and tested in the field. Not only past developments but also new developments, such as integrating programming, specifications, and proofs as is done in type theoretic languages such as Agda and Idris, and other systems such as Dafny [42] and Why3 [10]. Likewise, in the opposite direction, programming language design probably already have been and will be influenced by specification languages. Furthermore, it seems that program visualization techniques (of static structure as well as of executions) could help bringing modeling and programming closer together. Finally, extensible programming languages supporting the development of domain-specific language (DSL) constructs in addition to or restricting a programming language seems to be an important topic. The next section goes into more detail on the topic of DSLs.

4   Domain-Specific and Aspect-Oriented Languages

The perhaps major difference one could identify between programming and modeling languages is the level of abstraction: modeling languages explicitly support the focus on a specific aspect while ignoring others. Section 2 mentions computability, complexity and performance as examples. This difference essentially vanishes when looking at aspect-oriented [40] and domain-specific programming

[23,39]. In particular, aspect-oriented programming aims at a modular treatment of (so-called crosscutting) concerns, whereas domain-specific languages (DSLs) can be considered a means to generalize this form of modularity, both conceptually and technically:

– conceptually, one can consider a certain aspect as a particular domain, e.g., the domain of a specific kind of security, dependability, or traceability.
– technically, weaving can be considered as a very specific feature of a code generator that, e.g., merges a domain-specific/aspect program into code of the overall system.

In this sense, DSLs are much more than a way for supporting efficient programming by, e.g., factoring out boilerplate code. E.g., the *Language-Oriented Programming* [18,64] approach (LOP) as followed by the Racket team [21] is based on DSLs to support what they call the ultimate goal of programming language research, namely to deliver *software developers tools for formulating solutions in the languages of problem domains.*" (cf. Fig. 1).

```
01 #lang video
02
03 (image "splash.png" #:length 100)
04
05 (fade-transition #:length 50)
06
07 (multitrack (blank #f)
08             (composite-transition 0 0 1/4 1/4)
09             slides
10             (composite-transition 1/4 0 3/4 1)
11             presentation
12             (composite-transition 0 1/4 1/4 3/4)
13             (image "logo.png" #:length (producer-length talk)))
14
15 ; where
16 (define slides
17   (clip "slides05.MTS" #:start 2900 #:end 80000))
18
19 (define presentation
20   (playlist (clip "vid01.mp4")
21             (clip "vid02.mp4")
22             #:start 3900 #:end 36850))
23
24 (fade-transition #:length 50)
25
26 (image "splash.png" #:length 100)
```

Fig. 1. A script in the Racket-based *Video language* (reprinted from [4]).

Clearly, the racket team addresses programmers, or even super-programmers, capable of mastering various (programming) languages. This requirement is a little bit relaxed in the projectional editing approach [62] as most prominently provided by JetBrains' Meta Programming Systems (MPS) [35], which allows one to integrate DSLs that are not purely textual, e.g., spreadsheets and tables.

Language-Driven Engineering (LDE) goes even further by considering DSLs as a new way to impose a new kind of modularity which enables the cooperative development even of non-programmers with different mindset and education [60]. These people can be enabled to participate in the development process using adequate DSLs perhaps designed as enrichments of well-known application-level modeling languages, like P&ID diagrams, timing diagrams, process models, electrical wiring diagrams, timed automata, Markov chains, or whatever such users wish to use to support full code generation. Figure 2 displays a few of the languages we used in our industrial projects.

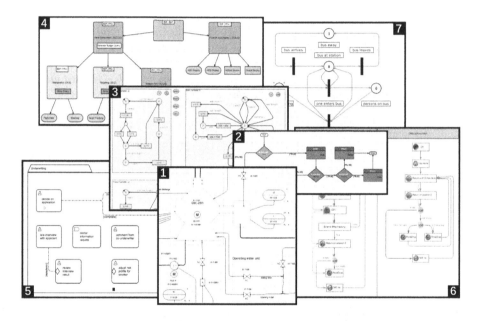

Fig. 2. Examples of DSLs: (1) Piping & Instrumentation Diagram [66], (2) Flow Graph [66], (3) Probabilistic Timed Automata [48], (4) Hierarchical Scheduling Systems [16], (5) OMG's Case Management CMMN [65], (6) EasyDelta Pick and Place DSL [7], and (7) Place/Transition Net [47] (reprinted from [60]).

While the LDE approach aims at enriching typically graphical domain languages[1], like the ones shown in Fig. 2, in order to define an external DSL for which full code can be generated, the LOP approach, as presented in [21], aims at capturing domain-specific features by establishing tailored internal domain-specific languages (there called *embedded DSLs* or *eDSLs*) on top of LISP/Racket

---

[1] Which are very popular in practice, as *"pictures are (often) worth a thousand words"*.

(see, e.g., Fig. 1)[2]. As a consequence, the addressed software developers are clearly programmers, while it is the goal of LDE to provide tailored (graphical) languages that allow application experts without programming knowledge to act themselves as software developers. In this sense, the Racket approach appears as a programming approach, LDE as a modeling approach, and the projectional editing approach as a hybrid. This illustrates the flexibility of DSLs to support the system development both at the modeling and the programming level. The work presented in [12] goes even at step further by considering DSLs as a means for transforming typical programming tasks into modeling activities which blurs the difference between modeling and programming.

5 Contributions to ISoLA 2018

The papers submitted to the UVMP track are introduced below, grouped into subsections according to the sessions of the track. Within each session the papers are ordered to provide a natural flow of presentations. Section 5.1 (*On Modeling and Programming*) provides an overview of the concepts of modeling and programming, and presents a wide spectrum of views of their relationship. Section 5.2 (*Formal Methods and Proofs*) focuses on the role of proofs, which establish the formal relationship between modeling and programming. Section 5.3 (*Modeling as Programming*) examines more closely the degree to which modeling can be considered as a programming activity. Section 5.4 (*The Application Perspective*) relates the discussion of modeling versus programming to real world phenomena. Section 5.5 (*Tailoring Languages*) discusses the role of domain-specific languages.

5.1 On Modeling and Programming

Jones [36] (*On Modeling and Programming*), argues that the term 'model' is used in several very different ways in computer science: analytic, in fields like physics to explain observed natural phenomena to reproduce results, experiments and insights; synthetic, as in computer science and engineering addressing constructed artifacts built to satisfy problem specifications; and in mechanization of established hand procedures. He argues that all three views are defensible and productive, but lead to very different ways of thinking. He focuses on modeling as used in the analytic and synthetic contexts. The paper introduces the concept of programming and different types of modeling but then concentrates very much on classical models related to formal systems and to programs. It treats issues of computability and complexity and discusses also the paradigms of computer science including the empirical, the mathematical, and the engineering paradigm. It concludes by saying that modeling has several meanings and purposes.

---

[2] The difference between internal and external DSLs can be sketched as follows: an internal DSL is added (e.g. via API functionality) to a host language, which is usually a general-purpose programming language, while an external DSL comes with its own syntax that is completely independent of already existing languages.

Elaasar [20] (*Definition of Modeling vs. Programming Languages*), explains how mainly graphical modeling languages and programming languages have originated in different communities, with different requirements. This has lead to differences in how modeling languages and programming languages are defined. This discussion is centered around the concepts of abstract syntax, concrete syntax, semantics, and software APIs, and the point is e.g. made, that the differences have lead to different tooling. A main observation is that while programming language developers usually focus on concrete syntax, modeling language developers focus on an abstract syntax, which may have numerous concrete syntaxes, such as a textual syntax and a graphical syntax. The points are illustrated with a case study, the definition of an ontology modeling language. It is finally argued, that modeling and programming languages seem to move towards a common point, with interesting perspectives what concerns e.g. common tooling.

Hallerstede, Larsen, and Fitzgerald [26] (*A Non-unified View of Modeling, Specification, and Programming*), argue that modeling and programming serve different purposes, and that care should be taken to distinguish them during development. They argue that a unified notation and method would become overly complex. Especially with many stakeholders it would be unrealistic to impose a unified set of methods and languages. The view is presented that executability is in tension with specification abstraction, and that using specification abstractions in programs makes them inefficient and limits their usefulness. Specific features mentioned, that are seen in specification languages but not explicitly in programming languages, include looseness (allowing many implementations) and quantification over infinite sets. It is mentioned, that formal methods tools with advantage can interact with traditional programs, e.g. a program can call a constraint solver.

Lethbridge and Algablan [43] (*Using Umple to Synergistically Process Features, Variants, UML Models and Classic Code*), describe a methodology for modeling variants such as product lines, and features, using the same master syntax as design models that are used for modeling classes, states, and composite structures. The extension to Umple is achieved by introducing mixset, that allows for creation of mixins composed from multiple locations in a textual codebase. Impressively, this approach allows for multiple programming languages to be embedded and generated from the design models. This work enables improved analysis, documentation generation, and reviewing/testing of models, design and code. It is particularly impressive that the work presented also allows for separation of concerns between various aspects of models to exist, while maintaining benefits of modeling, analysis, and code generation.

5.2 Formal Methods and Proofs

Börger [11] (*Why Programming Must Be Supported by Modeling and How*), argues that including abstract modeling concepts in terms of high-level programming language constructs into programming environments is not sufficient to bridge the numerous abstraction levels that software development typically passes on its way from requirements to code. Rather, an appropriate modeling framework (a design and analysis method and a language) is required that allows one to successively refine *ground models* comprising the user-level requirements in order to bridge the gap between descriptions understandable by the main stakeholders to executable code realizing the expected behavior. This is concretized in the realm of Abstract State Machines.

Huisman [31] (*On Models and Code - A Unified Approach to Support Large-Scale Deductive Program Verification*), points out that despite substantial progress in the area of deductive program verification over the last years, it still remains a challenge to use deductive verification on large-scale industrial applications. The classical reasons for why this is the case are mentioned, including the size of applications, and the need for users to provide loop invariants. However, in addition to these issues, problems are mentioned such as the need to reason about missing components, and the need for other specification formalisms than traditional pre-postcondition-style specifications. The suggestion is an approach based on a provable refinement relation defined between different levels in a model/program. Amongst important research topics are mentioned code generation from higher level models, support for optimization refinement, derivation of models from code, and support for compositional modeling and programming.

Ionescu, Jansson, and Botta [33] (*Type Theory as a Framework for Modelling and Programming*), propose type theory as a suitable framework for both modeling and programming. They show that it meets most of the requirements put forward in [14]. First and foremost, type theory supports specifying program properties as types, and programming and proving that (functional) programs meet their types. Type theory is compared to ZFC set theory, which is recalled to be a problematic foundation for computer science. Examples mentioned of systems based on type theory include NuPRL, Coq, Agda, Idris, and Lean. Type theory is not only considered as a foundation for programming but for mathematics in general, and as such can be used for example to encode continuous mathematics, useful for modeling of cyber physical systems. It is emphasized that type theory is particularly well suited for meta-programming, including definition of embedded DSLs.

O'Connor, Chen, Susarla, Rizkallah, Klein, and Keller [51] (*Bringing Effortless Refinement of Data Layouts to COGENT*), states that the COGENT systems programming language has enabled modeling of certain aspects of operating systems very effectively, but the gap between the current implementations and modeling capabilities/approaches is vast. The work attempts to solve an extremely difficult, and relevant problem with modeling for operating systems by narrowing the gap between the C data structures that are used profusely in operating systems, and the algebraic data types of COGENT. The data description language presented enables the programmer and modeler to effectively model the system and then verify properties about the system. The work presented is not only combining the various aspects of modeling, programming, and most importantly, verification, but, it is also paving the way for potentially creating operating systems using a waterfall design methodology, which, has mostly been a holy grail for system engineers and designers.

5.3   Modeling as Programming

Cleaveland [17] (*Programming is Modeling*), argues that programming is, in particular in the domain of embedded systems, a modeling activity, as it typically happens at a quite high level of abstraction, far away from the physical level. This tendency is supported by development languages that increasingly provide domain-specific features further abstracting from the physical reality. On the other hand he argues that modeling is much more general than programming, here seen as merely addressing the operational behavior, emphasizing that he regards the 'is' in the title as clearly asymmetric. The paper closes with discussing the implications of viewing programs as models, programming languages as meta models, and abstraction as a way to enforce structure.

Sestoft [57] (*Programming Language Specification and Implementation*), is presenting two examples concerned with programming language specification and implementation, illustrating the differences and similarities between modeling and programming. The first example is that of spreadsheets, and the evaluation of cell formulas. An operational+axiomatic semantics is presented, and it is shown how the operational semantics can be programmed in F#. It is shown that non-determinism in the specification may reflect run-time non-determinism in the implementation as well as under-specification. A cost semantics (specification) of spreadsheets is then presented, which would be difficult to represent in F#. The second example is a semantics of Ada written in VDM in the 1980ties, which is shown to be representable in F#, thus making the point that what was considered a specification in VDM in 1980 now looks much like an implementation in a functional language.

Havelund and Joshi [28] (*Modeling in Scala*), present two examples in using the Scala programming language for modeling. The first example is a reformulation in Scala of a conceptual model of what a relational database is, first formalized four decades ago in the VDM specification language. The similarity between the two formalizations is used as an argument that a modern programming language today has the a large intersection with what considered a formal specification language then. The second example is a reformulation of a spacecraft controller, first formalized two decades ago in the Promela language of the SPIN model checker. The modeling illustrates the use of an internal DSL for hierarchical state machines, and a randomized scheduler written in 50 lines of code, that detects the same four errors detected by SPIN. The argument is made that a high-level programming language can be used for modeling, and that further integration of modeling and programming is desirable, with support for DSL development, visualization, and verification.

Madsen and Møller-Pedersen [44] (*This is Not a Model*), argue for merging modeling and programming within the same language, and mention the object-oriented (modeling and) programming languages SIMULA and Beta as examples of languages designed with this objective. It is pointed out that one of the original advantages of object-orientation, introduced with SIMULA, was that the same concepts and language mechanisms could be used for analysis, design, and programming. This is contrasted to mainstream modeling and programming approaches where different languages are used for modeling and for programming. The paper defines a model as being the execution of a program, where the program itself is the model description. This is in contrast to traditional modeling languages such as UML, where the collection of diagrams is considered the model. It is advocated that more focus should be on tool support for viewing program executions, including visual techniques such as e.g. sequence diagrams.

5.4   The Application Perspective

Hatcliff, Larson, Belt, Robby, and Zhang [27] (*A Unified Approach for Modeling, Developing, and Assuring Critical Systems*), present an architecture-centric approach for development of embedded real-time systems, that emphasizes the use of a formally specified architecture as the 'scaffolding' through which different modeling and programming activities are organized. An open-source medical device, a Patient-Controlled Analgesic (PCA) infusion pump, is used as a concrete example. The distinction between 'models', 'specifications', and 'programs' is blurred. The approach is specifically based on the Architecture and Analysis Definition Language (AADL). Behaviors of components can be expressed and verified, either in the state machine notation BLESS, or programmed in conventional style using Slang, a dialect of the Scala programming language supported by verification. BLESS state machines are translated into Slang. Slang is translated into C and C^{++}.

Smyth, Schulz-Rosengarten, and Hanxleden [58] (*Towards Interactive Compilation Models*), describe the impact of considering compilation between hierarchies of implementation languages as a domain that deserves its dedicated domain-specific development environment: Modeling the entire development process itself on a meta-model level extends the possibilities of the model-based approach to guide the developer not only by supporting the refinement of tools for model creation, but also debugging, optimization, and prototyping of new compilations. The paper reports on experiences gathered while working on the model-based reference compiler of the KIELER SCCharts project which, in particular, illustrates the impact of considering meta modeling as part of the program development.

Margaria [45] (*From Computational Thinking to Constructive Design with Simple Models*) argues that the most important aspect of the educational revolution imposed by Computational Thinking is the "doing" part in the sense of creating a habit of designing the logic of any project or endeavor in terms of simple models. The advocated modeling-oriented teaching approach is based on years of experience with middle and high school students, beginner students in computer science, and with students of other disciplines. They all have been introduced successfully to CS or programming via constructing simple, yet executable models in the form of short courses, bootcamps, and semester-long courses in various locations and settings. Unlike coding, the model-oriented approach promises to be scalable, and adequate to provide the general public of professionals with the kind of familiarity with computational concepts that can be a game changer for the societal diffusion of basic computing-related comprehension and design skills. This perspective identifies dissemination of Computational Thinking as a new criterion for separating programming from modeling.

5.5 Tailoring Languages

Selić [56] (*Design Languages: A Necessary New Generation of Computer Languages*) argues that with the increased demand for so-called 'smart' systems required to interact with the physical world in ever more complex ways, we are witnessing a corresponding growth in the complexity of their embedded software. The first part of this paper examines in detail the primary inadequacies of current mainstream programming technologies, which renders them unsuitable for addressing modern software applications. This is followed by a discussion of emerging trends in computer language development, which point to a new generation of programming languages, referred to herein as design languages.[3] The primary technical requirements for these new languages are explained. The paper tackles an important problem, namely that of the future development of programming languages in a world full of cyber-physical systems and distributed computer applications.

Karsai [38] (*From Modeling to Model-based Programming*), starts with contrasting the limitations of 'classical' model-based design, e.g., in the UML-style, with the strong support domain-specific modeling frameworks like Matlab/Simulink provide, in particular, to their non-IT users. Karsai then addresses the question why 'truly' domain-specific software development which enables application experts to participate in the development process is still far from being (widely) accepted. The two main reasons given are the typically enormous effort for developing domain-specific development environments and lack of corresponding educations. The author proposes to address the first problem by enhancing the corresponding tooling and the second by adapting the software engineering curricula. The paper focuses on concretizing the corresponding vision by reporting on first experiences and successes.

Voelter [63] (*Fusing Modeling and Programming into Language-Oriented Programming: Our Experiences with MPS*) argues that modeling and programming, considered from the model-driven perspective, where models are automatically transformed into the real system, cannot be categorically distinguished. However, the two have traditionally emphasized various aspects differently, making each suitable for different use cases. After introducing 10 criteria and weighting to what extent they apply to either direction (modeling or programming), language-oriented programming with JetBrains MPS is presented as a hybrid approach, whose projectional editing and language modularity features provide powerful means to building domain-specific modeling tools. The main body of the paper presents discussions and examples from various projects for how those 10 criteria are addressed in MPS. As MPS itself is largely bootstrapped

---

[3] Design languages are essentially DSLs, as discussed in Sect. 4.

(i.e., built with itself), the very same criteria also apply to the meta level, explaining the choice of acronym which stands for Meta *Programming* System.

Bosselmann, Naujokat, and Steffen [12] (*On the Difficulty of Drawing the Line*) discuss the relationship between modeling and programming as a continuously evolving entity. It is a general tendency that structures and categorizations considered obvious in the past often get blurred in the cause of deeper investigation. E.g., the separating line between control and data path, traditionally clearly defined, is today often profitably moved by changing the level of interpretation, and even the gender classification has recently moved from a binary to a continuous spectrum. Domain-Specific Languages (DSLs), assumed here to come with corresponding rich tooling, are considered as a driver for a similar tendency when it comes to distinguishing between descriptive and prescriptive models, between model and program, or even between developer and user. Conceptual underlying key is to view the system development as a decision process which increasingly constrains the range of possible system implementations, and DSLs as a means to freeze taken decisions on the way towards a concrete realization. This way naturally comprises programming and modeling aspects. In fact, considering all interactions that influence the behavior of the system as 'development' turns GUIs into DSLs and users into developers. The pragmatics of this approach is illustrated in the light of the development of the Equinocs system, Springer's new editorial service.

6 Conclusion

We provided an introduction to the ISoLA 2018 track: *Towards a Unified View of Modeling and Programming*, discussing the possible unification of modeling and programming, the arguments against it, the arguments for it, and the role of domain-specific languages versus general purpose languages. Finally, we provided a summary of the 19 contributions to the track. The arguments against a unification of modeling and programming focus on certain features that cannot be implemented, are hard to implement, or are usually not seen in programming languages, such as under-specification, non-determinism, quantification over infinite sets, or continuous mathematics as found in cyber physical systems. An important argument is, that many interest groups may have different views on what formalisms are useful, and that designing a 'silver bullet' will not work. The arguments for a unification center around the observation that high-level programming languages tend to get closer and closer to modeling languages due to their abstractions, and that support for domain-specific extensions of programming languages will address some of the concerns raised against a unification.

Whichever way one sees this question, one can probably agree that more unification is possible than what can be observed in current practice, as formalisms in the different communities – viewed at an abstract level – already share many language constructs. However, the question remains, whether a single unified approach or just a unification of concepts should be strived for. After all, there are many (potentially conflicting) concerns that need to be taken into account:

- Allow for high-level as well as low-level programming.
- State properties of programs, as predicates, or as refinement relations between levels of abstraction, supported by formal proofs and testing.
- Textual as well as graphical syntax for programs/models.
- Visualization of executions.
- Support for meta-programming and design of domain-specific languages.
- Harmonize tooling technologies used in the different communities.

Finding a good balance between all those aspects without overloading individual solutions clearly provides lots of challenges for future research.

References

1. Documents associated with Object Constraint Language (OCL), Version 2.4. http://www.omg.org/spec/OCL/2.4
2. Abrial, J.R.: Modeling in Event-B. Cambridge University Press, Cambridge (2010)
3. Agda. http://wiki.portal.chalmers.se/agda/pmwiki.php
4. Andersen, L., Chang, S., Felleisen, M.: Super 8 Languages for Making Movies (Functional Pearl). In: Proceedings of the ACM on Programming Languages 1(ICFP) (2017)
5. Barras, B., et al.: The Coq Proof Assistant Reference Manual: Version 6.1 (1997)
6. Bauer, F., Broy, M., Gnatz, R., Hesse, W., Krieg-Brückner, B.: Towards a wide spectrum language to support program specification and program development. In: Alber, K. (ed.) Programmiersprachen. Informatik - Fachberichte, vol. 12, pp. 73–85. Springer, Heidelberg (1978)
7. Berg, A., et al.: PG 582 - Industrial Programming by Example. Technical report, TU Dortmund (2015). http://hdl.handle.net/2003/34106
8. Bjørner, D., Jones, C.B. (eds.): The Vienna Development Method: The Meta-Language. LNCS, vol. 61. Springer, Heidelberg (1978). https://doi.org/10.1007/3-540-08766-4
9. Bjørner, D., Jones, C.B.: Formal Specification and Software Development. Prentice Hall International (1982). ISBN 0-13-880733-7
10. Bobot, F., Filliâtre, J.C., Marché, C., Paskevich, A.: Why3: shepherd your herd of provers. In: Boogie 2011: First International Workshop on Intermediate Verification Languages, pp. 53–64. Wrocław, Poland, August 2011
11. Boerger, E.: Why programming must be supported by modeling and how. In: Margaria, T., Steffen, B. (eds.) ISoLA 2018. LNCS, vol. 11244, pp. 89–110. Springer, Cham (2018)
12. Bosselmann, S., Naujokat, S., Steffen, B.: On the difficulty of drawing the line. In: Margaria, T., Steffen, B. (eds.) ISoLA 2018. LNCS, vol. 11244, pp. 340–356. Springer, Cham (2018)
13. Broy, M.: On architecture specification. In: Tjoa, A.M., Bellatreche, L., Biffl, S., van Leeuwen, J., Wiedermann, J. (eds.) SOFSEM 2018. LNCS, vol. 10706, pp. 19–39. Springer, Cham (2018). https://doi.org/10.1007/978-3-319-73117-9_2
14. Broy, M., Havelund, K., Kumar, R.: Towards a unified view of modeling and programming. In: Margaria, T., Steffen, B. (eds.) ISoLA 2016. LNCS, vol. 9953, pp. 238–257. Springer, Cham (2016). https://doi.org/10.1007/978-3-319-47169-3_17

15. Broy, M., Havelund, K., Kumar, R.: Towards a Unified View of Modeling and Programming (Track Summary). In: Margaria, T., Steffen, B. (eds.) ISoLA 2016, part 2. LNCS, vol. 9953, pp. 3–10. Springer, Cham (2016). https://doi.org/10.1007/978-3-319-47169-3_1
16. Chadli, M., Kim, J.H., Larsen, K.G., Legay, A., Naujokat, S., Steffen, B., Traonouez, L.M.: High-level frameworks for the specification and verification of scheduling problems. Softw. Tools Technol. Transfer (2017)
17. Cleaveland, R.: Programming is modeling. In: Margaria, T., Steffen, B. (eds.) ISoLA 2018. LNCS, vol. 11244, pp. 150–161. Springer, Cham (2018)
18. Dmitriev, S.: Language Oriented Programming: The Next Programming Paradigm. JetBrains onBoard Online Magazine 1 (2004). http://www.onboard.jetbrains.com/is1/articles/04/10/lop/
19. Eiffel (2015). http://www.eiffel.com
20. Elaasar, M.: Definition of modeling vs. programming languages. In: Margaria, T., Steffen, B. (eds.) ISoLA 2018. LNCS, vol. 11244, pp. 35–51. Springer, Cham (2018)
21. Felleisen, M.: A programmable programming language. Commun. ACM **61**(3), 62–71 (2018)
22. Fitzgerald, J., Larsen, P.G., Mukherjee, P., Plat, N., Verhoef, M.: Validated Designs For Object-oriented Systems. Springer, Santa Clara (2005). https://doi.org/10.1007/b138800
23. Fowler, M., Parsons, R.: Domain-Specific Languages. Addison-Wesley/ACM Press (2011). http://books.google.de/books?id=ri1muolw_YwC
24. George, C., et al.: The RAISE Specification Language. The BCS Practitioner Series. Prentice-Hall, Hemel Hampstead (1992)
25. Gurevich, Y., Rossman, B., Schulte, W.: Semantic Essence of AsmL. Theor. Comput. Sci. **343**(3), 370–412 (2005)
26. Hallerstede, S., Larsen, P.G., Fitzgerald, J.: A Non-unified view of modelling, specification and programming. In: Margaria, T., Steffen, B. (eds.) ISoLA 2018. LNCS, vol. 11244, pp. 52–68. Springer, Cham (2018)
27. Hatcliff, J., Larson, B.R., Belt, J., Robby, Zhang, Y.: A unified approach for modeling, developing, and assuring critical systems. In: Margaria, T., Steffen, B. (eds.) ISoLA 2018. LNCS, vol. 11244, pp. 225–245. Springer, Cham (2018)
28. Havelund, K., Joshi, R.: Modeling in Scala. In: Margaria, T., Steffen, B. (eds.) ISoLA 2018. LNCS, vol. 11244, pp. 184–205. Springer, Cham (2018)
29. Havelund, K., Visser, W.: Program model checking as a new trend. STTT **4**(1), 8–20 (2002)
30. Holzmann, G.: The SPIN Model Checker. Addison-Wesley, Boston (2004)
31. Huisman, M.: On models and code - a unified approach to support large-scale deductive program verification. In: Margaria, T., Steffen, B. (eds.) ISoLA 2018. LNCS, vol. 11244, pp. 111–118. Springer, Cham (2018)
32. Idris. https://www.idris-lang.org
33. Ionescu, C., Jansson, P., Botta, N.: Type theory as a framework for modelling and programming. In: Margaria, T., Steffen, B. (eds.) ISoLA 2018. LNCS, vol. 11244, pp. 119–133. Springer, Cham (2018)
34. Jackson, D.: Software Abstractions: Logic, Language, and Analysis. The MIT Press (2012)
35. JetBrains: Meta Programming System. https://www.jetbrains.com/mps
36. Jones, N.D: On modeling and programming. In: Margaria, T., Steffen, B. (eds.) ISoLA 2018. LNCS, vol. 11244, pp. 22–34. Springer, Cham (2018)
37. Jones, S.L.P.: Haskell 98 Language and Libraries: The Revised Report. Cambridge University Press, Cambridge (2003)

38. Karsai, G.: From modeling to model-based programming. In: Margaria, T., Steffen, B. (eds.) ISoLA 2018. LNCS, vol. 11244, pp. 295–308. Springer, Cham (2018)
39. Kelly, S., Tolvanen, J.P.: Domain-Specific Modeling: Enabling Full Code Generation. Wiley-IEEE Computer Society Press, Hoboken (2008)
40. Kiczales, G., et al.: Aspect-oriented programming. In: Akşit, M., Matsuoka, S. (eds.) ECOOP 1997. LNCS, vol. 1241, pp. 220–242. Springer, Heidelberg (1997). https://doi.org/10.1007/BFb0053381
41. Lamport, L.: Specifying Systems: The TLA+ Language and Tools for Hardware and Software Engineers. Pearson Education Inc., London (2002)
42. Leino, K.R.M.: Dafny: an automatic program verifier for functional correctness. In: Clarke, E.M., Voronkov, A. (eds.) LPAR 2010. LNCS (LNAI), vol. 6355, pp. 348–370. Springer, Heidelberg (2010). https://doi.org/10.1007/978-3-642-17511-4_20
43. Lethbridge, T.C., Algablan, A.: Using umple to synergistically process features, variants, UML models and classic code. In: Margaria, T., Steffen, B. (eds.) ISoLA 2018. LNCS, vol. 11244, pp. 69–88. Springer, Cham (2018)
44. Madsen, O.L., Møller-Pedersen, B.: This is not a model. In: Margaria, T., Steffen, B. (eds.) ISoLA 2018. LNCS, vol. 11244, pp. 206–224. Springer, Cham (2018)
45. Margaria, T.: From computational thinking to constructive design with simple models. In: Margaria, T., Steffen, B. (eds.) ISoLA 2018. LNCS, vol. 11244, pp. 261–278. Springer, Cham (2018)
46. Milner, R., Tofte, M., Harper, R. (eds.): The Definition of Standard ML. MIT Press (1997). ISBN 0-262-63181-4
47. Naujokat, S., Lybecait, M., Kopetzki, D., Steffen, B.: CINCO: a simplicity-driven approach to full generation of domain-specific graphical modeling tools. Softw. Tools Technol. Transfer (2017)
48. Naujokat, S., Traonouez, L.-M., Isberner, M., Steffen, B., Legay, A.: Domain-specific code generator modeling: a case study for multi-faceted concurrent systems. In: Margaria, T., Steffen, B. (eds.) ISoLA 2014. LNCS, vol. 8802, pp. 481–498. Springer, Heidelberg (2014). https://doi.org/10.1007/978-3-662-45234-9_33
49. Nipkow, T., Wenzel, M., Paulson, L.C. (eds.): Isabelle/HOL: A Proof Assistant for Higher-Order Logic. LNCS, vol. 2283. Springer, Heidelberg (2002). https://doi.org/10.1007/3-540-45949-9
50. OCaml. http://caml.inria.fr/ocaml/index.en.html
51. O'Connor, L., Chen, Z., Susarla, P., Rizkallah, C., Klein, G., Keller, G.: bringing effortless refinement of data layouts to COGENT. In: Margaria, T., Steffen, B. (eds.) ISoLA 2018. LNCS, vol. 11244, pp. 134–149. Springer, Cham (2018)
52. OMG: SysML. http://www.omg.org/spec/SysML/1.3
53. OMG: UML. http://www.omg.org/spec/UML/2.5
54. PVS. http://pvs.csl.sri.com
55. Scala. http://www.scala-lang.org
56. Selić, B.: Design languages: a necessary new generation of computer languages. In: Margaria, T., Steffen, B. (eds.) ISoLA 2018. LNCS, vol. 11244, pp. 279–294. Springer, Cham (2018)
57. Sestoft, P.: Programming language specification and implementation. In: Margaria, T., Steffen, B. (eds.) ISoLA 2018. LNCS, vol. 11244, pp. 162–183. Springer, Cham (2018)
58. Smyth, S., Schulz-Rosengarten, A., von Hanxleden, R.: Towards interactive compilation models. In: Margaria, T., Steffen, B. (eds.) ISoLA 2018. LNCS, vol. 11244, pp. 246–260. Springer, Cham (2018)

59. Spivey, J.M.: The Z Notation - a Reference Manual. International Series in Computer Science, 2nd edn. Prentice Hall, Hemel Hempstead (1992)
60. Steffen, B., Gossen, F., Naujokat, S., Margaria, T.: Language-driven engineering: from general-purpose to purpose-specific languages. In: Margaria, T., Steffen, B. (eds.) ISoLA 2018. LNCS, vol. 11244, pp. 546–564. Springer, Cham (2018)
61. UPPAAL. http://www.uppaal.org
62. Voelter, M., Siegmund, J., Berger, T., Kolb, B.: Towards user-friendly projectional editors. In: Combemale, B., Pearce, D.J., Barais, O., Vinju, J.J. (eds.) SLE 2014. LNCS, vol. 8706, pp. 41–61. Springer, Cham (2014). https://doi.org/10.1007/978-3-319-11245-9_3
63. Voelter, M.: Fusing modeling and programming into language-oriented programming. In: Margaria, T., Steffen, B. (eds.) ISoLA 2018. LNCS, vol. 11244, pp. 309–339. Springer, Cham (2018)
64. Ward, M.P.: Language oriented programming. Softw. Concepts Tools **15**(4), 147–161 (1994)
65. Weckwerth, J.: Cinco Evaluation: CMMN-Modellierung und -Ausführung in der Praxis. Master's thesis, TU Dortmund (2016)
66. Wortmann, N., Michel, M., Naujokat, S.: A fully model-based approach to software development for industrial centrifuges. In: Margaria, T., Steffen, B. (eds.) ISoLA 2016. LNCS, vol. 9953, pp. 774–783. Springer, Cham (2016). https://doi.org/10.1007/978-3-319-47169-3_58

On Modeling and Programming

Neil D. Jones[(✉)]

DIKU, University of Copenhagen, Copenhagen, Denmark
neil@diku.dk

Abstract. In computer science "model" is used with different meanings:

- **Analytic.** Analogous field: physics. Relevant "model" meaning: a *theory* to explain observed natural phenomena. Important: *adequacy* of the explanations; *reproducibility* by other researchers of results and experiments.
- **Synthetic.** Analogous fields: computer science and engineering. Relevant use of "model": a *constructed artefact* (software, hardware,...) built to satisfy a *problem specification*. Important: the *reliability* of the constructed artefact; and the *correctness* of the artefact with respect to the specification.
- **Mechanisation** of established hand procedures. Analogous fields: data processing; automation of hospital procedures. (Academically inelegant, but a large percentage of worldwide computer science expenditures.) Relevant: *predictability, completeness, reliability, degree of automation, common sense.*

All three are defensible and productive, but lead to very different ways of thinking. We focus on the analytic and synthetic meanings, since the mechanisation dimension is out of Isola scope.

1 Perspectives on "Modeling"

From Collins' dictionary:

Model 9. A simplified representation or description of a system or complex entity, esp. one designed to facilitate calculations and predictions.

Model 10. An interpretation of a formal system under which the theorems in that system are mapped onto truths.

Model 14. To plan or create according to a model or models.

Figure 1 illustrates Collins' definitions. The central box concerns concepts of equality, truth, falsity, etc. that are precisely and stably defined and "live in their own world". Examples include mathematical relations such as $F = ma, e = mc^2$, Mendelian genetics, neural networks, and computer circuits.

© Springer Nature Switzerland AG 2018
T. Margaria and B. Steffen (Eds.): ISoLA 2018, LNCS 11244, pp. 22–34, 2018.
https://doi.org/10.1007/978-3-030-03418-4_2

1.1   Models in the Natural Sciences

The left-right arrow (**Model 9**) shows the prime concern of the natural sciences. This is *analytical*, concerned with finding out what is true "out there" in the real physical or biological world (in contrast to mathematics, engineering, logic, or data processing.)

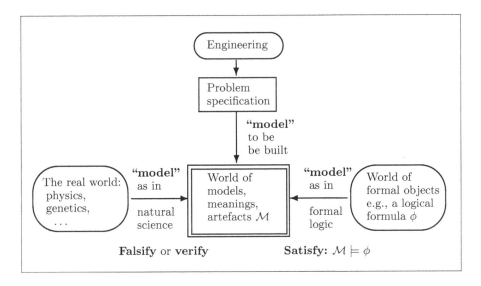

Fig. 1. Three different perspectives on modeling.

The left-to-right direction expresses a *hypothesis about nature* that may or may not hold in the long run. It is an attempt to discover and formulate properties of the real world. Well-known examples: Newton's laws, and the laws of Mendelian inheritance are both good models of the real world. Though not perfect, these "laws" survived long (and still do) since sufficiently precise for daily prediction and use. Subsequent new frameworks were developed with greater ability to explain observations made by physicists and biologists, and to predict the outcome of future experiments.

Limitations in a model of this sort arise if the model has poor predictive or explanatory power. If so, the model should be changed or scrapped.[1]

Collins 14: The top-down arrows in Fig. 1 are about specifications to be realised by humans and computers. The main goal is now to *implement* a desired behavior by building a physical or computer system to carry it out.

This is a quite different concept of "model", with goal "what can we build?" (rather than how to analyse the pre-existing world out there of the

---

[1] In an imperfect model, identifying the *places* where the model and reality differ can spur new developments. See Kuhn and Popper [10, 14] for much more on this topic.

natural sciences.) Much of a computer scientist's or engineer's work is first to *specify* a planned (but not yet existing) system's desired computational or physical/mathematical behavior[2]; and then to build a realisation.

From this viewpoint modeling is the relation between a specification of *what the designer wishes to be true* and what is actually true (in the center). Given a constructed system $\mathcal{M}$ in the central box, the correctness question is: does $\mathcal{M}$ satisfy the problem specification?

An implementation error arises if a model $\mathcal{M}$, e.g., a circuit or computer program, *does not behave as the designers intended*. Such errors can show a need to change the specification's implementation by hardware or software; but are not problems with the underlying nature of "the real world".[3]

In this context the natural science approach (experimental measurement of an already-constructed system) is not central, but can be useful for debugging: to see pragmatically whether a perhaps very large constructed system in fact has the properties its designers intended.

Remark: the very possibility of engineering, computer and circuit construction, etc. depends on well-understood properties of the physical world. Thanks to our engineering heritage we do not need to understand sophisticated aspects such as quantum phenomena, electron flow, etc. in order to grasp what a circuit or program does and how to use it. The reason is that hardware is *carefully designed* to function according to predictable laws of logic.

Collins 10: Model-checking (the right-left arrow in Fig. 1) is increasingly used to verify and debug hardware and software components. An iconic example: the disastrous launch of Ariane 5 was an expensive failure caused by a software error. Model-checking is now a significant interface between systems practice and mathematical logic. See Wikipedia for an overview.[4]

Logic relates a syntactic world with logical formulas ϕ to a world of meanings or artefacts $\mathcal{M}$ (also called "models"), over which the logical formulas are interpreted. Logic thus concerns what we can write in a formal language and the *relation between what has been specified and what is actually true* in a concrete implementation such as a program or circuit.

The field of *semantics* is about the connection $[\![\_]\!]$ between syntax, i.e., what is written in specification ϕ, and the meaning/operational effect of program or circuit $\mathcal{M}$.

Figure 2 shows some detail in the bottom right of Fig. 1. Remark: model-checking applies "after the fact", in the sense that it assumes that one is already given a specification ϕ, and a system $\mathcal{M}$ to be checked against ϕ. From this

---

[2] For example, by informal descriptions, or pre- and post-conditions, or formulas in temporal logic, or statecharts in UML [2,5,6].

[3] The error could also reveal that there is something wrong with the specification. Both error types are seen in practice, though specifications change less frequently than implementations.

[4] The bug might have been caught by computer-checking the control program, e.g., by theorem proving. Caveat: finite-precision arithmetic caused the Ariane bug; alas, a topic still beyond most current proving or model-checking technologies.

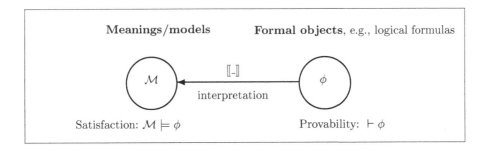

Fig. 2. Models as in model checking.

angle the model $\mathcal{M}$ itself (a program or circuit) is the object of study in model-checking. The point is to discover whether an alleged solution to a software or hardware construction problem actually satisfies the specification. This is in contrast to "model" as in Collins' definitions 9 or 14; there, the model captures a bit of the real world, or serves as a conceptual step towards constructing an artefact.

1.2 Models in Engineering and Computer Science

Both engineering and mathematics are *synthetic* rather than *analytic*. The top-down arrows express a third view of model: a stepping stone on the way between specifying requirements for a planned artefact, and actually building it. This is neither a fact about the world, nor an interpretation of a logical formula.

The starting point is a (top-down) *problem specification*. Next, a more operational *implementation* is developed: a step (bottom-up) towards constructing the final artefact. The specification and implementation phases usually need to be iterated, causing *a coevolution*: both are developed over time. This process has been called "stepwise refinement". (See [16] for more on top-down and bottom-up construction.)

Reliability of Constructed Artefacts. To gain perspective, compare the design and construction of a bridge, or the planning and launching of a satellite, with the construction and release of a program.

The *reliability* of the artefacts that have been constructed is very important in all three cases. However the task of *achieving* reliability for the three is very different, due to differences in "binding times" of construction phases [9].

Some relevant binding times are implementation; debugging; and usage. The three problem domains have large differences: how the artefact is implemented; how the end product is used; and our attitudes towards errors.

A bridge construction project may take years to finish, and uses (physical) models for in-advance error detection. The end result is stable and unchanging. Usage criteria include load-bearing ability, resistance to forces such as wind and weather and time, and maintainability. Usage occurs continuously, usually for many years. There are well-established procedures to detect and prevent errors before contruction begins, and well-understood criteria for success.

A satellite launch also involves much in-advance design and debugging, but with a difference: the launch occurs only once. Further, there is no realistic possibility to repair errors once the launch has happened.

Programs are much more malleable than bridges or satellites: the source program texts are (nearly) always available so updates can be made, and changes can be made online to correct errors. This gives great flexibility, but less motivation to eradicate all possible errors before the program is released.

On Half-Completed Artefacts: A statement that a half-completed bridge-building project is proceeding satisfactorily can be made with some confidence. The same is certainly *not* true of a half-completed program: it is hard to describe, to realise, and to assess progress on a software construction project that is under way.

A bottom-line difference is that bugs in bridge construction are unacceptable, and grounds for rejection of an entire project. Even worse, a bug in a satellite launch is usually catastrophic.

On the other hand, bugs in programs are expected and inevitable; but should all have been resolved once a software product has been delivered. Alas, this is very difficult to ensure. Program development is done by software experts working within a variety of programming language and system contexts, ones usually unrelated to the program's intended application area. As a result it can be hard to reach consensus with clients and even among program designers.

Not All Software Construction Problems Are Created Equal. *A not outrageously difficult case*: Implementing an abstract but well-defined problem, e.g., parsing, graph algorithms, satisfiability, compiling.

In contrast, *interaction and time-dependence* are central to computer science, but tools to describe and reason about them are far from mature. Some progress has been made, e.g., process algebra and temporal logic [4, 6, 12]; but much still needs to be done.

An especially difficult case: Mechanisation of established hand procedures. Two instances: business data processing, and managing hospital procedures. In these two areas, problem specifications are extremely difficult to evaluate, judge, and enforce; and even to formulate well in the first place. It is also challenging to ascertain whether a problem has been satisfactorily solved.

2   Models and Research Paradigms in Computer Science

"Model" notions relate to our ideas of what comprises research. Pioneers Newell, Perlis and Simon regarded computer science as the study of *phenomena related to computers* including digital computers, programming languages, algorithms and programs.

This was further developed into many subfields including the study and implementation of *algorithms* (Knuth's viewpoint); *abstractions* (automata,, complexity classes, temporal logic,. . .); *complexity* (Dijkstra,. . .); and *information structures* (e.g., ACM's Computing Curricula).

Empirical paradigm: (as in *natural sciences*, e.g., physics). The study of phenomena. The 1950s was a "data-gathering phase". In later years a model-based empirical approach became increasingly important because constructed systems were often too complex to understand a priori. As a result experimentation was sometimes needed to manage expansion, monitor errors, and improve interfaces.

Mathematical paradigm: The study of abstractions. The 1960s was an "elaboration and abstraction phase". Frequent topics: mathematical formulations of core ideas behind programs, circuits, computations, compilers,. . . Examples: programming language semantics, parsing and parser generation, computability and complexity theory.

Engineering paradigm: Construction of programs, systems, . . . We have since the 1970s been in a "technology phase". This paradigm deals with managing increasingly complex software-firmware-hardware systems. Goals are practical: building systems to meet user specifications, testing, verification . . . . Examples: software engineering, vision/robotics/animation, compiler construction, many more.

The Three Paradigms Support One Another. Wegner [15] concludes that, even though differing in approach and methods, progress in any of these paradigms aids and enables progress in others:

1. A computer scientist should be a "universalist", combining the enquiring mind and experimental aproach of the empirical scientist; the formalisation and abstraction ability of the mathematician; and the tool building and implementation ability of the engineer.
2. The ability to work at *different levels of abstraction*, and quickly to do *context shifts* is essential.
3. Computer science is rapidly expanding with many different viewpoints, approaches, and even perceptions. One effect, noted by Wegner and still true:

   This makes it very hard to come to a consensus on curriculum, research, etc. in order to educate future computer scientists.

3   On Building Models in Computer Science

3.1   Context Shifts Among Levels of Abstraction

Computer science has been called "general problem solving". A difference from most engineering and natural science is that computer scientists daily operate on a great many levels of abstraction; and frequently "shift level" (consciously or not). Some examples of abstraction levels:

- A specific *problem*
- An *algorithm* that solves a specific problem
- A specific *program* (or circuit, system,...)
- Study of *classes of algorithms* that solve a specific problem
- Study of *classes of problems* that can be solved in, say, polynomial time (as a function of input size)
- A compiler, that compiles *any source program* into a machine-language equivalent target program.
- A definition of a *programming language semantics*, e.g., Standard ML. Approaches: denotational, operational, or game semantics.
- A *framework for defining semantics* of various programming languages.

An architectural view of software engineering uses diagrams to represent *structural information*. An example: UML diagrams [3] can represent information about *behavior* or *interactions*. Higher levels of abstraction lead to *metamodeling*, e.g., UML's four-layered architecture (including UML itself, layer 2).

3.2   What Can Go Wrong?

1. Ill-posed problems (nasty if supported by large budgets and expectations).
2. Lack of clear *criteria for success*.
3. Not understanding in depth *what* a manual procedure accomplishes, before it is automated.
4. Lack of abstraction, e.g., seeing when and how can an earlier problem solution be re-used while solving a new problem.
5. *Unconsciously shifting* from one level of abstraction to another.

3.3   Managing Complexity in Software Development

This is not easy. As opposed to, say, bridge building, there are many competing but few well-developed and accepted successful practices in software development. UML is a notable step in what is a still very young field. Some things that help:

Hierarchical decomposition: *Reductionism* is often useful when constructing systems (despite its bad name in analytical science or philosophy).

Reducing the bandwidth of necessary inter-process or -thread communications.

Object-oriented program construction and extension approaches.

Many more: see any recent conference on software engineering. (However, there is no "design silver bullet" to control complexity and achieve reliability...)

4   On Executing Problem Specifications

"What" Versus "how". An **intensional** problem specification is *algorithmic*: it expresses *how* the problem is to be solved. Programming languages are very good for specifying "how": they are implementable and flexible (though not very abstract, and not well-suited for specifying user intentions).

On the other hand, an **extensional** problem specification expresses *what* is to be accomplished (in order to solve the problem), but says nothing about how this is to be done. There exist many different attempts to specify "what" by frameworks of varying generality; but none are wholly satisfactory. One reason is that "what" can be rather subtle.

4.1   Which Problems Can Be Specified?

The *sorting* problem is a simple, understandable example. A compact specification of what a sorting program must do: given input list ℓ_1, find list ℓ_2 such that

$$\text{permutation}(\ell_1, \ell_2) \text{ and nondecreasing } (\ell_2)$$

This intensional specification does not specify any one algorithm, and there exist a great many different but correct sorting algorithms. Examples: insertion sort, quick sort, merge sort, bucket sort, all with different characteristics (efficiency, stability,...).

Although the sorting specification cannot be used directly to sort anything, it can be used to check correctness of an alleged sorting program's output on a given input ℓ_1. In contrast, an answer "no" to the Turing machine halting problem cannot even be checked for correctness.

A more extreme view: a problem specification may be not at all directly executable, or even checkable. One reason: a specification may specify an impossible goal, e.g. "find an integer x such that $x^2 \bmod 4 = 3$". One cannot rule out all such possibilities, even by using a general theorem prover.

A classic unrealisable example: to decide the "halting problem" for a given Turing machine and input. In this example, the specified goal is mathematically well-defined, but algorithmically uncomputable.

4.2   Should Problem Specifications Be Executable?

An argument *against*: An executable specification formalism would have to have available at least one execution means available for *every* acceptable problem specification. Requiring executability in advance could limit algorithm expressivity, and thus limit the choice among alternatives of very different efficiencies. (For example, an executable "sort" would likely choose just one among many different but correct sorting algorithms.)

An argument *for:* the end result of stepwise refinement must be an executable program. Thus at least one development step must be executable. So why not the first one?

A related perspective: an implementation designer needs a solution that is asymptotically efficient enough (e.g., merge sort's $O(n \log n)$ time rather than $O(n^2)$). Asymptotic efficiency problems of this type are well understood, so a designer can choose from a general algorithm library, and so does not need to optimise from first principles.

4.3   A Programming Language Perspective

From a computer science view it is natural to think of two formalised languages:

- A language of *problem specifications* (concise, expressive); and
- A language of *programs* (efficiently executable on the computer).

This viewpoint naturally leads to thinking of a *compilation* task, from an executable specification language into a programming language.

A more systematic and automated approach can be made using the classical framework of *computability theory*, with a more operational viewpoint (partial evaluation is an example [9]).

4.4   Computability Theory

The classical field of computability theory[5] provides a crystal-clear distinction between *what* and *how* on the natural numbers $\mathbb{N}$. Its "what" is the set of (partial mathematical) functions $f : \mathbb{N} \to \mathbb{N}_\perp$ where $\mathbb{N}$ is the set of natural numbers and $\perp$ indicates nontermination.

Using this, the theory proves that one can precisely specify problems (what) that are not solvable by any computing device (how). Although abstract, this theory gives insights relevant to computational practice.[6]

A major 1930s breakthrough was the "grand confluence": realisation (and proof) that the notion of a computable function is *well-defined and invariant* for a very wide range of computing devices and data representations.[7]

The foundations of computability theory are easy to state, and recognisable to today's computer scientists. We write $[\![p]\!](d_1, \ldots, d_n)$ for the result (if any) of running program p on input data $d_1, \ldots, d_n$. The foundational axioms:

1. $f : \mathbb{N} \to \mathbb{N}_\perp$ is computable if and only if $f = [\![p]\!]$ for some program p.
2. A *self-interpreter* (or *universal*) program *univ* exists that satisfies, for any program p and data value d, the equation $[\![univ]\!](p, d) = [\![p]\!](d)$.
3. A *partial evaluator* program *s11* exists such that $[\![[\![s11]\!](p, s)]\!](d) = [\![p]\!](s, d)$ for any program p and data values s, d.

---

[5] Originally known as "recursive function theory", the field began in the 1930s.

[6] Computability theory does not concern *all functions* of type $f : \mathbb{N} \to \mathbb{N}_\perp$ for a simple reason: there exist too many of them. The number of functions of type $f : \mathbb{N} \to \mathbb{N}_\perp$ is $\aleph_1$, but the number of programs is $\aleph_0$.

[7] Nonterminating programs have to be allowed. There exists a computable partial function $f : \mathbb{N} \to \mathbb{N}_\perp$ such that no extension of f to a total function is computable.

These axioms involves *programs as data objects*: Axioms 2 and 3 use programs as *input* values. In Axiom 3, function $s11$ produces a program as output value.

The net effect: one can allow self-reference and metaprogramming without expanding the computability framework, provided we assume that programs are available as data objects, both as inputs to be interpreted and outputs to be generated.[8]

4.5 Partial Evaluation = Computability Plus Efficiency

Computability theory was motivated by questions in mathematical logic long before computers were invented; questions of computational efficiency were not yet relevant before complexity theory arose in the 1960s [7].

A partial evaluator $s11$ can be used to compile, generate a compiler, ind even generate a compiler generator. All this can be done by implementing the *Futamura projections*[9]. For details see [9] [remark: [9] uses mix in place of $s11$].

$$\begin{aligned} target &= [\![s11]\!](int, source) \\ compiler &= [\![s11]\!](s11, int) \\ cogen &= [\![s11]\!](s11, s11) \end{aligned}$$

4.6 Partial Evaluation of an Executable Specification Language

A natural goal is to develop an interpreter *specint* for a convenient and expressive specification language. Concretely, one would expect

$$output = [\![specint]\!](spec, input) = f(input)$$

for a specification *spec* of an input-output function f. Specialising *specint* to *spec*

$$target = [\![s11]\!](specint, spec)$$

would, by the first Futamura projection, compile the specification *spec* into a program to compute the input-output function f. Bottom line: for any express-ible problem specification *spec*, program $[\![s11]\!](specint, spec)$ satisfies *spec*, i.e., it computes f.

A simple example: this ambitious goal has been reached for specifications in the form of regular expressions. See, for example, [9] Sections 1.2, 1.2 (and

---

[8] Kleene anticipated the use of both recursive definitions and reflective programming already in 1938 by his *Second recursion theorem*: $\forall p \; \exists q \; \forall d \; . \; [\![p]\!](q, d) = [\![q]\!](d)$. ([8] is a recent article on this that considers efficiency).

[9] Here *target* is a program in the partial evaluator's output language; *int* interprets an input programming language; and *source* is a program in the interpreted language.

Section 9). Further, by the second Futamura projection, *specint* is transformed into a compiler *from* problem specifications *into* programs that satisfy them:

$$compiler = [\![s11]\!](s11, specint)$$

A recent advance in this direction: *optimal* partial evaluators have been built; see [1]. An optimal partial evaluator (as defined in [9]) removes *all interpretation overhead* if *int* is a self-interpreter. In this case

$$\forall d \in Data \ . \ time_{target}(d) \le time_{source}(d)$$

Thinking further: a universal specification language would require an interpreter that can efficiently solve a range of problems in the specification, including data types, interactive programs, nondeterminism, etc. The concept of optimality provides a useful measuring stick for quality of the partial evaluator involved.

5   Conclusions: Modeling in Relation to Programming

What is the purpose of programming? There are many possibilities including
problem understanding;
clarifying cause-effect relations in experimental contexts;
enlargng the playground: increasing the number of feasible experiments;
automation;
increased *reliability;* and
implementing and systematising informal data processing procedures.

Conclusions Depend on the Used Meaning of "model"

1. **An analytical goal** is to understand some aspect of the real world. Here, programming is not the end-result, but can be a valuable tool (as can mathematics, statistics, chemistry, etc.). Modeling is essential.
   A useful computer tool can be a domain-specific programming language that uses programs to try out a model of a natural phenomenon and see its consequences beyond those easily seen from the defining equations, e.g., with data too large or requiring too many steps for simulation by eye or by hand. This approach is common in nuclear physics, astronomy and genetics (among others)
2. **A synthetic goal** given a specification of a problem $\mathcal{P}$, find a solution in the form of a program π. This leads to further tasks, e.g.,
   - *systematically construct* program π from $\mathcal{P}$. This can be done informally or formally.[10]
   - If done formally, use some form of *modeling language* to relate proposed programs $\pi, \pi', \ldots$ to problem $\mathcal{P}$.
   - *verify* that program π indeed solves problem $\mathcal{P}$.

---

[10] Dijkstra pioneered this approach in [2].

3. **A recurrent complication:** One cannot always assume the definitive problem specification is given in advance. In practice, building a program to satisfy a specification almost always involves *coevolution* of both specification and program. How easy this is depends on the specification language, and the problem domain.
4. **Executable specifications:** The "systematic construction" line of thought suggests that a specification be thought of as a (meta-)program in an appropriate general-purpose model implementation language. On the other hand, the design and implementation of a general-purpose specification language seems quite challenging.
5. **Domain specific languages (DSLs):** In the opposite direction: both analytic and synthetic goals have led to design and implementation of a wide variety of special-purpose DSLs "tuned" to various application areas[11]. In many cases, new problems can be modeled in existing DSLs. However conceptually new problems frequently arise that are not solvable in an existing DSL, so a more general-purpose solution as in Sect. 4.6 seems desirable.

Acknowledgements. Remarks made by an anonymous referee, and D. Berezun and K. Havelund, led to substantial improvements to this paper.

References

1. Brown, M., Palsberg, J.: Jones-optimal partial evaluation by specialization-safe normalization. PACMPL **2**(POPL), 1401–1428 (2018)
2. Dijkstra, W.E.: A Discipline of Programming. Prentice-Hall, Englewood Cliffs (1976)
3. Fowler, M., Scott, K.: UML Distilled - A Brief Guide to the Standard Object Modeling Language, 2nd edn. Addison-Wesley-Longman, Boston (2000)
4. Grumberg, O., Veith, H. (eds.): 25 Years of Model Checking. LNCS, vol. 5000. Springer, Heidelberg (2008). https://doi.org/10.1007/978-3-540-69850-0
5. Harel, D.: Statecharts: a visual formalism for complex systems. Sci. Comput. Programm. **8**(3), 231–274 (1987)
6. Huth, M.R.A., Ryan, M.D.: Logic in Computer Science - Modelling and Reasoning About Systems. Cambridge University Press, Cambridge (2004)
7. Jones, N.D.: Computability and Complexity - From a Programming Perspective. Foundations of Computing Series. MIT Press, Cambridge (1997)
8. Jones, N.D.: A swiss pocket knife for computability. In: Semantics, Abstract Interpretation, and Reasoning about Programs, pp. 1–17 (2013). https://doi.org/10.4204/EPTCS.129.1
9. Jones, N.D., Gomard, C.K., Sestoft, P.: Partial Evaluation and Automatic Program Generation. Prentice Hall International Series in Computer Science. Prentice Hall, Upper Saddle River (1993)
10. Kuhn, T.S.: The Structure of Scientific Revolutions. University of Chicago Press, Chicago 2012 (1962)

---

[11] Many exist, for example specialised to database queries, differential equations, hardware design, parsing, typesetting, etc. Mernik et. al. give an overview in [11].

11. Mernik, M., Heering, J., Sloane, A.M.: When and how to develop domain-specific languages. ACM Comput. Surv. **37**(4), 316–344 (2005)
12. Milner, R.: Communication and Concurrency. Prentice Hall, PHI Series in Computer Science (1989)
13. Milner, R., Tofte, M.: Commentary on Standard ML. MIT Press, Cambridge (1991)
14. Popper, K.: The Logic of Scientific Discovery. Routledge, London (1959, 2002)
15. Wegner, P.: Research Paradigms in computer science. In: International Conference on Software Engineering (1976)
16. Wikipedia: Top-Down and Bottom-Up Design. Wikipedia (2018)

Definition of Modeling vs. Programming Languages

Maged Elaasar[✉]

Jet Propulsion Laboratory, California Institute of Technology,
Pasadena, CA 91109, USA
elaasar@jpl.nasa.gov

Abstract. Modeling languages (like UML and SysML) are those used in model-based specification of software-intensive systems. Like programming languages, they are defined using their syntax and semantics. However, both kinds of languages are defined by different communities, and in response to different requirements, which makes their methodologies and tools different. In this paper, we highlight the main differences between the definition methodologies of modeling and programming languages. We also discuss the impact of these differences on language tool support. We illustrate our ideas using examples from known programming and modeling languages. We also present a case study, where we analyze the definition of a new modeling language called the Ontology Modeling Language (OML). We highlight the requirements that have driven OML definition and explain how they are different from those driving typical programming languages. Finally, we discuss how these differences are being abstracted away using new language definition tools.

Keywords: Modeling · Programming · Syntax · Semantics · API Methodology

1 Introduction

Model-driven engineering (MBE) is a methodology that focuses on creating and exploiting models in the engineering of software-intensive systems. A model, expressed in a modeling language, is typically used to capture, communicate, and analyze the design of a software system. In a variant of the methodology, called model-driven development (MDD), the model is then transformed using a code generator into code in some programming language.

Both modeling and programming languages are computer languages that are defined in terms of their syntax and semantics. The syntax specifies the abstractions that can be used to describe a system, whereas the semantics specifies the meanings assigned to these abstractions. Moreover, the syntax can be specified in two levels: abstract and concrete. The abstract syntax specifies the abstractions or building blocks of expressions in a language (e.g., classes, fields, methods in the Java language) independently of their representations. The concrete syntax specifies the representations (using textual or graphical notation) of those abstractions. Both syntaxes are often

© Springer Nature Switzerland AG 2018
T. Margaria and B. Steffen (Eds.): ISoLA 2018, LNCS 11244, pp. 35–51, 2018.
https://doi.org/10.1007/978-3-030-03418-4_3

mappable to each other, although the typical direction and completeness of these mappings may vary between modeling and programming languages.

The syntax of a programming language like Java, Scala or C++ is typically specified using a context-free grammar expressed in a notation like Backus-Naur Form (BNF) [1]. A BNF grammar consists of a set of terminal symbols, non-terminal symbols, and production rules (in the form <non-terminal> ::= <expression>) that transform each non-terminal into a sequence of terminals and/or non-terminals. This specifies the concrete textual syntax of a programming language. Moreover, the abstract syntax is also (automatically) derivable from such grammar. It is represented as an abstract syntax tree (AST) that is made up of non-terminal nodes. However, such AST is context-free. Performing context analysis (gathering and checking semantics) on the AST is typically encoded manually in some imperative programming language.

On the other hand, the abstract syntax of a modeling language, like UML [2], SysML [3] or BPMN [4], is typically specified using a meta (higher-level) modeling language like Meta Object Facility (MOF) [5]. A MOF-based metamodel specifies the abstractions of a language as meta classes, that have properties, operations, relationships (e.g., generalizations, compositions, cross references) to other meta classes, and well-formedness rules, expressed in a rule language like the Object Constraint Language (OCL) [13]. Thus, unlike a BNF grammar, a MOF metamodel captures the semantic context of a modeling language (at least partially). Moreover, the concrete syntax of a modeling language is typically defined independently of the abstract syntax. There can be several concrete syntaxes for a language and each of them can be textual and/or graphical. While there are some standards that can be used to describe those concrete syntaxes, and their relationship to the abstract syntax, they are typically defined less formally using English prose. On the other hand, there exist some de facto frameworks that are widely used to specify those concrete syntaxes. (More on this in Sect. 2.2).

Furthermore, modeling languages differ from programming languages in terms of their tooling concerns and approaches. For example, modeling languages tend to have standard APIs, hence many general-purpose tools (e.g., query engines, transformation engines, visualizers) can be developed generically for them. Also, models are often stored in persistent storage in terms of their abstract syntax, as opposed (or in addition) to their concrete syntax. This persistence is often standardized (in XML or JSON). Also, models can grow in size dramatically and hence sometimes get persisted in databases (as opposed to files) to enhance their scalability. Also, in a collaborative editing environment, models often need to be compared and merged in terms of their AST as opposed to the persistent format. Models also often need to be visualized using a variety of notations and viewpoints.

In this paper, we show how the methodology of defining modeling languages often differ from that of programming languages, in terms of abstract syntax, concrete syntaxes and semantics. We also discuss the implications of these differences on language tooling concerns and approaches. We also report on a case study where a new modeling language, called the Ontology Modeling Language (OML) [6], has been defined. We highlight the requirements of OML, discuss how some of them may be different than typical ones for programming languages, and show how they have been addressed in the modeling language methodology. In addition, we reflect on the state of the practice in language definition today and highlight some technologies that have the potential to bring the two approaches closer together.

The rest of the paper is organized as follows. Section 2 describes the differences in the methodologies for defining programming vs. modeling languages. A discussion of the impact of these differences on language tooling is given in Sect. 3. Section 4 presents a case study where the OML modeling language has been defined. Some reflections on the state of the practice are offered in Sect. 5. Finally, Sect. 6 concludes the paper and outlines future works.

2   Definition of Modeling vs. Programming Languages

In this section, we describe the different methodologies of defining programming and modeling languages. We structure the description along three dimensions: abstract syntax, concrete syntax, and semantics.

2.1   Programming Language Definition

Concrete Syntax. The concrete syntax of a programming language is typically textual and specified with a context-free grammar that is expressed using a common notation like Backus-Naur Form (BNF) or Extended BNF (EBNF) [7] (which helps deal with some limitations of BNF like the definition of repeatable elements). Such notation allows specifying the textual syntax in two levels: a lexical level and a grammar level. The lexical level is specified with regular expressions that determine how characters form tokens (terminals). The grammar level is specified with production rules that determine how tokens (terminals) form phrases (non-terminals). For example, the following BNF grammar snippet specifies the syntax of simple algebraic expressions:

<expr> ::= <term> "+" <expr> | <term>
<term> ::= <factor> "*" <term> | <factor>
<factor> ::= "(" <expr> ")" | <constant>
<constant> ::= number

With such grammar, the expression '(1 + 2) * (3 + 5)' can be represented as a valid expression in the grammar. First, a lexer turns the sequence of characters into terminal tokens (e.g., '(', '1', '+', '2', etc.). Then, a parser groups the terminals into non-terminals that are added as nodes in an abstract syntax tree (AST) using the BNF production rules. For example, the AST of the above expression can be represented in memory as [term, [factor, [expr, constant, constant]], [factor, [expr, constant, constant]], where each node is represented as [parent, child1, child2, ...]. When such AST is printed, it can show as ['*', ['(', ['+', '1', '2'], ')'], ['(', ['+', '3', '5'], ')']]. Both the lexer and the parser for a programming language can usually be auto-generated from the BNF grammar of a language, as supported by tools like Lex-Yacc [8] or Antlr [9].

Abstract Syntax. As mentioned before, BNF is a context-free grammar, which means the AST produced based on it is also context free. This means that the AST just shows the composition of the non-terminals, without interpreting what they semantically mean nor how they are related semantically to each other. This is left to an interpreter that processes the AST and either adds to it semantic context, or produces another tree with semantic context. To clarify what is meant by this, consider the following example program file (example.java) expressed in the Java language:

> **package** a;
> **import** a.b.C;
> **public class** D **extends** C {
> }

This file could be parsed using a (pseudo) Java BNF grammar as ['example.java', [package, 'a'], [import, 'a.b.C'], [class, 'D', [super, 'C']]]. With this AST, we can see the structure of the Java file, but what we cannot see yet is how the nodes of that structure relate to each other. For example, the fact that class D belongs to package 'a', and that class C belongs to package 'a.b' is not automatically inferred by the parser. Rather, this information is added by the Java compiler that processes the AST to add the type information and creates the cross references. Only then, the AST of a program becomes ready to be checked for well-formedness. A compiler is usually coded manually as a visitor pattern over the AST.

Semantics. The semantics of a programming language refers to the formal meanings of the abstractions of a language. Three kinds of semantics can be identified:

- *Denotational semantics*: where language abstractions are mapped to mathematical objects that describe the meanings of those abstractions.
- *Axiomatic semantics*: where assertions about language abstractions and their relationships to other abstractions are specified
- *Operational semantics*: where abstractions are interpreted as transitions between state in some state machine.

While some of these semantics (e.g., axiomatic) can be checked by a compiler, others (e.g., operational) are checked at run-time. Bothe the compiler and the runtime system are different applications that are written separately.

2.2   Modeling Language Definition

Abstract Syntax. The abstract syntax of a modeling language is explicitly specified as a metamodel (a higher-level model) in a formalism such as the Meta Object Facility (MOF), defined by the Object Management Group (OMG). MOF is used to define many popular modeling languages like UML and BPMN. MOF is defined in two levels, Complete MOF (CMOF) and Essential MOF (EMOF). The latter is much simpler and has more adoption in the industry thanks to its popular Java implementation on the Eclipse platform called Ecore, which is provided by the Eclipse Modeling Framework (EMF) [11]. Moreover, Ecore itself has a textual syntax called Xcore [12].

A metamodel, defined in Ecore, specifies a modeling language as a set of interrelated classifiers. A classifier can either be a primitive type or a class. Primitive types, like Integer, Boolean, and String classify literal values. Classes, on the other hand, represent abstractions in the language. A class can have a number of structural features and operations and can specialize a number of other classes (in a taxonomy). A structural feature can either be an attribute, typed by a primitive type, or a reference, typed by a class. An operation, which may have a number of input parameters and a return type, represents behavior offered by the class. A class can also be constrained by a set of invariants expressed in a language called OCL, which supports a subset of first order predicate logic. In addition to invariants, OCL can also be used to specify body conditions of operations (i.e., conditions on the results of operations).

Unlike the abstract syntax of programming languages, which is generated in memory as a result of parsing and not persisted, that of modeling languages is typically persisted independently of the concrete syntax, and especially when the concrete syntax is only partial, i.e. does not represents all the information. A common specification for persisting MOF models is called the XML Metadata Interchange (XMI) [14], which maps the MOF syntax to XML.

It is also worth noting that MOF is not the only formalism to specify modeling languages in. Another common on is a UML profile, which is UML's extensibility mechanism. A UML profile creates a language with abstractions (called stereotypes) that are extensions of some meta classes of UML. One of those profile-defined languages is SysML, which extends UML to allow for modeling systems. An example of a SysML stereotype is called Block, which extends Class from UML to model a physical block.

Concrete Syntax. The concrete syntax of programming languages is usually defined as a view on its abstract syntax. Specifically, for meta classes in a metamodel, there could be rules in a concrete syntax specification that define how instances of those meta classes are depicted. A modeling language can have one or more concrete syntaxes, each of which can be textual or graphical.

Textual Concrete Syntax. While there is no dedicated specification for the specification of the textual syntax of a modeling language, there is a specification from OMG, called Model to Text (MTL) [15] that can be used to map the abstract syntax to some textual notation. The specification allows defining a textual template with embedded tags that have OCL expressions that query the model and convert the information into text. An implementation of this specification for EMF-based models exists and is called Acceleo [16]. However, MTL does not aim at producing a canonical mapping from an abstract syntax to its textual syntax, nor does not support the other mapping direction.

Furthermore, one technology that has become the defacto standard for defining the textual syntax of EMF modeling languages is called Xtext [17], which support bidirectional mapping between an EMF-based metamodel and an EBNF grammar for the language. Xtext supports both the generation of a metamodel from a given EBNF grammar and vice versa. Either way, Xtext provides the ability to specify a model using text that conforms to an EBNF grammar and automatically parses it in memory into the corresponding instance of the metamodel. The opposite direction is also supported.

Graphical Concrete Syntax. Modeling language specifications have historically described the graphical syntax informally using English prose. However, recently, an OMG specification, called Diagram Definition (DD) [18], emerged to address this limitation. DD allows the specification of a graphical syntax by specifying a unidirectional mapping from the abstract syntax metamodel of a modeling language to a graphical notation metamodel (e.g., of 2D graphics). This model-to-model mapping can be specified using a MOF-based mapping language like the Query/View/Transformation (QVT) [19]. An implementation of this specification is provided for EMF in the Papyrus modeling tool [20].

Furthermore, there exist several technologies that support the implementation of graphical syntaxes for EMF-based modeling languages. The first is the Graphical Modeling Framework (GMF) [21] and second is Sirius [22]. Both technologies support bidirectional mapping between an abstract syntax model and its graphical notation. However, GMF supports an imperative-style mapping, while Sirius supports a declarative-style mapping (using a mapping model).

Semantics. Unlike a BNF grammar for a programming language, the abstract syntax for modeling language is not context-free, but rather declaratively specifies the axiomatic semantics of the language. For example, the UML metamodel specifies that meta class UML::Class can reference another UML::Class as its superclass, contains one or more UML::Property as attributes, each of which references its UML::Type, etc. Also, the UML::Type meta class has a well-formedness rule expressed in OCL as '*not self-> closure(supertype)-> contains(self)*', which means a type cannot have cyclic inheritance. This means just by using the metamodel, we can check the conformance of a model to the abstract syntax, including its axiomatic semantics.

However, unlike programming languages, many modeling languages do not have (at least complete) denotational nor operational semantics. For example, the semantics of the UML has a fair amount of variability that is open to semantic interpretation. For example, the direction of the association arrows indicate that it is efficient to navigate from the source object to the target object of the association, but it is a variation point what this exactly means. The focus of those modeling languages is on communication of ideas rather than reasoning, simulation or execution. For example, the Business Motivation Model (BMM) [23] language is a way to describe the strategy for a business.

However, some modeling languages have formal semantics, and in those cases the (denotational and operational) semantics are specified similarly to programming languages. For example, Foundational UML (fUML) [24] is an executable language that provides well-defined operational (execution) semantics for a subset of UML.

3   Tooling of Modeling vs. Programming Languages

In this section, we discuss the differences between the tooling concerns of modeling and programming languages. These differences are mostly due to differences in language engineering requirements between the two. We structure the discussion along several axes, and relate them to the methodologies in Sect. 2 then it makes sense.

3.1   API

The API of a language refers to the interface through which a description specified in the language can be manipulated by tools on a given platform. Examples of such tools are editors, compilers, visualizers, interpreters, etc. In the case of a programming language, there is typically no specification of an API, at least not a single API. However, tools, like Antlr, can usually generate an API that corresponds to the context-free AST of the language, along with a visitor pattern that can be implemented to add semantic annotations (e.g., typing and cross references) or generate another context-specific API, which can used to perform further analysis like execution, visualization, etc.

On the other hand, modeling languages tend to have API that is fully derived from the metamodel, hence already incorporates all typing and cross referencing. Such API includes a factory pattern to instantiate every concrete class, getter and setter methods to access properties of classes and methods corresponding to the class operations. In addition, the generated API often extends an abstract (reflective) API provided by the tool (e.g., EMF) for all languages. Such API allows the definition of generic tools (e.g., editors, query engines, transformation engines) that work on different modeling languages in a consistent fashion.

3.2   Editors

An editor for a language allows creating descriptions in that language. They support features like content assist, auto completion, validation, syntax highlighting, formatting, refactoring, etc. Many of these features have some aspects that apply generically to all languages (in a given family), and some aspects that are specific to a language. Therefore, it is common to implement editors using frameworks that provide those generic aspects and can be extended to support the specific of a given language.

One such framework for programming languages is the Language Server Protocol (LSP) [25], which defines a protocol used between an editor and a language server that provides services like auto completion, go to definition, find all references, etc. The LSP has been implemented by several editors like Eclipse and Visual Studio Code for a variety of programming languages like Java, Python, and C++. In addition, editors for modeling languages with textual syntaxes, like those defined with Xtext, also implement the LSP. But, thanks to the reflective API provided by EMF, the implementation of LSP can be done in a generic way for all modeling languages.

Similarly, modeling languages with graphical syntaxes have editor frameworks (e.g., GMF and Sirius) that can support modeling languages generically thanks to the reflective API of EMF. For example, deleting an object from a model can almost always be implemented generically for any language, since removing an object from a model removes all its contained elements and their cross references.

It is also worth noting that since a modeling language can have multiple (textual or graphical) concrete syntaxes, that their editors or IDEs can allow working with those different concrete syntaxes or switching between them.

3.3 Persistence

Both programs and models can be stored in persistent storage. However, they differ in what gets stored and how it is stored. For a programming language, the concrete textual syntax is what get stored and it is almost always stored in files. The abstract syntax, on the other hand, is derived in memory when the files are parsed by compilers.

On the other hand, for a model, what gets stored can be either the abstract syntax only, the concrete syntax only, or both. For example, when a language has a textual concrete syntax, that syntax is what gets stored only, since the abstract syntax can unambiguously be derived upon parsing. However, when a language has a graphical syntax, both the graphical syntax and the abstract syntax are stored (together or in separate storage). In this case. the graphical syntax would contain its own details (layouts, styles) and reference the abstract syntax for the sematic details. Moreover, unlike a program, a model can also be defined exclusively using its abstract syntax APIs. In this case, only the abstract syntax is stored. When the model is stored in files, there are standards (e.g., XMI) that provide generic persistence rules based on the model's metamodel. This relieves the language developer from specifying a language-specific persistence format.

Furthermore, unlike a program, a model can also be stored in a database. While there are no standards for this, there are some technologies that support this like Connected Data Objects (CDO) [26], which is able to persist an EMF model in databases. This is possible thanks to the metamodel of the language and its EMF reflective API.

3.4 Configuration Management

Configuration Management (CM) refers to the ability to manage a program or a model in a repository that supports branching and version control. Many file-based CM systems, like Git [27], supports this generically. An important feature of those systems is the ability to compare versions of the files and calculate their differences. This supports auditing the change history of a file, but is also a prerequisite for merging changes to the same file by different contributors, which may have conflicts to resolve.

The compare/merge feature is therefore important to both programs and models since they are expected to have multiple contributors. In the case of programs and models with textual syntaxes, the typical support calculates textual differences. However, such support is not ideal because non-conflicting changes may sometimes appear on the same lines, hence often get misclassified as conflicts.

In the case of models that have abstract syntaxes, textual differencing is not effective as users do not typically work with the textual storage format directly. Instead, thanks to the reflective API of metamodels, there exist differencing and merging frameworks (e.g., EMF Compare [28]) that work on the model level, showing the users the changes in terms of the abstractions they work with. However, those changes are often at a lower level of abstraction than the actual editing operations that caused them in the editor. That is why some differencing frameworks offer ways to aggregate the lower changes into higher level changes. An example of this situation is when a model also has a graphical syntax that is stored separately. Changes in related abstract and graphical syntaxes can be correlated and presented together.

3.5   Extensibility

Extensibility refers to the ability of syntax or semantics of a language to be extended to cover other concerns. In the case of programming language, this is often a feature that needs to be built into the language. For example, Java supports the notion of annotations that can be put on its main abstractions (e.g., classes, attributes, methods) to add more information to them. In this case, interpreters can be developed to process those annotations (e.g., insert extra code in methods to implement a @precondition annotation).

Similarly, modeling languages can each have its own extensibility mechanism. For example, UML's extensibility mechanism is the UML profile, which provides a set of stereotypes that can apply to UML elements to tag them or possibly add new attributes. However, another extensibility mechanism may be defined by the meta language itself, thus inherited by all its languages. For example, EMF provides an abstract class that supports having key-value annotations. Meta classes inheriting from this abstract class give themselves this extensibility feature.

3.6   Integration Between Languages

It may sometimes be desirable to integrate different languages together. For example, one programming language may embed expressions from another programming language that is better able to address a concern (e.g., it is possible to embed expressions in Assembly within a C program). Another example is a modeling language that allows its elements to reference elements from another language (e.g., BPMN allows its elements to reference elements from any other model including UML). In both cases, the language definition can be designed to allow such support (both BNF and MOF allow a language to import definitions from other languages).

However, in modeling languages, this integration can also be free if one language is an extension of another (or of a common parent language). This is because when a class in a modeling language references another class, objects of the first class can reference objects of the second class or any of its subclasses, even if they are not defined by the same language. Moreover, if the reference is typed by the most abstract base class (defined by the meta language), then it can point to any object in any language.

4 Case Study

In this section, we report on a case study where we analyze the methodology of defining a new modeling language for a data warehouse system. We show how the language engineering requirements for this modeling language differ from those of a typical programming language, which also explains the differences in methodology and tool support. We first define the language requirements then analyze them. After that, we define the new language itself, specifically its abstract syntax, concrete syntax and semantics. Finally, we explain how this definition addresses the language requirements.

4.1 Language Requirements

The language we focus on is called the Ontology Modeling Language (OML), which was developed at the Jet Propulsion Laboratory (JPL) to be the lingua franca of a new data warehouse system for systems engineering. The basic requirements for the language include the ability to represent multi-viewpoint descriptions of a system that are authored in different system authoring tools, check the well-formedness and consistency of those descriptions, configuration manage them, and make them available for analysis and reporting.

4.2 Requirement Analysis

The main requirement of the language is support multi-view knowledge representation. Hence, the first candidate language that was considered for that was the Web Ontology Language (OWL) 2 [29]. OWL 2 has desirable characteristics that can help address this problem: (a) it supports organizing information as triples (subject, predicate, object) in different ontologies, which facilitates tracking the provenance of information coming from each authoring tool, and (b) supports storing the triples in textual files using multiple formats (e.g., XML, JSON, N-triples), which can be easily configuration managed in widely available file-based C/M systems (like Git).

Moreover, since OWL 2 supports multiple sublanguages, one of them was chosen, which was OWL 2 DL (Description Logic). This sublanguage (a) has description logic semantics, which provides good expressive power for system descriptions, (b) supports inference-based reasoning, which can help check the well-formedness and consistency of system descriptions, (c) has a defacto Java based API called Jena [30], and (d) supports an expressive pattern-based query language called SPARQL [31].

However, OWL 2 DL also has some undesirable characteristics for use on this problem, including: (a) there are multiple ways of using OWL 2 DL to encode the system descriptions, some of which can lead to unexpected results or cause scalability issues during the reasoning process, (b) the OWL syntax is at a lower level of abstraction making the system descriptions verbose, (c) the storage of triples in a file is not stable as the collection is not ordered, which may lead to unexpected deltas when ontologies (generated automatically from authoring tools) get committed to a C/M system, (d) the language has no visual notation that can help abstract out the information for users, (e) the Java API is mutable, which makes it harder to use to perform expensive analyses in a distributed computing environment (e.g., Spark [32]), and (f) the Java API cannot be used on an important tooling platform, which is a web browser.

4.3 OML Language Definition

The list of desirable and undesirable characteristics above has motivated the design of a new language, called OML, that retains the benefits of OWL 2 DL but also addresses its limitations in this context. In this section, we discuss the design of OML, specifically in terms of its abstract syntax, concrete syntax, semantics and API.

Abstract Syntax. OML is designed as a modeling language for ontologies, hence follows the common practice of defining the abstract syntax first with a metamodel. In this case, we chose to define it in Ecore (to leverage EMF's large ecosystem of tools), and in particular using its Xcore textual syntax. A simplified subset of the language metamodel in Xcore is shown in Fig. 1 (for brevity).

```
package oml {
    class Terminology {
        String iri
        Boolean isOpen
        contains Terms [*] terms
    }
    abstract class Term {
        String name
    }
    abstract class Entity extends Term {}
    class Aspect extends Entity {}
    class Concept extends Entity {}
    class Relation extends Term {
        refers Entity [1] source
        refers Entity [1] target
    }
}
```

Fig. 1. A simplified subset of the OML metamodel expressed in Xcore

The main abstractions (e.g., oml:Terminology, oml:Concept, oml:Aspect, oml: Relationship) are modeled as first class concepts in OML, as opposed to the much generic equivalent concepts in OWL 2 DL (e.g., owl:Ontology is used to represent either a terminology ontology or a description ontology, while owl:Class is used to represent a concept, an aspect, or a relationship between them). This makes modeling in OML more precise and also concise (more on this below).

Also, other desirable features of OWL 2 DL are maintained in OML. For example, the ability to preserve the provenance of information by keeping the information exported from every system tool in a separate OML terminologies is supported. Also, the ability to specify design patterns 10 in foundational (base) terminologies then specialize them in every discipline terminology is preserved. Moreover, the ability to create terminologies with open or closed world assumptions is retained in OML. Also, all the structural feature collections (e.g., Terminology:terms) in the metamodel are defined as ordered so that the persistence of an abstract model is stable.

Concrete Syntax. Several concrete syntaxes have been defined for OML to address different use cases. One of them is a textual syntax that was defined using an Xtext grammar (Fig. 2). The grammar is designed to work with the OML metamodel and is meant to be enable users to author ontologies with a text editor. This is mostly used to design terminologies representing the vocabularies of systems engineering disciplines. Such ontologies tend to be small in size, and configuration managed as text files.

```
grammar OML with org.eclipse.xtext.common.Terminals

generate oml "http://OML"

Terminology:
    (isOpen?='open')? 'terminology' iri=ID
    '{'
        (statements+=TerminologyStatement)*
    '}';

TerminologyStatement:
    Entity | Relation ;

Entity:
    Aspect | Concept;

Aspect:
    'aspect' name=ID;

Concept:
    'concept' name=ID;

Relation:
    'relation' name=ID '{'
        'source' '=' source=[Entity]
        'target' '=' target=[Entity]
    '}';
```

Fig. 2. A simplified subset of the OML textual syntax expressed in Xtext

An example of a model in OML representing a simple terminology of system structure is shown in Fig. 3. The terminology defines two concepts, a Block and an Interface and a relationship Exposes between them. An equivalent model defined in OWL 2 DL turtle format is shown in Fig. 4. Notice how the OML syntax is more readable, concise and accurate (all terms in the OWL 2 DL format are defined with owl: Class making it harder to understand the Exposes relationship for example).

```
open terminology structure {
   concept Block
   concept Interface
   relationship Exposes {
      source = Block
      target = Interface
   }
}
```

Fig. 3. A simple model in OML textual syntax showing a structure terminology

```
<structure> a owl:Ontology .
<#Block> a owl:Class .
<#Interface> a owl:Class .
<#Eposes> a owl:Class .
<#source>
    a rdfs:Property ;
    rdfs:domain <#Exposes> ;
    rdfs:range <#Block> .
<#target>
    a rdfs:Property ;
    rdfs:domain <#Exposes> ;
    rdfs:range <#Interface> .
```

Fig. 4. A simple model in OWL 2 DL syntax showing a structure terminology

Another concrete syntax that was designed for OML is the OML Zip representation. In this representation, elements of the same type in one OML ontology are represented together as a JSON array, ordered by 'iri', and stored in a JSON document (Fig. 5). Then all JSON documents that belong to one ontology are put together into a zip archive. This syntax is not meant for users to author in directly, but is rather constructed by API when system descriptions are read from system authoring tools and converted to OML in order to be managed by the data warehouse. This representation is efficient for this use case since terminologies in this case tend to be much larger in size than vocabulary ontologies, hence will have a smaller footprint in this compressed syntax. This format also allows writing an algorithm to detect differences between two OML models very efficient, as deltas can be reduced down to changed lines, as opposed to structural deltas that result from complex structural comparisons. Finally, this format allows every type to be stored as an array of objects of the same length and shape, which makes loading them into columnar databases efficient for analysis.

The last concrete syntax for OML is a high-level diagrammatic syntax that resembles a class diagram, and can be used to visualize the system description terminologies. This helps users understand the system design. Such diagrammatic syntax has been defined using the Sirius framework (Fig. 6). A terminology is shown with a box whose name appears in top left corner, a concept appears as a box within it with a centered text, and a relationship appears as an arrow from its source to its target with its name below.

```
"terminologies": {[
  {"iri": "structure", "isOpen": true}
]}

"concepts": {[
  {"iri": "structure#Block", "name": "Block"},
  {"iri": "structure#Interface", "name": "Interface"}
]}

"relationships": {[
  {"iri": "structure#Exposes", "name": "Exposes",
   "source": "structure#Block",
   "target": "structure#Interface"}
]}
```

Fig. 5. A simple model in OML JSON Zip format showing a structure terminology

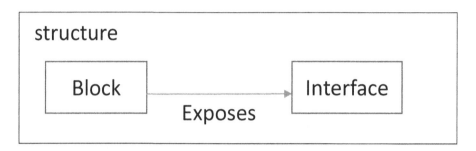

Fig. 6. A simple model in OML graphical notation showing a structure terminology

Semantics. The axiomatic semantics of OML has been encoded in the OML meta-model. However, its denotational semantics are defined by mapping its abstractions to those of OWL 2 DL, which has Description Logic semantics. This mapping (omitted here for brevity but alluded to by showing OML and OWL 2 examples in Figs. 3 and 4) is invoked before the OML ontologies is analyzed. The resulting OWL representation is loaded into a database (a triple store), then an inference engine is run on it to deduce new axioms from asserted axioms. Both sets of axioms can then be queried using a SPQRQL expression sent to a SPARQL query endpoint using the Jena API.

API. Defining the abstract syntax of OML with EMF provides it with a mutable Java API (e.g., factory pattern with named create methods, named getters/setter, etc.) that extends the framework-defined reflective API (e.g., EFactory::create, EObject:: eGet, EObject::eSet, etc.). Such API allows OML to leverage the large EMF ecosystem of tools. For example, a textual editor was developed using the Xtext framework and a graphical editor was developed using the Sirius framework. Both editors can be used by users to author vocabulary terminologies. The Java API also simplifies the implementation of extract-transform-load (ETL) interfaces to system tools, which can read system descriptions, transform them to OML, and persist them in the OML Zip syntax.

In addition to the default Java API, two other APIs were generated for OML based on the same abstract syntax metamodel (using custom code generators). One of them is an immutable functional API in Scala. This API is used to read and query OML data for analysis purposes. Thanks to the immutability of this API, it makes writing analysis scripts with it safer and easier to distribute (for example, on a distributed computing platform like Spark). The last API is a JavaScript API that allows manipulating OML data in web browsers, which is used to visualize OML data in web applications.

5 Reflection

After having discussed how the requirements of modeling and programming languages can be different, hence can affect the language definition methodologies and tooling concerns, the real question is whether the two approaches are fundamentally different.

One may be tempted to think of modeling languages as typically informal, highly abstract, and visual until they learn that some modeling languages have very well-defined execution semantics and textual notation (e.g., ALF [33]). On the other hand, one may think of programming languages as fundamentally low-level and general-purpose, until they learn about high-level programming languages that translates into other languages (e.g., Xtend [34] translating into Java, and JSX [35] translating into JavaScript) and learn about domain-specific languages (e.g., R for statistical computations [36]).

It is important to realize that the language engineering requirements of both families of languages are getting closer and hence their methodologies and tools will too. For example, the Xtext framework allows a domain specific language to have both a metamodel and an EBNF grammar. Which class would you classify such a language in? It is in both. Another example is the LSP framework, which allows an editor to support multiple programming and/or modeling languages.

6 Conclusions and Future Works

Modeling and programming languages are both computer languages. However, there are different language engineering requirements deriving both of them. These usually stem from the difference in priorities and objectives of the communities defining them. This explain why the methodologies and tools for these languages are different.

In this paper, we highlight and discuss the different methodologies of defining modeling vs. programming languages, especially in terms of their abstract syntax, concrete syntax and semantics. We also discussed the implications of these differences on the language tooling, in terms of API, editor, persistence, configuration management, extensibility and integration between languages. We then reported on a case study where we analyzed how a new language, called OML, was designed to satisfy its unique requirements. We then reflected on how these design decisions have addressed the requirements and influenced the language's tool support.

Going forward, we plan to investigate ways to bridge the gap between modeling and programming languages, especially in terms of tool support. We believe that each community can learn a lot from the other. For example, we think that programming language tools should have structural compare/merge support that is akin to that available to modeling languages. We also think that the semantic of modeling languages should be formalized in similar ways to programming languages.

Acknowledgement. The research was carried out at the Jet Propulsion Laboratory, California Institute of Technology, under a contract with the National Aeronautics and Space Administration.

Disclaimer. Reference herein to any specific commercial product, process, or service by trade name, trademark, manufacturer, or otherwise, does not constitute or imply its endorsement by the United States Government or the Jet Propulsion Labor.

References

1. Hopcroft, J., Ullman, J.: Introduction to Automata Theory, Languages, and Computation. Addison-Wesley, Reading (1979)
2. Object Management Group: OMG Unified Modeling Language, version 2.5.1 (2017). http://www.omg.org/spec/UML/2.5.1/
3. Object Management Group: OMG System Modeling Language, version 1.5 (2017). http://www.omg.org/spec/SysML/1.5/
4. Object Management Group: Business Process Model And Notation, version 2.0.2 (2014). http://www.omg.org/spec/BPMN/2.0.2/
5. Object Management Group: Meta Object Facility, version 2.5.1 (2016). http://www.omg.org/spec/MOF/2.5.1/
6. Jet Propulsion Laboratory: Ontology Modeling Language (OML) Workbench (2018). https://github.com/JPL-IMCE/gov.nasa.jpl.imce.oml.core
7. Scowen, R.: Extended BNF — A generic base standard. In: Software Engineering Standards Symposium (1993)
8. Levine, J., Mason, T., Brown, D.: `Lex & Yacc,' O'Reilly & Associates, October 1992. ISBN: 1565920007
9. Parr, T.: "ANTLR". http://www.antlr.org/
10. Gamma, E., Helm, R., Johnson, R., Vlissides, J.: Design Patterns: Elements of Reusable Object-Oriented Software. Addison-Wesley, Reading (1995)
11. Steinberg, D., Budinsky, F., Paternostro, M., Merks, E.: EMF: Eclipse Modeling Framework, 2nd edn. (2009)
12. Merks, E.: "Xcore". https://wiki.eclipse.org/Xcore
13. Object Management Group: Object Constraint Language, version 2.4 (2014). http://www.omg.org/spec/OCL/2.4/
14. Object Management Group: XML Metadata Interchange, version 2.5.1 (2015). http://www.omg.org/spec/XMI/2.5.1/
15. Object Management Group: MOF Model to Text Transformation Language, version 1.0 (2008). http://www.omg.org/spec/MOFM2T/1.0/
16. Obeo: Acceleo. https://www.eclipse.org/acceleo/

17. TypeFox: Xtext. https://www.eclipse.org/Xtext/
18. Object Management Group: Diagram Definition, version 1.1 (2015). http://www.omg.org/spec/DD/1.1/
19. Object Management Group: MOF Query/View/Transformation, version 1.3 (2016). http://www.omg.org/spec/QVT/1.3/
20. CEA-LIST: Papyrus. https://www.eclipse.org/papyrus/
21. Eclipse: Graphical Modeling Project (GMP). http://www.eclipse.org/modeling/gmp/
22. Obeo: Sirius. https://www.eclipse.org/sirius/
23. Object Management Group: Business Motivation Model, version 1.3 (2015). http://www.omg.org/spec/BMM/1.3/
24. Object Management Group: Semantics of a Foundational Subset for Executable UML Models, version 1.3 (2017). http://www.omg.org/spec/FUML/1.3/
25. Microsoft: Language Server Protocol. https://microsoft.github.io/language-server-protocol/
26. Eclipse: CDO Model Repository. https://projects.eclipse.org/projects/modeling.emf.cdo
27. Git. https://git-scm.com/
28. Eclipse: EMF Compare. https://www.eclipse.org/emf/compare/
29. W3C: OWL 2 Web Ontology Language Primer (2nd edn.) (2012). https://www.w3.org/TR/owl2-primer/
30. Apache: Apache Jena. https://jena.apache.org/
31. W3C: SPARQL Query Language for RDF (2008). https://www.w3.org/TR/rdf-sparql-query/
32. Apache: Apache Spark. https://spark.apache.org/
33. Object Management Group: Action Language for Foundational UML, version 1.1 (2017). http://www.omg.org/spec/ALF/1.1/
34. Eclipse: Xtend. https://www.eclipse.org/xtend/
35. React: Introducing JSX. https://reactjs.org/docs/introducing-jsx.html
36. R-Project The R Project for Statistical Analysis. https://www.r-project.org/

A Non-unified View of Modelling, Specification and Programming

Stefan Hallerstede[1(✉)], Peter Gorm Larsen[1], and John Fitzgerald[2]

[1] DIGIT, Department of Engineering, Aarhus University, Aarhus, Denmark
{sha,pgl}@eng.au.dk
[2] School of Computing, Newcastle University, Newcastle upon Tyne, UK
john.fitzgerald@ncl.ac.uk

Abstract. The languages used to express specifications, models and programs have much in common. However, in this paper we argue that because they serve different purposes, real care should be taken to distinguish them during development. Rather than seeking unification at the language level, we would recommend exploiting intersections between them where they arise. The main contribution of this paper is to point out the necessary differences and to offer evidence of situations in which common ground can be reached.

1 Introduction

We begin the discussion in this paper with a quote from the description of the 2018 ISoLA track *Towards a Unified View of Modeling and Programming*[1]: "It is the goal of the meeting to discuss the relationship between modeling, specification, and programming, with the possible objective of achieving an agreement of what a unification of these concepts would mean at an abstract level, and what it would bring as benefits on the practical level. What are the trends in the three domains: model-based engineering, formal specification and verification, and programming, and what can be considered to be unifying these domains."

We argue that such an enterprise should be pursued with great care. There is certainly potential in exploiting cross-cutting concepts, but at the same time *unification* could lead to methodologies that are impractical and limiting.

First we aim to clarify the central terms of our discussion: modelling, specification and programming. Furthermore, we need to discuss the related activities of verification and validation, and the objective of developing software in systems.

1.1 Software and Systems

Software increasingly forms a critical part of large-scale and potentially complex *systems*. We therefore begin by considering the systems engineering context.

---

[1] See http://www.isola-conference.org/isola2018/tracks.html.

© Springer Nature Switzerland AG 2018
T. Margaria and B. Steffen (Eds.): ISoLA 2018, LNCS 11244, pp. 52–68, 2018.
https://doi.org/10.1007/978-3-030-03418-4_4

We view a system as a "combination of interacting elements organised to achieve one or more stated purposes" [24]. Note that this concept of system requires the statement of purpose.

Systems engineering can be seen as the practice of creating and sustaining systems to improve the quality of life [26]. System elements are by no means all computational or susceptible to description in terms of the notations and tools employed by software engineers. However, the growing realisation that engineered systems are increasingly of cyber-physical in character has led to increasing interest in the successful synergy of software development activities with other engineering methods and tools [42].

Software is the medium in which the desired behaviour of some system elements may be expressed, in terms of both attributes and processes. Software engineering has evolved over the years to incorporate methodology from Systems Engineering (compare the editions of [48], for instance). Software is often developed in the context of systems that require multidisciplinary methodologies as illustrated by Fig. 1. To clarify the presentation we have added concrete components that are part of the self-balancing scooter model that is discussed in [11].

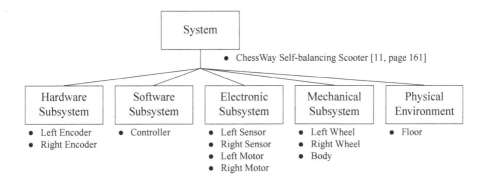

Fig. 1. Interdisciplinarity of systems engineering

Systems engineering processes encompass activities associated with agreement (such as procurement), organisational project-enabling processes (such as human resource and lifecycle management), technical management processes (such as configuration control), and technical processes from mission analysis through requirements definition to implementation, integration, validation, operation, maintenance and disposal [24]. Rigorous approaches to specification, modelling and programming can play a role in many of these processes. Figure 2 informally sketches the contribution of modelling, specification and programming to stages in a system life-cycle. There are cross-cutting concepts shared by modelling, specification and programming, but their different purposes suit their assignment to particular life-cycle phases.

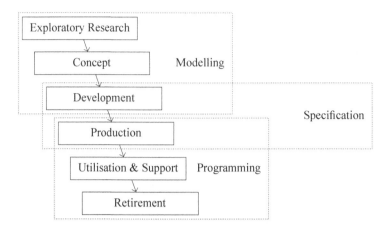

Fig. 2. Allocation of modelling, specification and programming to systems engineering phases

The need for modelling and specification arises at many points in the systems engineering life-cycle. These techniques may be applied by experts in different disciplines, working in different organisations, and using different tools on different platforms. In such an environment it would be unrealistic to impose a unified set of methods and languages top-down on each project. Such an approach would require the a priori agreement of the organisations involved, and an effort to identify the constraints this would impose on the diverse languages and methods involved.

In the remainder of this section we discuss the main concepts that are the focus of this paper: modelling, specification, programming, verification and validation. The different purposes have a strong influence on notation and methodology. Any attempt at unification must take this into account.

1.2 The Purpose of Modelling

A model is a "simplified or idealised description or conception of a particular system, situation, or process, often in mathematical terms, that is put forward as a basis for theoretical or empirical understanding, or for calculations, predictions, etc." [43], and modelling is the act of devising "a (usually mathematical) model or simplified description of (a phenomenon, system, etc.)" [43]. A model may be formal in the sense that it is represented in a notation that has a formal semantics. However, in systems and software engineering, models are frequently expressed using informal notations such as SysML [23]. In this paper we focus on formal models. Models are different from specifications in that they do not necessarily have implementation as their target objective.

1.3   The Purpose of Specification

The term *specification* may refer to "an act of identifying something precisely or of stating a precise requirement" [43], as well as the product of such an act. A specification may describe *what* a system should do without prescribing *how* the system should do it. It is considered good practice to ensure that specifications are abstract in the sense that they suppress detail that is not necessary to communicating the requirement. The term *formal specification* refers to the use of languages with mathematically described semantics in specification, permitting confirmation or refutation of properties within that semantic framework. The *purpose* of specification is thus to communicate an underlying requirement.

1.4   The Purpose of Programming

A program is a "combination of computer instructions and data definitions that enable computer hardware to perform computational control functions" [25]. Its *purpose* is to tell a machine *how* to perform a task in terms of the deployment of the particular computer's resources and capabilities. The need to work with a particular machine's characteristics means that the abstractions used in the program will often be closer to the needs of a particular architecture.

1.5   The Purpose of Verification

Verification is the "process of evaluating a system or component to determine whether the products of a given development phase satisfy the conditions imposed at the start of that phase" [25]. The most common approach to verification is *testing* where the conditions correspond to *test cases* [15]. The purpose of testing is "to show that a program does what it is intended to do and to discover program defects before it is put into use" [48]. Testing can be carried our manually or automated. Manual tests are necessary when human operators must be involved for their proper execution. Specifications may serve as the basis for testing. In fact, verification is also a "formal proof of program correctness" [25], which is in turn a "formal technique to prove mathematically that a computer program satisfies its specified requirements" [25]. Note the use of the term "specified requirements" in the latter definition. A better term would be specification in order to distinguish them from user requirements. Some ideas for unification may just be born out of an unfortunate choice of vocabulary.

1.6   The Purpose of Validation

Validation is the "process of evaluating a system or component during or at the end of the development process to determine whether it satisfies specified requirements" [25]. Validation is carried out at different stages of the development process spanning from the specification to the implementation as program. This is usually described by the V-model [45]; its upper layer deals with validation involving, in particular, user requirements and users. Its lower layer deals with verification that involves software specifications and programmers.

1.7 Brief Summary

In practice, modelling is seen as the production of abstract models that can be deployed in many development activities [26] such as in trade studies or design validation with the customer. These models are often focussed on early life-cycle stages, and make use of specific abstractions to analyse or demonstrate given types of property. Programming is seen as the production of software intended for an execution environment. A specification abstracts the aspects of the program that are related to execution, providing an abstract view of the software to be developed, restricting the possible implementations as little as possible. This is illustrated by Fig. 3.

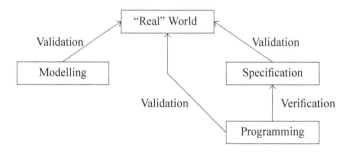

Fig. 3. Concepts and their relationships in software and systems engineering (We refer to the "Real World" but note that, in the development of a new product, this real world may not (yet) have been created!)

2 Differences Between Modelling, Specification and Programming

We have discussed the different *purposes* of modelling, specification and programming in Sect. 1. Also, the associated methods of validation and verification vary accordingly. This does not mean they have nothing in common, but the differences are important to observe because productive use depends on specific concepts being supported or available. In this section we discuss a collection of concepts important in modelling, specification and programming. Because they have a different meaning in the different areas, they might appear to be in agreement when they are not. Section 3 discusses some concrete cases in which modelling, specification and programming are mixed. The industrially successful applications appear to be those in which the differences have been exploited.

Systems. Specifications describe systems consisting of a program and its environment. The environment of a program is an essential part of a specification describing contextual assumptions about the program. The program itself is described as a component of a system causing some desired behaviour. Because an abstract description of a program and its environment are both part of the specification, we can demonstrate that they are consistent and exhibit certain desired behaviour. This can be done by evaluating the specification (if it is expressed in an executable form) or by formal proof or using both techniques. A specific technique of evaluation is *simulation* where the environment is executed and consequences of specific program designs can be explored. In programming the environment is not described explicitly. The "outside" of a program is described by isolated test cases or isolated logical assertions but this does not permit reasoning about their consistency.

Abstract models of systems often do not consider problems of implementation, and indeed do not target this. Such models may be used to obtain early feedback on the feasibility of a proposed solution (not yet thinking about software, hardware, electronics, etc.), or to explore the design space in the course of trade studies [14, 26]. The most appropriate way to specify the environment within a model may be a continuous description of its behaviour as is often the case in cyber-physical systems whereas controlling software components are described by discrete behaviour [37]. Most models are not used in later stages and the engineers building them are often not software engineers.

Abstraction. The concept of abstraction is ubiquitous in software engineering. As a consequence, what is understood by abstraction varies widely. In programming, abstraction usually refers to control abstraction and data abstraction [32]. By contract, in specification abstraction refers to the *omission* of control information or description of data representation. What is a set in a specification, might be an array, a list, a tree, etc. in a program. Usually, using programming representations in specifications makes them difficult to comprehend and analyse; using specification abstractions in programs makes them inefficient and limits their usefulness considerably. In modelling, of course, abstraction extends to the environment where different kinds of questions appear, e.g., concerning the fidelity of environment models with respect to physical reality. By contrast, concerning specification and programming one asks for correctness.

Properties. Properties specified in programs and specifications have vastly different abstraction levels. A related discussion evolving around the concept of "ground model" can be found in [5, Sec. 2.1.1]. The amount of detail in programs is usually so high that the kind of properties interesting in specifications are very hard to verify for programs. Refinement [1] bridges the gap between programs and specifications. Unfortunately, if more complicated systems are described, e.g., containing concurrency, real-time or mixed digital-analogue signals, refinement makes many program characteristics visible in the specification. Refinement is a useful proof technique but less suitable as an abstraction technique. In specifications properties are usually stated in such a way that they are close to requirements for the system. In programs they serve to a large degree to verify correctness properties for the programs. A unified approach risks mixing these problems and weaken the usefulness for specifiers and programmers alike.

Looseness. Specifications usually contain looseness (underdetermined or non-deterministic behaviour) [49]. The idea is to leave freedom to implementers when alternative realisations are equally good. The term "underdeterminedness" is only used in relation to specifications and it ensures deterministic behaviour whereas the term "non-determinism" has different meaning in specification and programming. In programming languages non-determinism is typically realised by some sort of search [21,44]. It can potentially be understood as declarative programming or as race conditions when we have concurrency. In specification languages non-determinism does not have an execution semantics in a conventional setting; it can describe a choice between (potentially) infinitely many possibilities (it is possible to either simulate with arbitrary choices or collect all possible choices [33]); it often abstracts behaviour of the environment. It is a facility to abstract away implementation detail.

Efficiency. Programming needs to be preoccupied with different kinds of efficiency depending on the target hardware. Of course, one needs to think about the trade off between run-time and memory consumption. In principle, specifications can deal with these issues, too. However, the number of factors that affect efficiency is very high, e.g., the cache layout and size, the presence of dedicated processors like graphics processors or the bandwidth of network connections. When writing programs we choose data representations that align with cache layouts, we set-up processors to carry out specific parts of computations like vector arithmetics, and we adjust the data that is transferred between nodes in a network to the available bandwidth. As the number of these concerns increases their consideration in specifications will raise the complexity and "pollute" the specification. Step by step this reduces the value of a specification given its purpose to capture core concepts and communicate them clearly. Whereas a specification at least describes software abstractly, in modelling one is not concerned with distinguishing software. Models often mix software with hardware, e.g. for communication interfaces, and abstracts behaviour by discrete models that are neither software nor hardware, e.g. the behaviour of a human operator who interacts with the system [28].

Data Structures. Data structures used in specifications and models are intentionally simple and unspecific with respect to their implementation [2]. They are numbers (with infinite domains), sets, maps and inductive types, for instance. This reduction is necessary for two main reasons: (1) it forces the specifier to focus on core concepts; (2) it frees the specifier from thinking about elaborate data-representations. Data structures used for programming are more specific like hash maps or arrays for representing maps. They also often require the programmer to think about stack or heap usage and about references or pointers passed around, possibly even aliasing. Data structures in models and specifications are geared towards reasoning. Those used in programs are geared towards efficiency.

Execution. Programs are limited in their expressiveness by what can be executed on a computer. A major feature of specifications is that they permit quantification over unbounded or infinite domains. Even if some of this can be executed on computer hardware, it can be hopelessly slow.

Specifications need not be executable, programs must be [13,20]. If specifications are made executable, they could not contain real numbers, for example. Instead they would have to use floating point or fixed point numbers. As a consequence, common algebraic laws will not hold, making reasoning about the specification difficult. Another problem with executable specifications is that their data representations will have to be close to those used for programming, and control constructs will be used to describe possible executions. This obscures specifications with much detail that is only needed for implementation but not for understanding and communicating what a system does.

In model-based systems engineering, we tend to distinguish simulation from execution more generally. Simulation is "The technique of imitating the behaviour of some situation or process (whether economic, military, mechanical, etc.) by means of a suitably analogous situation or apparatus" [43]). In the context of model-based systems engineering, simulation is the execution of a model, usually in an environment or tool specialised for the model's notation, often with the aim of validating the model against expectations or requirements [26]. Simulation usually makes simplifying assumptions, e.g., that a discrete transition does not take time, that are understood but do not detract from the simulation's purpose. A simulation permits predictions about aspects of the execution of an implementation but cannot be considered an execution by itself, because it abstracts from the physical reality and computer equipment. In models of cyber-physical systems, a simulation may integrate elements of models that are described in diverse discrete and continuous notations.

Stakeholders. Specifications and programs target very different groups of stakeholders. Whereas specifications are written at such a high level that its contents can be communicated with users and customers, programs are written for (other) programmers. This distinctions places a high demand for specifications to be a means of communication that programs do not need to satisfy. This permits programming to be far more technical including data structures, control flow and software architecture and design. These are necessary for effective programming but uninteresting for specification. In particular, in cyber-physical modelling stakeholders are from different disciplines. Modelling can permit them to communicate if it does not commit to terminology specific to only one discipline. A common language is a combination of continuous and discrete mathematics. Of course, some part described by discrete mathematics could correspond to a software specification or program, but to other stakeholders that is not important

3 Mixing Modelling, Specification and Programming

In this section we collect some evidence of different uses and combinations of modelling, specification and programming. They make different points about a unified view and do describe a unified view to various degrees. It appears difficult to generalise and make recommendations as to what a unified view should be. There is no coherent picture that would support this.

Integrated Modelling Tools. There are many examples of successful combined use of specifications with programming. In a VDM context work in the respect has been carried out in the 90's for VDMTools [34] enabling its VDM-interpreter to make use of legacy code [12]. This approach keeps a clean separation between programming and specification but permits specifications to rely on specific implementations in the C++ programming language when appropriate. This approach has been developed further in the Overture tool [35] where VDM and Java can be combined [39, 40], permitting VDM specifications to invoke Java programs and permitting Java programs to invoke VDM specifications.

Concrete Specification. The formal development support system MURAL [7] has a VDM specification [7, Appendix C] that is written in a form that could be executed. Specifications should be written on the abstraction level that is considered most appropriate for the purpose of the specification. Occasionally, this means specification is close to programming. Nevertheless, the VDM specification of MURAL permits reasoning about properties of MURAL (which is the main objective of a specification language) as opposed to the implementation in Smalltalk (where reasoning is not a concern). It has also been argued that specification and programming can be united by choosing suitable programming paradigms, e.g., for functional programming [50] or logic programming [31] or a mix of them [3]. This is of course true, if the required abstraction level permits this as in the case of the MURAL specification. But such conditions are not generally met.

Software Models. In [19] an industrial distributed train interlocking system is modelled that is responsible for ensuring safe control of routes for moving trains. The behaviour of the system is captured in the form of a co-model which combines discrete and continuous components of the system. The control logic, a distributed system, is described by an executable VDM specification. It interacts with the environment, i.e. the actual train movements, during execution and is validated by means of a co-simulation with the continuous environment model [16]. This co-model is an example where parts that are certainly not executable are mixed with parts that could be considered software. However, to become efficient software to be executed on devices of a deployed system with strong real-time and memory requirements the executable VDM specification would need to be replaced. It has been developed with a focus on clarity and understanding as one would expect for a specification, assuming the two mentioned requirements can be satisfied based on the experience of the participating domain engineers. Programming has a different focus that usually "hides" the purpose of specific program, good documentation is the common approach to describing the purpose, see e.g. [47].

Software Library. In [46] a formal B model is used directly as part of a finished software product. The model is "executed" without code generation by a constraint solver, in order to determine the feasibility of studying university courses and to generate time tables for students. The formal model itself can be viewed as a mixture of functional programming (computing derived data structures) and constraint programming. Parts of the software product, such as the graphical user interface, are still realised in Java. This approach is an example where conventional programming is combined with an executable specification in an end product. We believe that it is a necessity to support such approaches systematically because modelling, specification and programming always occur in a larger system context where appropriate technologies for different parts and components have to be chosen that are determined by constraints imposed by the system.

Multi-paradigm Programming. In [38] a formal specification is also directly "executed" in order to verify the correctness and integrity of configuration data of a railway network. This use of a formal specification for data validation exploits the mathematical abstractions offered by the B notation to describe safe network configurations abstractly. The tool loads network configuration data that is created by railway engineers and provides feedback on inconsistent data values with respect to the specified safe network configurations. Based on experience with [38,46] in [18] possible programming extensions of B are discussed and an integration with the Clojure programming language is proposed.

Mixed Monolithic Approaches. Approaches such as ProCoS [22] mix languages to provide a correctness-preserving development process. The main strength of mixed languages and methods of offering specification and programming from one hand is at the same time their major weakness when it comes to application. It is very attractive to have a seamless approach from design to code, however, for practical use in industrial projects some flexibility is needed. This usually requires bridging to existing legacy code or development methods where the strong soundness guarantees provided by a seamless approach no longer hold. It is difficult to strike a balance between theoretical and practical requirements for languages and methods that attempt to unify the different concepts. Alternatively, one has to make an early decision whether the impact of such work should be chiefly theory for science or of practical nature for engineering. Exploring the middle ground is challenging and should be done consciously with respect to the often opposing requirements.

4 Summary: Risks with Unified Approaches

Based on our experience, we briefly list several important issues that we have encountered when extending or unifying modelling, specification and programming languages.

Specifications Become Programs. Based on our experience, executability is nearly always in tension with specification abstraction [20]. There is a risk that programming concepts appropriate to the target machine, such as references and memory management, as well as considerations of execution performance, can pollute a specification to the extent that the scope of some analytic techniques can become restricted. Increasing the range of features in a specification language can make integration with other languages more difficult, although we would assert that the ability to form part of an integrated process is essential. The motivation of trying to offer specification and programming in a single package reduces the motivation to interface successfully to foreign approaches.

Insufficient Abstraction. Beginners at specification, whether practising professionals or university students, have to adopt a mental framework that focuses on understanding and analysing what is to be computed, and not how it is to be done. However, many of those entering the field have significant past experience and deep training as programmers. As a consequence, a common problem faced by beginners is the tendency to apply to specification techniques learned from programming. Typically, the result is a specification that is overly complicated [36] and difficult to reason about. There is a risk that approaches unified at the language level make it difficult to convey and practice the skills of good specification.

In order to describe the static semantics of a computer-based language the level of abstraction that enables reasoning would simply yield a boolean result. Even if such a specification was expressed using an executable subset and considered a "program" it would not be very helpful, since if an instance of the computer-based language had an error, one would get no guidance concerning its cause. In order to describe that it would be appropriate to yield instead a list of errors (and possibly warnings). This would be more helpful from a user's perspective but it does introduce noise compared to the abstract description.

Growing Methodologies. If one seeks a single unified method, there is a danger that each new application that challenges the expressibility of the language brings with it the temptation to add new features. Over time, the accumulation of features may well make it difficult for newcomers to master and moving effort from the solution of difficult engineering problems to coping with a complex language and methods. For example, in the context of the Unified Process and UML, Jacobsen states [29]: "If you take a unified process, the fundamental problem with that, you actually need to select what part of unified process you should use. The unified process is a framework, process framework comprises lots of things you can pick and choose; and you leave that to the project to identify what to pick and to choose. That takes time. You need to know the whole process to actually decide what I'm going to use. And that's not easy. Then you have to learn what to use, and you have to apply the knowledge. And finally you have to control it; it means change it because nothing is ever stable."

5   Concluding Remarks

This article argues neither in favour nor against unification, but rather to be conscious about the implications of attempts at unification. When compromises are made with respect to diverging objectives, one runs the risk of either complicating a unified approach or supporting at least one of them badly. In particular, we see the following risks:

- the unified notation and method becomes overly complex;
- the associated processes become rigid in order to cope with the complexity;
- one cannot opt in gradually because the notion, method and process become a monolithic whole;
- it becomes difficult to teach and understand.

Each of these points will reduce potential industrial impact and pick-up.

On the other hand, if these problems are avoided, a gain in productivity is possible because cross-cutting concepts can be exploited and, for instance, artefacts from design become available directly for implementation and vice versa. If this is done, one must ensure not to diminish the utility of modelling, specification and programming by attempting to cater for all needs at once.

Acknowledgments. We are grateful to our many collaborators and sponsors in projects such as DESTECS (FP7-248134), COMPASS (FP7-287829) and INTO-CPS (H2020-644047) as well as those mentioned in the appendices which collectively have formed our minds seeing the development of software in a more holistic fashion causing us to have the opinions presented in this article.

A   Mural

One of the earliest formal methods support environments, Mural, included basic facilities for constructing formal system descriptions expressed using a form of the VDM-SL notation, and validating them through manual formal proof [7]. At the core of Mural was a proof assistant implementing a logical framework supporting Natural Deduction proofs and populated with theories for the typed Logic of Partial Functions (LPF).

The logical framework was described in abstract mathematical terms and consequently could be easily modified and developed as the requirements for the support tool evolved. This mathematical description "allowed a separation of concerns, since we could concentrate solely on the issues of importance at that level of abstraction." [7] The description was manually rendered as a VDM specification and expanded to a complete functional specification of the Mural kernel. In order to permit validation of user interaction aspects, the formal specification was prototyped by manual translation to Smalltalk. Rather than developing the full implementation on the basis of the initial prototype, maintaining synchronisation of the specification and code was a priority for the team, and at least one major revision of the specification was accompanied by a reimplementation from scratch.

The approach used mathematical notations to express and explore requirements, a formal model-based language to express specifications, and an object-oriented language for implementations. The implementation of explicit operation specifications in VDM was straightforward in Smalltalk. Implementation of implicitly specified (pre-condition/post-condition) operations required documented design decisions with informally argued correctness arguments.

B   AGCO

In a research project supported by the Danish Innovation Foundation together with the company Agco, Aarhus University was involved with the development of a rather large VDM model which was combined with bits of Java realisations[2]. The idea behind this project is to optimise the logistics in relation to harvesting operations both offline before actually starting the operation as well as online while performing the operation. To a large extend this is a graph-theoretic problem but there are many interesting constraints that makes the optimisation challenging. Initially the VDM model encompassed the entire functionality but it turned out that this was very slow for the interpreter when using realistic fields [8,9]. Since Java already had large and efficient legacy libraries for graph traversal and Overture had a capability to bridge the gab between VDM and Java it was decided to move that functionality over to Java [40].

What is interesting about this application is that code generation to Java has been used [30]. This is even able to take the model/code blend into account in an efficient manner, and thus it is been possible to combine this with test automation with JUnit and perform continuous integration [10]. As a consequence this approach is actually also used in the current commercialisation efforts carried out. Thus, it can be said that this have been a strong integration between the VDM model and the parts that simply have been kept at Java level. However, as a consequence the VDM description is not really applicable for verification aspects, but purely used in a simulation context as a slightly more abstract "program". It is interesting to note however, that recently the VDM model have been moved from the VDM-RT dialect to the VDM-SL dialect which is significant simpler and has no notion of concurrency. Since the system use a publish/subscribe architecture it is possible to hide that part in such a Java based library. Interestingly the Java code generated from the new model is faster than the one generated from VDM-RT [41].

C   Communication Devices

In the EU research project PUSSEE (IST-2000-36103) Nokia proposed a case study to model and verify turbo codes, a technique for high-performance data transmission using block and convolutional codes [4]. The main interest in the case study was to create high quality (FPGA) implementations based on a verified model using the B Method [1] (resp. Event-B Method [2]). This has been studied conjointly by Nokia, KeesDA (a small start-up company that no longer exists), the University of Southampton and the University of Nancy. At first this looks like a straight forward problem. The maths of encoding and decoding block and convolution codes is not very hard. We have demonstrated this by modelling corresponding digital signal processing functions [17] and Hamming

---

[2] See   http://eng.au.dk/forskning/forskningsprojekter/electrical-and-computer-engineering-research-projects/off-line-and-on-line-logistics-planning-of-harvesting-processes/.

codes [6]. Unfortunately, the correctness of the mathematics at this level does not correspond to an abstraction that models data transmission between different stations. To express this property, error correction needs to be modelled. For the turbo codes this requires probabilistic modelling to attain the theoretical limit. In a practical situation, though, a few iterations of the turbo codes decoding are used to deal with the expected number of errors, thus not attaining the theoretical limit. That means, not all errors will be corrected. So, the value of a formal proof for the theoretical limit would be questionable. The alternative, is to model the non-deterministic possibility that faulty signals might be received. In the end, we did not find a strong argument in favour of a unified approach but accepted the need to use results concerning turbo codes that have been proven by other means. The complications and effort a full treatment within the B Method would have incurred would not have payed off in terms of improved quality.

Of course, not all communication is of this kind. A model we have produced with VOLVO in the same project for serial communication of heavy-duty vehicles [27] did not require additional techniques of verification [51]. In that model, we encountered different kinds of problems related to properties of electronic signal levels. These have been analysed by simulation and the results of the simulations have been used to improve the fidelity of the formal model with respect to the physical environment.

References

1. Abrial, J.R.: The B Book – Assigning Programs to Meanings. Cambridge University Press, Cambridge (1996)
2. Abrial, J.R.: Modeling in Event-B: System and Software Engineering. Cambridge University Press, Cambridge (2010)
3. Andrews, J.H.: Executing formal specifications by translation to higher order logic programming. In: Gunter, E.L., Felty, A. (eds.) TPHOLs 1997. LNCS, vol. 1275, pp. 17–32. Springer, Heidelberg (1997). https://doi.org/10.1007/BFb0028383
4. Berrou, C., Glavieux, A.: Near optimum error-correcting coding and decoding: Turbo codes. IEEE Trans. Commun. **44**(10), 1261–1271 (1996)
5. Börger, E., Stärk, R.: Abstract State Machines. Springer, Heidelberg (2003). https://doi.org/10.1007/978-3-642-18216-7
6. Cansell, D., Hallerstede, S., Oliver, I.: UML-B specification and hardware implementation of a Hamming coder/decoder. In: Mermet, J. (ed.) UML-B Specification for Proven Embedded Systems Design. Kluwer Academic Publishers, Boston (2004)
7. Jones, C., Jones, K., Lindsay, P.A., Moore, R. (eds.): mural: A Formal Development Support System. Springer, London (1991). https://doi.org/10.1007/978-1-4471-3180-9. ISBN 3-540-19651-X
8. Couto, L.D., Tran-Jørgensen, P.W.V., Edwards, G.T.C.: Combining harvesting operations optimisation using strategy-based simulation. In: Proceedings of the 6th International Conference on Simulation and Modeling Methodologies, Technologies and Applications (SIMULTECH), July 2016

9. Couto, L.D., Tran-Jørgensen, P.W.V., Edwards, G.T.C.: Model-based development of a multi-algorithm harvest planning system. In: Obaidat, M.S., Ören, T., Merkuryev, Y. (eds.) SIMULTECH 2016. AISC, vol. 676, pp. 19–33. Springer, Cham (2018). https://doi.org/10.1007/978-3-319-69832-8_2

10. Couto, L.D., Tran-Jørgensen, P.W.V., Larsen, P.G.: Enabling continuous integration in a formal methods setting (2018). Submitted for publication

11. Fitzgerald, J., Larsen, P.G., Verhoef, M. (eds.): Collaborative Design for Embedded Systems – Co-modelling and Co-simulation. Springer, Heidelberg (2013). https://doi.org/10.1007/978-3-642-54118-6

12. Fröhlich, B., Larsen, P.G.: Combining VDM-SL specifications with C++ code. In: Gaudel, M.-C., Woodcock, J. (eds.) FME 1996. LNCS, vol. 1051, pp. 179–194. Springer, Heidelberg (1996). https://doi.org/10.1007/3-540-60973-3_87

13. Fuchs, N.E.: Specifications are (preferably) executable. Softw. Eng. J. **7**, 323–334 (1992)

14. Gamble, C., Payne, R., Fitzgerald, J., Soudjani, S., Foldager, F.F., Larsen, P.G.: Automated exploration of parameter spaces as a method for tuning a predictive digital twin (2018). Submitted for publication

15. Gaudel, M.-C.: Testing can be formal, too. In: Mosses, P.D., Nielsen, M., Schwartzbach, M.I. (eds.) CAAP 1995. LNCS, vol. 915, pp. 82–96. Springer, Heidelberg (1995). https://doi.org/10.1007/3-540-59293-8_188

16. Gomes, C., Thule, C., Broman, D., Larsen, P.G., Vangheluwe, H.: Co-simulation: a survey. ACM Comput. Surv. **51**(3), 49:1–49:33 (2018)

17. Hallerstede, S., Zimmermann, Y.: Circuit design by refinement in EventB. In: FDL, pp. 624–637. ECSI (2004)

18. Hansen, D., Schneider, D., Leuschel, M.: Using B and ProB for data validation projects. In: Butler, M., Schewe, K.-D., Mashkoor, A., Biro, M. (eds.) ABZ 2016. LNCS, vol. 9675, pp. 167–182. Springer, Cham (2016). https://doi.org/10.1007/978-3-319-33600-8_10

19. Hasanagić, M., Fabbri, T., Larsen, P.G., Bandur, V., Tran-Jørgensen, P., Ouy, J.: Code generation for distributed embedded systems (2018). Submitted for publication

20. Hayes, I., Jones, C.: Specifications are not (necessarily) executable. Softw. Eng. J., 330–338 (1989). http://www.cs.man.ac.uk/csonly/cstechrep/Abstracts/UMCS-89-12-1.html

21. Hentenryck, P.V., Michel, L.: Constraint-Based Local Search. MIT Press, Cambridge (2005)

22. Hinchey, M., Bowen, J.P., Olderog, E.R. (eds.): Provably Correct Systems. NASA Monographs in Systems and Software Engineering. Springer, Cham (2017). https://doi.org/10.1007/978-3-319-48628-4

23. Holt, J., Perry, S.: SysML for Systems Engineering. IET (2008)

24. IEEE: International Standard ISO/IEC/IEEE 15288:2015(E), Systems and software engineering — System life cycle processes. ISO/IEC and IEEE Computer Society (2015)

25. IEEE Standards Board: IEEE standard glossary of software engineering terminology–IEEE std 610.12-1990 (1990)

26. INCOSE: Systems Engineering Handbook. A Guide for System Life Cycle Processes and Activities, Version 4.0. Technical report INCOSE-TP-2003-002-04, International Council on Systems Engineering (INCOSE), January 2015

27. SAE International: SAE J1708 revised OCT93, serial data communication between microcomputer systems in heavy-duty vehicle applications. http://www.sae.org

28. Jackson, M.: Problem Frames: Analysing and Structuring Software Development Problems. Addison-Wesley, New York (2001)
29. Jacobson, I.: Ivar Jacobson on UML, MDA, and the future of methodologies. InnoQ (2006). Interview
30. Jørgensen, P.W.V., Larsen, M., Couto, L.D.: A code generation platform for VDM. In: Battle, N., Fitzgerald, J. (eds.) Proceedings of the 12th Overture Workshop. School of Computing Science, Newcastle University, UK, Technical report CS-TR-1446, January 2015
31. Kowalski, R.: The relation between logic programming and logic specification. In: Hoare, C.A.R., Shepherdson, J. (eds.) Mathematical Logic and Programming Languages, pp. 11–24. Prentice-Hall, Upper Saddle River (1985)
32. Kramer, J.: Is abstraction the key to computing? Commun. ACM **50**(4), 37–42 (2007)
33. Larsen, P.G.: Evaluation of underdetermined explicit definitions. In: Naftalin, M., Denvir, T., Bertran, M. (eds.) FME 1994. LNCS, vol. 873, pp. 233–250. Springer, Heidelberg (1994). https://doi.org/10.1007/3-540-58555-9_98
34. Larsen, P.G.: Ten years of historical development: "Bootstrapping" VDMTools. J. Univers. Comput. Sci. **7**(8), 692–709 (2001)
35. Larsen, P.G., Battle, N., Ferreira, M., Fitzgerald, J., Lausdahl, K., Verhoef, M.: The overture initiative – integrating tools for VDM. SIGSOFT Softw. Eng. Notes **35**(1), 1–6 (2010). http://doi.acm.org/10.1145/1668862.1668864
36. Larsen, P.G., Fitzgerald, J., Brookes, T.: Applying formal specification in industry. IEEE Softw. **13**(3), 48–56 (1996)
37. Larsen, P.G., Fitzgerald, J., Woodcock, J., Nilsson, R., Gamble, C., Foster, S.: Towards semantically integrated models and tools for cyber-physical systems design. In: Margaria, T., Steffen, B. (eds.) ISoLA 2016. LNCS, vol. 9953, pp. 171–186. Springer, Cham (2016). https://doi.org/10.1007/978-3-319-47169-3_13
38. Lecomte, T., Burdy, L., Leuschel, M.: Formally Checking Large Data Sets in the Railways. CoRR abs/1210.6815 (2012)
39. Nielsen, C.B., Larsen, P.G.: Extending VDM-RT to enable the formal modelling of system of systems. In: Proceedings of the 7th International Conference on System of System Engineering, IEEE SoSE 2012. IEEE, July 2012. IEEE Systems Journal
40. Nielsen, C.B., Lausdahl, K., Larsen, P.G.: Combining VDM with executable code. In: Derrick, J. (ed.) ABZ 2012. LNCS, vol. 7316, pp. 266–279. Springer, Heidelberg (2012). https://doi.org/10.1007/978-3-642-30885-7_19. ISBN 978-3-642-30884-0
41. Nilsson, R.S., Lausdahl, K.G., Macedo, H.D., Larsen, P.G.: Transforming an industrial case study from VDM++ to VDM-SL. In: The 16th Overture Workshop, Oxford, July 2018
42. NIST, Cyber Physical Systems Public Working Group: Framework for cyber-physical systems: Release 1.0. Technical report National Institute of Standardards and Technology, May 2016
43. Oxford English Dictionary Online. Oxford University Press (2010)
44. Kowalski, R.: The relation between logic programming and logic specification. In: Mathematical Logic and Programming Languages, pp. 11–27 (1985)
45. Royce, W.: Managing the development of large software systems. In: WESCON, August 1970. Reprinted in the Proceedings of the 9th International Conference on Software Engineering (ICSE), Washington D.C. IEEE Computer Society Press (1987)

46. Schneider, D., Leuschel, M., Witt, T.: Model-based problem solving for university timetable validation and improvement. In: Bjørner, N., de Boer, F. (eds.) FM 2015. LNCS, vol. 9109, pp. 487–495. Springer, Cham (2015). https://doi.org/10.1007/978-3-319-19249-9_30

47. Sedgewick, R., Wayne, K.: Algorithms, 4th edn. Addison-Wesley, Boston (2011)

48. Sommerville, J.: Software Engineering, 10th edn. Pearson, Boston (2016)

49. Søndergaard, H., Sestoft, P.: Referential transparency, definiteness and unfoldability. Acta Inform. **27**, 505–517 (1990)

50. Turner, D.A.: Functional programming as executable specifications. In: Hoare, C.A.R., Shepherdson, J.C. (eds.) Mathematical Logic and Programming Languages, pp. 29–50. Prentice Hall, Upper Saddle River (1985)

51. Zimmermann, Y., Hallerstede, S., Cansell, D.: Formal modelling of electronic circuits using event-B, Case Study: SAE J1708 Serial Communication Link. In: Mermet, J. (ed.) UML-B - Specification for Proven Embedded Systems Design. Kluwer Academic Publishers, Boston (2004)

Using Umple to Synergistically Process Features, Variants, UML Models and Classic Code

Timothy C. Lethbridge$^{(\boxtimes)}$ and Abdulaziz Algablan

University of Ottawa, Ottawa K1N 6N5, Canada
{timothy.lethbridge,aalga075}@uottawa.ca

Abstract. We describe the synergies gained by enabling variants for product lines, or features, to be modeled in the same master syntax as design models (class diagrams, state diagrams, composite structure) and traditional source code. Our approach, using a construct we call mixsets, facilitates better analysis, documentation generation, diagram generation, reviewing and testing. It also solves problems related to tool dependency. We have implemented the approach in Umple, building on our previous work which merged design models with code. Our approach continues to allow multiple programming languages to be embedded and generated from the design models. Our extensions allow multiple approaches to separation of concerns (variants, traits, mixins, aspects) to co-exist, operating on models as well as code, and to synergistically enhance each other.

Keywords: Umple · Feature-oriented development · Separation of concerns
Aspect orientation · Traits · Mixins · Software modeling

1 Introduction

Since 2008, the open-source Umple technology has enabled developers to merge modeling and programming. It has allowed them to author and generate code for their software from one usable format that captures class models, state models and classic code in multiple programming languages [1–4].

In this paper, we describe how we have extended Umple to natively represent variant models (product lines, feature models). We add variant models by introducing the simple concept of the *mixset*, that allows creation of mixins composed from multiple locations in a textual codebase, along with constraints regarding usage of these mixins.

Our motivation for this research emerged from the need for a usable tool that made it easy to define variants or product lines consisting of both traditional code and textual model elements. When developing systems in Umple, we found we had to use external languages for specifying variants. These resulted in verbosity, didn't mesh nicely with the remainder of Umple syntax, and didn't allow for comprehensive analysis.

© Springer Nature Switzerland AG 2018
T. Margaria and B. Steffen (Eds.): ISoLA 2018, LNCS 11244, pp. 69–88, 2018.
https://doi.org/10.1007/978-3-030-03418-4_5

In the next section we present background regarding Umple as it existed prior to this work and other technologies for feature-oriented or product-line development that have informed our work.

In Sect. 3, we present the syntax and semantics of the feature-oriented extensions to Umple, and describe how they work synergistically with other capabilities of Umple. In Sect. 4 we give some simple case studies of our approach. In Sect. 5 we describe the benefits and compare our approach to alternatives. In Sect. 6 we conclude.

2   Background

The work described in this paper builds on a large body of research, which cannot all be described in a single paper. However, to help the reader we present highlights of the key background.

2.1   A Brief Look at Umple

Umple [4] is a technology for developing software that incorporates both traditional code (organized as classes with methods) as well as modeling abstractions such as class models (with UML attributes, associations and generalizations) and state machine models (events, hierarchical states, transitions). It generates code from the models and incorporates both generated code and user-supplied methods to build complete systems. It is notable that Umple can incorporate and generate code from multiple programming languages simultaneously.

Umple has been designed to be familiar-looking to developers, and to enable them to use it in conjunction with arbitrary text editors, version-control tools and build tools. Central to this is its textual form that looks like a C-family programming language, It has command-line, Eclipse plugin, and web-based tool support, so can be used in almost any toolchain. It has no external dependencies, nor does it require a specific runtime.

Features of particular relevance to this paper are Umple's multiple approaches to separation of concerns and modularity that all work synergistically together: Classes (with inheritance), files (with mixins – described later), traits [3] and aspects.

Like other object-oriented technologies, Umple organizes software primarily into *classes* and *interfaces*. Classes can contain methods as in Java and C++, but also attributes [5] (like variables but with richer semantics), associations [6], state machines [7] and various other entities.

In addition to classes and interfaces, Umple also has *traits* [3]. Traits can be used to *pull* in pieces of common functionality (methods, variables, state machines, and so on) into a class without the need for multiple inheritance. By 'pull', we mean that an entity (here a class, or another trait) requests inclusion of common functionality found in a trait.

Furthermore Umple also has *aspects*. These are used to *push* functionality into multiple methods. By 'push', we mean that the common functionality (in this context commonly called 'advice') has a mechanism (commonly called 'pointcuts') to include itself via pattern matching in other functionality (commonly called 'join points').

For simplicity we will refer to classes, interfaces and traits together as *classifiers*, following UML conventions

A system is also divided into *files*, but a file can have multiple classifiers; and multiple files can contain multiple parts of the same classifiers: these multiple parts are mixed together (the parts are called *mixins*), to create complete classifiers. The developer can therefore organize the files however, they want: Files could be organized so as to represent components, features, layers, or any other concern.

In Umple, each of the approaches to separation of concerns works with traditional code, with model entities, and with each other. This allows the developer great flexibility regarding how they structure their system.

The following is a simple example of Umple code. The class diagram generated from this is in Fig. 2

- Line 2 describes an association between Bank and Account, with the '1' and '*' being the multiplicities.
- Lines 6 and 10 describe a total of 4 attributes. Umple uses String as the default type if it omitted.
- Lines 9–11 describe a trait that is incorporated into LoanAccount in line 18, essentially enabling a form of multiple inheritance.
- The 'isA' keyword is used for all forms of specialization, including specifying superclasses, implemented interfaces and used traits. Here there are is statements on lines 14 and 18.

```
1    class Bank {
2        1 -- * Account;
3    }
4
5    class Account {
6        owner; Integer number; Integer balance;
7    }
8
9    trait InterestBearingAccount {
10       Float interestRate;
11   }
12
13   class DepositAccount {
14       isA Account;
15   }
16
17   class LoanAccount {
18       isA Account, InterestBearingAccount;
19   }
```

The Umple compiler works like other compilers in that it takes files in Umple syntax as input and generates various outputs including diagrams and code in target languages such as Java and C++. The compiler parses files (with suffix .ump) and builds an abstract syntax tree; this is then analyzed to extract an internal model (conforming to Umple's metamodel, available on its website) of the various classes and other model elements that are to be part of the system. Some of the items in the AST and model, are chunks of target-language code such as method bodies that Umple doesn't try to parse but merely passes through to the generated target language code. To create a final executable system, a target-language compiler must then be applied to the output generated by Umple; however, in most toolchains this step would be invisible to the Umple user.

Umple's incorporation of both models and code allow it to perform extensive analysis. The Umple compiler can detect many kinds of problems that could not be detected readily in technologies that just manage code or just manage models. During the Umple compiler's analysis phase, it detects hundreds of potential types of problems in the model. The target-language code generated by Umple is hence free of numerous types of defects that might otherwise be present if a developer was programming in the target language directly. The generated code may still have bugs in the chunks of passed-through target-language code, however Umple translates error messages raised by target-language compilers so they point at locations of such bugs in the original . ump files.

Code generated from Umple is not intended to be edited. It is supposed to be treated much like Java bytecode or machine code output from a typical C++ compiler. However, to raise the confidence of developers should they ever fear that Umple will disappear and to allow for inspection or auditing of code and models, the generated code in Umple is designed to be straightforward, self-contained and self-documenting. In particular, all comments present in the input Umple are output in the generated code.

In addition to executable systems, Umple also generates various web-based diagram formats and documentation. These allow the reader to trace system elements back to their originating files (e.g. to places in files where traits, aspects and mixins are defined). This not only helps the developer understand the code, but also helps overcome one of the hazards of separation-of-concerns: Confusion and errors resulting from *delocalization* of related information.

The motivation for the work described in this paper is to maintain and build on Umple's strengths outlined above. Although one can use previously-defined Umple separation-of-concerns mechanisms to build multiple variants of a system, a lot can be gained by incorporating key ideas from existing technologies for product-line and feature modeling. Umple's new *mixset* concept (to be described in Sect. 3.1) allows mixins to be composed from multiple locations in a textual codebase, and constrained in a simple way. This mechanism enables Umple developers to apply many of the feature modeling or product-line modeling approaches briefly reviewed in the next section.

2.2   Feature, Product-Line and Variability Modeling

Feature-oriented software development (FOSD) allows organizing of software by units of functionality [8]. The software architecture may have a small core, with each new capability being added as a feature. A feature might be represented as a set of software *deltas* (in a similar manner to deltas in a version-control system), using some kind of conditional-compilation preprocessor, as *aspects* that can be *woven* together with the core, as *mixins*, or using some other similar approach. FeatureIDE brings together many of these approaches into a usable tool [9].

Product-line (or product-family) technology has similarities to feature-oriented technology, with the key additional idea that it enables multiple versions of the software that effectively utilize shared assets, with different configurations of features [10]. Such product versions might be targeted for different customer groups or different hardware.

As a concrete example, imagine a company producing software to sell to banks. Different banks will want or need different feature sets. Some of the differences might be a function of the jurisdiction of the banks and hence different legal requirements; others might relate to the legacy of account types that various banks must accommodate. Still further differences might relate to each bank's desire to provide a suite of capabilities to attract customers, while not overwhelming customers and staff with too many choices or costs. To keep our example simple, we will later on model just two areas of variability: The first is whether a bank has more than one branch, and the second is whether overdrafts are allowed in deposit accounts.

2.3 Model-Driven Development and Product Lines

Model driven development (MDD) has two major connections with software product lines: modeling of diverse systems and modeling of the components of variants [11].

In the former, feature modeling (FM) is a common approach used to capture variability and to produce configurations, or variants in software product lines. Existing FM approaches are mostly derived from the work of Kang et al. on Feature-Oriented Domain Analysis (FODA) [12]. Research in feature modeling mainly focuses on the representation aspects, constraint precision and the derivation of valid configurations. Textual FM languages (e.g. TVL [13], and Clafer [14]) have the capability of being human-readable and offer rich syntax to handle feature modeling concerns such as cardinalities, feature attributes, and so on, in addition to making modeling more intuitive and concise. However, there is no standard way of mapping FM to other software artifacts such as design, or source code [15].

For the second role, MDD seeks to model variants of SPL via decomposing product line features to reusable pieces, or feature fragments. Usually there is considerable overlap between feature fragments which form different variants. Superimposition, "is the process of composing software artifacts by merging their corresponding substructures" [16], in other words, it merges fragments based on their names and position within nested structures. Because it is comparatively simple, the superimposition technique is a prevalent approach to compose feature fragments at the source code level. Approaches such as AHEAD (algebraic hierarchical equations for application design) [17] and FEATUREHOUSE [16] use superimposition to handle feature composition. As we will explain in this paper, Umple uses the notion of mixsets as an expressive yet simple approach, with similarities to superimposition as defined above.

Several approaches utilize aspects to model variants of SPL. Noda et al. proposed an aspect-oriented modeling mechanism that utilizes concerns by separating them from their functionality and then managing the relationships among them [18]. Umple mixsets extend the capability of aspect modeling by allowing aspects to be attached to several modeling constructs, in addition to merging them with traits and mixins.

Another approach to feature modeling is delta modeling in which a delta allows *deletion* – as well as addition – of modeling elements during reuse. ABS extends the delta programming concept to enable SPL by offering different sub-languages, or language layers, targeting feature modeling, delta modeling, configuration and selection of variants [19]. A class in ABS is used solely to generate objects although class-based inheritance is not allowed. Instead, ABS utilizes trait composition to model class hierarchical relationships. Umple supports trait composition in a similar manner, however, Umple fully falls in the object-oriented paradigm and allows class-based inheritance.

A recent industrial survey found that an average software engineer uses three different notations ranging from informal to formal representation to specify variability in her/his SPL projects [20]. Using various notations is often a significant impediment to the progress of software projects since it causes overhead for software engineers to keep several representations updated and also requires handling integration issues. This notation-diversity gap calls for novel approaches to effectively reduce it to lower levels. An objective of Umple is to reduce the need for such diversity by creating a single notation that has the combination of benefits most needed by developers. We will discuss Umple notation diversity further in Sect. 6.

The above survey also shows that annotative approaches, which describe variants within a single model, are less used for specifying variability in practice. On the other hand, *separate* variability models, which dedicate specific models to manage variability, are increasingly common. Umple's mixset capability can be used like an annotative variability approach or as a separate variability approach.

3   Umple Extensions to Incorporate Mixsets

In this section we introduce in a concise manner the enhancements we have made to Umple in the current work

Key top level entities in any Umple file prior to the work reported in this paper were class *name* {...}, interface *name* {...} and trait *name* {...}. The three dots (...) represent internal contents such as attributes, associations, state machines and methods; but we do not need to consider the details of these.

Any repeated occurrence of any top level entity with a matching name adds content to the entity (i.e. *mixes* it in). Thus class A {a;} class A {b;} results in class A {a; b;}. The redefinitions can be in the same file, or in separate files. When in separate files, the possibility of selective inclusion of mixins exists, hence allowing production of different system variants.

Umple traits [3] have additional semantics: They can be incorporated wholly or in part in other traits and classes with potential renaming of internal elements, and enforcement of the presence of various required (dependent) elements.

3.1   Mixsets

In this paper, we introduce the notion of *mixsets*, to provide variability modeling for both structural and behavioral models in Umple. Mixsets are a new type of top-level entity in Umple. Umple's other top-level entities include classes, interfaces, traits, standalone state machines, use statements, and enums.

The basic syntax for introducing a mixset is: `mixset mixsetName {...}`. A mixset contains a set of Umple top-level entities. But since top level entities can be specified in pieces, or mixins, that are composed to form the final entity, each mixset statement need only describe one of these mixins. A mixset is therefore a set of mixins.

Members of the set can be fragments of any of Umple's valid top-level entities including other mixsets. Mixsets allow these members and their contents to be combined to build a potentially optional feature or part of a system. Different combinations of mixsets would give rise to different *variants* perhaps targeted for a particular customer group or hardware platform.

Mixsets can enable structural model variability by adding new classes, attributes or associations to a model. They can provide behavioral model variability by adding alternative implementations of methods, or alternative states, transitions, and actions in state machines. In this paper, we will focus on structural variability.

The contents declared in the curly brackets of a mixset will only ever be incorporated in the variant if the Umple compiler encounters the syntax `use mixsetName;`. This is the same as the syntax used for incorporating separate Umple files, so a filename ending in .ump is actually a special case of a mixset name.

Since mixins are top-level entities, subject to being composed using Umple's mixin capability, parts of a given mixset can be found in different files or other mixsets

Basic Mixset Cases. The following are the four simplest cases for the definition and use of mixsets to specify fragments of Umple classes. Wherever a class definition is shown in these cases, several classes could be given, and elements such as interfaces and traits can also appear. Specifying fragments of other entities such as interfaces and traits works the same way.

Case   1:   Basic   mixset   definition   and   inclusion. `mixset M1 {class A {a;}}` means include this class with attribute A only if somewhere else the statement `use M1;` appears, or if M1 appears in a command argument to compile the system. From now on by *including* a mixset we mean by either via a use statement or a command argument. For syntactic simplicity, if only a single entity is contained in the mixset definition, the outer braces can be omitted, so the above becomes `mixset M1 class A {a;}`.

Case   2:   A   class   defined   partly   in   a   mixset. `mixset M2 class A{a1;}` `class A {a2;}` results in class A always being present with attribute a2, but the class will also have attribute a1 *only* if M2 is included.

Case   3:   Parts   of   a   mixset   defined   separately. `mixset M3 {class A{}}mixset M3 {class B{}}` has the same effect as `mixset M3{class A{} class B{}}`. In other words, the two declarations of M3 are mixed together using Umple's standard mixin approach.

Case 4: Mixset definition containing elements internal to classes, traits and interfaces. Such elements (e.g. methods, attributes) can be wrapped in mixset notation, as can blocks of code, wherever code is allowed in Umple (e.g. state machine actions, and so on). The syntax `class X { a; mixset M4 b;}` is equivalent to `class X {a;} mixset M4 class X{b;}` and will result in class X having attribute b only if a statement use M4; is encountered. Case 4 items will be transformed to case 3 as described later. We allow case 4 to reduce the verbosity of the language.

Grammar for Mixsets. The following is an extract of the Umple grammar rules describing mixsets. This is taken directly from the Umple user manual, which in turn is extracted from Umple's source code. In the Umple EBNF grammar notation, terminal constant symbols are shown in red; placeholders for alphanumeric identifiers are show in green with single square brackets; nonterminal rule names are in blue, and references to rules are in double square brackets. Three dots means that an existing rule has been modified to add the item.

Rule 1 indicates that require and mixset statements are newly introduced as top level entities. Rule 2 shows that they can also be added within classes (similar rules showing they can be added to interfaces, states, and state machines are omitted for brevity).

Rules 4 and 5 show how the 'extra code' comprising each mixset snippet is specified. Lines 6 through 12 define the require statement grammar. Note that the reference to multiplicity is to an existing Umple rule.

1	**entity-** : ... [[requireStatement]] | [[mixsetDefinition]] ...
2	**classContent-** : ... | [[mixsetDefinition]] ...
3	**mixsetDefinition** : mixset [mixsetName] ([[mixsetInnerContent]] | [[mixsetInlineDefinition]])
4	**mixsetInnerContent-** : { [[extraCode]] }
5	**mixsetInlineDefinition-** : ([entityType] [entityName] ([[mixsetInnerContent]])
6	**requireStatement** : require ([[requireBody]] | ([[multiplicity]] of { [[requireTerminal]] [[requireMultiplicityList]] }))
7	**requireBody-** : [(([[requireLinkingOptNot]])? [[requireTerminal]] [[requireList]]])]
8	**requireList-** : ([[requireLinkingOp]] [[requireTerminal]])*
9	**requireMultiplicityList-** : (, [[requireTerminal]])*
10	**requireLinkingOp** : ([[requireLinkingOptNot]] | [=and:&|&&|and|,] | [!or:(| | || |or|;)])
11	**requireLinkingOptNot** : (opt | not)
12	**requireTerminal** : [targetMixsetName]

General Algorithm for Processing Mixsets. To understand how mixsets work, it is helpful to understand how they are processed when Umple parses its source text. In the original Umple prior to this work, upon encountering a use statement, Umple would immediately parse the referenced file, with an error being raised if the file were not found, and there being no effect of repeated use statements referring to the same file.

Essentially, mixsets are treated as dynamically-generated virtual files – the Umple compiler only holds them in memory, rather than writing them to the file system. The compiler adds the contents between the mixset definition's braces (which we refer to as a snippet) to the relevant virtual file, without parsing it (other than to balance braces, quotes and comments), but also recording its location in the original.ump file to allow for debugging and to help solve the delocalization problem.

Use statements work essentially the same with mixset virtual files as with real files. Virtual files containing mixset contents are processed when a matching use statement is encountered just as though the file was real.

The pseudocode below (Algorithms A-D) describes the process that occurs when mixset and use statements are encountered. The nuances of this process that differ from processing of real files are:

1. If the Umple compiler encounters a use statement of a mixset *before* encountering a matching mixset declaration, Umple creates an empty virtual file for that mixset, by recording that a reference to the mixset name has been encountered (Lines C6-C7).
2. There is the possibility of (additional) snippets of a mixset being created *after* a matching use statement. In that case, a (new) snippet is added to the mixset virtual file and is processed *immediately* (Line A5 below). In other words, upon encountering such a mixset snippet, Umple first looks to see whether a use statement for it has already been encountered; if so, it processes that snippet immediately.
3. When mixset content is found *inside* a top-level entity, it is rewritten to the Case 3 form, as shown in Case 4 above before being processed (Algorithm B below).
4. Detection and reporting of a missing mixset (used without a matching definition, Lines D4-5 below) or other constraint violations (associated with require statements, Lines D8-9 below) can only occur at the end of parsing.
5. Reporting of errors and warnings refers to the original location in the.ump file, rather than to the location in the virtual file (Line A7 below).

A1	**Algorithm A handleBasicMixsetStatement(**
	mixsetName, _codeBlock_)
A2	-- Invoked when Umple parser encounters
A3	-- mixset **_mixsetName_** {**_codeBlock_**}
A4	If (use statement for **_mixsetName_** has been encountered)
A5	Parse **_codeBlock_** in the same way as a new Umple file
A6	Else
A7	Record with codeBlock the line in the .ump file
	where the mixset statement was found
A8	Add **_codeBlock_** to the ordered set of snippets
	associated with **_mixsetName_**
A9	End if
A10	End

B1	**Algorithm B handleMixsetInsideEntity(**
	mixsetName, _codeBlock_, entity, _entityName_)
B2	-- Invoked when Umple parser encounters
B3	-- **entity _entityName_ {** … mixset **_mixsetName_** {**_codeBlock_**}}
B4	Add `**entity   _entityName_** {` to the start of **_codeBlock_**
B5	Add } to end of **_codeBlock_**
B6	Process modified **_codeBlock_**
	using **handleBasicMixsetStatement**
B7	End

C1	**Algorithm C handleUseStatement(_mixsetName_)**
C2	-- Invoked when Umple parser encounters
C3	-- use **_mixsetName_;**
C4	-- and also if **_mixsetName_** is a command line argument
C5	If(a use statement for **_mixsetName_**
	has NOT already been encountered)
C6	Record that a use statement was encountered
	for **_mixsetName_**
C7	If (no snippets are associated with **_mixsetName_**)
C8	Do nothing
C9	Else
C10	Parse any snippets associated with **_mixsetName_**
	in the same way as an Umple file
C11	End if
C12	End if
C13	End

D1	**Algorithm D endOfParsingHandling()**
D2	-- Invoked after all parsing is complete
D3	For each (mixset referred to in a use statement)
D4	If (no snippet has been encountered for it)
D5	Emit a warning
D6	End if
D7	End for
D8	If(the logical condition of any require statement
	evaluates to false)
D9	Emit a warning
D10	End if
D11	End

Nesting, Combination and Constraints on Mixsets. Mixsets can be nested as follows: `mixset P {class M{}; mixset Q {class N{}}}` says that if P is included only, then class M will exist. If Q is included only, then neither class N or M will be created by this code because the system only 'sees' Q if P is included. If both P and Q are included, then both classes will appear.

Combinations and constraints among mixsets can be specified in the following ways, where M1 ... Mn are mixsets:

`use M5, M6;` means include both M5 and M6. If either doesn't exist it is an error.

`use M5; use M6;` is same as the above, just in two separate statements.

`mixset M7 {use M8, M9;}` means that if M7 is incorporated, then incorporate M8 and M9 as well. In other words, M7 requires both M8 and M9. This is just a simple combination of a regular mixset statement and regular use statements.

The *require* statement constrains a feature or product family model. These are illustrated in the examples later, but the following gives an overview:

`require [M10 or M11];` means that somewhere there must be a use statement for M10 or M11, or both. Standard Boolean logic is allowed with the keyword `xor` meaning at most one, `and` and `not` having the usual meanings, and parentheses being used for grouping.

The `of` operator is also available in the require statement. This can be used to require a certain number of mixsets selected from a set specified by a multiplicity, such as 1..* (meaning one or more). An example would be: `1..2 of {M12, M13 ...}` meaning that only one or two of the listed Mixsets is allowed, The notation `opt M14` is syntactic sugar for `and 0..1 of {M14}`, in other words marking a mixset as optional.

Taken together the above allow a rich way of embedding feature models within arbitrary Umple code. A feature model can be described all in one place in a single file, or the dependencies and inclusions can be distributed among multiple files. This flexibility is one of the hallmarks of Umple. However, Umple also prevents delocalization confusion by allowing automatic drawing of standard feature model diagrams.

4 Examples of Mixsets

In this section we illustrate some of the power of combining the mixset and requirements features into Umple through two illustrative examples. The aim is to show how mixsets are used to precisely express model variability and to configure software product variants.

4.1   Bank Example

This example describes generic software that can be used by various small banks. Some have multiple branches, so we can allow the feature MultiBranch for them. Also, some banks will want to allow overdrafts on their deposit accounts and others will not.

The following is an Umple model showing the use of two mixsets. The third line of class Bank specifies that there will be an association with a Branch class only if the Multibranch mixset is included. Instances of the Account class are also linked to a particular branch only in the case of Multibranch, and the entire Branch class is present only if Multibranch is included. If OverdraftsAllowed is included, then the InterestBearingAccount trait is included in DepositAccount, as is overdraftLimit.

```
1    class Bank {
2      1 -- * Account;
3      mixset Multibranch 1 -- 1..* Branch;
4    }
5
6    mixset Multibranch class Branch {
7      Integer id; String address;
8    }
9
10   class Account {
11     owner; Integer number; Integer balance;
12     mixset Multibranch * -- 1 Branch;
13   }
14
15   trait InterestBearingAccount {
16     Float interestRate;
17   }
18
19   class DepositAccount {
20     isA Account;
21     mixset OverdraftsAllowed {
22       Integer overdraftLimit;
23       isA InterestBearingAccount;
24     }
25   }
26
27   class LoanAccount {
28     isA Account, InterestBearingAccount;
29   }
```

Figure 1 (generated by Umple) shows the system with both mixsets included such as by compiling the system with umple Bank.ump OverdraftsAllowed Multibranch. Figure 2 shows the system if neither of these mixsets are included.

4.2   Alternative Code Arrangement for the Bank Example

The code presented in the last section distributed parts of the MultiBranch mixset among relevant entities. Some developers may instead prefer to group all the contents of the mixset in one place. This alternative is shown below, and illustrates the flexibility of the approach. The resulting system would be identical.

```
1   class Bank {
2     1 -- * Account;
3   }
4
5   class Account {
6     owner; Integer number; Integer balance;
7   }
8
9   trait InterestBearingAccount {
10    Float interestRate;
11  }
12
13  class DepositAccount {
14    isA Account;
15    mixset OverdraftsAllowed {
16       Integer overdraftLimit;
17       isA InterestBearingAccount;
18    }
19  }
20
21  class LoanAccount {
22    isA Account, InterestBearingAccount;
23  }
24
25  mixset Multibranch {
26    class Bank {1 -- 1..* Branch}
27    class Branch {Integer id; String address;}
28    class Account {* -- 1 Branch}
29  }
```

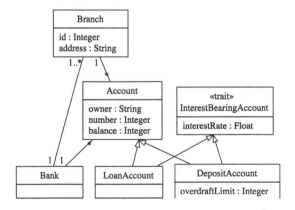

Fig. 1. Bank system with MultiBranch and OverdraftsAllowed

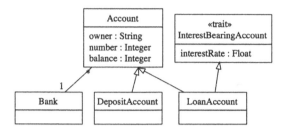

Fig. 2. Bank system with neither optional feature

4.3   Mobile Phone Example

This illustrates potential pre-smartphone mobile phone software configurations, and is taken from the literature [15] so can be used to compare Umple with other notations. A diagram of the feature model is shown in Fig. 3. The Umple code for the actual feature model, constraining the possible configurations is the following:

```
1    require [GSMProtocol opt Mp3Recording
2       and Playback and AudioFormat opt Camera];
3    mixset GSMProtocol require [GSM1800 opt GSM1900];
4    mixset AudioFormat require [1..2 of {Mp3,Wav}];
5    mixset Mp3Recording require [Mp3];
6    mixset Camera require [Resolution];
7    mixset Resolution
8       require [1 of {Res21MP, Res31MP, Res50MP}];
9    use GSMProtocol, GSM1900, Playback, AudioFormat;
```

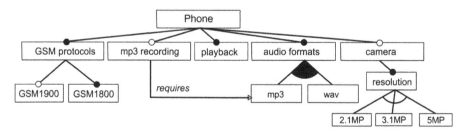

Fig. 3. Feature model diagram for the mobile phone example, from [15]

The final line above allows us to immediately meet the constraint associated with always-required features, to avoid having to specify these on the command line.

The above is as far as many feature modelling technologies go. However, Umple easily allows modeling at a detailed level such that code can be generated. The following shows some details of one approach to structuring the audio-related code in for the above.

```
1    mixset AudioFormat {
2      class AudioCodec { /* other details omitted */}
3    }
4    mixset Mp3 class Mp3Codec {
5      isA AudioCodec; /* other details omitted */
6    }
7    mixset Wav class WavCodec {
8      isA AudioCodec {/* other details omitted */
9    }
```

Note that rather than using mixsets, files could have been used instead; the feature model (require statements) above would have been the same, except with '.ump' suffixes.

To build a system with some combination of features, the user could specify the following as the command arguments, assuming Phone, ump is the top level file: `umple Phone.ump GSM1900 Wav Camera Res31MP`. Alternatively a file called Config.ump could be created containing use `GSM1900, Wav, Camera,Res31MP`; and the command arguments would then be `umple Phone.ump Config.ump`.

5   Comparison with Other Approaches

Due to space constraints, we will limit our comparison to a small number of approaches that can be used as alternatives to the work described in this paper.

- **C-Preprocessor directives (#define, #ifdef, #include)**. This is the classic way variants have been managed for decades in languages such as C and C++. It has a tendency to make code very complex, however.
- **Clafer** [14]. This is a textual language used to describe feature models. It also supports certain modeling capabilities such as state machines and parts hierarchies. It does not support management of source code.
- **Pure::Variants** [21]. This is a sophisticated commercial tool that plugs in to Eclipse and works with a variety of other tools, enabling managing of variants. It allows generation of variants of executable systems in a language-independent way; for example it can generate C-Preprocessor directives.
- **Git Branches**. It is possible to manage versions of software in branches in a configuration management system, merging only certain sets of changes into branches that correspond with a particular variant.
- **Aspect Orientation**: This is a group of technologies that can inject code into other code to add features. Most examples of its practical use are for simple features like logging.

- **Alternate file inclusion with mixins**: This is Umple's state before the extensions described in this paper. The approach is also used in technologies like Ruby.

In Table 1 we characterize the above approaches, along with Umple, based on the criteria listed below. Capitalized items in the table are strengths. Lowercase, italicized items are weaknesses.

- **Free and open source**. This is self-explanatory. Only Pure::Variants is commercial.
- **Weight**. This is judged based on the number of syntactic elements in the language and in the commands and software footprint needed to control the use of the language. The lower the weight, the more quickly and easily can the technology be learned and applied. A technology will naturally be heavier if it can do more; the challenge in technologies is to be able to do more with less through synergy. Umple and the C preprocessor are clearly the lightest. The C Preprocessor's capabilities are centered around the #define and #ifdef keywords, whereas Umple's capabilities are centered around the mixset, use and require keywords. At the opposite end is Pure:: Variants, which requires installation of a powerful but heavy-weight tool.
- **IDE agnosticism**: If a tool requires a particular IDE (such as Eclipse), then it is marked 'No' here. Only Pure::Variants is IDE-dependent. The remaining tools can be used with Eclipse, on the command-line or in a variety of other IDEs. Without IDE agnosticism the scope of usage of a technology is clearly limited.
- **Feature Model Usability/Visibility**: This is judged based on whether the feature model can be viewed by the developer as a distinct entity, separate from other information managed by the technology, and also the extent to which the user can clearly see what aspects of the system's design and source code correspond to each feature. Tools such as Git and the C-Preprocessor were not designed with visibility of the feature model in mind, so are ranked low here. We have tried to make this one of the strengths of Umple: Umple can generate a feature model diagram and allows easy searching for the elements of each mixset. Pure::Variants also has a lot of strength in this area.
- **Representational power**: This is high if all the most important constraints among features can be described by the technology. This includes constraints indicating that one feature requires another, some features are optional, and so on. The C Preprocessor, Git and Umple prior to the changes described in this paper had no capability for representing such constraints. Clafer, Pure::Variants and the new Umple with mixsets and require statements, explicitly allow such representation so are rated high. If pointcuts are well-described, some of the needed representational power can be harnessed, so we have rated aspect orientation as moderate in this regard.
- **Textual Notation**: Textual notations allow developers to use arbitrary text editors, to search easily, and to apply numerous text-manipulation tools. If the feature model has a textual notation, then this is tagged as follows: *Separate* indicates that the model is a distinct language separate from source code of the rest of the system. *Superimposed* means that it is a distinct language that can be added to source code (as is classically done for the C pre-processor, in some literature this is referred to as *annotative*). *Blended* extends the idea of superimposition, such that the language is integrated with source code (and other models if relevant). This has been one of the

Table 1. Advantages of certain approaches to managing variants and product lines

	Free and Open Source	Weight for variation management	IDE agnostic	Feature model usability/visibility	Representational power	Textual notation	Can manage traditional code?	Can manage UML models?	Analysis sophistication for variants
C Pre-Processor	YES	VERY LIGHT	YES	*low*	*low*	Superimposed	YES	*only indirectly*	*None*
Clafer	YES	LIGHT	YES	Moderate	HIGH	Separate	*no*	Partly	HIGH
Pure::Variants	*no*	*Heavy*	*no*	HIGH	HIGH	*no*	YES	*only indirectly*	HIGH
Git Branches	YES	Moderate	YES	*low*	*low*	Separate	YES	*only indirectly*	*Low*
Aspect Orientation	YES	Moderate	YES	*low*	Moderate	Separate	Block level	In some cases	*Low*
Alternate file inclusion with mixins	YES	VERY LIGHT	YES	*low*	*low*	BLENDED	File level	DIRECTLY	*Low*
Umple	YES	**VERY LIGHT**	**YES**	**HIGH**	**HIGH**	**BLENDED**	**Block level**	**DIRECTLY**	Moderate

key design goals of Umple. Umple, in particular, allows mixsets and require statements to be manipulated by other mixsets, and blends them tightly with other language features.

- **Can manage traditional code**: This indicates whether the technology can be used to control features that differ only with respect to elements of code in languages such as Java and C++. Umple and aspect-orientation are intermediate in this: They can manage variations among blocks of code, but not, differences within any arbitrary line of code. The ability to manage traditional code is important for several reasons: The need to express detailed algorithms will always exist, and variants may need different algorithms. This ability is also important so existing bodies of code can be managed when describing variants.
- **Can manage UML models**: This indicates whether the technology can manage variants in full class models (including associations), state machines and other modeling elements. It is important in order to raise the abstraction of a system's description. Of the tools listed, only Umple is designed to do this directly and reasonably comprehensively. Clafer does have a growing capability in this direction but doesn't generate code from its models. The notation 'only indirectly' means that the technology can manage other languages, so could be made to manage a textual modeling language (including managing Umple).
- **Analysis sophistication for variants**: This is judged based on the capabilities of the logic language used to describe the constraints among features, and the deduction engine available to find conflicts or other problems. This is a strength of Clafer and Pure::Variants. The ability to analyze variants is important to prevent errors such as inclusion of conflicting features.

Overall, Umple has been designed to have a high rating in almost all of the above criteria. In particular it is the only open-source tool that can textually and directly manage variants in both source code and models.

Umple is currently not the strongest tool when it comes to analysis: Our assessment is that the high level of sophistication available in other tools is not commonly needed, however.

Umple also cannot control variations in traditional code at the line-of-code level. However, it is almost always possible to refactor Umple code (e.g. by extracting methods) so that Umple can control code variability at any needed granularity.

6   Conclusions and Future Work

We have described a textual approach to managing optional and alternative features in a textual language that encompasses both abstract models and traditional code. This has been designed as an extension to Umple and allows both feature-oriented and product-line development. The key additions are:

- The *mixset* keyword, used to tag any set of Umple elements as parts of features that can optionally be included.
- Extension of the *use* keyword to operate with mixsets.

- The *require* keyword (and several associated operators), used to describe constraints among features, and therefore keep the system logically consistent.

Umple's capabilities for feature and product-line modeling allow code and model to be arranged in a variety of ways, and have a set of advantages that bring together the strengths found in competing technologies.

A key objective of Umple has been to allow developers to create software using a large variety of abstraction and separation-of-concerns mechanisms without excessive notation diversity. Existing solutions often require completely different languages to handle variants, models and traditional code, whereas Umple provides a harmonized syntax that allows these to be blended together. That doesn't however, prevent using Umple together with other languages. For example since Umple is a textual language a user could use some other tool for variants; they aren't limited to Umple's native variant capability based on mixins and mixsets. Similarly, Umple makes it easy to link Umple-generated modules to external libraries or jar files. The user can therefore choose the level of notation diversity they want to live with.

As future work, we intend to develop extensions to the approach described. Firstly, we want to allow renaming, selection and deletion operators on mixset inclusion, as is currently supported in Umple traits. This would allow generic features to be included in somewhat-different base systems and would enable Umple to gain the capabilities of delta-oriented product-line tools. We would also like to enhance the feature model with automated analysis capabilities to detect conflicted constraints, invalid configurations and dead features. We also plan to conduct a comprehensive empirical study of the effectiveness of the approach. Finally, we plan to incorporate requirements modeling into Umple, which can then also synergistically use mixsets, and other Umple features.

References

1. Lethbridge, T.C., Abdelzad, V., Husseini Orabi, M., Husseini Orabi, A., Adesina, O.: Merging modeling and programming using umple. In: Margaria, T., Steffen, B. (eds.) ISoLA 2016. LNCS, vol. 9953, pp. 187–197. Springer, Cham (2016). https://doi.org/10.1007/978-3-319-47169-3_14
2. Husseini-Orabi, M., Husseini-Orabi, A., Lethbridge, T.C.: Component-Based Modeling in Umple Modelsward 2018, pp. 247–255 (2018)
3. Abdelzad, V., Lethbridge, T.C.: Promoting traits into model-driven development. Softw. Syst. Model. **16,** 997–1017 (2015)
4. Umple. http://www.umple.org. Accessed 17 May 2018
5. Badreddin, O, Forward, A., Lethbridge, T.C.: Exploring a Model-Oriented and Executable Syntax for UML Attributes. In: Lee, R. (eds.) Software Engineering Research, Management and Applications. Studies in Computational Intelligence, vol. 496. Springer, Heidelberg, pp. 33–53 (2013). https://doi.org/10.1007/978-3-319-00948-3_3
6. Badreddin, O, Forward, A., Lethbridge, T.C.: Improving Code Generation for Associations: Enforcing Multiplicity Constraints and Ensuring Referential Integrity", SERA 2013, Springer SCI 496, pp. 129–149 (2013)
7. Badreddin, O., Lethbridge, T.C., Forward, A., Elasaar, M., Aljamaan, H., Garzon, M.: Enhanced code generation from UML composite state machines. MODELSWARD 2014, Portugal, INSTICC, pp. 235–245 (2014)

8. Apel, S., Kästner, C.: An overview of feature-oriented software development. J. Obj. Technol. **8**(5), 49–84 (2009)
9. Thüm, T., Kästner, C., et al.: FeatureIDE: an extensible framework for feature-oriented software development. Sci. Comput. Programm. **71**(1), 70–85 (2014)
10. Pohn, K., Böckle, G, van Der Linden, F.J.: Software Product Line Engineering: Foundations, Principles and Techniques. Springer, Heidelberg (2005). https://doi.org/10.1007/3-540-28901-1
11. Apel, S., Janda, F., Trujillo, S., Kästner, C.: Model superimposition in software product lines. In: Paige, Richard F. (ed.) ICMT 2009. LNCS, vol. 5563, pp. 4–19. Springer, Heidelberg (2009). https://doi.org/10.1007/978-3-642-02408-5_2
12. Kang, K.C., Cohen, S.G., Hess, J.A., Novak, W.E., Peterson, A.S.: Feature-oriented domain analysis (FODA) feasibility study (No. CMU/SEI-90-TR-21). Carnegie-Mellon Univ Pittsburgh Pa Software Engineering Inst (1990)
13. Classen, A., Boucher, Q., Heymans, P.: A text-based approach to feature modelling: syntax and semantics of TVL. Sci. Comput. Programm. **76**(12), 1130–1143 (2011)
14. Bąk, K., Diskin, Z., Antkiewicz, M., Czarnecki, K., Wąsowski, A.: Clafer: unifying class and feature modeling. Softw. Syst. Model. **15**(3), 811–845 (2016)
15. Czarnecki, K., Grünbacher, P., Rabiser, R., Schmid, K., Wąsowski, A.: Cool features and tough decisions: a comparison of variability modeling approaches. In: Sixth International Workshop on Variability Modeling of Software-Intensive Systems, pp. 173–182. ACM (2012)
16. Apel, S., Kastner, C., Lengauer, C.: FEATUREHOUSE: language-independent, automated software composition. In: Proceedings of the 31st International Conference on Software Engineering, pp. 221–231. IEEE Computer Society, May 2009
17. Batory, D., Sarvela, J.N., Rauschmayer, A.: Scaling step-wise refinement. IEEE Trans. Softw. Eng. **30**(6), 355–371 (2004)
18. Noda, N., Kishi, T.: Aspect-oriented modeling for variability management. In: 12th International Software Product Line Conference SPLC 2008, pp. 213–222. IEEE (2008)
19. Clarke, D., et al.: Modeling spatial and temporal variability with the HATS abstract behavioral modeling language. In: Bernardo, M., Issarny, V. (eds.) SFM 2011. LNCS, vol. 6659, pp. 417–457. Springer, Heidelberg (2011). https://doi.org/10.1007/978-3-642-21455-4_13
20. Berger, T.: A survey of variability modeling in industrial practice. In: Seventh International Workshop on Variability Modelling of Software-intensive Systems, p. 7. ACM (2013)
21. Pure: variants User's Guide. https://www.pure-systems.com/fileadmin/downloads/pure-variants/doc/pv-user-manual.pdf. Accessed 18 May 2018

Why Programming Must Be Supported by Modeling and How

Egon Börger[(✉)]

Dipartimento di Informatica, Università di Pisa, 56125 Pisa, Italy
boerger@di.unipi.it

Abstract. The development of code for software intensive systems involves numerous levels of abstraction, leading from requirements to code. Having abstract modeling concepts available as high-level programming constructs helps to define the code and to make sure that when the system runs with the software executed by machines, the software components behave in the expected way. We explain in this paper that nevertheless, there remains a gap, which cannot be closed by mere programming methods, but which can be closed if programming is supported by an appropriate modeling framework (a design and analysis method and a language).

1 Introduction

The title of this paper is a shorthand. Since (the meaning of) every program is a model of a part of the real world, programming is a form of modeling. Therefore, a more explicit formulation of the title is: Why and how much of programming in today's programming languages must be supported by modeling at higher levels of abstraction than that of the programming language. We use the term programming as short hand for programming *reliable complex* systems. So we speak about the development of code for complex software systems or for software intensive systems where it is critical that the software components do what they are supposed to do. Software intensive systems comprise systems where the software and the machines which execute it are only a part of the overall system, where for the code executing computer(s) the other parts appear as environment—technical equipment, physical surrounding, information systems, communication devices, external actors, humans—upon which the behavior of the software components depends and which they affect.

It is characteristic for the development of code for software intensive systems to involve descriptions at numerous levels of abstraction, leading from requirements through high-level design to machine executable code. For such descriptions, besides natural language (which is normally used to describe the requirements) a huge variety of dedicated (often ad hoc) languages and frameworks are available, covering the wide spectrum from direct coding in a programming language to pictorial (as such possibly not executable, 'abstract') models, consisting essentially of visual (graphical) descriptions which are then

© Springer Nature Switzerland AG 2018
T. Margaria and B. Steffen (Eds.): ISoLA 2018, LNCS 11244, pp. 89–110, 2018.
https://doi.org/10.1007/978-3-030-03418-4_6

transformed into more detailed textually described models and finally executable code. Well known examples of such graphical language constructs can be found, for example, in the OMG-languages UML, BPMN, SysML. In between one finds a myriad of textual, logic-based, formal specification languages, but also domain-specific languages and the interesting development of programming languages which directly offer constructs to express frequently occurring abstract modeling concepts. High-level programming constructs, like data types, collections, etc. clearly help to define the desired code and to justify that when the system runs, with the code executed by computer(s), the software components in fact behave the expected way. One finds them, to mention a few examples, in Java and C#, Scala (https://www.scala-lang.org/), Kotlin (https://kotlinlang.org/), K (http://www.theklanguage.com), etc.

However, natural language cannnot be avoided because it is the 'mother tongue' in which human stakeholders communicate to ensure a common understanding to capture the requirements correctly and completely. In particular, there remains a gap between requirements and code which for reasons of principle cannot be closed by mere programming constructs or model transformations. It appears prominently at the beginning of the chain which links the understanding by application domain experts (customers, users) of the system to-be-built to the behavior of the system when it runs under the control of the software. The question is how to relate in a controllably reliable way real-world items and behavior (objects, events and actions) to corresponding items in a textual or graphical description, whether directly by code or by an abstract model that is transformed in a correctness preserving manner to code.

In this paper we explain the three main facets of this epistemological problem:

- a *communication problem*,
- an *evidence problem*,
- an *experimental validation problem*.

We characterize the intrinsic properties of a language one needs to solve this problem. First, such a language must be **understandable** by the main parties involved, namely application domain experts (users, customers, who are not necessarily engineers) and software developers (designers and programmers). They need it as vehicle to intellectually grasp and transmit an adequate comprehension of complex systems. Second, to permit unambiguous system descriptions which are on the one side abstract enough and on the other side accurate enough, the language must allow the stakeholders to **calibrate the degree of precision** of descriptions (read: their level of abstraction) to the given problem and its application domain. Last but not least, the language must allow the software engineers to **link descriptions at different levels of abstraction**—transform models, lifting what compilers do to the given levels of abstraction—in a controllably correct and well documented way to code, using a practical refinement method that is supported by techniques for both, experimental validation and mathematical verification (whether informal, rigorous or formal and machine supported).

In Sect. 2 we explain the 'Why' in the title of the paper. It concerns the special epistemological status of *ground models*—the 'blueprints' through which domain experts and software developers must reach a common understanding of 'what to build' [28, p. 14]—and what this status implies for their validation as basis for the justification that the system, once it is built, behaves as intended.[1] In Sect. 3 we explain the 'How' in the title of the paper, namely how and in which sense the intended behavior, as defined by the ground model, can be shown to be 'preserved', in an objectively controllable and well documented way, by the software components developed for the system. This preservation of 'behavioral correctness' can be obtained via a set of either independent or successive refinement steps, which piecemeal implement abstract modeling terms by code, providing the details of the 'how to build', and are closely accompanied by corresponding validation and verification steps. It is here that high-level programming languages which offer support for frequently occuring modeling concepts are extremly helpful. We conclude in Sect. 4 with an explanation of the challenging problem to define practical, tool supportable patterns for stepwise refinements coming with corresponding stepwise verification techniques.

2 Ground Models

The development of reliable software, whose execution does—and can be explained to do—what it is supposed to do, needs a correct understanding and formulation of the project's real-word problem, including the context where the code executing computer is one among multiple components which together are expected to realize the desired overall system behavior. Such a problem description contains three parts:

- The domain experts (customers) are responsible for the **requirements**, which have to be turned into a sufficiently *precise and complete description of the intended system behavior* ('what to build' [28, p. 14]), at the level of abstraction and rigor of the given application domain.
- Given the requirements document, the design engineers must distill a **software specification**, that is a sufficiently precise[2] abstract description of the expected behavior of the software when executed by a computer in the system environment.
- Furthermore, the domain experts must provide a complete description of those **domain assumptions**, on the structure and behavior of the system components, on which the system designers can rely when it comes to guarantee

---

[1] To avoid a misunderstanding of the term 'ground' in 'ground model', we point out already here that during the development *process*, the ground models may be incomplete or incorrect and typically do change, usually incrementally; however, in each development phase there is one well-defined ground model which has to be related to its implementing code. This holds also in a more general sense for system evolution over time, as explained below.

[2] Here and above, what it means to be 'sufficiently precise' depends on the given problem and problem domain. The degree of precision must permit to perform the model inspection described in Sect. 2.2.

that the specification (and later also its implementation) behaves as system component the way the requirements demand to solve the given problem (*correctness property*). This document must make the underlying portion of implicit application-domain knowledge explicit which the software experts need to understand to make sure their understanding of the ground model is correct.

These three documents constitute what I call a *ground model*, although sometimes the term is also used to refer only to the software specification, which is what will be turned into the code to-be-built. The code development can start from these three documents; it also *must* start from them, if only because it is errorprone and expensive to start coding before the requirements are formulated correctly and put into an inspectable document. But be aware that the ground model is not only an initial model,[3] as used for example in the B-method [1]; it serves a heterogeneous group of stakeholders as the most abstract complete and correct model of the system to-be-built or of its evolutionary change due to new requirements that are requested to be incorporated. As a consequence, the ground model is subject to change during the code development process or during system evolution (often also called system maintenance), typically when additional or changed requirements appear; see the caveat below which explains why the three documents can be considered as finalized only at the end of the project, when the code is defined.

Whereas the system requirements and the domain assumptions are primarily under the responsibility of the domain experts, the software specification is shared by the two parties, standing between the application-domain-focussed requirements with the related domain assumptions and the software which has to be developed.

What is the special character of a ground model? Its constituents are targeted to support a common, objectively checkable understanding by humans—experts of different fields—of some desired behavior in the real world. This has three consequences:

- The descriptions must be formulated in a common language both domain and software experts understand. This *communication problem* has implications for the language in which ground models are formulated, showing a possible gap between such a language and programming languages, the latter being targeted to support the execution of programs by machines, see Sect. 2.1.
- To 'explain how the solution (read: the software specification) relates to the affairs of the world it helps to handle' [67, p. 254] presents an *evidence problem* we discuss in Sect. 2.2, evidence upon which every further system verification and validation is based. The problem arises because the real-world part involved in a ground model justification has no precise contour, so that mathematical reasoning does not apply.

---

[3] This is the reason why we changed the initially chosen name 'primary model' [9, p. 392] into 'ground model'.

- The experimental character of ground model verification implies the model *validation problem* we discuss in Sect. 2.3, which is about executability of models.

Ground model software specifications represent what in other engineering disciplines are called *blueprints*, for good reasons called 'golden models' in the semiconductor industry. It is general engineering practice that the stakeholders, together, analyze a system blueprint, reason about its features, test its appropriateness, maybe change it repeatedly, before proceeding in common agreement to the realization of the system. This is an effort to make sure that the system to-be-developed is well understood and, via its ground model, recognized as correct and complete. In [84] it is explained why 'there does not seem to be any compelling reason to treat the handling of models in software engineering in a radically different way than what is done in engineering in general'. In fact, as in classical engineering disciplines, also in software engineering a ground model serves as blueprint, providing the authoritative basis—a 'contract'—the software experts (designers and programmers) can rely upon for the software development via an appropriate refinement of model abstractions by code. Note that the use of ground models as software blueprints is not common practice and contradicts coding-alone forms of agile software development.

Remark on Agile Model Development. We remind the reader that the evolutionary character of the ground model design *process* usually implies frequent changes (additions, deletions, modifications) of the model, in particular in early development stages; but at each stage there is one binding ground model. It is here that agile development techniques can be adopted for ground model design, in particular in connection with the executable character of ground models described further in Sect. 2.3 and taking care that each ground model version is kept in sync with its executable counterpart.

For an example we can refer to the FALKO project at Siemens [21] which shows the industrial viability of this approach. In this project a central but defective railway process component (ca. 20 000 lines of handwritten, undocumented $C++$ code) of the system had to be reengineered. We used Abstract State Machines [26] to first define a ground model and then compile it to C^{++}, thus producing the code which was shipped to the Vienna Subway Operator. The definition of various ground model versions took 51 person weeks out of 66 of the entire project. In this first project phase we collected and modeled requirements, defined tentative ground models, inspected, tested and debugged them, using the ASM Workbench [31] to run the models on the given set of scenarios— until a model was reached which treated all scenarios in the expected way and satisfied all stakeholders. In the second phase of the project, it took 4 person weeks to write a compiler [83], for compiling the obtained ground model ASM to C^{++} code, and 11 person weeks to integrate the obtained Railway Process Model into the FALKO system (of ca. 300 000 lines of C^{++} code). Notably, (a) the developers and reviewers had no problem to understand the ASM models, (b) the tests performed with the ASM ground model versions uncovered bugs also in other components of the package, (c) the 'correctness' of the code has been obtained by the coherence of the ground model and its compilation. In fact, for the 4 installations of the system used by the Vienna Subway Operator since March 1999, one of them in daily use, until the entire system was replaced no failures or bugs were reported. When later additional requirements showed up, we introduced them into the ground model and the newly compiled code was shipped to Vienna.

Another non trivial example which illustrates the evolutionary character of ground model design can be found in the series of models in the literature which eventually led us to the ground model ASMs for Java and the Java Virtual Machine in [86]. Based upon these experiences, during my sabbatical at MS Research I suggested to the C# Development Group at Microsoft[4] to design ground model ASMs for defining and testing the desired semantics of C# constructs, prior to their implementation, and to use them for a precise documentation in the user manuals. Unfortunately, it was judged to be too risky to replace the traditional development process by a novel approach, so that the proposal has not been followed. However, two years later the Cambridge branch of Microsoft Research asked us to develop, within the Rotor project,[5] an ASM interpreter for C# programs [17] which defines a ground model for the semantics of the Ecma standard (which became the ISO standard) of C#. This work essentially turned out to be a *ground model reuse* project, adapting the Java/JVM ground model ASMs to C#/CLR ground model ASMs, see [27, 44]: an instance of evolutionary ground model development.

Returning to the special character of ground models, to be usable the way blueprints are used in other engineering disciplines, a ground model for the code one has to develop must have the following four properties, namely to be:

- *Precise* at the level of abstraction and rigor of the problem and of the application domain the model belongs to. This means that it contains no ambiguity which could lead the software developer to miscomprehend how the domain expert understands the model, in particular in its domain knowledge related features (which usually are not the principal domain of expertise of a software expert). See the discussion of the communication problem in Sect. 2.1.
- *Correct* in the sense that the model elements reliably and adequately convey the meaning of what in the real world they stand for. See the discussion of the evidence problem in Sect. 2.2.
- *Complete* in the sense that the model contains every behaviorally relevant system feature, but no elements which belong only to the implementation.
  - This completeness property is relative to the current understanding of the desired system and/or its implementation. It does not contradict the fact that most systems evolve over time, for example by adding more and more requirements: each system incarnation comes with its charateristic

---

[4] See my talk *A modular high-level definition of the dynamics of C sharp* to the group on September 27, 2000.

[5] See my talk *Abstract Operational Model for the Semantics of C#* delivered at the Microsoft Research Rotor Workshop, 23.-26.7.2002 (Queen's College, Cambridge).

complete set of features. A typical example are programs of a Product Line: the set of features in a Product Line usually increases with time, but every Product Line program instance has its defining complete set of features. In Sect. 3 we explain that the evolution of ground models must go hand-in-hand with a corresponding evolution of the code implementing them.

- *Consistent* in the sense that conflicting objectives, which may have been present in the original requirements, are resolved in the model.

It is important to be aware that the degree of detail which is required for a ground model depends on the given problem and problem domain. There is no absolute notion of precision, not even for logical systems. One cannot stress enough that what a ground model is concerned about is first of all **full understanding of what to build**, an understanding that must be shared by the stakeholders and the experts involved. In [84, Sect. 2.4] such models are called *descriptive* and distinguished from *prescriptive* models, whose role is to guide the implementation (by ground model refinements, as explained in Sect. 3). For example, the ground model ASMs for an interpreter of Prolog [23], Occam [15], Java [86, Part I] and C# [17] programs are descriptive models which explain the semantics of their language at the level of programming. The corresponding virtual machine models for the WAM [24], the Transputer [14], the JVM [86, Part II-III] and the .NET CLR [44] are of prescriptive character, representing a step towards the language implementation.

Note that completeness at the ground model level means that the model contains all elements which are relevant to guarantee the intended behavior, including descriptions of what in [84, Sect. 2.4] is called *primary functionality* together with the supporting system *infrastructure* (as far as relevant for the correct realization of the primary functionality), avoiding however to introduce details which are relevant only for the implementation.

Note that for epistemological reasons, the correctness and completeness properties cannot be established by purely model-relating means, since they relate precise conceptual features to phenomena in the real world, as further investigated in Sect. 2.2. In contrast, when a description is precise, its consistency, a logical, system-internal property, can be checked by rigorous, scientific, for software models typically by mathematical means.

2.1 Communication Problem

Why are **ground model descriptions** usually not directly programmed, but **must come prior to programming**?

Remember that a ground model, as blueprint of the code one has to develop, must be understandable for the two parties involved, for the software developers and for the experts of the corresponding application domain. This is a *communication problem* which is not taken seriously enough in current software engineering practice, although a thorough analysis of major accidents with software-intensive systems showed that 'The extra communication step between the engineer [read: the domain expert] and the software developer is the source of the most serious problems with software today' [63, Sect. 2.5]. The communication problem becomes only stronger where the domain experts are not familiar with mathematical notations, experts of their field but not used (neither willing to learn) to express their knowledge or reasoning in any formal logic, programming or mathematical language. This problem must be solved because domain experts and software engineers have to interact to define ground models, given that there are very few specialists who know the two fields involved so that they could define adequate ground models without further assistance.

To overcome the communication problem, the language in which ground models are formulated must have the capability to calibrate the degree of precision of descriptions to the given (any) application domain, so that a direct relation can be established between the real-world items and the linguistic counterparts which represent those items in the model. This is what Leibniz called 'proportio quaedam inter *characteres* ('symbols') et *res* ('things')' and considered to be the basis of truth: 'Et haec proportio sive relatio est *fundamentum veritatis*' [62]. A ground model must allow one 'to represent the concepts of the application domain at an adequate level of abstraction such that the specialities of the applications are directly represented and not covered by awkward implementation concepts' [29, Sect. 4].

To establish such a direct association of items in the world with linguistic expressions[6], the language must allow the modeler to **express directly**, without extraneous encoding, the following:

- every kind of real-world objects with their predicates (attributes and relations), which together constitute arbitrary system **states**,
- arbitrary actions to change the set of objects or some of their properties or relations, actions which constitute arbitrary **state changes**,
- **agents** (also called actors, or in [43] subjects) which perform the state changing actions following given (any) problem dependent rules.

In other words, contrary to a widely held view in the Formal Methods community, to be general enough the ground model language must be a portion of natural language which is

- generally understood,
- appropriately extendable by specific application domain concepts, where needed,
- clearly defined,

a language of the kind used in rigorous scientific and engineering disciplines, made up from precise and simple but general enough basic constructs to unambiguously and directly represent arbitrary real-world facts (states of affairs) and state changing events. Even high-level programming languages do not suffice for that, despite of the impressive progress modern programming languages made

---

[6] In [57, p. 163] such expressions are called 'ground terms' whose meaning is established by 'designations', relating the ground terms directly to phenomena one can observe in the real world. Note that designations are expressed in natural language.

to offer the programmers abstract concepts as commonly used in the language of mathematics, in particular logic and set theory. The reason is that each programming language is necessarily bound to a specific abstraction level, which is determined by the basic data structures, types and operations it offers.

Furthermore, modern (in particular object-oriented) programming languages, but also widely used OMG languages like UML, SysML, BPMN and other modeling languages, tend to put from the very beginning much attention on classes, their operations and structure, types, libraries, etc. which are of less importance for (and often hindering in the first phase of) system modeling (see [61] for a discussion). A similar observation has been made during the recent discussion whether coding is the new literacy, namely that 'programming as it exists now forces us to model, but it does so in an unnatural way' [49]. Also through analysing accidents of software intensive systems the need became clear that we must become 'able to grasp ... problems directly, without the intermediate muck of code' [85], to achieve an appropriate intellectual understanding of the system, given that 'Nearly all the serious accidents in which software has been involved in the past twenty years can be traced to requirements flaws, not coding errors.' [63, Sect. 2.5].

In particular, in a ground model language it must be possible to formulate in application-domain terms rules which govern the intended state changes. In its simplest and at the same time most general form, the underlying fundamental linguistic concept of 'commands' stating when and how to change the current state can be described by instructions of the following form:

$$\textbf{if } condition \textbf{ then do } action$$

to express that

- **if** in a given situation (read: in the current state) the *condition* (the expression of a statement) is true,
- **then** any actor which follows (read: executes) the instruction performs the *action*, thereby changing the state.

Instructions of this form are a well-understood fundamental element of natural language and present in any process description. Programming languages define specific instances of such instructions, those the programmer can use to form programs. Also to PROVE a *statement* in a system of logic is an instance of this scheme, namely **if** *condition* **then** PROVE(*statement*) where *condition* describes the axioms of the logic and PROVE the application of the deduction rules the underlying proof calculus offers to perform the proof for the *statement*. Under the name of 'guarded actions' or 'rules' such instructions appear also in various specification frameworks, each of which comes with a specific definition of what is allowed to appear as *condition* and *action*, see for example [2,4,33]. Concerning the understandability of ground models, the problem with such specific formal languages is that typically they are understood only by a rather restricted group of stakeholders, though formal languages contribute in an excellent way to do the work in appropriately circumscribed domains (see the role of domain-specific languages discussed below) and for specifically trained stakeholders.

In contrast, the distinguishing feature of the ASM method [26] is that it uses just the above abstract form of rules and nothing else,[7] rules with a rigorously defined yet intuitive and easy-to-grasp meaning which offer however the following:

- to refer without encoding to arbitrarily complex, application-domain specific structures as states,
- to use arbitrary state conditions and arbitrary actions which in application-domain terms (*'directly'*) update complex structured data,
- to be executed by concurrently running [25] actors.

This natural language character of ASM rules, in combination with their precise form and meaning, makes them suitable to solve not only the communication problem but also the evidence problem explained in the next Sect. 2.2. Note also that it is easy and mechanisable to turn an ASM into a behaviorally equivalent (though much larger!) natural language text; for a concrete illustration see [18].

2.2 Evidence Problem for Ground Models

The fact that a ground model must establish a relation between the real-world problem and the design of the code which has to be developed brings us to the *evidence problem* for ground models, mentioned in the introduction.[8] The real-world counterpart of a ground model does not exist as an object of study, to a wide extent it resides only in the heads of the domain experts. As a consequence, there is no way to 'prove' by whatever mathematical means the appropriateness of the association of real-world objects and relations with model elements. But **model inspection** can help to provide evidence of the needed adequate correspondence between on the one side ground model elements and events, and on the other side what happens in the part of the world the model expresses. This correspondence is what in [58] is called 'fidelity of models'. Such a review of the blueprint's fidelity must be performed in cooperation between the application-domain and the software experts, whereby the two parties can check in particular the correctness and completeness of the software specification, from where the code development has to start.

Model inspection is similar to code inspection, as commonly used in current software development practice, but (a) it involves not only programmers, but also domain and software design experts, (b) it happens at a higher level of abstraction than that of executable code, (c) it compares model elements to items and phenomena in the real world, and (d) it uses domain-specific knowledge and reasoning, which only in very special cases will be formally defined. To cite a practical example, such model inspections were critical for the development of the ground model ASM for the railway process model component of FALKO,

---

[7] The epistemological reason for this at first sight surprising conceptual comprehensiveness of ASMs is what is known as ASM Thesis, see [40,41,80,81] for recent work and detailed references to the literature on the thesis.

[8] In earlier publications we have called this a verification method problem, but since the word 'verification' carries a connotation of mathematical justification method, we move here to the more appropriate term 'evidence'.

the railway timetable validation and construction system [21] mentioned above. The feasability of model inspection has been tested during the Dagstuhl Seminar 'Practical Methods for Code Documentation and Inspection' [19], where the ground model [20] and the source code (see [65]) for the (rather simple, industrial) Production Cell case study [64] have successfully passed an inspection session.

The epistemological role of ground model inspection, to solve the evidence problem, shows one more reason why the language to formulate ground models must provide means to express states and state changes performed by actors *directly*, as explained in Sect. 2.1. The appropriateness check, of the link the inspection has to investigate between the model and the world, is strongly supported by coding-free expressability, which in turn necessitates linguistic support of descriptions at whatever abstraction level.

2.3   Validation Problem

The experimental character of ground model inspection brings us to the *validation problem* for ground models, which concerns models in general, including ground model refinements (see Sect. 3). A practically useful inspection procedure needs analysis support by repeatable experiments, aiming to falsify, in the Popperian sense [70], expected model behaviour (read: actions performed by agents), so that the model can be debugged before building the system. This is customary in traditional engineering disciplines. To make such an experimental validation possible for software models, these **software models should be executable**, conceptually or by machines (or be easily transformable into a machine executable version), so that runtime verification and testing become available at the application-domain level of abstraction. Model executability supports 'rapid prototyping of systems as part of the interative specification of requirements', as advocated in [28, p. 15].

To support ground model inspection often the very *concept of run of a model* suffices, e.g. to check scenario behavior (confirming its correctness or revealing a conceptual mistake). A characteristic recent example for this is the process algebra model developed in [39] (or its ASM version in [22, Ch. 6]) for the widely used Ad hoc On-Demand Distance Vector routing protocol AODV [68]. The model allowed their authors to exhibit some conceptual misbehavior in well-known implementations of the protocol, e.g. concerning the fundamental loop freedom and route correctness.

However, if the runs can be performed mechanically, by machines and not only intellectually, that increases the debugging potential considerably. We used both techniques with advantage for analyzing the Java and JVM ground models in [86], mathematically investigating runs of the ASM models and comparing them with the corresponding AsmGofer [82] runs of the refined executable model versions and with runs of Sun's code (see [86, Ch. A]). All the bugs we discovered in this process were reported to and corrected by Sun. Another interesting example is the above mentioned development of the ground model ASM for the railway process model component of the FALKO system [21]. In this project the requirements came as a set of scenarios so that no mathematical verification was possible, but the scenarios could be checked to validate the 'correctness' of the ground model. In fact, we validated it through AsmWorkbench [31] executions which confirmed the expectations of the scenarios. This was BEFORE compiling the ground model ASM to C^{++} code [83] (which, as mentioned already above, has worked for years in the Vienna subway system and never failed!).

This request for executability of software models is contrary to the still widely held view that software specifications should not be executable. The main reason which is usually given for this is that executability would imply a limitation of the expressiveness of the specification language [56]. Instead, declarative specifications are advocated,[9] using logic—axiom systems (algebraic approach) or equational theories (denotational approach)—to define the requirements, in an attempt to make specifications 'completely independent of any idea of computation' [50, p. 89], 'ideally ... *predicates* on solutions' [29, Introduction]. In particular, using descriptions where abstract assignment statements $f(s_1, \ldots, s_n) := t$ occur (as is typical for ASM models [26]) were declared by highly respected colleagues to belong to implementations (see the discussion in [10]). But the question is not whether descriptions are declarative or operational,[10] but at which level of abstraction they are formulated, as becomes clear also when one looks at B [1] or Event-B [2] or TLA+ [60] models (which formally are logical formulae but mimic the operational character of the described actions (assignments) by the x/x' notation). Different degrees of detailing serve the multiple roles of abstraction, such as providing an accurate and checkable overall system understanding, or isolating the hard parts of a system, or communicating and documenting design ideas, etc., depending on the role of every model, namely to serve a particular purpose, as emphasized in various systematic investigations of the general concept of 'model', see for example [42,87].

All in all, model executability offers high-level debugging which allows one to detect conceptual problems low-level code inspection easily misses. For a nice (famous and surprising) illustrating example about threads which concurrently run a termination detection protocol without central control see [46] (or [22, 3.2]). Model executability also helps to save on the enormous cost of late code-level testing or runtime verification. Model executability also supports exploratory software development processes.

---

[9] In [45], which contains a detailed evaluation of the pro and contra for executable specifications, it is rightly pointed out that 'non-executable' and 'declarative' are really different terms, as illustrated by the programming interpretation of Horn clauses in logic programming languages. Note also that since Horn clauses are a reduction class of first-order logic [16, Ch. 5.1], their computational interpretation is Turing complete so that using them implies no limitation of expressivity, at least in principle.

[10] For example, in the ASM method [26] one often uses purely declarative descriptions for complex back components, separating their definition from the abstract operational model of the system core under study.

3 Refinement Method

A critical, though software-engineering focussed, technical (not epistemological) question is how to transform a ground model in a correctness preserving way to code. There are at least three different ways to do this.

- **Direct Programming.** Here one proceeds from the ground model right away to programming in an appropriate programming language, using the ground model as the specification of the code functionality. Justifying the correctness of the implementation is supported by code inspection which checks and documents the design-intent-relation between high-level ground model and implementing code features.

  If the specification language supports modeling for change, this helps to identify and to perform the needed changes in the ground model and the corresponding code when during the maintenance phase, new requirements appear. The price to pay is to keep the ground model and the code in sync, the gain is that the design-intent-relation is kept, linking ground model objects and actions to code data and code segments. This results in less maintenance cost. For this approach, high-level languages which offer explicit expressions or instructions for abstract modeling concepts simplify the programming and justification task enormously. A strong support, as advocated by Language Oriented Programming [34,88] and supported by the Meta Programming System [66], comes also from domain-specific languages (DSLs) whose constructs directly reflect specific application domain concepts. This holds also if the DSL is directly implemented in a high-level programming language, see some characteristic examples in [3,54,55].

  Note that plugins in CoreASM [30] provide support for (also domain-specific) extensions of executable ASM models. One reviewer rightly expressed the concern that 'perhaps there are simply too many specialist fields in order for a generic method to be able to use anything except natural language'. The ASM method does not offer silver bullets for software development. It is generic not as a 'universal formalism', but only in offering an abstraction potential that allows the designer to use *arbitrary* structures and operations to *directly* and accurately model, validate and verify whatever specific application domain features.[11] Therefore, one can use this direct expressability by an ASM model, which is a description in the portion of natural language the domain experts use, to avoid having to define 'a DSL just to be able to talk to specialist stakeholders in a certain field once only'. In such once-only cases it is appropriate to directly program the ground model if its concepts and actions are easily implementable by those the programming language offers. Furthermore, in such cases the conceptual executability of ground model ASMs must suffice for their inspection because it would probably be too expensive to create plug-ins for the language extension by the domain specific features which appear in the model.

---

[11] In fact, the use of the ASM method is compatible with and integratable into most software development frameworks.

- **Compilation.** In this approach one writes a compiler for a class of ground models that includes the variety one has to expect in the given application domain where requirements keep changing. Having a compiler at hand, to capture the system evolution it suffices to adapt the models and then compile them to produce the code for the new system. For two examples see [6,21]. In this case, justifying the correctness of model implementations consists in showing that the compiler translates ground model items (objects, events, actions) correctly to code. This compiler correctness needs to be shown only once, by verification experts, so that the correctness problem for the code which implements a concrete ground model is reduced to the ground model correctness problem—a fruitful application of the divide-and-conquer principle.
- **Stepwise Refinement.** This approach can be combined with the compilation and the direct programming approach. Here one uses stepwise model refinement to turn the descriptive ground model into a prescriptive implementation model (term we borrow from [84]), leading through a set of intermediate more and more detailed models to a class of compilable ASMs or to (compilable) code.[12] This approach is appropriate if the gap between the ground model abstractions and the level of detail needed for the target code is large and mediated by multiple design decisions. In such cases it is helpful—and often leads to a natural component structure for the code—to split the implementation into multiple steps, making each of the various design decisions explicit by a corresponding refinement step. We mention various examples in the conclusion section. To guarantee the preservation of the design intent, each refinement step has to be checked to be correct; the verification should be documented to be controllable. Executability of refined models supports their experimental validation by simulations.

  The refinements (and their justification) are work of the software engineer, including the special case where a refinement step reveals the necessity to correct or complete the ground model in cooperation with the domain experts. The application-domain expert has to rely upon the professionality of the implementor who understands all the details of the language used for model refinements and code. The practicality of this approach depends on the refinement concept (see Sect. 4). To be practical, a refinement notion must allow the software engineer to express, apply and document any design decision clearly and controllably, without being restricted by a priori syntactical or verification method constraints. As pointed out in [58], this holds in particular for refinements used when modeling the interaction between software and the related part of the real world in cyber-physical systems.

---

[12] In the ASM method these refinements are called *vertical* refinement, which implement abstractions, as distinguished from *horizontal* refinements which extend a system by additional functionalities.

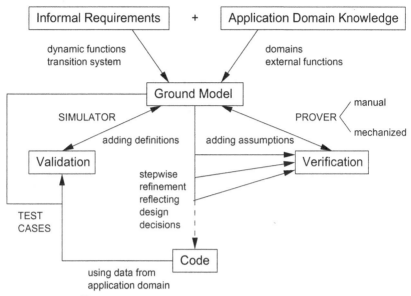

The figure above[13] illustrates the structure of such a software development process, as supported by the ASM method [26].

Caveat. It is a common experience that inconsistencies and conflicts between different design proposals and missing or incorrect requirements often are only detected in fine-grained models. Their resolution has to backtrack in the refinement hierarchy (which is more often a set of largely independent implementation steps than a chain), possibly coming back to the ground model. For this reason, the completeness and correctness of the ground model are guaranteed only once the final code is ready; the *process* of building the ground model and its refinements is by no means linear. But to support the maintenance and above all the evolution of software efficiently, it is important that all models involved by the code, each one reflecting some particular design decision, are fully documented and kept in sync. Each code version should come with its ground model and the refinement steps which link the two. Such a documentation of software evolution and maintenance avoids to create a legacy code problem.

4   Conclusion: Refinement Patterns

This is not the place to evaluate to which degree which modeling methods support building satisfactory ground models and refining them to code. The above investigation of the epistemological and the technical problems concerning the relation between programming and modeling does not depend on any specific modeling framework, though most illustrating examples in this paper refer to

---

[13] © 2003 Springer-Verlag Berlin Heidelberg, reprinted with permission, copied from [26].

ASMs. There is no reason to hide that, by now for three decades, I have formed, applied and advocated the ASM method. It comes with a (for models of computing) arguably most comprehensive[14] and at the same time simple and precise concept of 'model', namely ASMs,[15] and has been used with success to build ground models and their refinements for various complex software intensive systems, industrial standards and semantics of programming languages (for surveys see [26, Ch. 9], [22, p. 4] and [12], respectively).

However, I want to comment upon a doubt expressed by one reviewer who wonders whether ASMs are 'really adequate' to satisfy the requirements for ground models stated in Sect. 2, pointing out that their expressivity comes 'at the price of quite some conceptual complexity, which, to my experience, is far beyond the capabilities of typical domain experts'. My personal experience is different, but this may depend on the kind of domain experts one works with. More importantly, an adequate ASM model of a system will always reflect the inherent functional complexity of that system and cannot reduce it, but an ASM model can be fine-tuned to exactly the given application-domain-determined level of complexity, without complicating matters by any form of formal overhead. If the conceptual complexity of a system to be built is beyond the capabilities of a domain expert, this lack of system specific application-domain expertise has to be filled before the person can act as a professional cooperation partner for formulating the requirements, as the basis for *building* the system, and for checking that the ground model satisfies them. Note that if we speak only about a correct *use* of an existing system, this may be possible without specific domain-knowledge; e.g. no particular technical knowledge is required to use credit cards.

To conclude, I want to formulate a challenging problem, hoping that it may attract somebody. It concerns mainly, but not only, the ASM method [22,26] for software development.

A characteristic feature of the ASM method is its refinement notion [11], which has been developed originally for a modular definition of the semantics of Prolog (see [7–9]). ASM refinements allow one to refine not only data, but also operations (rules) and more generally entire segments of computation. This feature offers the designer ways to describe design ideas directly in terms of ASM refinement steps, but it also makes the notion considerably more general and harder to implement than the various refinement concepts in other state-based specification methods, e.g. B [1], Event-B [2], TLA$^+$ [60] and Z [32] (among others). These methods come with carefully restricted refinement definitions so that the refinements are supported by the corresponding proof tools.

There is an unavoidable trade-off between generality of the refinement notion and the degree to which it can be supported by theorem provers. Schellhorn has investigated the ASM refinement notion thoroughly in [71–75] and has implemented it in the KIV [59] theorem prover. The original goal was to machine check, using KIV [76,77], the WAM correctness proof in [24]; this proof proceeds via a hierarchy of a dozen proven-to-be-correct ASM refinement steps,

---

[14] See the footnote above on the various forms of the ASM Thesis.

[15] For an investigation of other modeling concepts see [42,87].

starting with a ground model ASM [23] (which was used to define the ISO standard of Prolog [13]) and leading to a complete model of the WAM. In the sequel, KIV verification has been applied to various other ASM models using the ASM refinement mechanism. Two major examples are the electronic purse case study Mondex [52] and the flash file system verification [78]. The Mondex example illustrates the practical feasibility of the ASM refinement approach for code verification: the refinement from the transaction to the protocol level [79] deals with the original Mondex case study, but the authors could also add a refinement to the security level (with crypto primitives) [51,53] and a refinement from there to Java code [48]. It is interesting to note that for the verification of the flash file system the refinement theory had to be developed further to handle not only functional correctness, but also crash safety, down to the level of code (see [36,69]). In particular [37], which further refines the high-level models in [38], illustrates the crucial role of finding appropriate intermediate models to verify that low-level features, like recovery from unexpected power cuts, are guaranteed.

The ASM refinement notion has been implemented also in PVS [35] where it has been used for compiler correctness proofs, starting with ASM ground models for source and target languages [47,89].

Here is the challenge: is it possible to distill practically useful *refinement patterns* which come with corresponding tool supported proof patterns, using the general ASM refinement concept?[16] I addressed this question to colleagues in the theorem proving community when in [5] we realized that the Java2JVM compilation correctness theorem, as stated and proved for stepwise refined ASM models of Java/JVM in [86], could have been proved by instruction-wise refinement steps where each new instruction is accompanied by a modular proof extension. This supports modeling for change and software product lines in a rather strong way. Can such a modular (in logical terms 'conservative') proof extension which corresponds to an ASM refinement step be supported by current theorem provers and to what extent?

Acknowledgement. We thank the following colleagues for a critical reading of various drafts of the paper: Don Batory, Heinz Dobler, Albert Fleischmann, Uwe Glässer, Daniel Jackson, Michael Jackson, Alexander Raschke, Klaus-Dieter Schewe and two anonymous referees.

---

[16] In the theoretical literature the prevailing view is determined by a search for *compositional* design and proof patterns, but it will be hard to find patterns for composing complex systems out of a large number of small simple models and a fortiori compositional refinement patterns in practice, in particular for modeling cyber-physical systems, simply because, as has been observed in [58], 'Compositionality is not found in the real physical world'.

References

1. Abrial, J.-R.: The B-Book. Cambridge University Press, Cambridge (1996)
2. Abrial, J.-R.: Modeling in Event-B. Cambridge University Press, New York (2010)
3. Artho, C., Havelund, K., Kumar, R., Yamagata, Y.: Domain-specific languages with scala. In: Butler, M., Conchon, S., Zaïdi, F. (eds.) ICFEM 2015. LNCS, vol. 9407, pp. 1–16. Springer, Cham (2015). https://doi.org/10.1007/978-3-319-25423-4_1
4. Back, R., Kurki-Suoni, R.: Decentralization of process nets with centralized control. Technical report Ser. A, No. 58, Department of Computer Science at Abo Akademi, Abo, Finland, February 1988
5. Batory, D., Börger, E.: Modularizing theorems for software product lines: the Jbook case study. J. Univers. Comput. Sci. **14**(12), 2059–2082 (2008)
6. Berry, G.: Formally unifying modeling and design for embedded systems - a personal view. In: Margaria, T., Steffen, B. (eds.) ISoLA 2016. LNCS, vol. 9953, pp. 134–149. Springer, Cham (2016). https://doi.org/10.1007/978-3-319-47169-3_11
7. Börger, E.: A logical operational semantics of full Prolog. Part I: selection core and control. In: Börger, E., Büning, H.K., Richter, M.M. (eds.) CSL 1989. LNCS, vol. 440, pp. 36–64. Springer, Heidelberg (1990). https://doi.org/10.1007/3-540-52753-2_31
8. Börger, E.: A logical operational semantics of full Prolog. Part II: built-in predicates for database manipulations. In: Rovan, B. (ed.) MFCS 1990. LNCS, vol. 452, pp. 1–14. Springer, Heidelberg (1990). https://doi.org/10.1007/BFb0029592
9. Börger, E.: Logic programming: the evolving algebra approach. In: Pehrson, B., Simon, I. (eds.) IFIP 13th World Computer Congress. Technology/Foundations, vol. 1, pp. 391–395. Elsevier, Amsterdam (1994)
10. Błlorger, E.: Review of E. W. Dijkstra and C. S. Scholten. Predicate Calculus and Program Semantics. Springer, Heidelberg (1989). https://doi.org/10.1007/978-1-4612-3228-5; Science of Computer Programming 23, 1–11 (1994)
11. Börger, E.: The ASM refinement method. Form. Aspects Comput. **15**, 237–257 (2003)
12. Börger, E.: The abstract state machines method for modular design and analysis of programming languages. J. Logic Comput. **27**(2), 417–439 (2014)
13. Börger, E., Dässler, K.: Prolog: DIN papers for discussion. ISO/IEC JTCI SC22 WG17 Prolog Standardization Document 58, National Physical Laboratory (1990)
14. Börger, E., Durdanović, I.: Correctness of compiling Occam to Transputer code. Comput. J. **39**(1), 52–92 (1996)
15. Börger, E., Durdanović, I., Rosenzweig, D.: Occam: specification and compiler correctness. Part I: simple mathematical interpreters. In: Montanari, U., Olderog, E.R. (eds.) Proceedings of the PROCOMET 1994, IFIP Working Conference on Programming Concepts, Methods and Calculi, North-Holland, pp. 489–508 (1994)
16. Börger, E., Grädel, E., Gurevich, Y.: The Classical Decision Problem. Perspectives in Mathematical Logic. Springer, Heidelberg (1997). Second printing in "Universitext", Springer 2001
17. Börger, E., Fruja, G., Gervasi, V., Stärk, R.: A high-level modular definition of the semantics of C#. Theor. Comput. Sci. **336**(2–3), 235–284 (2005)
18. Börger, E., Gargantini, A., Riccobene, E.: Abstract state machines. A method for system specification and analysis. In: Frappier, M., Habrias, H. (eds.) Software Specification Methods: An Overview Using a Case Study, pp. 103–119. HERMES Sc. Publ. (2006)

19. Börger, E., Joannou, P., Parnas, D.L.: Practical Methods for Code Documentation and Inspection, vol. 178. Dagstuhl Seminar No. 9720, Schloss Dagstuhl, International Conference and Research Center for Computer Science, May 1997
20. Börger, E., Mearelli, L.: Integrating ASMs into the software development life cycle. J. Univers. Comput. Sci. **3**(5), 603–665 (1997)
21. Börger, E., Päppinghaus, P., Schmid, J.: Report on a practical application of ASMs in software design. In: Gurevich, Y., Kutter, P.W., Odersky, M., Thiele, L. (eds.) ASM 2000. LNCS, vol. 1912, pp. 361–366. Springer, Heidelberg (2000). https://doi.org/10.1007/3-540-44518-8_20
22. Börger, E., Raschke, A.: Modeling Companion for Software Practitioners. Springer, Heidelberg (2018). https://doi.org/10.1007/978-3-662-56641-1. For Corrigenda and lecture material on themes treated in the book see http://modelingbook.informatik.uni-ulm.de
23. Börger, E., Rosenzweig, D.: A mathematical definition of full Prolog. Sci. Comput. Program. **24**, 249–286 (1995)
24. Börger, E., Rosenzweig, D.: The WAM - definition and compiler correctness. In: Beierle, C., Plümer, L. (eds.) Logic Programming: Formal Methods and Practical Applications. Studies in Computer Science and Artificial Intelligence, vol. 11, Chapter 2, pp. 20–90. North-Holland (1995)
25. Börger, E., Schewe, K.-D.: Concurrent abstract state machines. Acta Informatica **53**(5), 469–492 (2016). https://doi.org/10.1007/s00236-015-0249-7. Listed as Notable Article in ACM 21th Annual BEST OF COMPUTING, see http://www.computingreviews.com/recommend/bestof/notableitems.cfm?bestYear=2016
26. Börger, E., Stärk, R.F.: Abstract State Machines. A Method for High-Level System Design and Analysis. Springer, Heidelberg (2003). https://doi.org/10.1007/978-3-642-18216-7
27. Börger, E., Stärk, R.F.: Exploiting abstraction for specification reuse. The Java/C# case study. In: de Boer, F.S., Bonsangue, M.M., Graf, S., de Roever, W.-P. (eds.) FMCO 2003. LNCS, vol. 3188, pp. 42–76. Springer, Heidelberg (2004). https://doi.org/10.1007/978-3-540-30101-1_3
28. Brooks, F.P.: No silver bullet: essence and accidents of software engineering. Computer **20**(4), 10–19 (1987)
29. Broy, M., Havelund, K., Kumar, R.: Towards a unified view of modeling and programming. In: Margaria, T., Steffen, B. (eds.) ISoLA 2016, Part II. LNCS, vol. 9953, pp. 238–257. Springer, Cham (2016). https://doi.org/10.1007/978-3-319-47169-3_17
30. The CoreASM Project. http://www.coreasm.org and https://github.com/coreasm/, since 2005
31. Del Castillo, G.: The ASM Workbench. A Tool Environment for Computer-Aided Analysis and Validation of Abstract State Machine Models. Ph.D. thesis, Universität Paderborn, Germany (2001). Published in HNI-Verlagsschriftenreihe, vol. 83
32. Derrick, J., Boiten, E.A.: Refinement in Z and Object-Z. Springer, London (2001). https://doi.org/10.1007/978-1-4471-0257-1
33. Dijkstra, E.: Guarded commands, non-determinacy and formal derivation of programs. Commun. ACM **18**(8), 453–457 (1975). Also documented as EWD 472
34. Dmitriev, S.: Language oriented programming: The next programming paradigm. onBoard Electronic Monthly Magazine, April 2010. http://www.onboard.jetbrains.com/articles/04/10/lop/index.html
35. Dold, A.: A formal representation of Abstract State Machines using PVS. Verifix Technical report Ulm/6.2, Universität Ulm, Germany, July 1998

36. Ernst, G., Pfähler, J.: Modular, crash-safe refinement for ASMs with submachines. Sci. Comput. Program. **131**, 3–21 (2016). Alloy, B, TLA, VDM and Z (ABZ 2014)
37. Ernst, G., Pfähler, J., Schellhorn, G., Reif, W.: Inside a verified flash file system: transactions and garbage collection. In: Gurfinkel, A., Seshia, S.A. (eds.) VSTTE 2015. LNCS, vol. 9593, pp. 73–93. Springer, Cham (2016). https://doi.org/10.1007/978-3-319-29613-5_5
38. Ernst, G., Schellhorn, G., Haneberg, D., Pfähler, J., Reif, W.: Verification of a virtual filesystem switch. In: Cohen, E., Rybalchenko, A. (eds.) VSTTE 2013. LNCS, vol. 8164, pp. 242–261. Springer, Heidelberg (2014). https://doi.org/10.1007/978-3-642-54108-7_13
39. Fehnker, A., van Glabbeek, R., Hoefner, P., McIver, A., Portmann, M., Tan, W.L.: A process algebra for wireless mesh networks used for modelling, verifying and analysing AODV. Technical report 5513, NICTA, Brisbane, Australia (2013)
40. Ferrarotti, F., Schewe, K.-D., Tec, L.: A behavioural theory for reflective sequential algorithms. In: Petrenko, A.K., Voronkov, A. (eds.) PSI 2017. LNCS, vol. 10742, pp. 117–131. Springer, Cham (2018). https://doi.org/10.1007/978-3-319-74313-4_10
41. Ferrarotti, F., Schewe, K.-D., Tec, L., Wang, Q.: A new thesis concerning synchronised parallel computing - simplified parallel ASM thesis. Theor. Comp. Sci. **649**, 25–53 (2016)
42. Fleischmann, A., Oppl, S., Schmidt, W., Stary, C.: Ganzheitliche Digitalisierung von Prozessen. Springer, Heidelberg (2018). https://doi.org/10.1007/978-3-658-22648-0. Open Access Book
43. Fleischmann, A., Schmidt, W., Stary, C., Obermeier, S., Börger, E.: Subject-Oriented Business Process Management. Springer, Heidelberg (2012). https://doi.org/10.1007/978-3-642-32392-8. http://www.springer.com/978-3-642-32391-1 (Open Access Book)
44. Fruja, N.G.: Type Safety of C# and .NET CLR. Ph.D. thesis, ETH Zürich (2006)
45. Fuchs, N.E.: Specifications are (preferably) executable. Softw. Eng. J. **7**, 323–334 (1992)
46. Gervasi, V., Riccobene, E.: From English to ASM: on the process of deriving a formal specification from a natural language one. In Integration of Tools for Rigorous Software Construction and Analysis, volume 3(9) of Dagstuhl Report, pp. 85–90 (2014). Dagstuhl Seminar 13372 organized by Uwe Glässer, Stefan Hallerstede, Michael Leuschel, Elvinia Riccobene, 08.–13 September 2013. https://doi.org/10.4230/DagRep.3.9.74, URN: urn:nbn:de:0030-drops-43584, http://drops.dagstuhl.de/opus/volltexte/2014/4358/
47. Goerigk, W., et al.: Compiler correctness and implementation verification: The Verifix approach. In: Fritzson, P. (ed.) International Conference on Compiler Construction, Proceedings Poster Session of CC 1996, IDA Technical Report LiTH-IDA-R-96-12, Linköping, Sweden (1996)
48. Grandy, H., Bischof, M., Stenzel, K., Schellhorn, G., Reif, W.: Verification of Mondex electronic purses with KIV: from a security protocol to verified code. In: Cuellar, J., Maibaum, T., Sere, K. (eds.) FM 2008. LNCS, vol. 5014, pp. 165–180. Springer, Heidelberg (2008). https://doi.org/10.1007/978-3-540-68237-0_13
49. Granger, C.: Coding is not the new literacy, January 2015. http://www.chris-granger.com/2015/01/26/coding-is-not-the-new-literacy/. Consulted 01 December 2017
50. Hall, J.A.: Taking Z seriously. In: Bowen, J.P., Hinchey, M.G., Till, D. (eds.) ZUM 1997. LNCS, vol. 1212, pp. 87–91. Springer, Heidelberg (1997). https://doi.org/10.1007/BFb0027285

51. Haneberg, D., Grandy, H., Reif, W., Schellhorn, G.: Verifying smart card applications: an ASM approach. In: Davies, J., Gibbons, J. (eds.) IFM 2007. LNCS, vol. 4591, pp. 313–332. Springer, Heidelberg (2007). https://doi.org/10.1007/978-3-540-73210-5_17
52. Haneberg, D., Moebius, N., Reif, W., Schellhorn, G., Stenzel, K.: Mondex: engineering a provable secure electronic purse. Int. J. Softw. Inform. **5**(1), 159–184 (2011). http://www.ijsi.org
53. Haneberg, D., Schellhorn, G., Grandy, H., Reif, W.: Verification of Mondex electronic purses with KIV: from transactions to a security protocol. Form. Aspects Comput. **20**(1), 41–59 (2008)
54. Havelund, K.: Data automata in scala. In: Leucker, M., Wang, J. (eds.) Proceedings of the 8th International Symposium on Theoretical Aspects of Software Engineering (TASE), pp. 1–9. IEEE Computer Society Press (2014)
55. Havelund, K., Joshi, R.: Modeling and monitoring of hierarchical state machines in scala. In: Romanovsky, A., Troubitsyna, E.A. (eds.) SERENE 2017. LNCS, vol. 10479, pp. 21–36. Springer, Cham (2017). https://doi.org/10.1007/978-3-319-65948-0_2
56. Hayes, I.J., Jones, C.B.: Specifications are not (necessarily) executable. Softw. Eng. J. **4**(6), 330–33 (1989)
57. Jackson, M.: Problem Frames. Addison-Wesley, Boston (2001)
58. Jackson, M.: The right-hand side problem: Research topics in RE. In: RE Silver Jubilee, RE 2017, Lisbon, 6 September 2017
59. The KIV System. http://www.informatik.uni-augsburg.de/lehrstuehle/swt/se/kiv/
60. Lamport, L.: Specifying Systems: The TLA+ Language and Tools for Hardware and Software Engineers. Addison-Wesley (2002). http://lamport.org
61. Lamport, L., Paulson, L.C.: Should your specification language be typed? ACM Trans. Program. Lang. Syst. **21**(3), 502–526 (1999)
62. Leibniz, G.W.: Dialogus de connexione inter res et verba. Leibniz, G.W.: Philosophische Schriften, August 1677. Edited by Leibniz-Forschungsstelle der Universität Münster, vol. 4 A, n.8. Akademie Verlag (1999)
63. Leveson, N.G.: Engineering a Safer World: Systems Thinking Applied to Safety. Engineering Systems. MIT Press, Cambridge (2012)
64. Lewerentz, C., Lindner, T. (eds.): Formal Development of Reactive Systems. LNCS, vol. 891. Springer, Heidelberg (1995). https://doi.org/10.1007/3-540-58867-1
65. Mearelli, L.: Refining an ASM specification of the production cell to C++ code. J. Univers. Comput. Sci. **3**(5), 666–688 (1997)
66. Meta Programming System. https://www.jetbrains.com/mps/
67. Naur, P.: Programming as Theory Building. Microprocessing and Microprogramming, vol. 15 (1985)
68. Perkins, C., Belding-Royer, E., Das, S.: Ad hoc on-demand distance vector (AODV) routing. Technical report RFC 3561, Copyright (C) The Internet Society, Network Working Group, July 2003. http://tools.ietf.org/html/rfc3561
69. Pfähler, J., Ernst, G., Bodenmüller, S., Schellhorn, G., Reif, W.: Modular verification of order-preserving write-back caches. In: Polikarpova, N., Schneider, S. (eds.) IFM 2017. LNCS, vol. 10510, pp. 375–390. Springer, Cham (2017). https://doi.org/10.1007/978-3-319-66845-1_25
70. Popper, K.: Logik der Forschung. Springer, Heidelberg (1935)
71. Schellhorn, G.: Verification of ASM refinements using generalized forward simulation. J. Univers. Comput. Sci. **7**(11), 952–979 (2001)

72. Schellhorn, G.: ASM refinement and generalizations of forward simulation in data refinement: a comparison. Theor. Comput. Sci. **336**(2–3), 403–436 (2005)
73. Schellhorn, G.: ASM refinement preserving invariants. J. UCS **14**(12), 1929–1948 (2008)
74. Schellhorn, G.: Completeness of ASM refinement. Electr. Notes Theor. Comput. Sci. **214**, 25–49 (2008)
75. Schellhorn, G.: Completeness of fair ASM refinement. Sci. Comput. Program. **76**(9), 756–773 (2011)
76. Schellhorn, G., Ahrendt, W.: Reasoning about abstract state machines: the WAM case study. J. Univers. Comput. Sci. **3**(4), 377–413 (1997)
77. Schellhorn, G., Ahrendt, W.: The WAM case study: verifying compiler correctness for Prolog with KIV. In: Bibel, W., Schmitt, P. (eds.) Automated Deduction - A Basis for Applications, volume III: Applications, pp. 165–194. Kluwer Academic Publishers, Dordrecht (1998)
78. Schellhorn, G., Ernst, G., Pfähler, J., Haneberg, D., Reif, W.: Development of a verified flash file system. ABZ 2014. LNCS, vol. 8477, pp. 9–24. Springer, Heidelberg (2014). https://doi.org/10.1007/978-3-662-43652-3_2
79. Schellhorn, G., Grandy, H., Haneberg, D., Moebius, N., Reif, W.: A systematic verification approach for Mondex electronic purses using ASMs. In: Abrial, J.-R., Glässer, U. (eds.) Rigorous Methods for Software Construction and Analysis. LNCS, vol. 5115, pp. 93–110. Springer, Heidelberg (2009). https://doi.org/10.1007/978-3-642-11447-2_7
80. Schewe, K.-D., Ferrarotti, F., Tec, L., Wang, Q.: Distributed adaptive systems: theory, specification, reasoning. In: Butler, M., Raschke, A., Hoang, T.S., Reichl, K. (eds.) ABZ 2018. LNCS, vol. 10817, pp. 16–30. Springer, Cham (2018). https://doi.org/10.1007/978-3-319-91271-4_2
81. Schewe, K.-D., Ferrarotti, F., Tec, L., Wang, Q., An, W.: Evolving concurrent systems: behavioural theory and logic. In: Proceedings of the Australasian Computer Science Week Multiconference (ACSW 2017), pp. 77:1–77:10. ACM (2017)
82. Schmid, J.: Executing ASM specifications with AsmGofer. https://tydo.eu/AsmGofer
83. Schmid, J.: Compiling abstract state machines to C++. J. Univers. Comput. Sci. **7**(11), 1069–1088 (2001)
84. Selic, B.: Programming ⊂ Modeling ⊂ Engineering. In: Margaria, T., Steffen, B. (eds.) ISoLA 2016. LNCS, vol. 9953, pp. 11–26. Springer, Cham (2016). https://doi.org/10.1007/978-3-319-47169-3_2
85. Somers, J.: The coming software apocalypse. The Atlantic, 26 September 2017. Email newsletter, consulted on 11 November 2017
86. Stärk, R.F., Schmid, J., Börger, E.: Java and the Java Virtual Machine: Definition, Verification, Validation. Springer, Heidelberg (2001). https://doi.org/10.1007/978-3-642-59495-3
87. Thalheim, B., Nissen, I. (eds.): Wissenschaft und Kunst der Modellierung: Kieler Zugang zur Definition, Nutzung und Zukunft. Philosophische Analyse/Philosophical Analysis. vol. 64, De Gruyter (2015)
88. Ward, M.P.: Language oriented programming. Softw. Concepts Tools **15**(4), 147–161 (1994)
89. Zimmerman, W., Gaul, T.: On the construction of correct compiler back-ends: an ASM approach. J. Univers. Comput. Sci. **3**(5), 504–567 (1997)

On Models and Code
A Unified Approach to Support
Large-Scale Deductive Program Verification

Marieke Huisman[(⊠)]

University of Twente, Enschede, The Netherlands
m.huisman@utwente.nl

Abstract. Despite the substantial progress in the area of deductive program verification over the last years, it still remains a challenge to use deductive verification on large-scale industrial applications. In this abstract, I analyse why this is case, and I argue that in order to solve this, we need to soften the border between models and code. This has two important advantages: (1) it would make it easier to reason about high-level behaviour of programs, using deductive verification, and (2) it would allow to reason about incomplete applications during the development process. I discuss how the first steps towards this goal are supported by verification techniques within the VerCors project, and I will sketch the future steps that are necessary to realise this goal.

1 The Problem: Scaling Deductive Program Verification

Deductive program verification is a technique to prove the correctness of a program w.r.t. its specification, which is given in terms of pre- and postconditions of the methods occurring in the program, following the Design-by-Contract principle [20]. Typically deductive program verification uses (an extension or variant of) Hoare logic [12] or dynamic logic [8] as its underlying verification technique.

Over the last years, enormous progress has been made on the use of such deductive program verification techniques for non-trivial examples, such as for example the discovery of a bug in Timsort [11], the verification of a Linux's USB keyboard driver [25], the verification of avionics software [7], and the various VerifyThis challenges (see *e.g.*, [14,17]). There are many different factors that have contributed to this progress, such as:

- the increase in power of automated provers,
- efficient use of multi-core hardware for formal verification tools,
- developments in specification languages, and
- the development of new verification theories, such as the use of concurrent separation logics to reason in a modular way about concurrent programs [3, 18,21].

Of course, there exist other formal analysis techniques that provide a much higher level of automation than deductive program verification, but the attractiveness of deductive program verification lies in that (1) it can be used to reason

© Springer Nature Switzerland AG 2018
T. Margaria and B. Steffen (Eds.): ISoLA 2018, LNCS 11244, pp. 111–118, 2018.
https://doi.org/10.1007/978-3-030-03418-4_7

about a very large and flexible class of program properties, and (2) it allows to reason about programs with an unbounded state space, and in particular about parametrised programs, i.e., it is possible to prove that a method void m (int n) respect its specification for any possible value of its parameter n.

Therefore, I believe it is important to investigate why the use of deductive program verification on large-scale industrial examples remains difficult, and what can be done to improve this situation. To understand why the use of deductive program verification remains difficult, many different reasons can be given, but I believe the most important ones are the following.

- Applications are often simply *too large* to handle, and the verifier lacks the overview of the complete application. Deductive program verification is traditionally quite closely connected to the concrete code, and as a result, it can be difficult to reason about the application at a suitable level of abstraction, because too many low-level details have to be dealt with.
- Deductive program verification typically requires a high number of auxiliary annotations (loop invariants, intermediate assertions), which require a detailed understanding of the code and of the verification process.
- For large applications, if we wish to use deductive program verification *during* the development process, when not all components are available yet, typically the deductive program verification tools require at least some stubs (for example, method contracts for the unimplemented methods) for the missing parts before the available components can be verified.
- To reason about *global* system properties (which is necessary if we wish to show that the program requirements are fulfilled) we need to have some way to reason about the missing components as well.
- As mentioned above, deductive program verification techniques are developed for pre-postcondition-style specifications, which usually do not match well with how high-level program requirements are expressed. We need formal techniques to connect these two levels of specifications.

In this position paper, I propose to work on the unification of models and code, to provide a solution to this problem. I will then sketch the first steps towards this solution, which we are currently developing within in the VerCors tool set. Finally, I will conclude by outlining further research challenges that need to be addressed to fully achieve my proposed solution.

2   The Solution: Unification of Models and Code

I believe that to make the use of deductive program verification on large-scale industrial examples possible, we need to soften the border between program and model (or global/high-level specification). Ideally, one can have different views on the components of an application, see Fig. 1 for a visualisation. First of all, there should of course be a code view, which is executable and deterministic, and which provides many low-level details. But one also needs to have a specification view on the same component, which is high-level, declarative and abstract, possibly

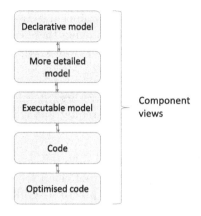

Fig. 1. Multiple views on a system component

non-deterministic, and leaves out many details. And many more different views for the same component should be possible: a high-level specification view can be refined into a more detailed, but still declarative model, which can further be refined into an executable model and finally into a code view. And this code view might be further refined, into a program that is further optimised, e.g. for performance or memory usage.

When we take this approach, there are two crucial requirements:

1. we need techniques to *connect* the views at all the different levels, and this connection needs to be *provably correct*, and
2. we need to be able to *compose* the components at all different view levels, i.e. it should be possible to "build" an application, where some of its components are only described by a high-level specification, and to combine these with code-level components, in order to reason about properties of the application as a whole, as visualised in Fig. 2.

There already exists some work on refinement between different views, such as done in VDM [5,10,15], Z [16], or EventB [1]. However, most of these approaches focus on refinement between different models, and if they go all the way to executable code, typically the code is extracted from a low-level model description, which is close to the code in spirit, but the connection between the code and the low-level model is not proven correct. Two exceptions that I am aware of are:

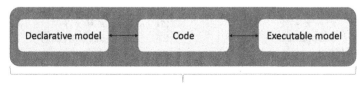

Fig. 2. Global verification with multiple component views

(1) the work by Dalvandi et al. [9], which aims at extracting code and annotations from an Event-B-model and then proving these correct using Dafny, and (2) the work of Tran-Jörgensen et al. [26], which generates JML annotations from VDM specifications.

Also, in the nineties early ideas on the transformation from models to programs, and from program to program have been developed, see e.g. [6,22,24]. These existing ideas need to be studied carefully, and it needs to be investigated if and how they can be incorporated in the current state-of-the-art deductive program verification tools.

Finally, also the work on the CompCert project, see e.g. [4,19] can be a source of inspiration. In this project, a verified tool chain for C is developed in Coq. However in the approach I advocate, also practical verification and applicability to different programming languages should be a major driving force.

3   First Steps: The VerCors Approach

Within the VerCors tool set, we have started to develop techniques to support this idea. In particular, we allow to specify an abstract model view of a component using process algebra, and then we use an extension of concurrent separation logic to prove that the concrete code behaves according to this model [23], while model checking technology can be used to derive global properties of the program from the process algebra models.

To illustrate this idea, let us consider the small code example in Fig. 3. Suppose we have a shared variable x protected by a lock lck, and two threads that manipulate x: one thread multiplies x by 4, the other thread adds 4 to x. The specifications of the two threads capture the thread's behaviours abstractly: assuming that the behaviour of the thread before this method call was equal to the process algebra term H (written $Hist(H)$), execution of the method adds the action $mult(4)$ or $add(4)$ to this behaviour (where $H.a$ denotes a process algebra term H, followed by action a, see the thread postconditions in lines 4 and 16).

```
1   class Mult extends Thread {          13   class Add extends Thread {
2                                         14
3   //@ requires Hist(H);                 15   //@ requires Hist(H);
4   //@ ensures Hist(H.mult(4));          16   //@ ensures Hist(H.add(4));
5   public void run() {                   17   public void run() {
6       //@ action mult(4) {              18       //@ action add(4) {
7         lock(lck);                      19         lock(lck);
8         x = x * 4;                      20         x = x + 4;
9         unlock(lck);                    21         unlock(lck);
10      //@ }                             22      //@ }
11  }                                     23  }
12  }                                     24  }
```

Fig. 3. Example: abstract behaviour specifications

```
1  //@ assume true;
2  //@ guarantee x == \old(x) * k;
3  action mult(k);
4
5  //@ assume true;
6  //@ guarantee x == \old(x) + k;
7  action add(k);
```

Fig. 4. Example action specifications

The *action* annotations (lines 6–10, and lines 18–22) inside the method body indicate the concrete code fragments that corresponds to the abstract actions. Given the action specifications that describe the effect of the actions *mult* and *add* in Fig. 4, we use our program logic to prove that the action implementations behave as specified.

Moreover, the program logic can also be used to verify that a process algebra term describes the global behaviour of the program. Suppose we have a `main` method, which starts the two threads and then waits for them to terminate. We can prove that the behaviour of this `main` method is to execute the *mult* and the *add* action in any order (see the postcondition in line 2 below, where $P + Q$ denotes a non-deterministic choice between P and Q and *empty* denotes an empty history). Finally, we can use existing model checking technology to reason about this abstract model, combined with the action specifications, to derive that the possible final values of variable x are 4 and 16.

```
1  //@ requires Hist(empty) & x == 0;
2  //@ ensures Hist(mult(4).add(4) + add(4).mult(4));
3  public void main(...) {
4    Thread t1 = new Mult(); Thread t2 = new Add();
5    t1.fork(); t2.fork();
6    t1.join(); t2.join();
7  }
```

This example is very simple, but we have used the same approach on larger and non-terminating programs [2,23,27].

4 Future Steps

The approach described above is still in its early stages. To fully realise the goal to have a seamless integration of code and models, more work is needed. I believe that the theory of how to make a connection between different levels of abstract models is reasonably well-understood [1,5,15,16], but to make a provably correct transformation from model (or high-level specification) to code is less clear. There are approaches to generate a model from code, but correctness of the extraction is then typically a meta-property, and cannot be proven for the model and code directly (and thus, in particular depends on whether the extraction is correctly implemented[1]). There also exists work on (provably correct) model-to-code generation, see e.g. [28], but the generated code is still very close to the model, and needs to be improved to achieve a reasonable performance.

Therefore, I believe we need to address the following research challenges:

- we need to further develop refinement techniques that from an abstract model can generate annotated and verifiable code, where it is important that the generated code can be executed efficiently;
- we need techniques to prove that a program that is transformed to optimise it for performance remains correct after the transformation, see [13] for further ideas;
- we need to consider whether it is possible to automatically derive a model or abstract view from a concrete program; and
- we need to further develop the abstract model theory for concurrent software, in particular making the abstract models compositional, such that it is possible to reason about the global behaviour of a system that is composed of both abstract models and concrete code components.

Acknowledgements. The author is supported by NWO VICI 639.023.710 Mercedes project.

References

1. Abrial, J.-R.: Modeling in Event-B – System and Software Engineering. Cambridge University Press (2010)
2. Amighi, A., Blom, S., Huisman, M.: VerCors: a layered approach to practical verification of concurrent software. In PDP, pp. 495–503 (2016)
3. Amighi, A., Haack, C., Huisman, M., Hurlin, C.: Permission-based separation logic for multithreaded Java programs. LMCS **11**(1) (2015)
4. Appel, A.W.: Verified software toolchain. In: Barthe, G. (ed.) ESOP 2011. LNCS, vol. 6602, pp. 1–17. Springer, Heidelberg (2011). https://doi.org/10.1007/978-3-642-19718-5_1
5. Bjørner, D.: The vienna development method (VDM). In: Blum, E.K., Paul, M., Takasu, S. (eds.) Mathematical Studies of Information Processing. LNCS, vol. 75, pp. 326–359. Springer, Heidelberg (1979). https://doi.org/10.1007/3-540-09541-1_33
6. Bowen, J.P., Olderog, E.-R., Fränzle, M., Ravn, A.P.: Developing correct systems. In: Fifth Euromicro Workshop on Real-Time Systems, RTS 1993, Oulu, Finland, 22–24 June 1993, Proceedings, pp. 176–187. IEEE (1993)
7. Brahmi, A., Delmas, D., Essousi, M.H., Randimbivololona, F., Atki, A., Marie, T.: Formalise to automate: deployment of a safe and cost-efficient process for avionics software. In: Embedded Real-Time Software and Systems (ERTS[2]) (2018)
8. Burstall, R.M.: Program proving as hand simulation with a little induction. In: Information Processing 1974, pp. 308–312. Elsevier, North-Holland (1974)

---

[1] Of course, a similar argument can be made here, but the advantage is that if the annotated code is available, correctness can be reverified by other tools.

9. Dalvandi, M., Butler, M.J., Rezazadeh, A.: Transforming Event-B models to Dafny contracts. In: Proceedings of the 15th International Workshop on Automated Verification of Critical Systems (AVoCS 2015), Volume 72 of Electronic Communications of the EASST (2015)
10. Dawes, J.: The VDM-SL Reference Guide. Pitman (1991)
11. de Gouw, S., Rot, J., de Boer, F.S., Bubel, R., Hähnle, R.: OpenJDK's Java.utils.Collection.sort() is broken: the good, the bad and the worst case. In: Kroening, D., Păsăreanu, C.S. (eds.) CAV 2015. LNCS, vol. 9206, pp. 273–289. Springer, Cham (2015). https://doi.org/10.1007/978-3-319-21690-4_16
12. Hoare, C.A.R.: An axiomatic basis for computer programming. Commun. ACM **12**(10), 576–580 (1969)
13. Huisman, M., Blom, S., Darabi, S., Safari, M.: Program correctness by transformation. In: Margaria, T., Steffen, B. (eds.) ISoLA 2018. LNCS, vol. 11244, pp. 365–380. Springer, Cham (2018)
14. Huisman, M., Klebanov, V., Monahan, R., Tautschnig, M.: VerifyThis 2015 a program verification competition. Int. J. Softw. Tools Technol. Transfer (2016)
15. International Organisation for Standardization. Information technology–Programming languages, their environments and system software interfaces–Vienna Development Method-Specification Language–Part 1: Base language, December 1996. ISO/IEC 13817–1
16. International Organisation for Standardization. Information technology–Z Formal Specification Notation-Syntax, Type System and Semantics (2000). ISO/IEC 13568:2002
17. Joosten, S.J.C., Oortwijn, W., Safari, M., Huisman, M.: An exercise in verifying sequential programs with VerCors. In: Summers, A.J. (ed.) 20th Workshop on Formal Techniques for Java-like Programs (FTfJP) (2018)
18. Jung, R., et al.: Iris: monoids and invariants as an orthogonal basis for concurrent reasoning. In: POPL, pp. 637–650. ACM (2015)
19. Kästner, D., et al.: CompCert: practical experience on integrating and qualifying a formally verified optimizing compiler. In: ERTS 2018: Embedded Real Time Software and Systems. SEE (2018)
20. Meyer, B.: Object-Oriented Software Construction, 2nd Edn. Prentice-Hall (1997)
21. O'Hearn, P.W.: Resources, concurrency and local reasoning. Theor. Comput. Sci. **375**(1–3), 271–307 (2007)
22. Olderog, E.-R., Rössig, S.: A case study in transformational design of concurrent systems. In: Gaudel, M.-C., Jouannaud, J.-P. (eds.) CAAP 1993. LNCS, vol. 668, pp. 90–104. Springer, Heidelberg (1993). https://doi.org/10.1007/3-540-56610-4_58
23. Oortwijn, W., Blom, S., Gurov, D., Huisman, M., Zaharieva-Stojanovski, M.: An abstraction technique for describing concurrent program behaviour. In: Paskevich, A., Wies, T. (eds.) VSTTE 2017. LNCS, vol. 10712, pp. 191–209. Springer, Cham (2017). https://doi.org/10.1007/978-3-319-72308-2_12
24. Partsch, H.: Specification and Transformation of Programs - A Formal Approach to Software Development. Texts and Monographs in Computer Science. Springer, Heidelberg (1990). https://doi.org/10.1007/978-3-642-61512-2
25. Penninckx, W., Mühlberg, J.T., Smans, J., Jacobs, B., Piessens, F.: Sound formal verification of Linux's USB BP keyboard driver. In: Goodloe, A.E., Person, S. (eds.) NFM 2012. LNCS, vol. 7226, pp. 210–215. Springer, Heidelberg (2012). https://doi.org/10.1007/978-3-642-28891-3_21
26. Tran-Jørgensen, P.W.V., Larsen, P.G., Leavens, G.T.: Automated translation of VDM to JML-annotated Java. STTT **20**(2), 211–235 (2018)

27. Zaharieva-Stojanovski, M.: Closer to reliable software: verifying functional behaviour of concurrent programs. Ph.D. thesis, University of Twente (2015)
28. Zhang, D.: From concurrent state machines to reliable multi-threaded Java code. Ph.D. thesis, Technische Universiteit Eindhoven (2018)

Type Theory as a Framework for Modelling and Programming

Cezar Ionescu[1], Patrik Jansson[2](✉), and Nicola Botta[3]

[1] University of Oxford, Oxford, UK
`Cezar.Ionescu@conted.ox.ac.uk`
[2] Chalmers University of Technology, Gothenburg, Sweden
`patrik.jansson@chalmers.se`
[3] Potsdam Institute for Climate Impact Research, Potsdam, Germany
`botta@pik-potsdam.de`

Abstract. In the context provided by the proceedings of the UVMP track of ISoLA 2016, we propose Type Theory as a suitable framework for both modelling and programming. We show that it fits most of the requirements put forward on such frameworks by Broy et al. and discuss some of the objections that can be raised against it.

Keywords: Software technology · Specification
Functional programming · Dependent types
Domain-specific languages

1 Introduction

The present paper was written as a contribution to the ISoLA 2018 track entitled "Towards a Unified View of Modeling and Programming". The basic question to be discussed there was that of the relation between "modelling"[1] and "programming". In one of its stronger forms, the question was formulated as

what are the arguments for and against the statement:
modeling is programming?

Such a question needs to be addressed in a certain context, one which would exclude certain possible meanings of "modelling", e.g., "To display (clothes) as a fashion model" (9th entry in the current Oxford Dictionary of English under "modelling"), and of "programming" (e.g., "To arrange by or according to a programme; to include or name in a programme; to draw up a scheme or itinerary of; to plan or schedule definitely", first entry under "programming" – the computer-oriented meaning only comes in fourth place). In order to obtain this context, we made a review of the definitions of modelling and programming used in the previous edition of this track, hosted at ISoLA 2016. The results

---

[1] We have used the British spelling throughout the document, except in literal quotes.

© Springer Nature Switzerland AG 2018
T. Margaria and B. Steffen (Eds.): ISoLA 2018, LNCS 11244, pp. 119–133, 2018.
https://doi.org/10.1007/978-3-030-03418-4_8

of this review are presented in the next section. As a result of this review, we were led to propose Type Theory as a unified framework for modelling and programming. We present a brief description of Type Theory, and show that the proposal is consistent with most of the requirements for such an framework put forward during ISoLA 2016 by Broy et al. We then discuss some possible objections, followed by some of the wider implications of this proposal.

2   ISoLA 2016 Definitions of Modelling and Programming

Seven of the sixteen contributions published within the "Towards a Unified View of Modeling and Programming" section of the ISoLA 2016 proceedings [38] contain a more or less explicit definition for both "modelling" and "programming".

– Selić [51]:
  - An *engineering model* is a selective representation of some system intended to capture accurately and concisely all of its essential properties of interest for a given set of concerns.
  - A program is a human-readable textual representation of the binary data that is actually stored and executed in a computer.

  Remark: since a program is itself a "selective representation", it follows that it is also a model (cf. the given definition), but Selić argues that this is misleading, since "programming languages are intended primarily and almost exclusively for prescriptive purposes".

– Seidewitz [50]:
  - A model is always about something, which I term the system under study (SUS). For our purposes here, we can consider a model to consist of a set of statements about the SUS expressed in some modeling language. These statements make assertions about certain properties of the SUS, but say nothing about other properties that are not mentioned.
  - Programs [...] are precise models of execution (where, for simplicity, I consider both data and algorithmic aspects to be included in the term "execution").

  Remark: Seidewitz considers that models are more general than programs: "From this point of view all programs are actually models. And all executable models are actually programs. But there are, of course, software models that are not programs."

– Elaasar and Badreddin [15]:
  - A model is a simplified representation of a more complex system. It is frequently used to abstract and analyze a system by focusing on one or more aspects. Models are used to understand, communicate, simulate, calibrate, evaluate, test, validate and explore alternatives for system development. Modelers use a wide variety of models to explore different aspects of the system such as requirements, structure, behavior, event, time, security, flow, process, activity, performance, quality, usability, etc. These models can be expressed in many forms including textual and visual representations.

- Programming, on the other hand, is the activity of developing executable software. Programs are written in a programming language, which is a set of rules for expressing computations in a human-readable form that can be translated unambiguously to a machine-readable form.

- Prinz et al. [46]:
  - Modelling is the activity to describe a real or imagined (part of a) system using a language with a semantics. The model does not provide a full match of the real system, but an abstraction.
  - Programming is the activity to prescribe a new (part of a) system using a language with a well-defined execution semantics. The program determines the system.

- Lethbridge et al. [36]:
  - Three criteria for what it means to "look and feel like a model", attributed by the authors to Ludewig [37, p. 196] and summarised as
    * (m1) There is a mapping between the model and the system being modeled, or part of it. The system is called the 'original' by Ludewig.
    * (m2) This mapping abstracts some properties of the system, hence providing a simplified view. Typical abstractions focus on behavioural properties or structural properties, but the same model may include both, as well as other types of abstractions.
    * (m3) The model is useful in that one can do things with the model instead of having to have access to the full (executable) system. Key things one can do with a model under m3 include analyzing it to measure it or to find defects, and transforming it into other forms. Models are therefore useful in early stages of design, but in some cases can also be used to generate some or all of the system.
  - Three criteria for what it means for a system to "look and feel like code":
    * (c1) The system, or parts of it, are composed of a set of units (files in the case of Umple), which can be edited using a text editor supporting syntax highlighting.
    * (c2) The textual syntax is designed to be usable by programmers.
    * (c3) When it is processed (compiled in the case of Umple), feedback such as warnings and errors is produced, highlighting issues on specific lines.

- Naujokat et al. [42]:
  At a conceptual level, modeling and programming can be regarded as two sides of the same medal: the WHAT and the HOW descriptions of a certain artefact. This duality of WHAT and HOW has a long tradition in engineering, where models were built to predict certain WHATs, like the aerodynamics of an envisioned car or its visual appearance, in order to optimize vital aspects, before entering the costly HOW-driven production phase, where modifications become extremely expensive. [...] In classical engineering, there is typically

a very clear and agreed upon distinction between a model (a WHAT)
and an implementation (the HOW), frequently connected to distinct
abstraction layers and different natures of the respective description
means. [...] the understanding of what is a HOW (an implementation or a program) and what a WHAT (a model or a specification) in
software becomes quite situation dependent.

– Broy et al. [12]:

Models are meant to describe a system at a high level of abstraction
for the purpose of human understanding and analysis. Programs, on
the other hand, are meant for execution. However, programming languages are becoming increasingly higher-level, with convenient notation for concepts that in the past would only be reserved for formal
specification languages.

Of the remaining nine papers, Berry [4] defines programming ("As an activity, programming is quite easy to define: one writes texts or graphics that are
compiled into some machine language and executed by some computer."), but
not modelling ("Modeling is not as clear-cut, because it deals with many more
concepts and objects.").

The remaining eight papers contain no definitions of modelling or programming. Rybicki et al. [49], and Larsen et al. [31] use the terminology of the model-
based engineering community (see, e.g., [40]), Rouquette [48] that of UML [43],
Elmqvist et al. [16] that of Modelica [18], Haxthausen and Pelska [20] "model"
both in the sense of modelling languages and in that of model theory. Lattmann
et al. [33] discuss domain-specific modelling languages. Kugler [28] refers to
"a combination of programming, modelling languages, specification formalisms
and methodologies", but there are no details in his brief contribution. Finally,
Leavens et al. [34] do not mention modelling at all, discussing instead *specifications*, i.e., partial descriptions of a software system against which the correctness
of *implementations* is to be assessed. This last treatment of modelling might seem
quite limited when compared to the others, but we believe that in this context
it is, in fact, quite natural.

2.1   Models and Specifications

The picture that emerges from a study of the definitions and of the most important references given in the ISoLA 2016 proceedings is, broadly speaking, the
following: a model of a system is a partial description of that system. The particular form of the partial description depends on the means we have, on the
system to be modelled, on what we plan to do with the description, etc. In
general, the relationship between the description and the system is not fully
formalised (and often not fully formalisable). There is a great variety of kinds
of description (scale models, mathematical models, narratives, pictures, formal
models, software models, ...). The systems being modelled do not necessarily
exist "in reality". For example, architectural blueprints can be seen as partial

descriptions of buildings that have yet to be built. In such cases, the relationship to the system can be quite formal[2], as blueprints are part of contracts and it must be decidable whether the buildings have been constructed correctly or not.

This variety of possible models can seem quite daunting, but there is one definite constraint in the context of ISoLA: the only models being considered are those that describe programs. In other words, the only models considered are *specifications*, which justifies the point of view implicitly adopted by Leavens et al. in [34].

This constraint is obvious in most of the articles above, but what about the models of real systems considered by Kugler, Printz et al., and others? In these cases, the models are meant to describe *simulations* of the real systems, but simulations are the result of the execution of programs. This is explained in Printz et al. when they discuss correctness: a model of a system (called the reference system) is correct if programs described by the model produce a simulation of that system.

In their contribution, Broy et al. call for "a single universal formalism for modeling and programming any form of system", but, again, the context makes clear that what is meant are software systems (object-oriented, functional, imperative, etc.). The unification being sought is at the level of the *framework* used, ideally, for both activities. Most of the ISoLA 2016 papers refer to such a framework, sometimes called *environment* (as in Elmqvist et al. [16]) or thought of as a high-level programming language (as in Seidewitz [50]).

3   A Brief Introduction to Type Theory

If the above analysis is correct, and we can therefore equate modelling with specification of software systems, then that is good news, for we do have a unified framework for modelling and programming, one that is mature (several decades old), with solid implementations (NuPRL, Coq, Agda, Idris, Lean), and impeccable mathematical credentials: *Type Theory*.

Type Theory, sometimes referred to as Dependently Typed Theory, is a pure functional programming language with a static type system. It is similar to Haskell, and stands in roughly the same relation to it as predicate logic to propositional logic. Type Theory was developed by the Swedish mathematician and philosopher Per Martin-Löf, who intended it to have the same foundational role for intuitionistic mathematics that set theory expressed in predicate logic had had for classical mathematics.

This is not the place for a presentation of Type Theory, especially since nowadays there are many very good ones available (for a particularly accessible one, see [1]). What we want to do here is to provide an intuition for why Type Theory is able to provide an environment for both specifications and implementations, and for the various "types as ..." analogies.

---

[2] Here, *formal* is in the OED's sense 5.a: "Done or made with the forms recognized as ensuring validity; explicit and definite, as opposed to what is matter of tacit understanding".

We start by recalling that set theory derives its foundational role in classical mathematics from its ability to represent properties in several different (equivalent) ways, within a first-order language. For example, given a property P over a set A, expressed as a formula in the first-order language of sets, we can view it as a

- set $P = \{ a \mid P\ a \}$: $a \in P$ iff a has the property P
- Boolean-valued function P: $P\ a = True$ iff a has the property P
- set-valued function P: $P\ a$ not empty iff a has the property P

In the third representation we can think of $P\ a$ as the set of *witnesses* to a having the property P.

All these allow us to talk about the property within the theory: it becomes an element of the universe of discourse. In contrast, the formula expressing the property is not an element of the universe of discourse.

These are consequences of the axiom of comprehension, which, in particular, directly legitimises the view of properties as sets. Other axioms of set theory introduce new ways of building sets from existing ones, by means of taking the powerset, unions and intersections.

If we take types in programming languages to be the analogues of sets in set theory, we can see that the available means for their construction are more restricted. Like many other programming languages, Type Theory allows the construction of inductive types. For example:

$$\frac{}{Z : Nat} \qquad \frac{n : Nat}{S\ n : Nat}$$

and

data $Nat : Type$ **where**
  $Z : Nat$
  $S : Nat \rightarrow Nat$

are two equivalent ways of expressing the rules for the construction of natural numbers, one in "natural deduction" style, the other in the style of Haskell, Agda, or Idris.

In most programming languages, we can usually represent properties as Boolean-valued predicates. For example:

$isEven : Nat \qquad \rightarrow Bool$
$isEven\ Z \qquad = True$
$isEven\ (S\ Z) \qquad = False$
$isEven\ (S\ (S\ n)) = isEven\ n$

In most cases, however, we cannot represent the associated set (here, the set of even numbers) as a datatype or as a type-valued function. Therefore, if a function requires its argument to be even, then the best we can do is to guard the call of the function with a run-time check. This leads to expressing requirements or specifications as tests, as in test-driven development methods or design by contract.

In contrast, in Type Theory, we have the additional possibility of representing a property by a type-valued function (or type family), which corresponds to the set-valued version in set theory. For example

$$\frac{k : Nat}{MkEven \ k : Even \ (2 * k)}$$

and

> **data** $Even : Nat \rightarrow Type$ **where**
> $MkEven : (k : Nat) \rightarrow Even \ (2 * k)$

are equivalent ways of expressing the type-valued function version of *isEven*. For every natural number n, $Even \ n$ is a type. If n is not even, then the type will be empty. Otherwise, the type will have one element, namely $MkEven \ (n \ / \ 2)$. Perhaps the best way to think of an element $e : Even \ n$ is that it represents *evidence* that n is even, by showing that n is made out of the doubling of a natural number.

If a function requires its argument to be even, we can now formulate this requirement at the level of its type, for instance

$$f : (n : Nat) \rightarrow Even \ n \rightarrow X$$

The function f is here in *curried* form, allowing partial application: $f \ n$ is a function of type $Even \ n \rightarrow X$, $f \ n \ e$ is a value of type X, assuming n and e have the appropriate types. This notation is standard in functional programming languages, but also, e.g., in VDM (see the VDM-10 manual ([32]), Sect. 3.2.8, page 29).

In order to call f with an argument n, we have to supply another argument of type $Even \ n$. We can only do that if n is $Even$, since otherwise $Even \ n$ would be empty. This additional argument must be reducible to the form $MkEven \ k$, where $k = n \ / \ 2$, and this can be checked at compile time (or, rather, at "type-checking time"). This ensures that f will never give rise to a run-time error, a much stronger guarantee than we can enforce by means of tests.

The ability to define inductive datatypes and type families lends Type Theory a surprisingly strong expressive power, equal to that of classical higher-order logic. In particular, we can formulate all the notions in current mathematics. Note, however, that the only formulas we can prove are those of constructive mathematics: the logic of Type Theory is intuitionistic.

When it comes to specifications of programs, this is not a bug, but rather a feature. The requirements on a program can be expressed at the level of types, for example

$$f : (x : X) \rightarrow Pre \ x \rightarrow \Sigma \ (y : Y) \ (Post \ x \ y)$$

is the type of a function that takes as input elements of a type X having the property *Pre*, and delivers elements of a type Y which are in the relation *Post* with the input. An implementation of f that satisfies the type checker will fulfil this specification.

This approach to specification and implementation in Type Theory has been successfully used in e.g., producing a verified C compiler, CompCert [35]; developing database access libraries which statically guarantee that queries are consistent with the schema of the underlying database [44]; implementing secure distributed programming [52]; implementing resource-safe programs [11,41]; and many others.

As a modelling framework, modelling in Type Theory has the advantage of mathematical consistency over using UML or similar approaches. As such, it is closer to formal methods like VDM, but we find it easier to express high-level, domain-specific properties in Type Theory. For example, we can formulate types for "resource-safe operations", "privacy-ensuring protocols", but also for "avoidable states" [6] or even "measures of vulnerability to climate change" [22].

4   Type Theory as a Framework for Modelling and Programming

In [12], Broy et al. put forward ten requirements for a unified framework for modelling and programming. We give a brief overview of how Type Theory fares with respect to them.

1. *Target domains:* can the formalism account for "modeling; programming of non-embedded systems, such as web applications, including scripting; and finally programming of embedded and cyber-physical systems"? Type Theory has been successfully used in all these domains, for example: modelling using dynamical systems [6,23], implementing typed web client applications [27], programming embedded systems [47].
2. *Predicate specifications:* "A formalism must generally support specifying properties as predicates rather than only as algorithms." As explained above, we can use types to express arbitrarily complex predicates.
3. *Programming in the large:* "A formalism must support programming in the large, and in general provide good modularization and component-based development." Types are a natural structuring mechanism for programs, especially when supplemented with higher-order constructs such as type classes. Most implementations of Type Theory provide support for modules, separate compilation units, packages, etc. In the context of "programming in the large", Broy et al. emphasise *concurrency*, both at the level of programming and that of modelling. Concurrent programming is difficult in any framework, and Type Theory is no exception, but it is the topic of active research (see, for example, [10,21,27]) that can build on the high-quality Haskell implementations of concurrency [39].

4. *High-level programming:* "A formalism must support high-level programming as found in modern programming languages." Type Theory *is* a high-level programming language, so this requirement could be considered satisfied "by definition". However, the explanation of this requirement notes: "A formalism should be statically typed, although with type inference, and with allowance for going type less in clearly defined regions to support scripting." While it is not obvious to us that scripting necessarily implies dynamic typing (especially in the presence of type inference), we do believe that there are situations in which the type checker must be forced to accept a given typing. This is the case, for example, when integrating with external programs written in a different language, or for which the source code is not available. Most (all?) implementations of Type Theory provide such a mechanism, usually by means of *postulates*.

5. *Low-level programming:* "A formalism must support low-level programming." The dependently-typed language Low* has been used to implement efficient low-level programs [47], and there are many other similar applications of implementations based on Type Theory. However, it is correct that at the current stage, implementations of Type Theory do not generate programs with the same performance characteristics as C.

6. *Continuous mathematics:* "A formalism can support modeling of cyber-physical systems." As a system originally designed for the formalisation of mathematics, Type Theory fulfils this requirement "by construction". The modelling capabilities of constructive mathematics have been amply demonstrated, e.g., by Bishop and Bridges [5], and the ForMath project [17].

7. *Domain-specific languages:* "A formalism must support definition of domain-specific languages." Like most functional programming languages, Type Theory is an excellent vehicle for embedding domain-specific languages (see, for example, Brady [9]).

8. *Visualization:* "A formalism must be visualizable.". This requirement is the only one that is currently not satisfied. Providing visual representations of formal specifications such as those represented by types in Type Theory is a problem that not only has not been solved, but, as far as we know, is not currently being tackled in a systematic way (say, in the framework of a Horizon 2020 project). The activities that come nearest to the mark are those involving diagrammatic reasoning, such as string diagrams [14]. These offer visual representations of the relationships of various entities in a categorical setting, and come with rules that allow rigorous proofs by means of manipulations of the diagrams. There exists a software tool that implements this kind of reasoning with string diagram, available at http:// globular.science/ [2], but it is unclear whether this kind of presentation would be appropriate for the proofs normally conducted in Type Theory. Perhaps the main difficulty here is that of coming up with the "right kind" of visualisation of type-based specifications, which will require the joint effort of HCI experts, modellers, programmers, and specialists in Type Theory.

9. *Analysis:* "A formalism must be analyzable." This requirement refers to "basic built-in support for unit testing, over advanced testing capabilities,

including test input generation and monitoring, to concepts such as static analysis, model checking, theorem proving and symbolic execution", which the more popular implementations of Type Theory support. However, the requirement asks that "the main emphasis should be put on automation. The average user should be able to benefit from automated verification, without having to do manual proofs." Tactics implemented in, e.g., Idris or Coq, attempt to automate certain parts of proofs, and are quite successful when dealing with properties that fit a certain pattern (which is often the case in DSLs, [11]). However, the moment one strays from the beaten path, proof obligations can no longer be filled-in automatically, thus we can only claim partial satisfiability of this requirement.

10. *What modelers do that programmers don't:* "A central question is how a model/program is represented." This requirement refers to the need for "a more sophisticated approach than the text-based source code repositories often used by programmers", since modelers "have the habits of querying models, transforming models, and generally consider models as data, in contrast to the programming community where data usually are separated from programs", and notes that "from within a program one can usually not get access to the entire AST of the program itself, although often limited forms of reflection are possible". Frameworks based on Type Theory are among the leading environments for *meta-programming* (a term that covers both reflection and code generation), which has been considered one of the "killer applications" for dependent types (e.g., by Chlipala in [13]), so we consider that this requirement is satisfied. Broy et al. point out that this requirement is connected to that of visualisation: this link might provide a starting point for projects aiming to satisfy the latter.

Type Theory fully satisfies most of the requirements, with partial scores for "programming in the large", "analysis", and "what modelers do". The only requirement that is not satisfied is "visualisation", which we hope will be a topic of future research.

5   Potential Objections

In this section, we consider some potential objections to using Type Theory as a unified framework for modelling and programming.

Three of the papers of the ISoLA 2016 proceeding, Haxthausen and Peleska [20], Larsen et al. [31], and Naujokat et al. [42], argue against the feasibility and usability of a unified framework for modelling and programming. In all three, the argument is that multiple formalism are needed to do justice to the wealth of potential goals, requirements, stakeholders etc.

All three papers point out the necessity of relating the various formalisms, in order to combine them to create more complex models, or to translate between them in order to reuse common aspects. We believe that the best way to do this is to implement the various formalisms as DSLs embedded in a common language, and that Type Theory is the most adequate candidate for such a language.

We will, however, very quickly admit that it is not a *perfect* candidate. The required level of precision can sometimes become a burden. For example, since each value has a unique type, we have difficulties working with subtypes. This can create problems when building *hierarchies* of models, since the familiar "subset" relation turns out to be quite awkward in a type-theoretical context. Similar remarks apply to other common set-theoretical constructions, such as that of *quotient sets*, which amount to introducing a new equality relation on a set. In Type Theory, the canonical equality on the elements of a type, namely the identity relation, has a privileged status, and working with a different equivalence relation instead is much more cumbersome.

Type Theory is an area of active research, and we hope that these difficulties will gradually be alleviated. In particular, the developments in the area of *homotopy type theory* seem to hold the key to the problem of working with different equivalence relations.

6   Conclusions

We have presented several arguments for the use of Type Theory as a framework for unified modelling and programming, where we have interpreted "modelling" to refer to (partial) descriptions of software systems, i.e., specifications of software systems.

In these concluding remarks, we would like to explain why we believe that Type Theory is a more adequate such framework than others, such as VDM or the B-method. It is quite likely that, with some additions and modifications, these too could meet the requirements put forward by Broy et al. After all, VDM and similar frameworks have been developed for the exact purpose of covering the spectrum from software specification to implementation in a formal, systematic fashion. Moreover, they have the same mathematical foundation as all (or at least most) of classical mathematics: set theory.

Indeed, all the standard mathematical theories can be "compiled down" to the first-order language of ZFC (Zermelo-Fraenkel with the Axiom of Choice). However, ZFC is far from actual mathematical practice. Instead, what one usually sees is a usage of "naive" set theory, as presented in the books of Halmos [19] and Bourbaki's summary [7] (but *not* in Bourbaki's extended treatment of set theory [8]!). This is then combined with some form of "naive" (and mostly implicit) type theory, to prevent set-theoretical "excesses", such as taking the intersection of π with the square root function. This has been pointed out again and again, and has led to the search for alternative foundations, e.g., based on category theory. For the computer scientist, this comes as no surprise: after all, just because every programming language must eventually be compiled down to machine code, it does not at all follow that the best way to understand programming languages is through the prism of machine code.

Thus, perhaps surprisingly, being based on ZFC offers little advantage when it comes to modelling actual mathematical concepts (see the requirement labelled *continuous mathematics* in Broy et al.'s list). On the contrary, the awkwardness in formulating and working with notions such as "continuous function", "differentiable function", "linear operator", etc., makes it difficult for such systems to make inroads into the area of scientific computing.

ZFC is also at a disadvantage when it comes to the foundations of computing science, for example, in giving an account of the semantics of programming languages. In fact, the study of the relationships between various programming languages has led to the introduction in computing science of the lambda calculus [30] and its various typed variants [3,45]. This has influenced the current style in computing science, which emphasises the distinction of syntax versus semantics, the introduction of names and structure [29], encourages calculational proofs and the creation of DSLs, all using types as the main structuring mechanism.

The mathematician Charles Wells used the term "computer science perspective" in an article published in the American Mathematical Monthly [54], in which he was arguing that this style could also be valuable in teaching mathematics. This "perspective" is perhaps one of the most valuable contributions that computing science can make to the larger intellectual landscape, and we have witnessed its effectiveness during the lectures given within the *Domain-Specific Languages of Mathematics* course taught in Chalmers from 2015/16 on [24–26].

Type Theory provides a natural foundation for both the computer science perspective and for constructive mathematics. When extended with classical postulates, resulting in a *typed predicate logic* [53], it brings us much closer to the language of mathematical practice than ZFC. Thus, Type Theory turns out to be a suitable vehicle for both mathematics and computing, at least in part because it was *not* created with any connection to software development.

A final remark: we have consciously decided to talk about "Type Theory" rather than any one of its implementations, because the most important unification that can be achieved is at the *conceptual* level, rather than the software level. The existing implementations have their strengths and weaknesses, and readers should make their choice based on their goals, needs, and background.

Acknowledgements. The work presented in this paper heavily relies on free software, among others on Idris, Agda, GHC, git, vi, Emacs, LATEX and on the FreeBSD and Debian GNU/Linux operating systems. It is our pleasure to thank all developers of these excellent products. This work was partially supported by the CoeGSS project (grant agreement No. 676547), which has received funding from the European Union's Horizon 2020 research and innovation programme.

References

1. Altenkirch, T.: Naive type theory (2017). http://www.cs.nott.ac.uk/~psztxa/mgs-17/notes-mgs17.pdf. Lecture Notes for a course at MGS 2017
2. Bar, K., Kissinger, A., Vicary, J.: Globular: an online proof assistant for higher-dimensional rewriting. Logical Methods Comput. Sci. **14**(1) (2018). https://doi.org/10.23638/LMCS-14(1:8)2018. http://arxiv.org/abs/1612.01093

3. Barendregt, H.P.: Lambda calculi with types. In: Abramsky, S., Gabbay, D.M., Maibaum, S.E. (eds.) Handbook of Logic in Computer Science, vol. 2, pp. 117–309. Oxford University Press Inc., New York (1992). http://dl.acm.org/citation.cfm?id=162552.162561

4. Berry, G.: Formally unifying modeling and design for embedded systems - a personal view. In: Margaria and Steffen [38], pp. 134–149. https://doi.org/10.1007/978-3-319-47169-3_11

5. Bishop, E., Bridges, D.: Constructive Analysis. Springer, Heidelberg (1985). https://doi.org/10.1007/978-3-642-61667-9

6. Botta, N., Jansson, P., Ionescu, C.: Contributions to a computational theory of policy advice and avoidability. J. Funct. Program. **27**, 1–52 (2017). https://doi.org/10.1017/S0956796817000156

7. Bourbaki, N.: Éléments de mathématique: Fasc. I. Livre 1, Théorie des ensembles; [5], Fascicule de résultats. Hermann (1964)

8. Bourbaki, N.: Théorie des ensembles. Springer, Heidelberg (2006). https://doi.org/10.1007/978-3-540-34035-5

9. Brady, E.: The IDRIS programming language – implementing embedded domain specific languages with dependent types. In: Central European Functional Programming School - 5th Summer School, CEFP 2013, Cluj-Napoca, Romania, 8 July–20 2013, Revised Selected Papers, pp. 115–186 (2013). https://doi.org/10.1007/978-3-319-15940-9_4

10. Brady, E.: Type-driven development of concurrent communicating systems. Comput. Sci. **18**(3) (2017). https://doi.org/10.7494/csci.2017.18.3.1413. https://journals.agh.edu.pl/csci/article/view/1413

11. Brady, E., Hammond, K.: Resource-safe systems programming with embedded domain specific languages. In: Russo, C., Zhou, N.F. (eds.) PADL 2012. LNCS, vol. 7149, pp. 242–257. Springer, Heidelberg (2012). https://doi.org/10.1007/978-3-642-27694-1_18

12. Broy, M., Havelund, K., Kumar, R.: Towards a unified view of modeling and programming. In: Margaria and Steffen [38], pp. 238–257. https://doi.org/10.1007/978-3-319-47169-3_17

13. Chlipala, A.: Ur: Statically-typed metaprogramming with type-level record computation. In: Proceedings of the 31st ACM SIGPLAN Conference on Programming Language Design and Implementation, PLDI 2010, pp. 122–133. ACM, New York (2010). https://doi.org/10.1145/1806596.1806612

14. Coecke, B., Kissinger, A.: Picturing Quantum Processes: A First Course in Quantum Theory and Diagrammatic Reasoning. Cambridge University Press, Cambridge (2017)

15. Elaasar, M., Badreddin, O.: Modeling meets programming: a comparative study in model driven engineering action languages. In: Margaria and Steffen [38], pp. 50–67. https://doi.org/10.1007/978-3-319-47169-3_5

16. Elmqvist, H., Henningsson, T., Otter, M.: Systems modeling and programming in a unified environment based on Julia. In: Margaria and Steffen [38], pp. 198–217. https://doi.org/10.1007/978-3-319-47169-3_15

17. ForMath project team: Papers and slides from the "formalisation of mathematics" (ForMath) project. http://wiki.portal.chalmers.se/cse/pmwiki.php/ForMath/PapersAndSlides

18. Fritzson, P.: Principles of Object-oriented Modeling and Simulation with Modelica 2.1. Wiley, Hoboken (2010)

19. Halmos, P.: Naive Set Theory. Van Nostrand (1960). Reprinted by Springer-Verlag, Undergraduate Texts in Mathematics (1974)

20. Haxthausen, A.E., Peleska, J.: On the feasibility of a unified modelling and programming paradigm. In: Margaria and Steffen [38], pp. 32–49. https://doi.org/10.1007/978-3-319-47169-3_4

21. Igried, B., Setzer, A.: Programming with monadic CSP-style processes in dependent type theory. In: Proceedings of the 1st International Workshop on Type-Driven Development, TyDe 2016, pp. 28–38. ACM, New York (2016). https://doi.org/10.1145/2976022.2976032

22. Ionescu, C.: Vulnerability modelling and monadic dynamical systems. Ph.D. thesis, Freie Universität Berlin (2009)

23. Ionescu, C.: Vulnerability modelling with functional programming and dependent types. Math. Struct. Comput. Sci. **26**(01), 114–128 (2016). https://doi.org/10.1017/S0960129514000139

24. Ionescu, C., Jansson, P.: Domain-specific languages of mathematics: presenting mathematical analysis using functional programming. In: Proceedings of the 4th and 5th International Workshop on Trends in Functional Programming in Education, TFPIE 2016, Sophia-Antipolis, France and University of Maryland College Park, USA, 2nd June 2015 and 7th June 2016, pp. 1–15 (2016). https://doi.org/10.4204/EPTCS.230.1

25. Jansson, P., Einarsdóttir, S.H., Ionescu, C.: Examples and results from a BSc-level course on domain specific languages of mathematics. In: Proceedings 7th International Workshop on Trends in Functional Programming in Education. EPTCS, Open Publishing Association (2018, in submission). Presented at TFPIE 2018

26. Jansson, P., Ionescu, C.: Domain specific languages of mathematics: Lecture notes (2018). https://github.com/DSLsofMath/DSLsofMath

27. Jeffrey, A.: Dependently typed web client applications. In: Sagonas, K. (ed.) Practical Aspects of Declarative Languages (PADL), pp. 228–243. Springer, Heidelberg (2013). https://doi.org/10.1007/978-3-642-45284-0_16

28. Kugler, H.: Unifying modelling and programming: a systems biology perspective. In: Margaria and Steffen [38], pp. 131–133. https://doi.org/10.1007/978-3-319-47169-3_10

29. Lamport, L.: How to write a 21st century proof. J. Fixed Point Theor. Appl., November 2011. https://doi.org/10.1007/s11784-012-0071-6. https://www.microsoft.com/en-us/research/publication/write-21st-century-proof/

30. Landin, P.J.: The next 700 programming languages. Commun. ACM **9**(3), 157–166 (1966)

31. Larsen, P.G., Fitzgerald, J.S., Woodcock, J., Nilsson, R., Gamble, C., Foster, S.: Towards semantically integrated models and tools for cyber-physical systems design. In: Margaria and Steffen [38], pp. 171–186. https://doi.org/10.1007/978-3-319-47169-3_13

32. Larsen, P.G., et al.: VDM-10 Language Manual. Technical report TR-001, The Overture Initiative, April 2013. www.overturetool.org

33. Lattmann, Z., Kecskés, T., Meijer, P., Karsai, G., Völgyesi, P., Lédeczi, Á.: Abstractions for modeling complex systems. In: Margaria and Steffen [38], pp. 68–79. https://doi.org/10.1007/978-3-319-47169-3_6

34. Leavens, G.T., Naumann, D.A., Rajan, H., Aotani, T.: Specifying and verifying advanced control features. In: Margaria and Steffen [38], pp. 80–96. https://doi.org/10.1007/978-3-319-47169-3_7

35. Leroy, X.: Formal verification of a realistic compiler. Commun. ACM **52**(7), 107–115 (2009). https://doi.org/10.1145/1538788.1538814

36. Lethbridge, T.C., Abdelzad, V., Orabi, M.H., Orabi, A.H., Adesina, O.: Merging modeling and programming using Umple. In: Margaria and Steffen [38], pp. 187–197. https://doi.org/10.1007/978-3-319-47169-3_14
37. Ludewig, J.: Models in software engineering - an introduction. Softw. Syst. Model 2, 5–14 (2003). https://doi.org/10.1007/s10270-003-0020-3 .
38. Margaria, T., Steffen, B. (eds.): ISoLA 2016. LNCS, vol. 9953. Springer, Cham (2016). https://doi.org/10.1007/978-3-319-47169-3
39. Marlow, S.: Parallel and concurrent programming in Haskell. In: Zsók, V., Horváth, Z., Plasmeijer, R. (eds)Central European Functional Programming School: 4th Summer School. LNCS, vol. 7241, pp. 339–401. Springer, Heidelberg (2012). https://doi.org/10.1007/978-3-642-32096-5_7
40. MBE Visual Glossary project: Model-based engineering visual glossary (2017). http://modelbasedengineering.com/glossary/
41. Morgenstern, J., Licata, D.: Security-typed programming within dependently-typed programming. In: International Conference on Functional Programming. ACM (2010). https://doi.org/10.1145/1863543.1863569
42. Naujokat, S., Neubauer, J., Margaria, T., Steffen, B.: Meta-level reuse for mastering domain specialization. In: Margaria and Steffen [38], pp. 218–237. https://doi.org/10.1007/978-3-319-47169-3_16
43. Object Management Group (OMG): Unified modeling language. OMG Document Number formal/17-12-05 (2017). https://www.omg.org/spec/UML/2.5.1/
44. Oury, N., Swierstra, W.: The power of Pi. In: Proceedings of ICFP 2008, pp. 39–50. ACM (2008). https://doi.org/10.1145/1411204.1411213
45. Pierce, B.C.: Types and Programming Languages, 1st edn. MIT Press, Cambridge (2002)
46. Prinz, A., Møller-Pedersen, B., Fischer, J.: Modelling and testing of real systems. In: Margaria and Steffen [38], pp. 119–130. https://doi.org/10.1007/978-3-319-47169-3_9
47. Protzenko, J., et al.: Verified low-level programming embedded in F*. In: Proceedings of the ACM on Programming Languages 1(ICFP), pp. 17:1–17:29, August 2017. https://doi.org/10.1145/3110261. http://arxiv.org/abs/1703.00053
48. Rouquette, N.F.: Simplifying OMG MOF-based metamodeling. In: Margaria and Steffen [38], pp. 97–118. https://doi.org/10.1007/978-3-319-47169-3_8
49. Rybicki, F., Smyth, S., Motika, C., Schulz-Rosengarten, A., von Hanxleden, R.: Interactive model-based compilation continued - incremental hardware synthesis for SCCharts. In: Margaria and Steffen [38], pp. 150–170. https://doi.org/10.1007/978-3-319-47169-3_12
50. Seidewitz, E.: On a unified view of modeling and programming position paper. In: Margaria and Steffen [38], pp. 27–31. https://doi.org/10.1007/978-3-319-47169-3_3
51. Selic, B.: Programming ⊂ modeling ⊂ engineering. In: Margaria and Steffen [38], pp. 11–26. https://doi.org/10.1007/978-3-319-47169-3_2
52. Swamy, N., Chen, J., Fournet, C., Strub, P.Y., Bhargavan, K., Yang, J.: Secure distributed programming with value-dependent types. Proc. ICFP 2011, 266–278 (2011). https://doi.org/10.1145/2034773.2034811
53. Turner, R.: Computable Models. Springer, Heidelberg (2009). https://doi.org/10.1007/978-1-84882-052-4
54. Wells, C.: Communicating mathematics: useful ideas from computer science. Am. Math. Monthl., 397–408 (1995). https://doi.org/10.2307/2975030

Bringing Effortless Refinement of Data Layouts to COGENT

Liam O'Connor[1]([⊠]), Zilin Chen[1,2], Partha Susarla[2], Christine Rizkallah[1], Gerwin Klein[1,2], and Gabriele Keller[1]

[1] UNSW Australia, Sydney, Australia
liamoc@cse.unsw.edu.au
[2] Data61, CSIRO (Formerly NICTA), Sydney, Australia
{zilin.chen,partha.susarla,gerwin.klein}@data61.csiro.au

Abstract. The language COGENT allows low-level operating system components to be modelled as pure mathematical functions operating on algebraic data types, which makes it highly suitable for verification in an interactive theorem prover. Furthermore, the COGENT compiler translates these models into imperative C programs, and provides a proof that this compilation is a refinement of the functional model. There remains a gap, however, between the C data structures used in the operating system, and the algebraic data types used by COGENT. This forces the programmer to write a large amount of boilerplate marshalling code to connect the two, which can lead to a significant runtime performance overhead due to excessive copying.

In this paper, we outline our design for a data description language and data refinement framework, called DARGENT, which provides the programmer with a means to specify how COGENT represents its algebraic data types. From this specification, the compiler can then generate the C code which manipulates the C data structures directly. Once fully realised, this extension will enable more code to be automatically verified by COGENT, smoother interoperability with C, and substantially improved performance of the generated code.

1 Introduction

In the context of end-to-end functional correctness verification of operating system components, the integration of modelling and programming presents a significant challenge.

Models are typically designed to enable concise specification and to reduce verification effort. In verifications using interactive proof assistants, such as that of the seL4 operating system[1], a *purely functional* model is ideal, as programs are modelled in terms of mathematical functions: objects for which proof assistants have significant built-in support and automation. On the other hand, programs are designed to be efficiently executable. Operating systems, and their kernels in

---

[1] The seL4 microkernel: https://sel4.systems (accessed on August 31, 2018).

© Springer Nature Switzerland AG 2018
T. Margaria and B. Steffen (Eds.): ISoLA 2018, LNCS 11244, pp. 134–149, 2018.
https://doi.org/10.1007/978-3-030-03418-4_9

particular, are usually written in relatively low-level languages such as C in order to achieve ideal performance and predictable run-time behaviour. Existing programming languages that support directly programming in a purely functional style such as HASKELL are not well-suited to systems programming, because of their reliance on extensive run-time support for memory management and evaluation.

The COGENT programming language [13] allows purely functional models to be compiled into efficient C code suitable for systems programming. It achieves this through the use of a sophisticated type system, which allows allocations to be replaced with efficient destructive update, and eliminates the need for a garbage collector. Furthermore, this compilation process is proven correct by translation validation—in addition to C code, the compiler generates a formal proof that any correctness theorem proven about the purely functional model also applies to the generated C code. Section 2 describes COGENT, its type system, and the associated verification framework in more detail.

COGENT programs do not exist in isolation, however. Typically, a COGENT program constitutes a component of a larger operating system, written in C. When integrating a COGENT component into this larger context, we see that there remains a gap between COGENT functional programming and typical systems programming used for the rest of the system.

In COGENT, programs are defined as pure functions operating on *algebraic data types*, such as product types (e.g. records, tuples) and sum types (also known as variants or tagged unions). The exact structure of these data types in memory is determined by the compiler. Many of the data structures in operating systems such as Linux could be represented as algebraic types, however their exact memory layout differs from that used by the COGENT compiler. Therefore, the file systems implemented in COGENT as a case study [1] must maintain a great deal of marshalling code to synchronise between the two copies of the same conceptual data structure. As COGENT code can only interact with the COGENT representation of the data, this synchronization code must be written in C. This code is tedious to write, wasteful of memory, prone to bugs, has a significant performance cost, and requires cumbersome manual verification at a low level of abstraction.

In this paper, we propose a new framework for data abstraction in COGENT programs. Rather than maintain two copies of data, we define a domain specific data description language, DARGENT, to describe the correspondence between COGENT algebraic data types and the bits and bytes of kernel data structures – what we call the *layout* of the data. As with COGENT itself, this framework reduces the gap between modelling and programming, in the sense that the programmer can write code as normal, manipulating ordinary COGENT data types, and after compilation the generated C code will manipulate kernel data structures directly, without constant copying and synchronisation at run-time. This will improve performance by eliminating redundant work, dramatically simplify the process of integrating C and COGENT code, and make it possible to verify more code with COGENT rather than using cumbersome C verification frameworks. Our vision for the DARGENT data description language is outlined in Sect. 3.

A number of extensions must also be made to COGENT itself to accommodate this new data refinement framework, outlined in Sect. 4:

1. The *type system* needs to be extended to incorporate these data layouts.
2. The *code generator* needs to compile each abstract read and write operation on COGENT data types to the equivalent concrete operation in C, according to DARGENT layouts.
3. The *verification framework* must be updated to once again automatically verify that the compiler output is a correct compilation of the compiler input.

At the time of writing, we have implemented the prototype data description language in the COGENT compiler, however the extensions to COGENT itself to take DARGENT layouts into account are still in development.

```
1  type Heap
2  type Bag = Ptr {count : U32, sum : U32}

3  newBag : Heap → ⟨Success (Heap, Bag) | Failure Heap⟩
4  freeBag : (Heap, Bag) → Heap

5  addToBag : (U32, Bag) → Bag
6  addToBag (x, b {count = c, sum = s}) =
7      b {count = c + 1, sum = s + x}

8  averageBag : Bag! → ⟨Success U32 | EmptyBag⟩
9  averageBag (b {count = c, sum = s}) =
10     if c == 0 then EmptyBag else Success (s / c)

11 type List a
12 reduce : ((List a) !, (a!, b) → b, b) → b

13 average : (Heap, (List U32)!) → (Heap, U32)
14 average (h, ls) = newBag h
15   | Success (h', b) →
16         let b' = reduce (ls, addToBag, b)
17         in averageBag b' !b'
18             | Success n → (freeBag (h', b'), n)
19             | EmptyBag → (freeBag (h', b'), 0)
20   | Failure h' → (h', 0)
```

Fig. 1. An example COGENT program, using heap-allocated data to compute the average of a list.

2 Overview of COGENT

COGENT is a purely functional programming language, in the tradition of languages such as HASKELL or ML. Programs are typically written in the form of mathematical functions operating on algebraic data types. Unlike HASKELL or ML, however, COGENT is designed for low-level operating system components, and therefore it does not require a garbage collector, and memory management is entirely explicit. Despite this, COGENT is able to guarantee memory safety through the use of a strict *uniqueness type* system. This static type discipline ensures that variables that contain references to heap objects or other singular resources such as files and disks cannot be duplicated or disposed of implicitly. It achieves this with a cheap syntactic criteria—any variable of such a type must be used *exactly* once. This means that it is impossible to leak memory, as this would mean such a variable would be left unused; nor is it possible to access memory after it has been freed, as this would require accessing the same variable twice. A similar type discipline is used to ensure memory safety in the programming language RUST[2].

Figure 1 gives a full example of a COGENT program, computing the average of a list, storing the running total and count in a heap-allocated data structure called a *Bag*. Line 2 defines the *Bag* as a Ptr to a heap-allocated record (a *product type*) containing two 32-bit unsigned integers. Lines 3 and 4 introduce allocation and free functions for *Bag*s. Definitions of types and of functions may be omitted from the COGENT source and provided externally via the C foreign function interface. Currently, heap memory management functions and loop iterators must be provided using this mechanism, although relaxing these requirements is part of ongoing work. The newBag function returns a *variant* (or *sum type*), indicating that *either* a bag and a new heap will be returned in the case of Success, or, in the case of allocation Failure, no new bag will be returned. The addToBag function (lines 5–7) demonstrates the use of pattern-matching to destructure the heap-allocated record to gain access to its fields, and update it with new values for each. The averageBag function (lines 8–10) returns if possible the average of the numbers added to the *Bag*. The input type *Bag*! indicates that the input is a *read-only*, freely shareable view of a *Bag*, called an *observer* in COGENT or a *borrow* in RUST. An observer can be made of any variable using the ! notation, as seen on line 17 where averageBag is called. Lines 11 and 12 introduce a polymorphic abstract *List* type, as well as a reduce function, which aggregates all data from the list using the provided function and identity element. Lastly, lines 13–20 define the overall average function, which creates a *Bag* with newBag, pattern matches on the result, and, if allocation was successful, adds every number in the given list to it, and then returns their average.

2.1 Uniqueness Types

Uniqueness types allow us to model imperative, stateful computations as pure mathematical functions, as the static type discipline ensures that each mutable heap object has exactly one usable reference at any point in time. This means

---

[2] The Rust programming language: https://www.rust-lang.org (accessed on August 31, 2018).

that a well-typed program can be given two interpretations: an imperative *update* semantics that mutates heap objects and a "pure" *value* semantics with no notion of a heap, that treats all objects as immutable values. As it is impossible to alias mutating objects, the equational reasoning by which we would reason about the pure interpretation applies just as well to the imperative interpretation, as the lack of aliasing makes it impossible to observe the mutation of an object from any reference other than the one used to mutate it.

Such equational reasoning is highly suitable for verification in a proof assistant such as Isabelle/HOL, as the pure denotation of a COGENT function is simply a mathematical function – objects for which most proof assistants have significant built-in support.

2.2 The COGENT Verification Framework

In addition to a programming language, COGENT is also a verification framework realised in Isabelle/HOL, based on *certifying compilation*. This means that apart from compiling a COGENT program to C, the compiler also generates an Isabelle/HOL shallow embedding of the program in terms of simple functions, and a proof that the generated C code is a *refinement* of that embedding. This entails that any functional correctness theorem proven about the simple shallow embedding also applies to the generated C code.

In prior work [1], we developed two Linux file systems in COGENT, and proved key correctness theorems about one of them. The equational semantics drastically reduced the effort required to verify these systems, and their performance was comparable to other Linux file systems that were hand-written in C.

Figure 2 gives an overview of the COGENT framework. The overall proof that the C code refines the purely functional shallow embedding in Isabelle is broken into a number of sub-proofs and translation validation phases. Three embeddings are generated: a top-level shallow embedding in terms of pure functions; a deeply-embedded representation of the abstract syntax of the COGENT program, which can be interpreted using either the *value* or *update* semantics; and an Isabelle/HOL representation of the C code generated by the compiler, imported into Isabelle/HOL by the same C parser used in the seL4 project [11]. As can be seen in the diagram, the compiler also generates a proof that the pure interpretation of the deep embedding is a refinement of the top-level shallow embedding, and that the C code is a refinement of the imperative interpretation of the deep embedding. These refinement proofs, along with the refinement theorem between the two semantic interpretations proven by [13], can be composed to produce a refinement proof stretching from the C code all the way up to the pure shallow embedding.

2.3 The C Model

To give a formal meaning to our C code in Isabelle/HOL, we make use of the same C-Parser framework [18] used by the seL4 project [10]. This framework

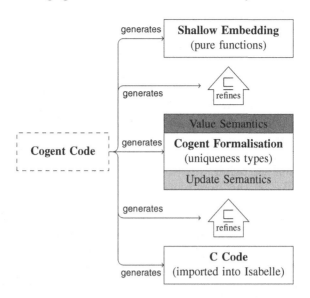

Fig. 2. The COGENT refinement framework. Boxes represent Isabelle/HOL embeddings of the COGENT program, arrows represent refinement proofs.

imports a large subset of C99 code into HOL by translating it into the embedded language SIMPL [16], which has a full formal definition of its operational and axiomatic semantics for use in proofs. This semantics could be viewed denotationally as a *relation on states*, describing what final states could result from a given initial state. The exact structure used to represent a state is a *parameter* to the definition of SIMPL, and therefore the C-Parser is free to choose a structure that mirrors the C code closely. Typically, the state structure is an Isabelle/HOL *record* with fields for each of the stack-allocated local variables used in the code, along with a field for the heap, represented using the memory model of Tuch [17].

A consequence of this representation is that, while the heap memory model used allows for pointer arithmetic, unions, and type-casting of *heap* memory, the view of the *stack* is significantly abstracted. With this state definition, it is not well-defined to take a pointer to a stack-allocated variable, or to reinterpret stack memory as a different type. C code that performs such operations is rejected by the C-Parser.

2.4 Data Refinement

A program C *refines* a program A if every observation of C is also a possible observation of A. If $[\![\cdot]\!]$ maps programs to sets of observations, then the refinement of A by C is expressed by $[\![C]\!] \subseteq [\![A]\!]$.

Seeing as observations in our case take the form of relations on states, such a refinement would entail that any partial correctness property proven for all executions in $[\![A]\!]$ will also apply to those executions in $[\![C]\!]$.

In our refinement proofs between the update semantics and C, however, the state spaces of the two programs are different, and thus the relations are not immediately comparable.

The COGENT memory model in the update semantics includes a mutable heap, however this heap contains values of *algebraic data types*, such as records (product types) and variants (sum types). The C memory model, on the other hand, is ultimately defined in terms of bits and bytes, not rich data types, to allow for pointer arithmetic and type-casting operations in C.

As our state spaces differ in this way, a simple subset relationship does not quite capture what we require of refinement; we need a notion of correspondence of states. We get this from some additional machinery from the world of *data refinement* [15]. We introduce a *refinement relation* R that relates abstract and concrete states, and show that each step our program takes preserves this relation; the relation represents the desired correspondence. We must show that our abstract program behaves analogously to the concrete program given corresponding initial states. That is, if R relates our initial abstract and concrete states, then every final state of a concrete program conc will be related by R to a final state of a corresponding abstract program abs:

$$R; [\![\text{conc}]\!] \subseteq [\![\text{abs}]\!]; R$$
(where; is composition of relations)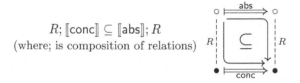

In our framework, the compiler generates the definition of this refinement relation by describing how the code generator lays out these rich data types in memory. Rizkallah et al. [14] describe in more detail the techniques we have developed to automatically prove these refinement theorems for COGENT programs.

These relation preservation proofs only imply refinement given the assumption that the relation R holds initially. A similar assumption is made for the verification of seL4, and proving this is the subject of ongoing research.

2.5   Memory Layouts in COGENT and Linux

Because of the restrictions on stack memory outlined in Sect. 2.3, the COGENT compiler chooses very straightforward memory layouts to represent algebraic data types. For record (product) types, each field is laid out in memory as a C struct. For variant (sum) types, a special value called the *tag*, which indicates the constructor used for the variant, is stored in a struct along with several sub-structures for the constructor parameters, only one of which will contain meaningful data.

The Linux kernel, on the other hand, typically chooses much more exotic data representations, using techniques such as:

Bitfields Several boolean flags are very often represented using the individual bits of a machine word.

Type tags The value of one part of a data structure can determine how to interpret/type-cast another part of a data structure, for example with tagged unions or tagged void pointers.

Container pattern Kernel-defined structures are often nested within component-specific structures at offset zero. This means that a component-specific object can be safely cast to the more general kernel-defined type for use within the kernel, and then cast back to the component-specific type when returned to the component by the kernel.

Padding and Alignment Often, blank space is left in the object intentionally to account for architecture-specific alignment considerations.

Dynamically sized objects Kernel data types often contain values that determine the size of other objects. For example, an array is often paired with its length as an integer.

Seeing as none of these techniques can currently be used by the COGENT compiler when laying out types in memory, Linux types such as these are typically modelled as abstract "black box" types in COGENT. Conversion functions from Linux data structures and COGENT data types must be manually written in C and painstakingly verified in Isabelle. These functions are very tedious to write, frustratingly error prone, and have a negative impact on performance.

The focus of our present work is therefore to extend the compiler and verification framework of COGENT to better support these kinds of memory layouts, transparently representing them as algebraic data types.

3   DARGENT, the Data Description Language

We are in the process of designing a data description language, called DARGENT, that describes how a COGENT algebraic data type may be laid out in memory, down to the bit level. Data descriptions in this language will influence the definition of the refinement relation to C code generated by the compiler. Eventually, we hope to make this language flexible enough to accommodate any conventional representation of an algebraic data type in memory. Section 4 describes in more detail the extensions necessary to COGENT to accommodate DARGENT descriptions.

Figure 3 gives a grammar for the syntax of DARGENT descriptions, which are made of one or more **layout** declarations, which give names to particular *layout expressions*. Each such expression describes how to lay out a data type in memory. Primitive types such as integer types, pointers, and booleans are laid out as a contiguous block of memory of a particular size. For example, a layout consisting of a single 4 bytes would only be appropriate to describe COGENT types that occupy four contiguous bytes of memory, such as U32 or pointer types.

$$\textbf{layout } \textit{FourBytes} = 4\text{B}$$

sizes	s	$::= n\mathrm{B} \mid nb \mid n\mathrm{B} + mb$	
layout expressions	ℓ	$::= s$	(block of memory)
		$\mid L$	(another layout)
		$\mid \ell$ at s	(offset operator)
		$\mid$ record $\overline{\{f_i : \ell_i\}}$	(records)
		$\mid$ variant $(\ell)\,\overline{\{A_i\,(n_i) : \ell_i\}}$	(variants)
declarations	d	$::=$ **layout** $L = \ell$	
layout names	L		
record field names	f		
variant constructors	A		
numbers	$n, m \in \mathbb{N}$		

(lists are represented by $\overline{\text{overlines}}$)

Fig. 3. The grammar of our DARGENT prototype.

Layouts for record types use the record construct, which contains subexpressions for the memory layout of each field. Seeing as we can specify memory blocks down to individual bits, we can naturally represent records of boolean values as a bitfield:

$$\textbf{layout}\ \textit{Bitfield} = \text{record }\{x : 1b, y : 1b\ \text{at}\ 1b, z : 1b\ \text{at}\ 2b\}$$

Here the at operator is used to place each field at a different bit offset, so that they do not overlap. If two record fields reserve overlapping blocks, the description is rejected by the compiler.

Layouts for variant types use the variant construct, which firstly requires a layout expression for the *tag* data, which encodes the constructor in the variant which is being used. Then, for each constructor in the variant, a specific tag value is given as well as a layout expression for any additional data provided in the variant type for that constructor.

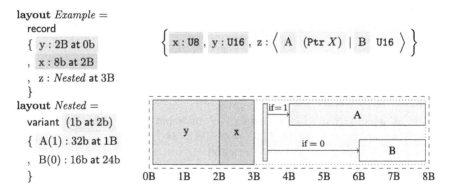

Fig. 4. A COGENT type (upper-right) laid out (lower-right) according to a DARGENT spec (left).

Figure 4 gives an illustrative example of a DARGENT description in our current prototype. We describe a memory layout for a COGENT record type containing two numbers and a variant, $\{x : U8, y : U16, z : \langle A (Ptr\ X) \mid B\ U16 \rangle\}$. As can be seen from the ordering of the fields y and x, fields may be placed in any order and at any location. This allows us to accommodate data layouts where certain parts of the data type must appear at particular offsets, such as with the container pattern mentioned in Sect. 2.5. It also makes it possible to leave unreserved space in between fields, accommodating data layouts which do this to respect padding or alignment constraints in the architecture.

The variant field z is represented according to the *Nested* description, offset by three bytes. That *Nested* description reserves the third bit of the first byte (the fourth byte of the original object) to determine which of the two constructors A and B is active. If the bit is 1, the constructor A is active, with the additional Ptr X payload stored at a one-byte offset (the fifth to eighth bytes of the original object). If the bit is 0, the constructor B is active, with the U16 payload stored at a three byte offset (the seventh and eighth byte of the original object).

4   Extensions to COGENT Type System

A COGENT type τ represented on the heap using a particular DARGENT layout ℓ will result in different C code than the same type τ represented using a different layout ℓ'. While they are identical on the abstract level, on the concrete level they are not interchangeable. Therefore, we must extend the COGENT type system such that identical types represented differently are distinguished, by *tagging* types with their representation.

Seeing as our DARGENT descriptions only apply to objects allocated on the heap, and COGENT pointer types (Ptr τ) only ever point to objects on the heap (both due to the restrictions described in Sect. 2.3), the natural place to add these tags is to the pointer type itself. We will add an additional representation parameter ℓ to the pointer type, written Ptr $\tau\ \ell$. This type indicates that the heap object of type τ pointed at by the pointer is laid out in memory according to the description ℓ. The type checker is then responsible for ensuring two properties:

1. That the layout ℓ is well-formed, i.e. that it does not reserve overlapping blocks of memory, and that it does not reference any unknown **layout** declarations.
2. That the type τ can be represented according to the description ℓ. For example, a 32-bit word U32 or a pointer on a 32-bit architecture could both be represented by the description *FourBytes* from Sect. 3, but a U64 value could not.

These descriptions are then used to generate the correspondence relation for each pointer type used in the program, which forms the basis of the refinement proof from COGENT to C.

4.1　Marshalling and Unmarshalling

Cogent programs often copy (parts of) heap allocated objects to the stack. For example, when pattern matching on particular fields of a heap allocated record, local variables are introduced for each field being matched, thus copying each matched field to the stack.

Without Dargent, this copying was straightforward, as the memory representations on the heap and on the stack were the same. With Dargent, however, the layouts may differ, and thus the compiler must also generate code to convert between the stack and heap representations of each heap-allocated type. We expect that this conversion code will be straightforward to generate as all the necessary information is provided to us by Dargent data descriptions.

4.2　Extended Pattern Matching

Currently, to match on a heap-allocated variant type, Cogent programs first copy the variant to the stack, and then match on the stack-allocated variant. This is not ideal, as large amounts of copying may be required if the variant contains a lot of data. To remedy this, we plan to make use of Dargent descriptions to perform pattern matching on heap-allocated variant types in-place.

Additionally, we plan to extend the currently limited pattern matching features available in Cogent to allow for *nested* patterns, so that a variant can be matched in-place inside a heap-allocated record, for example.

By reducing the amount of copying to the stack that needs to take place, we expect well-designed Cogent programs augmented with Dargent descriptions to require very little marshalling or unmarshalling at all, instead transparently manipulating the existing operating system data structures while viewing them as algebraic data types.

5　Future Work

The prototype data description language and framework envisioned here only scratches the surface of the potential use cases of Dargent. In addition to several syntactic improvements, such as allowing offsets and sizes of objects to be computed relatively to the offsets and sizes of other objects, we plan to extend our initial prototype of Dargent to support a number of additional semantic features.

5.1　Tighter C Integration

In our prototype, to access a data structure defined in C, one must define a highly platform-specific Dargent layout that matches the alignment, padding, integer size, and pointer size of the architecture and C compiler being used.

Ideally, we would like to be able to automate this process, replicating the exact layout decisions made by the C compiler so that C definitions can automatically be converted into Dargent for each compiler and architecture being used.

5.2   Constraints and Validation

Currently, data in memory is assumed to be *valid*, that is, to conform to the schema laid out by a DARGENT layout. Thus, to verify a COGENT program incorporating some external C code, it is necessary to prove that the C code does not violate the invariants of the data structure. Therefore, our framework is designed to only deal with *trusted* data, where deserialisation is a total function. Extending the framework to deal with potentially-invalid data must be done with great care, as our data refinement theorem requires that the refinement relation maps *every* concrete state in the execution of our program to a corresponding abstract state.

Even with the relatively simple data descriptions in our prototype, however, it is possible to have invalid data: for example, if the tag field for a variant type contains a value that does not correspond to any of the constructors in the type.

To address this, we intend to add a new totally abstract pointer type to COGENT, written `APtr`, which does not have any associated type or layout information. This type will be used to represent data on the heap that is potentially invalid. We will add a language construct to operate on values of type `APtr`, written **validate** $e \ \ell \ \tau$, which performs a dynamic check that the given `APtr` value e can be represented as the type τ using the representation ℓ, with the following typing rule:

$$\frac{\ell \text{ matches } \tau \qquad e : \texttt{APtr}}{\textbf{validate } e \ \ell \ \tau : \langle \text{Valid } (\texttt{Ptr } \tau \ \ell) \mid \text{Invalid } \texttt{APtr} \rangle}$$

This rule indicates that the **validate** operation returns a fully typed `Ptr` only if validation is successful. Because of the uniqueness type system, this conversion makes the previous `APtr` value inaccessible, making it impossible to interpret the same data structure in multiple ways. Thus, once validated, data will remain valid, even if mutated by COGENT programs.

This validation mechanism could be extended in a number of ways to support domain-specific error handling and validation constraints. For example, kernel data structures for file systems often include a "magic number" field that is hard-coded to be a specific unusual value, to detect buffer overruns early, and to debugging memory dumps easier. Some data structures, such as those found in file formats, also may include error detection mechanisms such as checksums.

We intend to allow the user to define these domain-specific constraints and attach them to a DARGENT descriptions using a subset of COGENT. Other embedded data description languages, such as PADS [6,8], take a similar approach where the host programing language of the data description language is used to attach domain-specific constraints about the data descriptions.

5.3   Wire Formats

While COGENT was originally conceived to ease the verification of file systems [9], we have long considered network stacks as another systems area which could benefit from the COGENT approach to verification.

To better support network stacks, we intend to extend DARGENT to support *wire formats*, which describe the layout of data as it is transmitted over a network link. Typically, network protocols specify bit and byte-level endianness for all values, which may differ from the architecture-defined endianness used for in-memory data structures. We plan to incorporate endianness annotations to DARGENT descriptions to accommodate this.

Typically, network protocols also incorporate various error checking and correction mechanisms for data. There is a wealth of existing work on data description languages for network protocols (see Sect. 6), and we plan to draw on this work to inform our design for error-checking in DARGENT, potentially integrating it into our constraints and validation framework.

5.4 Dynamically Sized Data

Right now, our prototype only supports data structures of statically-known size. Dynamically sized arrays, for example, must be left as abstract types, manipulated by externally-provided functions.

Typically, a dynamically-sized data structure contains *header* information from which the size of the *payload* data structure can be computed. This is a natural fit for dependent types, which is why the core calculus of PADS, the Data Description Calculus, is based on a dependent type theory [7].

In a concurrent project, we are working on bringing simple indexed or dependent types to COGENT [4]. This would allow dynamically sized arrays to be given a safe interface where only indices that are provably in-range can be used. By making DARGENT descriptions dependent, just as the types are, we could support dynamic structures that carry their size as a separate field very naturally, in a manner similar to PADS.

5.5 Layout Polymorphism

By taking a COGENT program and adding DARGENT layout descriptions, we mix the abstract functional model with concrete implementation details. Thus we cannot simply run the same program with different heap layouts without changing either the program or the layout.

A COGENT program that does not make use of kernel APIs or foreign C functions can be defined *independently* of the layout used. For this reason, we plan to extend COGENT to support *layout polymorphism*. Such a feature would allow COGENT functions to be defined generically for any layout, and instantiated to particular layouts by the compiler, based on their call-sites.

6   Related Work

The are numerous data description languages which generate access, serialisation and de-serialisation code, as well as code to transparently access the data without translating between representations. However, to the best of our knowledge, apart from the seL4 bitfield generator [5], there are no systems which also provide a machine-checked correctness proof for the generated code. This bitfield generator is subsumed by our work, as bitfields are just one of the capabilities of DARGENT.

The aforementioned PADS family of languages [6], particularly PADS/Haskell [8], serve as inspiration for parts of DARGENT. These languages, unlike DARGENT, are aimed at non-binary formats such as ASCII encodings, and focus entirely on data marshalling: parsing and pretty printing. By contrast, DARGENT prefers to rely on transparent data refinement, only translating data between representations when absolutely necessary.

DataScript [2], like DARGENT, is targeted at binary formats. Rather than algebraic data types, however, it is designed to generate object-oriented class definitions in Java for a given binary format, along with marshalling routines.

PacketTypes [12] and Protege [19] are both data description languages for describing wire formats for network protocols. They are focused on C implementations, and therefore do not provide the sort of data abstraction we see in DARGENT. Instead, they generate C code to serialise to and deserialise from wire formats.

Nail [3] is a very powerful tool for parsing and generating data formatted according to a grammar. Using Nail's description language, the tool generates an in-memory structure for the data, along with serialisation and deserialisation code. Nail supports a wide range of features, including recursive grammars, dependent fields, checksums, and dynamically sized data. Nail greatly reduces the effort in handling the conversion between data formats and their internal representations, backed by a semantic bijection. However, to the best of our knowledge, Nail lacks any formal semantics or proofs of correctness.

7   Conclusion

There is a fundamental tension between models, which are artefacts designed for *reasoning*, and programs, which are artefacts designed for *execution*. High level programming languages promise to ease this tension by allowing programs to resemble models more closely, and automating the process of refinement from model to executable.

Many traditional techniques for high level programming language implementation, such as run-time support for data representation and memory management, become unsuitable in the context of end-to-end formal verification. In order to minimise the assumptions made to support verification, we must adopt fully static, fully formalised techniques to describe the compilation process and the proof of its refinement.

At the same time, when developing operating system components, we need efficient and predictable performance—we must avoid sacrificing performance for verifiability.

COGENT, to a certain extent, already manages this balancing act, as it allows programs to be written in a purely functional style, while compiling to efficient C code without relying on any run-time support. The limitations of COGENT only begin to show once larger systems are implemented in it, where the mismatch of data representations can lead to severely under-performing systems.

The DARGENT data description language we have envisioned in this paper is the last piece in this puzzle. By allowing the programmer to control the compilation and refinement process, specifically in terms of data layouts, we widen the applicability of the COGENT framework to new domains such as network stacks, improve interoperability with existing systems code, and take another significant step towards achieving a *verified* unification of modelling and programming.

References

1. Amani, S., et al.: Cogent: verifying high-assurance file system implementations. In: International Conference on Architectural Support for Programming Languages and Operating Systems, Atlanta, GA, USA, pp. 175–188, April 2016
2. Back, G.: DataScript- a specification and scripting language for binary data. In: Batory, D., Consel, C., Taha, W. (eds.) GPCE 2002. LNCS, vol. 2487, pp. 66–77. Springer, Heidelberg (2002). https://doi.org/10.1007/3-540-45821-2_4
3. Bangert, J., Zeldovich, N.: Nail: a practical tool for parsing and generating data formats. In: Proceedings of the 11th USENIX Symposium on Operating Systems Design and Implementation, pp. 615–628. USENIX Association, Broomfield (2014). https://www.usenix.org/conference/osdi14/technical-sessions/presentation/bangert
4. Chen, Z.: COGENT⇑: giving systems engineers a stepping stone (extended abstract). In: The 2017 ACM SIGPLAN Workshop on Type-driven Development (ICFP TyDe 2017) (2017). https://www.cse.unsw.edu.au/~zilinc/tyde17.pdf
5. Cock, D.: Bitfields and tagged unions in C – verification through automatic generation. In: Proceedings of the 5th International Verification Workshop, Sydney, pp. 44–55, August 2008
6. Fisher, K., Gruber, R.: PADS: a domain-specific language for processing ad hoc data. In: Proceedings of the 2005 ACM SIGPLAN Conference on Programming Language Design and Implementation, pp. 295–304. ACM, New York (2005). http://doi.acm.org/10.1145/1065010.1065046
7. Fisher, K., Mandelbaum, Y., Walker, D.: The next 700 data description languages. J. ACM 57(2), 10:1–10:51. http://doi.acm.org/10.1145/1667053.1667059
8. Fisher, K., Walker, D.: The PADS project: an overview. In: Proceedings of the 14th International Conference on Database Theory, pp. 11–17. ACM, New York (2011). http://doi.acm.org/10.1145/1938551.1938556
9. Keller, G., et al.: File systems deserve verification too! In: Workshop on Programming Languages and Operating Systems (PLOS), Farmington, Pennsylvania, USA, pp. 1–7, November 2013
10. Klein, G., et al.: seL4: formal verification of an OS kernel. In: ACM Symposium on Operating Systems Principles, pp. 207–220. ACM, Big Sky, October 2009
11. Klein, G., Sewell, T., Winwood, S.: Refinement in the formal verification of the seL4 microkernel. In: Hardin, D. (ed.) Design and Verification of Microprocessor Systems for High-Assurance Applications, pp. 323–339. Springer, Boston (2010). https://doi.org/10.1007/978-1-4419-1539-9_11

12. McCann, P.J., Chandra, S.: PacketTypes: abstract specification of network protocol messages. In: Proceedings of the ACM Conference on Communications, pp. 321–333. ACM, New York (2000). http://doi.acm.org/10.1145/347059.347563
13. O'Connor, L., et al.: Refinement through restraint: bringing down the cost of verification. In: International Conference on Functional Programming, Nara, Japan, September 2016
14. Rizkallah, C., et al.: A framework for the automatic formal verification of refinement from COGENT to C. In: Blanchette, J.C., Merz, S. (eds.) ITP 2016. LNCS, vol. 9807, pp. 323–340. Springer, Cham (2016). https://doi.org/10.1007/978-3-319-43144-4_20
15. de Roever, W.P., Engelhardt, K.: Data Refinement: Model-Oriented Proof Methods and their Comparison. No. 47 in Cambridge Tracts in Theoretical Computer Science. Cambridge University Press, Cambridge (1998)
16. Schirmer, N.: Verification of sequential imperative programs in Isabelle/HOL. Ph.D. thesis, Technische Universität München (2006)
17. Tuch, H.: Formal memory models for verifying C systems code. Ph.D. thesis, UNSW, Sydney, Australia, August 2008
18. Tuch, H., Klein, G., Norrish, M.: Types, bytes, and separation logic. In: ACM SIGPLAN-SIGACT Symposium on Principles of Programming Languages, Nice, France, pp. 97–108. ACM, January 2007
19. Wang, Y., Gaspes, V.: An embedded language for programming protocol stacks in embedded systems. In: Proceedings of the 20th ACM SIGPLAN Workshop on Partial Evaluation and Program Manipulation, pp. 63–72. ACM, New York (2011). http://doi.acm.org/10.1145/1929501.1929511

Programming Is Modeling

Rance Cleaveland[(✉)]

Department of Computer Science, University of Maryland,
College Park, MD, USA
rance@cs.umd.edu

Abstract. This paper considers the relationship between modeling and programming in the context of embedded-software development. In this domain, design and development techniques such as model-based development and model-driven design are often used to improve the efficiency with which software is produced and to broaden the class of engineers who can develop it. This has led some to suggest that modeling has become, or is becoming, programming. The argument advanced in this paper is that the converse is in fact true: programming should rather be considered a form of modeling, with the programming language constituting an executable metalanguage in which models of dynamical systems are encoded and simulated, or "run". Modeling instead plays a design role, with some models used as a basis for the generation of code, although this is not a requirement: models for which code cannot be generated still play a valuable role in design processes. The basis for this perspective is presented, and research questions based on this viewpoint are given.

Keywords: Programming · Modeling · Model-based development
Model-driven engineering

1 Introduction

Software has become an indispensable component of many engineered systems, and the development of this software often constitutes a significant share of the cost of building these systems. For example, modern automobiles include 10s of millions of lines of code, and current estimates suggest that 10% of the cost vehicle is related to the development of the software in the vehicle, with this figure projected to rise to 30% by 2030 [14].[1] This excludes the costs of

---

[1] Other commentators give higher figures than this, although obtaining specific cost breakdowns from automotive manufacturers is historically difficult because software costs have traditionally been folded into "electronics costs" for vehicles [15]. These costs also depend on the vehicle technology: hybrid models such as the Toyota Prius rely much more on software and electronics than traditional internal-combustion-based ones, and estimates as high as 50% in the case of early models of the Prius have been given cited by engineering executives in presentations I have attended.

© Springer Nature Switzerland AG 2018
T. Margaria and B. Steffen (Eds.): ISoLA 2018, LNCS 11244, pp. 150–161, 2018.
https://doi.org/10.1007/978-3-030-03418-4_10

automotive recalls attributable to software defects, which in 2015 were projected to be the cause of 15% of all vehicle recalls [20].

To control the resulting costs associated with the creation of this software, organizations have pursued strategies, often based on *model-based development* or *model-driven design/engineering*, whose goal is to raise the level of abstractions used in software development and enable its implementation to be undertaken by domain experts who are not computer scientists. In these approaches, modeling languages such as MATLAB®/Simulink®/Stateflow®[2] or the Unified Modeling Language (UML) are used to develop models of the application; automated tools may then be used to synthesize the source code to be compiled and deployed in the system being designed. Industries such as automotive have begun to invest heavily in these so-called *autocoding* processes, and companies such as dSPACE have third-party tools for streamlining the autocoding process.

In many respects the emergence of these modeling languages can be seen as a logical extension of the development of programming languages, whose purpose is to insulate programmers from the vagaries of the specific platforms on which their applications are to run. Specifically, these modeling languages include constructs (integration and differentiation, state machines, matrices, vectors, event-processing, etc.) that are more abstract than those provided by general-purpose programming languages, and are intended to simplify the development of applications in the domains targeted by the modeling languages. This observation can naturally lead to the conclusion that modeling languages "are" next-generation programming languages, and that modeling should be seen as programming.

This perspective has a number of attractive aspects. Because of the syntactic fragility and complexity of source code, software developers have an extensive array of automated tools for producing, analyzing and managing their code bases, from text editors, syntax checkers and version managers to type checkers, debuggers and static analyzers. Repurposing these tools for model development enables similar levels of care to be taken in the management of models, which have traditionally not been received the same level of attention as source code. Similarly, imbuing the training of modelers with some of the craft used in the training of programmers would yield benefits to the engineering of models.[3] Having said that, I believe that in fact the inclusion relationship is incorrectly stated, and that programming is really modeling, rather than vice versa. Moreover, I contend there are good reasons to prefer this perspective, and that even as some programming is done via modeling, there are good reasons not to equate the two activities. In the remainder of this note I will explain this point of view,

---

[2] MATLAB®, Simulink® and Stateflow® are registered trademarks of The Math-Works, Inc.

[3] I recall working with a first-year engineering student who was developing a model for his university's mandatory one-credit course in MATLAB programming for engineers. I asked him why he was not using indentation to make his MATLAB code easier to read. His uncomprehending gaze spoke volumes to me about the possibilities for improving model development using tried-and-true techniques from coding.

and suggest implications it has for research on both modeling and programming languages.

2   The Advent of Model-Based Software Development

The use of modeling in embedded-software development derives from the inclusion of purpose-built software in physical devices, such as automobiles, aircraft and medical devices. Such *embedded software* is typically responsible for implementing the control strategies developed by engineers in these domains for ensuring desired behavior of the over-all system, whether it involves anti-lock braking, aileron control or heart-rhythm maintenance.

Engineering design in general is in the midst of a *virtualization revolution*, in which increasing parts of design and development involve the use of computing to assess initial design specifications. Computer-Aided Design (CAD) tools have been in the forefront of this revolution, and more recently simulation environments such as MATLAB and Modelica have been used to study aspects of the behavior of the designs [32] and not just their static characteristics. These *virtual* components (virtual because they do not have a physical existence) can also be tested in the context of existing physical devices, using so-called "hardware-in-the-loop" testing tools [23], thereby enabling the analysis of proposed designs for system components in the physical setting in which the actual components would be deployed.

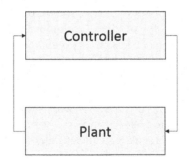

Fig. 1. A classical closed-loop control diagram.

The same advances in computational infrastructure that have enabled the use of automated modeling in engineering design have also provoked a second revolution in the design of for controllers for such systems: the use of digital hardware, and software, to implement control strategies. Returning to the virtualization narrative from above, when the system being designed includes an embedded-control unit, it is natural to include a model of the controller in the system design. The over-all structure of such a system is depicted in Fig. 1. The purpose of the controller is to modify the behavior of the physical part of the system, or "Plant", based to its physical state in order to provide desired functionality. In the model-based setting, the controller model interacts with models of physical components being controlled so that the efficacy of different control strategies can be analyzed at design time, without the need to construct prototypes.[4]

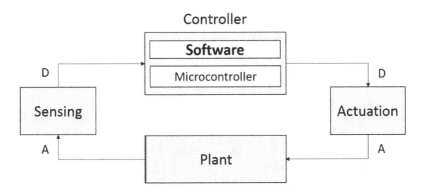

Fig. 2. Architecture of a digitally controlled system. The "D" and "A" labels reflect whether the data on the given lines is digital or analog.

Traditionally, these controllers would in turn be implemented using purpose-built mechanical or electronic linkages to convert feedback from the plant into forces used to alter the behavior of the plant. The advent of cheaper digital microprocessors since the 1970s, however, had led to the widespread use of *digital control systems* consisting microprocessors (often called *microcontrollers*) running software that computes the control strategy developed by the design engineers. This software is responsible for reading input data from the sensors and computing signals to send to the actuators that cause the desired changes in the plant, and it must be written, compiled and downloaded onto the microcontroller as part of the implementation of the actual controller. Figure 2 shows how this perspective alters the traditional closed-loop control diagram given in Fig. 1.

This emergence of so-called control software has had a profound impact on control-system design, since controllers can now be experimented with, debugged, and modified independently of the underlying microcontroller hardware. However, it does present engineering challenges absent from traditional control-system realization: the control software must be written and verified, and the organizations developing these devices often lacked the in-house expertise for this task. Because of their yearly product cycles and highly competitive

---

[4] Of course, the use of modeling does not obviate the need for eventual physical testing. However, it does change the nature and scope of that testing, whose goal becomes to confirm the fidelity of the modeling, and assess aspects of the physical aspects of the system not captured in the models.

marketplace, automotive companies have felt this pressure especially keenly, and it was in this industry that the interest in so-called *autocoding* first emerged [31]. Specifically, automotive-engineering teams were making increasing use of CAD and simulation modeling to make their design flows more efficient, and tools such as MATLAB and Simulink employed generation of C code from their models to improve performance of the model simulations [1]. A natural next step was to consider how to use the C code generated from the controller part of these models as the deployed control software. Tool vendors such as The Math-Works responded by developing tools, such as Real-Time Workshop (now called Simulink Coder^{TM}) [4] and Embedded Coder [3], for generating deployable code from models, and automotive companies (and most especially, their suppliers) have been adopting these tools increasingly aggressively as a means of making their software development processes more efficient.

This use of models as a basis for code generation also prompted studies of other uses for these models in the software development process. In particular, models of controllers came to be seen as specifications of the software to be deployed on the microcontroller, and this led to the develop of testing tools, such as Reactis®[5] [5,29] and BTC EmbeddedTester[6] [2], that generate test cases from models for application to source code and other downstream system artifacts. Other work focused on the use of inspections, modeling standards and other traditional software-engineering techniques for assessing model quality [19]. The resulting approaches have become referred to in industry as *model-based development* (MBD) [12].

An ongoing criticism of MBD as practiced is that modeling notations such as MATLAB and Simulink are proprietary. A complementary development in the research community has been to develop model-based engineering methods, including autocoding but also a rich array of model-verification and -analysis techniques, around open-source modeling languages such as UML [26,28]. The general term of art encompassing these approaches is *model-driven development* (MDD) or *model-driven engineering* [11,27]. Significant attention has also been paid to the metatheory of modeling in MDD research and its use as a basis for translating between modeling languages [9,24], so that models developed in different languages can be composed and interoperate.

3   Modeling Versus Programming

The previous section noted the industrial drive to raise the level at which programming, especially of embedded controllers, is undertaken, and the use of modeling languages such as MATLAB, Simulink and others as a basis for doing this. Given current trends, a natural question that arises is this: how "close" is

---

[5] Reactis® is a registered trademark of Reactive Systems, Inc.

[6] BTC EmbeddedTester is a product of BTC Embedded Systems AG.

modeling to programming? This question is often posed in a simplified form as follows: is modeling programming?[7]

The thesis of this paper is that, in order to be answered in the affirmative, the question in fact needs to be inverted. I argue that, rather than modeling becoming programming, programming is, and has always been, modeling, albeit a restrictive form of modeling undertaken in a specific meta-theory, namely a programming language with an executable semantics. In this sense, there are useful, widely employed forms of modeling, including requirements capture, architectural diagrams and human-factors design, that typically are not executable (although sometimes they are) and hence should not generally be considered programming. This point may be seen as controversial and will be returned to later in this section.

To clarify this thesis it will be helpful to define more precisely some of the terminology used. For modeling, the following definition of *scientific modeling* from [6] represents a useful starting point.

Scientific modelling is a scientific activity, the aim of which is to make a particular part or feature of the world easier to understand, define, quantify, visualize, or simulate by referencing it to existing and usually commonly accepted knowledge.

This definition presents modeling as explaining a particular aspect of the world in reference to existing accepted knowledge. One way to do this is to develop *encodings* that specify the precise relationship between the aspect of the world being modeled and currently understood phenomena. In mathematical approaches one constructs these encodings using a *metalanguage*, which contains a collection of well-understood entities as well as an agreed-upon collection of precisely defined operations for manipulating entities.

Seen in this setting, programming is indeed modeling! The programming language in which the programming is being undertaken satisfies the requirements of a meta-language; the basic data types and data structures of the programming language, and their associated built-in operations, represent "existing knowledge"; the layering of abstractions on top of these built-in programming-language features, which is the act of programming, amounts to the construction of an encoding, hence model, of entities not already represented in the language.

As a concrete example, consider a program in, say, C that implements operations on binary search trees. Binary search trees are not part of the core C programming language, but they do exists independently of C, as mathematical entities satisfying certain properties and with operations, such as insert, delete and lookup, that have can be defined mathematically. An implementation of binary search trees in C involves developing an encoding of the tree structure

---

[7] It is difficult to find references for questions like this, but I did hear Grady Booch, one of the designers of UML, give a talk in the Washington, DC area in the 2002–2003 time frame in which he posed this question in relation to the development of Executable UML. His take at that time was that Executable UML was not yet a programming language, although his reasoning differs from that in this paper.

using more primitive C constructs, then coding operations on these encodings as functions/subroutines in C. The net effect can be seen as developing a model of binary search trees, with C playing the role of the metalanguage governing what operations are allowed in the model encodings and how they work in terms of existing, lower-level operations in C. Since C is executable, the operations defined in this implementation of binary-search trees can be applied to binary-search tree objects in, with the result of the operation evaluated purely automatically. Seen in this light, many programming-language libraries, including ones that implement commonly used concepts in control theory (e.g. differentiation, integration, etc.) can be seen as encodings of models of the relevant mathematical theories.

This perspective—programming as modeling—can also be seen as explaining some aspects in the evolution of programming-language design. Arguably the first high-level programming language, FORTRAN, derives its name from the phrase "FORmula TRANslating system" [10], which in turn explains a key role to be played by the language: a metalanguage into which formula-based models of physical phenomena could be encoded. Similarly, what is (are) often called the first object-oriented language(s), Simula-1/67 [18], was (were) conceived of as languages for simulations and included constructs for simplifying the encoding of simulation models. Other, so-called "general-purpose" languages, such as Java, can be seen as devoted to generalized modeling, while more specialized languages, such as MATLAB or R [22], provide constructs aimed at simplifying the encodings of models given in more specialized settings. Still other approaches to programming, such as logic and functional programming, provide constraints on the operations that can be performed on models. Nevertheless, in all cases, programming languages are used as a basis for building abstractions, which can be seen as another way of saying "building models." These languages also permit code to be executed, meaning that the models, once embedded in the language, can be in effect be queried, or simulated, by providing sample inputs and initial conditions and inspecting the results produced by the model.

Earlier in this section I said that system modeling includes aspects that are not programming, and I listed three examples of such modeling: requirements, architectural, and human-factors. Some may complain about this, since, for example, tools exist for generating code from some architectural models in particular. My point, however, is that programming requires a fixed, executable metalanguage (the programming language itself). Many modeling notations, especially some of the more abstract ones in UML, such as Use-Case Diagrams [8], lack this crucial aspect; for this reason, I say they are not programming notations, although certainly subsets of them could be seen as such. This is not to disparage the utility of such diagrams, but rather an attempt to temper expectations about what they in fact are not required to be: programs.

4   Research Implications

The previous section explained my perspective on the relationship between modeling and programming, namely, that programming is a form of modeling, but not necessarily vice versa. In this section I explore some of the consequences of this perspective by giving two research themes that this understanding leads to.

Programming-Language Research. When using modeling to develop an understanding of a system, a modeler stays within the ontology of the modeling notation; that is, one uses concepts defined by the modeling notation. New concepts can be layered on top of existing modeling constructs, but one generally cannot redefine existing constructs.

Viewed as modeling languages, programming languages generally lack this ability to enforce adherence to specific base abstractions defined by programmers. While substantial work has been done on abstraction and information-hiding in the programming-language research community [25], to the best of my knowledge there has been almost no work on how to require programmers to use existing abstractions that have been defined by others.[8] This results in numerous practical problems: programmers re-invent abstractions already developed, leading to code bloat and lack of uniformity in coding policies; desired changes in standardized data structures become very difficult to enforce because of the possibility of different implementations of these data structures existing within a code base; and code maintenance becomes more of a headache because of the profusion of syntactic and semantic "clones" of abstractions.

In my view, what programming languages need to serve as better modeling languages is a suite of mechanisms for enforcing *sublanguage* adherence. Specifically, if L is a programming language, a sublanguage L' of L has the property that any program P' written in L' is also a valid program in L. A sublanguaging mechanism would restrict programs written by programmers to ones in such an L', with the definition of L' then enforcing adherence to a desired set of abstractions.

As an example of an existing (mostly human-enforced) sublanguaging mechanism, let me explain a set-up for engine-control software that I witnessed firsthand in a large international automotive company. That company's software was written in C and involved contributions by a large team of developers spread over several locations, with different teams responsible for different features of the system. To help with issues of code maintainability, especially in an environment in which there was ongoing staff turnover, the company enforced a variable-naming policy: the only variable names that could be used were ones on a master list (about 500 names long), with the names encoding what could be seen as *type information* about the values that would be stored in the variables. As a notional example, `currentAmps` might be the name of a variable encoding electrical current in amps, while `currentMilliamps` would represent the same physical measurement in terms of milliamps. As part of the build process for

---

[8] Even the work done on so-called *embedded domain-specific languages (DSLs)* [16] typically allows programmers to "jump into" the programming language in which the DSL is embedded, thereby permitting the potentially undisciplined definition and use of new abstractions. Embedded DSLs are, it must be noted, targeted at non-expert programmers who may not be able to exercise the features of the language the DSL is embedded in, yielding an analogue of "security by obscurity".

their code base, the company had an analyzer that rejected code using unapproved variable names. In this case, the sublanguage L' effectively consisted of programs whose variable names were required to come from the approved list.

One can imagine other useful sublanguaging ideas. For instance, disabling the use of pointers could be a way of ensuring that programmers do not build their own dynamic data structures and instead use ones provided in the code base. Another possibility would be to disable use of the assignment operator, so as to prevent users from inadvertently circumventing state-updating constraints the existing code base needs to enforce. Disabling certain constructs, such as bitwise boolean operations, might also be useful to enforce in certain settings, as would the disabling of the use of some operations, such as casting, on primitive data types.

How to implement and use sublanguaging would require research, of course. Nevertheless, I believe that a robust sublanguaging feature, designed with the viewpoint of making programming languages more robust and customizable as modeling languages, would benefit developers and the organizations that employ them.

Modeling Languages. If programming is a form of modeling, but modeling is not necessarily a form of programming, then what implications does this perspective have for research in modeling languages *vis à vis* code? I believe that a fruitful research theme to pursue would involve the explicit study of *synthesizability*, and more specifically the identification of subsets of modeling languages from which source code targetting different platforms can automatically be generated.

Synthesizability has been a topic of research in the digital-design community for a number of years [13]. Commonly used design languages, such as VHDL and Verilog, are like modeling languages in that not every design can be converted automatically to hardware. Significant research, and resulting tool support, has been devoted to identifying synthesizable fragments of these languages, based on the supporting infrastructure (data-type support, etc.) provided by the environment in which the synthesized circuitry is to run. Developing a theoretical framework for synthesizability for modeling languages used in MBD/MDD would provide benefits similar to those afforded by research on this topic in the hardware community: automated generation of implementations when this is possible, and alerts as to when it is not.

A concrete example of a synthesizability problem in the area of MBD involves the use of so-called fixed-point arithmetic[9] in coding [21]. In many control applications the target hardware lacks floating-point capability, both for reasons of cost and also of accuracy. Generating fixed-point implementations from generic MATLAB/Simulink/Stateflow models is generally not possible, because modelers using these notations frequently employ floating-point numbers in their modeling. In practice, what currently happens in such scenarios is that versions of the floating-point models are converted by hand to fixed-point

---

[9] Fixed-point arithmetic stands in counterpoint to floating-point arithmetic, and is not related to the theory of fixed points for functions.

models, with attendant issues relating to fixed-point design (e.g. scaling and over-flows) addressed then [30]. Specialized tools, such as The MathWoks' Embedded-Coder [3] or dSPACE's Targetlink [7], are then used to generate code from these hand-crafted fixed-point models. Developing frameworks and tools for extending the synthesizability frontier in this case, so that some fixed-point code can automatically be generated, would yield significant benefits in the practice of fixed-point controller design.

As the previous example suggests, synthesizability is not an absolute criterion; the target platform on which the generated code is to run plays a major role in what is synthesizable and what is not. Work on model-transformation frameworks [17] by the MDD community represents a possible starting point for developing adaptable synthesis frameworks that can be employed by synthesis tools.

5   Conclusions

In this paper I have explored the relationship between programming and modeling in the context of embedded software. After giving my perspectives on the model-based development (MBD) and model-driven design (MDD) approaches, I have advanced a thesis on the relationship between modeling and programming: programming is a form of modeling, but not vice versa. I have then offered what I see are interesting research directions arising from this perspective: sublanguaging for programming languages, so that modeling-based abstractions can be enforced, and synthesizability for modeling languages, so that it can be determined when code can be extracted efficiently and automatically from models given in modeling languages. I believe that these two general topics offer a number of interesting technical problems for researchers, and that accompanying automated tools will lead to better modeling and programming practices.

References

1. Accelerating Simulink Models. https://www.mathworks.com/help/vision/ug/accelerating-simulink-models.html. Accessed 30 Aug 2018
2. BTC EmbeddedTester. https://www.btc-es.de/en/products/btc-embeddedtester/
3. Generate C and C++ Code Optimized for Embedded Systems. https://www.mathworks.com/products/embedded-coder.html. Accessed 30 Aug 2018
4. Generate C and C++ Code from Simulink and Stateflow Models. https://www.mathworks.com/products/simulink-coder.html. Accessed 30 Aug 2018
5. Software Testing and Validation with Reactis. https://www.reactive-systems.com/. Accessed 30 Aug 2018
6. Scientific Modelling. https://en.wikipedia.org/wiki/Scientific_modelling. Wikipedia Accessed 30 Aug 2018
7. Targetlink. https://www.dspace.com/en/pub/home/products/sw/pcgs/targetli.cfm. Accessed 30 Aug 2018
8. Adolph, S., Cockburn, A., Bramble, P.: Patterns for Effective Use Cases. Addison-Wesley Longman Publishing Co., Inc., Boston (2002)

9. Atkinson, C., Kuhne, T.: Model-driven development: a metamodeling foundation. IEEE Softw. **20**(5), 36–41 (2003)
10. Backus, J.: The history of FORTRAN I, II, and III. ACM SIGPLAN Not. **13**(8), 165–180 (1978)
11. Balasubramanian, K., Gokhale, A., Karsai, G., Sztipanovits, J., Neema, S.: Developing applications using model-driven design environments. Computer **2**, 33–40 (2006)
12. Bauer, A., et al.: AutoMoDe - notations, methods, and tools for model-based development of automotive software. Technical report, SAE Technical Paper 2005-01-1281 (2005)
13. Brayton, R.K., et al.: VIS: a system for verification and synthesis. In: Alur, R., Henzinger, T.A. (eds.) CAV 1996. LNCS, vol. 1102, pp. 428–432. Springer, Heidelberg (1996). https://doi.org/10.1007/3-540-61474-5_95
14. Burkacky, O., Deichmann, J., Doll, G., Knochenhauer, C.: Rethinking Car Software and Electronics Architecture. Automotive & Assembly Insights, February 2018. https://www.mckinsey.com/industries/automotive-and-assembly/our-insights/rethinking-car-software-and-electronics-architecture
15. Charrette, R.: This car runs on code. IEEE Spectr. **46**, 3 (2009). https://spectrum.ieee.org/transportation/systems/this-car-runs-on-code
16. Cuadrado, J.S., Molina, J.G.: Building domain-specific languages for model-driven development. IEEE Softw. **24**(5), 48–55 (2007). ISSN 0740–7459. https://doi.org/10.1109/MS.2007.135
17. Czarnecki, K., Helsen, S.: Classification of model transformation approaches. In: Proceedings of the 2nd OOPSLA Workshop on Generative Techniques in the Context of the Model Driven Architecture, USA, vol. 45, pp. 1–17 (2003)
18. Dahl, O., Nygaard, K.: SIMULA: an ALGOL-based simulation language. Commun. ACM **9**(9), 671–678 (1966)
19. Deissenboeck, F., Wagner, S., Pizka, M., Teuchert, S., Girard, J.-F.: An activity-based quality model for maintainability. In: IEEE International Conference on Software Maintenance, ICSM 2007, pp. 184–193. IEEE (2007)
20. Halvorson, B.: Software Now to Blame for 15 Percent of Car Recalls. Popular Science, June 2016. https://www.popsci.com/software-rising-cause-car-recalls
21. Hanselmann, H.: Implementation of digital controllers, a survey. Automatica **23**(1), 7–32 (1987)
22. Ihaka, R., Gentleman, R.: R: a language for data analysis and graphics. J. Comput. Graph. Stat. **5**(3), 299–314 (1996)
23. Isermann, R., Schaffnit, J., Sinsel, S.: Hardware-in-the-loop simulation for the design and testing of engine-control systems. Control. Eng. Pract. **7**(5), 643–653 (1999)
24. De Lara, J., Vangheluwe, H.: AToM^3: a tool for multi-formalism and meta-modelling. In: Kutsche, R.-D., Weber, H. (eds.) FASE 2002. LNCS, vol. 2306, pp. 174–188. Springer, Heidelberg (2002). https://doi.org/10.1007/3-540-45923-5_12
25. Parnas, D., Clements, P., Weiss, D.: The modular structure of complex systems. IEEE Trans. Softw. Eng. **3**, 259–266 (1985)
26. Rumbaugh, J., Jacobson, I., Booch, G.: The Unified Modeling Language Reference Manual. Pearson Higher Education, New York (2004)
27. Schmidt, D.: Model-driven engineering. Computer **39**(2), 25 (2006)
28. Selic, B.: Using UML for modeling complex real-time systems. In: Mueller, F., Bestavros, A. (eds.) LCTES 1998. LNCS, vol. 1474, pp. 250–260. Springer, Heidelberg (1998). https://doi.org/10.1007/BFb0057795

29. Sims, S., DuVarney, D.: Experience report: the reactis validation tool. In: ACM SIGPLAN Notices, vol. 42, pp. 137–140. ACM (2007)
30. Smith, S.: Digital Signal Processing: A Practical Guide for Engineers and Scientists. Elsevier, Dordrecht (2013)
31. Toeppe, S., Ranville, S., Bostic, D., Wang, Y.: Practical validation of model based code generation for automotive applications. In: 18th Digital Avionics Systems Conference, Proceedings, vol. 2, p. 10.A.3. IEEE (1999)
32. Zeigler, B., Kim, T.G., Praehofer, H.: Theory of Modeling and Simulation. Academic Press, Orlando (2000)

Programming Language Specification and Implementation

Peter Sestoft[(✉)] [ID]

Computer Science Department, IT University of Copenhagen,
Copenhagen, Denmark
`sestoft@itu.dk`

Abstract. The specification of a programming language is a special case of the specification of software in general. This paper discusses the relation between semantics and implementation, or specification and program, using two very different languages for illustration. First, we consider small fragments of a specification of preliminary Ada, and show that what was considered a specification in VDM in 1980 now looks much like an implementation in a functional language. Also, we discuss how a formal specification may be valuable even though seen from a purely formal point of view it is flawed. Second, we consider the simple language of spreadsheet formulas and give a complete specification. We show that nondeterminism in the specification may reflect run-time nondeterminism, but also underspecification, that is, implementation-time design choices. Although specification nondeterminism may appear at different binding-times there is no conventional way to distinguish these. We also consider a cost semantics and find that the specification may need to contain some "artificial" nondeterminism for underspecification.

Keywords: Specification · Implementation
Programming languages · Nondeterminism · Underspecification

1 Introduction

This paper investigates the relation between specification (or modeling) and programming in the special case where the specification describes a programming language and its implementations, rather than some other software artefact. We study two examples of programming language specification to make several observations.

We first use a large but incomplete specification (of an Ada language subset) to make two observations. One observation is that the 1980 VDM formal specification looks very much like a functional program today. This indicates that the distinction between specification and programming may be one of degree, contingent on (specification and programming) language sophistication and notational support for the use of sets, maps, sequences and other useful structures. The other observation is that although the VDM specification is incomplete and has

© Springer Nature Switzerland AG 2018
T. Margaria and B. Steffen (Eds.): ISoLA 2018, LNCS 11244, pp. 162–183, 2018.
https://doi.org/10.1007/978-3-030-03418-4_11

some formal deficiencies, it enabled its authors to subsequently develop a validated compiler for full Ada. Hence the value of an attempted formal specification may lie as much in the knowledge that its authors acquire through developing the specification as in the resulting formal text itself.

We next use a small but complete example specification (of simple spreadsheet formulas) to discuss the role of nondeterminism in specifications. We observe that specification nondeterminism may reflect desired run-time nondeterminism in the implementation; or it may reflect language aspects left unspecified and hence open to implementation-time choices; or both. The first case is illustrated by the spreadsheet RAND function which is expected to produce a new pseudorandom number at each evaluation. The second case is illustrated by unspecified argument evaluation order in function calls, where a sequential implementation may choose left-right or right-left or any other fixed order. The third case is illustrated by the run-time nondeterminism exhibited by truly parallel implementations of argument evaluation order. We note that there is no standard way to describe the intended binding-time (run-time or implementation-time) of specification nondeterminism. We further observe that a richer instrumented semantics eg. accounting also for the cost of expression evaluation may need to have additional nondeterminism so as not to overconstrain the possible implementations.

2   Example: A Formal Description of Ada

In this section we study the book "Towards a Formal Description of Ada" [3] from 1980 and present some reflections on it. That book uses the VDM specification language [2] to give a formal description of a preliminary version of the Ada programming language, at the time a novel, advanced and complex but rather well-designed language. The bulk of the 630-page book is based on MSc theses written by five software students (Bundgaard, Schultz, Pedersen, Løvengreen, Dommergaard) at the Technical University of Denmark, under the supervision of Dines Bjørner and Hans Bruun. It represents an impressive amount of work.

We make the following observations:

– The formal description of Ada from 1980 can today be considered a (very large) functional program, an implementation of the language. We discuss this in Sect. 2.1 and show some concrete examples of a transliteration of the VDM specification into the F# programming language [23].
– From a purely formal viewpoint, the Ada description in [3] is incomplete and inconsistent, and most likely wrong in several details. Some functions are not defined, names are misspelt, types are wrong, and so on. In Sect. 2.2 we show and discuss some examples.
– However, to consider the specification a failure would be to completely misunderstand its significance and utility. Some of the authors of the specification went on to develop a full-fledged Ada compiler, the first European one to be validated, and founded the company DDC International, now DDC-I, to sell it [4]. We discuss this in Sect. 2.3.

2.1   The Ada Formal Description as a Functional Program

The 1980 formal description of Ada consists of VDM *domain definitions*, which are type definitions in modern functional programming terms, and VDM *formulae*, which are function definitions. The specification consists of hundreds of such formulae, most of which are admirably short and comprehensible, representing a careful factorization of the many interacting aspects of the Ada language.

In this section we consider a few fragments (around two percent) of the VDM description of the Ada static semantics and show how some of the advanced constructs used in the VDM formulae can be expressed in a modern functional programming language. Specifically, we express them in F#, developed at Microsoft Research Cambridge UK [23], but we might have used the Haskell or Scala languages instead. Historically, F# descends from the ML programming language which was created in the 1970es and whose first description was published in 1979 [9]. It is possible that the designs of VDM and of ML may have inspired each other at the time, and hence not necessarily a surprise that VDM can be translated into F#.

Nevertheless, the translation supports our point of view that what was considered a specification in 1980 can be considered an implementation in 2018, thanks to advances in programming language design and implementation.

For space reasons we present only fragments of the VDM formulae, and no domain definitions, so we do not expect the reader to understand all details of the examples.

Figures 1 and 2 show how VDM record update, record field selection, pattern matching and lambda expressions can be expressed in F#.

```
.0  lookup-base-type(btype)(sur) =
.1  let ds = sel-ds(btype)(sur) in
.2  btype + (s-ds:-> cases ds:
.3            (mk-Access(fct,compl)->
.4                mk-Access(Ld.lookup-base-type(fct(d))
.5                          (sur+(s-dict:->d)),compl) ,
.6           T -> ds) ,
.7         s-sub:-> cases ds:
.8           (mk-Array()   -> nil,
.9            mk-Record() -> nil,
.10           T           -> s-sub(btype)) )

.11 type: Type -> Surroundings -> Type
```

Fig. 1. Fragment of the Ada static semantics [3, page 148] expressed in VDM. The VDM notation "btype + ..." represents record field update, and "cases ds:" represents pattern matching. Due to typesetting limitations at the time, a lambda expression $\lambda d.e$ was written as Ld.e in line 4. The formula can be expressed in a functional language such as F#, see Fig. 2.

```
let rec lookup_base_type (btype : Type) (sur : Surroundings) : Type =
    let ds = sel_ds(btype)(sur)
    { btype
      with
        s_ds =
          match ds with
            | Access { s_map = fct; s_com = compl } ->
              Some (Access { s_map =
                function d -> lookup_base_type (fct(d)) { sur with s_dict = d };
                            s_com = compl });
        s_sub =
          match ds with
            | Array _ -> Nil
            | Record _ -> Nil
            | _ -> btype.s_sub
    }
```

Fig. 2. An F# version of the VDM formula in Fig. 1. Record update is expressed as "{btype with ...}", and pattern matching as "match ds with". A constructor such as Array is written without the mk- prefix that is customary in VDM.

```
.0 lookup-all-name(name)(sur) =
.1 let mk-All-name(name') = name              in
.2 let descr-list = lookup-name(name')(sur) in
.3 conc <cases descr-list[i]:
.4    (mk-Obj-descr(typ, ) ->
.5        cases sel-ds(typ)(sur) :
.6        ( mk-Access(fct) -> <mk-Obj-descr(fct(s-dict(sur)),nil)>,
.7          T -> <>),
.8      T -> <>) | i E ind descrl>

.9 type: All-name -> Surroundings -> Descr*
```

Fig. 3. Fragment of the Ada static semantics [3, page 194] in VDM. The notation "< e | i ∈ ind descrl>" spanning lines 3–8 evaluates VDM expression e for each index i into sequence descrl. (The latter is a misspelling of descr-list in line 2). This creates a sequence of zero- or one-element sequences, flattened into one sequence using the conc VDM function. This can be expressed in F# as shown in Fig. 4.

Figures 3 and 4 show how VDM list comprehension and iteration over indices can be expressed elegantly using F# sequence expressions, and how F#'s nested pattern matching can be used to good effect.

Figures 5 and 6 show how the VDM combination of choice of an element, recursion, and production (or not) of a value can be expressed using F# sequence expressions.

Figures 7 and 8 show how the VDM nondeterministic construction "such that" (s.t.), which here simply produces a list without duplicates, and be expressed in F# using its Set module in combination with sequence expressions.

```
let lookup_all_name (All_name(name') : All_name) (sur : Surroundings)
                : seq<Descr> =
    seq { for di in lookup_name(name')(sur) do
          match di with
          | Obj_descr { s_tp = { s_ds = Some (Access {s_map = fct }) } }
              -> yield Obj_descr { s_tp = fct(sur.s_dict); s_con = None }
          | _ -> ()
        }
```

Fig. 4. An F# version of the VDM formula in Fig. 3. An F# sequence expression "seq { ...}", similar to list comprehensions in Haskell and to mathematical set comprehensions, neatly expresses the more complicated construct in the original's lines 3–8. Also, the original's nested **cases** expressions can be expressed concisely by nested patterns in the argument to the **Obj-descr** constructor match.

```
.0 get-available-obj-list(parms)(pset)(sur)=
.1 if pset = { } then <> else
.2 let d E pset in
.3 let mk-Subprgr-descr( ,,entrance) = d   in
.4 ((if s-return(entrance) ≠ nil and
         parameter-checker(parms)(entrance)(sur)
.5     then <mk-Obj-descr(s-return(entrance),CONSTANT)>
.6     else <> )) ^
.7  get-available-obj-list(parms)(pset\d)(sur) ) )

.8 type: Act-parm* -> ( Subprgr-descr)-set ->Sur -> Obj-descr*
```

Fig. 5. Fragment of the Ada static semantics [3, page 195] expressed in VDM. This VDM formula uses recursion to process the elements of the set **pset** one at a time, producing a zero- or one-element sequence for each, and concatenating the results into a single sequence using sequence concatenation ($\hat{\ }$). The formula can be expressed concisely in F# as shown in Fig. 6.

```
let get_available_obj_list (parms : seq<Act_parm>) (pset : Set<Subprgr_descr>)
                (sur : Surroundings) : seq<Descr> =
    seq { for Subprgr_descr(_, _, entrance) in pset do
          match entrance.s_return with
          | Some typ when parameter_checker(parms)(entrance)(sur) ->
              yield Obj_descr { s_tp = typ; s_con = Some CONSTANT }
          | None -> ()
        }
```

Fig. 6. An F# version of the VDM formula in Fig. 5. In the sequence expression, "for ... in pset" combines the nondeterministic choice of **d** (original line 2) with decomposition (original line 3). The **match** expression with side condition (**when**) neatly expresses the conditional and selection in the original lines 4–5.

```
.0   extract-name-types( name ) (sur) =
.1   let descrl = lookup-name(name) (sur) in
.2   conc < cases descrl[i]:
.3           ( mk-Obj-descr(otype, )   -> <otype> ,
.4             mk-Overload-descr(ds)   ->
.5               ( let list E Type* be.s.t
.6                   card elems list = ln list and
.7                   elems list = {ltype |
                                    mk-Literal-descr(ltype)E ds }) in
.8               list)                   ,
.9             mk-Number(val)          -> <mk-Pseudotype(val)> ,
.10            T                        -> <> )
.11    | i E ind descrl>

.12  type: Name -> Surroundings -> ( Type | Pseudotype )*
```

Fig. 7. Fragment of the Ada static semantics [3, page 197] expressed in VDM. The "conc < ...| i *in* **ind** descrl>" in lines 2–11 works as in Fig. 3 to create a sequence of Types or Pseudotypes from a sequence of descriptions. Lines 5–8 nondeterministically choose a list of Types such that (s.t.) it has no duplicates and it has one element for each type appearing in a Literal-descr in the sequence ds of descriptions. This can be expressed equally concisely in F# as shown in Fig. 8.

```
let extract_name_types (name : Name) (sur : Surroundings)
                   : seq<TypeOrPseudoType> =
    let descrl = lookup_name(name)(sur)
    seq { for di in descrl do
            match di with
            | Obj_descr { s_tp = otype } -> yield (TOPT_Type otype)
            | Overload_descr(ds) ->
                yield! Set.ofSeq(Seq.choose
                    (function | Literal_descr(ltype) -> Some (TOPT_Type(ltype))
                              | _ -> None) ds)
            | Number(v) -> yield TOPT_Pseudotype(v)
            | _ -> ()
    }
```

Fig. 8. An F# version of the VDM formula in Fig. 7. The outer sequence expression corresponds to lines 2–11 in the original. The construct Set.ofSeq(Seq.choose(...)) corresponds to the nondeterministic choice of list in the original's lines 5–8. The type TypeOrPseudoType and constructors such as TOPT_Type are artefacts of F#'s type system being more picky about subtypes than VDM is.

2.2 Some Flaws in the 1980 Formal Description of Ada

This section shows that from a purely formal point of view, the Ada description in [3] has some flaws. The purpose is not to blame the authors of that specification, who did an admirable job given the tools of the time; there is little value in finding hairs in the soup four decades later. The VDM specification was developed without tool support, so even misspelt variable names and type names, wrong argument order, wrong declared return type of a function, and similar fairly trivial mistakes would have to be discovered by human proofreading. Given the magnitude of the work, the number of such errors is modest.

One drawback of the Ada formal description is that it is incomplete:

- First of all, the formal description covers a subset of preliminary Ada called A6, and does not claim to be complete. The static semantics chapter has a list of "aspects of Ada not covered" [3, page 131], and several sections called "Missing functions" [3, pages 176, 185, 190, 202].
- The dynamic semantics chapter has a list of "functions used in this model but not defined" [3, page 305].

Also, when investigating the formulae shown in Sect. 2.1 we came across a few mistakes:

- Formula `lookup-unitname` [3, page 148], not shown here, is declared to have return type `Dict`, but the correct type is `Descr`.
- Formula `parameter-checker` [3, page 163], not shown here, is declared to have parameter order `entrance actual-parm-list sur` but in formula `get-available-obj-list`, shown in Fig. 5, it is called with the opposite argument order `parms entrance sur`.
- Some constructors and types are spelled inconsistently, for instance `Simp_name` versus `Simple_name` [3, pages 139 and 191], as well as `Sub_prgr_descr` versus `Subprgr_descr` [3, pages 141 and 195].
- Some local variables are spelled inconsistently, for instance `descr_list` versus `descrl`, as shown in Fig. 3.

Flaws such as those listed above are of course easily fixed, but from a purely formal point of view they show that the description is not a consistent formal object. Moreover, given what we know about human fallibility, it is reasonable to assume that in addition to these superficial inconsistencies there are more substantial, semantically important, mistakes in the description.

The next section argues that the specification is valuable and useful anyway.

2.3   Formal Specification, Valuable Despite Formal Flaws

This section argues that a "formal" specification may be valuable and useful even though, from a purely formal point of view, it is incomplete and even inconsistent. One indication is that, thirty-eight years after the publication of [3], the DDC-I Ada compiler and the DDC-I company still exist [25], in contrast to most competitors from that time. It is clear that to develop the specification in [3] the authors had to scrutinize the informal description of Ada, develop and discuss illustrative examples, and so on, and thereby gained a deep understanding, invaluable when subsequently developing the Ada compiler.

One of the authors, Hans Henrik Løvengreen, said: "It has been shown how the Ada Compiler [...] can be systematically derived from the formal definition.

The idea is that problems should be revealed and solved at the abstract level, such that the implementation will be straightforward." [3, page 318].

Also, a 1988 US Institute for Defense Analyses assessment says "[...] the formal definition was not mechanically transformed into a compiler. Rather, the formal definition was used by the compiler writers as the reference instead of a natural language requirements document. DDC personnel with whom we have spoken claim that the extra up-front effort taken to first formalize the definition of Ada led to efficiencies in the long run." [19, page 8].

Hence the chief value of a formal specification may be that the very work of developing it forces and motivates the authors to immerse themselves in the domain (whether a programming language or an application) and its intricacies, thereby building a comprehensive mental model of it. This viewpoint was suggested by Naur in 1985 concerning programming: "programming in this sense must be the programmers' building up knowledge of a certain kind, knowledge taken to be basically the programmers' immediate possession, any documentation being an auxiliary, secondary product" [17, page 253]. Replacing "programming" with "writing a formal specification", the view would be that much of the value of writing a formal specification lies in "building up knowledge" in the minds of the specification's authors, and that the resulting formal text or model may actually not be the most significant outcome of this activity. The story of the 1980 Ada description [3] seems to corroborate this view: The value of (attempted) formalization may to a large extent lie in forcing the specification's authors to pay attention to details that would be more easily glossed over if writing (only) in English or another natural language.

Nevertheless, despite its utility in subsequently implementing a validated Ada compiler, it must have been recognized at the time that the Ada description [3] had some shortcomings. Several of its authors became involved in a subsequent 1984–1987 European project to develop a more complete formal specification of Ada [4, Sect. 3.2] [19, Sect. 1.2]. The more complete specification of (revised) Ada resulting from this effort is difficult to locate today, having been published mostly as technical reports. The above-mentioned US assessment laments the complexity of the latter more complete formal specification, the high level of computer science theory background required to understand it, and the poor English of the exposition [19, Sect. 4].

The early, less complete and less formal 1980 Ada specification [3] appears in the end to have been the more useful one.

3   Example: Spreadsheet Semantics

Here we consider a simple "programming language", namely spreadsheet formulas. We use a combination of operational semantics and axiomatic semantics. The former specifies evaluation of the formula in a single spreadsheet cell. The latter specifies the expected consistency of all cells.

3.1   Formulas, Cells and Sheets

In our simplified spreadsheet model, a spreadsheet consists of a grid of cells. Each cell is either blank or contains a formula =e where e is an expression as shown in Fig. 9. Each non-blank cell in addition contains its formula's computed value, which is shown to the spreadsheet user.

$$
\begin{array}{llll}
e ::= & \texttt{n} & \text{number constant} \\
  | & \texttt{ca} & \text{cell reference} \\
  | & \texttt{IF}(e_1,e_2,e_3) & \text{conditional expression} \\
  | & \texttt{RAND}() & \text{volatile function} \\
  | & \texttt{F}(e_1,\ldots,e_n) & \text{built} - \text{in function call}
\end{array}
$$

Fig. 9. Syntax of the simplified spreadsheet formula language.

3.2   Characteristics of Spreadsheets

Spreadsheets and spreadsheet formulas have some peculiar characteristics:

(a) Consistency after recalculation: A cell's computed value after a recalculation must be the result (or rather, a possible result) of evaluating the cell's formula, given the computed values of all other cells. A reference to a cell such as A2 must have the same value wherever it appears, so A2=A2 must be true.

(b) Error values: An expression always has a value; there is no notion of exception or failed evaluation. Thus some expressions, such as 1/0 and ASIN(2), must evaluate to error values such as #DIV/0! and #NUM!.

(c) Error strictness: If an argument to a built-in function evaluates to an error value, then the function call evaluates to that error value.

(d) Volatile functions and cells: Some functions (RAND(), NOW()) are nondeterministic: each evaluation may produce a different result, so RAND()=RAND() may be false. Any cell that involves a nondeterministic function must be recomputed in a recalculation.

(e) Non-strictness of IF(e1,e2,e3): The "then" branch e2 should not be evaluated unless e1 evaluates to true; and similarly for the "else" branch e3.

(f) Cyclic cell reference dependencies: The evaluation of formula in a cell may refer to the value of that cell itself, directly or indirectly. In that case, no ordinary number value may be found for the cell, but an error value such as #CYCLE! may be found instead.

(g) Side effect freedom: The evaluation of a formula has no side effects.

These characteristics are not accidents of design, but essential for the practical utility of spreadsheets. They do have some non-trivial consequences for implementations.

It follows from (a) that the value held in a cell may need to be recalculated after an update to any cell on which it depends, directly or indirectly.

By (d), (e) and (f), if cell A2 contains the formula =IF(RAND()<0.2,A2+1,42) then there may or may not be a cyclic dependency of A2 on itself, depending on the value of RAND() in this particular recalculation. Hence cycles must be detected during evaluation, not by a preceding topological sorting of cells.

It follows from side effect freedom (g) that it is not observable whether a formula is evaluated once or twice or not at all, or whether it is evaluated before, at the same time as, or after, another formula. This allows an implementation to choose evaluation order (sequential or parallel), evaluate a cell zero times (reuse cached cell value), once (when precedents are up to date), or multiple times (evaluate it speculatively, maybe in parallel on multiple processors). It also allows cell areas with copy-equivalent formulas to be replaced by map-reduce style bulk array operations [1].

3.3   Formal Evaluation Semantics

The formal semantics of spreadsheet evaluation given here is from our book [22, Sect. 1.8]. It uses operational semantics [14, 18] to specify the local evaluation of each cell's formula (Sect. 3.3) and an axiomatic semantics to specify the global consistency of a spreadsheet after a recalculation (Sect. 3.4).

This gives fine control over formula evaluation, accounting for spreadsheet characteristics (b) through (e) in Sect. 3.2, while leaving completely unconstrained the recalculation mechanism required to obtain spreadsheet characteristics (a) consistency of the recalculated spreadsheet and (f) detection of reference cycles.

Operational Semantics of Expressions. We describe a spreadsheet's formulas using a map $\phi : Addr \rightarrow Expr$ so that when $ca \in Addr$ is a cell address, $\phi(ca)$ is the formula in cell ca. If cell ca is blank, then $\phi(ca)$ is undefined. The domain $dom(\phi)$ of ϕ is the set of non-blank cells. The ϕ function is not affected by recalculation, only by editing the formulas in the spreadsheet.

We describe the evaluation of expressions (Fig. 9) using the semantic sets and functions in Fig. 10. For instance, $Value = Number + Error$ is the set of values, and $Addr$ contains cell addresses ca such as B2.

We describe the result of a recalculation by a function $\sigma : Addr \rightarrow Value$ so that $\sigma(ca)$ is the computed value in cell ca. The σ function gets updated by each recalculation and must satisfy consistency requirements described in Sect. 3.3.

We describe the evaluation of an expression e by an evaluation judgment of the form $\sigma \vdash e \Downarrow v$, which says: When σ describes the calculated values of all cells, then formula e may evaluate to value v. The "may" is important because, in general, an expression may evaluate to multiple different values. For instance, RAND() may evaluate to any number between 0.0 (included) and 1.0 (excluded). Hence, 7+1/RAND() may evaluate to some number greater than 8 or to the error value #DIV/0! in case RAND() produces 0.0.

The complete set of inference rules that describe when a formula evaluation judgment $\sigma \vdash e \Downarrow v$ holds are given in Fig. 11.

$$
\begin{aligned}
n &\in Number = \{ \text{ proper numbers } \} \\
& Error = \{ \text{\#NUM!},\text{\#DIV/0!},\text{ \#CYCLE! } \} \\
ca &\in Addr = \{ \text{ cell addresses } \} \\
v &\in Value = Number + Error \\
e &\in Expr = \{ \text{ formulas, see Fig. 9 } \} \\
\phi & \in Addr \rightarrow Expr \\
\sigma & \in Addr \rightarrow Value
\end{aligned}
$$

Fig. 10. Sets and maps used in the spreadsheet semantics: *Number* is the set of proper floating-point numbers, excluding NaNs and infinities; *Error* is the set of error values; *Addr* the set of cell addresses; *Value* the set of values (either number or error); and *Expr* the set of formulas.

$$
\frac{}{\sigma \vdash \mathbf{n} \Downarrow n} \quad (e1)
$$

$$
\frac{ca \notin dom(\sigma)}{\sigma \vdash \mathbf{ca} \Downarrow 0.0} \quad (e2b)
$$

$$
\frac{ca \in dom(\sigma) \quad \sigma(ca) = v}{\sigma \vdash \mathbf{ca} \Downarrow v} \quad (e2v)
$$

$$
\frac{\sigma \vdash e_1 \Downarrow v_1 \in Error}{\sigma \vdash \mathtt{IF}(e_1,e_2,e_3) \Downarrow v_1} \quad (e3e)
$$

$$
\frac{\sigma \vdash e_1 \Downarrow 0.0 \quad \sigma \vdash e_3 \Downarrow v}{\sigma \vdash \mathtt{IF}(e_1,e_2,e_3) \Downarrow v} \quad (e3f)
$$

$$
\frac{\sigma \vdash e_1 \Downarrow v_1 \quad v_1 \neq 0.0 \quad \sigma \vdash e_2 \Downarrow v}{\sigma \vdash \mathtt{IF}(e_1,e_2,e_3) \Downarrow v} \quad (e3t)
$$

$$
\frac{0.0 \leq v < 1.0}{\sigma \vdash \mathtt{RAND}() \Downarrow v} \quad (e4)
$$

$$
\frac{\sigma \vdash e_i \Downarrow v_i \in Error}{\sigma \vdash \mathtt{F}(e_1,\ldots,e_n) \Downarrow v_i} \quad (e5e)
$$

$$
\frac{\sigma \vdash e_1 \Downarrow v_1 \notin Error \quad \ldots \quad \sigma \vdash e_n \Downarrow v_n \notin Error}{\sigma \vdash \mathtt{F}(e_1,\ldots,e_n) \Downarrow f(v_1,\ldots,v_n)} \quad (e5v)
$$

Fig. 11. Evaluation rules for simplified spreadsheet formulas. From [22].

The formula evaluation rules in Fig. 11 may be explained as follows:

– Rule (e1) says that a number constant $\mathbf{n}$ evaluates to that constant's value.
– Rule (e2b) says that a reference ca to a blank cell evaluates to 0.0.

- Rule (e2v) says that a reference ca to a non-blank cell evaluates to the value $\sigma(ca)$ calculated for that cell. This value may be a number or an error.
- Rule (e3e) says that the expression IF(e_1,e_2,e_3) may evaluate to error v_1 if the condition e_1 may evaluate to error v_1.
- Rule (e3f) says that IF(e_1,e_2,e_3) may evaluate to v provided the condition e_1 may evaluate to zero and the "false branch" e_3 may evaluate to v.
- Rule (e3t) says that IF(e_1,e_2,e_3) may evaluate to v provided e_1 may evaluate to some non-zero number v_1 and the "true branch" e_2 may evaluate to v.
- Rule (e4) says that function call RAND() may evaluate to any number v greater than or equal to zero and less than one. Hence, this rule models nondeterministic choice.
- Rule (e5e) says that a call F(e_1,...,e_n) to a built-in function F may evaluate to error v_i if one of its arguments e_i may evaluate to error v_i. If more than one argument may evaluate to an error, then the function call may evaluate to any of these. Hence, the semantics does not prescribe an evaluation order for arguments, such as a left to right, or right to left, or all in parallel.
- Rule (e5v) says that a call F(e_1,...,e_n) to a function F may evaluate to value v if each argument e_i may evaluate to non-error value v_i, and applying the actual function f to arguments $(v_1,...,v_n)$ produces value v. The final result v may be a number such as 5, for instance, if the call is $+(2,3)$; or it may be an error such as #DIV/0!, for instance, if the call is /(1.0, 0.0).

There are five groups of rules (e1), (e2x), (e3x), (4), (e5x), in Fig. 11, each corresponding to one of the five kinds of formulas in Fig. 12. One can easily write a program whose five cases of the match correspond exactly to the five groups of rules; see the F# program in Fig. 12: the distance from specification (operational semantics in Fig. 11) to program (implementation) is short.

However, the various appearances of nondeterminism in the specification have been treated differently in the implementation. Whereas the (e4) RAND rule's nondeterminism has been explicitly retained in the interpreter, the (e5e) rule's nondeterminism has been quietly eliminated through the use of the F# tryFind function, which searches a list sequentially from the head for a value that satisfies the predicate isError.

It is not at all clear from the specification (Fig. 11) whether nondeterminism in a given rule is essential and must be retained in an implementation (as in e4), or whether it is merely underspecification intended to provide some implementation freedom (as in e5e).

3.4   Axiomatic Semantics of Recalculation

The previous subsection describes how to evaluate a formula, given values (via σ) of all cells in the worksheet. Now we can describe the requirements on a recalculation: It must find a value for every non-blank cell ca in the sheet, and that value $\sigma(ca)$ must be a possible result of evaluating the formula $\phi(ca)$ in that cell. These consistency requirements on a recalculation are stated in Fig. 13.

```
let rec eval (sigma : env) (e : expr) =        // Rule:
    match e with
    | Const d -> Num d                          // e1
    | CellRef (c,r) ->
        match Map.tryFind (c,r) sigma with
        | None    -> Num 0.0                    // e2b
        | Some v -> v                           // e2v
    | If (e1, e2, e3) ->
        let v1 = eval sigma e1
        match v1 with
        | Error _ -> v1                         // e3e
        | Num 0.0 -> eval sigma e3              // e3f
        | Num _   -> eval sigma e2              // e3t
    | Rand -> Num (random.NextDouble())         // e4
    | Func (f, es) ->
        let vs = List.map (eval sigma) es
        match List.tryFind isError vs with
        | Some vi -> vi                         // e5e
        | None    -> evalBuiltin f vs           // e5v
```

Fig. 12. An interpreter (in F#) for simple spreadsheet expressions, closely following the operational semantics in Fig. 11. The left-hand side of (->) in a match case corresponds to the conclusion of a rule group, and the right-hand side's conditions and recursive calls correspond to rule premises.

$$(1)\ dom(\sigma) = dom(\phi)$$
$$(2)\ \forall ca \in dom(\phi).\ \sigma \vdash \phi(ca) \Downarrow \sigma(ca)$$

Fig. 13. The consistency requirements, or axioms, for spreadsheet recalculation. Requirement (1) says that a recalculation must find a value $\sigma(ca)$ for every non-blank cell ca. Requirement (2) says that the computed value $\sigma(ca)$ must agree with the cell's formula $\phi(ca)$. Considered as a "definition" of σ it is circular in that σ appears both on the left of the ($\vdash$) and on the right. This is necessary, since the evaluation of a formula $\phi(ca)$ may depend on the value $\sigma(ca')$ of any cell ca'.

These requirements leave it completely unspecified how a spreadsheet recalculation works: whether it recalculates all cells or only some cells; whether it calculates a cell only once or multiple times; whether it does so sequentially, and if so in what order, or in parallel; whether it guesses the values or computes them; and so on. This underspecification is intentional: it is essential to permit a range of implementation strategies and optimizations.

While it is entirely obvious that formula evaluation can be implemented as specified in Sect. 3.3, it is much less clear how to implement recalculation, and whether it can be implemented as specified. A simple sequential (single-threaded) approach is to equip each non-blank cell with a state that is either Dirty (the initial state), Computing or Uptodate. Then while there is at least one Dirty cell, pick one, change its state to Computing, evaluate its formula, and if successful, set the cell's computed value to the formula's value and its state to Uptodate. A cell reference encountered during evaluation may be handled like this: If the referred-to cell is Uptodate, use its computed value; if it is Dirty, recursively compute its value; and if it is Computing, there is dependency cycle in the spreadsheet. This procedure performs a form of depth-first traversal of the depends-on (or precedents) graph, with cycle detection. However, this describes a mechanism, not a specification, and is heavily biased towards single-threaded evaluation. How to make a parallel multi-threaded version of this mechanism so that it correctly discovers (dynamic) dependency cycles is far from clear, and certainly not something one would want to put into a specification.

Hence in this case, the distance from the specification (axiomatic semantics in Fig. 13) to a program (implementation) is considerable and not easily overcome.

One could nevertheless imagine an specification language with a general fix-point construct that would find a σ satisfying Fig. 13 with reasonable efficiency. When in the next section we extend the semantics to further specify the cost of spreadsheet evaluation, this seems less plausible.

4   Example: Spreadsheet Cost Semantics

In this section we extend the evaluation semantics from Sect. 3.3 to a cost semantics, which in addition to a possible computed value of the expression describes the possible cost of computing it. More precisely, the semantics describes the *work*, that is, uni-processor cost [5], of the computation. In a parallel implementation, some of that work may be performed in parallel.

The cost semantics presented here was developed to enable a (static) cost analysis of spreadsheets, for the purpose of partitioning and scheduling parallel evaluation of spreadsheets; see [6].

The cost of a computation is described by a non-negative integer representing a number of computation steps, for instance the number of evaluation rule applications, plus some measure of the cost of calling a built-in function. This notion of work can reasonably be assumed to be within a constant factor of the actual number of nanoseconds required to evaluate an expression.

4.1   Cost Semantics for Expressions

The evaluation judgment $\sigma \vdash e \Downarrow v$ gets extended to $\sigma \vdash e \Downarrow v, c$, which states that when σ describes the calculated values of all cells, then formula e may evaluate to value v at computational cost c. As in Sect. 3.3, the semantics is nondeterministic ("may") in the sense that the evaluation of an expression e could produce many different values v at many different costs c.

The inference rules defining the cost judgment $\sigma \vdash e \Downarrow v, c$ are given in Fig. 14.

$$\frac{}{\sigma \vdash \mathtt{n} \Downarrow n, 1} \ (c1)$$

$$\frac{ca \notin dom(\sigma)}{\sigma \vdash \mathsf{ca} \Downarrow 0.0, 1} \ (c2b)$$

$$\frac{ca \in dom(\sigma) \qquad \sigma(ca) = v}{\sigma \vdash \mathsf{ca} \Downarrow v, 1} \ (c2v)$$

$$\frac{\sigma \vdash e_1 \Downarrow v_1, c_1 \qquad v_1 \in Error}{\sigma \vdash \mathtt{IF}(e_1,e_2,e_3) \Downarrow v_1, 1 + c_1} \ (c3e)$$

$$\frac{\sigma \vdash e_1 \Downarrow 0.0, c_1 \qquad \sigma \vdash e_3 \Downarrow v, c_3}{\sigma \vdash \mathtt{IF}(e_1,e_2,e_3) \Downarrow v, 1 + c_1 + c_3} \ (c3f)$$

$$\frac{\sigma \vdash e_1 \Downarrow v_1, c_1 \qquad v_1 \neq 0.0 \qquad \sigma \vdash e_2 \Downarrow v, c_2}{\sigma \vdash \mathtt{IF}(e_1,e_2,e_3) \Downarrow v, 1 + c_1 + c_2} \ (c3t)$$

$$\frac{0.0 \leq v < 1.0}{\sigma \vdash \mathtt{RAND}() \Downarrow v, 1} \ (c4)$$

$$\frac{\begin{array}{c} J \subseteq \{1, \ldots, n\} \\ \forall j \in J.\ \sigma \vdash e_j \Downarrow v_j, c_j \qquad v_i \in Error \text{ for some } i \in J \end{array}}{\sigma \vdash \mathtt{F}(e_1,\ldots,e_n) \Downarrow v_i, 1 + \sum_{j \in J} c_j} \ (c5e)$$

$$\frac{\begin{array}{c} \sigma \vdash e_1 \Downarrow v_1, c_1 \qquad \ldots \qquad \sigma \vdash e_n \Downarrow v_n, c_n \\ \forall i.\ v_i \notin Error \end{array}}{\sigma \vdash \mathtt{F}(e_1,\ldots,e_n) \Downarrow f(v_1,\ldots,v_n), 1 + \sum_{j=1,n} c_j + work(f, v_1, \ldots, v_n)} \ (c5v)$$

Fig. 14. Cost semantics rules for simplified spreadsheet formulas. From [6].

These rules are mostly straightforward extensions of the formula evaluation rules in Fig. 14:

- Rule (c1) says that evaluating a number constant n requires 1 computation step, and similarly for cell references by rules (c2b) and (c2v).
- Rule (c3e) says that if e_1 may evaluate to error v_1 in c_1 computation steps, then IF(e_1,e_2,e_3) may evaluate to error v_1 in $1 + c_1$ computation steps.
- Rule (c3f) says that if e_1 may evaluate to zero in c_1 computation steps and the "false branch" e_3 may evaluate to v in c_3 computation steps, then IF(e_1,e_2,e_3) may evaluate to value v in $1 + c_1 + c_3$ computation steps.
- Rule (c3t) is similar, for when e_1 may evaluate to some non-error non-zero number v_1 in c_1 computation steps.
- Rule (c4) says that function call RAND() may evaluate to any (non-error) number v between zero and one, in one computation step.

- Rule (c5e) is quite different from the corresponding evaluation rule (e5e) in Fig. 11. It says that an implementation may choose to evaluate just a subset $\{e_j \mid j \in J\}$ of the arguments when some e_i with $i \in J$ evaluates to an error v_i, and then let v_i be the result of the function call. Also, it says that the total cost of this is the cost $\sum_{j \in J} c_j$ of evaluating that subset of arguments, plus one. The rationale for this is discussed in Sect. 4.2.
- Rule (c5v) says that if each argument e_i may evaluate to non-error value v_i in c_i computation steps and applying the actual function f to argument values $(v_1, \ldots, v_n)$ produces value v at a cost of $work(f, v_1, \ldots, v_n)$ computation steps, then the call $\mathrm{F}(e_1, \ldots, e_n)$ may evaluate to value v using a total of $1 + \sum_{j=1,n} c_j + work(f, v_1, \ldots, v_n)$ computation steps.
  Here $work(f, v_1, \ldots, v_n)$ describes the cost of applying function f to argument values $(v_1, \ldots, v_n)$. For instance, one would expect $work(+, v_1, v_2) = 1$ since the cost of addition is independent of the numbers added.

Since each cost rule adds 1 to the cost incurred by subexpression evaluations, the cost semantics essentially counts the number of rule applications.

4.2   Rationale for Cost of an Error Argument

While most of the cost semantics rules in Fig. 14 are obvious extensions of the evaluation rules in Fig. 11, this is not the case for rule (c5e) which is quite different from rule (e5e). Here we discuss why.

It is possible to imagine a cost rule (c5bad) as a trivial extension of rule (e5e), like this:

$$\frac{\sigma \vdash e_i \Downarrow v_i, c_i \qquad v_i \in Error}{\sigma \vdash \mathrm{F}(e_1, \ldots, e_n) \Downarrow v_i, 1 + c_i} \ (c5bad)$$

This rule says that if one of the arguments e_i may evaluate to an error v_i using c_i computation steps, then the call $\mathrm{F}(e_1, \ldots, e_n)$ to a function F may evaluate to error v_i in $1 + c_i$ computation steps. However, this cost is unrealistically low: a conforming implementation would have to correctly guess which (if any) argument expression e_i can evaluate to an error, and then evaluate only that expression. Such an implementation would seem implausibly clever.

A more realistic rule might stipulate instead that the cost is the sum of the costs of evaluating all argument expressions. However, this is needlessly pessimistic since an implementation may stop evaluating arguments once one of them evaluates to an error.

Another realistic cost rule might correspond to implementations that evaluate argument expressions $e_1, e_2, \ldots$ from left to right until one of them (if any) evaluates to an error. However, this restricts the possible implementations and would preclude or complicate parallel evaluation of arguments.

Instead we propose rule (c5e) in Fig. 14 which corresponds to implementations that may evaluate the argument expressions in any order (or in parallel) but may avoid evaluating all of them in case one evaluates to an error. This corresponds to choosing a subset $J \subseteq \{1, \ldots, n\}$ of the argument indexes and evaluating only those e_j for which $j \in J$, to values v_j at costs c_j, where one of the v_j is an error, and then stating that the total cost of the call is the sum $\sum_{j \in J} c_j$ of the costs of the arguments actually evaluated, plus one. Through different choices of J, rule (c5e) subsumes all three alternative rules discussed above.

Since the set J may be chosen in many ways, this introduces nondeterminism in the evaluation cost, in addition to nondeterminism in the computed value.

Clearly the choice of the set J is a specification artefact of little interest to a spreadsheet implementer, not to speak of a spreadsheet user. Yet apparently the J set is necessary for the specification to permit realistic implementations without favoring any particular ones. See also the discussion in Sect. 5.1.

4.3 Cost Semantics for Recalculation

Sections 4.1 and 4.2 above gave evaluation-and-cost rules for evaluation of spreadsheet formulas. How do we describe the cost of recalculation in terms of these?

First, we introduce a cost environment $\gamma : Addr \to Nat_0$ such that $\gamma(ca)$ is the cost of evaluating the formula at cell address ca. Then we slightly change the recalculation consistency requirements from Fig. 13 to also record the cost of evaluation for each cell, as shown in Fig. 15.

$$(1)\ dom(\sigma) = dom(\gamma) = dom(\phi)$$
$$(2)\ \forall ca \in dom(\phi).\ \sigma \vdash \phi(ca) \Downarrow \sigma(ca), \gamma(ca)$$

Fig. 15. Recalculation consistency requirements recording also evaluation cost, for simple formulas. The judgment $\sigma \vdash e \Downarrow v, c$ is defined in Fig. 14. Compared to Fig. 13, requirement (2) has been extended to record the evaluation cost of cell ca in $\gamma(ca)$.

Using the cost environment γ we can now express the cost of a full recalculation of a spreadsheet described by ϕ. This is simply the cost of evaluating the formula of every non-blank cell once:

$$fullcost = \sum\nolimits_{ca \in dom(\phi)} \gamma(ca)$$

In general, it is wasteful to perform full recalculation after only a single cell has been edited by the spreadsheet user. This does not matter here.

5 Specification and Implementation

5.1 Nondeterminism Versus Underspecification

It should be clear from the discussion in Sect. 4.2 of the Fig. 14 rule (c5e) that rule nondeterminism in the specification may reflect either run-time nondeterminism in an implementation (rules e4 and c4) or underspecification, that is, implementation-time design choices (rules e5e and c5e), or a mixture of those.

The difference is one of binding-time (as in language implementations and in partial evaluation): when is the nondeterministic choice made, and the chosen value henceforth fixed? Should there be a (formal) way to describe stages (implementation design stage, program linking stage, load-time stage, run-time stage, ...) and to describe when a given choice should be made? For instance, a RAND() function whose value gets fixed at 0.500 at the implementation design stage would disappoint many spreadsheet users.

Yet it is not so easy to separate the implementation design stage and the run-time stage even in the simple case of rule (c5e) discussed Sect. 4.2. At what stage does it make sense to choose the set J?

If one has decided on a sequential (singlethreaded, uniprocessor) implementation, one would probably decide at implementation design time on an evaluation order (maybe left to right) for actual arguments. Also, one may or may not stop evaluation once an argument evaluates to an error value. In any case this leaves no nondeterminism at run-time, but corresponds to J always having the form $\{1, 2, \ldots, i\}$ or $\{1, 2, \ldots, n\}$. In this case, the choice of the set J in rule (c5e) represents underspecification, or an implementation-time design choice.

By contrast, if one has decided on a parallel (multithreaded, multiprocessor) implementation, one may evaluate function argument expressions in parallel on multiple threads. Any thread that evaluates an argument to an error value v_i may cancel other argument evaluation threads and make the function call return v_i, discarding the remaining argument evaluations. In this case, the choice of the set J in rule (c5e) represents an implicit nondeterministic run-time choice in the implementation. However, the apparently nondeterministic choice is not made by explicitly choosing a set J, but by the run-time system's scheduler, which appears random due to other loads on the machine, outside interrupts, and truly unpredictable races between multiple cores accessing the same memory.

5.2   Does a Cost Semantics Make Sense?

The cost semantics may seem to be overly specific in prescribing the cost of a computation in addition to its result. Is it sensible for a formal specification to do that?

We believe that this is useful and meaningful for two reasons: First, a cost semantics may be abstracted to a (static) cost analysis, which can then be used in programmer feedback, scheduling decisions and the like [6]. Second, a semantics with additional detail may provide better understanding of the specified language. For instance, a call-by-name semantics for lazy evaluation may correctly specify the values that an implementation of lazy evaluation must compute, but give the wrong impression of time and memory consumption. A slightly more complicated semantics that properly models arbitrary data graphs in memory will prescribe the same computed values but additionally provide insight into time and memory consumption, and into possible implementations. Indeed, we have previously shown that a proper such semantics for lazy evaluation [15] may be rich enough that an abstract machine and an implementation can be derived from it [21].

In the late 1980es several researchers proposed "instrumented" versions of denotational semantics for programming languages. An abstract interpretation based on the instrumented semantics would then be used to provide static reference count analysis, variable escape analysis, and the like. Thus the instrumentation built some implementation-related properties, or expectations, into the denotational semantics [20, Sect. 2.4]. Of course it is possible for an "instrumented" specification to go overboard and specify something that cannot be implemented, witness the unrealistic cost rule (c5bad) discussed in Sect. 4.2. This problem is not specific to instrumented semantics; an ordinary semantics may well be unimplementable, for instance by specifying a fair nondeterministic choice between infinitely many possibilities.

However, an "instrumented" semantics is likely to contain some internal redundancy, and therefore more likely to be contradictory. For instance, rule (c5v) specifies both that all of a function's arguments must be evaluated once before calling the function *and* that the cost of a function call includes the sum of the costs of the argument evaluations. By mistake or design the rule might leave out one of these aspects and thereby specify a language that has only strange implementations.

5.3   The Distance from Specification to Implementation

The plain spreadsheet evaluation semantics in Sect. 3 remained reasonably close to an implementation. It is imaginable that even the axiomatic specification of recalculation in Fig. 13 could be handled by a specification language with a general fixpoint computation mechanism.

For the spreadsheet cost semantics in Sect. 4, this is much harder to imagine, since the semantics specifies a property of the implementation besides the computed value, namely the time (or number of computation steps) that the implementation consumes to compute the value. Even when the cost semantics is consistent and admits reasonable implementations (as we believe the one in Sect. 4 does), it is hard to imagine a general and usable specification/programming language mechanism that can that guarantee both correct result and correct time consumption.

6   Related Work

The view that programming languages are becoming so expressive that they can conveniently be used as specification languages is certainly not new [7,10]. Already the liberation from manual memory management in Lisp (1960) and the liberation from explicit evaluation order in Prolog (1972) must have given these languages the flavor of "describing what, not how" relative to other programming languages at the time, making programs in those languages look like specifications. In a 1994 experiment with prototyping, a working Haskell program, solving a programming challenge, was so concise and elegant that it was mistaken for "a mixture of requirements specification and top-level design" by a group of highly experienced software engineers [12, page 14].

The study of the Ada formal description in Sect. 2 is just further evidence that one decade's specification may be a later decade's program.

Also the research on semantics-directed compiler generation [8,13] in the 1980es and 1990es implicitly conflated specification and implementation. If a programming language implementation can be automatically generated from a sufficiently detailed semantics or specification, then that specification is itself just a program (in a sophisticated language) that can be transformed or compiled into an implementation of the language it specifies. This view is explicit in Tofte's work [24], which also expressed skepticism as to the feasibility and generality of this approach.

Our study in Sect. 2 was loosely inspired by Naur's critique [16, Sects. 4 and 5] of Jones and Henhapl's VDM semantics for Algol 60 [11]. But where Naur's paper broadly questions the presumed advantages of formal specifications, taking flaws in Jones and Henhapl's specification as evidence, our view is that even a (formally) flawed formal specification may be valuable because of the insight acquired while developing it.

As mentioned in Sect. 2.3, this view is in fact similar to the 1985 view proposed, in the realm of programming, by Naur himself [17].

7   Conclusion

This paper investigated the relation between specification (or modeling) and programming in the special case where the specification describes a programming language (semantics) and its implementations.

We observed that an Ada formal description written in VDM in 1980 looks very much like a functional program today, suggesting that the difference between specification and program may be one of degree. We also argued that while from a formal point of view the specification is incomplete and flawed (and hence its text not usable for purely formal purposes), it was still highly valuable, due to the knowledge acquired by its authors in the process of developing it.

We observed that nondeterminism in a specification may reflect either intended run-time choice in implementations, or permissible choice between possible implementations, but that there is no conventional way to distinguish these roles or binding-times of specification nondeterminism. We also observed that while operational and denotational semantics specification often suggest an implementation, and even axiomatic specifications can sometimes be implemented (for instance using search or inference), this is much harder when the semantics specifies also the computational cost of the implementation.

Hence there are still simple cases where it is truly hard to regard a semantics (specification) as an implementation (program), or to see how one could mechanically produce an implementation from the semantics.

References

1. Biermann, F., Dou, W., Sestoft, P.: Rewriting high-level spreadsheet structures into higher-order functional programs. In: Calimeri, F., Hamlen, K., Leone, N. (eds.) PADL 2018. LNCS, vol. 10702, pp. 20–35. Springer, Cham (2018). https://doi.org/10.1007/978-3-319-73305-0_2
2. Bjørner, D., Jones, C.B. (eds.): The Vienna Development Method: The Meta-Language. LNCS, vol. 61. Springer, Heidelberg (1978). https://doi.org/10.1007/3-540-08766-4
3. Bjørner, D., Nest, O.N. (eds.): Towards a Formal Description of Ada. LNCS, vol. 98. Springer, Heidelberg (1980). https://doi.org/10.1007/3-540-10283-3
4. Bjørner, D., Gram, C., Oest, O.N., Rystrøm, L.: Dansk datamatik center. In: History of Nordic Computing 3 - Third IFIP WG 9.7 Conference, HiNC 3, Stockholm, Sweden, pp. 350–359, 18–20 October 2010. Springer (2011)
5. Blelloch, G.: Programming parallel algorithms. CACM **39**(3), 85–97 (1996)
6. Bock, A., Bøgholm, T., Leth, L., Sestoft, P., Thomsen, B.: Concrete and abstract cost semantics for spreadsheets. Technical report. ITU-TR-2018-203, IT University of Copenhagen (2018). (to appear)
7. Broy, M., Havelund, K., Kumar, R.: Towards a unified view of modeling and programming. In: Margaria, T., Steffen, B. (eds.) ISoLA 2016, Part II. LNCS, vol. 9953, pp. 238–257. Springer, Cham (2016). https://doi.org/10.1007/978-3-319-47169-3_17
8. Ganzinger, H., Jones, N.D. (eds.): Programs as Data Objects. LNCS, vol. 217. Springer, Heidelberg (1986). https://doi.org/10.1007/3-540-16446-4
9. Gordon, M.J., Milner, A.J., Wadsworth, C.P.: Edinburgh LCF: A Mechanised Logic of Computation. LNCS, vol. 78. Springer, Heidelberg (1979). https://doi.org/10.1007/3-540-09724-4
10. Havelund, K.: Closing the gap between specification and programming: VDM++ and Scala. In: HOWARD-60: A Festschrift on the Occasion of Howard Barringer's 60th Birthday. EPiC Series in Computing, vol. 42, pp. 210–233 (2014)
11. Henhapl, W., Jones, C.B.: A formal definition of ALGOL 60 as described in the 1975 modified report. In: Bjørner, D., Jones, C.B. (eds.) The Vienna Development Method: The Meta-Language. LNCS, vol. 61, pp. 305–336. Springer, Heidelberg (1978). https://doi.org/10.1007/3-540-08766-4_12
12. Hudak, P., Jones, M.P.: Haskell vs. Ada vs. C++ vs. Awk vs. ...: An experiment in software prototyping productivity. Technical report. YALEU/DCS/RR-1049, Yale University, Department of Computer Science, October 1994
13. Jones, N.D. (ed.): SDCG 1980. LNCS, vol. 94. Springer, Heidelberg (1980). https://doi.org/10.1007/3-540-10250-7
14. Kahn, G.: Natural semantics. In: Brandenburg, F.J., Vidal-Naquet, G., Wirsing, M. (eds.) STACS 1987. LNCS, vol. 247, pp. 22–39. Springer, Heidelberg (1987). https://doi.org/10.1007/BFb0039592
15. Launchbury, J.: A natural semantics for lazy evaluation. In: Twentieth ACM Symposium on Principles of Programming Languages, Charleston, South Carolina, January 1993, pp. 144–154. ACM (1993)
16. Naur, P.: Formalization in program development. BIT **22**(4), 437–453 (1982)
17. Naur, P.: Programming as theory building. Microprocess. Microprogram. **15**, 253–261 (1985)
18. Nielson, H., Nielson, F.: Semantics with Applications: An Appetizer. Springer, London (2007). https://doi.org/10.1007/978-1-84628-692-6

19. Platek, R.A.: The European formal definition of Ada. A U.S. perspective. IDA Memorandum Report M-389, Institute for Defense Analyses (1988)
20. Sestoft, P.: Analysis and Efficient Implementation of Functional Programs. Ph.D. thesis, DIKU, University of Copenhagen, Denmark (1991). DIKU Research Report 92/6
21. Sestoft, P.: Deriving a lazy abstract machine. J. Funct. Program. **7**(3), 231–264 (1997)
22. Sestoft, P.: Spreadsheet Implementation Technology: Basics and Extensions, 325 p. MIT Press, Cambridge (2014). ISBN 978-0-262-52664-7
23. Syme, D., Granicz, A., Cisternino, A.: Expert F#, 4th edn. Apress, New York (2015)
24. Tofte, M.: Compiler Generators. In: What They Can Do, What They Might Do, and What They Will Probably Never Do. Monographs in Theoretical Computer Science. Springer, Heidelberg (1990). https://doi.org/10.1007/978-3-642-61504-7
25. Wikipedia: DDC-I. https://en.wikipedia.org/wiki/DDC-I

Modeling with Scala

Klaus Havelund[(⊠)] and Rajeev Joshi

Jet Propulsion Laboratory, California Institute of Technology, Pasadena, USA
{klaus.havelund,rajeev.joshi}@jpl.nasa.gov

Abstract. The activities and the associated formalisms for modeling and programming have many commonalities. In this paper we emphasize this point of view by modeling two examples in the programming language Scala, which have previously been modeled in the VDM specification language, and the Promela modeling language of the SPIN model checker respectively. The latter Scala model uses an internal DSL for hierarchical state machines, and a simple randomized testing framework exposing the same errors as found with SPIN. We believe, as the examples illustrate, that this use of a modern programming language for modeling is promising, especially if utilizing internal DSLs.

1 Introduction

Numerous formalisms exist for modeling systems before their development (prescriptive modeling) or as they exist (descriptive modeling). These formalisms have either a textual form or a graphical form, or both. Graphical formalisms can sometimes be grounded in a corresponding user friendly textual formalism, but not always, as is the case for example for UML and SysML in their standardized versions (XML cannot be considered user friendly). Meanwhile, modern high-level programming languages have evolved in recent years with several features that make them suitable for modeling, especially if supported by visualization, as we argue in this paper, and illustrate with two examples. Similar arguments were presented in [4,5]. One such high-level programming language is SCALA [19], which combines object-oriented and functional programming. We present two formal modeling activities performed twenty years apart: one in 1979 using the VDM specification language [3,6], and the other in 1997 using the PROMELA modeling language of the SPIN model checker [14]. We show how these models can be formalized in SCALA with little impact on size or readability.

The VDM specification is for a relational database model, formalized in [2] in a functional subset of VDM. The modeling in SCALA is almost one-to-one. For a more detailed comparison between VDM and SCALA we refer the reader to [8]. It is interesting to note that VDM was originally used just for describing systems on paper, with no support for execution or even parsing and type checking.

The research performed was carried out at Jet Propulsion Laboratory, California Institute of Technology, under a contract with the National Aeronautics and Space Administration.

T. Margaria and B. Steffen (Eds.): ISoLA 2018, LNCS 11244, pp. 184–205, 2018.
https://doi.org/10.1007/978-3-030-03418-4_12

The PROMELA model is that of the Remote Agent spacecraft controller, first formalized in PROMELA in [13]. This latter example is interesting in two respects. First, several errors were detected in the original PROMELA model, one of which later caused an actual deadlock in flight, and which also was detected in the SCALA model using a simple testing approach. Second, the SCALA model uses a Domain-Specific Language (DSL) - an internal SCALA DSL - for modeling with Hierarchical State Machines (HSMs), as a larger effort to explore how such an HSM DSL can be used for modeling flight software for modern spacecraft.

The paper is organized as follows. Section 2 presents the relational database model in VDM and SCALA. Section 3 presents the Remote Agent model in PROMELA and SCALA, and describes its testing. Finally, Sect. 4 concludes the paper.

2   Relational Databases

The example presented here is the concept of relational databases, as modeled in VDM by Bjørner in [2], and reproduced here. We shall not illustrate how a database is updated, but will, as in [2], focus on how they are queried. This is not a description of how a database is implemented, but rather the definition from a user's abstract point of view. It is a conceptual model as argued by Bjørner in [2], meant to convey the concept of a relational database to a reader.

2.1   An Informal Description

A *relational data base* consists of an unordered collection of distinctly *named relations*. Each relation consists of an unordered collection of unnamed *tuples*. A tuple is a sequence of *fields*, the data of the database, identified by their position in the tuple[1]. All tuples of a particular relation are of the same length, and for a particular position, the fields in that position in all tuples of a relation are of the same type. The fields in tuples are of primitive type, such as integers, floating point numbers, Booleans, and strings.

The query language offers a collection of *commands*, all of which from the database will produce an unnamed relation, which is stored in a particular *working space*, which also can be referred to in the commands. Relations are referred to by their name, or if no name is provided, the reference is to the relation in the working space. The following four commands must be supported[2]. *Selection*: operates on a single relation (the origin relation) and delivers the relation containing all those tuples from the origin relation, whose field in a given position stands in a given relation to a given value. *Projection*: operates on a single relation, and delivers the relation of tuples each of which is a sub-tuple of a tuple in the origin relation, containing only selected fields. *Join*: operates on two relations. It forms the concatenation of those tuples from the two relations which in

---

[1] The paper [2] also presents a model where fields of a tuple are named by character strings, probably a more correct model.

[2] We have for space considerations omitted the division command from [2].

respective positions have fields which stand in a certain relation to each other. *Store*: stores the unnamed relation in the working space as a named relation. A *session* is a sequence of commands.

2.2   Relational Database Model in VDM

In the following, VDM specifications, Figs. 1, 2, and 3, are shown in boxes with rounded corners, whereas SCALA programs, Figs. 4, 5, and 6, are shown in boxes with square corners. The first set of VDM definitions are shown in Fig. 1. These are the essential types of the specification[3]. The type RDB is that of a relational database, consisting (a cartesian product) of a set of relations RELS and a working space WS. The RDB type is defined as a constructed type using the :: symbol. The elements of this type are constructed by calls of an implicitly defined constructor mk−RDB(rels,ws), which in turn can be referred to in pattern matching. The type RELS represents the named relations as a mapping (function with finite domain) from relation names (type Rid) to relations of type REL. A workspace WS is a relation REL, which itself is a set of tuples TPL. A tuple is a finite non-empty list of fields of type *Field*. The type Field is the union of various primitive types, such as integers.

1	RDB :: RELS WS
2	RELS = Rid $\vec{m}$ REL
3	WS = REL
4	REL = TPL-set
5	TPL = Field^{+}
6	Field = INTG | ...

Fig. 1. Domains in VDM.

1	Cmd = Sel | Proj | Join | Sto
2	Sel :: [Rid] N_1 ROp Field
3	Proj :: [Rid] $N_1{}^{+}$
4	Join :: ([Rid] N_1) ROp ([Rid] N_1)
5	Sto :: Rid
6	ROp = $\underline{EQ}$ | $\underline{NEQ}$
7	
8	Sess = Cmd*

Fig. 2. Commands in VDM.

The next set of VDM definitions are shown in Fig. 2, and model the commands that can be issued against a relational database. The Cmd type is defined as the union of a collection of constructed types, each representing a kind of command: selection, projection, join, and storing the workspace as a named relation. Each of these commands carry arguments.

The Sel command carries an optional relation identifier ([Rid] = Rid ∪ {**nil**}), a positive (non-zero) natural number, comparison operator of type ROp, and a field value. The semantics is: select those tuples from the relation where the field identified by the positive number is related to the field argument as indicated by the relational operator. When the relational identifier is **nil** the relation referred to is that in the unnamed working space. The relational operator type

---

[3] It is very common in VDM to approach a problem by starting defining such type definitions.

```
1    E−Sess(cl)(mk−RDB(rs,ws)) =
2      if cl = ⟨ ⟩
3        then mk−RDB(rs,ws)
4        else
5          (let (rs ', ws') =
6             cases hd cl :
7               mk−Sel(r,i,o,f) →
8                 (rs, {t | t ∈ ((r=nil) → ws, T → rs(r)) ∧ t[i] = f}),
9               mk−Pro(r,il) →
10                (rs, {⟨t[il [i]] | 1 ≤ i ≤ len il ⟩ |
11                      t ∈ ((r=nil) → ws, T → rs(r ))}),
12               mk−Join((r₁,i₁),o,(r₂,i₂)) →
13                (rs, { t₁ ⌢ t₂ |
14                  t₁ ∈ ((r₁=nil) → ws, T → rs(r₁)) ∧
15                  t₂ ∈ ((r₂=nil) → ws, T → rs(r₂)) ∧
16                  cases o : (EQ → t₁[i₁] = t₂[i₂],
17                            NEQ → t₁[i₁] ≠ t₂[i₂ ])}),
18               mk−Sto(r) →
19                (rs + [r ↦ ws], ws)
20          in
21            E−Sess(tl cl )(mk−RDB(rs',ws')))
22
23   type: Cmd* ⁻̃→ (RDB ⁻̃→ RDB)
```

Fig. 3. Evaluation function in VDM.

is the union of two singleton types containing the constants respectively $\underline{EQ}$ (for *equal*) and $\underline{NEQ}$ (for *not equal*). The format of the other commands should now be clear: projection maps a set of tuples in a relation to a set of tuples only containing a certain subset of columns indicated by a list of column numbers. A join combines tuples from two relations where one column value in one relation is related to another column value in the other relation in a certain way. Storing stores the working space as a named relation. Finally, a session Sess is a (possibly empty) list of commands.

Finally, the recursively defined function E−Sess in Fig. 3 interprets a session on a relational database, resulting in a new relational database, as indicated by the type of the function at the bottom of the figure ($A \xrightarrow{\sim} B$ is the set of partial functions from A to B). We shall not go into much details of this function definition, except for some notation explanation: line 8 contains a set comprehension of tuples t which belong to either the working space if the relation id is **nil** or to the relation denoted by the relation id: rs(r), and which satisfy the equation[4]: t[i] = f. The set comprehension in lines 10-11 is the set of tuples, each of which itself is generated by a tuple comprehension expression projecting to only those tuple elements identified by column ids in the list il. The term ... + [... ↦ ...] in line 19 is a finite map update. This definition is written

---

[4] This is actually wrong as will be discussed later.

in a functional style. However, VDM also supports an imperative style where expressions can have side effects.

2.3 Relational Database Model in Scala

The SCALA model (a program) of the relational database concept is shown in Figs. 4 (types), 5 (commands), and 6 (applicative evaluation function). We have written the functions as closely as reasonable to the VDM version, except that we introduced a couple of auxiliary functions for looking up a relation id and for comparing fields. Commands in Fig. 5 are defined using class inheritance, and using so-called **case** classes that allows for pattern matching over objects of the classes. We see in Fig. 6 the **for−yield** construct, the general form of which is:

for $(x_1 \leftarrow exp_1; \ldots; x_n \leftarrow exp_n$ **if** $\mathsf{p}(x_1, \ldots, x_n)$ **yield** $\mathsf{f}(x_1, \ldots, x_n)$

This construct is used to model the set and list comprehensions in the VDM specification. It denotes a collection of values. The expressions $exp_1, \ldots, exp_n$ must themselves denote collections (lists, sets, maps, ...). For each $x_1 \in exp_1$, $x_2 \in exp_2$, etc, where the Boolean expression $\mathsf{p}(x_1, \ldots, x_n)$ is true, the value denoted by the expression $\mathsf{f}(x_1, \ldots, x_n)$ is added to the resulting collection. The type of the resulting collection is that of the first expression exp_1. So if it is a list, the result will be a list, if a set, the result will be a set. For example, if exp_1 is a set, it corresponds to VDM's set comprehension:

$$\{ \mathsf{f}(x_1, \ldots, x_n) \mid x_1 \in exp_1 \wedge \ldots \wedge x_n \in exp_n \wedge \mathsf{p}(x_1, \ldots, x_n) \}$$

```
1    type Rid
2    type RDB = (RELS, WS)
3    type RELS = Map[Rid, REL]
4    type WS = REL
5    type REL = Set[TPL]
6    type TPL = List[Field]
7    type Field = Any
```

Fig. 4. Domains in Scala.

It should be clear that the VDM model and the SCALA program are very similar. One might prefer the more mathematical notation of the VDM specification. The topic of displaying programs with a mathematical appearance was addressed elegantly in the FORTRESS programming language [7]. The VDM specification in [2] was written before the appearance of syntax and type checkers for VDM. We did indeed find six errors, including two syntax errors, and four type checking/static analysis errors. All of these were fixed in our presentation of the VDM model, except for line 8 in Fig. 3, where the test $\mathsf{t}[\mathsf{i}] = \mathsf{f}$ ignores the operation o in the pattern $\mathsf{mk-Sel}(\mathsf{r,i,o,f})$. This is changed in the SCALA version.

```
1    trait Cmd
2    case class Sel( rid : Option[Rid], fieldNr : N1, o: ROp, field : Field ) extends Cmd
3    case class Proj( rid : Option[Rid], fieldNrs : List1 [N1]) extends Cmd
4    case class Join( l : (Option[Rid], N1), o: ROp, r: (Option[Rid], N1)) extends Cmd
5    case class Sto( rid : Rid) extends Cmd
6
7    trait ROp
8    case object EQ extends ROp
9    case object NEQ extends ROp
```

Fig. 5. Commands in Scala.

```
1     def E_Sess( cl : List [Cmd])(rdb: RDB): RDB = {
2       val ( rs , ws) = rdb
3       if ( cl == Nil) rdb
4       else {
5         val ( rs_ , ws_) =
6           cl .head match {
7             case Sel( r , i , o , f) ⇒
8               ( rs , for (t ← getRel( r , rdb) if comp(o)(t(i),f)) yield t)
9             case Proj( r , il ) ⇒
10              ( rs , for (t ← getRel( r , rdb)) yield (for ( i ← il ) yield t( i )))
11            case Join ((r1, i1 ), o , (r2, i2 )) ⇒
12              ( rs ,
13                for (t1 ← getRel( r1 , rdb); t2 ← getRel( r2 , rdb)
14                  if comp(o)(t1(i1),t2(i2 ))) yield (t1 ++ t2)
15              )
16            case Sto( rid ) ⇒
17              ( rs + (rid → ws), ws)
18          }
19        E_Sess( cl . tail )( rs_ , ws_)
20      }
21    }
```

Fig. 6. Evaluation function in Scala.

One interesting observation, however, would not be highlighted by a syntax or type checker, static analyzer, or theorem prover. This concerns the Join command, which simply concatenates the tuples from each relation, see line 13 in Fig. 3 and line 14 in Fig. 6. This means that common columns are duplicated, which is not the standard "natural join" operator[5], where such columns are merged into one. We noticed this discrepancy only upon executing the model. It may be a minor issue, but it illustrates how executable models can reveal otherwise undiscovered properties.

---

[5] https://en.wikipedia.org/wiki/Relational_algebra.

3   The Remote Agent

In this section we shall demonstrate a SCALA model of a space software module previously (in 1997) modeled in the PROMELA language of the SPIN model checker [14]. SPIN supports verification of finite state asynchronous process systems communicating via message passing and/or shared variables. Models are formulated in the PROMELA language, which has similarities to a simple programming language, although without much support for regular programming with data structures. Efficient verification has been given priority over convenient modeling language features in some cases. Properties to be verified are stated as assertions in the model, or in the linear temporal logic LTL. The SPIN *model checker* automatically determines whether a model satisfies a property, and generates a counter example in the form of an error trace if this is not true.

The particular system being modeled is the multi–threaded *plan execution module* of the *Remote Agent* (RA) [16], which itself was programmed in LISP. The Remote Agent was an artificial intelligence based spacecraft control system architecture. In addition to the plan execution module modeled in this section, it also contained a *planning module*, which generated plans based on goals received from Earth, sending these plans to the plan execution module for execution. A third module, the *mode identification and recovery module*, constantly monitored the state of the spacecraft and would attempt to recover in case of anomalies. The Remote Agent was one of 12 technologies tested on the DEEP-SPACE 1 (DS-1) spacecraft, launched October 1998. The Remote Agent itself was initiated during May 1999, demonstrating the complete control of a spacecraft by artificial intelligence based software for the first time in NASA's history.

The plan execution module is a classic multi-threaded application vulnerable to classic concurrency errors such as data races and deadlocks. The SPIN effort, described in [13], consisted of hand translating parts of the plan execution LISP code into a model in the PROMELA language of SPIN, and then verifying two properties formulated by the Remote Agent programmers. Both properties turned out to be broken in the model, revealing a total of 4 errors. The effort was at the time considered very successful before flight. It, however, further gained reputation since one of the errors, after having been fixed in the code, was later re-introduced in a different part of the plan execution module by a different programmer through a copy-and-paste operation, but without copying the fix (a critical section). This caused a data race that lead to a deadlock during flight. Because of the deadlock, thrusting did not turn off when required, and the spacecraft was unable to recover by itself. The craft was put in stand-by mode by the ground crew until a repair was made.

3.1   The Remote Agent in Promela

In this section we shall present the Remote Agent plan execution module in more (although not full) detail, as well as its modeling in PROMELA. The full description of the Remote Agent can be found in [13]. The Remote Agent Executive, Fig. 7, supports execution of *tasks*. A task may be, for example, to operate a camera. A task often requires that specific *properties* hold during its execution. For example, the camera-operating task may require the camera to be turned on throughout task execution. When a task is started, it first tries to *achieve* the properties on which it depends, whereafter it starts performing its main function. E.g. the camera-operating task may try to turn on the camera before running the camera. Properties may, however, be unexpectedly broken (e.g., the camera may turn off) and tasks depending on such broken properties must then be informed about this (aborted).

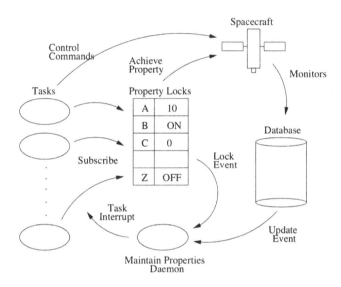

Fig. 7. The Remote Agent executive.

The Database. The state of the spacecraft at any particular point can be considered as an assignment of values to a set of variables, each corresponding to a component sensor on board the spacecraft. As an example, the variable CAMERA may have one of the values ON or OFF. A particular assignment of a value to a variable is called a *property*, where the variable is called the *property name* and the value is called the *property value*. The actual state of the spacecraft is constantly monitored, and stored in a *database*.

The Lock Table. When a task requires a certain property to hold, e.g. (RADIO, ON), it adds the property in a *lock table*. During this locking, other tasks with incompatible properties, e.g. (RADIO, OFF), cannot execute. Two properties are incompatible if they require different observed values of the same variable. The lock table in addition for each locked property stores which tasks rely on it (there can be multiple), and in addition contains a flag *achieved*, which is set to true when the property has been achieved to hold in the database.

The Daemon. Executing concurrently with the tasks is a *property maintenance daemon* that monitors the lock table and the database. If there is an *inconsistency* between the database and the locks – meaning that a locked property no longer holds in the database while the *achieved* flag is true – the daemon aborts all tasks *subscribing* to the property, and subsequently it tries to re-achieve the property (if a task has not already done so). The daemon remains inactive unless certain *events* occur, such as a change of the database (a DB_EVENT) or lock table (a LOCK_EVENT). Once awakened, the daemon examines all locks in the property lock table. For each lock where the achieved field is *true*, it checks whether the property holds in the database. If this is not the case, all tasks in the lock's subscribers list are aborted and a recovery procedure is initiated to re-achieve the property. After examining all locks, the daemon goes into sleep mode again by waiting for another DB_EVENT or LOCK_EVENT event.

The Tasks. Before a task executes its main job, it will try to achieve the properties that the execution depends on. The first step is to lock the properties in the lock table. Locking a property will only succeed if it is compatible with the existing locks; otherwise, the task aborts. If there are no conflicting locks and the lock does not already exist, the task will create it. Note that some other task may have already locked the same property, which is not defined as a conflict. If it succeeds, the task also puts itself into the subscribers list of the lock, indicating that the task depends on this property.

The creator task of a lock is called the *owner*, in contrast to tasks that subscribe later to the same property. The owner is responsible for achieving the property, resulting in the database being updated. Upon successful achievement, the achieved-field in the lock is set to *true* by the task. If the achievement fails, the task aborts. Other tasks that subscribe later than the owner must wait for the owner to achieve the property. This is done by simply waiting for a DB_EVENT, and the indication that the property was successfully achieved.

Once a task has first locked and then achieved its required properties, it executes its main job, relying on the properties to be maintained throughout job execution. Before a task terminates, it releases its locks. That is, it removes itself from the subscribers list, and if the list then becomes empty (no other subscribers), it removes the lock completely. In case there are other subscribers, the lock must of course be maintained.

Modeling in Promela. The modeling in PROMELA required some ingenuity due to the lack of modern programming language concepts. E.g. PROMELA's concept of asynchronous communication channels (introduced with keyword **chan**) was used to model lists, the basic data structure of LISP. All communication between processes in this model takes place via *shared variables*, reflecting the LISP implementation. Figure 8 shows the top level task process and Fig. 9 shows the top level daemon process. Each of these in turn call functions that perform further operations. The PROMELA code in total is 332 uncommented lines of code. The LISP module it was modeled after was 3000 lines of code. The model only deals with a limited number of tasks and properties in order to limit the search space the SPIN model checker has to explore. Abstractions were made in an informal manner.

A task (Fig. 8) will want to achieve a property p before executing its main task, here named closure. Before that, it locks the property in the lock table. During execution of the closure, it may get aborted in case the daemon discovers an inconsistency between the lock and the database. The task is thrown to the program point in line 10, whereafter it will release its lock.

```
1   proctype Achieving_Task(TaskId this)
2   { Property p;
3       . . .
4     bool err = 0;
5     {
6        lock_property ( this ,p, err );
7        achieve_lock_property ( this ,p, err );
8        closure ()
9     } unless {err || active_tasks [ this ]. state == ABORTED};
10      active_tasks [ this ]. state = TERMINATED;
11      { release_lock ( this ,p)} unless { active_tasks [ this ]. state == ABORTED}
12  }
```

Fig. 8. Promela model of tasks.

The daemon (Fig. 9) will initially (first_time == **true**) check all locks and then (line 17) wait for the database or lock table to be updated. Upon being awakened, it will first check all locks and interrupt tasks subscribing to violated locks (line 6). The daemon maintains a counter event_count holding the value of the sums of two counters being increased when respectively the database is updated and the lock table is updated. It will execute a conditional statement (lines 11–18) which will repeat the procedure if these counters have changed, otherwise the daemon will wait for new changes.

The Properties to be Verified. The PROMELA model was verified against the following two properties (delivered to us after the model had been created):

RELEASE property: *A task releases all of its locks before it terminates.*

ABORT property: *If an inconsistency occurs between the database and an entry in the lock table, then all tasks that rely on the lock will be terminated, either by themselves or by the daemon.*

The RELEASE property was stated as an assertion after line 11 in Fig. 8. The ABORT property was stated as the Linear Temporal Logic (LTL) formula, focusing on just one of the tasks (task 1):

```
[] (task1_property_broken -> <>task1_terminated).
```

```
1   proctype Daemon(TaskId this) {
2      bit   lock_violation ;
3      byte event_count  = 0;
4      bit   first_time  = true;
5      do
6      :: check_locks( lock_violation );
7         if
8         :: lock_violation   → do_automatic_recovery()
9         :: else
10        fi ;
11        if
12        :: (! first_time  &&
13           Ev[DB_EVENT].count + Ev[LOCK_EVENT].count ≠event_count ) →
14              event_count = Ev[DB_EVENT].count + Ev[LOCK_EVENT].count
15        :: else  →
16           first_time  = false;
17           wait_for_events ( this ,  DB_EVENT,LOCK_EVENT)
18        fi
19     od
20   };
```

Fig. 9. Promela model of the daemon.

The definitions of the terms `task1_property_broken` and `task1_terminated` are not shown here, see [13] for details. The property states that it is always ([]) the case that if task 1's property is broken, then eventually (<>) task 1 is terminated.

The model, consisting of two tasks, each attempting to lock the same variable but with different conflicting values, a daemon, and an environment that randomly can damage a database entry, was verified exhaustively by SPIN. It turned out that both properties were violated. in the model as well as in the LISP code according to the programmer. The error numbering below follows the numbering in [13].

- *Error 1*: The RELEASE property was violated since the task in Fig. 8 may not only get aborted by the daemon during its main task, but also during releasing the lock, which causes the lock releasing to be abandoned. This error is somewhat obvious from the code, but was not detected by the programmer, nor by us during modeling since we did not know the properties at that point.
- *Error 2*: The ABORT property was violated since the daemon in Fig. 9 in line 15 makes the decision to wait for new events if the event counters have not changed. However, if the environment corrupts the database in between this decision has been taken and the actual wait in line 17, the daemon will not wake up to detect the damage.
- *Error 3*: The ABORT property was violated since the daemon in Fig. 9 in the function check_locks contains two pieces of sequentially composed code: one

where tasks depending on violated properties are aborted, and one where the daemon repairs the database. In case the environment damages the database in between these two sections of code, the tasks will not get aborted.

- *Error 4*: The ABORT property was violated since when a task achieves a property and then subsequently sets the *achieved* flag to true, the environment may damage the database in between these two statements, and hence the daemon may not detect the damage since the *achieved* flag his false (a lock is only defined as violated if this flag is true).

All these errors were classical concurrency errors where the environment damages the database in between two sections of code not protected by a critical section. The pattern of Error number 2 was the one causing a deadlock during flight in a sibling module to where the code was copied without copying the fix.

3.2 The Remote Agent in Scala

In this section, we show our model of the Remote Agent using a SCALA DSL for Hierarchical State Machines (HSMs), using the same naming conventions as in [13]. HSMs [18] are an extension of traditional state machines: they allow declaration of mutable state variables (which can be used in transition guards, and updated in transition actions), hierarchical nesting of states (a child state inherits all transitions from its parent, but can override any subset), entry and exit actions (which are triggered when control enters or leaves a state), and support for orthogonal regions (multiple child states executing in parallel - not currently supported by the DSL). Figure 10 shows a graphical depiction of the HSM for a Remote Agent task, automatically generated from the SCALA program using the SCALAMETA [20] and PLANTUML [17] frameworks. Following standard notation, the filled out black circles indicate the initial child substate that is entered whenever a parent state is entered. Associated with each state are also optional code fragments called the *entry* and *exit* actions, which are executed whenever the HSM transitions into or out of a state respectively. A transition between two states is shown using a labeled arrow, where the label is of the form EVENT if guard/code, which indicates that the HSM reacts to the given EVENT only if the given guard holds, and then it executes the given code and transitions to the target state. The hierarchical nature of the state machine means that a child state inherits transitions from its parent state, unless it explicitly overrides the transition. For instance, all substates of the lock_and_execute state inherit the transitions on ABORT and ERROR events that take the HSM into the state release_lock. Thus, when a remote agent task is first started, it starts in the state enterCriticalSection, and executes the entry action send(STEP) which sends the STEP event to itself[6]. In state enterCriticalSection, the HSM responds to a

---

[6] The idiom of an HSM sending an event to itself is commonly used in HSMs to implement sequential behavior, and is used extensively in our modeling. Breaking up a sequence of steps using this idiom allows us to check system executions where task behaviors are interleaved with each other.

STEP event only if the associated guard condition is true. When this condition is true, and the HSM is scheduled for execution, it executes the enterCritical() code block, and transitions to the state fail_if_incompatible_property.

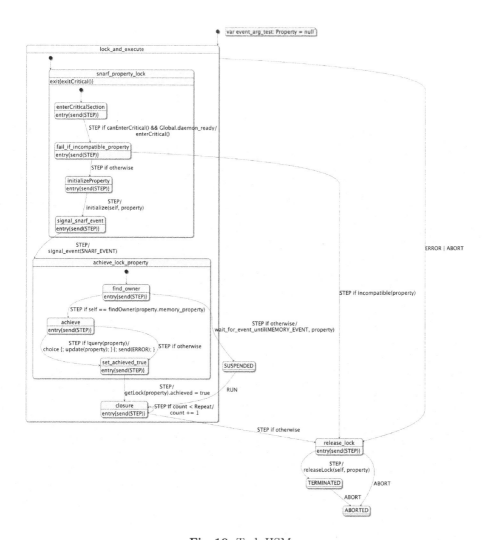

Fig. 10. Task HSM.

Figure 11 shows the HSMs for the daemon and the environment (which can inflict damage by corrupting the database). An attractive feature of modeling HSMs in SCALA is that transition guards and actions can be written using a full-fledged programming language. For instance, in state check_counter, the daemon calls the SCALA function newCount() to test if the sum of the counts of updates to the database and the lock table differs from its own local count. If they are

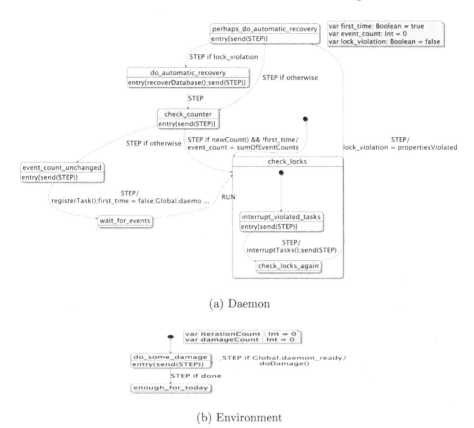

(a) Daemon

(b) Environment

Fig. 11. Daemon and environment HSMs.

different, it updates its event count and transitions to check_locks; but if they are the same, it transitions to event_count_unchanged, and subsequently waits in the next step. As we describe later (see Sect. 3.3), this logic is flawed as the daemon can miss a race condition that can lead to database corruption.

Figure 12 shows how the task state machine is expressed in our SCALA HSM DSL (in space saving format). Each HSM kind is implemented as a class, which extends the RaHSM class, which itself extends the HSM trait defined in [12]. The RaHSM class adds e.g. prioritized event queues. The Task class is parameterized with a monitor, which checks properties of interest as the system is running. Each state in the HSM is a SCALA object that extends the underlying state class, optionally passing it the name of its superstate (if any), and an optional Boolean value true if it is the initial state of the superstate. Entry and exit blocks are defined as shown, e.g. lines 11 and 8, as calls of functions that each can take an arbitrary block of SCALA code (call-by-name) that is executed on entry or exit. HSM transitions are defined using the when construct, with each event transition defined using SCALA pattern matching. Each transition has the form when E **if** grd $\Rightarrow$ S exec code, which denotes a transition that executes on receiving event E if condition grd is true, and then the given code is executed, and the HSM changes to state S. For instance lines 18 and 19 show two HSM transitions on the STEP event, depending on whether a guard condition is true or not. The form '**if** otherwise', meaning negation of all other guards, makes diagrams more readable. The use of pattern matching allows compact representation of many transitions where different events have the same target state and the same behavior, see for instance line 5 where the ERROR and ABORT events are handled in one statement.

The SCALA model is 556 lines of uncommented code (assuming all definitions are in one file as in the PROMELA case), compared to the 332 lines of uncommented PROMELA model and the 3000 lines of original LISP code. The additional code compared to the PROMELA model reflects a more detailed and natural programming of the data structures, such as the lock table, and the modeling of the Remote Agent processes as HSMs is somewhat verbose.

3.3 Monitoring and Randomized Scheduling

In this section we describe how the SCALA model is tested.

Monitoring. The properties to be monitored are formulated in the DAUT SCALA DSL [9,10], supporting a formalism combining temporal logic and programming. DAUT is a part of an effort defining monitoring DSLs in SCALA, including also the works described in [1,11,15]. A DAUT monitor is a SCALA class extending the class Monitor[E], parameterized with the type of events E it can monitor. The Monitor class offers a method verify (event: E), which updates the monitor for a new event, issuing an error if the monitor is violated on a safety property, and a method end() terminating the monitor, and issuing an error if a liveness property is violated (some event did not occur that should have occurred). The events we shall monitor here are called EVRs (EVent Reports), and are defined by the type definitions in Fig. 13. There are four kinds of EVRs, all subclassing the EVR trait. There is an EVR reporting an HSM entering a state, exiting a state, sending a message to another HSM, and finally an action reporting any other kind of event.

We define two monitors, shown in Fig. 14. Class RaMonitor defines some utility functions specific for the Remote Agent scenario. The ReleaseMonitor implements the RELEASE property from Sect. 3.1. It reads: *"it is always the case, that when an EnterState(task, state) is observed, i.e. the task enters state, and this state is either the TERMINATED state or the ABORTED state, then the task has released the property it was locking (a function call on the task)"*. As can be seen, this is a temporal logic formula of the form $\Box(e \rightarrow p)$, where e is an event and p is a state predicate.

The AbortMonitor implements the ABORT property. A variable abortedTasks is introduced to store all tasks that have received an ABORT message, and is updated upon each observed ABORT message (the first **case** statement). The

```
 1   class Task(. . .) extends RaHSM(monitor)
 2   {  initial (lock_and_execute)
 3
 4     object lock_and_execute extends state() {
 5       when { case ERROR | ABORT ⇒ release_lock } }
 6
 7     object snarf_property_lock extends state(lock_and_execute, true) {
 8       exit {  exitCritical () } }
 9
10     object enterCriticalSection extends state(snarf_property_lock, true) {
11       entry { send(STEP) }
12       when {
13         case STEP if canEnterCritical() && Global.daemon_ready ⇒
14           fail_if_incompatible_property  exec { enterCritical () } } }
15
16     object fail_if_incompatible_property extends state(snarf_property_lock) {
17       entry { send(STEP) }
18       when {case STEP if incompatible(property) ⇒ release_lock
19             case STEP if otherwise ⇒ initializeProperty } }
20
21     object initializeProperty extends state(snarf_property_lock) {
22       entry { send(STEP) }
23       when {case STEP ⇒ signal_snarf_event exec {initialize( self ,property)}}}
24
25     object signal_snarf_event extends state(snarf_property_lock) {
26       entry { send(STEP) }
27       when {case STEP ⇒ achieve_lock_property exec {signal_event(LOCK_EVENT)}}}
28
29     object achieve_lock_property extends state(lock_and_execute)
30
31     object find_owner extends state(achieve_lock_property, true) {
32       entry { send(STEP) }
33       when {case STEP if self == findOwner(property.memory_property) ⇒ achieve
34             case STEP if otherwise ⇒ SUSPENDED exec {waitfor_event(DB_EVENT,property)}}}
35
36     object achieve extends state(achieve_lock_property) {
37       entry { send(STEP) }
38       when {case STEP if !query(property) ⇒ setachieved_true exec {
39             choice { update(property) } { send(ERROR) }}
40             case STEP if otherwise ⇒ setachieved_true }}
41
42     object set achieved_true extends state(achieve_lock_property) {
43       entry { send(STEP) }
44       when {case STEP ⇒ closure exec {getLock(property).achieved = true}}}
45
46     object closure extends state(lock_and_execute) {
47       val Repeat = 2; var count: Int = 0
48       entry {send(STEP)}
49       when {case STEP if count < Repeat ⇒ closure exec {count += 1}
50             case STEP if otherwise ⇒ release_lock}}
51
52     object release_lock extends state() {
53       entry { send(STEP) }
54       when {case ABORT ⇒ ABORTED
55             case STEP ⇒ TERMINATED exec { releaseLock(self, property) }}}
56
57     object ABORTED extends state()
58
59     object TERMINATED extends state() {
60       when { case ABORT ⇒ ABORTED }}
61
62     object SUSPENDED extends state() {
63       when { case RUN ⇒ closure }}
64   }
```

Fig. 12. The task HSM in Scala.

```
1   trait  EVR
2   case class  EnterState(task:  RaHSM, state: String)  extends EVR
3   case class  ExitState(task:  RaHSM, state: String)  extends EVR
4   case class  Message(sen: RaHSM, event: EventId, rec: RaHSM)  extends EVR
5   case class  Action(name: Any*)  extends EVR
```

Fig. 13. The monitored event reports.

property (the second **case** statement) then reads: *"it is always the case, that when an Action(DB_EVENT) or an Action(LOCK_EVENT) is observed, i.e. either the database or the lock table is modified, then for each violated task (i.e. relying on a property that has been broken in the database), for which we have not in the past observed a Message(_, ABORT, target), where target denotes that task, we must observe such an abort message in the future"*. This is effectively the equivalent to a temporal logic formula of the form: $\square(e_1 \rightarrow \forall t \in S . (\neg \blacklozenge e_2(t) \rightarrow \Diamond e_2(t)))$, where e_1 is an event and e_2 is an event parameterized with a task t, universally quantified over the finite set S (the violated tasks). Here $\blacklozenge e_2(t)$ means that $e_1(t)$ occurred in the past, and $\Diamond e_2(t)$ means that $e_2(t)$ will occur in the future. In DAUT a *hot* state must match a future event, otherwise the end() method will issue an error. The SCALA construct **for** $(t \leftarrow S$ **if** $P (t))$ **yield** hot $\{...\}$ results in a list containing a hot state for each t in S for which $P(t)$ holds. As can be seen, DAUT does not directly support past time logic, thus requiring the auxiliary variable abortedTasks.

Randomized Scheduling. The four HSMs (two tasks, the daemon, and the environment) execute by sending each other messages, including the STEP messages to themselves. A scheduler will in each step have to pick a state machine which is enabled (e.g. there are messages in its queue) and execute the state machine on the first message in the queue. We shall use the SCALA concept of an *iterator* to select enabled machines to execute. The MachineSelector class in Fig. 15 extends Iterable [RemoteAgentHSM], which requires us to define an iterator method, which in turn returns an Iterator [RemoteAgentHSM] object, which itself defines the hasNext and next methods. Each call of next(), assuming that hasNext is true, returns an enabled machine that can execute one step. SCALA's (effectively JAVA's) random number generator is used to pick a machine randomly. In addition, a user-defined function canRun parameterized with a machine and all the machines, can be used to select which machine to run. This function is useful for steering the scheduler around errors already detected, in order to detect different errors, as illustrated in the next subsection.

Given an instance of the MachineSelector, we can iterate over the machines it generates, calling the run() method on each machine making it potentially perform one transition, as shown in the scheduler in Fig. 16. This class resets and re-executes the state machines from their initial state numerous times, defined by the upper limit maxResets provided as parameter to the class. The second

```
 1 │ class RaMonitor extends Monitor[EVR] { ...}
 2 │
 3 │ class ReleaseMonitor extends RaMonitor {
 4 │   always {
 5 │     case EnterState(task, state) if state == "TERMINATED" ||
 6 │                                     state == "ABORTED" ⇒
 7 │       task.asInstanceOf[Task].hasReleasedProperty()
 8 │   }
 9 │ }
10 │
11 │ class AbortMonitor extends RaMonitor {
12 │   var abortedTasks: Set[RaHSM] = Set()
13 │
14 │   always {
15 │     case Message(_, ABORT, target) ⇒
16 │       abortedTasks += target
17 │     case Action(DB_EVENT) | Action(LOCK_EVENT) ⇒
18 │       for (task ← violatedTasks() if !abortedTasks.contains(task)) yield hot {
19 │         case Message(_, ABORT, target) if target.hsmName == task.hsmName ⇒ ok
20 │       }
21 │   }
22 │ }
```

Fig. 14. Monitors for the release and abort properties.

```
 1 │ class MachineSelector(
 2 │     machines: List [RemoteAgentHSM],
 3 │     canRun: (RemoteAgentHSM, List[RemoteAgentHSM]) ⇒ Boolean)
 4 │   extends Iterable [RemoteAgentHSM]
 5 │ {
 6 │   val random = new scala.util.Random
 7 │
 8 │   override def iterator : Iterator [RemoteAgentHSM] =
 9 │     new Iterator [RemoteAgentHSM] {
10 │       def isEnabled(machine: RemoteAgentHSM): Boolean = {
11 │         machine.enabled() && canRun(machine, machines) && ...
12 │       }
13 │
14 │       override def hasNext: Boolean = machines.exists(isEnabled(_))
15 │
16 │       override def next(): RemoteAgentHSM = {
17 │         val enabledMachines = machines.filter(isEnabled(_))
18 │         val nextMachine = random.nextInt(enabledMachines.size)
19 │         enabledMachines(nextMachine)
20 │       }
21 │     }
22 │ }
```

Fig. 15. The machine selector.

class parameter is the function reset, which is user defined, and which generates a new list of machines and a new instance of the monitor (so we can call the method end() on it). The third parameter is the user defined canRun method used to control the machine selection.

```scala
1   class Scheduler(
2     maxResets: Int,
3     reset : () ⇒ ( List [RemoteAgentHSM], Monitor[EVR]),
4     canRun: (RemoteAgentHSM, List[RemoteAgentHSM]) ⇒ Boolean)
5   {
6     def run (): Unit = {
7       for (i ← 0 until maxResets) {
8         val (machines, monitor) = reset ()
9         val generator = new MachineSelector(machines, canRun)
10        for (machine ← generator) { machine.run() }
11        monitor.end()
12      }
13    }
14  }
```

Fig. 16. The scheduler.

Test Results. The monitors were executed with a flag causing them to terminate on the first error encountered. For each error an error trace is produced. For example for error number 2, the error trace in Fig. 17 is produced after 1.1 seconds on reset number 2,453 of the HSMs to their initial state. It shows that task 1 first (step 12) locks the property and achieves it in the database. Then the daemon (step 14) wakes up. The daemon later (steps 24 and 25) determines that there are no new events, and it gets ready to wait for new events. The environment (step 26) then destroys the database. Finally (step 29) the daemon goes to sleep, as a result of the previous counter check, and therefore misses the database corruption that happened in between.

We ran the test harness with one property at a time. For each found error, we had to route the scheduler around that error, in order to find the next one (as an alternative to fixing the errors which we did not). This was done by defining the canRun functions (see Fig. 15). For example, the function avoidError2 in Fig. 18 defines a thread as schedulable if either it is not the environment, or if it is, the daemon is not in state event_count_unchanged, where it has taken the *decision* to wait but not waited yet. All four errors mentioned in Sect. 3.1 were detected using the monitors and the randomized scheduling. The approach was also useful in getting the SCALA model and monitors correct. Figure 19 shows the data for the different verifications, comparing the verification performed with SPIN in [13] in 1997. The testing of the SCALA model was performed on a MacBook Pro 15 inch laptop running macOS Version 10.13.5, with a 2.8 GHz Intel Core i7, and 16 GB of memory. A Sun workstation was used for the SPIN verification.

```
...
12. Task1   : achieve -STEP-> set_achieved_true
...
14. Daemon  : wait_for_events -RUN-> interrupt_violated_tasks
...
24. Daemon  : perhaps_do_automatic_recovery -STEP-> check_counter
25. Daemon  : check_counter -STEP-> event_count_unchanged
26. Env     : do_some_damage -STEP-> do_some_damage
...
29. Daemon  : event_count_unchanged -STEP-> wait_for_events
```

Fig. 17. Extract from counter example for error 2 containing 29 transitions, detected after 1.1 seconds on reset number 2,453.

```
1  def avoidError2(machine: RaHSM, machines: List[RatHSM]): Boolean = {
2    !machine.isInstanceOf[Env] || {
3      val daemon = machines.find { case machine ⇒
4        machine.isInstanceOf[Daemon]
5      }.get.asInstanceOf[Daemon]
6      !daemon.inThisState("event count unchanged")
7    }
8  }
```

Fig. 18. User defined scheduler control method avoiding error 2.

For each of the four errors, we indicate the property violated, the number of states explored by SPIN, the memory consumption in Mb used by SPIN, the time spent by SPIN (seconds), the number of resets of the SCALA model (and average over 10 runs in parentheses), and the time spent testing the SCALA model (and average over 10 runs in parentheses). The last two rows show data for a "correct" model, i.e. after fixing errors and/or proper re-routing the scheduler around errors 1–4. Here the PROMELA model was proved correct by SPIN. For the SCALA model, no further errors were found during 1 million resets. This does of course not exclude the possibility of further errors in the SCALA model, due to the randomness of the approach, in contrast to SPIN, which performs an exhaustive exploration of the given model's state space. However, since both are models, abstracting the real 3000 line LISP program, both approaches may have missed errors. Note finally, that SPIN in its current form (year 2018), which has evolved considerably since 1997, on a modern multi-core machine would be much faster than indicated in Fig. 19. The comparison is not intended to illustrate any speed advantages of the SCALA scheduler, only that one in a high-level programming language quickly can write a relatively effective test engine.

Error nr.	Kind	States SPIN	Memory SPIN (Mb)	Time SPIN (sec)	Iterations SCALA	Time SCALA (sec)
1	RELEASE	2,963	2.6	0.3	8,283 (26,682)	1.9 (2.88)
2	ABORT	49,038	3.7	5.3	2,453 (122,338)	1.1 (8.44)
3	ABORT	45,705	3.6	4.9	3,357 (63,264)	1.2 (5.08)
4	ABORT	48,858	3.7	5.4	283,899 (329,039)	16.1 (20.31)
✓	RELEASE	222,840	7.1	21.2	1,000,000	57.7
✓	ABORT	107,479	5.0	11.6	1,000,000	54.5

Fig. 19. Verification data.

4 Conclusion

We have shown how a high-level programming language can be used for modeling. The modeling of the Remote Agent used an internal DSL for modeling HSMs, supported by automated visualization of these from their text representation. Such an approach should furthermore be supported by formal verification, possibly through a refinement relation between levels of abstraction, with mathematical specifications over infinite domains at the top level. Note, that internal DSLs, in providing the expressiveness of the host language, require the user to be a programmer in the host language, in contrast to external DSLs. This conflict between expressiveness of internal DSLs, versus notational convenience of external DSLs, can be a dilemma for DSL implementers. Note finally, that the systems modeled here are discrete systems, in contrast to continuous systems such as cyber-physical systems, which seem more challenging.

References

1. Barringer, H., Havelund, K.: TraceContract: a Scala DSL for trace analysis. In: Butler, M., Schulte, W. (eds.) FM 2011. LNCS, vol. 6664, pp. 57–72. Springer, Heidelberg (2011). https://doi.org/10.1007/978-3-642-21437-0_7
2. Bjørner, D.: Formalization of data base models. In: Bjørner, D. (ed.) Abstract Software Specifications. LNCS, vol. 86, pp. 144–215. Springer, Heidelberg (1980). https://doi.org/10.1007/3-540-10007-5_37
3. Bjørner, D., Jones, C.B. (eds.): The Vienna Development Method: The Meta-Language. LNCS, vol. 61. Springer, Heidelberg (1978). https://doi.org/10.1007/3-540-08766-4
4. Broy, M., Havelund, K., Kumar, R.: Towards a unified view of modeling and programming. In: Margaria, T., Steffen, B. (eds.) ISoLA 2016. LNCS, vol. 9953, pp. 238–257. Springer, Cham (2016). https://doi.org/10.1007/978-3-319-47169-3_17
5. Broy, M., Havelund, K., Kumar, R., Steffen, B.: Towards a unified view of modeling and programming (track summary). In: Margaria, T., Steffen, B. (eds.) ISoLA 2016. LNCS, vol. 9953, pp. 3–10. Springer, Cham (2016). https://doi.org/10.1007/978-3-319-47169-3_17
6. Fitzgerald, J., Larsen, P.G., Mukherjee, P., Plat, N., Verhoef, M.: Validated Designs for Object-Oriented Systems. Springer-Verlag TELOS, Santa Clara (2005)

7. Fortress. https://en.wikipedia.org/wiki/Fortress_(programming_language)
8. Havelund, K.: Closing the gap between specification and programming: VDM^{++} and Scala. In: Korovina, M., Voronkov, A., (Eds.), HOWARD-60: Higher-Order Workshop on Automated Runtime Verification and Debugging, vol. 1 of EasyChair Proceedings, Manchester, UK, December 2011
9. Havelund, K.: Data automata in Scala. In: Proceedings of the 8th International Symposium on Theoretical Aspects of Software Engineering (TASE 2014) (2014)
10. Havelund, K.: Monitoring with data automata. In: Margaria, T., Steffen, B. (eds.) ISoLA 2014. LNCS, vol. 8803, pp. 254–273. Springer, Heidelberg (2014). https://doi.org/10.1007/978-3-662-45231-8_18
11. Havelund, K.: Rule-based runtime verification revisited. Softw. Tools Technol. Transf. (STTT) **17**, 143–170 (2015)
12. Havelund, K., Joshi, R.: Modeling and monitoring of hierarchical state machines in Scala. In: Romanovsky, A., Troubitsyna, E.A. (eds.) SERENE 2017. LNCS, vol. 10479, pp. 21–36. Springer, Cham (2017). https://doi.org/10.1007/978-3-319-65948-0_2
13. Havelund, K., Lowry, M.R., Penix, J.: Formal analysis of a space-craft controller using SPIN. IEEE Trans. Softw. Eng. **27**(8), 749–765 (2001)
14. Holzmann, G.: The SPIN Model Checker. Addison-Wesley, Boston (2004)
15. Kauffman, S., Havelund, K., Joshi, R.: **nfer** – a notation and system for inferring event stream abstractions. In: Falcone, Y., Sánchez, C. (eds.) RV 2016. LNCS, vol. 10012, pp. 235–250. Springer, Cham (2016). https://doi.org/10.1007/978-3-319-46982-9_15
16. Pell, B., Gat, E., Keesing, R., Muscettola, N., Smith, B.: Plan execution for autonomous spacecrafts. In: Proceedings of the International Joint Conference on Artificial Intelligence, Nagoya, Japan, August 1997
17. PlantUML. http://plantuml.com
18. Samek, M.: Practical UML Statecharts in C/C++, Second Edition: Event-Driven Programming for Embedded Systems, 2nd edn. Newnes, MA (2009)
19. Scala. http://www.scala-lang.org
20. Scalameta. https://scalameta.org

This Is Not a Model

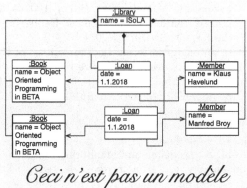

Ceci n'est pas un modèle

On Development of a Common Terminology for Modeling and Programming

Ole Lehrmann Madsen[1,2] and Birger Møller-Pedersen[3(✉)]

[1] Aarhus University, Aarhus, Denmark
olm@cs.au.dk
[2] The Alexandra Institute Ltd., Aarhus, Denmark
olm@alexandra.dk
[3] Department of Informatics, University of Oslo, Oslo, Norway
birger@ifi.uio.no

Abstract. SIMULA and Beta are object-oriented languages intended for modeling and programming. This is in contrast to mainstream where different languages are used for modeling and programming. In previous papers, it has been argued that there are a number of advantages in developing a unified language. In order to do this, a consistent terminology for modeling and programming is needed. The notion of *model* is essential in this respect. In UML, the diagrams are considered models. For SIMULA and Beta the program executions are considered models. We argue for the latter and discuss the implications for the design of a unified language.

Keywords: Modeling · Programming · Languages

1 Introduction

The goal of this paper is to contribute to the development of a unified language for modeling and programming as suggested in [1, 2]. As pointed out in [1], one of the strengths of object-oriented programming as originally introduced by SIMULA [3] was that it provided a unified approach to modeling and programming. However, since the advent of languages for object-oriented analysis, design and modeling [4–7],

© Springer Nature Switzerland AG 2018
T. Margaria and B. Steffen (Eds.): ISoLA 2018, LNCS 11244, pp. 206–224, 2018.
https://doi.org/10.1007/978-3-030-03418-4_13

the modeling and programming communities have diverged. The modeling community seems to have focused mainly on modeling whereas the programming community seems to have ignored modeling. In [1] we argued for going back to the future and get inspiration from SIMULA to develop a unified language.

In order to develop a unified language, it is necessary to obtain a consistent terminology for modeling and programming, which is the subject of this paper. A key question here is a common understanding of the notion of a model. In UML [8] the diagrams constitute the models. In object-oriented programming[1], the program execution is the model, and the program is considered a description of the program execution[2]. In this paper, we will argue that the program execution should be considered the model and that UML diagrams and the program text should be considered descriptions of the design of the model, i.e. the program execution.

As discussed here and in [1], the main scope for modeling is object-oriented modeling as represented by UML [3]. The scope for modeling in [2] is mainly with respect to formal specifications. In this paper, we mainly consider object-oriented modeling as represented by SIMULA, Beta [9] and UML, but we will return to specifications later in this paper. Ultimately, the work represented by [1, 2] and in this paper may lead to a unified language for UML-like modeling, formal specifications and programming. This vision is shared by others, see e.g. [10], and to a certain extent [11], although the answer there is to make UML executable by adding an action language. This will eventually imply that Executable UML [12] becomes a programming language and thus an example of a unified language.

The diagram in the picture of the title is obviously not a model but - as the reader may have already guessed - just **a picture**[3] **of a model**. The object diagram depicts the state of matters of a library at a given point in time: the ISoLA library has two loans, two members and two books.

This picture is not a picture of the real library, the real members or the real book. It is a **picture** of a **dynamic system of objects** with attributes with values and references to each other at a given point of time. Each object **models** (or **represents**) a real member or a real book, and the system of objects together is a **model** of a given library. By observing the dynamic system of objects with values of attributes and references, an observer will get an understanding of how real libraries work.

The diagram in the title picture is an object diagram in UML. The object symbols in the figure are pictures of the objects in the dynamic system. The objects are usually defined by classes (or singular object descriptors as in Beta and Self [13]), and none of these are part of the diagram.

The diagram in the picture in Fig. 1 is obviously not a model either. We have just established that the above system of objects is the model of a given library, so the diagram in Fig. 1 is simply a (partial) **description** of the model (i.e. of the classes of the above objects).

---

[1] As represented by the Scandinavian School of Object-Orientation with SIMULA and Beta.

[2] With program execution we mean the family of executions based upon a given program.

[3] https://en.wikipedia.org/wiki/The_Treachery_of_Images.

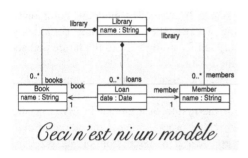

Fig. 1. 'This is neither a model'

If more details had been added to the diagram in Fig. 1, or to a different, but associated description, the complete description could have included the description of the generation of the objects that are depicted in the title picture. It could also include the setting of values of attributes and making the references between objects.

Such details would typically be part of a description in terms of a **program** with the same classes as those that describe the objects in Fig. 1. A **program execution** would generate (and thereby consist of) the system of objects depicted in the title picture, and a **debugger** for the corresponding programming language could show the state of matters at a given point of execution, as the diagram in the title picture does. So, for programming the **program execution is the model** of the given library, while the **program is the description** of the model.

From the above there are three different artifacts of modeling and programming that need to be distinguished:

- The dynamic system of objects as generated by a program in the form of a program execution or the imagination of a model execution described by UML diagrams.
- The description of the design of the dynamic system of objects by means of a program and/or UML diagrams.
- Descriptions of *required properties* developed during analysis and design of the system and descriptions of *observed properties* during execution of the system.

As pointed out in [1, 2, 14], programming is modeling, and the similarities between modeling languages and programming languages call for a unified language. This, however, requires a consistent view on modeling, model, description of a model, picture (snapshot) of a model, program execution, program, etc. This paper is a contribution to this clarification.

In Sect. 2, we further elaborate on the similarities and differences between artifacts of modeling and programming. In Sect. 3, we discuss modeling in general. In Sect. 4, we discuss modeling and programming. In Sect. 5, we discuss implications for the design of unified languages. Finally, Sect. 6 is the conclusion.

2   Current Situation with Respect to Terminology

As mentioned above, in order to develop a unified language, it is necessary to obtain a consistent terminology for modeling and programming. We therefore have a look at what is the current situation and what it takes to get at a unified and consistent terminology.

2.1   Artifacts and Terminology

The ultimate goal of both modeling and programming is to develop systems (applications). System development involves many other things like e.g. work processes and project management, but for modeling and programming there are currently three different kinds of artifacts:

- The dynamic **system** consisting of objects.
  In programming this is called **program execution**.
  In modeling - at least for executable models - this is called **model execution**.
- The **description** that is used to *generate* the system.
  In programming these generative descriptions are called **programs**, while in modeling with executable models these are called **models** (in terms of a mixture of diagrams and text). Executable UML [12] uses a combination of class diagrams and activities (in Java). Recently, state machines in UML have got a precise semantics, [15], that makes it possible to use state machines for executable UML models. The same applies to composite structures [16].
- The **descriptions** of *required* or *observed properties* of the system.
  Required properties are the properties required by different stakeholders and concerns, sometimes given by requirements specifications of various forms, ranging from textual documents to scenario descriptions with e.g. required interactions between users/other systems and the system, or between parts of the system (for design requirements).
  Observed properties are the properties observed when testing, debugging and finally running the production version of the generative system description.
  The goal, of course, is that the observed properties are consistent with the required properties.
  In programming required properties are typically described using *snapshots*, general snapshots (introduced early [17] by Peter Naur), assertions, invariants, etc. and by *scenario descriptions* using Message Sequence Charts [18], sequence diagrams or similar.
  In modeling, required properties are described by means of object diagrams for simple snapshots, use case models and sequence diagrams for scenarios. State machine and activity models may also be used for requirements specification.

Tools like debuggers also provide descriptions by using a combination of snapshots and scenario descriptions to describe the state of the system at a given stage of execution and the sequences of actions leading to this state. In programming, these descriptions could be better aligned with the mechanisms of the programming language, and for modeling the situation is also surprisingly bad. In [19] a comparison of tools for executable UML has been made and it is reported that only a few tools for Executable UML provide support for model-level interactive debugging.

It is an advantage if generative and property descriptions are aligned. While Message Sequence Charts is a separate language, sequence diagrams as part of UML make it possible to check that e.g. class diagrams and sequence diagrams are consistent. e.g. that the messages of sequence diagrams are matched by corresponding properties of the classes involved.

This is also the case for descriptions of required and observed properties, which can be made using the same language mechanisms. This is obviously the case for sequence diagrams. The following is a quote from the introduction to sequence diagrams of UML:

> 'Interactions are used in a number of different situations. They are used to get a better grip of an interaction situation for an individual designer or for a group that needs to achieve a common understanding of the situation. Interactions are also used during the more detailed design phase where the precise inter-process communication must be set up according to formal protocols. When testing is performed, the traces of the system can be described as interactions and compared with those of the earlier phases.'

Programmers rely on semantics of programming languages, defined e.g. by formal definitions or reference implementations. Users of executable UML should expect the same and, in fact, there is a precise definition of it. The fUML standard defines an execution semantics for a large subset of standard UML. However, according to [19], the majority of tools for Executable UML do not conform to this definition.

2.2 Practice

Most programmers will claim that they are not modeling, and modelers will claim that they are not programming.

Still, in programming e.g. a reservation system, programmers will do a minimum of modeling by introducing *objects that model phenomena* from the application domain. Passenger objects will model real passengers; Flight objects will model real flights etc. A consequence of this is that it is natural to consider the dynamic system of objects to be a model of the application domain.

In modeling, objects are not said to be models of the corresponding real application domain entities. The term model is used for descriptions.

When it comes to the description of objects - typically by means of class descriptions - many programmers do not take the implied step of regarding these as representations of the corresponding domain concepts, and most textbooks on programming are also silent about this. With classes as representations of domain concepts follows that subclasses are representations of specialized concepts, but in programming this is not an established fact (consensus). Some programmers regard classes merely as implementations of interfaces, and subclassing as a means for code reuse. Some even argue for a type concept in addition to a class concept.

Modelers, however, are well aware that class diagrams define classes as representations of domain concepts and subclasses as representations of specializations of these domain concepts

Modeling is not just making executable models. In fact many developers (including pure programmers) believe that it is valuable to make informal, sketchy property descriptions as part of specifying requirements, analyzing domains and systems, and for designing systems. Some kinds of property descriptions are really not meant for execution such as use case descriptions, sequence diagrams and object diagrams.

3   Modeling in General

Modeling is used in a number of areas such as architecture, science, engineering, entertainment, and system development. Models are used for different purposes depending on the area being considered. One class of models is constructed to understand properties of systems, including parts of nature. Another class of models is made to analyze properties of a system design, before the system is built, and to check that the system design has certain expected properties. A third class of models is just used as toys, like a toy railroad. Finally, models may be used to communicate properties of systems between scientists, engineers, designers, and others.

Architecture. In architecture, physical models are made of planned or existing buildings. A possible technical use of an architectural model is to facilitate visualization of internal relationships within the structure, or external relationships of the structure to the environment. Architects make models of new buildings to communicate their ideas about the form of the building.

Science. In science, modeling is used for *understanding* parts of nature. In biology, physical models of molecules are examples of this. Newton's Laws and Einstein's Theories of Relativity are examples of models expressed by mathematics.

Engineering. Engineers make models of bridges, cars, airplanes, roads, etc. to check physical properties, like performance of a entity/system at an early stage without the expense of building a full-sized prototype. Such models are mainly expressed as mathematical models. However, physical models may be used for communicating the design of the artifact being constructed.

Geography. Maps[4] of part of the world are examples of models that most people are familiar with. There are many kinds of maps serving different purposes. A map is a

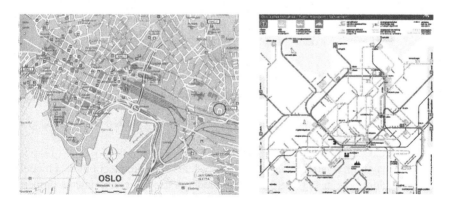

Fig. 2. A model is made from a particular *viewpoint* and for a given purpose

---

[4] The book: 'Maps of the Imagination – the writer as a cartographer' by Peter Turchi is an excellent exploration of the relationships between creative writing, making maps, and creativity. Turchi gave an inspiring keynote on this subject at OOPSLA'2007.

model of a geographic area and it is made with a specific purpose, and for this purpose some properties are relevant, whereas other properties are irrelevant, see Fig. 2.

Toys. Many forms of toys are examples of physical models. This includes everything from toy railroads, cars, ships, dolls, houses, kitchens, etc.

Primitive Models. In [20] Hoare mentions the curiosum that in primitive societies, the model[5] is sometimes useful in its own right, because it was believed that manipulation of the model might cause corresponding changes in the real

Fig. 3. Modeling in primitive societies

world. In Voodoo, it is common practice to make dolls being models of enemies and stick needles into the doll to cause pain to a real person (Fig. 3).

We use the following definition of model[6]:

DEFINITION. A *model* refers to a small or large, *abstract* or *actual*, *representation* of a *planned* or *existing* entity or system from a particular *viewpoint*.

A model may be an *abstract* representation; mathematical models are examples of abstract representations. A mathematical model is usually a set of equations describing properties of a given system. This can be in the form of differential equations, etc. Mathematical models are an important class of models.

A model may be an *actual* representation. Models of molecules, the solar system, buildings, and bridges can be made of cardboard, wood, plastic, wire, plaster, LEGO bricks, or other substances. They are examples of actual representations. In other words, an actual representation is a physical representation of a system.

(a) Model of **planned** building   (b) Model of **existing** solar system

Fig. 4. A model may be of a planned or an existing system

Models may represent *planned* or *existing* systems. The architect builds a model of a planned building (as in Fig. 4(a)), and the model is used to communicate properties such as form and visual appearance to the customer before the house is built. The

---

[5] Hoare does not talk about models, but *representations* of abstractions.

[6] Inspired by Webster [6] and Wikipedia [model, physical model, computer simulation, abstraction, etc.].

astronomer may create a model of an existing system (as in Fig. 4(b)) of the solar system to illustrate orbits of the planets and moons to be used for teaching.

As illustrated by Fig. 2, a model is always made from a particular viewpoint in the sense that the modeler selects the properties of the system that are relevant for the use of the model. The purpose of the map in the left side of the figure is to show the physical form and names of the roads and rail roads in Oslo. The purpose of the map in the right side is to show the lines and stops of public transport in Oslo, but the actual physical form of the routes is not represented. In general, a model only represents a fraction of the properties of a given system. For a given model, we thus (only) represent the properties that are relevant for the purpose of the model. The only complete model of a given system is the system itself as pointed out by Carl Adam Petri and others.

The definition also says that a model may be small or large – for large systems such as the solar system the model is small, but for small systems such as an atom, the model may be large. We will later see that *abstract representation*, *actual representation*, *planned system*, *existing system*, and *viewpoint* are relevant for modeling of software systems, whereas this is not the case for *small* and *large*.

In the following we examine what are the key advantages of models as actual representations in order to provide an analogy for viewing software systems as actual representations as it will be presented in Sect. 4.

Ask any child what is the model of a car in Fig. 5, and you will get the answer that the LEGO car is the model, and not the description of how to build the car. The reason for this is clear, since the *LEGO car is the matter of interest* – not the description of how to build it.

Even grown-ups will agree – most of them have been exposed to physical models of molecules, the solar system, buildings, and bridges made of cardboard, wood, plastic, wire, and plaster.

LEGO bricks are, like cardboard, wood, etc., examples of material (with *substance*) that can be used to make models as actual representations. An actual representation is a **physical** (substantial) **model** of a system. A physical model may include a single entity (for example, a bolt) or a large system (for example, the Solar System). The model itself is a system, and it allows us to simulate or visualize something about the system it models. In Sect. 4, we will argue that objects in analogy with LEGO bricks are the physical entities of which computerized models are made.

The LEGO car in Fig. 5 obviously represents a phenomenon from the domain of vehicles. And elements of the LEGO car – wheels, doors, motor, etc., represent corresponding elements of the real car.

For a model as an actual representation, it should be clear from the domain what the elements of the model represent. For a model of a building, it is usually obvious what the elements represent. For the solar system, there may be a need to put labels on the elements of the model to indicate which planets or moons they represent.

A LEGO car as the one in Fig. 5 has the dynamics given to it by children playing with them. More advanced cars may have motors; however, they still have to be operated, e.g. by remote controls. The description only describes the capabilities of a car.

Description   **Model**

Fig. 5. Description and Model

4 Modeling and Programming

'To program is to understand'
Kristen Nygaard

As mentioned in [1, 21], SIMULA [3, 22, 23] was a language intended for modeling (at that time called 'system description') as well as for programming. As pointed out in [21], this was one of the original advantages of object-orientation: that the same concepts and language mechanisms could be used for analysis, design and programming. When object-oriented analysis, design and programming were defined based upon this advantage, this was in contrast to the (at that time) mainstream tools and techniques that were based on Structured Analysis and Structured Design and programming (in Cobol, and C) – leading to problems of keeping descriptions in three different languages up-to-date and consistent. SIMULA as a unified language for modeling and programming was thus a big step forward.

Software systems are complex entities, so programming is not just a matter of getting the job done. An important part of program development is to understand, describe and communicate about the application domain – *to program is to understand*. It is therefore important that program executions and programs reflect phenomena and concepts from the application domain – i.e. that programming is modeling, see [9, 24].

A software system for administrating libraries will e.g. need representations of the same elements with the same properties as the model of the library, so a model description may readily become part of the software. This will be facilitated especially well if both model descriptions and implementations are made in a unified language.

The 'actual representation' of the Webster definition of model is in line with the above understanding of the dynamic system of objects to be the model of a library. The following section 'formalizes' this in the definition of object-oriented programming.

Modeling and Object-Oriented Programming. In [24] we introduced a definition of object-oriented programming where the emphasis was that the program execution is a physical model, e.g. capturing the analogy of objects to physical entities such as LEGO bricks, wood and cardboard. Our definition below is a slightly revised version of the definition in [24] to be more aligned with the Webster definition above:

DEFINITION. *Object-oriented programming*. A program execution is regarded as a *physical model*, representing the behavior of either an *existing* or *planned* system (in an application domain) from a particular *viewpoint*.

In this definition of object-oriented programming, objects are the physical entities of which models are made. The main purpose was to make programmers (and modelers) think in terms of designing a physical system of objects. In his "Ten Things I hate about Object-Oriented Programming" [14], Oscar Nierstrasz makes the point that efforts on Object-Oriented Programming are too focused on classes and their descriptions, while objects should be the focus.

Real libraries are dynamic systems with changing sets of books, loans, and members, so when making models of these in order to understand libraries, obviously models of such systems must be dynamic systems of objects representing the real books, loans and members.

In addition to identifying objects and their properties in the application domain, it is of course important to identify the domain specific concepts in order to understand and organize our knowledge about the domain. For the library system, the Book-objects in the program execution model books from the domain of libraries. The Book-class, on the other hand, does not represent the books but is rather a representation of the concept of a Book – a domain specific concept.

The process of identifying domain specific concepts is called *abstraction* and the resulting concepts are often also referred to as *abstractions*. Abstraction is thus an important part of modeling but we will not discuss abstraction in this paper – Hoare is a good reference here [20, 25].

A program execution may model an *existing* system, which may be a simulation of the existing system or a digital twin – see further below. A program execution may also model a *planned* system, which may be a prototype or production version of a new software. This is analogous to architects making models of planned buildings. As we shall see below, it is even a good idea to combine simulation and planned systems.

As for modeling in general, an object-oriented model is also made from a particular *viewpoint* where objects, classes, attributes, etc. are selected in order to represent the relevant properties of the system being modeled. This is even the case for models of planned systems: part of planning a system is to select the viewpoint and thereby the purpose of the system. Concepts are modeled by classes, and subclasses model concept hierarchies – a subclass is thus a specialization of its superclass.

From models via prototypes to final products. In traditional disciplines such as engineering and architecture, models are quite separated from the real systems, in the sense that if you have a model of a planned building you cannot reuse the model when constructing the building.

In some areas, you may start with a model and then construct a series of prototypes – here you may perhaps reuse elements of a prototype in the next prototype and perhaps in the final product. In programming, you have the advantage that one may more or less continuously develop a series of prototypes that eventually converge into a production version.

Simulation. As mentioned, object-oriented programming was originally intended for simulation of real systems (SIMULA I [26]), and this is of course still an application area for object-oriented programming. Simulation is an important methodological tool in the study of systems. A description of the system is made in terms of a simulation program. An execution of the program will create a model that simulates part of the behavior or the system.

Simulation is in general a much wider discipline than computer simulation. In many professions physical simulators are used for training purposes. This is e.g. the case for training of airplane pilots.

In his talk[7] at the SIMULA 50 Years Anniversary in 2017, James Gosling presented an interesting approach to take simulation a step further towards implementing real systems. The example was the development of a system of sea robots. An object-oriented system of the planned application was made with objects representing the sea robots. The model was part of a large simulation model of the sea and the physical sea robots. It was therefore possible to experience if they behaved according to specifications: spreading in the sea and avoiding collisions with other objects in the sea, etc. Eventually, the code of the simulation sea robot objects was deployed in the physical sea robots without any changes. A similar approach for embedded systems is described in [27]. This approach might be worth to explore as a general approach to develop systems that have to be deployed in a complex real-world setting.

Digital Twin. The notion of a **Digital Twin** has developed in relation to Internet-of-Things (IoT). Digital Twins are digital representations of things, spanning from whole products to physical items (like sensors) connected to the Internet. We believe that the notion of a Digital Twin may benefit from being considered a model in the above sense, in the form of an actual representation.

A Digital Twin may observe the state of the twin product/item (by means of sensors), analyze data from the twin, and influence the behavior of the twin (by means of actuators or by modifying the software in the twin). These capabilities of the Digital Twin are in addition to the parts of the Digital Twin that directly represent the corresponding Twin.

This distinction between *representative* and *non-representative* parts is not special for Digital Twins. A program in a unified modeling and programming language will have elements that describe representative parts (model specific elements), and it will have implementation specific elements.

In a section above, we mention Hoare's reference to primitive models that people believed could influence the real world. With Digital Twins we do have a notion of models that may influence the real world – although not primitive ☺.

Descriptions. The description of the LEGO car is of course needed both to build and operate the car. In a similar way, the program text is a description of how to generate the program execution in terms of a dynamic system of objects. For executable UML, the analogy to the program text and the program execution is evident. In any case, a program and/or a UML diagram describe the design and structure of a dynamic system of objects.

The Webster definition of a model includes an abstract as well as actual representations and a program text and/or UML-diagram may be considered a model in the

---

[7] https://www.youtube.com/watch?v=ccRtIdlTqlU.

form of an abstract representation. We do not claim that one view of what should be called a model is more correct than the other. However, we believe that for modeling and programming it is most useful to consider the program execution to be the model – i.e. an actual representation.

Abstract representations may be useful for making formal analysis, as with verification tools for programs, or formal specifications of new systems. Modeling as in formal specification is one viewpoint on this, see [2]. It is, however, important to distinguish between the generative descriptions (program text and/or UML-diagram), the program execution, and the property descriptions.

5 Implications for Unified Language Design and Tools

The approach with program execution considered the model (and the program just the description) has implications for a language for both modeling and programming, and also for specification. In addition to the advantages illustrated above, there are also some practical implications: 'models' and programs will no longer be inconsistent – it is well-known that using different languages for modeling and implementation makes it hard to retain consistency between the two different kinds of descriptions. In addition, having different languages implies that the same language mechanisms have to be developed and implemented twice, and supported by tools. Programmers will expect that such a language will have the well-known mechanisms of programming languages, as e.g. generics, so in that respect Executable UML is not yet the answer. Programmers will also expect that tools for a unified language will be of the same quality as tools for mainstream programming languages.

Below we will comment on what we consider the overall implications for the design of a unified language and supporting tools.

5.1 Programmers Must Learn to Model and Modelers Must Learn to Program

Most text books on programming focus on the technical aspects of programming and programming languages, and modeling is at best just treated superficially.

In the design of software systems, programmers should have focus on phenomena and concepts from the application domain being represented respectively as objects and classes. This has been essential for the design of the Beta language – and we refer to Chapter 18 in the Beta book [9] for a presentation of the conceptual framework for modeling and programming underlying Beta.

5.2 The Program Execution Should Have More Focus

As argued above, the program execution is the primary matter of interest when developing a software system. At present the program text is the primary matter of interest and the dynamic system of objects generated during program execution is not treated as an important artifact in itself.

This does not mean that the program text and/or design diagrams are not important. After all, it is the program that describes the design and structure of the program execution – as also emphasized by Andrew Black [28], page 36.

5.3 Language Mechanisms Should Support Modeling as Well as Programming

In the design of the Beta language, a modeling as well as a technical argument were required for including a new mechanism in the language.

Class/subclass represents concept hierarchies. As an example, let us take the class/subclass mechanism. In SIMULA, Beta and UML, there is no doubt that a class represents a concept in the application domain and a subclass represents a specialized concept.

Unfortunately, many programming language designers [29, 30] consider a class to be an implementation mechanism and a subclassing to be a reuse (code grabbing) mechanism. The use of the term inheritance has unfortunately contributed to this misunderstanding of the class/subclass mechanism.

We also see that many textbooks explain virtual methods by means of dynamic dispatch – i.e. at a very technical level without relating virtual methods to modeling. A subclass adds new attributes (properties) to the intension of a class and thus restricts the extension of objects covered by the subclass. A virtual attribute that is further defined in a subclass should be viewed as a specialization of the corresponding attribute in the superclass. In addition to virtual methods, Beta also has virtual classes [31], which further extends the modeling capabilities of Beta.

No need for a separate type concept. This reuse-view of class/subclass has the implication that language designers (primarily in the type theory community) often add a type mechanism to the language to represent concepts (although they rarely talk about concepts – types are usually viewed from a mathematical point of view). This results in a language with both class and type, which clearly adds to the complexity of the language.

The reason that the class/subclass mechanism not being considered a type mechanism may be traced to the use of classes in e.g. Smalltalk [32] where you often see subclasses that do not have a proper subclass (subtype) relation to its superclass.

Behavioral compatibility. Another reason may be that the subclass mechanism cannot guarantee that a given subclass is behaviorally compatible with its superclass. By overriding methods in a subclass, one may completely change the behavior of the superclass. In SIMULA, it was quite clear that an instance of a subclass should be compatible with the superclass. A reference in SIMULA qualified by (of type) say Vehicle should be able to refer instances of any subclass of Vehicle without breaking the code. Thus Subtype Substitutability was inherent in the design of SIMULA, but it was later reinvented as the Liskov Substitution Principle [33].

As mentioned, behavioral compatibility cannot be guaranteed by a language mechanism. In Beta, a method cannot be redefined in a subclass but only specialized with respect to the sequence of actions being executed. This implies that actions in the supermethod are always executed but may be supplemented (via the inner mechanism) in submethods. In [34] we presented this as specialization of methods or inheritance also for methods.

Still behavioral compatibility cannot be guaranteed. This will require a proof, and the use of invariants and pre- and post-assertions for methods as well as inner may be useful here. This is an example of non-executable specifications that may be useful for programming – but nothing new in this.

Concurrency. Another implication of programming as modeling is how to select language mechanisms for supporting concurrency. Concurrency is inherent in most domains and must be properly modeled in program executions. This obviously requires language mechanisms for modeling active entities in the application domain.

Concurrency was central in SIMULA, which originally was designed as a simulation language and here it was essential to be able to model active entities. Objects in SIMULA are active and technically they are coroutines used to define the notion of pseudo-parallel systems – at the time when SIMULA was designed, state-of-art of language design was not ready for designing a real concurrent language.

No mainstream programming language has included active objects in the style of SIMULA. For Beta the notion of active objects has been further developed [9, 35]. UML has also active objects.

Low-Level Primitives. Since a programming language has to be implemented on a low-level platform, there will of course be primitives and other low-level mechanisms that may not be useful from a modeling perspective. But the language designers must be aware of the distinction between low-level primitives and higher-level mechanisms, including abstraction mechanisms such as class, subclass, and virtual.

5.4   One-to-One Correspondence Between Textual and Graphical Syntax

Most modeling languages have a syntax in the form of diagrams whereas most programming languages have a textual syntax. A diagrammatic syntax is often to be preferred in the early phases of analysis and design and is better suited for communication with users. In a later phase, a textual syntax may be preferred since it is more compact. We believe that modeling is not synonymous with graphical notation. In many situations a textual notation is superior.

A unified language must have a diagrammatic as well as a textual syntax and it should be possible to switch freely between these. We had this for the graphical syntax for Beta [9, 21]; [10] also demonstrates that this is possible.

5.5   Language Support for Describing Properties

One of the advantages of UML is that language mechanisms for describing required or observed properties of the software system in the form of scenarios using interaction diagrams and snapshots of the state of objects at a given point in time using object diagrams are defined within UML. And as mentioned above, one of the goals of UML is that scenarios and snapshots generated during execution may be verified against the design scenarios.

This implies that the syntax for describing the design of the system is consistent with the syntax describing properties.

No mainstream programming language includes mechanisms for describing properties, but a unified language should certainly follow the UML line and include such mechanisms.

5.6   Observation of Properties of the Program Execution

A high-level debugger for an object-oriented language should be able to present snapshots and/or method invocation sequences of the program execution in terms of a combination of sequence diagrams and object diagrams. This will support the approach where the system of objects during execution is really the model. In addition, it will provide a missing link between the design of a system and the execution/debugging of the system; debugging will take place at the same conceptual level as design.

One of the authors has implemented a prototype of such a high-level debugger for a language derived from Beta, [36]. This debugger generates sequence diagrams and displays object diagrams and method activation diagrams, while the program is executed. The debugger supports the usual debugging actions such as step, step-over, breakpoints etc. For objects and method activations, you may inspect data items such as arguments and local variables.

5.7   Other Modeling Elements from UML

As mentioned above, Executable UML supports associations and activities, and it will eventually have support for composite structures and state machines. A unified language for modeling and programming should obviously also support associations, composite structures and state machines in some form. Few mainstream programming languages have direct support for these mechanisms, and it is unfortunately not obvious how to do it. There have been proposals for introducing associations, e.g. [37, 38]. State machines are usually implemented by means of design patterns [39–41] or state machines frameworks (e.g. Spring Statemachine[8]), but that is not good enough when it comes to providing feedback at the right level. A few programming languages such as Plaid [42, 43] have direct support for state machines in what is called 'State-Oriented Programming'. An early approach to this was programming with 'Modes', [44] and its counterpart in Beta [45]. Especially state machines should be supported with its well-known graphical syntax, while this is of less importance for e.g. activities as they are used in fUML. From programming languages there is a lot of experience in designing languages mechanisms for the algorithmic part of a language.

5.8   Non-executable Specifications

In some communities e.g. [2], modeling is often associated with formal specifications of software systems. As already mentioned, [2] argues for a unification of modeling and

---

[8] https://projects.spring.io/spring-statemachine/.

programming languages since a vast majority of the language mechanisms are the same. Formal specification languages do, however, contain non-executable mechanisms such as assertions and constraints.

In [7], Tony Hoare introduced the notion of abstract data types, and he used SIMULA classes to describe such abstract data types. He also introduced the notions of class invariant and pre- and post-conditions for methods to prove the correctness of such a data type. The object-oriented language Eiffel [28] is an early language with explicit support for invariants and pre- and post-conditions, and other languages support these as well.

Assertions may be used to prove the correctness of a given program but they may also be used as debugging aids to be checked during run-time. Non-executable mechanisms are thus not new to programming languages, so the vision of a unified language including modeling, programming and formal specification is definitely feasible.

Inspired by the experience with SIMULA, Nygaard and associates in the early seventies developed a language, DELTA [46] that was meant as a pure specification language. DELTA has most of the language constructs of SIMULA, but has also predicates that may enforce state changes. So in general, DELTA is not executable.

5.9 Generative Descriptions Versus Description of Properties

In programming, it is quite clear that the program is a description used to generate a program execution. And since programming languages in general do not have mechanisms for describing required or observed properties, these are described using other languages including informal diagrams.

UML contains both forms of descriptions, and as mentioned this is quite useful. However, it should be clear to the designer/programmer which mechanisms describe the program execution and which mechanisms describe the properties.

A similar issue holds for specification languages, which according to [2] have many 'programming' mechanisms. Assertions, invariants, etc. are in most languages used to describe properties that may be tested at runtime. In DELTA [46], assertions may be used to describe state changes, which implies that DELTA in general is non-executable.

6 Conclusion

As argued in [1, 2] the software development process will benefit from a unified language for specification, modeling and programming. Specification languages, (UML-like) modeling languages, and programming languages have major language elements in common.

A unified language will greatly support the transitions between modeling (and specification) and programming in an iterative process.

For this to work, a common understanding and a common terminology for modeling and programming is needed. And in this paper, we have argued that the final artifact of the software development process - the program execution - should be considered the model. This notion of model corresponds to a model as an actual representation according to Webster and others.

Programs, UML diagrams and formal specifications should all be considered descriptions of program executions. Such descriptions may be considered models in the form of abstract representations according to Webster. And as mentioned above, one may of course consider such descriptions to be models, but for modeling and programming we believe it is most useful to consider the program execution to be the model.

In general, there needs to be more focus on the program execution in the software development process. Most tools focus on diagrams and program text and less on the program execution. We have argued that a debugger based on a combination of sequence diagrams and object diagrams will support the view that the program execution is the model.

UML contains elements like object diagrams and sequence diagrams that may be used to present snapshots and properties of the program execution. This might bring the debugger to the level of UML and provide a link between design and debugging.

One of the original benefits of object-oriented programming was that the same concepts and language mechanisms could be used for analysis, design and programming instead of alternating between Structured Analysis, Structured Design and programming in Cobol and/or C. However, as pointed out in [1] the modeling communities and programming communities are diverging. This paper is a further contribution to the development of a unified language for modeling and programming.

Acknowledgements. We would like to thank the organizers (especially Klaus Havelund) for inviting us, the reviewers for constructive criticism, Hans Petter Dahle, Eyvind W. Axelsen and Arne Maus for valuable comments, and Susanne Brøndberg for proofreading.

References

1. Madsen, O.L., Møller-Pedersen, B.: A unified approach to modeling and programming. In: Petriu, Dorina C., Rouquette, N., Haugen, Ø. (eds.) MODELS 2010. LNCS, vol. 6394, pp. 1–15. Springer, Heidelberg (2010). https://doi.org/10.1007/978-3-642-16145-2_1
2. Broy, M., Havelund, K., Kumar, R.: Towards a unified view of modeling and programming. In: Margaria, T., Steffen, B. (eds.) ISoLA 2016. LNCS, vol. 9953, pp. 238–257. Springer, Cham (2016). https://doi.org/10.1007/978-3-319-47169-3_17
3. Dahl, O.-J., Myhrhaug, B., Nygaard, K.: SIMULA 67 Common Base Language (Editions 1968, 1970, 1972, 1984). Norwegian Computing Center, Oslo (1968)
4. Coad, P., Yourdon, E.: Object-Oriented Analysis. Prentice-Hall, Englewood Cliffs (1991)
5. Rumbaugh, J., et al.: Object-Oriented Modeling and Design. Prentice Hall, Englewood Cliffs (1991)
6. Booch, G.: Object-Oriented Analysis and Design with Applications. Benjamin/Cummings, Redwood City (1991)
7. Booch, G., Rumbaugh, J., Jacobson, I.: The Unified Modeling Language Reference Manual. Addison Wesley, Essex (1998)
8. OMG, UML 2.5 (2015)

9. Madsen, O.L., Møller-Pedersen, B., Nygaard, K.: Object-Oriented Programming in the BETA Programming Language. Addison Wesley, New York (1993)

10. Lethbridge, T.C., Abdelzad, V., Husseini Orabi, M., Husseini Orabi, A., Adesina, O.: Merging modeling and programming using Umple. In: Margaria, T., Steffen, B. (eds.) ISoLA 2016. LNCS, vol. 9953, pp. 187–197. Springer, Cham (2016). https://doi.org/10.1007/978-3-319-47169-3_14

11. Neubauer, P., Mayerhofer, T., Kappel, G.: Towards Integrating Modeling and Programming Languages: The Case of UML and Java (2014)

12. OMG, Semantics of a Foundational Subset for Executable UML Models (fUML), Version 1.3 (2017)

13. Ungar, D., Smith, R.B.: Self: the power of simplicity. In: Object-Oriented Programming Systems, Languages and Applications, OOPSLA 1987, Orlando, Florida, USA. ACM Press (1987)

14. Nierstrasz, O.: Ten things I hate about object-oriented programming. In: The JOT Blog (2010)

15. OMG, Precise Semantics of UML State Machines (PSSM) Version 1.0 Beta (2017)

16. OMG, Precise Semantics of UML Composite Structure (PSCSTM) - Version 1.1 (2018)

17. Naur, P.: Proof of algorithms by general snapshots. BIT **6**, 310–316 (1966)

18. ITU, Message Sequence Charts (MSC), Recommendation Z.120, Geneva (1999)

19. Ciccozzi, F., Malavolta, I., Selic, B.: Execution of UML models: a systematic review of research and practice. Softw. Syst. Model., 1–48 (2018)

20. Hoare, C.A.R.: Notes on Data Structuring, in Structured Programming. Academic Press, London (1972)

21. Kristensen, B.B., Madsen, O.L., Møller-Pedersen, B.: The when, why and why not of the BETA programming language. In: The Third ACM SIGPLAN Conference on History of Programming Languages, HOPL III, San Diego (2007)

22. Dahl, O.-J., Nygaard, K.: SIMULA–A Language for Programming and Description of Discrete Event Systems. Norwegian Computing Center, Oslo (1965)

23. Birtwistle, G.M., et al.: Simula BEGIN. Studentlitteratur/auerbach, Philadelphia (1973)

24. Madsen, O.L., Møller-Pedersen, B.: What object-oriented programming may be - and what it does not have to be. In: Gjessing, S., Nygaard, K. (eds.) ECOOP 1988. LNCS, vol. 322, pp. 1–20. Springer, Heidelberg (1988). https://doi.org/10.1007/3-540-45910-3_1

25. Dahl, O.-J., Dijkstra, E.W., Hoare, C.A.R.: Structured Programming. Academic Press, London (1972)

26. Dahl, O.-J., Nygaard, K.: SIMULA: an ALGOL-based simulation language. Commun. ACM **9**(9), 671–678 (1966)

27. Fischer, J., Møller-Pedersen, B., Prinz, A.: Modelling of systems for real. In: Proceedings of the 4th International Conference on Model-Driven Engineering and Software Development (MODELSWARD 2016), pp. 427–434. SCITEPRESS – Science and Technology Publications, Rome (2016)

28. Black, A.P.: Object-oriented programming: some history, and challenges for the next fifty years. Inf. Comput. **231**, 3–20 (2013)

29. Black, A.P., Bruce, K.B., Noble, J.: The Grace Programming Language Draft Specification Version 0.3.1303 (2013)

30. Cook, W.R., Hill, W., Canning, P.S.: Inheritance is not subtyping. In: 17th ACM SIGPLAN-SIGACT Symposium on Principles of programming Languages, POPL 1990, San Francisco, California. ACM, New York (1990)

31. Madsen, O.L., Møller-Pedersen, B.: Virtual classes–a powerful mechanism in object-oriented programming. In: Object-Oriented Programming, Systems Languages and Applications, OOPSLA 1989. ACM Press, New Orleans (1989)

32. Goldberg, A., Robson, D.: Smalltalk-80: The Language and Its Implementation. Addison-Wesley Longman Publishing Co., Inc., Boston (1983)
33. Liskov, B.H., Wing, J.M.: A behavioral notion of subtyping. ACM Trans. Program. Lang. Syst. **16**(6), 1811–1841 (1994)
34. Kristensen, B.B., Madsen, O.L., Møller-Pedersen, B., Nygaard, K.: Classification of actions or Inheritance also for methods. In: Bézivin, J., Hullot, J.-M., Cointe, P., Lieberman, H. (eds.) ECOOP 1987. LNCS, vol. 276, pp. 98–107. Springer, Heidelberg (1987). https://doi.org/10.1007/3-540-47891-4_10
35. Madsen, O.L.: Building safe concurrency abstractions. In: Agha, G., et al. (eds.) Concurrent Objects and Beyond. LNCS, vol. 8665, pp. 66–104. Springer, Heidelberg (2014). https://doi.org/10.1007/978-3-662-44471-9_4
36. Madsen, O.L.: Using object sequence diagrams for defining object semantics or just another high-level debugger. Technical report, Aarhus University (2018, in Preparation)
37. Rumbaugh, J.: Relations as semantic constructs in an object-oriented language. In: Object-Oriented Programming, Systems Languages and Applications, OOPSLA 1987. ACM Press, Orlando (1987)
38. Østerbye, K.: Associations as a Language Construct. In: TOOLS 1999, Nancy (1999)
39. Gamma, E., et al.: Design Patterns: Elements of Reusable Object-Oriented Software. Addison-Wesley Professional Computing Series. Addison-Wesley, Reading (1995)
40. Chin, B., Millstein, T.: An extensible state machine pattern for interactive applications. In: Vitek, J. (ed.) ECOOP 2008. LNCS, vol. 5142, pp. 566–591. Springer, Heidelberg (2008). https://doi.org/10.1007/978-3-540-70592-5_24
41. Andresen, K., Møller-Pedersen, B., Runde, R.K.: Combined modelling and programming support for composite states and extensible state machines. In: MODELSWARD 2015 - 3rd International Conference on Model-Driven Engineering and Software Development. SciTePress, ESEO, Angers (2015)
42. Aldrich, J., et al.: Typestate-oriented programming. In: Onward 2009, OOPSLA 2009, Orlando, Florida, USA (2009)
43. Sunshine, J., et al.: First-class state change in plaid. In: OOPSLA 2011, Portland, Oregon. ACM, USA (2011)
44. Taivalsaari, A.: Object-oriented programming with modes. J. Object Oriented Program. **6**(3), 25–32 (1993)
45. Madsen, O.L.: Towards integration of state machines and object-oriented languages. In: Technology of Object-Oriented Languages and Systems, pp. 261–274 (1999)
46. Holbæk-Hanssen, E., Håndlykken, P., Nygaard, K.: System Description and the DELTA Language. Norwegian Computing Center, Oslo (1973)

A Unified Approach for Modeling, Developing, and Assuring Critical Systems

John Hatcliff[1]([⊠]), Brian R. Larson[1], Jason Belt[1], Robby[1], and Yi Zhang[2]

[1] Kansas State University, Manhattan, USA
hatcliff@ksu.edu
[2] US Food and Drug Administration, Silver Spring, USA

Abstract. Developing and assuring safety- and security-critical real-time embedded systems is a challenging endeavor that requires many activities applied at multiple levels of abstraction. For these activities to be effective and trustworthy, they must be grounded in a common understanding of the system architecture and behavior.

We believe that these activities are best addressed in a unified framework of modeling and programming that enables developers, analysts, and auditors to freely move up and down layers of abstraction, shifting their viewpoints to suit the activities at hand, while maintaining strong traceability across the different layers and views. In this approach, the distinction between "models", "specifications", and "programs" is often blurred.

In this paper, we summarize an architecture-centric approach to critical system development and assurance that emphasizes the use of formally specified architectures as the "scaffolding" through which many different activities are organized and synchronized. We provide examples of: (a) analyses, behavioral constraints, and implementations, (b) important abstraction transitions, and (c) key traceability relationships within the framework. We discuss how these features are being used to develop systems on time and space partitioned execution and communication platforms for systems in the medical domain. We use an open-source medical device that we are developing – Patient-Controlled Analgesic (PCA) infusion pump as a concrete example.

1 Introduction

Developing and assuring safety- and security-critical real-time embedded systems is a challenging endeavor that requires many activities applied at multiple

This work is sponsored in part by US National Science Foundation Food and Drug Administration Scholar-in-Residence program (CNS 1238431, 1355778, 1446544, 1565544), the Department of Homeland Security (DHS) Science and Technology Directorate, Homeland Security Advanced Research Projects Agency (HSARPA), Cyber Security Division (DHS S&T/HSARPA/CDS) BAA HSHQDC- 14-R-B0005, the Government of Israel and the National Cyber Bureau in the Government of Israel via contract number D16PC00057.

© Springer Nature Switzerland AG 2018
T. Margaria and B. Steffen (Eds.): ISoLA 2018, LNCS 11244, pp. 225–245, 2018.
https://doi.org/10.1007/978-3-030-03418-4_14

levels of abstraction. Use cases are often developed to informally document the intended behavior of the system in terms of the user's (or broader system context's) view of the system inputs and outputs. Requirements are developed that, among other things, establish relationships and constraints between inputs and outputs. System and component interfaces and architecture are specified, and component behavioral interface specifications derived from requirements. Many forms of design-level analysis are performed including dependence analysis, hazard analysis, and control loop analysis. The results of these analyses drive specification of risk controls and functional safety concepts, which are expressed in terms of the architecture and reflected in behavioral requirements. When security is a concern, system dependencies resulting from data and control flow analysis may be used for information flow analyses to establish conformance to confidentiality and integrity objectives. Component implementations are developed, often using partitioned execution and communication services that align with the architecture. Component implementations must be integrated, and interface contracts of the respective components must be verified to be compatible at integration points. Verification is performed to establish conformance between the implementation and requirements at key points within the architecture, e.g., inputs and outputs and interfaces.

While there are other important aspects of system development and assurance, we have highlighted those above because they are strongly tied to the *system architecture* and associated interactions and constraints on interfaces captured in the architecture. Establishing the overall integrity of the development and assurance process relies on each of these aspects having a common and consistent view of the architecture and interfaces.

The centrality of architecture to development and assurance has led to many lines of work on *modeling approaches* (e.g., [4]) as well as more formal architectural definition languages [24]. While these approaches have numerous benefits for general purpose development, for our purposes they are inadequate for several reasons. Primarily, they do not provide modeling elements and patterns of interaction that align with those commonly found in embedded systems, and they typically fail to offer the structure and semantic precision needed to link the development and assurance aspects above.

In this paper, we summarize an *architecture-model-centric* approach to critical system development and assurance that emphasizes the use of formally specified architectures as the "scaffolding" through which many different activities are organized and synchronized. We provide examples of analyses relevant to embedded real-time systems, declarative interface contracts and assertions, and implementations. *A key theme of our approach is the deep integration of architectural models and programming leading to the following features:*

- component code skeletons and realization of communication between components are automatically generated from architectural models, leading to strong traceability between models and deployed executables,
- configuration of underlying platform aspects including real-time threading policies, communication quality-of-service policies, which are often specified

at the programming language level and thus difficult to understand or reason about from a system perspective, are now specified at the modeling level,
– analyses shift freely between the different abstraction levels provided by models and conventional programming languages.

To demonstrate the capabilities of our unified view of modeling and programming, we provide a walk-through of some of the development artifacts of the Open Patient Controlled Analgesic (PCA) Pump – freely-available design artifacts for a safety-critical medical device created at the behest of the US Food and Drug Administration, funded by the NSF/FDA Scholar in Residence program. The Open PCA Project website provides a hundreds of pages of realistic artifacts including user needs and use cases, requirements, architectural models, behavioral specifications, hazard analyses, and assurance cases (http://openpcapump.santoslab.org). In this paper, we provide a brief overview of the following aspects:

– using specifications in the Architecture and Analysis Definition Language (AADL) [7, 30] to define the structure of an embedded system (Sect. 4),
– illustrating simple forms of flow analyses that freely shift abstraction levels between models and code (Sect. 6),
– demonstrating how models form an abstraction of the system to support various forms of analysis–especially hazard analyses for risk management (Sect. 7)
– specifying component behavior contracts formally and declaratively that support rigorous model-based system design and integration tasks as well as systematic code-level verification of conformance to contracts (Sect. 8),
– "programming" system behaviors at the AADL model level using state-transition machines (Sect. 8.1),
– verifying that state machine behavior specifications conform to contracts (Sect. 8.2)
– illustrating the alignment of executable implementation with the architectural-centric, model-based design (Sect. 9).

2   Open PCA Pump Background

A PCA infusion pump is used to infuse pain medication into a patient's blood stream through an intravenous (IV) line (Fig. 1). Pain medication is prescribed by a licensed physician, placed into a labeled drug vial by the hospital pharmacy, and the vial is loaded into the PCA pump at the patient's bedside. By interacting with the pump's operator interface, the clinician enter parameters that indicate the prescribed drug, dose, and rates of infusion during different infusion modes. The pump infuses a prescribed basal flow rate (basal infusion mode) which may be augmented by a patient-requested bolus (this mode is activated when the patient presses a hand-held button) or a clinician-requested bolus (this mode is activated by the clinician via the device operator interface). When entering parameters, the clinician also set limits on total drug volume that can be infused

Fig. 1. Example PCA pump (Color figure online)

over a set time period (e.g., one hour) and also sets a "lock out interval" indicating a time period that must elapse between each patient bolus dose. These limits provide safeguards against overinfusion of the drug – which is a significant hazard associated with a PCA Pump.

PCA pumps, unfortunately, have been associated with a large number of adverse events [5,14]. The FDA notes [6] that while PCA pumps (and infusion pumps in general) have allowed for a greater level of control, accuracy, and precision in drug delivery—thereby reducing medication errors and contributing to improvements in patient care—infusion pumps have been associated with persistent safety problems. From 2005 through 2009, 87 infusion pump recalls were conducted by firms to address identified safety problems. Infusion pump problems have been observed across multiple manufacturers and pump types. Through analysis of pump-related adverse event reports and device recalls, the FDA has concluded that many of these problems appear to be related to deficiencies in device design and engineering [6].

2.1 Open PCA Pump Project Goals and Artifacts

The Open Patient Controlled Analgesic (PCA) Pump project [32] was created, in part, to illustrate how rigorous development processes may address some of the safety issues discussed above, as well as broader challenges in certified systems [13] and risk management in interoperable medical systems [10,26]. The Open PCA includes an interrelated set of publicly-available medical device design artifacts: requirements, architecture, formal behavioral specifications, risk analyses, implementation, and assurance case. One theme of the artifacts is the unification of architecture model, behavior specification, and behavior implementation.

The project is a joint research effort between Kansas State University researchers, US Food and Drug Administration (FDA) engineers, and industry experts. Drawing on the broad experience of the team in medical device engineering, tools for safety and security critical development, safety and security standards development, and reviewing medical safety and security, the project aims to illustrate advanced engineering and assurance technologies in the context of realistic development processes and work products used to support safety and security reviews.

The Open PCA Project currently provides the following artifacts.

Concept of Operations A concept of operations documents stakeholders, user needs, and an extensive collection of use cases addressing normal operations and response to fault conditions and other safety/security-related events. Use case diagrams capturing important device/patient/operator interactions are defined and simulated with jUCMNav [2].

Requirements Following the US Federal Aviation Administration (FAA)'s Requirements Engineering Management Handbook [23], a requirements document provides functional, safety, and security requirements, tracing of the requirements to stakeholders, goals, and use- or exception-cases, and allocation of requirements to functional architecture component(s) [21].

Architecture The system architecture is specified in the Architecture Analysis and Design Language (AADL).

Formal Behavior Specifications Specifications are attached to the architecture using the Behavior Language for Embedded Systems with Software (BLESS) [18,19], which define the behavior of each component.

Implementation Real-time thread behaviors are specified using state machines attached as BLESS annex sub-clauses and are fully implemented using KSU's Sireum Slang (a Scala programming language subset designed for analysis and verification) from which C code suitable for embedded systems is generated.

Correctness Proof Inductive proofs showing that implementations conform to corresponding specifications are stated and proved using the BLESS framework.

Risk Management Error behavior (i.e., the emergence and propagation of potential errors within the system) is modeled with AADL's error modeling annex (EMV2) [15,17] for hazard analysis and risk controls.

Assurance Case An assurance case arguing the Open PCA Pump's safety and effectiveness is specified using NOR-STA [25], which references the above artifacts.

For more information on the goals and artifacts of the Open PCA Project, see the overview paper [11] and the project web site [32].

3   AADL Background

An architecture modeling framework that: (a) provides computational model for real-time embedded systems, and (b) enables strong traceability between models and deployed systems is key to our approach for integrating modeling and programming. In this section, we provide motivation for using the AADL modeling language as our architecture modeling framework.

3.1 AADL Goals and Modeling Emphases

AADL was created in response to the high cost associated with (far too frequent) failed subsystem integration attempts due to ambiguous or incompletely documented component interfaces. AADL is now used in several industrial development settings. For example, on the System Architecture Virtual Integration (SAVI) effort [3,8], aircraft manufacturers together with subcontractors use AADL to define a precise system architecture using an "integrate then build" design approach. In this approach, important interactions are specified, interfaces are designed, and integration is verified before the internals of components are built. Once correct integration is established, contractors provide implementations that are compliant with the architecture. The virtual integration approach is an example of how a tightly integrated modeling and programming paradigm enables a shifting of development focus between different levels of abstraction to better suit development needs; integration activities are: (a) emphasized at the modeling level instead of the source code level, and (b) shifted earlier in the development process due to the ability to leverage models.

SAE International standard AS5506C [16] defines the AADL core language expressing the structure of embedded, real-time systems to precisely define components, their interfaces, and their communication. The AADL modeling elements include software components, execution platform components, and general components. The categories of software components are data, subprogram, subprogram group, thread, thread group, and process. Execution platform component categories that represent computing hardware are processor, virtual processor, memory, bus, virtual bus, and device (which is used to model sensors, actuators, or custom hardware). A system component represents an assembly of interacting application software and execution platform components. One could use system components to model everything (like SysML does), but the other component categories provide useful semantics when architecting embedded systems. An abstract component can later be refined into a specific component category, or model non-machine entities like people. A *feature* is a part of a component type definition that specifies how that component interfaces with other components in the system. In typical embedded systems, AADL *ports* are the most commonly used class of features. A port can be classified as providing either an *event port* (typically used to model interrupt signals or other notification-oriented messages without payloads), a *data port* (typically used to model shared memory between components or distributed memory services where an update to a distributed memory cell is automatically propagated to other components that declare access to the cell), or an *event data port* (typically used to model asynchronous messages with payloads as are commonly found in publish-subscribe frameworks).

The AADL standard provides a description of the intended semantics for real-time threading and port-based communication in what it terms *run-time services*. While the description is informal, it is sufficiently precise to enable a run-time system to be designed that provides threading and communication APIs that are utilized by application code. This enables a useful separation between application code (which varies across systems) and platform-oriented threading and communication infrastructure (which remains the same and can be reused across different systems). In some sense, the AADL run-time services establish a computational model of the threading and communication commonly found in real-time embedded systems. The alignment of the AADL modeling language and associated analyses with the computational model can enable development and analysis activities that might typically be carried out at the source code level to be carried out in the modeling language itself. Moreover, the AADL run-time services can provide an abstraction layer than enables realization of the services on multiple platforms – enabling applications to more easily be transitioned to different platforms.

Unfortunately, the above vision of flexibly combining modeling and programming has been impeded by the fact that the AADL run-time services are somewhat underspecified in the standard, and only limited work has been done on providing implementations of the services (and associated application code generation from AADL). The OCARINA framework [22] and the Slang framework described Sect. 9 provide some of the most complete implementations to date. Providing a more rigorous description of the AADL run-time services is part of the current AADL committee work plan. One of the purposes of the Open PCA project and the summary provided in this paper is to illustrate the integrated modeling and programming development paradigm that can be supported by a full specification and realization of the AADL run-time services.

In the specific case of the AADL run-time services for port-based communication, our overall approach builds on well-developed lines of research (e.g., [29]) in which architectural connection modeling elements have a well-defined semantics (or even multiple, selectable semantic interpretations), that provide abstractions for underlying implementations. Chosing a particular connector with a specific semantic interpretation can be seen as "programming step" in which a particular underlying implementation is chosen and integrated into the system executable during the build process.

The AADL core language can be extended with properties and annex sublanguages. Properties can be understood as named attributes (i.e., key/value pairs) that can be attached to a model element. The property declaration mechanism allows one to specify the particular categories of modeling elements to which the property can be attached. AADL provides many pre-declared properties, and allows definition of new properties through user defined property sets. Examples of pre-declared properties include thread properties (e.g., specifying dispatch protocol such as periodic, aperiodic, sporadic, etc., and various properties regarding scheduling), communication properties (e.g., capturing queuing policies on particular ports, communication latencies between components, rates on periodic communication, etc.), memory related properties (e.g., capturing sizes of queues and shared memory, latencies on memory access, etc.). User-specified property sets enable one to define labels for various implementation choices available on underlying platforms (e.g., choice of middleware realization of communication channels, configuration of middleware policies, etc.). In summary, the property mechanism allows key attributes of the underlying implementation to be exposed to enable model-level analysis and model-level selection of implementation options. In particular, many definitions of attributes and many forms of attribute selection that might conventionally be defined at the source code level can be defined at the model level – blending the notions of "modeling" and "programming".

Whereas the property mechanism enables reusable sets of attributes to be defined, AADL's Annex mechanism allows the core modeling language to be extended with sub-languages of wide-ranging syntactic and semantic complexity. Elements of annex models can be introduced in AADL's textual core language models using delimiter syntax of the form `annex MyAnnex {** ... **};`. Annex sublanguages can be standardized via the SAE standards process. Standardized annexes that are relevant to the work described in this paper are described below.

- The Behavior Annex (BA) extends AADL with the ability of defining component behavior via state machines that contain states, state variables and (guarded) state-transitions with associated actions written in a simple imperative language.
- The *Error Model* Annex extends the AADL core language with error tokens and associated propagation descriptions for specifying different types of faults, fault behavior of individual system components, fault propagation affecting related components in terms of peer to peer interactions and deployment relationship between software components and their execution platform, and aggregation of fault behavior and propagation in terms of the component hierarchy.
- The *Code Generation* Annex, defines a mapping between the AADL core language and programming languages. It specifies, for each AADL component type, how to map it into executable code. As the AADL language targets safety-critical systems, the annex focuses on defining such a mapping for programming languages that are typically used to implement such systems.

Annexes can also be defined for dedicated specification languages for particular analysis and verification approaches. For example, we use the annex mechanism to For example, we use the annex mechanism to in our work to provide a behavioral interface specification language (BISL) [12] for AADL called BLESS [19]. BLESS provides component behavioral specifications that can be analyzed by formal deduction tools. BLESS, inspired from BA, improves and extends the state-transition formalism and, more importantly, introduces assertions that can be inserted into state-transitions. BLESS also provides a component interface contract language that can be used to phrase assume-guarantee reasoning for AADL components and systems. BLESS's verification condition generation framework enables one to verify that component implementations captured in BLESS's state transition system language conform to BLESS assertions and contracts, and that BLESS interface contracts of composed components are compatible.

Regarding the theme of blending modeling and programming, BLESS state-transition systems can be seen as "programs" at the AADL level from which lower-level conventional "source code" can be automatically generated. Alternatively, they can be viewed as specifications to which manually developed source code should comply. In a development workflow, component interface specifications can first be captured in BLESS at the AADL model level and then translated down to source-code level interface specifications.

4   Open PCA Pump Architecture Overview

Figure 2 depicts the top-level structure of the Open PCA Pump's functional architecture. The full architecture includes 20+ AADL components, with the additional components not shown here being nested in one or more layers inside the top-level components. Figure 2 illustrates the architecture using AADL's graphical view. In contrast to other popular UML-based modeling languages, AADL also has textual view of the architecture that is somewhat similar in syntactic appearance and abstraction level to the CORBA Interface Definition Language (IDL).[1] The emphasis of the AADL textual models in AADL tooling and work flows aids in the blending of modeling and programming (which is also centered around textual representations).

The architecture shown in Fig. 2 has some physical components (power bus, internal bus, processor, and memory), but it is mostly a functional architecture having four subsystems: safety, operation, power, and fluid.

There is an intuitive connection to programming conveyed by the graphical view in Fig. 2: (a) the software and system components denoted by the rounded ovals have interfaces denoted by the triangle icons (AADL ports), and (b) the realization of the behavior of the components includes programmed interactions through the interfaces of the components. The lines connecting AADL ports (AADL connections) represent communication pathways represented by reusable, application independent communication mechanisms such as real-time event/message services or middleware. Solid dark triangles represent data ports, white triangles represent event ports, while triangles with a white outline with dark fill represent event ports with data payloads. In AADL's textual representation, these ports have declared data types (similar in style to the use of data types in a programming language), and the AADL property mechanism is used to express attributes of the communication (e.g., such as the rate of periodic communication).

For our research emphasis on assurance, the safety subsystem of Fig. 2 is most important. The design of the safety subsystem is based on principles for a

---

[1] Note that the breadth of AADL descriptions is much greater than CORBA IDL's.

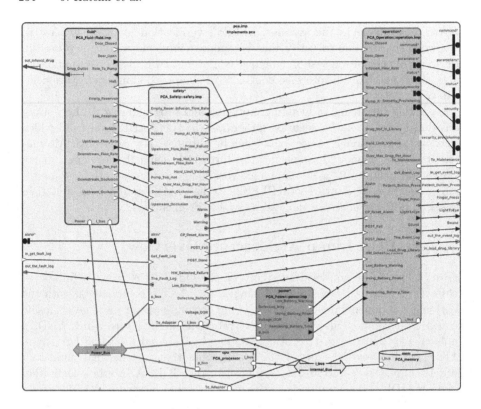

Fig. 2. Open PCA pump functional architecture

medical device safety architecture presented in [20]. It independently monitors other subsystems for unsafe conditions and malfunctions. For example, the safety subsystem has a hardware error detector and an error logger that will detect and record faults that may prevent the system from operating normally. The independence of the safety subsystem from the rest of the system is supported by an independent safety core processor and separated safety buses, which allows the subsystem to execute even when the main processor is inoperative. A LED is illuminated to indicate an error that cannot otherwise be displayed.

The fluid subsystem includes the components that hold, move, or measure the liquid drug. The thick blue line indicates the path of the drug from reservoir to patient.

The operation subsystem decisions regarding pumping, but can be overridden by the safety subsystem. It contains two devices: a patient button requesting an additional bolus of pain medication, and a scanner for reading the patient's wristband, clinician badge, and drug vial label. The scanner could be optical, reading bar or QR codes, or RFID.

A security subsystem (not shown) provides functionality to authenticate the patient, clinician, and drug to ensure that the right drug is infused into the right patient, and to ensure that the pump is attended by a trained, authorized clinician. A control panel (not shown) provides the user interface on the PCA pump itself; another user interface could be a nurses' station connected via a network.

The power subsystem conditions DC voltage from either mains source or battery backup, and provides information and warnings about the power supply. Though comparatively simple, the power subsystem requires careful engineering for dependable power supply and ordering during power-on.

In the sections that follow we illustrate how this architecture description forms a scaffolding for integrating different forms of analysis, behavioral specification, and development of component implementations.

5   Real Time Configuration

AADL provides predefined properties that can be used to specify the real time configuration of the underlying runtime environment. Schedulability, timing and resource utilization analysis can then be performed using existing tools like FAS-TAR or Cheddar. The following specification shows some of these properties applied to an AADL thread contained in the PCA Pump model.

```
1   thread Patient_Bolus_Checker
2     features
3       Minimum_Time_Between_Bolus: in data port ICE_Types::Minute
4         {BLESS::Assertion => "<<:=MINIMUM_TIME_BETWEEN_BOLUS>>";};
5       Patient_Button_Request: in event port;
6       Patient_Request_Not_Too_Soon: out event port
7         {BLESS::Assertion => "<<PATIENT_REQUEST_NOT_TOO_SOON(now)>>";};
8       Patient_Request_Too_Soon: out event port
9         {BLESS::Assertion => "<<PATIENT_REQUEST_TOO_SOON(now)>>";};
10    properties
11      Thread_Properties::Dispatch_Protocol => Sporadic;
12      Timing_Properties::Compute_Execution_Time => 1 ms .. 2 ms;
13      Timing_Properties::Period => 5 ms;
14      Timing_Properties::Deadline => 10 ms;
15  end Patient_Bolus_Checker;
```

The **Period** property specifies, for sporadic threads, the minimum interval between successive dispatches. **Compute_Execution_Time** specifies the amount of time a thread will execute after it has been dispatched. **Deadline** specifies the maximum amount of time allowed between a thread dispatch and the time that thread begins waiting for another dispatch.

6   Flows

If modeling and programming are to be tightly integrated, then analysis of models and programs, as well as reporting and visualizations of analysis results, should be tightly integrated. With strong alignment between system architecture models and system realizations in our approach, several forms of analysis can be seamlessly shifted between architecture artifacts and code artifacts, where the architecture artifacts and associated analysis information can be seen as an abstraction of the code-level artifacts and associate system realization.

One example of such an analysis is information flow analysis, which is typically derived from data and control dependence information. This analysis information supports multiple concerns such as security (can one ensure that information that a component's secret information does not flow to unauthorized clients). Other examples include impact analysis (if the implementation of a particular feature of the system changes, what other portions of the system might be affected by the change – this information may be used to scope re-certification efforts or to optimize regression testing), and latency analysis (capturing worse case time delays involved in communicating information from one part of the system to another).

At the model level, AADL provides a *flow* construct to represent intracomponent flows (e.g., information flowing into component port $P1$ flows out through ports $P2$ and $P3$) as well as "end-to-end" flows through multiple components and connections. Flows can be used to model both information flows as well as physical flows (such as the drug flow throughout the PCA pump). In the Open PCA Pump artifacts, information flows model access to maintenance functions solely through the physical maintenance jack (behind a locked door holding the drug reservoir) and restrictions on key-pair generation for security provisioning through the maintenance jack. Figure 3 shows a physical flow of drug through the fluid subsystem with thick blue lines.

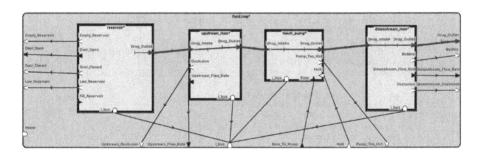

Fig. 3. Fluid subsystem

Model-level information flows can be used as specifications, and code-level tools are used ensure that all code-level information flows conform to those specifications. Alternatively, code-level information flow analysis can automatically discover flows and present the results in terms model-level flows. Our research efforts in these directions build off of our previous work on analysis and flow contracts for SPARK Ada [1,31] and data/control dependence for Java [28], including ensuring non-interference properties of dynamically created threads in the presence of heap-allocated data [27].

7   Error Modeling

Hazard analysis is a key activity in the development of most safety critical systems. A hazard is an intrinsic property or condition that has the potential to cause harm or damage. Example hazards in the PCA Pump include over-infusion of an opioid and infusion of air bubbles within the opioid. Hazard identification is the process of recognizing that a hazard exists and defining its characteristics, including the specific harm that might result. Hazard analysis examines possible component failures as well data flow, control flow, and other system dependencies in an effort to determine possible root causes. The system design is then modified to mitigate hazards by removing root causes, or detecting states related to root causes and taking corrective action.

Existing industry practice typically performs hazard analysis informally and records the results in text-based documents or spreadsheets. However, since AADL enables a formal architecture description of the system, many aspects of hazard analysis can be carried out directly within the model – including identifying root causes, identifying paths along which errors resulting from root causes may propagate, and identifying system interactions with the environment that potentially cause harm. Due to the alignment of implementations with models, this enables much stronger traceability from implementations to hazard analysis artifacts than conventional approaches.

The Error Modeling Annex (version 2) of AADL (EMV2) provides model annotations and tool support for model-based hazard analysis (see [17] for an illustration of the different types of activities and analysis supported by EMV2). Error tokens, classified according to error types, are abstractions of error conditions that model the effects of faults within a system. Connecting to well-known concepts from the programming language community, error tokens and associated propagation rules form an abstract interpretation of the fault-related behaviors of a system. The EMV2 standard pre-declares many useful error types, but allows users to define their own. The listing below shows a few of the error types defined for Open PCA Pump.

```
annex EMV2 {**
  error types
      --the actual drug flow differs from prescribed, may injure patient
    DrugFlowError : type;
      --the flow rate may be incorrect, but it's zero, so it's safe
    DrugStopped : type extends DrugFlowError;
      --the flow rate may be incorrect, and possibly harmful
    DrugRateError : type extends DrugFlowError;
      --when someone other than the patient presses the patient button
    ThirdPartyPress : type;
    AlarmError : type;    --the class of alarm errors
    FalseAlarm : type extends AlarmError;    --alarm erroneously sounded
    MissedAlarm : type extends AlarmError;    --alarm missed
  . . .
```

The principal cause of patient harm is improper volume of drug infusion, modeled as `DrugFlowError`, which is further subdivided into `DrugStopped` for loss of therapy, and `DrugRateError` for continued infusion, but at a wrong rate. An `AlarmError` could be a `FalseAlarm` or a `MissedAlarm`.

Of particular concern for PCA pumps is someone other than the patient pressing the bolus request button. This is modeled as `ThirdPartyPress`.

EMV2 annex libraries can also define error state machines, which can be referenced by EMV2 annex subclauses of particular components. The `FailStop` error state machine (AADL source not shown) referenced in the next listing has two states, `working` and `failed`, and a single error event `fail` which causes transition from `working` to `failed`.

The patient button listing below provides a simple example of error modeling. It uses the `FailStop` error state machine, and assigns an (estimated) failure rate to the `fail` error event. When in the `failed` state no bolus requests are transmitted resulting in the propagation of a `EarlyServiceTermination` error. Otherwise, a `ThirdPartyPress` error on `Button_Press` is propagated through `Request_Bolus`. Note, we cannot *know* whether a button press is by the patient or not, but we can model the existence of such errors, which can then be mitigated by enforcing a minimum time between boluses.

```
device patient_button
  features
    Request_Bolus: out event port; --patient has pressed the button
                                    --requesting a bolus
    Button_Press: in event port; --physically depressing the button
end patient_button;

device implementation patient_button.imp
  annex EMV2 --button passes along third-party presses
  {**
  use types ErrorLibrary, PCA_Error_Model;
  use behavior PCA_Error_Model::FailStop;
  error propagations
    --button passes along third-party presses
    Button_Press: in propagation {ThirdPartyPress};
    --button may also be broken
   Request_Bolus: out propagation {EarlyServiceTermination,ThirdPartyPress};
  flows
    --no output when button fails
    fail_silent: error source Request_Bolus{EarlyServiceTermination}
      when failed;
    --flow through errors
    third_party:  error path Button_Press{ThirdPartyPress}->Request_Bolus;
  end propagations;
  properties
  EMV2::OccurrenceDistribution => PCA_Properties::PatientButtonFailureRate
      applies to fail;
  **}; --end of EMV2
end patient_button.imp;
```

Many analyses can be performed using EMV2 for risk analysis such as failure modes and effects analysis (FMEA), fault-tree analysis (FTA), and reliability block diagram (RBD). In particular, because EMV2 annotations are including directly in the architecture model, the automation of various analysis and reporting tasks can be improved.

8   BLESS Specification, Behavior, and Proof

Development of high assurance systems benefits from being able to formally specify desired system and component behaviors. When modeling and programming are integrated, formal component interface specifications should be applicable at both the model and code levels.

BLESS was created to be an annex sublanguage for AADL to specify, implement, and verify behavior. Behavior is declaratively specified by BLESS::Assertion properties attached to ports to express what is assumed to be true about events and/or data arriving on in (incoming) ports, or what is guaranteed to be true about events and/or data leaving from out (outgoing) ports. Additionally, components may have an invariant property. The combination of port assertions and an invariant (if any) constitute a component's specification.

The Patient_Bolus_Checker thread in the following listing enforces a minimum time between boluses. The minimum time value is communicated to the pump along with the drug prescription and helps to prevent the patient from getting too much painkiller. The Patient_Bolus_Checker determines if a patient pushes the bolus request button too soon after the previous bolus was administered.

```
1  thread Patient_Bolus_Checker
2    features
3      Minimum_Time_Between_Bolus: in data port ICE_Types::Minute
4        {BLESS::Assertion => "<<:=MINIMUM_TIME_BETWEEN_BOLUS>>";};
5      Patient_Button_Request: in event port;
6      Patient_Request_Not_Too_Soon: out event port
7        {BLESS::Assertion => "<<PATIENT_REQUEST_NOT_TOO_SOON(now)>>";};
8      Patient_Request_Too_Soon: out event port
9        {BLESS::Assertion => "<<PATIENT_REQUEST_TOO_SOON(now)>>";};
10 end Patient_Bolus_Checker;
```

A BLESS::Assertion property is just a string enclosed within double angle brackets, << >>. BLESS assertions themselves are temporal logic formulas that extend first-order predicates with simple temporal operators that determine when a predicate should be evaluated. p@t means predicate p evaluated at time t. Line 4 says that the value received on the Minimum_Time_Between_Bolus is MINIMUM_TIME_BETWEEN_BOLUS, a 'ghost' variable used to represent the true value of the minimum time between boluses. Line 7 says that when an event is emitted from port Patient_Request_Not_Too_Soon, then the formula PATIENT_REQUEST_NOT_TOO_SOON(now) will be true.

PATIENT_REQUEST_NOT_TOO_SOON is the label of an assertion with a single parameter now that is the current instant, and can be thought of as the timestamp taken when the event is emitted.

```
<<PATIENT_REQUEST_NOT_TOO_SOON:x:
  Patient_Button_Request@x and not
  (exists t:time in x-MINIMUM_TIME_BETWEEN_BOLUS,,x
    that Patient_Request_Not_Too_Soon@t)>>
```

Here, x is a formal parameter, replaced by the actual parameter now. It says that the patient pressed the bolus request button, and there has not been a patient bolus administered in the open interval (,,) between now and now - MINIMUM_TIME_BETWEEN_BOLUS.

In our current research, we are developing a framework for translating BLESS specification down to code-level contracts in Slang. This integrated framework tracks verification conditions associated with these specifications, and enables verification conditions to be discharged either in model-level activities or code-level activities.

8.1   BLESS Behaviors

In our approach, behaviors of components can be expressed either in model-oriented state machine notations or programmed in conventional style using Slang (see Sect. 9).

The listing below illustrates the use of the BLESS state transition notation to provide the implementation of the `Patient_Bolus_Checker.imp` thread:

```
1   thread implementation Patient_Bolus_Checker.imp
2     annex BLESS
3     {**
4     invariant <<LPB()>>
5     variables
6       last_patient_bolus: time:=0
7         <<LPB: :Patient_Request_Not_Too_Soon@last_patient_bolus and
8           not (exists t:time in last_patient_bolus,,now
9             that Patient_Request_Not_Too_Soon@t)>>;
10    states
11      start: initial state
12        <<last_patient_bolus=0 and now=0 and LPB()>>;
13      run: complete state
14        <<LPB()>>;
15      check_last_bolus_time: state
16        <<LPB() and Patient_Button_Request@now>>;
17      done: final state;
18    transitions
19      go: start-[ ]-> run{};
20      button: run -[on dispatch Patient_Button_Request]->
21              check_last_bolus_time{};
22      nottoosoon: check_last_bolus_time -[(now-Minimum_Time_Between_Bolus?)
23              > last_patient_bolus]-> run
24      { <<LPB() and Patient_Button_Request@now and
25          (now-MINIMUM_TIME_BETWEEN_BOLUS@now) > last_patient_bolus>>
26        Patient_Request_Not_Too_Soon!
27        ; <<Patient_Request_Not_Too_Soon@now>>
28        last_patient_bolus:=now
29        <<Patient_Request_Not_Too_Soon@now and last_patient_bolus=now>>};
30      toosoon: check_last_bolus_time -[(now-Minimum_Time_Between_Bolus?)
31              <= last_patient_bolus]-> run
32      { Patient_Request_Too_Soon! };
33      quit: run-[on dispatch stop]->done{};
34    **};
35  end Patient_Bolus_Checker.imp;
```

Line 4 says that the predicate `LPB()` is invariant (always true), and defined on lines 7–9 giving the meaning of persistent variable `last_patient_bolus` as the timestamp of the most recent, delivered patient bolus. There are four states (lines 10–17) illustrating the different categories of AADL Behavior Annex states. (1) **initial** exactly one state in which thread behavior starts (no incoming transitions); (2) **complete** suspend until next dispatch; (3) **execution** (no label) transitory state; (4) **final** has no outgoing transitions. States may have assertions indicating what is true about the system when in that state.

Transitions have labels (l), source (s) and destination (d) states, condition (c) that allows the transition, and an action (a) performed before entering the destination state: `l:s-[c]->d{a};` Transitions leaving complete states have dispatch conditions. Transitions leaving initial and execution states have boolean expressions for conditions. The only actions in this example are port output (!), assignment (:=), and sequential composition (;). Assertions may be interspersed within actions to be proof outlines.

8.2   BLESS Verification

BLESS behaviors are formally verified to conform to their specifications by transforming proof outlines into inductive proofs.

Proofs that behavior meets specification are created by generating verification conditions (VCs), and then solving them by transforming them into axioms by repeated application of human-selected tactics. The verification condition for a subprogram is that, if the subprogram is invoked with a precondition that holds, then the subprogram will terminate with its postcondition holding. BLESS thread behaviors require many more VCs:

- the assertion of each complete state must imply the thread invariant;
- the assertion of each execution state must imply the disjunction of conditions or transition leaving that state; and,
- a verification condition for each transition.

One VC is generated for each transition. If the transition lacks an action, the VC asks whether the conjunction of the source state's assertion and the transition condition implies the destination state's assertion. Otherwise, the VC has the conjunction of the source state's assertion and the transition condition as the precondition for the action, and the destination state's assertion as the postcondition (a.k.a., Hoare Triple).

Compound components (those that have subcomponents) are also specified by assertions on their features (usually ports), and a component invariant. Connections between subcomponents and between subcomponents and the containing component's features (ports) have assume-guarantee VCs. The assertion property of an out port must imply the assertion property of any in port to which it is connected. Most assume-guarantee VCs are of the form $P \to P$, and thus are axiomatically solved.

Invariants of compound components also get VCs; they must be implied by the disjunction of their subcomponents' invariants.

The procedure for solving VCs is too involved for inclusion here, but relies on human selection of tactics to transform VCs into axioms. Generally, the tactics are selected interactively, but are recorded as a tactic script that can invoked with a file-selection pop-up.

9   Code Generation and Slang

Slang is a subset of Scala under development at KSU. Slang has its own means of formal verification separate from BLESS. Proved correct BLESS behaviors are translated into Slang for simulation, further verification, and code generation into deployment languages like C and C++. Less safety-critical threads can be programmed directly in Slang – though outside of the AADL architecture using source code property references. KSU is working with Adventium Labs on the ISOSCELES platform for security-robust platforms for medical devices [9]. Part of our effort is code generation from the unification of model and program from AADL+BLESS to executable code on ISOSCELES. Part of this effort implemented the standard AADL runtime services on ISOSCELES to match the semantics for component communication defined by the AADL standard.

9.1   Implementing the Component "Business Logic"

In the Slang Embedded development environment, the developer programs behaviors of AADL- derived threads. Alternatively, Slang thread implementations can be auto-generated from AADL- level **BLESS** specifications. The example below shows a portion of the Slang code that was generated from the **BLESS** transition system from Sect. 8.1.

```
1   var currentState : CompleteState.Type = CompleteState.start
2   var last_patient_bolus : Art.Time = z"0"
3
4   def Compute_Entrypoint(): Unit = {
5     currentState match {
6       case CompleteState.start =>
7       case CompleteState.run =>
8         if (api.getPatient_Button_Request().nonEmpty) { do_button() }
9         ...
10    }
11  }
12
13  def do_button(): Unit = {
14    executionState_check_last_bolus_time()
15  }
16
17  def executionState_check_last_bolus_time (): Unit = {
18    val t1 = Conversions.toArtTime(api.getMinimum_Time_Between_Bolus())
19    if (Art.time()-t1 > last_patient_bolus) { do_nottoosoon() }
20    else if (Art.time()-t1 <= last_patient_bolus) { do_toosoon() }
21  }
22
23  def do_nottoosoon(): Unit = {
24    api.sendPatient_Request_Not_Too_Soon()
25    last_patient_bolus = Art.time()
26    currentState = CompleteState.run
27  }
28
29  def do_toosoon(): Unit = {
30    api.sendPatient_Request_Too_Soon()
31    currentState = CompleteState.run
32  }
```

On line 8, it uses the custom API that was generated for `Patient_Bolus_Checker.imp` to check if an event arrived on the `Patient_Button_Request` event port. The current data value on the `Minimum_Time_Between_Bolus` data port is retrieved on line 20 in order to determine if the required amount of time has elapsed since the last `Patient_Button_Request` event had occurred. It then sends out the appropriate event on lines 26 or 32.

10   Conclusion

In this paper, we have illustrated an approach for deeply integrating modeling and programming. Some of the key enablers of our approach are a specific domain (embedded systems) in which a specific computation model (real-time threads with port-based communication) – around which architectural and computational structures can be designed that can be central to both modeling and programming. With this approach, there is very strong traceability between models, source code, and deployed executables, with architectural models forming abstractions around which many analysis and configuration activities can be performed.

In our ongoing research, the biggest challenge we are working on is dependable code generation so that the verification of the model applies also to the deployed system. Towards this end, we are developing Slang, both as an intermediate form for translating BLESS programs into object code, and as a means of directly programming a thread's business logic in Slang. Performing formal verification of Slang generated from BLESS provides a double formal verification.

In partnership with Adventium Labs on the ISOSCELES project, we are developing code generation down to native code that can be deployed in real medical devices.

The Open PCA Pump artifacts have helped to achieve the vision of formally-verified fusion of model and programming, and to provide means to communicate this vision.

It is important to note that the focus of Sects. 8.1, 8.2 and 9 is on software and its verification (aligning with the overall emphasis on "programming"). However, overall system assurance also relies on the correctness of both software and hardware elements. One of the reasons that AADL includes both hardware and software modeling elements is to address the full spectrum of system modeling and assurance. While behavior contracts can be used in some cases to summarize the behavior of hardware elements (e.g., sensors and actuators) invoked by software, further work is necessary to provide a deeper integration of hardware assurance within the paradigm that we have described.

References

1. Amtoft, T., et al.: A certificate infrastructure for machine-checked proofs of conditional information flow. In: Degano, P., Guttman, J.D. (eds.) POST 2012. LNCS, vol. 7215, pp. 369–389. Springer, Heidelberg (2012). https://doi.org/10.1007/978-3-642-28641-4_20
2. Amyot, D.: jUCMNav - Eclipse Plugin for the User Requirements Notation (2018). http://jucmnav.softwareengineering.ca/foswiki/ProjetSEG/WebHome
3. AVSI: System Architecture Virtual Integration (SAVI) Initiative (2012). https://wiki.sei.cmu.edu/aadl/index.php/Projects_and_Initiatives#AVSI_SAVI
4. Booch, G., Rumbaugh, J., Jacobson, I.: The Unified Modeling Language User Guide, 2nd edn. Addison-Wesley, Boston (2005)
5. Joint Commission: Preventing patient-controlled analgesia overdose. Joint Commission Perspectives on Patient Safety, p. 11, October 2005
6. US FDA Infusion Pump Improvement Initiative, April 2010
7. Feiler, P., Gluch, D.: Model-based engineering with AADL. In: An Introduction to the SAE Architecture Analysis and Design Language. Addison-Wesley, Boston (2013)

8. Feiler, P.H., Hansson, J., de Niz, D., Wrage, L.: System architecture virtual integration: an industrial case study. Technical Report CMU/SEI-2009-TR-017, CMU (2009)
9. Harp, S., Carpenter, T., Hatcliff, J.: A reference architecture for secure medical devices. Biomed. Instrum. Technol., September 2018. Association for the Advancement of Medical Instrumentation (AAMI)
10. Hatcliff, J., Vasserman, E.Y., Carpenter, T., Whillock, R.: Challenges of distributed risk management for medical application platforms. In: 2018 IEEE Symposium on Product Compliance Engineering (ISPCE), pp. 1–14, May 2018
11. Hatcliff, J., Larson, B., Carpenter, T., Jones, P., Zhang, Y., Jorgens, J.: The open PCA pump project: an exemplar open source medical device as a community resource. In: Proceedings of the 2018 Medical Cyber-Physical Systems (MedCPS) Workshop (2018)
12. Hatcliff, J., Leavens, G.T., Leino, K.R.M., Müller, P., Parkinson, M.: Behavioral interface specification languages. ACM Comput. Surv. **44**(3), 16:1–16:58 (2012)
13. Hatcliff, J., Wassyng, A., Kelly, T., Comar, C., Jones, P.L.: Certifiably safe software-dependent systems: challenges and directions. In: Proceedings of the on Future of Software Engineering (ICSE FOSE), pp. 182–200 (2014)
14. Hicks, R.W., Sikirica, V., Nelson, W., Schein, J.R., Cousins, D.D.: Medication errors involving patient-controlled analgesia. Am. J. Health-Syst. Pharm. **65**(5), 429–440 (2008)
15. SAE International: SAE AS5506/1, AADL Annex E: Error Model Annex. SAE International (2015). http://www.sae.org
16. SAE International: SAE AS5506 Rev. C Architecture Analysis and Design Language (AADL). SAE International (2017). http://www.sae.org
17. Larson, B., Hatcliff, J., Fowler, K., Delange, J.: Illustrating the AADL error modeling annex (v.2) using a simple safety-critical medical device. In: Proceedings of the 2013 ACM SIGAda Annual Conference on High Integrity Language Technology, HILT 2013, pp. 65–84. ACM, New York (2013)
18. Larson, B.: Behavior language for embedded systems with software (BLESS). http://bless.santoslab.org
19. Larson, B.R., Chalin, P., Hatcliff, J.: BLESS: formal specification and verification of behaviors for embedded systems with software. In: Brat, G., Rungta, N., Venet, A. (eds.) NFM 2013. LNCS, vol. 7871, pp. 276–290. Springer, Heidelberg (2013). https://doi.org/10.1007/978-3-642-38088-4_19
20. Larson, B., Jones, P., Zhang, Y., Hatcliff, J.: Principles and benefits of explicitly designed medical device safety architecture. Biomed. Instrum. Technol., September 2018. Association for the Advancement of Medical Instrumentation (AAMI)
21. Larson, B.R., Hatcliff, J., Chalin, P.: Open source patient-controlled analgesic pump requirements documentation. In: Proceedings of the 5th International Workshop on Software Engineering in Health Care, pp. 28–34. IEEE, Piscataway (2013)
22. Lasnier, G., Zalila, B., Pautet, L., Hugues, J.: OCARINA: An environment for AADL models analysis and automatic code generation for high integrity applications. In: Kordon, F., Kermarrec, Y. (eds.) Ada-Europe 2009. LNCS, vol. 5570, pp. 237–250. Springer, Heidelberg (2009). https://doi.org/10.1007/978-3-642-01924-1_17
23. Lempia, D., Miller, S.: Requirement engineering management handbook. Technical Report DOT/FAA/AR-08/32, US Federal Aviation Administration (2009)
24. Medvidovic, N., Taylor, R.N.: A classification and comparison framework for software architecture description languages. IEEE Trans. Softw. Eng. **26**(1), 70–93 (2000)

25. Gdansk University of Technology: NOR-STA: Support for achieving and assessing conformance to norms and standards (2018). http://www.nor-sta.eu/en

26. Procter, S., Hatcliff, J.: An architecturally-integrated, systems-based hazard analysis for medical applications. In: 2014 Twelfth ACM/IEEE International Conference on Formal Methods and Models for Codesign (MEMOCODE), pp. 124–133. IEEE (2014)

27. Ranganath, V.P., Hatcliff, J.: Pruning interference and ready dependence for slicing concurrent java programs. In: Duesterwald, E. (ed.) CC 2004. LNCS, vol. 2985, pp. 39–56. Springer, Heidelberg (2004). https://doi.org/10.1007/978-3-540-24723-4_4

28. Ranganath, V.P., Hatcliff, J.: Slicing concurrent Java programs using Indus and Kaveri. Int. J. Softw. Tools Technol. Transf. **9**(5), 489–504 (2007)

29. Ray, A., Cleaveland, R.: Architectural interaction diagrams: Aids for system modeling. In: Proceedings of the 25th International Conference on Software Engineering, ICSE 2003, pp. 396–406 (2003)

30. SAE International: SAE AS5506/2. Architecture Analysis & Design Language (AADL) Annex, vol. 2 (2011)

31. Thiagarajan, H., Hatcliff, J., Belt, J., Robby, R.: Bakar Alir: supporting developers in construction of information flow contracts in SPARK. In: 2012 IEEE 12th International Working Conference on Source Code Analysis and Manipulation, pp. 132–137 (2012)

32. Kansas State University: Open PCA pump project (2018). http://openpcapump.santoslab.org

Towards Interactive Compilation Models

Steven Smyth[(⊠)], Alexander Schulz-Rosengarten, and Reinhard von Hanxleden

Real-Time and Embedded Systems Group, Department of Computer Science,
Christian-Albrechts-Universität zu Kiel, Olshausenstr. 40, 24118 Kiel, Germany
{ssm,als,rvh}@informatik.uni-kiel.de,
www.informatik.uni-kiel.de/rtsys/

Abstract. A chain of model-to-model transformations prescribes a particular work process, while executing such a chain generates a concrete instance of this process. Modeling the entire development process itself on a meta-model level extends the possibilities of the model-based approach to guide the developer. Besides refining tools for model creation, this kind of meta-modeling also facilitates debugging, optimization, and prototyping of new compilations. A compiler is such a process system. In this paper, we share the experiences gathered while we worked on the model-based reference compiler of the KIELER SCCharts project and ideas towards a unified view on similar prescribed processes.

1 Introduction

In our previous publications towards a unified view of modeling and programming [9, 13] we focused on the program/model that should be compiled. Using the model-based approach, we showed how a model-based compiler can transform a program to the desired target platform step-by-step while preserving the intermediate results. The approach, named SLIC for Single-Pass Language-Driven Incremental Compilation, was used to create the compiler for the synchronous language SCCharts [18].

While working on the model-based compiler, we since recognized that providing meaningful guidance for and resources to the developer does not solely depend on the artefact that should be compiled, but also on the process which performs the transformations. Instead of using a compiler that is particularly developed for a specific use case, we built upon the experiences we gained during the development of the SLIC approach to model the entire compilation process. Modeling the process provides us with new possibilities to aid the developer in their pursuit to create complex products, such as (1) arbitrary annotated intermediate models, and (2) the ability to change the compilation model at any time. We will demonstrate our generic framework in the following sections. For more concrete information on the compiler implementation and two technical use cases, we refer the interested reader to the associated technical report [15].

To illustrate the process and to continue the story told previously [9, 13], we use the Kiel Integrated Environment for Layout Eclipse Rich Client (KIELER)[1]

---

[1] http://rtsys.informatik.uni-kiel.de/kieler

© Springer Nature Switzerland AG 2018
T. Margaria and B. Steffen (Eds.): ISoLA 2018, LNCS 11244, pp. 246–260, 2018.
https://doi.org/10.1007/978-3-030-03418-4_15

SCCharts language implementation as running example. KIELER is an academic open-source project that serves as a proof-of-concept platform. However, the approach presented here is not restricted to the SCCharts compiler, SCCharts, or KIELER, since every system of consecutive processes may be modeled and executed in a similar way. For example, our reference implementation within the KIELER project also includes compilers for languages such as C, Esterel, and various domain-specific languages as well as non-compilation tasks such as simulation of compiled artefacts.

Contributions and Outline

We here propose *process systems* that lift the concept of modeling such that models are not only used to specify some system under development, but also to specify *how* the modeling tool synthesizes an artefact that can be simulated and, finally, deployed. This approach not only gives the modeler full control over what the modeling tool should do, but also allows to inspect what it actually does for a specific functional model, along each step of the synthesis process. We introduce process systems in Sect. 2, beginning with an exemplary, abstract user story on classical programming and modeling. Section 3 takes a more detailed view of process system models, illustrated with our exemplary realization in the KIELER project. This demonstration serves as an example for similar process system modeling and is not restricted to the work done within KIELER. Further technical use cases can be inspected elsewhere [15]. Subsequent to related work in Sect. 4 we conclude in Sect. 5.

2   A Generic User Story

In this section we take a closer look at three alternative development processes sketched in Fig. 1. We assume that the developer uses an Integrated Development Environment (IDE) to work on a particular software project. Usually, the build process and/or project has to be configured by either the developer themselves or by another build expert Typically, the developer works directly on the artefact in question. However, the work foci differ.

2.1   Programming vs. Modeling

Figure 1a gives an abstract view on a **classical programming** development process, which is fairly straightforward. The IDE might be the Eclipse CDT[2]. The developer often has to be a programming expert and generally also configures the build process. While they usually work on one file at a time, they must keep an eye on the whole project, which is usually a collection of files, because it might influence the compilation. When they complete a development step, they issue a compilation command. An embedded (often external) compiler then compiles the source files to binary code that can be executed or embedded elsewhere if

---

[2] https://www.eclipse.org/cdt

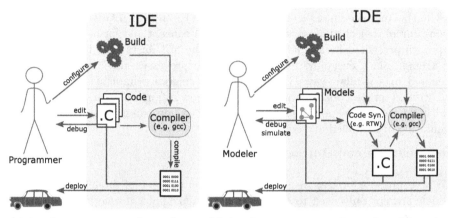

(a) An abstract view on classical programming development process

(b) An abstract view on classical modeling development process

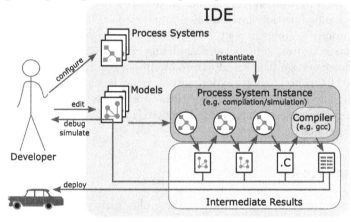

(c) Development story with interactive process system instances

Fig. 1. Three alternative development processes

the source code is error free. Errors and warnings are fed back to the editor inside the IDE. They mark the erroneous line and give more or less processed information about the actual error or warning.

The **classical modeling** work-flow (Fig. 1b) looks actually quite similar. The modeler has to configure their project and can explore the project's files. Instead of editing a text file, the modeler usually works on a domain-specific, often graphical, model. The IDE, which may be something like Eclipse or a classical modeling tool, such as Matlab/Simulink or Ptolemy, uses an integrated code synthesis, such as the Real-Time Workshop (RTW) in Matlab/Simulink, to synthesize code. Similar to the classical programming paradigm, as soon as a development step is finished, the source models are compiled to a classical, general purpose language, such as C. Afterwards, they are compiled to binary code like before, with the addition that the user feedback often includes some sort of simulation. Here it depends on the concrete design choices if the simulation runs inside the IDE or on the compiled product.

Although the development processes are quite similar, there is a subtle shift in the focus on the developer. In the first case, the developer has to be a programmer, whereas the models in the second case are typically maintained by a domain expert. However, even in the second case programming experts are sometimes required to aid the modeler with special requirements or IDE extensions.

2.2   Interactive Process Systems

Figure 1c depicts the more interactive approach that we advocate here. With *interactive process systems*, operating procedures, such as compilation or simulation, can be created and modified by the developer. Here, these process systems are simply models just like the working artefact, but perhaps models of another meta-model. When the modeler wants to compile (resp. simulate) the actual status of the model, the respective process system gets instantiated. Afterwards, the issued command can be processed by that system's instance. The feedback, including errors, *intermediate*, and *final results*, is directly available as individual model instances of appropriate meta-models. They can be inspected by the modeler or used as source for further systems. In the figure, we see an instantiated process system. The artefact is processed sequentially by single processors, e.g., model-to-model transformations, of the instance. All intermediate steps are observable. Eventually, the user wants to deploy binary code and one of the intermediate results may be general purpose source code that can be sent to an external compiler as before. Conceptually, the compiler call is just another process in the system's sequential chain.

Note that this approach is agnostic to the question whether the intermediate results (or, in fact, the original model) are graphical or textual. If the syntax is graphical, a key enabler to be able to represent the artefacts is the integration of automatic layout facilities into the modeling tool. In KIELER, we make use of the Eclipse Layout Kernel (ELK)[3] to synthesize the views. We argue that this is also an example of *pragmatic modeling* concepts [5,19], which aim to enhance modeler productivity by allowing to seamlessly switch between textual and graphical representations tailored to specific use cases. To quote a practitioner: "In our experience over many years my colleagues and I concluded that textual modeling is the only practical way, but that a graphical view of the models is a must-have as well. [KIELER] closes exactly that gap."[4]

The interactivity of the approach becomes apparent in the ability to observe all intermediate steps, to run system instances as they are needed and to create new or change existing systems all during run-time. There is no need to go through long re-build and re-start cycles. As described before, a process system can basically perform any kind of job. As an example, the figure depicts a

---

[3] https://www.eclipse.org/elk
[4] Dr. Andreas Seibel, BSH Hausgeräte GmbH, E-Mail from Oct. 6, 2017.

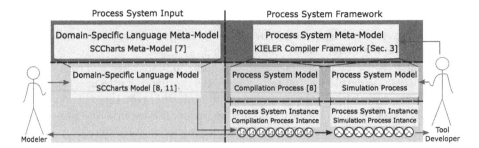

Fig. 2. Process system's different model layer and user roles

model-to-model (M2M) compilation. Here, technically, the term *interactive* subsumes the dynamic nature of the approach, meaning that instances of systems are generated dynamically as they are needed. These instances carry dynamic properties on their own and live as long as they are required. This also resembles the classical class-object hierarchy of the object-orientated paradigm.

Another take on this is to view process systems as a—rather abstract—data flow model. Traditionally, data flow models are collections of *actors* that consume and produce *data* [7]. Conceptually, the processors of a process system correspond to actors, and the data they consume and produce correspond to the intermediate results generated along a synthesis chain. One difference is that in process systems, each actor typically "fires" only once, and the"schedule" that governs how the process system is executed/instantiated is rather simple, usually just a single sequential execution of all processors. However, more complex, dynamic execution schemes are also possible, as alluded to later in Sect. 3.2. Alternatively, if we want to focus on the schedule of the processors, we can also view process systems as control-oriented state machines, where one processor can be "active" at a time, and when it is finished, control advances to the next processor. This view can be helpful for example to define more elaborate schedules, but hides what is actually produced and consumed by the processors, which is why we consider the data-flow analogy typically more fitting than the state-oriented analogy.

Due to the interactivity of the approach, tool developers and modelers can easily create, explore, and modify different aspects of the whole development process. The difference is not disparate work-flows, but the diverse work-flow artefacts that are being worked on. Figure 2 shows the different layers of models and the two main roles of users. On the left side, the modeler mainly works on the system's input, e. g., a particular model in a specific domain-specific language (DSL). The model's meta-model also belongs to the system's input, but is usually outside of the modeler's scope w.r.t. making changes during a particular project. In the example in the figure, the modeler works on an SCCharts model, whose syntax is defined in the corresponding meta-model. Again, it is not important here wheter the syntax is textual or graphical. This decision can be made as the case arises depending on the preference of the domain expert. At this, the form of editor must not be the same as the graphical view of the model. Transient view and automatic layout technologies [14] may help the modeler to explore the model without getting distracted by tedious tasks, such as placement and alignment of graphical elements.

On the framework's side on the right, there is also the framework's meta-model for defining system models. Derived from this, different systems can be created that hold the necessary instructions. These systems can be instantiated to be applied on a specific artefact. In the example shown, the created SCCharts model is fed into an compilation system instance. During compilation, several observable intermediate results are created. The result of the whole context also serves as input for a simulation instance.

In general, the modeler will be more interested in the actual project's model and the systems' results, whereas the tool developer's focus will lie on the systems and the underlying framework, including the relevant meta-models. However, both can utilize all aspects of the development process to drive their work. For example, the modeler may also change a particular system to toggle optimizations if necessary. More obviously, the tool developer can use different model inputs to test and extend the framework. This could also lead to closer feedback loops between domain experts and tool developers.

3   Process Systems in KIELER

In the KIELER Compiler (KiCo) the smallest compilation unit is called a *processor*. We moved away from the specific term *transformation* to emphasize that a processor does not have to perform a transformation. Instead processors are categorized into *transformer*, *optimizer*, and *analyzer* to specify their role. A variety of tasks can be implemented as processors, such as M2M transformations, optional optimizations, and, e. g., object counting, but this should be restricted to this atomic task to facilitate modularity and reuse.

3.1   Static Process Systems

A list of processors forms a *process system*. These systems describe a single compilation from a certain source type down to the desired target. When compared to the object-orientated programming paradigm, process systems can be seen as classes. They can be instantiated to perform a task for a concrete artefact. In the previous publications we described two compilation approaches, the netlist-based and the priority-based approaches, for SCCharts [9,18]. Each of

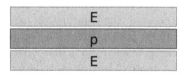

Fig. 3. The atomic compilation unit, a processor p, receives a source and a target environment when instantiated.

these is an own process system, more specifically a *compilation system*.

When a system is instantiated, an instance for every processor within the system is created. A *processor instance* is then connected to a *source environment* from which it will receive input data and a *target environment* to work on

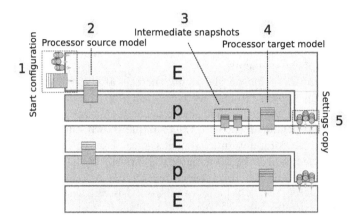

Fig. 4. Concept of a compilation context with two processors.

and store data for the next processors. The simplest system possible is shown in Fig. 3. It consists of a single processor with its corresponding source and target environments. Once the system is fully instantiated, a new *compilation context* (gen. process context) exists, which can be used to compile an artefact. While the context, including all environments and all data, is observable during compilation, it will remain accessible even after the compilation finished until discarded, so that all data and results can be inspected as long as desired.

Conceptionally, the developer is free to choose the nature of their environments. In KIELER we use typed, but arbitrary data storages. Hence, processors may store arbitrary (ancillary) data in the environments, but have a form of type-safety when accessing it.

The developer does not have to bother with all the instances and environments. The KiCo framework will do most of the work. In general, when invoking a compilation programmatically, one only needs two lines of code. First, a *context* has to be created. The context needs to know which system model it should use and on which artefact the compilation should be invoked. Once the context is created, the compilation can be executed. Listing 1 shows an excerpt from the KIELER project where a compilation is started asynchronously as soon as the user presses a particular button. The programmer could make adjustments to the context before the compile method is executed, but in this case, it is not necessary.

```
1 val context = Compile.createCompilationContext(view.activeSystem, model)
2 context.compileAsynchronously
```

Listing 1. Compilation invocation excerpt from the KIELER project

Usually a compilation system includes more than one processor. Figure 4 shows how processors interact with their environments to orchestrate the entire compilation. As described before, once a context has been created, it needs an input artefact and can be configured if necessary. The first environment in the

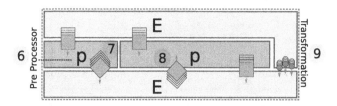

Fig. 5. To save resources several processors can be grouped together. Generally, everything that happens between two environments is commonly called a transformation.

context receives the *start configuration* [1] as can be seen in the figure. After the invocation of the compilation, the first processor begins its work. It fetches the model from its source environment [2] and begins its computations. That model is the *source model* from the processor's perspective. While working on the model, the processor can do several snapshots of the current state and store them in its *target environment* [3]. These intermediate states can be inspected during or after the compilation. At the end of the processor's job, the result is saved [4]. In the example, the graphic indicates that the result is of the same meta-model as the source model. However, any type can be used. E. g., as targets are often other programming-languages, the backends usually give simple text as results. Once the processor terminates, the next processor starts its job. From its perspective, the former target environment now becomes the source environment and the processor can work on the next one. The framework takes care that all settings, model references, and additional auxiliary data get copied to the new environments if necessary [5].

To facilitate modularity and consume less resources, processors often perform pre- or post-processing jobs for transformers without the need of dedicated environments as depicted in Fig. 5. Hence, a processor can run with the same environments as another one [6]. In the example, the job saves a second model with a different meta-model in the environment [7]. This secondary model may store ancillary data (e. g. loop information from a loop analyzer), which can be picked up by subsequent processors [8]. Usually, what is commonly called *transformation* is everything that happens between the source and the target environments [9]. The result that is stored in the last environment represents the result of the whole compilation. \

Note that pre- or post-processors also store these data in the target environment of the main processos as they are not allowed to change the source environment. However, the developer is not required to handle these inputs differently as the framework will ensure correct accesses. In fact, technically, KiCo processors internally always only work on the target environment. The framework automatically creates a copy from the source environment before a processor is called.

To be even more resource-saving, a compilation can be set to *in-place*. Compiling in-place does not create new model instances to work on. The processors all work on the same models, hence intermediate results are only observable

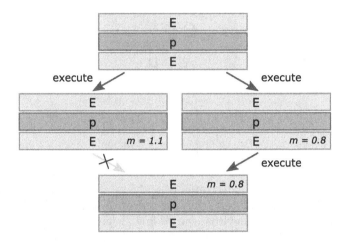

Fig. 6. When joining different branches, model measures rate the quality of the preceding results to determine the new source environment.

during compilation and only one at a time. At the end of the compilation, only the final result remains. Conceptually, this would also look like the schema in Fig. 5 where only two environments exist and all processor instances live in between.

3.2   Dynamic Process Systems

The KiCo framework can also handle branching. As we tend to create small, concise systems and this mechanic is rarely used at the moment, we will only sketch the two predominant concepts of KiCos decision-making. Succeeding processors are always executed in KiCo. In the first approach, when joining different branches, KiCo compares quality measures (m) inside the joining environments to decide which result will be the source for the joining processor as can be seen in Fig. 6. The measure is determined by a post-processor and can be handled and customized like every other processor. Which characteristics of the model are used to determine the value is up to process system. By definition, a smaller value generally means a better result, e. g., model size. In the figure two paths branch from a source. On both paths, a processor performs its job. The result is then judged by a *measuring processor*. Compared to the source model, the result on the left branch is greater, i. e. worse. Subsequently, the right branch is chosen for the joining processor. Note that this mechanism can also be used to exclude invalid paths. An invalid model results in an infinite measure (∞) and is discarded. This, however, depends on the task of the processor. For example, if an optimizer fails, it should simply return the source model with $m = 1.0$ as a failed optimization should not change the artefact semantically.

In the second approach, as a process system is also a model and accessible from the contained processors, a processor can alter the process system and, therefore, affect the succeeding processors. Hence, it is also possible to decide for the next processor during run-time. This is particularly helpful when a static schedule is not determinable, as has been shown by Rahimi-Barfeh [12].

3.3 SCCharts Compilation

The default version of the netlist-based compilation system uses 33 processors. Listing 2 shows a shortened description for the netlist-based compilation of SCCharts. Every processor has its own unique identifier. However, compilation systems are often composed of other systems, which can be referenced. Here, the downstream compilation builds upon the standard high-level SCCharts compilation (line 4–5) and nine further processors identified by their identifiers.

```
1  public system de.cau.cs.kieler.sccharts.netlist
2      label "Netlist−based␣Compilation"
3
4  system de.cau.cs.kieler.sccharts.extended
5  system de.cau.cs.kieler.sccharts.core
6  de.cau.cs.kieler.sccharts.scg.processors.SCG
7  post process de.cau.cs.kieler.scg.processors.threadAnalyzer
8  de.cau.cs.kieler.scg.processors.dependency
9  de.cau.cs.kieler.scg.processors.basicBlocks
10 post process de.cau.cs.kieler.scg.processors.expressions
11 de.cau.cs.kieler.scg.processors.guards
12 de.cau.cs.kieler.scg.processors.scheduler
13 de.cau.cs.kieler.scg.processors.sequentializer
14 de.cau.cs.kieler.scg.processors.codegen.c
```

Listing 2. Model description of the netlist-based SCCharts compilation

As these descriptions define compilation models interactively, we use concepts such as transient views [14] to visualize the system graphically and, if necessary, point to problems such as unknown processors or type incompatibility between processors. *Interactively* means that we can inspect, change, and save the model during runtime to invoke altered compilation runs without the need of long re-configure and re-start cycles. Figure 7a shows the automatically generated graphical representation of the netlist-based compilation system during editing. This view is synchronized with the editor of the model's description and instantaneously re-generated upon change. The referenced high-level SCCharts systems can be expanded and collapsed for readability. Problems appear in red. The generated views are also used as control panel in the KIELER project to invoke the compilations and to select intermediate results.

In the example depicted in Fig. 7a, the Surface / Depth processor creates an SCCharts model which is then transformed to its corresponding Sequentially Constructive Graph (SCG), a sequentially constructive variant of a control-flow graph, by the SCG processor. The subsequent Dependency processor expects an SCG as input. If one would swap the SCG and Dependency processors, the compilation chain becomes type incompatible, as depicted in Fig. 7b.

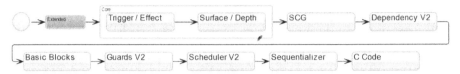

(a) SCCharts netlist-based compilation system. In this view, the **Extended** system is collapsed and the **Core** system is expanded.

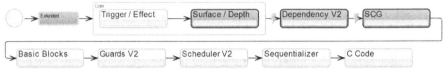

(b) While modeling, errors, such as type incompatibility, can be highlighted immediately.

Fig. 7. Example of an automatically generated graphical (view) of a compilation system (Color figure online)

Figure 8 shows a complete example of a running KIELER instance during simulation. In the SCCharts editor tool, the abstract model is described with a textual syntax [1]. A graphical view of the model is instantaneously generated by the transient view framework [14] [2]. The user can further influence the visualization of the presented data via options on the right sidebar [3]. However, these options consist mainly of rather coarse convenience settings to set the current focus to specific points of interests. [4] – [6] show examples of different information views. These can be configured (and saved per perspective) individually. Together with the transient live visualization [2], they resemble the systems and intermediate result regions from the previous figures. The selected compilation system is depicted in [4]. A view to manipulate the running simulation is open in [5]. Selected data observers can be inspected in [6]. Note that information of the running simulation is visible in the model diagram [2], the simulation view [5], and the observers [6] simultaneously. The variable states and current active model elements can be highlighted directly in the model. The user can input new environment settings in the simulation view. Here, one can also control single forward and backward steps of the simulation. Furthermore, the actual and past data of selected variables can also be visualized in the data observer [6].

4   Related Work

Steffen already showed a close relation between compilation and modeling back in 1997 [16]. He proposed to use *consistency models* to detect inconsistencies between different model descriptions. This relates to giving a semantics to a programming language by translation into an intermediate language. Over the years, a number of modeling compilation approaches have been developed such as CINCO [10], a meta-level modeling tool generator, and MARAMA [6], which provides metatools for language specification and tool creation. KICO's process

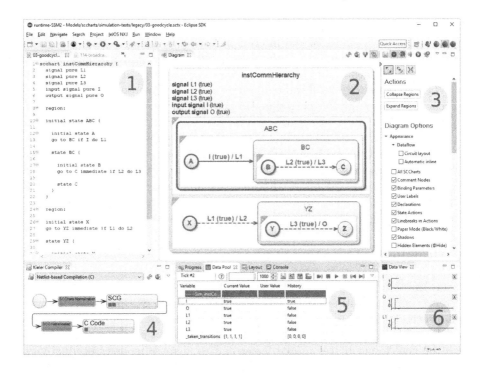

Fig. 8. Complete example of a running KIELER instance during simulation.

categorization into specialized work units is in line with ETI's process system [17]. While targeting a slightly different group of experts, such an even more generic process synthesis approach could also be implemented in KiCo. We discuss further possible future routes in the conclusion in Sect. 5. In our approach we provide the modeler with generic, interactive tools to orchestrate compilation processes. These are divided into atomic steps that aid the modeler to refine the process and to find errors without the need for long development cycles. The source, intermediate, target, and additional models are presented in well-readable graphical views using transient view and automatic layout technologies [14].

The proposed process systems can be seen as a variant of *scientific workflows* [4], as implemented in tools such as TAVERNA [11], for M2M transformations combined with state-of-the-art pragmatic modeling techniques. While there are similarities, such as a loose processor concept and type-checking, the focus of KiCo lies on M2M transformations where every intermediate result is a fully functional artefact. The processor system itself, including the environments in a running context, is also considered a simple model here. There is no need for a specialized description language or special data storages, e.g., for processor meta-data such as processor run-time. In our approach, the system's model can be influenced during design- and run-time, which includes alterations by the contained processors. Furthermore, as long as the transient view framework supports the meta-model of the intermediate results, views can be generated instantaneously and there is no difference between the different artefacts, even if they are positioned on distinct meta-levels.

When it comes to general compilation techniques, numerous well-understood approaches (e. g. Copy Propagation [1] and Register Allocation [3]) can be applied to our compiler to improve the results. However, as classical compilers are more or less a *blackbox*, working with intermediate results becomes difficult. For example, as depicted elsewhere [15], the gcc[5] possesses settings to toggle different optimizations or to print out intermediate representation of the basic blocks [2] of a source program. However, the interplay between the different modules and the textual representation of data seems to only target compiler experts and is arguably rarely useful for the common user.

5   Conclusions

We presented how the compiler framework works that was used to create the reference implementation for the synchronous language SCCharts. We showed that process systems, such as compilation or simulation, themselves are also models and how this can help both, the domain expert and the tool developer, with the goal to get better results faster and to increase modeler productivity. While both may have different foci during a project's lifetime, both can use a similar framework to drive their development and to help each other.

For us, in Model-driven Software Development (MDSD), programming with models does not only mean to model a program with, e. g., a sophisticated IDE that provides us with new tools to construct the program. For example, modern programming IDEs provide features such as syntax highlighting, code completion, reference counting, refactoring, etc. Many of these features focus on creating the model and then they are done. In our approach, the whole process is modeled. The user can inspect and change every part of it interactively. They can influence the compilation improving the final result or add new processors that provide new models and views to give better feedback. We thus argue that MDSD is not solely about modeling a particular artefact. It is also about the way to get to the final deployable software.

Besides further improvements for the SCCharts compiler and streamlining the MDSD user experience, we see further future work. For example, the KIELER project includes several modules that still use dedicated components that perform dedicated model transformations to prepare the models for specific tasks. As illustrated in Sect. 2, we are currently working on the compilation and simulation systems. However, the KiCo framework could also be used to generalize even more of these processes, e. g., deployment tasks. This would also facilitate the re-usability of the approach beyond the classical compilation task. Furthermore, we want to combine our approach with the continuing trends of mobile location-independent technologies, such as mixed web/desktop applications using tools

---

[5] https://gcc.gnu.org

such as electron[6]. We are optimistic that this will further increase the possibilities for and flexibility of prototyping and team-driven software development.

References

1. Aho, A.V., Sethi, R., Ullman, J.D.: Compilers — Principles, Techniques, and Tools. Addison-Wesley, Reading (1986)
2. Allen, F.E.: Control flow analysis. In: Proceedings of a Symposium on Compiler Optimization, pp. 1–19. ACM, New York (1970)
3. Chaitin, G.J., Auslander, M.A., Chandra, A.K., Cocke, J., Hopkins, M.E., Markstein, P.W.: Register allocation via coloring. Comput. Lang. **6**(1), 47–57 (1981)
4. Curcin, V., Ghanem, M., Guo, Y.: The design and implementation of a workflow analysis tool. Philos. Trans. R. Soc. Lond. A Math. Phys. Eng. Sci. **368**(1926), 4193–4208 (2010)
5. Fuhrmann, H., von Hanxleden, R.: On the pragmatics of model-based design. In: Choppy, C., Sokolsky, O. (eds.) Monterey Workshop 2008. LNCS, vol. 6028, pp. 116–140. Springer, Heidelberg (2010). https://doi.org/10.1007/978-3-642-12566-9_7
6. Grundy, J.C., Hosking, J., Li, K.N., Ali, N.M., Huh, J., Li, R.L.: Generating domain-specific visual language tools from abstract visual specifications. IEEE Trans. Softw. Eng. **39**(4), 487–515 (2013)
7. Lee, E.A., Neuendorffer, S., Wirthlin, M.J.: Actor-oriented design of embedded hardware and software systems. J. Circ. Syst. Comput. (JCSC) **12**(3), 231–260 (2003)
8. Motika, C.: SCCharts–Language and Interactive Incremental Implementation. Number 2017/2 in Kiel Computer Science Series. Department of Computer Science: Dissertation, Faculty of Engineering, Christian-Albrechts-Universität zu Kiel (2017)
9. Motika, C., Smyth, S., von Hanxleden, R.: Compiling SCCharts—a case-study on interactive model-based compilation. In: Margaria, T., Steffen, B. (eds.) ISoLA 2014, Part I. LNCS, vol. 8802, pp. 461–480. Springer, Heidelberg (2014). https://doi.org/10.1007/978-3-662-45234-9_32
10. Naujokat, S., Lybecait, M., Kopetzki, D., Steffen, B.: Cinco: a simplicity-driven approach to full generation of domain-specific graphical modeling tools. Int. J. Softw. Tools Technol. Transf. **20**(3), 327–354 (2018)
11. Oinn, T., et al.: Taverna: a tool for the composition and enactment of bioinformatics workflows. Bioinformatics **20**(17), 3045–3054 (2004)
12. Rahimi-Barfeh, M.: Incremental compilation of SCEst. Bachelor thesis, Kiel University, Department of Computer Science, September 2017. http://rtsys.informatik.uni-kiel.de/~biblio/downloads/theses/mrb-bt.pdf
13. Rybicki, F., Smyth, S., Motika, C., Schulz-Rosengarten, A., von Hanxleden, R.: Interactive model-based compilation continued – interactive incremental hardware synthesis for SCCharts. In: Proceedings of the 7th International Symposium on Leveraging Applications of Formal Methods, Verification and Validation (ISoLA 2016). LNCS, vol. 8802, Corfu, Greece, pp. 443–462, October 2016

---

[6] https://electronjs.org

14. Schneider, C., Spönemann, M., von Hanxleden, R.: Just model! – Putting automatic synthesis of node-link-diagrams into practice. In: Proceedings of the IEEE Symposium on Visual Languages and Human-Centric Computing (VL/HCC 2013), San Jose, CA, USA, pp. 75–82, September 2013
15. Smyth, S., Schulz-Rosengarten, A., von Hanxleden, R.: Watch your compiler work — compiler models and environments. Technical report 1806, Christian-Albrechts-Universität zu Kiel, Department of Computer Science, July 2018. ISSN 2192-6247
16. Steffen, B.: Unifying models. In: STACS 1997, 14th Annual Symposium on Theoretical Aspects of Computer Science, Lübeck, Germany, pp. 1–20, March 1997
17. Steffen, B., Margaria, T., Braun, V.: The electronic tool integration platform: concepts and design. Int. J. Softw. Tools Technol. Transf. 1(1), 9–30 (1997)
18. von Hanxleden, R., et al.: SCCharts: sequentially constructive Statecharts for safety-critical applications. In: Proceedings of ACM SIGPLAN Conference on Programming Language Design and Implementation (PLDI 2014), Edinburgh, UK, pp. 372–383. ACM, June 2014
19. von Hanxleden, R., Lee, E.A., Motika, C., Fuhrmann, H.: Multi-view modeling and pragmatics in 2020 — position paper on designing complex cyber-physical systems. In: Calinescu, R., Garlan, D. (eds.) Monterey Workshop 2012. LNCS, vol. 7539, pp. 209–223. Springer, Heidelberg (2012). https://doi.org/10.1007/978-3-642-34059-8_11

From Computational Thinking to Constructive Design with Simple Models

Tiziana Margaria[✉]

Chair of Software Systems, University of Limerick, and Lero, Limerick, Ireland
tiziana.margaria@ul.ie

Abstract. Computational Thinking has advocated for a decade the importance of a kind of education that elicits and fosters the understanding of computational concepts that are deemed "natural", thus widely learnable and adoptable, but not supported or at least not explicitly featured nor named in traditional education.

In this paper we argue that the most important aspect of this educational revolution is actually the "doing" part, in terms of creating a habit of designing the logic of any project or endeavour in terms of simple models. Simple models, especially if formally underpinned, analyzable, executable, and amenable to code generation for the orchestration of services, are the missing link between computational thoughts and the programming level.

Our approach is based on years of experience with middle and high school students, beginner students in Computer Science aged from 17 to over 50, and with students of other disciplines. They have been introduced successfully to *CS* or *programming* via constructing simple, yet executable models in the form of short courses, bootcamps, and semester-long courses in various locations and settings.

We are convinced that, unlike the widespread push towards *coding*, this approach is scalable. We also advocate its adequacy to provide the general public of professionals with the kind of familiarity with computational concepts and the level of confidence in practical *making* of applications and designs that can be a game changer for the societal diffusion of basic computing-related comprehension and design skills.

1 Introduction

The production and evolution of IT are expected to grow to levels of speed, scale, affordability and collaborative effort that will truly make IT enter the fabric of every economical and societal endeavour. This is the projected future of our society in the next decade. For it to happen, the ease of learning, understanding, and applying new disruptive technologies must drastically improve. While the need to educate users is generally agreed, it is much less generally agreed that the production of complex and sophisticated applications and systems must drastically change as well.

© Springer Nature Switzerland AG 2018
T. Margaria and B. Steffen (Eds.): ISoLA 2018, LNCS 11244, pp. 261–278, 2018.
https://doi.org/10.1007/978-3-030-03418-4_16

We argue that the needs of the people, the economical sectors, and the large-scale trends can only be met if the IT professions embrace and adopt a new way of producing and consuming IT. We analysed in [31] briefly the various dimensions of this transformational change, with all the indicators pointing to a new, much more infrastructural role of IT competence. This means that if we wish indeed to achieve a better materialization of the knowledge intrinsic in the person of the domain experts, to make it accessible to other individuals and systems, and amenable also to access by IT systems, we need to develop a new understanding and a new practice of large scale IT education.

We also argue that this new way should be based on more formal descriptions, more models, more reasoning and analysis before expensive implementations are incurred, coupled with automatic transformations, generations, and analyses that take advantage of the models and the formalized knowledge. We also argue that this is possible, based on a new interpretation of the role and relevance of knowledge, models, and code that shifts the accent from programming to the ability to produce running artefacts and systems.

Computational Thinking [55] has advocated for a decade the importance of a kind of education that elicits and fosters the understanding of computational concepts that are deemed "natural", thus widely learnable and adoptable, but not supported or at least not explicitly featured nor named in traditional education.

The most important aspect of this educational revolution is however actually the "doing" part, in terms of creating a habit of designing the logic of any project or endeavour in terms of simple models. *Simple models*, especially if formally underpinned, analyzable, executable, and amenable to code generation for the orchestration of services, are *the missing link* between computational thoughts and the programming level.

In this paper, Sect. 2 presents what we mean with computational doing and briefly presents the existing literature on more or less closely related approaches. Section 3 presents our flavor of simple models for constructive design along withe the description of the curriculum of a module recently introduced in the common entry 1st year course in Computer Science. Section 4 discusses generative approaches as the means to educate at large scale, and finally Sect. 5 draws some perspectives and concludes.

2   Computational Doing

The need for engineers and specialists is growing much faster than their production along the established paths. The "producers" of IT specialists are increasingly detached from universities and the universities of applied science: vocational courses and dual education combining formal education with a training on the job component are increasingly advocated as *just in time* sources of right-skilled personnel. The dream of the employers is an agile workforce training, on demand, supportive of workforce evolution, that provides competence building by means of blended or online capability-oriented approaches. It may sound as a collection of buzzwords, and it is today only partially satisfied by expensive MOOCs, online offerings that are compatible with a demanding job, and other local initiatives like, in Ireland, the National MSc in Artificial Intelligence, or the Higher Diploma courses.[1]

These aspiring software developers, like the novice students in our traditional Computer Science courses, need to acquire a thorough understanding of fundamental computational concepts like sequential execution, conditional branching, loops, modularisation, hierarchy and reuse. This understanding and "computational thinking" is deepened when they encounter the concepts in different contexts and environments, as opposed to only in one traditional programming language. In [10] we described how we used the Cinco Adventure Game Tool, a tool that allows students to model simple browser games in an intuitive graphical framework, to train basic computational concepts in a creative and engaging, learning-by-doing fashion. In that effort, as well as in the module on Introduction to Model Driven Development offered jointly to the incoming BSc and the HDip students, we consciously steered away from traditional programming languages, in order to separate the use of the concepts and constructs from the hurdle of a programming language syntax and development environment. This distinction provides a scaffolding step for those who would struggle with the concepts and syntax at once, more clarity for those who are comfortable with both conceptualization and operationalization in a coding concept, equipping them with literacy in a further language layer (the models and their properties) at which to design, validate, and communicate their thoughts. At the same time, this provides also a possible path to the "production" at large scale of skilled domain experts, who are sufficiently trained when they are able to compose themselves the solutions to their professional needs on the basis of a comfortable DSL that is implemented in a service-oriented fashion. Indeed the demand for these "application engineers" is rising. They need to understand and operate at a domain specific level. In a traditional setting that goes straight to the programs, their coding concerns at most the glue code between calls to existing libraries. In our XMDD [36] approach, they compose Service Logic Graphs (SLGs) using functionalities from available SIB palettes, or more likely they modify existing SLGs for new needs and purposes, again using the SIB palettes of those domains.

Together with central concepts like algorithms and data, central skills that also these DSL users need to master are problem posing, analysing, generalizing, finding relationships, classifying, and investigating [58]. As shown in [20], training computational thinking skills with dedicated novice programming environments before approaching a standard programming language reduces the learning curve and increases the success rate for beginning programmers. While there is a rich literature about educational programming environments, like App Inventor [56, 57], Greenfoot [19,52] and Scratch [30,42], very little has been published on the

---

[1] These are 1 year courses that provide a title equivalent to the BSc. CSIS is running an HDip in Software Development and a HDip in Software Development and Data Analytics. They are approved on a yearly basis by the Irish Higher Education Authority according to the needs expressed by industry.

role of modelling in computing education. Reported individual success stories include graduate and postgraduate courses in model-driven engineering [8,51], teaching modelling with executable UML models before getting to program [43], and our use of eXtreme Model-Driven Development (XMDD) environments for educational purposes [25]. However, in spite of our having educated hundreds of students in this new educational paradigm, and having extensively published about this approach in a computer science education context [5,25] but also for Summer computer camps for girls, as reported in [24] and [38], even like-minded researchers are still unaware of it and lament the lack of diffusion and prominence of this pedagogy culture [17].

Our approach is based on years of experience with middle and high school students, beginner students in Computer Science aged from 17 to over 50, and with students of other disciplines. They have been introduced successfully to *CS* or *programming* via constructing simple, yet executable models in the form of short courses, bootcamps, and semester-long courses in various locations and settings. We are convinced that, unlike the widespread push towards *coding*, this is approach is scalable. We also advocate its adequacy to provide the general public of professionals with the kind of familiarity with computational concepts and the level of confidence in practical *making* of applications and designs that can be a game changer for the societal diffusion of basic computing-related comprehension and design skills.

3   Simple Models for Constructive Design

We use metaphors and Problem-Based Learning to ease a natural understanding of the concepts that is supported to a large extent by intuition, common sense, and just a little bit by formal discipline. We model, but we model aspects that are "logical" in the context of the case studies represented and analayzed. Abstracting and generalising is the second step: it swiftly follows from the motivating examples and it leads as quickly to the application to new settings and problems. Problem-Based Learning has proven successful also in the IT education of business information system students [41]. However the context of that study applied a multiplicity of design phases and tools that spanned the problem definition domain, traditional modelling formalisms and tools that are not executable, and realized the final design in hand-programmed code. In mechanical engineering the CDIO movement[2] follows a similar path, but oriented to the *making* of engineered artefacts.

In our setting, we face a large cohort of students in the first semester of university, who have not programmed before (computer science is not yet regularly included in the school programs of Ireland), and who faced in the past extremely severe difficulties in starting with beginner's level Java. The *Introduction to Model-Driven Design*' module has been designed to be run in a compact bootcamp format and in a completely coding-free fashion, in order to separate the hurdle of managing a complex syntax from the education in computational

---

[2] Worldwide CDIO Initiative, http://www.cdio.org.

Service Logic Graphs (SLGs)

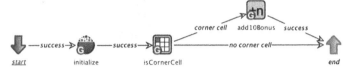

A **Service Logic Graph (SLG)** is a 4-tuple $T=(S, s_0, Act, Trans)$ with:

S	a set of SIBs
s_0	a unique „Start SIB"
Act	a set of possible branching conditions
$Trans = \{(s,a,s')\}$	a set of transitions where $s,s' \in S$ and $a \in Act$.

Fig. 1. Service Logic Graphs and SIBS as a DSL for a strategy game and as a KTS.

thinking concepts, and the training in software production (and problem solving) in groups using the XMDD style of model-driven development along the lines of [25].

In the first weeks, we address in combination the different aspects that make a well rounded developer: models and working with models, expressing properties and purpose, querying models by model checking, familiarity with representation systems and with the software engineering lifecycle and values, and finally the abilities to manage, negotiate, explain and present that are today collectively called soft skills.

3.1 Models and Working with Models

Concerning the model understanding, interpretation, formalisation, and use, we address first how to use models to solve problems, i.e. in order to design solutions. In the first three weeks the students gain theoretical and practical experience with problem solving by designing and executing strategies of the board game Chain Reaction [1,2,21]. This happens as a laboratory project in pairs directly in Weeks 1–3. In order to solve the problem, they are introduced to the essential model primitives: sequence, decision, iteration, fork/join parallelism and hierarchy, which constitute the intuitive basis of the *simple models* we advocate.

eXtreme Model Driven Design (XMDD) is a software development paradigm that explicitly focuses on the What (solving problems) rather than on the How (the technical skills of writing code).

To give an impression of the models, the process model (called Service Logic Graph, or SLG) in Fig. 1 has been created by dragging workflow building blocks (called Service-Independent Building Blocks, or SIBs) from the Chain Reaction DSL library in a drag&drop fashion onto the canvas, and connecting these SIBs as appropriate through labeled branches representing the flow of control. Once

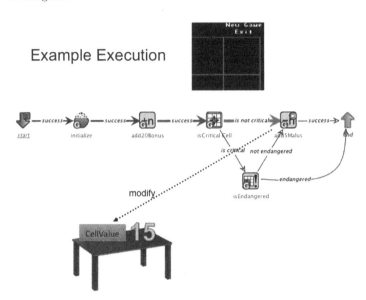

Fig. 2. SLG execution: Model tracing (interpreter), the Game's Board window, and an illustration of the side effects in memory

the parameters of the SIBs have been configured (in a dedicated SIB inspector) the workflow is ready for execution, shown in Fig. 2.

The control panel of the Tracer plugin steers the execution of the models. We see that it is currently executing the SIB **add5malus**: the green-colored branches of the model on the canvas visualize the path executed so far and where the execution has currently arrived. The upper window in the figure shows the result from the workflow execution on the game board: nothing is shown, as we are still before the first move. The students literally "follow" on the model all the initialisation functionality that is needed before the game even starts.

The computational concepts that students learn using the simple modelling language are in principle the same as in a general-purpose programming language, but presented to them in a different perspective, which helps to deepen their understanding. Table 1 compares how the most relevant concepts in our unit match the central concepts in general-purpose modelling languages and in common programming languages.

In order to still separate syntax from concepts, we introduce several behavioural modelling styles: UML Activity Diagrams in Weeks 1 and 2, and Service Logic Graphs in weeks 1 to 3. Mainly for historical reasons, last year we also introduced flowcharts, but it turned out that their more primitive notation confused the weaker students. For example, the notation for fork/join parallelism constructs does not have the now familiar fork node and join node, so many students missed the distinction of their AND-split/merge meaning w.r.t. a XOR-split/merge due to the absence in the flowchart notation of the

Table 1. Basic computational concepts in the simple models (XMDD) and in a general-purpose programming language.

	XMDD modelling language	General-purpose programming language
Sequential execution	Any single branch (fan-out = 1)	Sequential execution (line by line, or ";")
Conditional branching	Branches, (fan-out > 1)	If-statement, Switch-statement
Loop	Cyclic paths	while-loop, do-loop, for-loop
Memory	Inventory	Variables
Hierarchy	Submodel references	Function calls (procedural inlining, call and return)
Modularisation	Submodel references	Functions, Classes, Namespaces
Reuse	Submodel references, Subgraph reuse	Functions, Classes
Recursion	Self-referencing models	Self-invoking functions
Creating executable	Code generation	Compilation

characteristic "black bars". So this year we discontinued the flowchart notation as it proved not to be simple enough.

The Service Logic Graphs (SLGs) are introduced as an alternative behavioural notation aiming at similar purposes but with a clearer formal semantics. We discuss the difference between an action and a SIB, how a SIB with one or more outgoing branches is equivalent to an activity if there is only one outgoing branch, and to the grouping of an activity followed by a decision if there are 2 or more outgoing branches, so that we clarify the difference between semantics and representation. We also discuss which elements of a representation are essential or not, e.g. discussing the ability to overlay the standard SIB icon taken from the UML activity notation with custom icon symbols, because SLGs can distinguish "look" and "feel" of such symbols, while activity diagrams foresee only labels but no further customisation of the appearance.

In the practice sessions, SLGs are used from week 1 onward to design the executable strategies for the Problem Solving board game, Chain Reaction.

We introduce the mathematical concepts needed for analysis and verification in terms of abstract models: different types of models embody different intrinsic discrete structures. We talk about graphs and directed graphs, then proceed in weeks 2–4 to introduce Kripke Systems, Labelled Transition Systems, Kripke Transition Systems, and to link these with the Service Logic Graphs the students are already familiar with.

3.2   Properties and Purpose

Aiming at model checking, we address next how to express knowledge. The necessary knowledge concerns on one side the purpose of a system, from a requirement and holistic quality point of view, and on the other side the properties that can be established on a system, introducing the concepts of refinement (system refinement, model refinement, property refinement), model hierarchy and architecture, the distinction of system and context and their interplay, and a simple assume/guarantee approach to establishing truth and asking questions. Students discover logics as a means to express properties: how to encode knowledge and queries as properties, and ultimately as constraints. We start with boolean logic in week 3, and move on to properties about system executions in weeks 4 and 5. Taking the point of view of single runs we introduce paths and (P) LTL, taking then the point of view of the potential behaviour on all runs, as continuations, we introduce computation trees and CTL.

3.3   Querying Models: Model Checking

Model checking is experienced in action in week 4, in lab sessions with the GEAR model checker [3,4]. The practical model checking of system properties and local properties with GEAR is accompanied by intuitive LTL and CTL model checking by hand on small examples, and by the explanation of simple recursive algorithms for AG, AF in week 5. This is the first contact with recursion, in order to compute fixpoints. The principle of fixpoint computation by successive iterations is explained for maximal and minimal fixpoints.

3.4   Simple Introduction to Representation Systems

Concerning models, precision in the syntax is trained when drawing the graphical elements of graphs, flowcharts, activity diagrams, SLGs and discussing similarities and differences. Through the semantics of models students see the use of discrete mathematics concepts, via the definition and characterization of concrete models and model types in terms of sets, graphs, labels, and their relations. An example is the formal definition of an SLG in Fig. 1, that in class is first presented in its correspondence with the elements of an example graph, and then derived as a variation of a KTS, which itself combines the labellings of both a Kripke Structure and an LTS.

Concerning logics, we introduce logics as examples of textual languages. Accordingly, the syntax is presented as a grammar, in BNF. As simplifications for complex formulas we introduce derived language primitives, like Until. As shortcuts for recurring classes of properties we introduce the concept of patterns for property templates. These are used then to write requirements for the designed systems and algorithms. The semantics of the logic operators is presented first in an intuitive way, in terms of what does teach primitive mean on the models, and with examples. This is followed by the presentation of the formal definitions, which include the notation for semantics and satisfaction.

3.5 Elements of Software Engineering

On the learn-by-doing practical side, in spite of the short time the students are conceiving, modelling, verifying, compiling, deploying, executing and then repeatedly improving in groups two team projects. They also learn about the history of programming (even the Univac programmers used models!), the different phases of a program's design, waterfall vs. agile design, quality assurance, testing, rapid prototyping and iterative improvement. A fast turn around time for comprehension and modification was mentioned a number of times as a significant advantage of the model-based approach. Indeed, all three projects concern different aspects of model driven development.

In the Chain Reaction project (weeks 1–3) the students use an existing DSL for this game, in our environment a collection of SIB libraries, and preexisting wrapper SLG models, so that they just need to compose their own strategy as one or more SLGs that are composed using the provided DSL. There is online support [2] and literature [21], and support in class by peer teaching assistants who are 2nd year students. This is effectively the development of an algorithm in "pair modelling" fashion, the modelling analogue to pair programming. Some teams ended up with recursive algorithms and many with hierarchy. Rapid prototyping is encouraged by the quick turn around time, effectively delivering a model-based version of a Problem Based Learning with embedded agile CDIO approach (Conceive, Design, Implement, Operate). They learn the advantage of DSLs, and they appreciate the distance between the complexity of the algorithm they can obtain this way and what they would be able to program themselves in Java, the language that is taught in parallel in a dedicated module. They are supported in their transfer from the lecture to the project by the fact that we consistently use SLGs from the Chain Reaction example and DSL when illustrating concepts with SLGs in the classrooms. Figure 1 shows how we formally characterize an SLG using a specific model as example on which to illustrate and discuss the definition, and Fig. 2 shows that we use the same model to illustrate the concepts of execution, of interpretation (vs. compilation), of the Tracer as the interpreter in the jABC development environment for XMDD that they use, and the concept of a shared memory (the "table" metaphor) where the ongoing execution over time Generates, Uses, Modifies, and Kills the data types and data values of the variables the SIBs operate upon.

3.6 Model Checking with GEAR

In the model checking project, carried out individually, students use GEAR to familiarize with the structure of formulas and their meaning as local or global system properties. Thanks to the two working modes of GEAR, they can be initially just users of predefined properties, which in real life corresponds to a verification w.r.t a preexisting knowledge base of properties and constraints. In a second step they define themselves properties for some of their own Chain Reaction models, learn how to analyze the system bottom up, from the local atomic propositions to the temporal properties of the entire graph. The educational accent here is on the difficulty to come up a priori with all the "right" properties (akin in this case to specifications), and thus demonstrating how design is a continuous adjustment of system model on one side and set of properties on the other side, with the aim of keeping them consistent. Late discovered properties also make tangible the concept of incremental specification [47], that seems natural if embedded in this agile model driven approach to design.

3.7   Learning by Doing with the Cinco Adventure Game Tool

For a larger collaborative design experience where they design own executable applications we use the Webstory described in [29], in the laboratory in weeks 5–6, which is realized as a Cinco-product [39]. Cinco is the current reference implementation of the XMDD (eXtreme Model-Driven Development) paradigm [36] and of the One-Thing Approach (OTA) [34] which enforce the rigorous use of user-level models and refinement throughout the software development process and software life cycle. With the *Cinco Adventure Game Tool* we have introduced a CDIO-like component in this first semester experience, in order to combine the conceptual education with the "making" experience and provide the students with an experience of "ownership" that can strengthen their confidence, if successful, and if unsuccessful clearly outline the kind of project-like environment they are most likely to encounter in their future work experiences. The purpose is to go beyond the pure algorithm design contained, e.g., in [3], and go towards an own design as experienced in [22,23,28] with the scientific workflows in the area of expertise of the students. However, in our case the students do not have any specific area of expertise to draw from, thus the decision to use adventure games as an easily accessible and attractive domain. Details on this experience, including an analysis of the complexity of the models with a split concept per concept have been reported in [10]. The students have no problems in understanding and using the concepts, use the tools proficiently and enjoyed designing and modelling the games. Working together on a game project in small groups, they showed sustained engagement, developed a high level of confidence, and created quite complex games containing various fundamental computational constructs.

3.8   Soft Skills

Called also "graduate attributes", soft skills play a significant role in the entire course. They work individually for the two tests (midterm and end of term) and for the model checking lab project, but they also have a good 50% of the tasks in groups, learning to work in teams and to manage various goals and tasks in parallel.

- Breaking the ice (Day 1) foresees a short on-boarding session: the activities in the first lab hour make them get to know each other and interact naturally when building together a physical artefact in teams.

- Working in pairs: the Chain Reaction project in Weeks 1–3 makes them understand, communicate, work in pairs, as in pair programming. They use a complex pre-populated XMDD development environment (jABC4) in a concrete application setting: produce the most skilful chain reaction strategies. This is done in rounds of iterative improvement as in agile development and concludes with an oral presentation of the own final strategy to the lab group of ca 30 peers and some tutors. Pairs can continue to work on the strategies, improving them in their own time until Week 6, where there is an optional artefact delivery followed by an artefact competition in an evening final tournament, with all the course invited.
- Working in (small) teams for the Webstory project (Weeks 5–6). They learn to organize, coordinate, agree in teams of 3–5, manage teamwork with new team members, and to achieve creative *product*-design in a team. The final team presentation requires all members to present and to reflect on their journey with the technology and as a team, and the best projects are demonstrated and showcased at the final event, right after the chain reaction tournament.

4   Generative Approaches as the Means to Educate at Large Scale

As stated in [31], we believe that generative approaches based on models as first class citizens are the key to the next wave of large scale computer literacy. Mainstreams approaches to innovation, today, suggest to *eliminate waste* and *fail fast*. Additionally, along *lean* guidelines, every artefact one does not have to produce or manage is preferable to those that are produced, maintained, and can fail. The practice of XMDD as described in Sect. 3 shows its adequacy as paradigm along several aspects.

- The **structuring aspect** is based on a core of simple control patterns corresponding to the traditional *while-languages*, plus hierarchy [45,46]. These elementary structures plus the concept of feature and feature interaction like in [14,15,18,37,47] allow a nice and incremental factoring of well characterized system components. The reasoning about structure, behaviour and properties as entities that need to be kept coherent along the design and along evolution lead to discourse about the most opportune units of reuse (for development, evolution and testing), units of localized responsibility, e.g. for maintenance, evolution and support, and even contracts for abstraction and compositionality as in [11].
- Along the **cultural aspect**, accessibility, acceptance and buy-in for a model-driven IT are improved by resorting to work with IT artefacts within easily intelligible domain models, rather than code. Comprehension-oriented model driven design and development, as also recognized in [17] and [53], is essential if one wishes to reach the masses of engaged professionals rather than the coding elite. By appealing initially to common sense and intuition, newcomers are invited instead of scared, developing a level of confidence that allows them

to face later the formal parts and what's less intuitive from a much more positive attitude.

- The **dissemination aspect** is then taken care of by sharing such models (understandable to the domain experts) and possibly also the implementations of the building blocks, this by using for example the existing Open Source Software facilities and structures. Libraries of services have been in use in the telecommunication domain since the '80s [48]. They are increasingly adopted in bioinformatics and geo-information systems, which are examples of two communities where there is significant public funding. Indeed many public funding agencies at the national and European level promote open data, open access to publication and open sourcing the output artefacts (code or models).

- The **education aspect** benefits as well. The abysmal participation of women and minorities in Computer Science and Computer Engineering has been widely criticized all along the 30 years of my own career, yet it is still not solved one generation later, in spite of many factual proofs that women and minorities are not at all a-priori less able to become excellent technologists and programmers. This approach can offer a solution to the advantage of both the IT professionals, i.e those for whom IT literacy is a primary skill, and the non-IT professionals, i.e. the vast majority of those for whom IT literacy is useful and desirable, but ancillary and therefore it is acquired only if its acquisition can happen with a marginal effort and at a marginal cost.

Short trainings in "Computational Doing" with simple, but formally rich and executable models, like the 3 day Summer camps reported on in [24] can lower the individual barrier to trying out a career path in IT. We could have more young or mature students taking up courses leading them to an IT profession for which they also have to master the programming and coding skills.

Courses like the Introduction to MDD module, which is delivered in a compact form over 6 weeks, could be useful also for non-IT professionals, to make them feel at ease with some of the terminology and means that are essential to convey their ideas and wishes to the IT professionals responsible to implement them. Models, especially the simple models here described, have a good chance of being amenable to suit the "marginal cost yet significant benefit" population in education and in the professions. While traditional compact modules "Introduction to Computer Science" typically bring students to produce only tiny programs, learn-by-doing approaches based on models and ready components for existing DSLs can jumpstart efficiency and prowess. As described in detail in [23] from an educational point of view and then demonstrated in larger scale in the book [22] resulting from that course, the approach is well aligned to the technical background and requirements of Master students of interdisciplinary programs that include some share of applied computer science. Those students are enrolled in the Master programs in Bioinformatics and in Geovisualization. They already held a Bachelor's degree in a natural science discipline (such as biology or geography), thus could be regarded as application experts in their respective scientific domain, but they were not yet trained in computer science or programming. Like our 1st year students, they autonomously designed and implemented (based on adequate DSLs) complex software for their specific computational problems, which were different forms of scientific workflows.

5   Perspectives and Conclusion

If we wish to go *Towards a Unified View of Modeling and Programming*, we need to find an adequate bridge between those who live inside their own area of expertise and cannot program, thus possess MDSL-level skills, and those who are proficient programmers, who however have to understand and satisfy the needs of these MDSL-level stakeholders. In order to build a bridge that provides a common meeting ground for the concepts in solution and system design as well as a common practice in the art of design and development, eXtreme Model Driven Design based on simple models is a sweet spot.

If as a global society we are going to make IT truly pervasive, we will notice that a large part of the tasks the general population has to deal with, personally and in the profession, is nicely modellable with the simple models we work with. It starts with most of what is today modelled (or programmed?) in spreadsheets, like for example complex patient classifications in cancer-related research [32,54] modeled form an excel calculation form and from direct observation. The assessment procedures for dyslexia in Italy [7] were modelled from direct observation in an assessment centre and from the Italian national guidelines. The assessment processes for diabetic retinopathy [9] were modelled as an "As-is" process landscape aimed at improvement and automation in the Diabetic Centre of the Ospedale Molinette in Torino.

XMDD and its tools form the basis for a Service-oriented Continuous Engineering approach [35] to the formalization and definition of domain-specific languages. The concepts of SLG and SIB prove useful and understandable to all these stakeholders from different professions. They are not new: the basis was laid in the '80s in the telecommunication industry, in order to guarantee interoperability across vendors, national policies, and various technologies and platforms for the then emerging Intelligent Network architectures [12,13], followed by the concept of feature as user-level unit of behaviour reuse [15,18,47]. Actually this ITU standard marked the birth of service oriented computing with microservices, as we explained in 2005 [37], reinvented many years later in order to allow a "customer" view into programming, for those systems for which there is no accessibility to the code.

In terms of expressive power, simple models can be easily combined with Higher-Order Processes [40]. They can be analyzed by a game based model checking for full mu-calculus, with forward and backward modalities, that is geared toward explanation and visualization as in GEAR rather than towards vaste state space size that can only be represented implicitly. Process synthesis facilities from LTL specifications with various techniques as shown in [26,33,49] and more recently with PROPHETS [16,27] the MDSL users for example to lay down the main features of a complex process (i.e. the steps they know), and let the synthesis tool autocomplete the correct mediators, like adding the right connecting bridges to the islands of an archipelago. With Language Driven Engineering [44,50] it is additionally possible to add meta-levels to the model stack, designing languages as models and generating the tools that support those languages directly from the language descriptions. The Webstory editor [29], DIME [6], and Cinco [39] itself are all implemented this way.

From this collected experience, we are convinced that, unlike the widespread push towards coding, this approach is scalable, and can provide the general public of professionals with the kind of familiarity with computational concepts and the level of confidence in practical making of applications and designs that can be a game changer for the societal diffusion of basic computing-related comprehension and design skills.

Acknowledgment. This work was supported, in part, by Science Foundation Ireland grants 13/RC/2094 and 16/RC/3918 and co-funded under the European Regional Development Fund through the Southern & Eastern Regional Operational Programme to Lero - the Irish Software Research Centre (www.lero.ie) and Confirm, the Centre for Smart Manufacturing (www.confirm.ie)

References

1. Chain reaction game website. https://brilliant.org/wiki/chain-reaction-game/
2. Chain reaction resources on the jabc website. https://hope.scce.info/chainreaction/
3. Bakera, M., Jörges, S., Margaria, T.: Test your strategy: graphical construction of strategies for connect-four. In: Proceedings of the 2009 14th IEEE International Conference on Engineering of Complex Computer Systems, pp. 172–181. ICECCS 2009. IEEE Computer Society, Washington, DC (2009). https://doi.org/10.1109/ICECCS.2009.51
4. Bakera, M., Margaria, T., Renner, C., Steffen, B.: Tool-supported enhancement of diagnosis in model-driven verification. Innov. Syst. Softw. Eng. **5**, 211–228 (2009). https://doi.org/10.1007/s11334-009-0091-6
5. Bordihn, H., Lamprecht, A., Margaria, T.: Foundations of semantics and model checking in a software engineering course. In: Bollin, A., Margaria, T., Perseil, I. (eds.) Proceedings of the First Workshop on Formal Methods in Software Engineering Education and Training, FMSEE&T 2015, co-located with 20th International Symposium on Formal Methods (FM 2015), Oslo, Norway, 23 June 2015. CEUR Workshop Proceedings, vol. 1385, pp. 19–26. CEUR-WS.org (2015). http://ceur-ws.org/Vol-1385/paper4.pdf
6. Boßelmann, S., et al.: DIME: a programming-less modeling environment for web applications. In: Margaria, T., Steffen, B. (eds.) ISoLA 2016. LNCS, vol. 9953, pp. 809–832. Springer, Cham (2016). https://doi.org/10.1007/978-3-319-47169-3_60
7. Brullo, V.: Modellizzazione di processi per l'individuazione e il trattamento di disturbi specifici dell'apprendimento in bambini in età scolare e prescolare. Master thesis, Politecnico di Torino, Torino (Italy), July 2016
8. Cabot, J., Tisi, M.: The MDE Diploma: first international postgraduate specialization in model-driven engineering. Comput. Sci. Educ. **21**(4), 389–402 (2011). https://doi.org/10.1080/08993408.2011.630131

9. Cioè, C.: Software Requirements for a Diabetic Retinopathy Centre. Master's thesis, Politecnico di Torino, Torino, Italy (2016)
10. Gossen, F., Kühn, D., Margaria, T., Lamprecht, A.L.: Computational thinking: learning by doing with the cinco adventure game tool. In: 2018 IEEE 42nd Annual Computer Software and Applications Conference (COMPSAC), vol. 01, pp. 990–999. IEEE Computer Society (2018). ISSN 0730–3157
11. Graf, S.: Building correct Cyber-Physical Systems - can we improve current practice? In: Proceedings of 23rd International Conference on Formal Methods in Industrial Critical Systems (FMICS 2018). LNCS, vol. 11119 (2018)
12. International Telecommunication Union: CCITT Recommendation I.312 / Q.1201 - Principles of Intelligent Network Architecture, October 1992. https://www.itu.int/rec/T-REC-I.312-199210-I/en
13. International Telecommunication Union: ITU-T Recommendation Q.1211 - Introduction to Intelligent Network Capability Set 1, March 1993. https://www.itu.int/rec/T-REC-Q.1211-199303-I/en
14. Jonsson, B., Margaria, T., Naeser, G., Nyström, J., Steffen, B.: Incremental requirement specification for evolving systems. In: Calder, M., Magill, E.H. (eds.) Feature Interactions in Telecommunications and Software Systems VI (FIW 2000), pp. 145–162. IOS Press, May 2000
15. Jonsson, B., Margaria, T., Naeser, G., Nyström, J., Steffen, B.: Incremental requirement specification for evolving systems. Nord. J. Comput. **8**, 65–87 (2001). http://dl.acm.org/citation.cfm?id=774194.774199
16. Jörges, S., Lamprecht, A.-L., Margaria, T., Naujokat, S., Steffen, B.: Synthesis from a practical perspective. In: Margaria, T., Steffen, B. (eds.) ISoLA 2016. LNCS, vol. 9952, pp. 282–302. Springer, Cham (2016). https://doi.org/10.1007/978-3-319-47166-2_20
17. Karsai, G.: From modeling to model-based programming. In: Margaria, T., Steffen, B. (eds.) Proceedings of 8th International Symposium on Leveraging Applications of Formal Methods, Verification and Validation. LNCS, vol. 11244, pp. 295–308 . Springer, Cham (2018)
18. Karusseit, M., Margaria, T.: Feature-based modelling of a complex, online-reconfigurable decision support service. Electron. Notes Theor. Comput. Sci. **157**(2), 101–118 (2006). http://www.sciencedirect.com/science/article/pii/S1571066106002489
19. Kölling, M.: The greenfoot programming environment. Trans. Comput. Educ. **10**(4), 14:1–14:21 (2010). http://doi.acm.org/10.1145/1868358.1868361
20. Koulouri, T., Lauria, S., Macredie, R.D.: Teaching introductory programming: a quantitative evaluation of different approaches. Trans. Comput. Educ. **14**(4), 26:1–26:28 (2014). http://doi.acm.org/10.1145/2662412
21. Kühn, D., Neubauer, J.: Guided domain-specific tailoring of jABC4. In: Lamprecht, A.-L. (ed.) ISoLA 2012/2014. CCIS, vol. 683, pp. 113–127. Springer, Cham (2016). https://doi.org/10.1007/978-3-319-51641-7_7
22. Lamprecht, A.-L., Margaria, T. (eds.): Process Design for Natural Scientists - An Agile Model-Driven Approach. CCIS, vol. 500. Springer, Heidelberg (2014). https://doi.org/10.1007/978-3-662-45006-2
23. Lamprecht, A.L., Margaria, T.: Scientific workflows with XMDD: a way to use process modeling in computational science education. Procedia Comput. Sci. **51**(0), 1927–1936 (2015). http://www.sciencedirect.com/science/article/pii/S187705091501265X. 15th International Conference On Computational Science (ICCS 2015): Computational Science at the Gates of Nature

24. Lamprecht, A., Margaria, T., McInerney, C.: A summer computing camp using chainreaction and jABC. In: 40th IEEE Annual Computer Software and Applications Conference, COMPSAC Workshops 2016, Atlanta, GA, USA, 10–14 June 2016, pp. 275–280. IEEE Computer Society (2016). https://doi.org/10.1109/COMPSAC.2016.41

25. Lamprecht, A.L., Margaria, T., Neubauer, J.: On the use of XMDD in software development education. In: 39th Annual IEEE Computer Software and Applications Conference (COMPSAC 2015), vol. 2, pp. 835–844, July 2015

26. Lamprecht, A.-L., Margaria, T., Steffen, B.: Seven variations of an alignment workflow - an illustration of agile process design and management in Bio-jETI. In: Măndoiu, I., Sunderraman, R., Zelikovsky, A. (eds.) ISBRA 2008. LNCS, vol. 4983, pp. 445–456. Springer, Heidelberg (2008). https://doi.org/10.1007/978-3-540-79450-9_42

27. Lamprecht, A.L., Naujokat, S., Margaria, T., Steffen, B.: Synthesis-based loose programming. In: Proceedings of the 7th International Conference on the Quality of Information and Communications Technology (QUATIC 2010), Porto, Portugal, pp. 262–267. IEEE, September 2010

28. Lamprecht, A.L., Steffen, B., Margaria, T.: Scientific workflows with the jABC framework. Int. J. Softw. Tools Technol. Transf. 18(6), 629–651 (2016). https://doi.org/10.1007/s10009-016-0427-0

29. Lybecait, M., Kopetzki, D., Zweihoff, P., Naujokat, S., Steffen, B.: A tutorial introduction to graphical modeling and metamodeling with CINCO. In: Margaria, T., Steffen, B. (eds.) Proceedings of 8th International Symposium on Leveraging Applications of Formal Methods, Verification and Validation. LNCS, vol. 11244, pp. 519–538. Springer, Cham (2018)

30. Maloney, J., Resnick, M., Rusk, N., Silverman, B., Eastmond, E.: The scratch programming language and environment. Trans. Comput. Educ. 10(4), 16:1–16:15 (2010). http://doi.acm.org/10.1145/1868358.1868363

31. Margaria, T.: Generative model driven design for agile system design and evolution: a tale of two worlds. In: Howar, F., Barnat, J. (eds.) FMICS 2018. LNCS, vol. 11119, pp. 3–18. Springer, Cham (2018). https://doi.org/10.1007/978-3-030-00244-2_1

32. Margaria, T., Floyd, B.D., Gonzalez Camargo, R., Lamprecht, A.-L., Neubauer, J., Seelaender, M.: Simple management of high assurance data in long-lived interdisciplinary healthcare research: a proposal. In: Margaria, T., Steffen, B. (eds.) ISoLA 2014. LNCS, vol. 8803, pp. 526–544. Springer, Heidelberg (2014). https://doi.org/10.1007/978-3-662-45231-8_44

33. Margaria, T., Meyer, D., Kubczak, C., Isberner, M., Steffen, B.: Synthesizing semantic web service compositions with jMosel and Golog. In: Bernstein, A., Karger, D.R., Heath, T., Feigenbaum, L., Maynard, D., Motta, E., Thirunarayan, K. (eds.) ISWC 2009. LNCS, vol. 5823, pp. 392–407. Springer, Heidelberg (2009). https://doi.org/10.1007/978-3-642-04930-9_25

34. Margaria, T., Steffen, B.: Business process modelling in the jABC: the one-thing-approach. In: Cardoso, J., van der Aalst, W. (eds.) Handbook of Research on Business Process Modeling. IGI Global (2009)

35. Margaria, T., Steffen, B.: Continuous model-driven engineering. IEEE Comput. 42(10), 106–109 (2009)

36. Margaria, T., Steffen, B.: Service-orientation: conquering complexity with XMDD. In: Hinchey, M., Coyle, L. (eds.) Conquering Complexity, pp. 217–236. Springer, London (2012). https://doi.org/10.1007/978-1-4471-2297-5_10

37. Margaria, T., Steffen, B., Reitenspieß, M.: Service-oriented design: the roots. In: Benatallah, B., Casati, F., Traverso, P. (eds.) ICSOC 2005. LNCS, vol. 3826, pp. 450–464. Springer, Heidelberg (2005). https://doi.org/10.1007/11596141_34

38. McInerney, C., Lamprecht, A.-L., Margaria, T.: Computing camps for girls – a first-time experience at the University of Limerick. In: Tatnall, A., Webb, M. (eds.) WCCE 2017. IAICT, vol. 515, pp. 494–505. Springer, Cham (2017). https://doi.org/10.1007/978-3-319-74310-3_50

39. Naujokat, S., Lybecait, M., Kopetzki, D., Steffen, B.: CINCO: a simplicity-driven approach to full generation of domain-specific graphical modeling tools. Softw. Tools Technol. Transf. **20**, 327–354 (2017)

40. Neubauer, J., Steffen, B., Margaria, T.: Higher-order process modeling: product-lining, variability modeling and beyond. Electron. Proc. Theor. Comput. Sci. **129**, 259–283 (2013)

41. Paravati, G., Lamberti, F., Gatteschi, V.: Joint traditional and company-based organization of information systems and product development courses. In: 39th IEEE Annual Computer Software and Applications Conference, COMPSAC 2015, Taichung, Taiwan, 1–5 July 2015, vol. 2, pp. 858–867 (2015). https://doi.org/10.1109/COMPSAC.2015.83

42. Resnick, M., et al.: Scratch: programming for all. Commun. ACM **52**(11), 60–67 (2009). http://doi.acm.org/10.1145/1592761.1592779

43. Starrett, C.: Teaching UML modeling before programming at the high school level. In: Seventh IEEE International Conference on Advanced Learning Technologies (ICALT 2007), pp. 713–714, July 2007

44. Steffen, B., Gossen, F., Naujokat, S., Margaria, T.: Language-driven engineering: from general-purpose to purpose-specific languages. In: Steffen, B., Woeginger, G. (eds.) Computing and Software Science: State of the Art and Perspectives, LNCS, vol. 10000. Springer (2018)

45. Steffen, B., Margaria, T., Braun, V., Kalt, N.: Hierarchical service definition. Annu. Rev. Commun. ACM **51**, 847–856 (1997)

46. Steffen, B., Margaria, T., Claßen, A.: Heterogeneous analysis and verification for distributed systems. Softw. Concepts Tools **17**(1), 13–25 (1996)

47. Steffen, B., Margaria, T., Claßen, A., Braun, V.: Incremental formalization: a key to industrial success. Softw. Concepts Tools **17**(2), 78–95 (1996)

48. Steffen, B., Margaria, T., Claßen, A., Braun, V., Reitenspieß, M.: An environment for the creation of intelligent network services. In: Intelligent Networks: IN/AIN Technologies, Operations, Services and Applications - A Comprehensive Report, pp. 287–300. IEC: International Engineering Consortium (1996)

49. Steffen, B., Margaria, T., Freitag, B.: Module Configuration by Minimal Model Construction. Technical report, Fakultät für Mathematik und Informatik, Universität Passau (1993)

50. Steve Boßelmann, S.N., Steffen, B.: On the difficulty of drawing the line. In: Margaria, T., Steffen, B. (eds.) Proceedings of 8th International Symposium on Leveraging Applications of Formal Methods, Verification and Validation. LNCS, vol. 11244, pp. 340–356. Springer, Cham (2018)

51. Tekinerdogan, B.: Experiences in teaching a graduate course on model-driven software development. Comput. Sci. Educ. **21**(4), 363–387 (2011). https://doi.org/10.1080/08993408.2011.630129

52. Utting, I., Cooper, S., Kölling, M., Maloney, J., Resnick, M.: Alice, greenfoot, and scratch - a discussion. Trans. Comput. Educ. **10**(4), 17:1–17:11 (2010). http://doi.acm.org/10.1145/1868358.1868364

53. Voelter, M.: Fusing modeling and programming into language-oriented programming - our experiences with MPS. In: Margaria, T., Steffen, B. (eds.) Proceedings of 8th International Symposium on Leveraging Applications of Formal Methods, Verification and Validation. LNCS, vol. 11244, pp. 309–339. Springer, Cham (2018)

54. Wickert, A., Lamprecht, A., Margaria, T.: Domain-specific design of patient classification in cancer-related cachexia research. In: Gnesi, S., Plat, N., Spoletini, P., Pelliccione, P. (eds.) Proceedings of the 6th Conference on Formal Methods in Software Engineering, FormaliSE 2018, collocated with ICSE 2018, Gothenburg, Sweden, 2 June 2018, pp. 60–63. ACM (2018). http://doi.acm.org/10.1145/3193992.3194002

55. Wing, J.M.: Computational thinking. Commun. ACM **49**(3), 33–35 (2006). http://doi.acm.org/10.1145/1118178.1118215

56. Wolber, D., Abelson, H., Spertus, E., Looney, L.: App Inventor 2: Create Your Own Android Apps. O'Reilly Media (2014). https://books.google.nl/books?id=YjcCBQAAQBAJ

57. Wolber, D.: App inventor and real-world motivation. In: Proceedings of the 42nd ACM Technical Symposium on Computer Science Education, pp. 601–606. SIGCSE 2011. ACM, New York (2011). http://doi.acm.org/10.1145/1953163.1953329

58. Zendler, A., Spannagel, C., Klaudt, D.: Process as content in computer science education: empirical determination of central processes. Comput. Sci. Educ. **18**(4), 231–245 (2008). http://www.tandfonline.com/doi/abs/10.1080/08993400802390553

Design Languages: A Necessary New Generation of Computer Languages

Bran Selić[✉]

Malina Software Corp., Nepean, ON K2J 2J3, Canada
selic@acm.org

Abstract. With the increased demand for so-called "smart" systems, which are required to interact with the physical world in ever more complex ways, we are witnessing a corresponding growth in the complexity of the software that is at the core of such systems. Keeping pace with this rise in complexity is proving to be a challenge for current mainstream programming technologies, whose origins are typically rooted in increasingly outdated computing paradigms that can be traced to some of the earliest applications of computers (e.g., solving numerical problems). This paper first examines some of the salient shortcomings of current mainstream programming technologies; shortcomings that render them unsuitable for addressing modern software applications. This is followed by a discussion of emerging and necessary trends in computer language development, which point to a brand new generation of languages, called *design languages*. The primary technical requirements for these new languages are identified, and certain pragmatic and socio-economic issues associated with their introduction into industrial practice are reviewed. The paper concludes with a high-level summary of crucial research topics required to realize the full potential of these languages.

Keywords: Domain-specific languages · Programming languages Modeling languages

1 Introduction

As modern society increases its critical dependence on so-called "smart" systems[1], there are worrisome indications that current software technologies are proving inadequate to meet the technical challenges posed by such systems. One key characteristic that is common to all such systems is that they are becoming increasingly more integrated into the operational aspects of the functioning of today's society. Thus, smart electrical grids are expected to perform dynamic load balancing across multiple interconnected energy networks, smart cars assist humans in the operation of their vehicles with perspectives towards fully automated driving, smart buildings regulate various domestic functions such as heating, electrical power consumption, and home security, and so on.

---

[1] See, for example, the "Smart Anything Everywhere" initiative that is part of the European Commission's Horizon 2020 Programme (https://smartanythingeverywhere.eu).

© Springer Nature Switzerland AG 2018
T. Margaria and B. Steffen (Eds.): ISoLA 2018, LNCS 11244, pp. 279–294, 2018.
https://doi.org/10.1007/978-3-030-03418-4_17

Clearly, the software to control these types of systems must have an effective means for interacting with the physical world. This means not only sensing the state of that world but also responding in "real-time"; i.e., providing timely responses to changes in the state of the physical environment and the systems that it regulates.

Real-time and embedded systems programmers are well aware of the often overwhelming complexity that interworking with the physical world involves. After all, the physical world is inherently concurrent, multifaceted, and often unpredictable. It is, therefore, not uncommon for code designed to cope with "exceptional" situations to be significantly larger and more complex than the code required for realizing a system's primary functionality. (In fact, part of the problem may lie in the very fact that such phenomena are classified as exceptions, rather than as less likely but still integral aspects of overall real-world behavior). And, as commercial demands for software with ever more sophisticated functionality grows, the degree of complexity will only increase.

Unfortunately, as illustrated by numerous examples, some of which are described in this paper, current mainstream programming technologies are less and less capable of responding to this explosion in complexity. Much of this is due to the fact that most of them are still rooted in a classical and somewhat idealistic but highly outdated view of the nature and role of computers, which is biased in favor of numerical computation. Thus, for example, Edsger Dijkstra, generally recognized as one of the core ideologues of today's computer science, lamented the introduction of hardware interrupts into computing technology because they introduced non-determinism into computations:

"[The interrupt] was a great invention, but also a Pandora's Box ... essentially, *for the sake of efficiency*[2], concurrency [became] visible ... and then all hell broke loose" [1].

However, although efficiency may have been the primary motivation for adding interrupts in this particular case, it is just one example of the growing need for computers (and, hence, for software) to interact effectively with their physical surroundings. In yet another of his notes, Dijkstra states:

"I see no meaningful difference between programming methodology and mathematical methodology" [2].

These statements reflect a mathematician's idealized view of software and software design as an exercise in applied mathematics rather than as an engineering problem[3]

Another telling example of this "Platonist" approach to the theory of software can be seen from the way that time is treated. As Edward Lee notes:

"[t]ime has been systematically removed from theories of computation. 'Pure' computation does not take time and has nothing to do with time" [3].

---

[2] Author's emphasis.

[3] Mathematical approaches to software are often more focused on reaching qualitative conclusions that abstract out the quantitative aspects. However, in engineering the quantitative is often a fundamental concern.

Even the various temporal logics, devised to incorporate the notion of time into computational theory, only provide a very abstract notion of time, using qualitative terms such as "eventually" and "henceforth". But, as Lee points out further:

> "... much of the problem is that computation *does* take time. Even with infinitely fast computers, software will still have to deal with time because the physical processes with which it interacts, evolve over time" [3].

This idealized view of computing is perhaps not surprising given its history, its technological foundations based on mathematical logic, and its initially dominant application to numerical and other mathematically-oriented problems. (Even the very term "computing" attests to this bias.) It is, therefore, no accident that most mainstream programming languages favor a purely mathematical concept of value, with primitive data types such as integers, reals, Booleans, etc., which are (somewhat imperfect) analogs of corresponding mathematical concepts. As in formal mathematics these are, quite intentionally, decoupled from any physical connotations. Of course, it is still possible to associate physical dimensions (e.g., weight, length, time) and units (e.g., kilograms, meters, and milliseconds) with such values. But, crucially, as explained in Sect. 2.2, the physical semantics of such associations are not incorporated in the definition of these languages, and consequently, these semantics are not enforced by associated language support tools such as compilers and debuggers. For example, the C++ language and its compilers do not "know" the relationship between pounds and kilograms. Consequently, as the Mars Climate Orbiter example described in the Sect. 2 demonstrated, it is not possible to automatically detect invalid combinations of these two different types.

Today's mainstream programming languages, such as C++, Java, or C#, are intentionally designed to be "general purpose", which means that they are designed to primarily capture and enforce the semantics of common mathematical logic and arithmetic. The premise then is that capturing and ensuring problem-domain semantics (e.g., that pounds and kilograms are different types) are the responsibility of human programmers. But, as argued in this paper, this is a severe and unnecessary underutilization of the automation potential provided by modern computers. It has far-reaching negative consequences particularly for the coming wave of "smart" interactive applications. The solution being proposed here is to define a new generation of higher-level computer languages; one that allows more direct expression of problem-domain phenomena and design intent and one that takes much greater advantage of the automation potential of computers.

The advantages and shortcomings of the current generation of mainstream programming languages, are discussed in greater detail in the following section. Section 3 introduces and explores the notion of *design languages* as a crucial part of an advanced strategy for addressing the challenges of 21st century applications. The core requirements for this new generation of computer languages are highlighted, as are the pragmatic issues involved in their introduction into practice, including a discussion of potentially major socio-economic hurdles. The section closes with a brief overview of necessary research. Section 4 summarizes the arguments made in the paper.

2   The Successes and Failures of Mainstream Languages

There cannot be any doubt that the transition from second generation assembly languages to the higher-level third-generation languages was highly beneficial in terms of both programmer productivity and program quality. The reasons for this are discussed briefly in Sect. 2.1. However, Sect. 2.2, examines the primary shortcomings of current mainstream modeling languages, which are representative of the third (and still current) generation of computer languages that make them unsuitable for advanced interactive applications.

2.1   What Is Behind the Success of Third-Generation Languages

One of the primary advantages of third-generation programming languages was that their constructs were defined in such a way that it was possible to automatically prevent entire categories of common coding flaws and error-prone programming practices that plagued assembly language programming. This was possible because languages incorporated higher-level technology-independent *semantics* of their constructs in the language specification. As a result, semantically invalid formulations, such as invalid combinations of incompatible types, could be readily detected and flagged.

Complementing this important feature was the use of computer-based automation to enforce those semantics. This was provided through language-specific computer-based tools such as compilers, program editors, program validators of various kinds, debuggers. They bridged the gap between the higher-level semantics instilled in the language constructs and the underlying hardware technology used to realize them. In this text, the term *first-class* is used to denote language constructs whose semantics are recognized and enforced by language-specific tools. These stand in contrast to programmer-generated constructs, whose definition and semantics are the responsibility of the language user, with all the reliability and productivity problems that this entails.

The introduction of third-generation languages into practice had dramatic effects. Programs that would have taken months with assembly languages could now be realized in days and, moreover, these programs tended to be significantly more reliable. The obvious conclusion that can be drawn from this experience is that, if properly conceived and executed, an *increase in the level of abstraction* of a computer language when combined with a corresponding *increase in the use of automation* can provide major advances in both the quality of software produced and programmer productivity.

2.2   Critical Shortcomings of Current Mainstream Programming Languages

The benefits of higher levels of abstraction and automation are certainly well known and understood. However, what is surprising is how long it is taking the software community to reapply this eminently successful pattern. "Modern" mainstream programming languages, such as Java and C#, seem to be mired in a kind of third-generation sclerosis. Although some of them have undoubtedly introduced important technical improvements, such as object orientation and fewer error-prone constructs, compared to early third-generation languages such as FORTRAN or COBOL, they most definitely have not produced the same dramatic increases in productivity and quality as was experienced with the transition from second- to third-generation languages. In simple terms, a line of Java or C# code is not much more productive than a line of FORTRAN or COBOL.

It is, therefore, not surprising that we still use the term "coding", as synonym for programming. After all, both "code" and "coding" generally imply a transformation of some original formulation into a different and usually more cryptic form. This is the reason why programs written in these languages are not only difficult to write correctly but are also extremely difficult to understand. If, for example, my solution is best expressed as a state machine or a sequence diagram, the task of translating that into an equivalent third-generation language program is going to be both time consuming and susceptible to various *coding errors*. On the other hand, such a translation can be much more easily performed by a computer-based translator that "understands" the semantics of the original source specification, with the important added benefit that the resulting executable can be optimized for performance.

However, raising the level of abstraction to "recognize" the semantics of higher-level formalisms such as state machines is not sufficient for the new generation of "smart" software applications. The software in these systems has to interact in a *timely and appropriate manner* with the physical world, which means that it is also necessary to account for the semantics of the physical world.

The above discussion leads to the conclusion that there are multiple reasons why the current generation of mainstream languages needs to be replaced. In the remainder of this section, the following three categories of primary shortcomings of these languages are discussed in more detail:

- Inadequate support for interacting with the physical world
- Inadequate expressive power for modern software needs
- A volatile and inherently unsafe nature

Inadequate Support for Interacting with the Physical World. Lack of support for expressing physical world phenomena, such as time or physical quantities, was already mentioned. For example, when specifying time quantities, it is more or less common practice to specify these in program code in terms of purely numerical values (e.g., delay(100), force = 250). The physical nature and measurement units that these numbers represent are often implicit, based on an established shared convention. Consequently, if different units are being used for different parts of the system, it is up to human programmers to detect that conversions are necessary and to implement them. Needless to say, this is error prone. Notorious examples of software-based disasters that this can induce include the Ariane 5 rocket failure[4] and the Mars Climate Orbiter[5] disaster, both of which resulted in multi-million dollar damages.

In the Ariane 5 case, a floating-point value representing horizontal velocity was converted into a corresponding integer, whose value, unfortunately, exceeded the 16-bit hardware limit on integers. Despite careful scrutiny that such software is normally

---

[4] See http://www-users.math.umn.edu/~arnold/disasters/disasters.html.
[5] See https://en.wikipedia.org/wiki/Mars_Climate_Orbiter.

exposed to, the error went undetected. The rocket and its payload were destroyed shortly after launch.

The Mars Climate Orbiter failed because different development teams made different assumptions about the measurement units to be used in their software; one group used International Standard units whereas the other used US Standard units. This elementary type violation error somehow slipped through all the various code inspections and automated validations. The spacecraft carrying the Orbiter reached Mars but, because of the coding error, it was destroyed as soon as it was deployed.

While lack of meaningful support for "physical" data types is a clear example of what Fred Brooks Jr. refers to as *accidental* complexity [4], dealing with physically distributed software intensive systems also involves *essential* complexity. For example, there are critical phenomena inherent in physically distributed systems that software spanning such systems must contend with. For example, when dealing with time values in such systems, time readings may be provided by different physically distributed and possibly unsynchronized clocks. In time sensitive applications, it may be critical to understand and account for the relationships between the values measured by the different clocks, which are, after all, imperfect physical devices (e.g., differences in characteristics such as accuracy, resolution, drift, or jitter).

As Edward Lee pointed out, quantitative time values can be of crucial importance in real systems. Precise knowledge of the true values of deadlines, timestamps, computing times, and communication delays may be critical in many "smart" distributed applications. Even in modern business applications, such as stock market-related buy-sell activities, time differences in the order of microseconds may prove critical. While a qualitative analysis of time characteristics of such systems using temporal logics is likely to be useful, it is not always sufficient. In addition to problems with time values, other complex phenomena encountered in distributed systems include partial system failures and other types of malfunctions, variabilities in the nature and timing of physical cues, true physical concurrency[6], and so on. For software spanning such a system to be reliable to the desired degree, it is necessary that some or all of these complexities need to be understood and accounted for.

However, if these and other types of physical-world semantics were to be incorporated into the definition of computer languages designed for interactive software applications, the specification of software for such systems would not only be simplified but the likelihood of human error would be greatly reduced. For example, it might be useful to explicitly specify the necessary design minima for response times of an application. This can then be automatically matched against the timing capabilities of underlying platforms, so that potential mismatches (a kind of quantitative type violation) can be detected prior to deployment.

Inadequate Expressive Power for Modern Software Needs. A different category of shortcomings of mainstream languages involves the serious lack of expressive power in representing some critical facets of complex software systems. Expressive power can be defined as the ability to precisely specify some phenomenon or idea while minimizing the amount of information provided explicitly.

---

[6] In contrast to pseudo-concurrency, which can be controlled.

Perhaps the most glaring is their inability to specify, in a direct, precise, and comprehensible fashion, the high-level design of a complex software system, that is, its *architecture*[7]. This is because the early third-generation ancestor languages were designed primarily to express fine-grained detail, such as algorithms and low-level data structures. This fine-grained mindset has carried over into the design of more recent languages. Consequently, none of these languages provide first-class support for specifying layered structures or high-level end-to-end interaction sequences, both of which are fundamental to specifying the architecture of complex software systems. Instead, such things are specified indirectly, either through documentation or indirectly by various directives with very general semantics. For example, layering relationships can sometimes (but not always) be deduced by tracing usage dependencies between source files. These are typically specified by compiler directives, such as `#include` statements, which, unfortunately, can serve other purposes as well. Similarly, high-level end-to-end sequences between collaborating run-time software entities, can only be reconstructed by manually tracing through causally-connected invocation chains of procedure calls embedded in the code (akin to navigating by looking at map through a keyhole-sized aperture).

With the inability to formally capture core architectural intent, it is not surprising that it is practically impossible to guarantee that the architectural integrity of a system is maintained, both during initial development as well as in the course of subsequent maintenance. Seemingly minor difficult-to-spot coding errors can easily violate a high-level design decision, leading to the well-known phenomenon of "architectural decay".

Once again, the responsibility for ensuring that critical aspects of an application, such as its architecture, are properly interpreted and implemented is passed on to less than fully-reliable human programmers. This despite the fact that, in principle, such information can be formally captured and, therefore, automatically validated by a computer.

The same lack of expressiveness can be found when programming various problem-specific high-level formalisms commonly used in software design, such as finite state machines, or message sequence diagrams.

In many cases the text-based concrete syntax of these languages exacerbates the problem of lack of expressiveness. This is because many of the above formalisms as well as common architectural design patterns are typically specified in graphical form because this is generally more compact and easier to comprehend than equivalent textual renditions. While text has many advantages in terms of the ease with which computers can manipulate it, this is yet another example of the technology-centric bias inherent in mainstream programming languages.

The Volatile and Unsafe Nature of Mainstream Programming Languages. A famous example of an expensive software disaster is the case of the failure of the AT&T long distance telephone network in the United States in 1990 [5]. The problem started with the installation of a new software version into the network; a step that is always undertaken with great care, usually at night during times of low utilization. In

---

[7] While architectural description languages do exist, they are either informal or not formally coupled to the mainstream language programs that realize them.

this particular case, following the upgrade, one of the routing nodes in the network failed. But, because these systems are designed for high availability, it recovered relatively quickly. Due to the redundancy of the network, this glitch had little noticeable impact on the operation of the network. However, as it came back up, the software in the recovering node sent notifications to its immediate neighbors informing them that it was back in service. Unfortunately, due to a bug in the software, this "recovery" message caused each of the neighboring nodes to fail in turn. This initiated an endless cycle of failures and recoveries, effectively incapacitating the entire network. (To recover the network, the operators had to revert to the earlier version of the software). Since the long-distance network provides the core infrastructure for much government and business work, the cost of this failure was literally in the hundreds of millions of dollars.

Following a post mortem analysis, the root cause of the problem was uncovered in one small fragment of code: one of the branches of a multi-branch C-language "switch" statement had accidentally omitted to include a corresponding "break" statement. As a result, once the actions in that branch were completed, the code execution carried through to the branch immediately below it, executing inappropriate code that eventually led to the failure of the entire node and, from there, the entire network.

Most experienced programmers can sympathize with this, and many of them likely have encountered comparable cases in their own practice, although, one hopes with less dire consequences. What is particularly distressing about this situation, however, is how a small-scale coding flaw – one that could happen even to the most experienced programmer and one which can be easily overlooked even during careful code inspections or not caught during testing – could have such enormous consequences. The Ariane 5 incident mentioned previously was yet another example of this same syndrome. "Small" but difficult to detect coding errors of this nature are quite common in practice: uninitialized variables, misaligned pointers, and even type violations. Industry statistics suggest that there are, on the average, between 15 and 50 bugs in every 1000 lines of production code [6]. There is, unfortunately, no realistic way of predicting the consequences of all such errors. Exacerbating this issue is that, usually in the interest of efficiency, many programming languages provide various unsafe mechanisms, such as "cast" operators, that override compiler safety features.

There has been a lot of research effort invested in supporting formal analyses of such programs, so as to detect these problems before the code is put into service. However, third-generation programming languages exhibit a highly non-linear almost chaotic nature, wherein even the smallest flaw – such as a missing "break" statement – can lead to catastrophic results. This means that any formal treatment of programs must analyze the system at this most detailed of levels – which, unfortunately, quickly leads to a combinatorial explosion of possible executions even for small programs. Hence, it is often not practically feasible to use formal methods to ascertain with confidence the reliability of complex software systems.

In summary, computer languages should be free of constructs that can lead to such "butterfly effects", whereby a seemingly minor and difficult to spot implementation flaw can lead to unpredictable and potentially catastrophic consequences.

3   Design Languages: A Necessary New Generation of Computer Languages

Starting with the premise that dramatic gains in quality and productivity can only come from significant increases in levels of abstraction and automation, it is useful to analyze and be more precise about what this entails. Specifically, what exactly is meant by that much used phrase "raising the level of abstraction"?

Simply put, it means that we are trying to abstract away from the technical details of the underlying computing technology by overlaying a more problem domain-specific conceptual framework over them. This is often done incrementally, in multiple discrete steps through successive software layers (sometimes referred to as *layers of abstraction*), each presenting an application programming interface that is closer to the problem domain. Ultimately, the application should be provided with an environment that directly supports the semantics of the problem and solution domains (e.g., support for finite state machines).

A common third-generation language solution to this problem is to provide domain-specific *program libraries and frameworks*. For example, for software applications controlling physical devices, there might be program libraries that in some way directly support concepts from physics such a torque, force, and the like.

Unfortunately, the *domain-specific library approach is insufficient*. First of all, because such libraries are realized using general-purpose programming languages, the automation tools associated with those languages (e.g., compilers, editors, or validators) are unable to detect violations or misuse of the problem-domain specific semantics that they are intended to capture. The Mars Climate Orbiter disaster described earlier is a clear example of this shortcoming. Moreover, these libraries are often designed and created by error-prone human programmers, who may not even be domain experts.

Consequently, as explained in Sect. 2.1, to be truly effective, domain-specific concepts should be supported as first-class language concepts. For example, if a state machine formalism is an appropriate match for a domain, the specification for the corresponding language should include concepts such as "state", "transition", and the like and these should be directly available to the language user.

By instilling computer languages with domain-specific concepts in this way, it becomes much easier to express design intent in a standard, direct, and unambiguous manner. Furthermore, supported by corresponding infrastructure tools such as language-specific translators, editors, interpreters, etc., the unreliable and unproductive human element of the translation process can be reduced or even eliminated. The concepts supported by such languages are the ones that application designers use to specify their designs clearly and unambiguously in the most succinct form. Hence, they are referred to herein as *design languages*[8], although, it should be understood that they should be equally useful in problem analysis.

---

[8] This form is preferred to the more common "domain-specific language" because it more clearly identifies how the language is intended to be used and also avoids possible misinterpretations that the older term might carry in some circles.

3.1   Requirements for Modern Design Languages

The core requirements for fully-fledged design languages are summarized below. They are derived from practical experiences with a number of prototypical design languages as well as analyses of early attempts at transcending third-generation languages (see Sect. 3.2 below).

1. They should support domain-specific concepts and their semantics as first-class language constructs.
2. The semantics of the language concepts should be defined by means of a precisely-defined formalism that accurately captures the domain-specific semantics and which is suitable for formal (computer-supported) analyses based on those semantics. This formalism could be mathematical, but it could also be defined operationally. Whichever the case, it enables automatic analysis by language-specific tools.
3. As much as possible, the formalism underlying a language should not be prone to chaotic phenomena, whereby a small-scale flaw in a design specification could lead to unpredictable consequences (i.e., "the butterfly effect").
4. Despite the critical importance of precise formal specification, it should still be able to use the language in so-called "sketching" mode[9]; that is, it should be possible to use them to quickly create high-level specifications that may be incomplete, but which can still be usefully analyzed by formal means.
5. They should support one or more concrete syntaxes that provide direct and intuitive expression of design intent in a manner appropriate for their target domain. Specifically, it should be possible to have multiple different concrete syntaxes for a given design language each corresponding to a specific viewpoint (i.e., a specific set of concerns).
6. They should provide an extension mechanism to support evolutionary developments in the domain and in the underlying technologies. Any new extensions must be semantically aligned with the rest of the language concepts.
7. To eliminate the need for coding, at least some design languages should be such that specifications written in that language are sufficiently detailed that they can be automatically translated (i.e., *without human intervention*) into complete and final implementations. However, as indicated in item 3 above, to be qualified as true design languages, such languages must also support sketching modes. That opens up the possibility of a continuous evolution starting from a high-level specification and terminating on a fully-fledged implementation using a single language. This would minimize discontinuities in methods, tools, and expertise, which often lead to corruption of original design intent.
8. Because "domain" is a relative and recursive concept (i.e., one domain might incorporate multiple finer-grained domains), it should be possible to embed one design language into another design language that covers a broader scope. Clearly, this is only possible if the semantics of the two languages are compatible in some way. In fairness, what constitutes compatibility between two sets of semantics is still much of a research issue. This issue is discussed further in Sect. 3.3 below.

---

[9] https://martinfowler.com/bliki/UmlAsSketch.html.

3.2   Early Design Languages

Various higher-level languages devised to support the process of designing software have been around almost since the inception of programming, with basic flow charts[10] and Nassi-Shneiderman diagrams[11] among the earliest. These languages raised the level of abstraction by compressing multiple programming language instructions and corresponding flows into conceptually meaningful behavioral units that exposed design intent in a more direct manner using a graphically-based syntax.

Subsequently, in the late 80's and throughout the 90's, the term "fourth-generation programming language", was used to characterize a number of domain-specific languages[12]. Although they have some commonality with design languages as defined here, they do not meet all the requirements defined in Sect. 3.1. Nevertheless, they can be considered as ancestors of true design languages in that they were designed to overcome the limitations of the third-generation programming paradigm by raising the levels of abstraction and automation.

Certain more mathematically-oriented high-level formalisms, such as Petri nets and David Harel's statecharts [7], were subsequently re-cast as computer languages, that is, languages that could be usefully interpreted by a computer.

From such beginnings, the trend towards higher-level modes of expression supported by computers continued with a new generation of what are often called "modeling languages". This included a myriad of object-oriented notations, including some, such as UML and SysML, which were standardized by industry and which, as a result, gained significant currency. Despite much disagreement and pervasive industry pessimism about the real benefits of these languages, there is significant published evidence to the fact that, if applied properly, they can lead to significant gains in productivity and quality [8–10].

Most of these early modeling languages were informal tools created to facilitate quick and lightweight exploration of design alternatives through sketching. The importance of the ability to *clearly capture design intent with minimal effort* should not be underestimated, since it can increase productivity by expediting the critical process of design-space exploration. Unfortunately, the informal nature of these languages means that it is not possible to take advantage of computer-based automation to validate the resulting models. Clearly, the ability to combine a lightweight sketching mode with automated formal validation would be a highly advantageous characteristic of a computer design language. This is the motivation for requirement 4 above.

Another recognized drawback of early modeling languages was their concrete syntax, which was typically based on informal and unscientific principles [11]. While the importance of an appropriate concrete syntax for a computer language is often downplayed by professional programmers[13], in practice it is crucial, since it is the primary interface by which design intent is conveyed to human observers.

---

[10] See https://en.wikipedia.org/wiki/Flowchart.

[11] See https://en.wikipedia.org/wiki/Nassi%E2%80%93Shneiderman_diagram.

[12] See: https://en.wikipedia.org/wiki/Fourth-generation_programming_language.

[13] This can be deduced from the widely used term "syntactic sugar", which implies that syntax is merely a superfluous adornment that is not needed by "macho" programmers.

A well-chosen syntax will enable direct and intuitive expression of an idea in a way that maximizes comprehension with minimal intellectual effort.

Over time, some of the more widely used modeling languages, such as UML [12] and SDL [13], evolved into fully-fledged formal and even executable languages. These are computer languages that are capable of producing complete and final implementations. Specifications written in these languages can be translated automatically – without human intervention in the translation process – into executable computer programs. Hence, these can be deemed prototypical design languages, along with other executable high-level language examples such as AADL [14] and Simulink/Stateflow [15] from Mathworks Inc[14]. However, in contrast to fully-fledged design languages, they were designed to be used primarily as implementation languages rendering them less suitable for use in the earlier stages of design.

3.3   Some Pragmatics

Complex software systems are multifaceted, involving multiple domains, some of them nested within each other, as noted in Sect. 3.1. Invariably, some of these domains intersect with each other, so that some elements appear in multiple domains simultaneously. This results in the problem of ensuring that all the different representations of such elements, each expressed in a different language, must be consistent. If these languages are based on different formalisms, it may be difficult to ensure consistency or, even worse, to be able to detect inconsistencies. At the very least, these languages should not have semantics that are in direct contradiction. Detecting such incompatibilities is still very much a research topic.

One way of mitigating this problem is to define all the overlapping domain-specific languages as specializations of a common underlying base language. This ensures a single common semantics foundation for all. This is facilitated if the base language has a flexible extension mechanism (requirement 6 in Sect. 3.1 above). That such an approach is both feasible and practical has been proven by the case of UML and its profile mechanism[15]. Namely, UML profiles have been used successfully to create many different domain-specific languages, each sharing a common semantic foundation, but each adding its own domain-specific refinements[16].

The UML profile mechanism provides another example that can be emulated by new design languages: a highly flexible annotation mechanism. This allows a means for marking up a specification expressed in one domain-specific language to support its mapping (translation) to a different domain-specific language. For example, the UML MARTE profile [16] includes several domain-specific languages for annotating standard UML models for the purpose of various types of analyses, including performance and schedulability. The concepts defined in these profiles represent markings that identify target domain concepts and their properties. These are then used by a

---

[14] https://en.wikipedia.org/wiki/Fourth-generation_programming_language.

[15] This is not to say that the extension mechanism need necessarily be based on the UML profile mechanism, which is possibly not the best technical solution to language extensibility.

[16] https://www.omg.org/spec/category/uml-profile.

specialized model transformation algorithm to generate a corresponding target domain model, which can then be used for automated formal analysis.

Wherever practical, formal analyses should involve various mathematical methods, but they may also involve simulation. For simulation, it is extremely useful if the language and the corresponding tool infrastructure allow execution of high-level (i.e., abstract) and incomplete models, as specified in requirement 4 in Sect. 3.1. This can be further enhanced if the formal validation mechanisms built into the language can be applied selectively. One approach to high-level validation is to start with a relatively small but essential set of validations and then, as the design evolves and more detail is added, to gradually add more refined validations as necessary.

3.4   What Stands in the Way [17]

In addition to the technical and research challenges discussed previously, there are additional critical factors that need to be overcome before greater development and adoption of design languages can occur. There are both economic and cultural impediments.

From a cost perspective, it is important to remember that the development of a useful computer language requires major investments in time and resources: defining the language, developing and maintaining corresponding tools (e.g., compilers, editors, validators, and debuggers), developing and maintaining training materials for the language, training programmers, as well as developing a rich set of reusable program libraries. From that point of view, one can understand why, given the choice, many development groups opt for established "mainstream" languages, which "come for free", so to speak.

On the cultural front it should be recognized that practitioners who have invested much personal time and effort in mastering these mainstream languages are understandably reluctant to switch to a new programming paradigm or even a new language. The fact is that in today's highly competitive IT environment, software practitioners are mostly hired and judged based on their mastery of a particular configuration of programming technologies as opposed to having domain-specific expertise.

Consequently, if we are to emerge from the current slump in the evolution of computer languages, towards languages that are better attuned to domain-specific semantics, which implies defining domain-specific languages, it is absolutely fundamental to develop methods and automated means to minimize the cost of developing and maintaining a *language infrastructure* (tools, program libraries, training materials, etc.) that would support domain-specific languages. Some attempts have already been made to automate aspects of this (e.g., automatic generation of language-specific editors), but, overall, this is still a mostly open research topic.

3.5   Research Challenges Ahead

One of the two "pillars" that support the idea of design languages is the increased use of computer automation. Automation is used in many different functions: specification authoring, specification validation, transformations of specifications from one form to another, specification viewing, code generation, and so on. Current tools used for early design languages such as UML or SysML leave much to be desired in terms of efficiency, scalability, usability, and usefulness [17]. How should these and other shortcomings of current tools be eliminated? What should a toolchain that supports design languages look like? What are the use cases? These and other issues represent a major area of fruitful multi-disciplinary research.

On the language front there are also numerous areas that need to be systematically explored before we can have a clear understanding how to design these languages in a systematic and reliable way: What are the best ways of specifying the abstract syntax of a design language? How can we define the semantics of a new language in a way that can be correctly interpreted by language support tools? How do we detect semantically incompatible languages? What are the most appropriate patterns for mapping the semantics of one language to the semantics of another? How should we define concrete syntaxes in ways that are optimal from a human comprehension perspective? Which methods should be used for direct code generation (i.e., bypassing an intermediate third-generation language)? Given the definition of the semantics of a design language, how can we generate tests from specifications written in that language? How do we develop automated custom validators for individual languages?

There is some work already ongoing in most of these areas. However, it is fair to say that we are still very far from a comprehensive theoretical understanding of how to effectively define, implement, and use design languages. This presents significant opportunities for useful, interesting, and rewarding research in this domain are vast.

4 Summary

The starting thesis for this work is that the current generation of mainstream computer languages, that is, programming languages, is simply not powerful enough to deal with the challenges that are being posed for modern software systems. After all, as never before in history, there are immense commercial, economic, and social pressures to create ever more sophisticated technologies; technologies that are much more capable and more adaptive to society's needs than any to date. The foundations for this increased functional sophistication is expected to come through more "intelligent" software. Yet, given the current success rate of software projects[17], it seems that we are far from developing such sophisticated systems using current technologies and methods in a systematic and dependable manner. Therefore, it is argued here that many of the difficulties encountered in software systems stem from inadequacies of current mainstream programming languages. They are still much too primitive and much too distant from problem domains they are addressing. Worst of all, there is a widespread view that bridging this growing semantic gap should be the responsibility of human programmers, who are tasked with "manually" translating (i.e., coding) domain-specific concepts into computer-technology domain concepts.

---

[17] See for example: https://www.scrumalliance.org/community/articles/2016/october/what-we-really-know-about-successful-projects.

However, positive industrial experience with certain higher-level languages, that is, languages that transcend the third-generation, suggest that it is time to explore and develop a new generation of computer languages capable of more direct expression of problem-domain and solution-domain concepts, while transferring much more of the responsibility for validation and the production of the final implementation to computers. Consequently, these new design-oriented languages ("design languages") are likely to be increasingly more domain specific, but with precisely defined (i.e., formal) semantics, which allows them to take advantage of computer automation. In addition to being significantly higher on the abstraction scale and syntactically more comprehensible compared to mainstream third-generation languages, they are also distinguished by the capability to serve across the entire development cycle, from analysis through to implementation. Because they have precise formally defined semantics open to computer automation, specifications expressed using these languages can be validated, with the help of corresponding tool support, even though they are highly abstract and incomplete. This has the potential to dramatically reduce the time to explore and analyze different design alternatives, thereby improving both productivity and overall product quality compared to traditional methods.

This technological breakout from the confines of third-generation computer languages has already started, with numerous existence proofs even in large industrial projects. But, it is still in the early stages, as there is no systematic and reliable way of specifying and exploiting these languages. To achieve that requires a significant and well-coordinated research front.

Acknowledgement. The author would like to thank Dr. Manfred Broy for helpful suggestions on how the text could be improved.

References

1. Dijkstra, E.: My recollections of operating system design, E.W. Dijkstra Archive at the University of Texas (2001). https://www.cs.utexas.edu/users/EWD/ewd13xx/EWD1303.PDF
2. Dijkstra, E., Why American Computing Science seems incurable, E.W. Dijkstra Archive at the University of Texas (1995). https://www.cs.utexas.edu/users/EWD/ewd12xx/EWD1209.PDF
3. Lee, E.A.: Embedded software. In: Zelkowitz, M. (ed.) Advances in Computers, vol. 56. Elsevier Science (2002)
4. Brooks, F.: No silver bullet – essence and accident in software engineering. IEEE Comput. **20**(4), 91–94 (1987)
5. Lee, L.: The Day the Phones Stopped, Plume (1992)
6. McConnell, S.: Code Complete: A Practical Handbook of Software Construction, 2nd edn. Microsoft Press (2004)
7. Harel, D.: Statecharts: a visual formalism for complex systems. Sci. Comput. Program. **8**(3), 231–274 (1987)
8. Weigert, T., Weil, F.: Practical experience in using model-driven engineering to develop trustworthy systems. In: Proceedings of IEEE International Conference on Sensor Networks, Ubiquitous, and Trustworthy Computing (SUTC 2006), pp. 208–217. IEEE Computer Society (2006)

9. Corcoran, D.: The good, the bad and the ugly: experiences with model driven development in large scale projects at Ericsson. In: Kühne, T., Selic, B., Gervais, M.-P., Terrier, F. (eds.) ECMFA 2010. LNCS, vol. 6138, p. 2. Springer, Heidelberg (2010). https://doi.org/10.1007/978-3-642-13595-8_2

10. Hutchinson, J., Rouncefield, M., Whittle, J.: Model-driven engineering practices in industry. In: Taylor, R., et al. (eds.) Proceedings of the 33rd International Conference on Software Engineering (ICSE 2011), pp. 633–642. Association for Computing Machinery (ACM) (2011)

11. Moody, D., van Hillegersberg, J.: Evaluating the visual syntax of UML: an analysis of the cognitive effectiveness of the UML family of diagrams. In: Gašević, D., Lämmel, R., Van Wyk, E. (eds.) SLE 2008. LNCS, vol. 5452, pp. 16–34. Springer, Heidelberg (2009). https://doi.org/10.1007/978-3-642-00434-6_3

12. Object Management Group (OMG): Semantics of an Executable Subset for Executable UML Models, OMG document formal/17-07-02, OMG (2017)

13. International Telecommunications Union (ITU): Z.101: Specification and Description Language – Basic SDL-2010, ITU Recommendation Z.101, ITU (2010)

14. SAE International, Architecture Analysis and Design Language (AADL): Specification AS5506B (2012). https://www.sae.org/standards/content/as5506b/

15. Mathworks, Inc., Simulink (2018). https://www.mathworks.com/products/simulink.html

16. Object Management Group (OMG), UML Profile for MARTE, OMG document formal/11-06-02 (2011). https://www.omg.org/spec/MARTE/1.1/PDF

17. Selic, B.: What will it take? a view on adoption of model-based methods in practice. J. Syst. Model. **11**(4), 513–526 (2012)

18. LNCS Homepage. http://www.springer.com/lncs. Accessed 21 Nov 2016

From Modeling to Model-Based Programming

Gabor Karsai[(⊠)]

Institute for Software-Integrated Systems, Vanderbilt University,
Nashville, TN 37235, USA
gabor.karsai@vanderbilt.edu

Abstract. Modeling is a fundamental, analytical tool for engineering design. Programming is the synthesis (i.e. construction) of 'machines' that do something useful. Advances made during the past three decades showed how these activities are intertwined in systems development and cannot be separated. Arguably, the future of engineered systems shall encompass both, especially considering the design of cyber-physical systems where the computational is in continuous interaction with the physical. State-of-the-art industrial practice appears to focus on 'model-based programming' – programming with higher-level abstractions. In this paper we outline a broader picture for integrating modeling and programming, and what it means for engineering processes and engineering education.

Keywords: Model-driven development · Systems engineering
Software-intensive systems

1 Introduction

Model-driven software development and engineering (MDE) [1] is about 30 years old and it is a reasonable question to ask what role it plays today in the practice of building software-intensive systems and how its future may look like. While it is hard to pinpoint the exact start, it appears that MDE grew out from the experience with object-oriented analysis and design [2], when developers realized that software design can be represented on a higher-level of abstraction, using a graphical notation similar to the ones used various engineering disciplines (electrical, industrial, mechanical, etc.). In other words, software designers started using models of the engineering artifacts they were producing that abstracted away the details of the implementation.

Modeling is a fundamental engineering activity [3] that is widely practiced in all disciplines of engineering. Electrical circuit diagrams, maquettes of buildings, kinematic diagrams, and stoichiometric equations are well established design tools for engineers, and they are created and used *before* the engineering product is built, to perform analysis and verification. Once the models pass the rigorous analysis, the product is created – in a sense the model becomes a *blueprint* for the builder. Additionally, models are used in the operation of the engineered system, for instance model-predictive control is used in chemical plants and robots.

Software modeling is similar yet radically different from (conventional) engineering modeling. First, engineering models always relate to physical reality, while software

© Springer Nature Switzerland AG 2018
T. Margaria and B. Steffen (Eds.): ISoLA 2018, LNCS 11244, pp. 295–308, 2018.
https://doi.org/10.1007/978-3-030-03418-4_18

models are abstractions of abstractions, often representing a design idea or decision. Second, software models often become directly involved in the implementation, as they are used to generate code. In fact, some commercial products, like the Matlab toolsuite [4], are identified as 'model-based programming environments', as they are used to generate the implementation: executable code. Third, the language of engineering models is partly evolved from engineering practice mostly based on physics, and the semantics of the model is grounded in physical reality. For software models, the semantics is frequently less precisely defined, and often custom for a specific software engineering problem, for example object-oriented design.

Our main arguments of the paper are as follows. (1) Model-driven development in general and model-based programming in particular is practiced following distinct development styles, some of which we identify in the second section. (2) These styles are effective for various situations in development and it is necessary to understand which are best for a specific case. (3) Current software engineering education does not appear to communicate the development styles well, and if model-driven development is expected to gain wider acceptance a better approach is needed.

In the next section we discuss various model-based development styles, and this is followed by a section on their effectiveness. The next section introduces an example system with a domain-specific modeling language for architecting distributed, real-time, embedded applications. The final section summarizes the observation and outlines a vision for the next stage in model-driven development.

2   Model-Based Development Styles

In this section we introduce three development styles for model-based development that have been observed in practice. The important observation here is that there are multiple interpretations of the term 'model-based development'.

2.1   Models for OO Design and Analysis

The original concept of MDE has grown out from the object-oriented analysis and design techniques, as advocated by Grady Booch, James Rumbaugh, and Ivar Jacobson. Their work resulted in UML – a collection of modeling languages for the analysis and design of object-oriented systems [5]. Models represent requirements, structure, behavior, deployment, etc. of a software system, and thus they capture the high-level design aspects. Therefore, the main objective of models in this context is to document and communicate the high-level design of a system.

Communicating abstract design decisions via models helps software engineers to develop a common understanding of the system, hence they are useful. Models here are rather high-level, and many of the implementation details are abstracted away, which preserves flexibility for the implementation. However, imprecise (or informal) semantics of the modeling language used (such as UML) can lead to misunderstanding or incorrect interpretation, leading to an initiative to formally define the semantics of UML [6]. Often developers consider modeling as extra burden (as they have to build the implementation in any case), and therefore models often diverge (as they are left behind) from the implementation. Keeping models and implementation code consistent is a challenge. A number of UML tools offer code generation (often for a well-defined subset of the modeling language [7]), but the generated code is often just a skeleton for a full implementation, and a human needs to provide further details. The roundtrip between generated code and models is a challenge, often leading to the complete de-synchronization between models and code.

Nevertheless, models for design are useful as they can express properties of the software that is hard to see from the implementation code (or non-code artifacts). Understanding how a complex system works is essential for further evolution and maintenance of that system, hence models can be an invaluable resource, even if they are somewhat disconnected from the actual implementation.

2.2   Models for Higher-Level Programming in a Domain

MDE is often used in a well-defined, restricted domains. For example, signal processing and control, as well as simulation systems often have their own domain-specific language with well-defined semantics, the most prevalent examples being the Matlab toolsuite (Simulink/Stateflow) [8] and Modelica (a simulation language) [9]. The models here can be either the models of the signal processing and control system (Matlab) or models of a physical system (Modelica) and its environment. The models are executable by a simulation (or 'execution') engine and can be translated into efficient executable code as well.

Note that in these development environments models are equivalent to an implementation of the target: an engineered system, while they are also used to model the 'environment' of the target: the 'plant' to be controlled and its physical environment not under control. This is a very powerful paradigm, as the models capture not only what is being built but also the designer's assumptions about the world it is placed in. While in conventional development tests need to be created independently from the target system, here the tests can be produced executing the models of the environment. As a consequence, this style of model-driven development plays a major role in the cyber-physical system domain – most automotive software today is produced using this approach. Note that the implementation is never changed manually as models are used mainly for generating code that is not to be modified. As a consequence there is no need for round-tripping between model and code.

2.3   Models for Domain-Specific Programming

General purpose programming languages focus on algorithms and data structures, but this makes the translation of domain abstractions into lower level concepts mandatory. Conventionally this translation is performed by the developer and the main challenge in software engineering is to facilitate this process, to make it more effective and less error prone.

Domain-specific languages [10] provide to opportunity to address this challenge: if developers can directly use domain-specific abstractions (which are then automatically translated into efficient data structures and algorithmic implementations) they can, arguably, become more productive [11]. In this case models are constructed from pre-defined domain-specific abstractions, they are checked against domain-specific construction 'rules' (i.e. constraints), and translated into implementation artifacts.

Note that the notion of 'domain' here is quite arbitrary, and often not precisely defined or delineated. This implies that in a development project it is mandatory to perform a domain analysis, whereby the domain-specific abstractions are identified, and the translations of those abstractions (and their compositions) into implementation artifacts is developed. In other words, the domain-specific modeling language and is transformations need to be realized first. Only then can a developer become productive. To put it in perspective: the cost of developing the tooling for domain-specific models will have to be amortized over the entire development project.

The development style discussed here is distinct from the previous one in the sense that here the modeling language is custom for a (relatively small) domain and the tool construction (or customization) is part of the development process.

3 Effectiveness

The ultimate challenge of software engineering is to manage complexity, so that complex, engineered artifacts that satisfy some objectives of functionality, performance, and dependability can be produced with an acceptable level of effort. It is natural to ask the question: how effective are the model-based development styles described above in this respect?

In object-oriented modeling for analysis and design the effectiveness comes mainly from being able to capture and communicate ideas about requirements, the design, and, to a certain degree, the implementation. We can rely only on subjective and anecdotal evidence (from personal communications), but it is probably safe to state that the OO models are mainly used for documentation in real development projects. This is not to say that they are not relevant but they seem to play a role rather in representing analysis results and software designs than in other implementation activities: coding, debugging, etc.

For the second case: higher-level programming in a domain the picture is much different. As the models are the 'program' they are essentially implementations. Hence they are effectively contributing to the actual code artifacts that are produced and ultimately executed on a processor. There are two points to note here: (1) not all code can be generated from models, and (2) there is a typically significantly complex runtime environment that is needed to host the generated code on a particular software platform.

The cause of (1) is that the (graphical) modeling languages used are typically not Turing-complete (e.g. Simulink), and custom primitive operators must be implemented in an algorithmic language (e.g. S-functions or Matlab scripts). Models are used to describe structure (e.g. Simulink) or behavior (e.g. Stateflow), but the most elementary computations are still to be implemented procedurally. The deeper cause is pragmatics: while a graphical language *can* be Turing complete it is likely to be more cumbersome to use than textual languages, therefore we don't or rarely use them for specifying algorithms. Existing visual idioms appear to be more suited to express structure than algorithms.

The cause for (2) is the wide variety of execution platforms. The modeling language abstractions (e.g. signal flows or multi-rate, periodic control calculations) must be mapped into implementation abstractions (e.g. messages and periodic threads) – while carefully isolating the modeler/developer from such details. The result is that the run-time environment includes a complete 'virtual machine' that implements the modeling abstractions on a particular platform. This way the developer often loses control over the implementation details, but gains the benefit of productivity. Furthermore, the developers are at the mercy of the platform provider as the run-time environments are specifically crafted for the modeling abstractions (and the corresponding code generators), as well as for the lower-level (e.g. operating system, messaging framework abstractions) and they require significant effort and intricate knowledge of details to modify.

Note that execution platforms can (and should be) modeled as well, mainly for clarifying their semantics. The models for execution platforms represent a mapping from the high-level abstractions they provide (to the model-driven programs) to the lower-level implementation abstractions. However, these models, with the – very important – exception of formal definition for the semantics of the execution platform, are of little use in practice.

The third case: domain-specific programming with models is effective due to the advantages outlined for the previous two approaches. Domain-specific models are based on domain abstractions and the 'construction rules' for correct models, as defined in and enforced by the meta-model of the modeling language. Domain-specific models represent and document the design of system to be implemented, as well as its environment; and these models can (and should) be involved in generating code and other artifacts for the system to be built. Hence, domain-specific models can make a developer effective because (1) they are able to represent designs (as UML in the case of object-oriented modeling), and (2) they can be used in automatic generation of code (as Simulink/Stateflow).

While this third approach seems to be the most powerful and flexible, it comes with significant costs. Some of the issues are as follows.

- Significant effort is needed to build a domain-specific modeling language and its tools. Software engineers are trained to transform solutions to domain problems into concrete code but they are less trained to design domain-specific languages that capture domain abstractions and allow the expression of solutions as a composition. This is a skill that appears to be missing from traditional Computer Science curricula, perhaps because it necessitates a number of skills: domain and requirements analysis, meta-modeling of a domain, model transformation and code generation, etc. While tools are available, designing a useful modeling language – and implementing its 'semantics' (i.e. figuring out how to translate it into code artifacts) is a difficult task.
- The interface between the models and the conventional programming abstractions (algorithms, data structures, objects, run-time platform, and architecture) is difficult. It is clear that a domain-specific modeling language cannot (and should not) address all aspects of a system. On the other hand code and other artifacts are generated from the models, and these have 'live together' with hand-written code (or

artifacts). The interface between these two categories need to be carefully designed and developers must be able to understand the interface from both sides. This is an accidental complexity of domain-specific model-based development that needs attention.

- There is an important 'educational overhead' with domain-specific modeling languages. In this style of development modeling and (conventional) programming are interleaved and developers have to be skilled not only in an implementation language but also in the (often non-standard) modeling language. Note that designer of the modeling language and the developers of the actual system could be different persons, and probably there are much more developers than language designers. The syntax and semantics of the modeling language, and the interface between models and (conventional) implementation code has to be clearly communicated to the developers.

- During the lifetime of a development project (which, today, also includes operation time) the domain-specific modeling language tends to evolve. This places extra burden on the developers as they need to keep up with the changes in all parts of the system: models, implementation code, other model-generated artifacts, etc.

In summary, development with domain-specific models incurs a significant overhead that needs to be recovered by making developers more effective and productive overall.

4 The RIAPS Experience

Given the above observations and concerns, we show an illustrative example for using model-based development in a domain-specific case: distributed, real-time embedded application software for power systems. This example shows how the third style can be applied and be useful for non-expert developers.

The "Resilient Information Architecture Platform for Smart Grid" (RIAPS) [12] project[1] aims at developing a distributed computing platform – software infrastructure – for implementing various Smart Grid applications. The vision of Smart Grid [13] refers to a revolutionary change in how electrical energy is produced and distributed, where all the complex monitoring and control functions are implemented using distributed, embedded computing devices and communication networks. The classical 'radial' distribution model (where generators supply power to the grid that feeds consumers in a – generally – tree-like topology) is being replaced by a model where consumers are becoming 'prosumers' who sometimes consume sometimes produce energy, thereby changing the direction of power flows. The Smart Grid also includes Distributed Energy Resources (DER-s): local generators, photovoltaic cells, or batteries and other energy storage devices. The monitoring and control of such dynamic system necessitates a software system that, by necessity, has to be distributed: dues to network delays and the need for fault tolerance.

---

[1] Supported by the Advanced Research Projects Agency-Energy (ARPA-E), U.S. Department of Energy, under Award Number DE-AR0000666.

Developing software for such distributed real-time embedded system necessitates skills in distributed system programming under real-time and fault tolerance requirements. On the other hand, the actual algorithm development requires knowledge of electrical engineering, signal processing, and control. The typical situation is that very few developers have the necessary skills in all areas.

The concept of RIAPS is to provide a 'software platform' that eases the development of distributed, real-time, resilient software systems and allows developers knowledgeable in engineering to build complex applications. The envisioned developer of RIAPS applications is an electrical engineer who has some experience in developing algorithms for monitoring and control – but not necessarily an expert in distributed systems. Clearly, such developers need assistance from a model-based development environment that helps mitigate the complexity of distributed systems.

A typical example for RIAPS algorithms is as follows. Envision a power network, with networked, embedded computing ('RIAPS') nodes available at every transformer, substation, distribution feeder, wind turbine unit, or industrial or residential customer. The goal is to maintain the balance of power flows in the network: power produced (say, by the turbines of a wind farm) must match to power consumed by the customers. If we produce more power (say, because suddenly there is more wind) some of the generators need to be taken off line, as not to upset the balance. Assuming a full distributed, and decentralized system (where there is no central control room monitoring and making control decisions about everything), the communicating RIAPS nodes have to implement various functions. In the particular example at hand, the computing nodes have to execute a distributed state estimation algorithm followed by solving an optimization problem to decide which wind turbine(s) to take offline. For the state estimation, the nodes have to dynamically form groups of closely coupled nodes, elect a node that responsible for the state estimation within the group, gather all the data needed for the estimation algorithm, execute the estimation, and then relay the results to other, neighboring groups. As the examples shows, the process involves message exchanges, group formation, leader election (the algorithmic building blocks of distributed systems), as well as numerical algorithms like matrix inversion, etc.

4.1 Modeling in RIAPS

Out of the three approaches described earlier, clearly the third one is the only feasible. General purpose object-oriented model-based design and development is not very useful here. The use of models for higher-level programming in a domain is feasible, but: (1) it would have required a huge effort to build a completely new complex development environment for this purpose, and (2) existing technologies (e.g. Simulink/Stateflow) are not addressing well the needs of completely distributed systems. While electrical engineers can be familiar with Matlab, it is not clear how Simulink/Stateflow can be used to develop decentralized applications.

When designing RIAPS perhaps the most fundamental decision was about what to model. The main categories are the software (i.e. the distributed application), or the 'plant' (i.e. the power network), or possibly both. We decided to focus on the software, as the power system is already modeled in another system anyway. This is not to mean that the two are (or cannot be) related, but our primary goal was to help the (electrical engineer) developer. .

Distributed RIAPS applications are built from stateful algorithmic components ('objects') that interact with each other via messages sent through the communication network. They also interact with the power system devices through I/O devices attached to the embedded processors they are running on. In RIAPS we call the former as 'components' and the latter as 'device components'.

A component works like an object (in the classical, object-oriented sense) but they (1) are single-threaded, (2) interact with other components via *ports*, and (3) they can be triggered by time or events. The single-threaded nature means that there is only one thread executing the operations of a component, i.e. they are serialized. Ports are integral part of a component that have special operations to send and receive messages, and the platform framework is responsible for delivering the messages to the right recipients. Components can also have special ports called timers that can be periodic or one-shot that produce messages (like ports) for consumption by the component.

The algorithmic aspects of a component are implemented 'operations': essentially the methods of the component. These operations are triggered by events (when a message arrives at a port) or when a timer fires. Some operations are triggered by the framework, e.g. the component constructor and various operations that inform the component that it has been activate (or de-activated), and about some system-level issue (like, e.g. when a peer component got disconnected from the network).

Note that the above scheme for a component essentially defines the component in terms of its interfaces (ports) – and this is what we model about a component. Figure 1 shows an example for a component model.

```
// Local estimator component
component LocalEstimator (sT=1.0) { // sampleTime parameter
   // Subscriber port to trigger with SensorReady messages
   sub ready: SensorReady ;
   // // Request port to query sensor for last value
   req query: (SensorQuery , SensorValue ) ;
   // Publisher port to publish estimated value messages
   pub estimate : Estimate ;
}
```

Fig. 1. Model of a component with 3 ports

Components from applications through the interactions that are facilitated by ports. Therefore the model of an application is, essentially, the set of permitted component interactions in the application. The most trivial approach to model this is via a diagram with ported objects (like a digital circuit diagram) – but this is rather tedious to construct. Therefore we used a linguistic construct to model the application's interactions.

In the component model the (non-timer) ports are typed with the (data-) type of the message they are to handle. This message type is explicitly specified in the application model. When two ports are of the same type, then the system can infer an interaction between those ports, and this inference result establishes the 'wiring diagram' for the application.

In RIAPS ports are also marked with the type of interactions they are participating on. The allowed types are as follows.

- Publishers are output ports (i.e. a component can send messages through them, but not receive messages), and they are related to subscribers (of the same message type) that are input ports (i.e. a component can receive messages through them but not send). Publishers and subscribers establish a unidirectional flow of messages of the same type – the messages published get delivered to all (matching) subscribers, and all subscribers will receive messages from all (matching) publishers.
- Request and reply ports are for both send and receiving messages – they can be used for synchronous request/reply interactions. A component with a request port sends a message (of a specific type) that gets delivered to another component on its reply port. The second component, after reading the message from the request port computes an answer and sends it through the same reply port. This message gets
- delivered to the request port of the first component which triggers an operation on the component. The request/reply ports establish a bidirectional interaction between two components where send/receive operations are paired up with receive/send operations. Here, the ports are typed with a pair of message types, with the first element being the type of the message traveling in one direction and the second being the type for the other direction.

Figure 2 gives an illustration for an application's topology. Here, the Aggregator is receiving Estimate messages that are produced by the Estimator's LocalEstimator component. Within an Estimator the Sensor is pushing out SensorReady messages that are consumed by the LocalEstimator. The LocalEstimator issues SensorQueries that the corresponding Sensor responds to with SensorValue messages. Note that with this purely textual and declarative model we are able to describe in a compact way the architecture of a distributed application.

For performance reasons, RIAPS components are grouped into higher-level units called actors. Components in the same actor share an address space, so very efficient communication mechanisms (like shared queues) can be used to implement the message passing among them. Implementation-wise actors are processes, while components are threads – although developers will not expected work with these concepts.

The modeling approach described above is very compact and powerful, but it breaks down in one case: when messages need to be restricted to a set of components that are co-located in the same actor or in the same hosts. This is a common case in distributed applications: the scope of message delivery need to be restricted to a well-defined set of nodes. We achieve this by marking certain message types as 'local' (meaning local to a network host) or 'internal' (meaning local to an actor). Figure 3 shows an illustrative example: the model of a complete application. The local messages

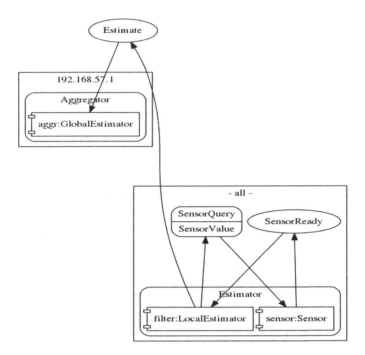

Fig. 2. Application topology

are defined in the Estimator actor, generating the application topology shown on the previous figure.

We argue that such textual description is not only more compact but simpler to construct than the equivalent graphical representation. Entering the text (especially with a syntax-driven editor, as described below) requires less effort than drawing the corresponding graph. A graphical form can be automatically constructed from the textual form for inspection (in fact, Fig. 2 was constructed automatically from a textual form).

For a distributed system, modeling the application's logical architecture (i.e. the 'wiring diagram') is only one part of the solution – we also need to model how the application software is to be deployed on the nodes of a network. One, trivial solution is to deploy each actor on each node (and have the interaction patterns be set up by the mechanism described above) – but this is probably not efficient or suitable for all cases. On the other end of the spectrum, one can deploy specific actors to specific hosts of the network, but this could be somewhat tedious to prepare.

Currently we have a modeling approach for these two cases, illustrated on Fig. 4, but we are working on a more advanced approach where the deployment model describes (1) what nodes with specific features (e.g. specific I/O interfaces) are needed, and (2) which actors need to be placed on those nodes. The goal is to provide an abstract description in the model, and then have a search algorithm figure out the specific details of the deployment. This is work in progress, but it illustrates how a domain-specific model can ease the details of deploying a complex distributed application on a network.

```
app DistributedEstimator {
   // Message types used in the app
     message SensorReady;
     message SensorQuery;
     message SensorValue;
     message Estimate;
   // Sensor component
     component Sensor {
       // Periodic timer trigger to trigger sensor every 1 sec
     timer clock 1000;
     // Publish port for SensorReady messages
       pub ready : SensorReady ;
     // Reply port to query the sensor and retrieve its value
       rep request : ( SensorQuery , SensorValue ) ;
     }
   // Local estimator component
     component LocalEstimator {
     // Subscriber port to trigger component with SensorReady messages
       sub ready : SensorReady ;
     // Request port to query the sensor and retrieve its value
       req query : (SensorQuery , SensorValue ) ;
     // Publish port to publish estimated value messages
       pub estimate : Estimate ;
     }
   // Global estimator
     component GlobalEstimator {
     // Subscriber port to receive the local estimates
       sub estimate : Estimate ;
     // Periodic timer to wake up estimator every 3 sec
       timer wakeup 3000;
     }
   // Estimator actor: performs local state estimation
     actor Estimator {
       local SensorReady, SensorQuery, SensorValue ;   //Local messages
       { // Sensor component
         sensor : Sensor;
         // Local estimator, publishes global message 'Estimate'
         filter : LocalEstimator;
       }
     }
   // Aggregator: collects estimates
     actor Aggregator {
       { // Global estimator, subscribes to 'Estimate' messages
         aggr : GlobalEstimator;
       }
     }
 }
```

Fig. 3. Model of a complete application

```
app DistributedEstimator {
  on all Estimator;
  on (192.168.57.1) Aggregator;
}
```

Fig. 4. Deployment model

4.2   The Model/Code Interface in RIAPS

One of the goals of RIAPS is simplicity: electrical engineer developers should be able to develop distributed applications quickly. For this reason, we chose Python and C++ as the primary implementation language for RIAPS components. The proposed workflow is to implement and test the application in Python, and if better performance is required the components can be re-implemented in C++. Note that Python as both a direct interface to C++ code, as well as typed variant of the language (Cython [14]) that could be compiled into efficient C++ code. Here we describe the Python interface implementation, but C++ is similar (although more elaborate).

RIAPS components are Python classes that need to inherit from a framework-defined base type called 'riaps.Component'. Each component must implement a method for each 'input-type' port as described in the model. A subscriber ports, timer ports, request ports and reply ports are all 'input-type' ports, while publisher ports are 'output-type' ports. The notion is that when a message (or a timer event) arrives at a component, the associated method will be called by the framework. The method is expected to read the message and react to it, possibly sending messages on 'output-type' ports. Note that request ports are both input-type and output-type: they can be used to send messages, as well as for receiving messages (and thus triggering the message handler method).

Each port object is bound to a variable within the component class, and the port object implements the actual send and receive operation that transfer the message from the component to the framework and vice versa.

Note that the RIAPS models do not specify the details of the messages (i.e. the actual data structure). This is left to the developer, and for Python components it is quite simple: messages can carry any type of serialized Python object. If C++ components are involved we can use various serialization methods, like CapnProto [15] or Google's protocol buffers [16].

The only strict requirement for the operations in the component code is that they have to be terminating. Note that they have to be also responsive: for example an operation should never block: i.e. wait on something forever. Some care is needed from the developer to avoid such situations. The framework has provisions for detecting timing violations and handling them appropriately.

4.3   Experience

RIAPS has been used by developers who have a strong electrical engineering background, but not professional software engineers. Especially the Python implementation was very effective and the users we able to develop distributed applications quite rapidly. The domain-specific modeling language for the architecture and deployment were found to be very useful and the Python interface to the framework simple.

The single-threaded nature of the components was somewhat challenging and developers had to learn how to encode a distributed algorithm in the required message passing style. Consider for instance the classical distributed averaging algorithm [17]:

$$x_i(k+1) = \sum_{j=1}^{N} a_{ij}(k)x_j(k)$$

where we consider a set of $i = \{1, 2, \ldots N\}$ of actors. Each actor i starts with a scalar value $x_i(0)$. At each nonnegative integer time k, node i receives from some of the other nodes j a message with the value of $x_j(k)$, and updates its value according to the above equation, and publishes that value for the others. As the component timers in the RIAPS nodes are not synchronized the implementation of the above algorithm presents some difficulty. For this reason, RIAPS has a time synchronization service that maintains a synchronized global system time for all the RIAPS nodes in the network, and the local component timers can be synchronized to that.

In summary, in RIAPS the models of the architecture and the deployment were quite helpful for the developer as they reduced the accidental complexity in configuring a complex architecture of computational objects and hardware resources. They were expressed in a readable language and were simpler than equivalent (diagrammatic) graphical models. They were not describing behavior as that was left to implementation code (Python or C++).

5 Conclusions and Vision

Clearly, model-driven software development and programming has come a long way from being a documentation tool for object-oriented design or a graphical tool for very specific programming tasks. Modern development environment, including but not limited to Eclipse and Microsoft's Visual Studio do have some support for model-driven development, and specific fields, like embedded software for control and signal processing, are supported by specialized model-driven development tools.

However, it is not clear that mainstream software development has unequivocally embraced the technology. Software development is about building abstractions to manage complexity but it appears that today we still use mainly programming languages for that. Arguably the world's largest source code repository is Github. Yet it is hard to find actual projects there that use model-driven techniques – there are many projects that build *tools* for model-driven development though.

What can this lack of impact attributed to? The pragmatic answer is: it is not clear for an average developer what benefits model-based programming will generate, given the cost: the arguably steep learning curve. Notwithstanding Matlab that has answered this question in a specific domain, software developers today build abstractions in code, not models.

We argue that this points to two problems: (1) lack of education and training materials for model-based development, (2) easy to use tools to support this paradigm. The first problem should be addressed by including the model-driven development techniques in Computer Science curricula. We argue that the conceptual foundations for model-based domain-specific programming – and especially how to construct and use domain-specific modeling languages should be taught to software developers. Some textbooks are already available, e.g. [18]. The second problem can only be addressed with concentrated effort in modern tool development. Two examples:

GEMOC [19] and work at Vanderbilt: WebGME [20] are steps in this direction. WebGME has been included as a core tool in a graduate-level CS course at Vanderbilt. However, the wide-spread incorporation of domains-specific model-driven development into the curricula remains a challenge.

References

1. Völter, M., Stahl, T., Bettin, J., Haase, A., Helsen, S.: Model-Driven Software Development: Technology, Engineering, Management. Wiley, New York (2013)
2. Booch, G.: Object-Oriented Analysis and Design. Addison-Wesley, Reading (1980)
3. Chapman, W.: Engineering Modeling and Design. Routledge (2018)
4. Mathworks homepage. https://www.mathworks.com/. Accessed 20 July 2018
5. Rumbaugh, J., Booch, G., Jacobson, I.: The Unified Modeling Language Reference Manual. Addison Wesley, Boston (2017)
6. Evans, A., France, R., Lano, K., Rumpe, B.: Meta-modelling semantics of UML. In: Kilov, H., Rumpe, B., Simmonds, I. (eds.) Behavioral Specifications of Businesses and Systems, pp. 45–60. Springer, Boston (1999). https://doi.org/10.1007/978-1-4615-5229-1_4
7. Vidal, J., De Lamotte, F., Gogniat, G., Soulard, P., Diguet, J.-P.: A co-design approach for embedded system modeling and code generation with UML and MARTE. In: Proceedings of the Conference on Design, Automation and Test in Europe, pp. 226–231. European Design and Automation Association (2009)
8. Carloni, L.P., Passerone, R., Pinto, A., Sangiovanni-Vincentelli, A.L.: Languages and tools for hybrid systems design. Found. Trends® Electron. Des. Autom. 1(1–2), 1–193 (2006)
9. Fritzson, P.: Principles of Object-Oriented Modeling and Simulation with Modelica 2.1. Wiley (2010)
10. Selic, B.: A systematic approach to domain-specific language design using UML. In: 10th IEEE International Symposium on Object and Component-Oriented Real-Time Distributed Computing, ISORC 2007, pp. 2–9. IEEE (2007)
11. Gray, J., Fisher, K., Consel, C., Karsai, G., Mernik, M., Tolvanen, J.-P.: DSLs: the good, the bad, and the ugly. In: Companion to the 23rd ACM SIGPLAN Conference on Object-Oriented Programming Systems Languages and Applications, pp. 791–794. ACM (2008)
12. Eisele, S., Madari, I., Dubey, A., Karsai, G.: RIAPS: resilient information architecture platform for decentralized smart systems. In: 2017 IEEE 20th International Symposium on Real-Time Distributed Computing (ISORC), pp. 125–132. IEEE (2017)
13. Farhangi, H.: The path of the smart grid. IEEE Power Energy Mag. 8(1) (2010)
14. Cython home page. http://cython.org/. Accessed 20 July 2018
15. Capnproto homepage. https://capnproto.org/. Accessed 20 July 2018
16. Protocol buffers homepage. https://developers.google.com/protocol-buffers/. Accessed 20 July 2018
17. Nedic, A., Olshevsky, A., Ozdaglar, A., Tsitsiklis, J.N.: On distributed averaging algorithms and quantization effects. IEEE Trans. Autom. Control 54(11), 2506–2517 (2009)
18. Voelter, M., Benz, S., Dietrich, C., Engelmann, B., Helander, M., Kats, L.C.L., Visser, E., Wachsmuth, G.: DSL engineering: designing, implementing and using domain-specific languages (2013). http://dslbook.org
19. The GEMOC homepage. http://gemoc.org/. Accessed 20 July 2018
20. The WebGME homepage. https://webgme.org/. Accessed 20 July 2018

Fusing Modeling and Programming into Language-Oriented Programming
Our Experiences with MPS

Markus Voelter[✉]

independent/itemis, Stuttgart, Germany
voelter@acm.org
http://voelter.de

Abstract. Modeling in general is of course different from programming (think: climate models). However, when we consider the role of models in the context of "model-driven", i.e., when they are used to automatically construct software, it is much less clear that modeling is different from programming. In this paper, I argue that the two are conceptually indistinguishable, even though in practice they traditionally emphasize different aspects of the (conceptually indistinguishable) common approach. The paper discusses and illustrates language-oriented programming, the approach to {modeling|programming} we have successfully used over the last 7 years to build a range of innovative systems in domains such as insurance, healthcare, tax, engineering and consumer electronics. It relies on domain-specific languages, modular language extension, mixed notations, and in particular, the Jetbrains MPS language workbench.

Keywords: Domain-specific languages · Language modularity
Function programming · Language engineering · Meta programming

1 Introduction

1.1 What This Paper Is (Not)

This paper describes the author's perspective on the differences between modeling and programming. It is not a scientific (and hence, complete and objective) survey of the literature on how modeling and programming relate.

In particular, in the paper, *modeling* is interpreted as the automated construction of software (source code and other artifacts) from prescriptive models. Of course the term modeling can be interpreted differently, which would lead to a completely different discussion of the subject. However, because of its large scope, such a discussion is either very superficial or even longer than the paper as it is now, which is why we focus on this particular interpretation of the term. We elaborate on the terminology below.

© Springer Nature Switzerland AG 2018
T. Margaria and B. Steffen (Eds.): ISoLA 2018, LNCS 11244, pp. 309–339, 2018.
https://doi.org/10.1007/978-3-030-03418-4_19

1.2 Definition of Terms

Before discussing our particular view on programming and modeling, we first define what *we* understand the term "modeling" to mean.

The Essence of Models. The generally agreed definition of a model is that a model abstracts from the reality of a system: certain properties of the system are ignored and others are approximated. Which properties are ignored and how others are approximated depends on the purpose of the model. A *good* model is one where the decisions about ignoring and approximating properties are well aligned with the model's purpose, i.e., the set of analyses, decisions or derivations performed on/with the model.

Descriptive vs. Prescriptive. Models can be descriptive or prescriptive. A *descriptive* model describes an *existing* system for the purpose of understanding how it works, communicating this understanding to stakeholders and to make predictions about how the modeled system's behavior will evolve as time passes or as a reaction to stimuli. Most models in science are descriptive models, because science is about understanding the (existing) world. Examples include climate models, the standard model of particle physics, models of how populations evolve, or finite element models in structural engineering. In contrast, a *prescriptive* model represents a plan for a system that *does not yet exist*. Its primary purpose is to guide the construction of that system. Of course one still analyses prescriptive models in order to ensure certain properties of the future system, and exploits the abstraction and/or notation to make the system accessible to particular stakeholders. Examples include the CAD models for cars, electrical plans for buildings, or models used in biology to synthesize new compounds.

Modeling in Software Engineering. In software engineering, we use both descriptive and prescriptive models. For example, in reverse engineering, when we represent the high-level structure of the code as components and visualize their dependencies, this is a descriptive model whose purpose it is to help estimate ("predict") how much effort it is to make particular changes to the software. However, prescriptive models are much more common:

- A PROMELA [9] model used to model check a state machine using Spin[1] before it is implemented.
- A state machine model that abstracts from the low-level details of implementing one in C using a `switch` statement.
- A decision table or decision tree used to analyze completeness and consistency of the decision criteria based on an SMT solver.
- A model of the rules that govern when a truck driver is required to take breaks that is used to generate a C implementation for a tachograph.
- A model of a component architecture that is used to generate middleware infrastructure in an AUTOSAR system.

For a prescriptive model in software engineering to be useful, it is critical that the behaviors expressed in the model are transferred faithfully into the to-be-built

---

[1] http://spinroot.com.

system; otherwise the predictions or analysis results derived from the model are of no use. This leads us to the notion of model-*driven*.

Model-Driven.[2] The "driven" expresses that the to-be-developed system is *automatically* constructed[3] from its prescriptive model. In other words, from the perspective of a user, only the model has to be adapted for the system to change. This can be achieved through (multi-step) transformation/generation/-compilation or through interpretation.

Automatic derivation of the real system from the model is usually not the *only* (or even the primary) reason why one uses a model-driven approach – all other reasons mentioned above might apply. But the automatic derivation is a crucial[4] to ensure consistency between the model and the system; otherwise models usually get outdated as the system evolves, or vice versa. Automatically deriving the real system is thus the defining characteristic of model-driven.

Separation of Concerns and Domain Logic. Most practical systems address many different concerns. In addition to the core functionality, concerns such as authentication and authorisation, encryption and privacy, transactions and persistence, or timing and throughput are common. Describing them all in one model or program is usually a mess.[5] Separation of concerns helps by allocating different concerns to different models, each of them expressed with a language that is suitable for the particular concern. To "prescribe" the complete system, all concern-specific models have to be created, aligned, and then fused during the construction of the final system. The more concerns have to be addressed, the more challenging is the construction process. In many systems there is one concern that is special, often called the domain logic:

- In a system that creates monthly salary and wage statements for employees [23], the domain logic comprises the rules that determine what counts as work time, as well as the laws that drive the deductions and benefits that apply to the employees' gross salary, plus their evolution over time.
- In a medical application that helps patients deal with the side effects of treatments [25], the domain logic is a set of data structures, algorithms, decisions procedures and correctness criteria that judge the criticality of side effects relative to the current phase of the treatment.
- In a tachograph, the device that monitors driving and break periods of truck drivers, the rules that govern when a driver has to take a break, and for how

---

[2] We intentionally omit the typically following word (Engineering, Development, Software Development or Architecture) because the supposed differences not relevant here.

[3] For the purpose of this paper, we ignore the question of how to ensure that this automatic construction process is correct. It is a problem where a theoretically satisfying answer is hard to give, but can be achieved relatively easily in practice.

[4] Alternatively, one could implement the system manually and then use tools to ensure consistency with ethe model. However, the author has never seen this approach used in practice.

[5] In fact, a major reason why it is so hard to understand and automatically migrate legacy software is exactly this mess.

long, depending on the driving history over days and weeks, make up the core domain logic of the system.

– In an observation planning system for a radio telescope, the domain logic is the parameters needed to perform a successful observation of a particular spot in the sky, including positioning, focus, filtering and image processing.

The reason why it is useful to treat the domain logic specially in the context of software engineering is that, in many systems, the domain logic is not naturally contributed by software engineers but instead by experts in the domain [21]. It is thus especially useful to extract it into a separate model, ideally one that uses abstraction and notations from that domain. This way, the models become accessible to domain experts, and they are potentially analyzable by tools that find problems that are relevant on the level of the domain.

Platforms. Whenever we construct the system from one or more concern-specific models, we expect that system to run on some kind of platform. The platform includes the operating system, middleware and application servers, but also libraries and frameworks available to us. Parts of most concerns are addressed by the platform, and the respective model only "instructs" the system how to use the platform – the models configure the platform.

~ ~ ~

This leads us to the following definition of model-driven:

> **Definition:** Model-driven refers to a way of developing a software system S where users change a set of prescriptive models M_i representing concerns C_i at an appropriate abstraction level in order to affect the behavior of S. An automatic process constructs a full implementation of S that relies on a platform P.

In the rest of this paper, we understand the term "modeling" to mean"model-driven" in the sense of this definition.

~ ~ ~

Notably, the definition does not use the words *declarative* or *executable*, even though they are widely used in this context. This is because the author considers both of these terms not useful.

Declarativeness. Using "declarative" [22] to characterise models is problematic because it implies that programs, in contrast, are not declarative. This is obviously not true, because there is a whole field called declarative programming.[6] More specifically, *declarative* is interpreted in two different ways. The strict interpretation says that a declarative program describes *the logic of a computation without describing its control flow*.[6] This is definitely not true for all kinds of models: state machines or workflow models (as in BPMN) model control flow explicitly. The less strict definition of *declarative* just means that something specifies the "what" but not the "how". Or in other words: avoid the details that

---

[6] https://en.wikipedia.org/wiki/Declarative_programming.

are not necessary (for a particular purpose). This makes the word synonymous with "abstraction", and so it also does not add anything to our understanding of models.

Executability. This term is problematic for two reasons. First, for a model that describes only the structure of a system (and can be used to automatically construct that system) the term "executable" makes little sense unless one treats it as a synonym for "driven" (which then also makes it meaningless). Second, execution itself is not well-defined. For example, the domain logic in the above salary/tax example can be executed in the sense that unit tests can be written against it to verify the correctness in terms of compliance with the salary and tax law. But the "real" system that is later executed in the data center requires addressing scalability and security, as well as other non-functional concerns. These cannot be automatically derived from the domain logic alone. So, is the model that describes the domain logic concern "executable"?

2   Comparing Programming and Modeling

Reading the definition of *model-driven* above, it is apparent that it (also) describes programming, with the construction part being the compiler. We might argue that the difference between modeling and programming is

- that compilers produce machine code (not true for the Java compiler, it produces bytecode, another "model"),
- that the semantic gap between input and output is bigger in case of model-driven (not true, consider an optimizing compiler for a functional language),
- that the opposite is the case (also not quite true, consider a Modelica compiler that creates efficient C code from differential equations),
- or that only in model-driven we use separation of concerns (not true, consider SQL + Java + HTML + JavaScript + CSS).

It is impossible to draw a hard line between programming and modeling[7] (in the sense of model-driven). However: programming and model-driven clearly have distinct histories, traditions and communities. As a consequence, although the two are fundamentally the same, they emphasize different aspects of a common approach. Figure 1 highlights this emphasis. Of course Fig. 1 paints with a broad brush, and for each of the criteria you will find a counterexample. However, we think the general trends are true; we elaborate below.

A Model-driven is often targeted at non-software domains, thus integrating more of this domain's concepts directly into the language (insurance contract,

---

[7] It should also be mentioned that we are comparing programming and modeling specifically because this was the "task" set by the ISOLA track. There are other related fields one could compare, such as scripting (Perl, awk, what sysadmins do) and end-user programming (often using Excel, Access or low-code environments). In our opinion these are also basically the same, but also emphasize different aspects because of their unique context and tradition.

		Model-Driven	Programming
A	High-level, domain-specific concepts	███	░░░
B	User-definable Abstractions	░░░	███
C	Focus on Behavior and Algorithms	░░░	███
D	Type Systems	░░░	███
E	Focus on Execution	░░░	███
F	Notational Freedom	███	
G	Separation of Concerns	███	░░░
H	Integration of Stakeholders	███	░░░
I	Powerful, productivity-focused IDEs	███	███
J	Liveness	░░░	░░░

Fig. 1. Comparison between Programming and Modeling (in the sense of the definition given at the end of Sect. 1). The darker the color, the more emphasis.

break period, image filter). Programming on the other hand emphasises orthogonal and flexibly composable concepts (function, class, module).

B Consequently, programming (and its languages) optimises for letting users build their own, new abstractions. In modeling, the abstractions are often predefined and can be assembled into programs only in very particular ways. For example, in the tachometer example, users can define rules (the purpose of the language), but cannot create their own abstractions for defining rules; break or driving period are predefined.[8]

C Programming almost always includes the specification of behavior, the notion of algorithms is fundamental. In model-driven, there are many useful languages that only specify structure (UML Class Diagrams, SysML material flow, ADLs) or specify behavioral patterns instead of formulating the behavior algorithmically (consider an async flag on a remote communication specification).

D As a consequence of focussing on behavior, algorithms and user-defined abstractions, programming languages usually rely on sophisticated type systems. In contrast, model-driven can often make do with much simpler constraint checks.

E Programming has a clear focus on execution: if it doesn't run, it's not a program. In model-driven, while execution is always a factor as per its definition, other aspects such as analysis or communication with stakeholders might be the primary reason for using models.

---

[8] Formal specification languages such as Z [30], VDM++ [4] or OBJ [7] provide sophisticated means for defining abstractions for downstream analysis. However, these are outside the scope of this paper because they not used in the context of model-driven as defined in this paper.

F For all intents and purposes, programming relies on textual notations (the odd graphical programming language, such as ASCET[9] or Scratch [12], is the exception). On the other hand, model-driven is more flexible in its use of other notations such as math, tables or diagrams. One could even argue that model-driven puts too much emphasis on graphical notations.

G Traditionally, a particular program has been written in *one* programming language, and concerns tended to be mixed. More recently, this has been changing for programming: SQL + Java + HTML + CSS + Javascript. Modeling has always had a tendency to describe the different concerns of the system separately, with different models and different languages.

H Partially because of the emphasis on separation of concerns, but also because of domain-specific abstractions and more diverse notations, model-driven is better at integrating non-programmers or domain experts into the software development process. The attempts at non-programmers reading source code (for example, to give feedback) are not very successful.

I Anybody who has ever used the "typical" tools for model-driven will probably agree that programming IDEs are more powerful and usable: from code navigation to refactorings to integrated test execution, model-driven tools cannot compete.

J Liveness broadly refers to removing the distinction between a program and its execution [17]. Since it is a relatively new trend, both fields are relatively weak. We suggest that modeling is slightly better, because in some cases the models are created specifically for analysis and rapid feedback, and because liveness can be supported more easily for more narrow domains (i.e., it is harder for general-purpose languages).

3   A Hybrid Approach

In our[10] work on domain-specific languages (DSLs) in the context of business and engineering software, we have combined characteristics from the programming and model-driven column in Fig. 1, further complicating an attempt at distinguishing the two. In this section we will illustrate, for each of the characteristics, what we have done, and why it is useful.

~ ~ ~

---

[9] https://www.etas.com/de/products/ascet-developer.php.

[10] This refers to a team of engineers at itemis Stuttgart who specialize in language engineering with MPS. Between 2010 and 2018, the team has grown from 2 to 15 people, and we have been developing languages in a wide variety of domains such as healthcare, automotive, aerospace, robotics, finance, embedded software, science and government.

All our work is based on JetBrains MPS.[11] MPS is a language workbench [6], a tool for developing ecosystems of languages. MPS supports a wide range of modular language composition approaches, in particular, extension and restriction are supported directly [20]. This is possible because of two fundamental properties of MPS. First, it relies on a projectional editor [29]. Projectional editors do not use parsing. Instead, a user's edit operations *directly* change the abstract syntax tree, from which an updated visual representation is then projected. This way, ambiguities that result from grammars and parsing cannot arise when independently developed languages are combined. This works for essentially any notation, including tables, diagrams, math symbols as well as structured ("code") and unstructed ("prose") text [27], a feature we exploit extensively in the construction of DSLs. Projectional editors have historically had a bad reputation regarding usability and editing efficiency. However, recent advances as implemented natively in MPS and in an extension called grammar cells [29] lead to good editor productivity and user acceptance [1]. Second, MPS has been designed from the start to not just develop one language at a time, but ecosystems of collaborating languages. The formalisms for defining structure, type systems and scopes have all been designed with modularity and composition in mind. We analyze MPS' suitability for modular language composition in [26] (the paper also evaluates MPS more generally).

While other language workbenches exist [5], none of them provides the unique properties, scalability and robustness of MPS, which is why the approach – at least currently – cannot be fully implemented with another language workbench.

~ ~ ~

In this section, we pick up the differences in emphasis discussed in the previous section, talk briefly about how in our approach we blur the distinction between programming and model-driven even further, and then provide lots of examples to make the case; in each section, examples follow after the separator (the three tildes). The examples center around three ecosystems:

mbeddr. mbeddr is an implementation of the C programming language in MPS, plus a set of 30+ modular language extensions for embedded software development [28]. Extensions include state machines, physical units and interfaces/components. mbeddr has been in development since 2011 and is used in several commercial projects, including a smart meter [24].

KernelF. KernelF is an extensible and embeddable functional language [23]. Its purpose is to serve as the core of DSLs. We have been using it in a variety of DSL projects, including in the finance, healthcare and smart contract domains.

IETS3. IETS3 is a set of languages for systems engineering, including a widely customizable language for component architectures as well as a feature modeling language. It is currently used in three different systems engineering projects, mostly in the automotive industry.

---

[11] https://www.jetbrains.com/mps/.

3.1 **A** High-level, Domain-Specific Concepts

In programming, new abstractions are provided through libraries,[12] developed with the language itself. In idiomatic use of MPS, new abstractions are provided through language extensions, defined outside the language, using MPS' language definition facilities. A language extension can be seen as a library plus syntax, plus type system and plus IDE support (and a semantics definition via an interpreter or generator). In other words, many more abstractions are first-class, with the resulting advantages in terms of analyzability and IDE support.

Libraries, in general, can be composed. For example, you can use the collections from the Java standard library together with the Joda Time[13] library for date and time handling and the Spring[14] framework for developing server-side applications. There is no need to explicitly compose the frameworks, the combination "just works". While this composability is not true for language modules in general (primarily because of syntactic ambiguities), it is true with MPS: for all intents and purposes, language extensions can be composed just like libraries. The composition also has similar limitations: one cannot statically prove that the composition will not have unintended side-effects, and the set of libraries/language extensions might not fit well in terms of their style. However, if language extensions are developed in a coordinated, but still modular way, as a stack of extensions, these limitations do not apply.

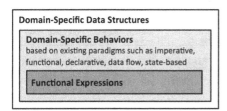 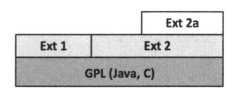

Fig. 2. Our two most important patterns for DSL design: a custom language with a (restricted) embedded functional language and base language that is incrementally grown towards a domain.

We rely on two primary patterns for language design, both shown in Fig. 2. The first one uses a three layer approach where the domain contributes the core structural abstractions and the coarse-grained behaviors, but the low-level expressions and functional abstractions are reused from an existing language; we use KernelF [23] for this purpose. In the second approach, we take a full existing language (such as Java, C or again, KernelF) and "grow" it towards a domain by adding more and more domain-specific abstractions (implemented as modular language extensions). In the first case, only selected parts of the

---

[12] In this context, we consider frameworks a form of library.

[13] http://www.joda.org/joda-time/.

[14] https://spring.io/.

embedded functional language are available to the user, which makes analysis of the whole program simpler. In the second case, one typically allows the full base language in user programs; this nicely supports gradual abstraction in the sense that users can always fall back to the base language if no suitable high-level abstraction exists. However, analyzability potentially suffers because low-level constructs can "pollute" high-level, analyzable abstractions (think: C pointer arithmetics embedded inside a state machine described first-class).

~ ~ ~

Decision Processes. In an extension of KernelF for Smart Contracts,[15] we have developed first-class support for collaborative decisions [19]; Fig. 3 shows examples. A `MultiPartyDecision` is a top-level declaration (like a record or a function) that supports a declarative configuration of the decision: which parties are involved, and can that list of parties be changed dynamically (at runtime, as the decision process runs), what is the decision procedure (unanimous, majority, specific threshold or completely custom), is a minimum turnout required, is there a time limit for making the decision, and can a party revoke their votes. The complete, potentially non-trivial implementation of this process is handled internally to the declarative specification. In addition, the IDE only allows those commands on a decision object that are valid based on its configuration.

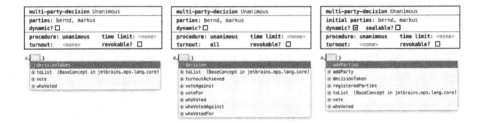

Fig. 3. Declarative decision procedures, each with a different configuration and resulting code completion proposals.

State Machines. As part of mbeddr's extensions for embedded programming, we have developed first-class support for state machines. They support the textual notation shown in Fig. 4, but also tabular and graphical notations; those can be switched by the user. As a consequence of state machines being first-class, mbeddr provides automatic model checking [2] support for properties such as reachability of states and activeness of transitions, but also allow users to define their own temporal properties which are then checked by the model checker.

Timelines. In a project in the context of tachographs, we built a DSL to describe the rules that determine when truck drivers have to make breaks. The

---

[15] https://en.wikipedia.org/wiki/Smart_contract.

```
statemachine HierarchicalFlightAnalyzer {          composite state airborne initial = flying {
  macro stopped(next) = tp->speed == 0 mps           on reset [ ] -> beforeFlight { points = 0; }
  macro onTheGround(next) = tp->alt == 0 m           on next [onTheGround && stopped] -> crashed
  in event next(Trackpoint* tp) <no binding>         state flying (airborne.flying) {
  in event reset() <no binding>                        on next [onTheGround && tp->speed > 0 mps] -> landing
  out event crashNotification() => raiseAlarm         on next [tp->speed > 200 mps] -> flying { points += VERY_HIGH_SPEED; }
  readable var int16 points = 0                        on next [tp->speed > 100 mps] -> flying { points += HIGH_SPEED; }
  initial state beforeFlight {                       } state flying
    entry { points = 0; }                            state landing (airborne.landing) {
    on next [tp->alt > 0 m] -> airborne                on next [stopped] -> landed
    exit { points += TAKEOFF; }                        on next [ ] -> landing { points--; }
  } state beforeFlight                               } state landing
  state crashed {                                    state landed (airborne.landed) {
    entry { send crashNotification(); }                entry { points += LANDING; }
  } state crashed                                    } state landed
                                                   } state airborne
```

Fig. 4. The textual notation for state machines in mbeddr.

language has first-class abstractions for timelines, driving periods, breaks and other abstractions core to that domain. The relationships between the various periods can also be described. The abstractions also come with a very particular notation shown in Fig. 9 A and discussed in Sect. 3.6. The language builds on top of mbeddr, and embeds C expressions in the timelines. From the rules, we generate executable C code that goes into the tachograph firmware.

3.2 B User-Definable Abstractions

Technically there is no reason why one could not build languages that allow users to build their own abstractions, just like any programming language. In fact, MPS ships with Java, mbeddr implements all of C, and KernelF is a full functional programming language. By growing a language incrementally towards a domain, users can choose if they want to use predefined abstractions (such as the mbeddr state machines mentioned above), or whether they want to define their own abstractions using the facilities of the base language.

~ ~ ~

mbeddr Components. mbeddr has an extension for component-oriented programming that includes interfaces with operations; hierarchical components with ports that provide and require those interfaces; interface polymorphism; and instantiation of components and wiring through connectors. The idea is similar to ADLs [13] and UML composite structures, but directly integrated into C. Similar to classes in C++, users can define their own abstractions using components. Section 5.1 and Fig. 1 in [24] illustrates the architecture of a Smart Meter built with mbeddr's components. itemis France is currently extracting a reusable platform from this architecture, again illustrating the ability to create user-defined abstractions. *Inside* the components, users can use low-level C code (or other extensions) to implement a components's behavior; an example of an abstraction gradient [8].

Functional Abstractions in KernelF. KernelF supports functions, function calls, currying, lambdas, higher-order functions and function references, as well as enums, tuples, collections and records. Similar to any other functional programming language, users can use these language concepts to create their own abstractions. However, KernelF does not support algebraic data types, a module system or function composition. This is because KernelF is intended to be embedded in (or extended towards) DSLs which typically supply their own first-class domain-specific abstractions instead for these.

3.3 C Focus on Behavior and Algorithms

Structure-only models are useful in the context of model-driven. For example, they can be used to generate distribution middleware, database schemas and access layers, or UIs. However, historically, the prevalence of structure-only models in model-driven is also a consequence of limitations in the tools: trying to graphically model the algorithmic parts of tax calculations really is a pain. With MPS, we can mix arbitrary notations, so algorithmic aspects are not problematic; in particular, we are not forced to represent them graphically. It turns out that in practice, lots of the business value in the domain logic of a system lies in the way *decisions* are made, and how values are *calculated*, the two main aspects of behaviors.

~ ~ ~

KernelF Utilities. KernelF supports various utilities for making decisions, such as graphically-rendered decision trees and various forms of decision tables (both shown in Fig. 5); all of these notations are fully editable. In addition, KernelF also has support for mathematical symbols to support concise notations for calculations (rightmost item in Fig. 5). "Regular" programming with (higher-order) functions are of course also supported for decisions and calculations.

Fig. 5. Decision trees and tables, as well as math symbols available in the KernelF util package. All are expressions, so they can be used widely in KernelF programs.

Insurance Math. Actuaries use many conventions when writing down their heavily numerical, recursive functions. For example, they distinguish between iterator variables and parameters, where parameters remain constant in (recursive) calls to functions that declare the same parameters (see Fig. 6). Sameness is established by relating them to a definition in a data dictionary, which is why the parameters do not declare types when used in functions; those types are in the data dictionary. The language, an extension of KernelF, also relies heavily on various forms of lookup tables, built as another extension.

D : Kommutationswerte		
Ergebnistyp:	**Laufvariable:**	**Parameter:**
number{3}	x	i
		geschlecht
		q

$$D_x := l_x * \frac{1}{(1 + i)^x}$$

l : Lebende im Jahr x		
Ergebnistyp:	**Laufvariable:**	**Parameter:**
number{0}	x	geschlecht
		q

$$l_0 := \text{startwertLebende}$$
$$l_x := l_{x-1} * (1 - q.\text{lookup}(x, \text{geschlecht}))$$

Fig. 6. A compact numerical functional notations for insurance math; parameter values do not have to be specified for calls to functions that take the same ones.

Temporal Data. A KernelF extension developed for a salary/tax calculations system has temporal types. The system supports bitemporal [10] data, and the temporal types shown here represent one of the two dimensions. The notation TT[U] represents a temporal version of a base type U. Temporality means that a variable ttu: TT[U] does not represent a single value; instead, ttu is a sequence of (date, U)-pairs, expressing that on date the particular value of ttu changed to a particular u: U. The following example states that on Jan 1, 2017 the salary became 5.000 EUR, and on May 1 it changed to 6.000 EUR.

```
val salary : TT[currency] = TT | 2017 01 01  =>  5.000 EUR |
                               | 2017 05 01  =>  6.000 EUR |
```

Fig. 7. Reslicing of temporal values. a and b are temporal values where the actual value (a1, a2, a3 and b1, b2) is different in subsequent time periods (represented by the slices); s is a regular scalar. When a temporal value is "operatored" with a scalar, the slices remain the same, but their values change. In the case of two temporal values, the slices intersect, and the values are computed per intersection.

The extension overloads the basic operators (+, -, * or /) for temporal types to "reslice" the temporal periods (Fig. 7); the semantics of the operators regarding their basic types U remain unchanged. These overloaded operators let users write arithmetic code that works with temporal data as if it was regular, scalar data. To effectively work with temporal data, more support is required. An example is the reduce operator: ttv.reduce(S, r) (where r is a daterange, a type that represents time periods) reduces a temporal value back to a scalar. The operation takes into account the slices within r (for example, the month for which taxes are calculated) and a reduction strategy S. The strategy includes LAST (the value of the last slice in r), SUM (sum of all slice values), and WEIGHTED_AVERAGE where the sum is weighted with the relative duration of each slice.

3.4 D Type Systems

Classical constraint checking is used in many of our languages: Are the names of states in state machines unique? A decision procedure that allows revocation of votes also requires a minimum turnout. Are there circular imports between mbeddr modules? However, we also use type checking. It is required once expressions, such as those from KernelF, are embedded into a DSL. Similarly, if full programming languages are implemented for the purpose of extension (as in mbeddr with C, or as Jetbrains did with Java), the full type system of this language must be available in MPS. On the other hand, we do not require type systems that support meta programming (reflection, type bounds, implicit operations and other "magic" that can be found for example in Scala), because we can use MPS' meta programming facilities to build language extensions.

~ ~ ~

Number Types in KernelF. The number type in KernelF is interesting because it has a range and a precision. This is very useful in many DSLs; for example, in a project in the healthcare domain, the ranges help validate domain-specific data such as blood pressure. The following patterns are supported:

```
number           => number[-inf|inf]{0}   // integer type, unlimited range
number[0|inf]    => number[0|inf]{0}      // positive integer
number[10|20]    => number[10|20]{0}      // integer type, range as specified
number{2}        => number[-inf|inf]{2}   // 2 decimal places, unlimited range
number[3.3|4.5]  => number[3.3|4.5]{1}    // range as specified, precision derived
```

KernelF operators perform basic arithmetic computations on the ranges of numeric types. However, we have not implemented a fully dependent type system [32] since this is too complicated for language implementors and for the developers of language extensions; ours is pragmatic in that gives up early on trying to compute the specific ranges and just assumes [-inf|inf], i.e., unlimited range.

```
42 + 33               ==> 75    <number[75|75]{0}>
42 + 2 * 3            ==> 48    <number[48|48]{0}>
aReal + anInt        ==> 75.33 <number[75.33|75.33]>
if aBool then 42 else 33 ==> 42    <number[33|42]{0}>

type tt: number[-10|10]
val n3, n4 : tt              = 0
val n34    : number[-100|100] = n3 * n4
```

Units in mbeddr. mbeddr supports physical units. Every numeric C type (short int, int, double and the like) and their literals can be annotated with a physical unit. The system ships with the SI base units (m, s, kg, K, A, mol, cd), and users can derive their own units from those base units. Figure 4 has a few examples in the state machine. Here are a few more:

```
derive N    as kg * m / s / s;      // defining a new unit for force
derive mps as m / s;                // defining a new unit for speed
int/m/   length = 20 m;             // variable definition with unit type
int/mps/ speed  = length / 20 s;    // performs computations with units
int/mps/ kaputt = 20 * length;      // error caught by the type system
```

Temporal Types. The two examples in this section are *only* type system extensions. During execution, they do not play a role: KernelF's number types are mapped to Java's `BigInteger` and `BigDecimal`, and mbeddr's physical units are completely elided during reduction to plain C. The temporal shown in the previous section also involves adaptations in the type system, but the execution semantics have to be adapted as well (to compute the sliced values).

3.5 E Focus on Execution

Because of the ability to add arbitrary abstractions as first-class concepts, it is easier to add meaningful (i.e., relevant to the user) analyses and verifications. We have exploited this in several projects and languages, as we show below. On the other hand, almost all of the DSLs we have built over the last years are executable; an exception is a set of languages for performance analysis and security assessments in embedded systems.

~ ~ ~

The KernelF Interpreter. KernelF ships with an interpreter that runs directly on the AST of the program in MPS. Thus, the effect of a change to a program or its input data can be seen immediately. The most used form of specifying inputs and observing outputs is as part of test cases. They can be executed automatically (technically, as part of MPS' type checking the program) or on demand. The actual value is rendered inline in the code, and the assertion/cases/suites are rendered in green/red, corresponding to test success or failure. Like the core language definition, the interpreter infrastructure is modular to allow language extensions to also supply an interpreter for that extension. For example, the decision processes (Sect. 3.1) and the temporal arithmetics (Sect. 3.3) come with modular interpreter extensions.

The mbeddr Build Infrastructure. mbeddr does not ship with an interpreter. Instead, the extensions, such as components or state machines, are reduced to plain mbeddr C by a multi-step reduction pipeline (see [24] for the performance of this generated code). The last step is then the generation of textual C code, and its compilation with a configurable C compiler (gcc by default). The whole process is completely integrated with MPS' build infrastructure; `Ctrl-F9` runs everything. Programs can also be executed directly from the IDE, their output rendered in the MPS console.

Scenario Testing and Simulation. In a medical project we developed a set of DSLs based on KernelF to model the algorithms in mobile phone apps that help patients with medicine dosage and the side effects of therapies [25]. One language supports given/when/then-scenario descriptions as well as their execution as tests using the interpreter. In addition, there is an interactive simulator, based on an in-IDE rendering of the final phone app, where healthcare professionals can interactively experiment with the algorithms they are currently developing.

Model Checking for mbeddr Components. mbeddr can check components for their compliance with the semantics defined with pre/postconditions on the operations in interfaces using model checking; see Fig. 8. The contract is translated to labels in the generated C code, and the integrated CBMC model checker [11] performs a reachability analysis for those labels. The results are lifted back to the level of the DSL in order to be meaningful to the developer. This approach combines the convenience of specifying the semantics via the DSL with verification of the final system, the generated C code [14, 15].

Fig. 8. Model checking component contracts. **Top Left:** an interface definition in mbeddr that expresses the semantics of the operations with pre/post conditions. **Bottom Left:** A component providing the interface and implementing the operations; implementation is arbitrary C code. **Top Right:** Verification results lifted from the raw CBMC result to the level of the DSL; a list of succeeded and failed pre/postcondition. Clicking on one selects the respective location in the code. **Bottom Right:** Execution trace for a failed check. Clicking selects corresponding location in code.

SMT Solving for KernelF Decision Tables. Several of KernelF's decision support abstractions support consistency checking based on an SMT solver. In particular, decision tables are checked for completeness (are all possible inputs handled) and overlap (for every particular set of inputs, will only one row/cell combination be valid). For multi decision tables, we also check coverage, and ensure that the condition in row i is either distinct from, or a subset of all lower rows i + k. This is important for the "shadowing" semantics of these tables. Results are reported as regular error markers on the code. The solver takes into account restrictions on the inputs from ranges in number types or other constraints; we are currently working on translating all of KernelF to the solver in order to take the complete context into account for these and other checks.

Performance Analysis using Simbench. Simbench relies on the system engineering-level component language we developed for IETS3 to model automotive E/E architectures. A modular extension of the components language allows systems engineers to model resources (such as CPUs, memory or disk storage) as well as the components' use of these resources (CPU instructions, memory amount or disk access bandwidth) during the execution of particular scenarios (such as the boot/startup of an in-car navigation system). Simbench then performs a discrete event simulation to analyze timing properties and detect resource bottlenecks and the resulting critical paths. This helps engineers optimize the system architecture for performance through improved scheduling of tasks.

Security Analyst. Also relying on IETS3 components to model E/E architectures, the tool is used to analyze the security properties of these architectures. In particular, users can model attack scenarios and risks regarding the component-based system architecture. The tool then computes risk/attack propagation vectors and lets users define mitigations. The result of the analysis is a set of reports that demonstrate how and why a particular set of security measures lead to a secure system relative to the previously defined risks and attacks. This tool is also example of purely structural models: no actual behaviors are described.

3.6   F Notational Freedom

The importance of the notation, or concrete syntax, cannot be overstated in the context of modeling languages: users initially always judge a language by the notation. Even if the concepts behind the language are great, users might not get to appreciate this if they cannot get past the "syntax they don't like". This becomes even more crucial for languages that address domain logic, and hence target people who may not be professional developers. Three ingredients allow us to use notations that are closely aligned with domains. First, the projectional editor can support essentially any notation; we have syntax libraries for structured and unstructured text, tables, math and diagrams. Second, because the modular language extensibility lets us easily define new first-class concepts, we have "hooks" to which we can attach specialized notations. Third, since MPS is bootstrapped, extending MPS with completely new notational primitives (that can then be used with multiple languages) is just a matter of modularly extending the notation meta language; we discuss the meta level in Sect. 4.

~ ~ ~

Many of the screenshots shown in this section are also examples of customized syntax, in particular Figs. 3, 5 and 6. More examples follow.

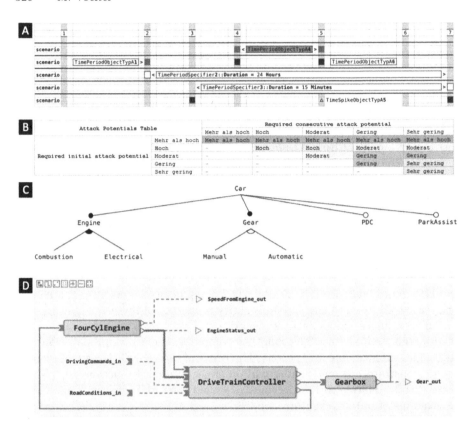

Fig. 9. Further examples of notational flexibility we use in MPS. **A:** a custom-developed notation for timelines; **B:** tabular notations inspired by Excel; **C:** decorated tree notation for feature models; **D:** box-and-line diagrams.

Timelines. The previously mentioned tachograph timelines are shown in Fig. 9A. Clearly, the notation it is very much inspired by Excel, which our customer had used to prototype the language. The timelines are an example of a project-specific notation: it is not built with our generic table notations framework, but has been built into MPS specifically for this project.

Excel-style. The previously mentioned Security Analyst relies mainly on tables, some of them rather large. Figure 9B shows a small one. While spreadsheets such as Excel are a good way for ad-hoc problem solving, they are rarely a good implementation technology for core domain logic, because of Excel's very limited support for managing complexity (the "Horror Stories" list at the European Spreadsheet Risk Group[16] provides ample evidence for this claim). However, they are often a good source from which to extract the core concepts, and sometimes also parts of the notation of DSLs.

---

[16] http://www.eusprig.org/horror-stories.htm.

Feature Models. Feature models are a widely used formalism for describing variability in systems [3]; an example is shown in Fig. 9C. From a notational perspective, the decorations on and between the lines are interesting – such decorations are also useful in other tree-based notations. Our tree notation language (which is different from the language to describe box-and-line notations described next) generically supports decorations "on both ends".

Box-and-Line Diagrams. Figure 9D shows the graphical notation for IETS3 components. Note that the diagrams are fully editable (through a palette, in-diagram buttons, intentions and drag/drop). The diagrams can embed textual notations with full IDE support (for example, one can use KernelF expressions to define values for component parameters in the diagram) and the diagram can itself be embedded in a textual editor. All our graphical editors have a textual secondary notation that can be enabled by users; often, bulk editing is much faster using a textual syntax. The integration between text and diagrams is maybe the most convincing demonstration of the benefits of a unified (projectional) editor architecture. Integrating diagram editors with parser-based text editors is significant work otherwise [18]. In addition to the components, we have used the box-and-line notation also for state machines, entity relationship-style data models, and for dataflow programming (in the Siemens ESD[17] tool).

Unstructured Text. Code that conforms to a well-defined language has a rigid structure, especially in a projectional editor. However, many parts of programs are best expressed as unstructured text: comments are the obvious example, but mixed content, such as markup (think: HTML) or requirements documents are also examples. To enable this, MPS supports rich text: rich text paragraphs are fundamentally unstructured, so users can use all the editing gestures known from regular text editors (which is unnatural to MPS' projectional editor, see [1]). However, the text is still stored in an AST (a list of Word nodes), and by implementing custom Words, one can embed arbitrary structured nodes into the text paragraph. This leads to full and extensible support for semi-structured content. The requirements document in Fig. 10 is an example.

3.7   G Separation of Concerns

In software engineering, concerns are separated[18] for many reasons. Among the most prevalent ones are:

1. Different stakeholders contribute different ingredients to a system, and each of them should be able to concentrate on their part, with an optimized language.
2. Different ingredients of a system are contributed at different times during the development process, so separating the respective artifacts is useful.

---

[17] https://www.plm.automation.siemens.com/de/products/lms/imagine-lab/embedded-software-designer.shtml.
[18] https://en.wikipedia.org/wiki/Separation_of_concerns.

4.1 | Price Depends on Country and Price Group
| priceDep /functional: status=accepted, @pricing

The price of the phone call depends on several factors, including the **#country** and the **#pricegroup**. The actual **#actMinPrice** is computed from the **#baseMinPrice** with the following equation: **#(actMinPrice = baseMinPrice ∗ priceFactor / 100)**. the **#priceFactor** is given by table:

		Countries				priceFactor	^words
		Germany	Italy	Spain	(	pricegroup	^words
Price‐groups	PLATINUM	10	8	7	1	actMinPrice	^words
	GOLD	11	10	9	10	baseMinPrice	^words
	SILVER	12	8 + B	8	8		

Fig. 10. Example from the mebddr requirements language. The number (4.1) is automatically computed from the nesting level and is not editable. The title is simple text. The /functional is one value from an enumerated type, same with the status. The @pricing is a predefined tag. The text paragraph is unstructured text with the # introducing embedded variable definitions. Those variables can contain an expression that can in turn reference other embedded variables, with full IDE and type system support. Finally, the table is a modular extension of the requirements language for data tables. The table supports full expressions as its data, as illustrated by the 8 + B, where B is a reference to a constant.

3. There is a 1:n relationship between instances of concern C_1 and concern C_2; separating the concerns allows having multiple instances of C_2 for a given single instance of C_1 (for example, having multiple UI definitions for a single data model definition).

A drawback of concern separation is that the concerns usually have to be recombined at some point, for example for an analysis or for constructing the full system; so some semantic connection is required between the models (and the underlying languages). It can also be hard for users to understand the interactions of the separated conderns; they have to recombine them in their head.

   The needs of use cases 1 and 2 (stakeholder/process-step specific abstractions and notations) often lead to the use of different tools for the different concerns, which, in turn, makes rejoining the separated concerns hard from a technical perspective (as opposed to the semantic perspective mentioned above). This problem does not exist in our approach: because of MPS' flexibility with abstractions and notations, we can credibly represent a very wide range of concerns within MPS[19], making reintegration technically trivial.

   Many of our DSLs are explicitly built to factor out domain logic from technical aspects: the models/languages capture the domain logic, and the generators/interpreters/platforms contribute the technical aspects. In this case, the

---

[19] Of course, in some projects it is necessary for organizational reasons to keep some concerns in different tools; typical examples are requirements, architecture models or low-level implementation. There are various ways of integrating external data into MPS, from actual import to stub models to using URLs or other pointers to reference data stored in non-MPS files or other resources.

models often mix the various concerns *within* the domain logic, while the technical ones handled separately by the infrastructure.

MPS supports annotations. An annotation can be used to add additional data (AST nodes) to a model *without the underlying language definition knowing about it*. This means that, on model level, concerns are not separated, because the annotation is structurally and synantically inlined in the model. However, on language level, concerns remain separated. We use this regularly, for example, to parametrize advanced analyses on models, to attach documentation or to attach presence conditions for product line variability.

Finally, as mentioned above, MPS supports multiple projections for the same underlying AST. In particular, a particular projection can *not* show parts of the AST. This can be used to render a model in a concern-specific way while the underlying AST stored all concerns' data in one integrated resource.

~ ~ ~

mbeddr's Build. mbeddr programs use a build configuration to specify how the executable is built from the source modules. It can be seen as a mix of makefile, compiler switches as well as instructions on how to reduce language extensions to plain C. For example, one can configure whether the components should support interface polymorphism (flexible) or not (faster, lower memory consumption). The main drivers for separating this concern are the above-mentioned reasons 2 (process) and 3 (`1:n` – many executables from the same sources).

Verification in mbeddr. CBMC-based verifications of C code in mbeddr requires non-trivial parametrization of the verifier: which default analyses should be performed (NaN, div-by-zero, array-bounds), how far should loops be unwound, should slicing be turned on or not. Setting these parameters sensibly requires experimentation and/or experience with CBMC. This is why the configuration is kept in a separate concern model (use cases 1 and 2).

Healthcare DSL. In the KernelF-based healthcare DSL mentioned earlier we separate four different concerns, mainly for reasons 1 and 2: complex decisions (defined and reviewed by healthcare professionals), overall execution of the algorithm (contributed by healthcare and software people), test scenarios (reviewed by healthcarers) and configuration of derived artifacts (contributed by software people, later in the process). There is also a use of multiple projections: states and transitions in the main algorithm state machine can be annotated as `good` and `exceptional` tags; a particular projection shows only the good case to allow reviewers to understand the essence of the algorithm.

Spacecraft Architecture based on mbeddr. Wortmann [31] describes an approach where the abstractions of ESA's reference architecture for spacecraft software[20] were directly integrated into C through mbeddr language extensions. This is an example of the integration (as opposed to separation) of concerns: in the traditional approach based on a UML modeling tool and a classical C IDE, integrating the architecture description (UML model) and the implementation

---

[20] http://savoir.estec.esa.int/SAVOIRDocuments.htm.

(C code) was *technically* hard, so they were separated. mbeddr, plus extensions, allowed OHB to create an integrated program/model of the two without losing the semantics of the abstractions defined in the reference architecture.

3.8 H Integration of Stakeholders

Integrating domain experts, who are typically not programmers, more directly into the development of software has been a long-standing goal of software engineering in order to get rid of inefficiencies in the development process. Domain-specific languages at the appropriate abstraction level that employ notations borrowed from the domain can make a significant contribution toward this goal. Bringing models "alive" through simulation and testing is another important ingredient.

~ ~ ~

Public Benefits. Another DSL that extends KernelF is used for public benefits calculations. It is quite different in style from the salary/tax calculation language in that it relies much more on first-class domain abstractions and uses a notation that more closely resembles forms, while still supporting expressions (with full tool support) inside form fields (see Fig. 11). Execution of the models for the purpose of testing is supported through extensions to KernelF's interpreter.

Healthcare. In the healthcare DSL, healthcare professionals and software engineers create algorithms collaboratively, essentially by pair programming. While the asynchronous, state-based main algorithm is harder for the medical personnel to get used to, the tabular and tree-based decisions procedures are very accessible. The overall algorithm is then validated by doctors through generated flowcharts, and through interactive simulations based on interpreters.

Salary/Tax. In the salary/tax DSL, one reason for acceptance by domain experts is that the language directly supports working with temporal data, which dramatically simplifies expressing idiomatic calculations. In addition, the language is designed in a way to support efficient, reactive execution; the domain experts, when writing calculation code, are isolated from this technical concern.

3.9 I Powerful, Productivity-Focused IDEs

MPS provides all the features known from programming-language IDEs: syntax highlighting, code completion, error markup, quick fixes (aka intentions), refactorings, goto definition, find references, search and replace, and version control integration including diff/merge *for all supported notations*. Most of these editor services work automatically once the language and its notation is defined, but all of them can also be customized. In addition, for non-textual notations, buttons, menus and palettes can be added to toolbars, views or inline in the notations themselves (such as little buttons to add new connections in diagrams, or buttons to add/delete rows/columns in tables). Below we discuss particular examples that go beyond these generic IDE features.

~ ~ ~

Unterhaltsvorschuss

```
Zeitangabe:        laufend
Häufigkeit:        monatlich einmal
Leistungskontext:
Leistungsart:      Leer
Zählart: uvg
Anspruch Beginn: Anfang - Unbegrenzt: junger Mensch.geburtsdatum
Anspruch Ende:     01.01.1800 ▥ - 31.12.9999 ▥  : min(junger Mensch.geburtsdatum + 12 Jahre ,
                                                       datum + 72 Monate - Anzahl Monate mit uvg)

Zeitraum für Berechnung: Anfang - Unbegrenzt: {standardzeitraum, standardzeitraum}
zweckgebundene Leistung: ☐
dem Grunde nach:         ☐
Zeitraumbezogene Daten
nullwerte Anzeigen : boolean = 01.01.1800 ▥    - 31.05.2016 ▥   : true
                               01.06.2016 ▥    - Unbegrenzt    : false
berechnungsart     : berechnungsarttyp = 01.01.1800 ▥ - 31.12.9999 ▥ : dreißigstel
Bezugsobjekte:
Attribute: bemerkung   : string wird validiert
           antragsdatum : Datum
```

Fig. 11. Public benefits calculations using a form-style DSL. The DSL is quite form-oriented; the yellow shaded parts are rigid, and cannot be edited. The parts shaded red are domain-specific expressions and types that play an important role in the usability of the DSL for the end users. Both shadings are not present in the actual tool.

Validity of Rules In the salary/tax language, calculation rules have a validity period in order to represent the evolution of the underlying law. For example, the church tax might be calculated in one particular way until the end of 2017, but then in another way starting from 2018; each rules specifies its validity period. Once the system has been used for a while, there will be different incarnations of calculation rules for each particular data item, and developers will have a hard time understanding the set of rules valid for a particular point in time. To solve this issue, the IDE allows users to select a date, and it then renders the program code in a way where only the rules relevant for this date are shown.

Context Navigation. MPS supports context actions, i.e., buttons in a palette that are specific to the currently selected program node. In the salary/tax language we use this to support context navigation (Fig. 12). For a given data item, the actions allow quick navigation to all rules that calculate that particular item, and to all downstream calculation rules that depend on the current data item. Similarly, when a rule is selected, all alternative rules (different validity period or different precondition) are shown.

Variants in mbeddr. In mbeddr, parts of programs can be annotated with presence conditions, i.e., Boolean expressions over features in a feature model (this can be seen as a structurally clean version of #ifdefs). Users can select a particular configuration (i.e., set of selected features), and the code can be projected to only show those parts that are present in this configuration, based on evaluating the Boolean expressions. In the full projection, parts that have the same presence condition are shaded with the same color to help users quickly identify parts that are in the same configuration

Tool as Language. In traditional languages and their IDEs, many added-value services, for example, those for program understanding, testing, and debugging, rely on service-specific UI elements (such as tool windows, buttons, or menus). Because of MPS' flexibility in how editors can be defined, we use languages and language extensions instead of these UI elements. Examples include the REPL and its rendering of structured values (Fig. 15), the overlay of variable values over the program code during debugging Fig. 14, test coverage and other reports over the program, generated test vectors and their validity state (Fig. 13) and the diffing of mutated programs vs. their original in the context of mutation testing. This leads to a less complex appearance of the IDE, which fits well with our domain expert users.[21]

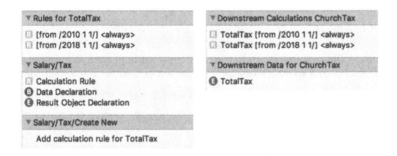

Fig. 12. Palette actions that support context-specific navigation for the currently selected program node in the salary/tax language.

3.10 J Liveness

Programs (or models that describe behavior) are essentially recipes of how something will behave once it is fed with particular inputs. In other words, the *program* is different from its *execution*: a program can "run". Special tools called debuggers help programmers understand the execution of their programs. Contrast this with a spreadsheet: a spreadsheet does not run (alternatively you can also say that it always runs). In any case there is no distinction between the recipe its execution for a particular set of inputs. This is generally helpful because during programming, users do not have to imagine how the program will run later.[22] Live programming is about removing the separation between a program and its execution, or at least using tools to help users bridge this gap more easily than

---

[21] We have to make more progress in this direction to make MPS suitable for a wider range of domain experts.

[22] On the other hand, it is hard to see how a spreadsheet-like approach can be generalized, and made to scale. It is well known that there are serious problems with the quality of spreadsheets. There is probably a reason for the recipe/execution separation.

by staring at program code. For example, the Live workshop[23] defines liveness as follows:

Live programming systems abandon the traditional edit-compile-run cycle in favor of fluid user experiences that encourages powerful new ways of "thinking to code" and enables programmers to see and understand their program executions.

According to this definition, we have made progress in this direction.

~ ~ ~

In-IDE Interpreter. We mentioned the in-IDE interpreter before. It is typically executed as part of the type system.[24] This means that any change to the input data, or the program itself, will instantly update the output, very much "abandoning the ... edit-compile-run cycle". With the projectional editor it is easy to render computed data, such as a program's outputs, directly into an editor. One use of this approach is with (generated or manually written) test vectors, as shown in Fig. 13. Since the programs (in this language) are functional, this setup is just like Excel – the computation state is "right there".

```
fun recAdd(base: number, arg: number): number where [ pre arg >= 0]
    = alt [ arg == 0  => base
            otherwise => 1 + recAdd(base, arg - 1)]

test case TestFunctions [fail] {
    vectors for recAdd ->
```

		base	arg	res	status
0:	valid	1	3	4	ok
1:	valid	0	0	0	ok
2:	valid	10	10	10	actual was 20
3:	valid	6	0	6	ok
4:	invalid input	6	-1		not executed

```
}
```

Fig. 13. Test vectors for testing a function `recAdd`; changing the function implementation or any of the inputs will immediately update the success status (incl. shade color) and the actual output value.

Debugger for KernelF. We also support a debugger for KernelF. Again, since (at least in its basic version) KernelF does not support effects, a computation can be shown as a "state" – no interactive stepping, as a means of representing the passage of time, is necessary. However, it is possible that the same piece of code is executed more than once because of loops (for example, through higher-order functions on collections) or through recursion. This is why the debugger

---

[23] https://2017.splashcon.org/track/live-2017.

[24] If the computation is big, it can also be triggered explicitly, avoiding slowing down the type system.

has two components: a tree view (Fig. 14B) shows the computation tree, where each tree node represents an *execution* of a program node and shows its value *in that execution*. In addition, the values of the program nodes in a particular execution can be overlaid over the source by double-clicking the execution node in the tree. This is shown in Fig. 14A.

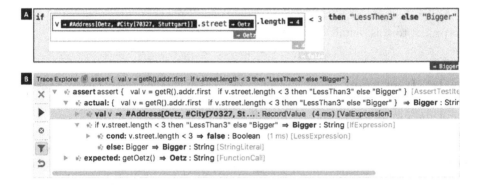

Fig. 14. KernelF's debugger. B: Tree view that represents *executions* of the underlying program nodes. A: An execution's value overlay over the corresponding source code.

REPL and Interactors. KernelF also comes with a REPL where users can enter expressions, see their values, and then use the value in downstream expressions (by referencing the i-th output by $i). Users can open a REPL for any expression via an intention. The REPL has special support for interactors, such as the decision procedures discussed earlier in the context of smart contracts. Interactors expose their (mutable) state through a generic API, so users can see the interactor evolve as they send commands via the REPL. In addition, because the state is represented in a homogeneous, structured way, the REPL can highlight the diff of the state between subsequent steps (Fig. 15).

4   The Meta Level

Large parts of MPS are bootstrapped: the facilities for language definition are built with MPS itself. In other words, the discussion about programming and modeling can also be applied to MPS itself. We do this briefly in this section.

A **High-level, Domain-Specific Concepts** MPS has first-class abstractions for many of the ingredients of languages including structure, notation or type systems. DSLs for expressing IDE services are also available. These are defined as MPS languages, and they can be extended like any other MPS language. For example, the grammar cells [29] that make it easier to define usable text editors are an extension of MPS' language for defining textual editors. The languages for defining tables and diagrams have also been developed by our team, as a non-invasive extension to MPS itself. The same is true for the DSL used to define

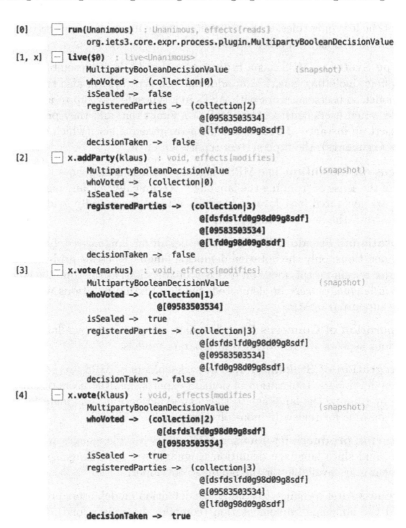

Fig. 15. A REPL session that modifies an interactor through commands; the REPL shows the state internal state of the interactor, as well as its evolution based on a diff.

interpreters. IncA [16] is a DSL for incremental program analysis built with MPS, deeply integrated into MPS to support analysis of MPS-defined languages.

B **User-definable Abstractions.** All language definition languages (except the structure) are extensions of BaseLanguage, MPS' version of Java. So while the DSLs for type systems, editors or constraints do not allow the definition of abstractions using these languages, users can always use BaseLanguage and factor behavior into classes.

C **Focus on Behavior and Algorithms.** The only language that is purely structural is the structure definition language. All others express some kind of behavior, be it typing rules, scope definitions or the interactive aspects of editors based on the various supported notations.

D **Type Systems.** MPS has a type system that basically resembles the Java type system, including generics. In addition, the type system also reflects MPS' meta model, so users can work with ASTs in a typesafe way (up to a point). For example, when users construct an AST of a `Function`, and they programmatically insert an instance of `Statement` in the `arguments` slot (which structurally expects `Arguments`), the type system reports an error.

E **Focus on Execution** The MPS language definition languages focus on execution in the sense of "running the language". Technically, all language definition models are generated into Java code which is then dynamically loaded and executed to "run" the new language in MPS.

F **Notational Freedom** The language definition languages rely largely on textual notations; only the notation definition languages uses a grid-style layout. The major reason for this focus on text is probably that, at the time the language definition languages were implemented, the non-textual notations were not yet reliably supported in MPS.

G **Separation of Concerns** Every language aspect has its own language, and the various aspects are also defined in separate models.

H **Integration of Stakeholders** The stakeholders of MPS are primarily the language developers. Integration of domain experts, i.e., the users of languages, is done by running the language so they can experience it. The meta languages are not suitable for review by non-software people.

I **Powerful, productivity-focused IDEs** Since MPS languages are developed in MPS, and since language definition languages are MPS languages, all MPS IDE features are available for the language developer.

J **Liveness** After a change to a language definition model, users press `Ctrl-F9` to build the language implementation (compile, dynamic reload). This is reasonably fast for realistically-sized languages. So while the edit-compile-run cycle still exists, it is fast enough for fluid work. Liveness in the stricter sense of the word is not supported.

5   Conclusions

Programming and modeling, in the sense of model-driven, where models are automatically transformed into the real system, cannot be categorically distinguished. However, the two have traditionally emphasized different aspects differently, making each suitable for different use cases.

Our approach to building (more or less) domain-specific modeling languages and environments combines ingredients from both fields in a novel way, relying on two pillars: projectional editing, which lets us use a wide range of notations, and language modularity, which allows us to reify library abstractions as language abstraction, which, in turn, leads to better analyzability and IDE support. Those two, plus the practice of growing a general-purpose base language towards a domain, give us the necessary range in abstraction to cover "typical" modeling and programming tasks, as the many examples in this paper demonstrate.

~ ~ ~

MPS' spiritual father, Sergey Dmitriev, calls this approach language-oriented programming; language-oriented programming can be seen as the 21st century version of model-driven. Based on the observation that it is essentially impossible to nail down the difference between a (prescriptive) model and a (suitably abstract) program, we propose the following, very pragmatic definition of "model":

> **Definition:** A model is an artifact expressed with a language defined in a language workbench that supports the features illustrated in this paper.

The reason for this definition is that, because of the language workbench's capabilities, one can incrementally add first-class abstractions, analyses, tool support and notations to "programs" to give them all the properties of a "model".

Acknowledgements. While I *wrote* the paper, the material discussed in the paper would not have been possible without the team at itemis. So I want to acknowledge everybody who contributed ideas, code, or validation. In addition, I want to thank the MPS team at Jetbrains for building an amazing tool and for helping us use it productively over the years. Finally, Tamas Szabo provided useful feedback on the paper, so I want to thank him specifically. The same thanks goes to my ISOLA reviewers.

References

1. Berger, T., Völter, M., Jensen, H.P., Dangprasert, T., Siegmund, J.: Efficiency of projectional editing: a controlled experiment. In: Proceedings of the 2016 24th ACM SIGSOFT International Symposium on Foundations of Software Engineering, pp. 763–774. ACM (2016)
2. Clarke, E.M., Grumberg, O., Peled, D.: Model Checking. MIT Press, Cambridge (1999)
3. Czarnecki, K., Eisenecker, U.W., Czarnecki, K.: Generative Programming: Methods, Tools, and Applications, vol. 19. Addison Wesley, Reading (2000)
4. Durr, E., Van Katwijk, J.: Vdm++, a formal specification language for object-oriented designs. In: 1992 Proceedings Computer Systems and Software Engineering, pp. 214–219. IEEE (1992)
5. Erdweg, S., et al.: The state of the art in language workbenches. In: Erwig, M., Paige, R.F., Van Wyk, E. (eds.) SLE 2013. LNCS, vol. 8225, pp. 197–217. Springer, Cham (2013). https://doi.org/10.1007/978-3-319-02654-1_11
6. Fowler, M.: Language workbenches: The killer-app for domain specific languages (2005)
7. Goguen, J., Meseguer, J.: Rapid prototyping: in the obj executable specification language. ACM SIGSOFT Softw. Eng. Notes **7**(5), 75–84 (1982)

8. Green, T.R.: Cognitive dimensions of notations. In: Sutcliffe, A., Macaulay, L. (eds.) People and Computers V, pp. 443–460. Cambridge University Press, Cambridge (1989)

9. Holzmann, G.: Spin model checker, the: primer and reference manual. Addison-Wesley Professional (2003)

10. Jensen, C.S., Snodgrass, R.T.: Temporal data management. IEEE Trans. Knowl. Data Eng. **11**(1), 36–44 (1999)

11. Kroening, D., Tautschnig, M.: CBMC – C bounded model checker. In: Ábrahám, E., Havelund, K. (eds.) TACAS 2014. LNCS, vol. 8413, pp. 389–391. Springer, Heidelberg (2014). https://doi.org/10.1007/978-3-642-54862-8_26

12. Maloney, J., Resnick, M., Rusk, N., Silverman, B., Eastmond, E.: The scratch programming language and environment. ACM Trans. Comput. Educ. (TOCE) **10**(4), 16 (2010)

13. Medvidovic, N., Taylor, R.N.: A classification and comparison framework for software architecture description languages. IEEE Trans. Softw. Eng. **26**(1), 70–93 (2000)

14. Molotnikov, Z., Völter, M., Ratiu, D.: Automated domain-specific C verification with mbeddr. In: Proceedings of the 29th ACM/IEEE International Conference on Automated Software Engineering, pp. 539–550. ACM (2014)

15. Ratiu, D., Schaetz, B., Voelter, M., Kolb, B.: Language engineering as an enabler for incrementally defined formal analyses. In: 2012 Formal Methods in Software Engineering: Rigorous and Agile Approaches (FormSERA), pp. 9–15. IEEE (2012)

16. Szabó, T., Erdweg, S., Voelter, M.: IncA: a DSL for the definition of incremental program analyses. In: 2016 31st IEEE/ACM International Conference on Automated Software Engineering (ASE), pp. 320–331. IEEE (2016)

17. Tanimoto, S.L.: A perspective on the evolution of live programming. In: Proceedings of the 1st International Workshop on Live Programming, pp. 31–34. IEEE Press (2013)

18. van Rest, O., Wachsmuth, G., Steel, J.R.H., Süß, J.G., Visser, E.: Robust real-time synchronization between textual and graphical editors. In: Duddy, K., Kappel, G. (eds.) ICMT 2013. LNCS, vol. 7909, pp. 92–107. Springer, Heidelberg (2013). https://doi.org/10.1007/978-3-642-38883-5_11

19. Voelter, M.: A smart contract development stack. Accessed 6 Dec 2017

20. Voelter, M.: Language and IDE modularization and composition with MPS. In: Lämmel, R., Saraiva, J., Visser, J. (eds.) GTTSE 2011. LNCS, vol. 7680, pp. 383–430. Springer, Heidelberg (2013). https://doi.org/10.1007/978-3-642-35992-7_11

21. Voelter, M.: An argument for the isolation of 'fachlichkeit' (2017). https://languageengineering.io/an-argument-for-the-isolation-of-fachlichkeit-3a67a939d23b

22. Voelter, M.: Thoughts on 'declarativeness' (2017). https://languageengineering.io/thoughts-on-declarativeness-fc4cfd4f1832

23. Voelter, M.: The design, evolution, and use of KernelF. In: Rensink, A., Sánchez Cuadrado, J. (eds.) ICMT 2018. LNCS, vol. 10888, pp. 3–55. Springer, Cham (2018). https://doi.org/10.1007/978-3-319-93317-7_1

24. Voelter, M., van Deursen, A., Kolb, B., Eberle, S.: Using C language extensions for developing embedded software: a case study. In: Proceedings of OOPSLA 2015, pp. 655–674. ACM (2015)

25. Voelter, M.: Using language workbenches and domain-specific languages for safety-critical software development. Softw. Syst. Model., 1–24 (2018). https://doi.org/10.1007/s10270-018-0679-0

26. Voelter, M., Kolb, B., Szabó, T., Ratiu, D., van Deursen, A.: Lessons learned from developing mbeddr: a case study in language engineering with mps. Softw. Syst. Model., 1–46 January 2017. https://doi.org/10.1007/s10270-016-0575-4
27. Voelter, M., Lisson, S.: Supporting diverse notations in MPS' projectional editor. In: GEMOC Workshop
28. Voelter, M., Ratiu, D., Kolb, B., Schaetz, B.: mbeddr: instantiating a language workbench in the embedded software domain. Autom. Softw. Eng. **20**(3), 1–52 (2013)
29. Voelter, M., Szabó, T., Lisson, S., Kolb, B., Erdweg, S., Berger, T.: Efficient development of consistent projectional editors using grammar cells. In: Proceedings of the 2016 ACM SIGPLAN International Conference on Software Language Engineering, pp. 28–40. ACM (2016)
30. Woodcock, J., Davies, J.: Using Z: Specification, Refinement, and Proof. Prentice Hall International. Pearson Education, UK (1996)
31. Wortmann, A., Beet, M.: Domain specific languages for efficient satellite control software development. In: DASIA 2016, vol. 736 (2016)
32. Xi, H., Pfenning, F.: Dependent types in practical programming. In: Proceedings of the 26th ACM SIGPLAN-SIGACT Symposium on Principles of Programming Languages, pp. 214–227. ACM (1999)

On the Difficulty of Drawing the Line

Steve Boßelmann, Stefan Naujokat[(✉)], and Bernhard Steffen

Chair for Programming Systems, TU Dortmund University, Dortmund, Germany
{steve.bosselmann,stefan.naujokat,steffen}@cs.tu-dortmund.de

Abstract. The paper considers domain-specific tool support as a means to turn descriptive into prescriptive models, and to blur the difference between models and programs, and even between developers and users. Conceptual underlying key is to view the system development as a decision process which increasingly constraints the range of possible system implementations and Domain-Specific Languages (DSLs) as a means to freeze taken decisions on the way towards a concrete realization. This way naturally comprises both programming and modeling aspects. In fact, considering all interactions that influence the behaviour of the system as development turns GUIs into DSLs and makes it even hardly possible to draw the line between developers and users. We will illustrate this viewpoint in the light of the development of the Equinocs system, Springer's new editorial service.

Keywords: Modeling · Metamodeling · Programming
Domain-specific languages · Language-oriented programming
Language-driven engineering · Code generation · Model transformation

1   Introduction

There is a general tendency that structures and categorizations considered obvious in the past often get blurred in the course of deeper investigation. E.g., the separating line between control and data path, traditionally clearly defined, is today often profitably moved by changing the level of interpretation, and even the gender classification has recently moved from a binary to a continuous spectrum. A similar trend can also be observed when considering the role, structure, and pragmatics of modeling/specification languages on the one, and programming languages on the other side: Originally, there was a quite clear distinction between the typically very abstract loose and descriptive modeling and the much more concrete and prescriptive programming. This distinction was also clearly reflected in their role: Modeling aimed at the description of WHAT a system is supposed to do (in particular, this description should not force the programmer to overspecify), and programming should aim at the description of an efficient solution, the HOW. Technically, this was reflected by modeling languages to support certain logics, whereas programming tended to be more imperative. With the evolution of more and more involved compilation and synthesis techniques

© Springer Nature Switzerland AG 2018
T. Margaria and B. Steffen (Eds.): ISoLA 2018, LNCS 11244, pp. 340–356, 2018.
https://doi.org/10.1007/978-3-030-03418-4_20

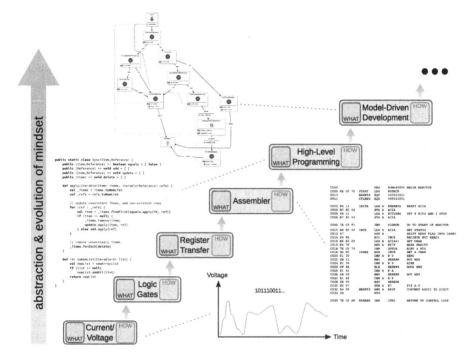

Fig. 1. Evolution of mindset in the past decades: from HOW to WHAT

this clear categorization got blurred.[1] Figure 1 sketches this evolution, which indicates the steady move towards more and more abstract system description organized in a HOW/WHAT cascade.

This cascaded abstraction influenced the development of increasingly higher-level modeling and programming languages as well as their support frameworks and infrastructures: defining a system's behavior at the level of electric current and voltage is almost impossible, leading to the introduction of numerous well-defined abstractions in the design of hardware components: transistor level, gate level, register transfer level, up to the instruction set level, which was the first abstraction offered to humans to "interact" with the machine by programming it. The instruction set of a CPU was in fact the basis for assembler languages, which in the fifties and sixties were regarded as extremely high-level abstractions of the underlying hardware. The successive raise from one level to the next built a systematic discipline to map the higher-level concepts stepwise down to the electrical level, where each program, each instruction, each clock cycle level operation are eventually executed. Assembler languages introduced the "thinking in commands" perspective, and thereby the imperative programming paradigm.

---

[1] In the hardware domain, synthesizing circuits from logical descriptions is actually standard since many decades! [11].

Today, they typically form the lowest abstraction level modern computer scientists are willing to consider.

The enormous development of programming and modeling languages [3,4] of the last 50 years equipped programming languages with concepts, metaphors, and mechanisms that allow programmers to focus more and more on describing the intended functionality (the WHAT) directly at the upper level, rather than having to deal with implementation details like inner structures, specific machine characteristics or the economic use of storage (the HOW). The more complex the addressed platform, the greater is the benefit of this approach. A good example here are modern Web applications which require the configuration of a complicated stack of technologies [1]. Another example are cross-cutting concerns like security and real time behaviour [2,18]. Enhanced development frameworks allow developers also here to focus on the required functionality, while the other concerns are taken care of during code generation and deployment, e.g., in an aspect-oriented fashion [13]. This ongoing development is, in fact, not so different from the well-established steps that decoupled programming from electrical level considerations.

In this paper we discuss a, in a sense, more radical trend and its impact: moving from universal languages to domain-specific or even purpose-specific languages. We illustrate that adequate specialization combined with tailored tooling allows one to simplify the required languages to a point that even application experts without any programming knowledge can express their intents in a way that corresponding solutions can be automatically generated without sacrificing non-functional properties like dependability, efficiency, and security. Conceptual backbone is our Language-Driven Engineering (LDE) [9,19] approach, which can be explained as a discipline of DSL orchestration.

After sketching the LDE background and philosophy in Sect. 2, Sect. 3 discusses LDE-oriented language refinement along the development of Springer's Equinocs system, before we conclude with a discussion of the approach and directions for future research in Sect. 4

2   LDE: Background and Philosophy

Modeling, specification, programming: drawing clear lines between these notions seems impossible. As clearly pointed out by Völter [23], usual criteria like executability, looseness, textual, graphical, and abstraction, give tendencies, but do not lead to accurate classification. We go even a step further and see the distinction between prescriptive and descriptive as a matter of purpose and perspective. Consider climate models, mentioned by Völter as clearly out of scope of prescriptive model-driven approaches: Good descriptive models for climate are naturally ideal prescriptive models for corresponding simulators, which, in a sense, make the original climate models even executable!

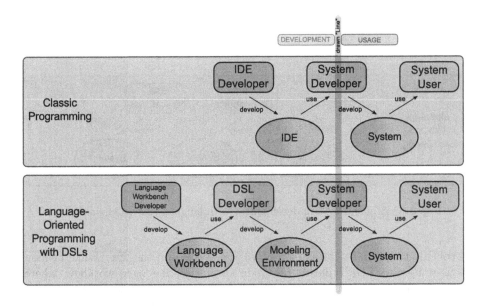

Fig. 2. Comparison: meta levels in classic programming vs. domain-specific approaches

In principle, also the most abstract descriptions[2] can become executable when regarded in a specific context: the graphical model of a calender turns into a prescriptive specification when, e.g., defining travel schedules, and typical (product) configurators use numerous similarly abstract and domain-specific descriptions as prescriptive modeling components for search and filtering.[3] In fact, the whole idea of domain-specific (modeling) languages (DSLs) [8,16] can be regarded as a way to automatically make abstract description *operational*.[4] Of course, this requires to establish adequate corresponding (execution) landscapes, powerful enough to adequately interpret the abstract input description.[5]

Language-Oriented Programming (LOP) [5,6,24] exploits this observation by offering to develop DSLs within appropriate meta environments – often called Language Workbenches [7] – in order to also address stakeholders without (explicit) programming expertise (cf. Fig. 2). Impressive is here the projectional editing functionality of JetBrains MPS [12], which allows, e.g., business people

---

[2] here to be understood as descriptive models, as any form of description can be interpreted that way.

[3] For a car configurator, (descriptive) images of a car, are often used to support the adequate selection (prescription).

[4] Please understand 'operational' as 'lives up to its purpose in a corresponding realization'.

[5] Traditional correctness-by-construction methods fit in here as well. In fact, there is no clear conceptual difference between this DSL-'enactment' and a compiler. Only the level of application is different.

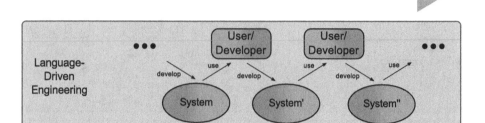

Fig. 3. Continuous system development with language-driven engineering

to contribute tabular data as part of a larger system in the 'Excel'-like fashion they are used to. LOP typically results in a waterfall-like 'meta workflow' where required additional DSLs are provided before the actual systems development starts.

Language-driven engineering (LDE) [9,19] goes a step further by considering the development of tailored DSLs as essential continuous part of the system development and evolution process (cf. Fig. 3). E.g., our LDE-based development of the Equinocs system[6] proceeds by co-evolution of the metamodeling environment CINCO [17] for easier generation of (graphical) domain-specific languages, of DIME [1], our dedicated (graphical) DSL-specific[7] integrated development environment (IDE),[8] and of Equinocs itself.

This co-evolution requires elaborate means for maintaining coherence, e.g., to allow one to (easily) migrate existing Equinocs versions into new versions of DIME and existing DIME versions into new versions of CINCO in a way that exploits the new features of DIME, an Eldorado for generative programming and model-to-model transformations.[9] In this context, it is important to distinguish three flavours of language evolution:

- In an upgrading form (e.g. Java 7 to Java 8). Often, at least when this happen as natural extension, migration is not an issue at all.
- As DSL specialization. In this case it makes a lot of sense to define the semantics of the specialized language via translation to the original language,

---

[6] The next version of Springers Online Conference Service.

[7] In [19] we introduced the term mindset-specific IDE, and the acronym mIDE to indicate that DSLs are more than just means for purpose-specific simplification. New mindsets are powerful means to reach 'out of the (traditional) box'.

[8] DIME comprises currently four graphical DSLs.

[9] This requirement may remind of the situation of frameworks that have to explicitly deal with round-trip engineering, a problem that is overcome by frameworks following a full (code) generation policy.

with the advantage that reusing the available code generator for that language immediately provides a code generator for the specialized language [21]. On the other side, migration is typically quite constraint and complicated, but typically also only required in a very restrictive fashion as part of a (major) refactoring activity.

– As service oriented extension with new dedicated languages in the way discussed in [19], which can be regarded as a light-weight language specialization technology generalizing the idea of component libraries, with an intent reminiscent of the ideal of projectional editing of MPS.

LDE considers all these forms of evolution as part of the product development/system life cycle. In a sense, this generalizes the idea of 'a software system is never finished' to its entire development and evolution scenario. Everything co-evolves, the meta-metamodels for defining tailored DSLs, the DSLs, the system itself, as well as the infrastructure the system is supposed to run on. In this highly agile approach, the roles of metamodels, models, specifications, and programs converge, however, as part of an overall scenario that is characterized by diversification: We envisage the number of languages involved in individual projects to radically grow. In particular, we envisage that the use of graphical notation will lead to a tighter integration of domain experts into the system/application development process, as it is typically more intuitive and helps supporting the intended mindsets and purpose. We will discuss our corresponding visions, options, and the state of the art along the Equinocs development in the remainder of this paper.

3   Application Example: The Equinocs Development

In the following, we sketch LDE-oriented language refinement in the context of the development of Equinocs – Springer's new online conference management system that handles all phases of a conference, from setup over submission to review and proceedings production. Equinocs is entirely developed in a model-driven way with DIME, a tool that provides dedicated modeling languages for the development of complex multi-user Web applications.

Modeling Web applications with DIME is done by defining user interactions, the presentation and organization of the GUI, as well as eventually required permissions to access data or perform actions. DIME provides specific modeling languages for the creation of these aspect-specific models:

– **Interaction processes** manage the user interactions with the application, like page transitions including the data flow between different pages.
– **GUI models** define the appearance of pages in the Web application. They comprise basic UI components to display various types of content (text fields, images, etc.) as well as structural components to define panels, blocks, grid layouts, etc. Furthermore, data input via forms can be modeled with respective components for content-specific form fields.

– **Data models** are used to model the actual domain by means of various data types with attributes as well as (bidirectional) associations between them.

The basic building blocks of models in DIME are based on a component model called Service-Independent Building Blocks (SIBs) [20] that either are basic components or reference hierarchically to other models in the workspace. While the so-called Native SIBs wrap native implementations like service calls to an API, those SIBs that hold references to other models in the workspace enable the reuse of models. In DIME, process models and GUI models can be nested inside each other in a hierarchical fashion, both mutually as well as within models of the same type. In the context of GUI models, this enables the easy creation and encapsulation of recurrent complex components, like forms. Regarding process models, a clean process architecture arises from the use of sub-processes via Process SIBs and the integration of user interfaces happens likewise via GUI SIBs.

From DIME models, the running application is fully generated by a powerful code generator. Beyond that, DIME is itself generated in a model-driven way from models of the domain 'modeling language development'. The tool that provides editors for those models, as well as the required code generator, is our CINCO framework, which provides specific modeling languages, the Meta Graph Language (MGL) and the Meta Style Language (MSL), for the definition of both the structure as well as the visualization of graph models. Finally, in this line of modeling and code generation, CINCO is built upon the frameworks provided by the Eclipse Modeling Project [10,22]. Already here, we see two things:

1. Modeling is used – like programming – for the development of a program, tool or system.
2. The user of one level can be a developer of another: users of DIME are developers of the Equinocs system and the developers of DIME are users of the CINCO framework.

Both observations show that trying to draw a clear line seems impossible. Should this even be tried? Or should we strive for more levels of language development, so that with each level, the domain of the target system is more and more narrowed until we reach the finally desired system? Of course, such a more fluent approach only works efficiently with a powerful support framework. Most of the challenges (some of which we will discuss in the following) are not yet solved with any of the available language workbench systems. We already address some with the CINCO ecosystem, but believe that the modeling/programming community needs to team up for this ambitious aim.

In the following, three examples from the context of Equinocs, which motivate the provision of new UIs as DSLs, will be presented.

3.1   Report Form Language

In the Equinocs system, reviewers fill out report forms to provide their assessment for each paper they have been assigned to. These reports can be accessed

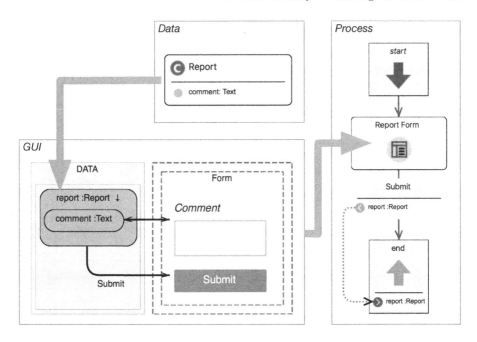

Fig. 4. DIME models for report creation

by the members of the conference committee and make up the basis for decision making. Hence, the UI created by the developers comprises a page for creating and editing a report (report form) as well as a page for presenting the actual result (report details). To keep the following example simple, let us assume that this report form consists of only a single field *Comment* to hold a free text. Figure 4 shows the required models in DIME for the realization of this report form in Equinocs. The GUI model holding the form is embedded in the interaction process. Both models reference the type *Report* from the data model. While the process model requires this reference for the definition of the data flow, the GUI model uses it to link the form field *Comment* with the data type's attribute *comment* to express where the field's value should be saved.

Let us now assume that we endeavour to extend the report form by introducing an additional field *assessment* to hold one of the discrete values *reject*, *accept* or *indifferent*. This would be helpful to provide a condensed overview for the conference committee. Based on the models so far, this is realized by the Equinocs developers through the following steps:

S1 Extend the data model of the application by means of adding a new attribute *assessment* to the data type *Report*.

S2 Add an additional input field to the UI model of the report form and link it with the newly created attribute *assessment*.

S3 Add an additional display field to the UI model of the report detail page.

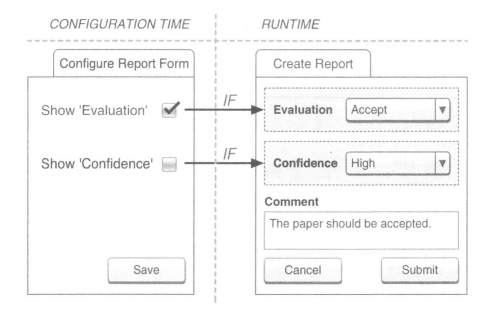

Fig. 5. Report form configuration

From a language-centric point of view, what we create and maintain this way, is a very restricted DSL for reports to be used by reviewers in the running Equinocs system. In particular, any request for new form fields actually is a change request for the report DSL communicated from system users to system programmers, i.e., a language management issue spanning the two layers of system runtime and system design. We will discuss some of the implications derived from this still simple example in more detail. In particular, we will illustrate how a user role morphs more and more into a developer role.

Implications Towards the System Level. The prominent disadvantage of the depicted approach of changing the report form on the system design level is that this would have immediate effect on all managed conferences after the re-deployment of the system, although not all organizers of all conferences would consider the changes as a welcome improvement. Typical management systems for conferences or journals have more complex forms, with often more than 10 fields like 'confidence of the reviewer', 'in scope for the topic of the conference', 'novelty in the field', or even 'quality of language'. The perception of these feature-rich solutions totally differs, as some may find it absolutely necessary, while others consider it highly annoying. However, it is almost natural to introduce conference settings to hold options for the organizers to turn these features on or off, either at initial configuration time or even on demand at runtime.

In the UI, these settings can be realized with a simple check box for each of the report form fields, named with something like 'Show <field.name>' (cf. Fig. 5).

From a language-centric point of view, what we just introduced, is a DSL for report forms to be used by system users like the conference organizers. Though we have already introduced a report DSL for reviewers above, the abstraction layer of this report form DSL differs, as the latter can be used to change the former. The ability to change the report DSL has so far been reserved for the system developers. But we shifted parts of the definition of the report DSL from programming level to the system level by introducing a new restricted DSL for that purpose and handing it over to the system users.

This is an excellent example to stress that switching the abstraction layer from the modeling language (report DSL) to the metamodeling language (report form DSL) does not necessarily mean to switch from system level to programming level. The language shift is more fluid and different parts of a language's definition might even be allocated on separate levels, as illustrated by this specific example.

Providing a DSL for report forms to be used by conference organizers adds flexibility for the latter at the cost of clarity and control on the programming level. While so far, the developers of the system had known exactly which fields exist in the report form, they now have to deal with the fact that some may not exist. Any business logic of the system that relies on values from one of the fields needs to be rebuilt in a more robust manner to not fail if they are missing. As an example, consider the logic of the system asserting that papers can only be accepted if at least one report exists whose value for *assessment* is other than *reject*. In general, if the system so far behaved differently depending on the current value of a specific field, it now has to first check whether such a value exists and behave predictable otherwise. The possible absence of a value imposes constraints for defining the corresponding business logic.

What if we continue to shift control over the report DSL from programming level to system level? Although the conference organizers can decide which fields are shown in the report forms, which fields are available at all is still predefined by the system developers. In particular, the workflow to add a completely new field on demand has not changed much. It still would require a change request addressed to the developers and the latter to run through the transformation steps listed above. As an alternative, we might transfer even more power to the system users by allowing them to create new form fields on demand, thereby extending the report DSL used by the reviewers. The required UI for the conference configuration (i.e., the report form DSL) would then need to be extended by a form for the organizers to change the list of available report form fields, including the feature to remove existing fields or create completely new ones (cf. Fig. 6). The latter can be achieved in multiple ways based on different restrictions. We might allow to only create fields of a specific type, e.g. those holding a pre-defined set of possible values (e.g., enum literals). In this case, providing a name for the field as well as the actual list of possible values is enough. Alternatively, we might hand over the definition of the value type of a form field, thus adding the definition options for text, boolean or integer values.

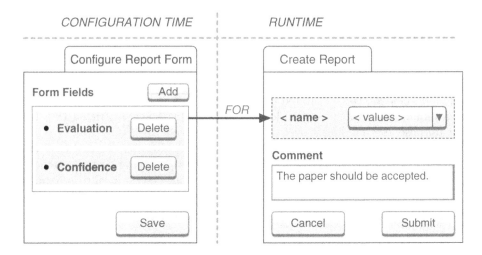

Fig. 6. Report form field creation

Again, these design decisions have so far been reserved for the system developers. And just like we discussed above, this transformation means more flexibility for the system users, but even less clarity and control for the system developers. While so far the developers had to respect that some fields of the report form may not be used at runtime, they now have to deal with the fact that (a part of) the report form is not even known at design time. What remains is kind of a meta-level perspective that tells them there may exist fields, the types they may have as well as the types of possible values. However, the remaining control over these features is hardly enough to be used as a basis to define meaningful business logic of the system. It is impossible to define system behavior based on the value of fields from which the developers do not know whether they exist. However, we might counteract this development by means of providing another specific DSL for the system users to define such behavior that depends on the actual values of report form fields. We will pick up this idea again in Sect. 3.3 where we exemplarily discuss the introduction of such a language.

From an abstract language-centric perspective, we have outlined a stepwise top-down transfer of control over a DSL from system design level to system level (cf. Fig. 7). It is easy to see that with increasing control comes increasing flexibility, in exchange for complexity. We have achieved that the report DSL can now be manipulated by the system users. But what would be an adequate way to do so? We argue that whether the increased complexity is manageable for the system users depends on the language they use. Using the instruments of the system developers requires knowledge and skills that span the handling of types and attribute definitions, i.e., knowledge that is traditionally associated with the programming domain. On the contrary, a DSL specialized to the definition of forms can provide an intuitive user interface and at the same time hide most of the complexity (type definitions, etc.) underneath. We might either create a DSL

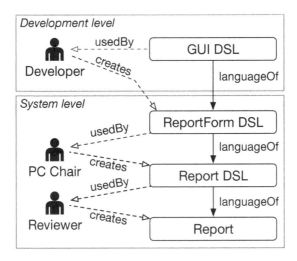

Fig. 7. Top-down DSL creation

by means of a Web form with distinct input fields, or a graphical DSL to build a visual model of the report form. However, both languages can be understood as restricted versions of the DSLs at system design level, as DIME's GUI models already comprise components for this very task. But the restricted versions focus solely on those components that are necessary to define a form by means of only including the different types of form fields that the conference organizers should be able to create.

Please note, the definition of data types must not be part of the report form DSL as there is no need to change the data model explicitly. Required data types as well as the relations between form fields and associated type attributes can be generated, as each form field matches a unique attribute of the already existing data type *Report*. New form fields can trigger the creation of new attributes automatically. However, these semantics have to be defined and assured by the Equinocs developers along with the definition of the form DSL, as the mapping of its language constructs on the applications' data model is still their responsibility.

Increase vs. Decrease of Expressive Power. The report form example describes a stepwise increase of the expressive power of the DSL, reaching from no control at all over configuration-based activation/deactivation of pre-defined form fields up to fully customized field types with respective sets of possible values. The driving motivation is restricting the DSL to ensure that the outcome, i.e., the model created by the user on the next level, represents a manageable artifact that can be integrated into the system. However, we could very well have chosen an opposite approach, i.e., starting with few restrictions and decreasing the expressive power by means of adding constraints on demand. Although we might hand over the full power of a general purpose programming language like Java, in practice, we would strive for a language that is more tailored to the application domain. For the report form example, the GUI DSL in DIME would have been a suitable starting point. With this, users on the system level can create components to extend the report form[10]. However, without additional constraints, they might as well create other UI components apart from those that fit into forms. Hence, it is advisable to restrict the GUI DSL to elements that actually can be integrated into forms, i.e., form fields and other content-related components like texts, images, etc. as well as components to add structure.

The difference between both approaches to create a DSL is apparent. A stepwise increase of expressive power aims at restricting the users of the language as much as possible, initially starting with only a few alternatives to choose from. In contrast, a stepwise decrease strives for providing as much freedom as possible, thereby trying to assure with appropriate constraints that the outcome is still valid by means of being integratable into the system context.

Implications Towards the Meta Level. We have just discussed the creation of a form DSL as a solution for the conference organizers to build their own report forms for reviewers. In this setting, we investigated the Equinocs application on the system level in relation to the modeling environment DIME on the development level. In the next subsection, we switch the perspective to investigate DIME on the system level in relation to CINCO on the development level.

3.2   Automatic Generation of Forms

To keep the example simple, let us consider the initial state of the Equinocs application as described at the beginning of the previous section. Here, changes to the report forms can only be done by the developers of Equinocs, i.e., within the DIME modeling environment. It is easy to see that in this scenario the transformation steps S1 to S3 listed above (changes to the data model, report form and report detail) would have to be repeated (or reverted) for any change requests regarding the extension (or reduction) of the report form fields, i.e., the report DSL. Although the development effort is relatively small, this approach means repetitive work for the developers. Reusing model elements like the UI components for the form fields would only reduce the effort but cannot eliminate the necessity of running through these steps over and over again. This is due to a mismatch between the intent of the Equinocs developers and what can be expressed in the DIME languages available for designing the Equinocs system. These languages let them define a *Report* data type with attributes (Data DSL) and form fields (GUI DSL), as well as *which* form field is related to *which* of these attributes.

However, what they actually need to express is that certain attributes of the *Report* data type are relevant for creating or editing reports and that respective form fields should be displayed at runtime for this exact purpose. But

---

[10] As Equinocs is a Web application, here we assume that a suitable Web editor for the GUI DSL exists to be easily integrated.

this requires addressing metamodel concepts of DIME's Data language, e.g., by means of a for-each construct in GUI models to iterate over attributes of data types. Additionally, as some attributes might be irrelevant in this specific context, some kind of filter mechanism would have to be established, along with a feature to enhance the Data model with some sort of 'UI cues'. Without going into further detail, we realize that a solution for this issue would definitely require changes to the modeling languages in DIME, i.e., changes on the metamodel level from the perspective of the Equinocs developers. Along with these additional syntactical elements, a model generator that generates GUI models for default forms might save the developers a great deal of work.

From this example, we can see that although the affected levels of abstraction differ, this constellation is very similar to the one depicted above regarding change requests for the report DSL. The only difference is the perspective, as now DIME is on the system level in relation to CINCO on the development level.

3.3   Conference Flow Language

The previous examples both show how the transfer of power over (parts of) a specific DSL can blur the line between development level and system level, as along with control over the DSL responsibilities are shifted from one level to the other. To illustrate this point further, we now introduce a new user role along with a new DSL into the system design process.

In the current implementation of Equinocs, the flow of a conference – i.e., which phases exist, when they are triggered, and what happens in each of them – is determined by the Equinocs developers in those process models that define the application's business logic. Additionally, some variation points are added into these processes, to reflect that the flow slightly differs depending on configuration parameters set by the conference organizers, like the minimum number of reviewers per paper or the decision for allowing a rebuttal phase.

As already discussed, the GUI for setting these configuration parameters can be understood as a DSL for the conference organizers to 'program' the behavior of the conference system. However, this DSL limits conference organizers to the options foreseen by the Equinocs developers and new demands regarding more expressive power result in increased complexity on both the system level as well as the development level. In fact, with more configuration parameters, the conference flow, which is spread across various process models already, becomes increasingly cluttered due to conditional branching to cover all possible conference flow alternatives.

The LDE way to address this problem is to introduce a dedicated DSL that is particularly tailored towards the definition of conference flows together with a code generator that guarantees the requirements on both the system level as well as the development level. In particular, this DSL may comprise constructs to decide on per-paper phase transitions based on the actual form field values of associated reports, as introduced in Sect. 3.1.

This scenario directly leads to the idea of also adding an additional role to the system design process: experts that know the domain of 'running conferences' and thus are suitable to define conference flows. This qualification profile, however, is neither matched by the typical conference organizer – as learning a dedicated DSL to run a conference is something that very few, if any, conference organizers are willing to do – nor by the typical developer, which in our scenario is expert for modeling Web applications with DIME.

Actually, for the future of Equinocs, we foresee that Springer's support team is capable of realizing the conference organizers' needs using such a dedicated flow DSL. But in which stage of the system design process would the definition of the conference flow be integrated? We can find good arguments for integrating this task into the development process, just as we do for shifting it to the system runtime. The best solution might even be to allow it into both levels. This illustrates that drawing a line between developers and users is as difficult as between programming and modeling, and that a corresponding distinction very much depends on the observer's perspective.

4   Conclusion and Perspectives

We have argued that domain-specific tool support has the potential to serve a means to turn descriptive into prescriptive models, and to blur the difference between models and programs, and even between developers and users. Underlying mindset is to view the system development as a decision process which increasingly constraints the range of possible system implementations and Domain-Specific Languages (DSLs) as a means to freeze taken decisions for future development and evolution. The corresponding development paradigm LDE (for Language-Driven Engineering), introduces a novel cooperative development paradigm that is tailored to specifically address all stakeholders, and it emphasizes that what is to be considered a model or a program is a matter of perspective.

We have illustrated the pragmatics of this viewpoint in the light of the development of the Equinocs system, Springer's new editorial service, by showing how the power of a user can incrementally be enhanced to turn her stepwise into a more and more powerful developer. In addition, we have sketched how the development of Equinocs could profit from the evolution of DIME, Equinocs' underlying development environment.

LDE and the imposed viewpoint on specifications, (meta) models, and programs has also reached (even undergraduate) teaching [15]. Experience shows that the traditional distinctions do not at all show up when confronting students directly with our perspective-driven viewpoint.

Currently, we are working on making LDE widely accessible, e.g., by providing a corresponding Web-based development environment [14], and by successively strengthening the domain-specific development support. Following the open-source philosophy, we hope to attract users and co-developers in order to establish an LDE community.

References

1. Boßelmann, S., et al.: DIME: a programming-less modeling environment for web applications. In: Margaria, T., Steffen, B. (eds.) ISoLA 2016. LNCS, vol. 9953, pp. 809–832. Springer, Cham (2016). https://doi.org/10.1007/978-3-319-47169-3_60
2. Boßelmann, S., Neubauer, J., Naujokat, S., Steffen, B.: Model-driven design of secure high assurance systems: an introduction to the open platform from the user perspective. In: Margaria, T., Solo, M.G.A. (eds.) The 2016 International Conference on Security and Management (SAM 2016). Special Track "End-to-end Security and Cybersecurity: From the Hardware to Application", pp. 145–151. CREA Press (2016)
3. Broy, M., Havelund, K., Kumar, R.: Towards a unified view of modeling and programming. In: Margaria, T., Steffen, B. (eds.) ISoLA 2016. LNCS, vol. 9953, pp. 238–257. Springer, Cham (2016). https://doi.org/10.1007/978-3-319-47169-3_17
4. Chatley, R., Donaldson, A., Mycroft, A.: The next 7000 programming languages. In: Steffen, B., Woeginger, G. (eds.) Computing and Software Science: State of the Art and Perspectives, LNCS, vol. 10000. Springer (2018, to appear)
5. Dmitriev, S.: Language Oriented Programming: The Next Programming Paradigm. JetBrains onBoard Online Magazine 1 (2004). http://www.onboard.jetbrains.com/is1/articles/04/10/lop/
6. Felleisen, M. et al.: A programmable programming language. Commun. ACM 61(3), 62–71 (2018)
7. Fowler, M.: Language Workbenches: The Killer-App for Domain Specific Languages?, June 2005. http://martinfowler.com/articles/languageWorkbench.html. Accessed 10 Apr 2018
8. Fowler, M., Parsons, R.: Domain-Specific Languages. Addison-Wesley/ACM Press, New York (2011)
9. Gossen, F., Margaria, T., Murtovi, A., Naujokat, S., Steffen, B.: DSLs for decision services: a tutorial introduction to language-driven engineering. In: Margaria, T., Steffen, B. (eds.) ISoLA 2018, LNCS 11244, pp. 546–564. Springer, Cham (2018)
10. Gronback, R.C.: Eclipse Modeling Project: A Domain-Specific Language (DSL) Toolkit. Addison-Wesley, Boston (2008)
11. Hachtel, G.D., Somenzi, F.: Logic Synthesis and Verification Algorithms, 1st edn. Springer, Boston (1996). https://doi.org/10.1007/0-387-31005-3
12. JetBrains: Meta Programming System. https://www.jetbrains.com/mps/. Accessed 10 Apr 2018
13. Kiczales, G., et al.: Aspect-oriented programming. In: Akşit, M., Matsuoka, S. (eds.) ECOOP 1997. LNCS, vol. 1241, pp. 220–242. Springer, Heidelberg (1997). https://doi.org/10.1007/BFb0053381
14. Lybecait, M., Kopetzki, D., Zweihoff, P., Fuhge, A., Naujokat, S., Steffen, B.: A tutorial introduction to graphical modeling and metamodeling with cinco. In: Margaria, T., Steffen, B. (eds.) ISoLA 2018, LNCS 11244, pp. 519–538. Springer, Cham (2018)
15. Margaria, T.: From computational thinking to constructive design with simple models. In: Margaria, T., Steffen, B. (eds.) ISoLA 2018, LNCS 11244, pp. 261–278. Springer, Cham (2018)
16. Mernik, M., Heering, J., Sloane, A.M.: When and how to develop domain-specific languages. ACM Comput. Surv. 37(4), 316–344 (2005)
17. Naujokat, S., Lybecait, M., Kopetzki, D., Steffen, B.: CINCO: a simplicity-driven approach to full generation of domain-specific graphical modeling tools. Softw. Tools Technol. Transf. 20(3), 327–354 (2017)

18. Naujokat, S., Neubauer, J., Margaria, T., Steffen, B.: Meta-level reuse for mastering domain specialization. In: Margaria, T., Steffen, B. (eds.) ISoLA 2016. LNCS, vol. 9953, pp. 218–237. Springer, Cham (2016). https://doi.org/10.1007/978-3-319-47169-3_16

19. Steffen, B., Gossen, F., Naujokat, S., Margaria, T.: Language-driven engineering: from general-purpose to purpose-specific languages. In: Steffen, B., Woeginger, G. (eds.) Computing and Software Science: State of the Art and Perspectives, LNCS, vol. 10000. Springer (2018, to appear)

20. Steffen, B., Margaria, T.: METAFrame in practice: design of intelligent network services. In: Olderog, E.-R., Steffen, B. (eds.) Correct System Design. LNCS, vol. 1710, pp. 390–415. Springer, Heidelberg (1999). https://doi.org/10.1007/3-540-48092-7_17

21. Steffen, B., Naujokat, S.: Archimedean points: the essence for mastering change. LNCS Trans. Found. Mastering Chang. (FoMaC) **1**(1), 22–46 (2016)

22. Steinberg, D., Budinsky, F., Paternostro, M., Merks, E.: EMF: Eclipse Modeling Framework, 2nd edn. Addison-Wesley, Boston (2008)

23. Voelter, M.: Fusing modeling and programming into language-oriented programming. In: Margaria, T., Steffen, B. (eds.) ISoLA 2018, LNCS 11244, pp. 309–339. Springer, Cham (2018)

24. Ward, M.P.: Language oriented programming. Softw. Concepts Tools **15**(4), 147–161 (1994)

X-by-Construction

X-by-Construction

Maurice H. ter Beek[1], Loek Cleophas[2,3], Ina Schaefer[4(✉)],
and Bruce W. Watson[3,5]

[1] ISTI–CNR, Pisa, Italy
m.terbeek@isti.cnr.it
[2] TU Eindhoven, Eindhoven, The Netherlands
l.g.w.a.cleophas@tue.nl
[3] Stellenbosch University, Stellenbosch, South Africa
{loek,bwwatson}@sun.ac.za
[4] TU Braunschweig, Braunschweig, Germany
i.schaefer@tu-bs.de
[5] CAIR, Stellenbosch, South Africa

Abstract. After decades of progress on Correctness-by-Construction (CbC) as a scientific discipline of engineering, it is time to look further than correctness and investigate a move from CbC to XbC, i.e., considering also *non-functional properties*. X-by-Construction (XbC) is concerned with a step-wise refinement process from specification to code that automatically generates software (system) implementations that *by construction* satisfy specific non-functional properties concerning security, dependability, reliability or resource/energy consumption, to name but a few. This track brings together researchers and practitioners that are interested in CbC and the promise of XbC.

1 Motivation and Aim

Correctness-by-Construction (CbC) sees the development of software (systems) as a scientific discipline of engineering. Originally intended as a mere means of programming algorithms that are correct *by construction* [4,8], the approach found its way into commercial development processes of complex software systems [6,7]. In this larger context, we can say that CbC advocates a step-wise correctness-preserving refinement process from specification to code, ideally by CbC design tools that automatically generate error-free (system) implementations from rigorous and unambiguous specifications of requirements. Afterwards, testing only serves the purpose of validating the CbC process rather than finding bugs.

A lot of progress has been made in this domain during the last four decades or so, implying the time has come to look further than correctness and investigate a move from CbC to XbC, i.e., considering also *non-functional properties*. *X-by-Construction (XbC)* is concerned with a step-wise refinement process from specification to code that automatically generates software (system) implementations that *by construction* satisfy specific non-functional properties concerning security, dependability, reliability or resource/energy consumption, etc.

© Springer Nature Switzerland AG 2018
T. Margaria and B. Steffen (Eds.): ISoLA 2018, LNCS 11244, pp. 359–364, 2018.
https://doi.org/10.1007/978-3-030-03418-4_21

Building on the highly successful track "Correctness-by-Construction and Post-hoc Verification: Friends or Foes?" at ISoLA 2016 [1], which focussed on the combination of post-hoc verification with CbC, the aim of the current XbC track at ISoLA 2018 is to bring together researchers and practitioners that are interested in CbC and the promise of XbC. Therefore, we invited researchers and practitioners working in the following communities to discuss moving from CbC to XbC:

- People working on system-of-systems, who address modelling and verification (correctness, but also non-functional properties concerning security, reliability, resilience, energy consumption, performance and sustainability) of networks of interacting legacy and new software systems, and who are interested in applying XbC techniques in this domain in order to prove non-functional properties of systems-of-systems by construction (from their constituent systems satisfying these properties).
- People working on quantitative modelling and analysis (e.g. through probabilistic or real-time systems and probabilistic or statistical model checking) in particular in the specific setting of dynamic, adaptive or (runtime) reconfigurable systems with variability. These people work on lifting successful formal methods and verification tools from single systems to families of systems, i.e., modelling and analysis techniques that need to cope with the complexity of systems stemming from behaviour, variability, and randomness—and which focus not only on correctness but also on non-functional properties concerning safety, security, performance or dependability properties. As such, they are likely interested in applying XbC techniques in this domain to prove non-functional properties of families of systems by construction (from their individual family members satisfying these properties).
- People working on generative software development, who are concerned with the automatic generation of software from specifications given in either general formal languages or domain-specific languages, leading to families of related software (systems). Also in this setting, the emphasis so far has typically been on functional correctness, but the restricted scope of the specifications—especially for domain-specific languages—definitely offers a suitable ground for reasoning about non-functional properties, and for using XbC techniques to guarantee such properties.
- People working on systems security, privacy and algorithmic transparency and accountability, who care about more than correctness. The application of XbC techniques could provide security guarantees from the outset when designing critical systems. It could also enforce transparency when developing algorithms for automated decision-making, in particular those based on data analytics—thus reducing algorithmic bias by avoiding opaque algorithms. For instance, people working on *Privacy by Design* start from the presupposition that any personal data processing environment should be designed such that privacy is taken into account already in the requirement elicitation and earliest design phases [3].

2   Contributions

In his keynote, Poll [12] discusses some positive and negative experiences in applying formal methods to security. Based on insights from the language-based security paradigm LangSec, he provides directions for leveraging formal methods to improve security.

Johnsen et al. [2] plead for a more central, high-level role of deployment decisions as part of a by-construction development process and call it *Deployment-by-Construction (DbC)*. According to this paradigm, deployment decisions should be expressed as part of a program's high-level model and evaluated in terms of how they affect program performance. To illustrate their proposal, the authors apply DbC in the context of parallel architectures with shared memory and caches. More concretely, they present a toolbox for evaluating deployment decisions for specific high-level parallel programs when interacting with existing memory structures. Based on the input, the toolbox scores the program execution with a performance indicator to compare different implementations and environments. The authors also provide a proof-of-concept implementation of the toolbox in Maude. Given a set of deployment decisions, this paper thus provides a means to abstractly represent and analyse a program's memory accesses with respect to their impact on runtime behaviour.

Steffen et al. [10] propose an approach to obtain a property X by construction via model transformations. The main idea of the approach is that an initial model is transformed into another model that guarantees the property X. The model transformations are very much into the spirit of aspect-oriented programming where an aspect is weaved into a base program such that the aspect implements a specific behaviour at certain base program points. As an instantiation of this idea, the authors consider their graphical modelling language framework CINCO with which graphical modelling languages and transformations can easily be specified and implementations thereof can be generated and generate models that guarantee the properties of model checkability and learnability.

Méry [11] describes a procedure for formal system modelling and step-wise refinement of algorithms using Event-B. He distinguishes several best practices for modelling as *design patterns*. The idea is to provide an abstract specification of the problem in Event-B, which is then refined progressively and transformed into an algorithm which is correct-by-construction in the sense that it satisfies the properties defined in the abstract specification. The patterns are categorised in paradigms (Inductive, Call-as-Event, Call-as-Service), and for each category a pattern is described in an abstract way, together with an example in the form of a problem solution developed using the introduced pattern. The crucial refinement steps are shown on an abstract level during the description of the pattern, but the actual application of a pattern is given by showing the resulting algorithm, invariants and properties.

Steinhöfel and Hähnle [15] describe an approach for compilation that is verified to be correct, but done in a modular way. This is achieved by a rule-based approach, relating each source language construct to the corresponding target language construct. The translation between the two is done at the level of symbolic execution trees, and proving the correctness of the translation can be done automatically provided both source and target language have been formalised in terms of symbolic execution (SE) rules. Proving the correctness is done via a program logic that is capable of SE of abstract programs. A new source or target language can easily be added by formalising such a language in terms of SE rules. The authors exemplify this by re-using a previously available SE formalisation of a subset of the Java language, and define one for the LLVM IR.

Huisman et al. [9] consider deductive program verification in contexts where high-level programs need to be refined to lower-level programs as a compilation step or for performance reasons such as introducing multi-core computing constructs, e.g., loop parallelizations. The authors argue for not just transforming program code in such cases, but to transform existing program annotations in concert. This is proposed to ensure that the result of the transformation is suitably annotated, i.e., to ensure the result can be proven correct provided the original program with its annotations could be. The authors sketch a diverse range of example settings for such annotation-aware transformations, and provide a research agenda of the open questions that need to be answered for a fully-fledged methodology around such annotation-aware transformations, including automation and genericity beyond the settings discussed in the paper.

Tribastone [16] provides an interesting perspective on software performance and ensuring it by construction. The main idea of this extended abstract is to extract a software performance model from the code, analyse it and propose fixes to the code if the performance properties are not met. Open research challenges for this approach are discussed which include which quantitative models to use and how to derive those performance models faithfully from the code base.

Schneider [14] discusses the idea of privacy-by-design (PbD) as one of the biggest challenges in finding suitable ways to handle personal data. Current legislation makes it mandatory to comply with the privacy requirements set in the regulation. PbD is one approach to build a system in a way such that it satisfies those privacy requirements from the inception of the system and also is a possibility to show to regulators that the privacy requirements are met. Schneider asks the question how much privacy can effectively be achieved by PbD, and if it cannot, if there are other ways to achieve privacy by construction.

Legay et al. [5] consider a move from correctness-by-construction to security-properties-by-construction via calculi for reasoning about such properties. The authors begin with straightforward password-entry code (in C), in which a Boolean access control variable is set depending on password correctness. The resulting calculus expresses the equivalence of that variable with the validity of the entered password. That example is neatly extended to capture timing properties which form some of the well-known attacks on such C code. The calculus is also seamlessly combined with the correctness argument. A considerably more complex example is also worked out, in which AES-style cryptography is considered. While the standard code in that example is remarkably compact, it hides a number of security vulnerabilities. Again, the calculus allows for reasoning about the known potential problems.

Schaefer et al. [13] propose an approach to confidentiality-by-construction (C14bC). The main idea is to recast information flow control properties in a CbC-style set of refinement rules. Hence, a program observing information flow control properties can be derived in a constructive fashion that preserves the desired security policy *ab initio* rather than rejecting a program as non-compliant *ex post facto*. The authors give a set of those refinement rules for a simple guarded command language and also consider the notion of declassification in order to build a more expressive constructive framework. This work paves the way for future extensions to more generic information flow policies also considering trust-by-construction.

3   Conclusion

The X-by-Construction track shows that a number of different, complementary approaches can be used to ensure that non-functional (X-)properties are guaranteed to hold in a system by construction. Formal methods for classical functional correctness can be extended to apply to X-properties as well [5,12,14]. Refinement-based approaches from classical functional CbC can be extended to X-properties [13], or model transformations can be used to introduce an X-property into the transformed model [10]. Refinement-based approaches can be generalised by using patterns capturing well-established design decisions to incorporate X-properties into a deployed system [2,11]. Correctness of those transformations can be ensured by correctly transforming annotations that are used for verification of the transformed program [9] or by proving the transformation rules correct themselves [15]. In the other direction, models extracted from implementation artifacts can be used for analysis of X-properties and results can be used to fix the implementation [16]. It remains a challenge for future research to see which of these approaches is applicable to what kind of X-property and which additional ideas are necessary to arrive at a holistic development approach for X-by-Construction.

References

1. ter Beek, M.H., Hähnle, R., Schaefer, I.: Correctness-by-construction and post-hoc verification: friends or foes? In: Margaria, T., Steffen, B. (eds.) ISoLA 2016. LNCS, vol. 9952, pp. 723–729. Springer, Cham (2016). https://doi.org/10.1007/978-3-319-47166-2_51
2. Bijo, S., Johnsen, E.B., Pun, K.I., Seidl, C., Tarifa, S.L.T.: Deployment by construction for multicore architectures. In: Margaria, T., Steffen, B. (Eds.) ISoLA 2018, LNCS 11244, pp. 448–465 (2018)
3. Cavoukian, A.: Privacy by design. IEEE Technol. Soc. Magaz. **31**(4), 18–19 (2012)
4. Dijkstra, E.W.: A constructive approach to the problem of program correctness. BIT Numer. Math. **8**(3), 174–186 (1968)
5. Given-Wilson, T., Legay, A.: X-by-C: non-functional security challenges. In: Margaria, T., Steffen, B. (eds.) ISoLA 2018. LNCS, vol. 11244, pp. 486–501. Springer, Cham (2018)

6. Hall, A.: Correctness by construction: integrating formality into a commercial development process. In: Eriksson, L.-H., Lindsay, P.A. (eds.) FME 2002. LNCS, vol. 2391, pp. 224–233. Springer, Heidelberg (2002). https://doi.org/10.1007/3-540-45614-7_13

7. Hall, A., Chapman, R.: Correctness by construction: developing a commercial secure system. IEEE Softw. **19**(1), 18–25 (2002)

8. Hoare, C.A.R.: Proof of a program: FIND. Commun. ACM **14**(1), 39–45 (1971)

9. Huisman, M., Blom, S., Darabi, S., Safari, M.: Program correctness by transformation. In: Margaria, T., Steffen, B. (eds.) ISoLA 2018. LNCS, vol. 11244, pp. 365–380. Springer, Cham (2018)

10. Lybecait, M., Kopetzki, D., Steffen, B.: Design for 'X' through model transformation. In: Margaria, T., Steffen, B. (eds.) ISoLA 2018. LNCS, vol. 11244, pp. 381–398. Springer, Cham (2018)

11. Méry, D.: Modelling by patterns for correct-by-construction process. In: Margaria, T., Steffen, B. (eds.) ISoLA 2018. LNCS, vol. 11244, pp. 399–423. Springer, Cham (2018)

12. Poll, E.: (Some) security by construction through a LangSec approach. In: Margaria, T., Steffen, B. (eds.) ISoLA 2018. LNCS, vol. 11244, pp. xx–yy. Springer, Cham (2018)

13. Schaefer, I., Runge, T., Knüppel, A., Cleophas, L., Kourie, D., Watson, B.W.: Towards confidentiality-by-construction. In: Margaria, T., Steffen, B. (eds.) ISoLA 2018. LNCS, vol. 11244, pp. 502–515. Springer, Cham (2018)

14. Schneider, G.: Is privacy by construction possible? In: Margaria, T., Steffen, B. (eds.) ISoLA 2018. LNCS, vol. 11244, pp. 471–485. Springer, Cham (2018)

15. Steinhöfel, D., Hähnle, R.: Modular, correct compilation with automatic soundness proofs. In: Margaria, T., Steffen, B. (eds.) ISoLA 2018. LNCS, vol. 11244, pp. 424–447. Springer, Cham (2018)

16. Tribastone, M.: Towards software performance by construction. In: Margaria, T., Steffen, B. (eds.) ISoLA 2018. LNCS, vol. 11244, pp. 466–470. Springer, Cham (2018)

Program Correctness by Transformation

Marieke Huisman[1(✉)], Stefan Blom[2], Saeed Darabi[3], and Mohsen Safari[1]

[1] University of Twente, Enschede, The Netherlands
m.huisman@utwente.nl
[2] BetterBe, Enschede, The Netherlands
[3] ASML, Veldhoven, The Netherlands

Abstract. Deductive program verification can be used effectively to verify high-level programs, but can be challenging for low-level, high-performance code. In this paper, we argue that compilation and program transformations should be made *annotation-aware*, i.e. during compilation and program transformation, not only the code should be changed, but also the corresponding annotations. As a result, if the original high-level program could be verified, also the resulting low-level program can be verified. We illustrate this approach on a concrete case, where loop annotations that capture possible loop parallelisations are translated into specifications of an OpenCL kernel that corresponds to the parallel loop. We also sketch how several commonly used OpenCL kernel transformations can be adapted to also transform the corresponding program annotations. Finally, we conclude the paper with a list of research challenges that need to be addressed to further develop this approach.

1 Introduction

Over the last decade, substantial progress has been made in the development of techniques for deductive program verification. By now, it is possible to verify non-trivial programs effectively, as illustrated for example by the attempt to verify the TimSort algorithm [12], as well as by the advent of logics to reason about concurrent software, see e.g. [9,14,15,18]. However, there still is a gap to bridge between the programs that can be verified effectively, and the actual code that is running on systems – even when the deductive verification tool at hand actually supports reasoning about a real programming language.

For deductive program verification to be successful, one needs to understand the algorithm, and the invariants that are preserved by the algorithm. As a consequence, verification is typically most suited when the verified program is written at a relatively high-level, using high-level data structures to abstract the program's state space. However, when code is implemented, for performance reasons often low-level implementation choices are made, which might obfuscate the high-level algorithm, and can make verification of the actual implemented code much more challenging than the verification of the high-level algorithm.

Therefore, in this paper we argue that verification should be done step-wise, and that we should extend compilers and program transformations in such a way

© Springer Nature Switzerland AG 2018
T. Margaria and B. Steffen (Eds.): ISoLA 2018, LNCS 11244, pp. 365–380, 2018.
https://doi.org/10.1007/978-3-030-03418-4_22

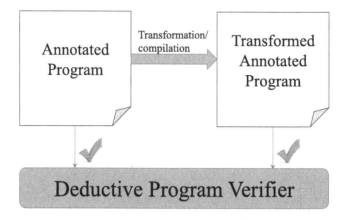

Fig. 1. Annotation-aware program transformation and compilation

that they can preserve *provability of correctness*. Thus, we do not aim at proving that the compilation process or a program transformation preserves correctness, but instead we argue that the compilation or transformation process should be extended to include the extra information that is needed to make sure that the resulting program can be proven correct.

In the particular case of this paper, we look at deductive program verification. As deductive program verification techniques require code to be annotated with intermediate properties, we argue that compilation and program transformation should become *annotation-aware*, i.e. they should not only transform the program, but also the corresponding program annotations, as illustrated by Fig. 1. If this annotation transformation is done properly, then the low-level, high-performance code can be verified (provided the original high-level program was verified). Ideally, this process is done fully automatically, i.e, the high-level program is annotated and verified, and subsequently the developer applies a collection of different program transformations, searching for optimal performance, while the correctness is preserved fully automatically.

We believe that such an approach to correctness preservation by compilation and program optimisation is a necessary step to make verification of high-performance low-level code feasible and scalable. We discuss first steps in this direction, as well as the research challenges that need to be addressed to realise this scenario. In particular, we show how the verification of compiler directives for the parallelisation of loops can be used to compile the loop into an OpenCL kernel (suitable for GPU architectures), such that the loop specification is compiled into a kernel specification (based on ideas we presented in [4]). We also discuss various program transformations that can be used to improve the performance of OpenCL kernels, and sketch how the annotations of a verified kernel should be adapted to ensure that the result of the program transformation can be verified again. In this paper, we focus on transformations that are suitable to OpenCL kernels, but similar techniques also should be applicable to transformations that improve performance of a program running on a CPU.

The ideas presented in this paper are currently partly supported by our Ver-Cors tool set, which supports the verification of concurrent software for multiple input languages, such as Java, C with OpenMP annotations, OpenCL kernels, and our own prototype language PVL [5]. Support for OpenCL at the moment is still lacking some features, in particular to reason about barriers. However, this is only an implementation issue: for the PVL language we can reason about parallel blocks, using barriers for synchronisation. Therefore, in this paper, where suitable we give annotated OpenCL examples as should be verifiable in the near future (and where we currently can verify the corresponding PVL version).

The remainder of this paper is organised as follows. Section 2 provides the necessary background on permission-based separation logic. We discuss in particular how we use this to verify loop parallelisations, and OpenCL kernels. Next, Sect. 3 discusses how loops and their specifications are compiled into OpenCL kernels with corresponding specifications. Section 4 then sketches how similar ideas can be used when transforming the OpenCL kernels to improve their performance, while Sect. 5 concludes with the open research challenges that we believe need to be addressed to fully realise this scenario.

2   Background

Before discussing how program specifications are preserved by compilation and transformation, we first give a brief introduction to our programming specification language, and discuss the basics behind our verification approach. In particular, we discuss loop iteration contracts, which is a technique that we use to reason about high-level programs, and we discuss the main ingredients of our verification technique for OpenCL programs.

2.1   Program Specification Language

Our program specification language is based on permission-based separation logic [1,7], combined with the look-and-feel of the Java Modeling Language (JML) [16]. In this way we exploit the expressiveness and readability of JML, while using the power of separation logic to support thread-modular reasoning. We briefly explain the syntax of formulas and how it extends the standard JML program annotation syntax, where JML annotations are expressions in first-order logic. For the precise semantics of our formulas, we refer to [8,10].

Every thread holds permissions to access memory locations. These permissions are encoded as fractional values (cf. Boyland [8]): any fraction in the interval $(0, 1)$ denotes a *read permission*, while 1 denotes a *write permission*. Permissions can be split (by subtraction) and combined (by addition), and soundness of the program logic ensures that for every memory location the total sum of permissions over all threads to access this location does not exceed 1. This guaranty is sufficient to ensure data race freedom of any verified program: if a thread holds a write permission to a location, no other thread will have access to this location; if a thread holds a read permission to a location, any other thread also can have at most a read permission. The set of permissions that a thread holds is typically called its *resources*.

Formulas F in our program specification language extend first-order logic formulas with the following expressions: permission predicates $\mathsf{Perm}(e_1, e_2)$, conditional expressions $(\circ?\circ : \circ)$, separating conjunction $\star$, and universal separating conjunction $\bigstar$ over a finite set I. The syntax of formulas is formally defined as follows:

$$F ::= b \mid \mathsf{Perm}(e_1, e_2) \mid b?F : F \mid F \star F \mid \bigstar_{i \in I} F(i)$$
$$b ::= \mathbf{true} \mid \mathbf{false} \mid e_1 == e_2 \mid e_1 \leq e_2 \mid \neg b \mid b_1 \wedge b_2 \mid \dots$$
$$e ::= [e] \mid v \mid n \mid e_1 + e_2 \mid e_1 - e_2 \mid \dots$$

where b is a side-effect free boolean expression, e is a side-effect free arithmetic expression, $[\circ]$ is a unary dereferencing operator – thus $[e]$ returns the value stored at the address e in shared memory – v ranges over variables and n ranges over numerals. Wellformedness requires that the first argument of the $\mathsf{Perm}(e_1, e_2)$ predicate is always an address, while the second argument is a fraction. We use the array notation $a[e]$ as syntactic sugar for $[a + e]$ where a is a variable containing the base address of the array a and e is the subscript expression; together they point to the address $a + e$ in shared memory.

For the semantics of the formulas we refer to [10], but as an example we define the semantic of universal separating conjunction as $\bigstar_{i \in I} F(i) \equiv F(p) + F(p+1) + \dots + F(q)$ (if $I = \{p, \dots, q\}$).

2.2   Iteration Contract

To reason about loop parallelisations, and to show that the parallelisation of a loop does not change its behaviour, we introduced the notion of *iteration contracts* [4,11]: an iteration contract specifies a contract that should hold for every iteration of the loop. This iteration contract should specify at least which variables are read and written by one iteration of the loop, but it can be extended with functional properties. Information about the variables read and written can be used directly to verify whether a loop can be parallelised (because all iterations are independent), or whether a loop can be vectorised (i.e., it can be safely parallelised in lock step). In the latter case, the verification requires us to add some additional annotations that indicate the minimal synchronisation that is necessary between the different iterations. Note that this is different from a loop invariant, where a condition must hold immediately before (and after) each iteration. Loop invariants do not give us any insights in how to parallelise a loop.

Example 1. Suppose we have the following loop:

```
//@ requires a.length == b.length;
for (int i = 0; i < a.length; i++) {
        a[i] = 2 * b[i];
}
```

We can prove that this loop respects the following iteration contract:

```
/*@
requires Perm(a[i], 1) ** Perm(b[i], 1/2);
ensures Perm(a[i], 1) ** Perm(b[i], 1/2);
ensures a[i] == 2 * b[i];
@*/
```

where the *requires* and *ensures* keywords indicate the pre- and postcondition, respectively, and ** is the ascii-notation for *. From the fact that we can verify this iteration contract, we can conclude that this loop can be safely parallelised without changing its behaviour [4]. Moreover, from this iteration contract we can also conclude that after successful termination of this (parallelised) loop, we have (\forall int i; 0 <= i && i < a.length; a[i] == 2 * b[i]).

Example 2. Now suppose that we have the following loop (with forward dependencies), where all arrays a, b and c have length N:

```
//@ requires a.length == N;
//@ requires b.length == N;
//@ requires c.length == N;
for (int i = 0; i < N; i++) {
      b[i] = c[i] * 2;
      if (i > 0) {
         a[i] = b[i-1];
      }
}
```

Also for this loop we can give an iteration contract:

```
/*@
Perm(a[i], 1) ** Perm(b[i], 1) ** Perm(c[i], 1/2);
ensures Perm(a[i], 1) ** Perm(b[i], 1/2) ** Perm(c[i], 1/2);
ensures i > 0 ==> Perm(b[i -1], 1/2);
ensures i == N - 1 ==> Perm(b[i], 1/2);
@*/
```

However, in order to verify this iteration contract, we need to add an extra annotation, indicated by the keyword send, in the loop that indicates that a read permission on b[i] is transferred from one iteration to another. The annotation that we need here is:

```
for (int i = 0; i < N; i++) {
      b[i] = c[i] * 2;
      //@ send i < N - 1 ==> Perm(b[i], 1/2), 1
      if (i > 0) {
         a[i] = b[i-1];
      }
}
```

This send-annotation captures that after the first assignment, the permission to access b[i] is transferred to iteration i + 1 as indicated by the ",1'. Thus, if we execute the loop instructions in parallel, at this point synchronisation will be needed. We can either vectorise the loop (i.e., execute the instructions in a lock-based manner) or parallelise it by using appropriate synchronisations. For clarity we can add the matching receive-annotation, but this is not strictly necessary:

```
//@ receive i > 0 ==> Perm(b[i - 1], 1/2);
```

Note that also in this case, the iteration contract can be extended with functional properties expressing how the contents of the different arrays are updated. For this loop, one could prove that (\forall int i; 0 <= i && i < N; i > 0 ==> a[i] = c[i - 1] * 2) holds afterwards. However, in order to prove this, also knowledge about the contents of c[i-1] would be necessary, thus also a (read) permission on c[i] would have to be transferred from iteration i to i+1.

2.3   Verification of OpenCL Kernels

One possibility to improve the performance of a program is to compile into a GPU-compliant kernel program (using e.g. the PENCIL compiler, developed within the CARP project [3]). Also OpenCL programs can be verified using permission-based separation logic. We briefly describe the main ideas of the verification approach, for full details we refer to [6].

An OpenCL kernel program divides the work over a group of work groups. Each work group consists of a fixed number of threads. Each thread executes the same, sequential program. To avoid data races, each thread should only access its own part of the shared data. Threads within a work group synchronise by means of a barrier.

To verify an OpenCL kernel, the behaviour of each thread should be specified with a pre- and postcondition. The specification of a work group is the universal separating conjunction of all its thread specifications. The specification of a kernel is the universal separating conjunction of all its work group specifications. Note that wellformedness of the universal separating conjunction expressions guaranties that the total sum of all accesses to a location never exceeds 1, thus guarantying data race freedom. Each thread is verified using standard sequential program verification techniques. Barriers need a specification that indicates how they transfer permissions. When a thread invokes a barrier, it has to fulfil the barrier precondition, and then can assume the barrier postcondition. Additionally, it has to be shown that the barrier only re-distributes the resources that are handed in by the threads upon entering the barrier.

Example 3. As an example, we show the annotated version of a simple kernel that rotates the elements of an array to the right[1]. The invariant property specifies a property that holds throughout the execution. Further we specify the behaviour of a single kernel thread (the specification of the work group and

---

[1] As mentioned above, currently the VerCors tool set does not support all OpenCL features. Therefore we have actually verified a PVL variant of this kernel.

kernel can be derived from this). The precondition just indicates the necessary permissions, the postcondition also specifies the rotation. Read permissions are split over all threads; for readability therefore we simply write read instead of giving the precise fraction. Each thread, which is responsible for one array location, first reads the location on the left of this one, then it synchronises at the barrier (where it gives up the read permission on its left location, and obtains a write permission on its own location) and subsequently it writes the value read before to the location it is responsible for.

```
/*@
    invariant array != NULL;
    requires get_global_id(0) != 0 ==>
            Perm(array[get_global_id(0) - 1], read);
    requires get_global_id(0) == 0 ==> Perm(array[size - 1], read);
    ensures Perm(array[get_global_id(0)], 1);
    ensures get_global_id(0) != 0 ==>
            array[get_global_id(0)] == \old(array[get_global_id(0) -
                1]);
    ensures get_global_id(0) == 0 ==>
            array[get_global_id(0)] == \old(array[size - 1]);
@*/
__kernel void rightRotation(int array[], int size) {
    int tid = get_global_id(0);  // get the index
    int temp;
    if (tid != 0) { temp = array[tid - 1]; }
    else { temp = array[size - 1]; }
    /*@
        requires tid != 0 ==> Perm(array[tid - 1], read);
        requires tid == 0 ==> Perm(array[size - 1], read);
        ensures Perm(array[tid], 1);
    @*/
    barrier(CLK_GLOBAL_MEM_FENCE);
    array[tid] = temp;
}
```

3 From Loop to Kernel Program

This section shows the connection between loops specified with iteration contracts and annotated OpenCL kernels (as also discussed in [4]). We assume that the code is compiled using a basic parallelising compiler, without further optimisation. In the next section, we will look into how further optimisations can be applied, while still preserving correctness.

Independent Loops. Given an independent loop, the basic compilation to kernel code is simple: create a kernel with as many threads as there are loop iterations and each kernel thread executes one iteration. Moreover, the iteration contract can be used as the thread contract for each parallel thread in the kernel directly. The size of the work group can be chosen at will, because no barriers are used.

Example 4. Consider the simple loop in Example 1. This can be compiled into the following annotated OpenCL kernel[2].

```
/*@
    invariant a != NULL;
    invariant b != NULL;
    requires Perm(a[get_global_id(0)], 1);
    requires Perm(b[get_global_id(0)], 1/2);
    ensures Perm(a[get_global_id(0)], 1);
    ensures Perm(b[get_global_id(0)], 1/2);
    ensures a[get_global_id(0)] == 2 * b[get_global_id(0)];
@*/
__kernel void example1(int a[], int b[]) {
    int tid = get_global_id(0);
    a[tid] = 2 * b[tid];
}
```

Forward Loop-Carried Dependencies. Given a loop, we consider loop-carried dependency as: if there exists two statements S_{src} and S_{dst} in the body of the loop and there exists two iterations i and j such that first $i < j$, second, in iteration i an instance in S_{src} and in iteration j an instance in S_{dst} access to the same location and third, at least one of them is a write. In this case we have loop-carried dependency and if S_{src} syntactically appears before S_{dst} we call it forward loop-carried dependency.

If the loop has forward dependencies, the kernel must ensure that its body respects these dependencies. Thus in particular, any **send**-annotation that is necessary to verify the iteration contract results in a barrier, where the barrier specification is derived from the **send** (and corresponding **receive**) annotation.

```
for(int j=0; j < N; j++)          /*@
/*@                                 requires φ(tid);
  requires φ(j);                    ensures ψ(tid);
  ensures ψ(j);                   @*/
@*/                                __kernel loop(...)
{                            ⇒     {
    L₁: if(g₁(j)) { I₁(j); }           C₁(tid);
        ⋮                                 ⋮
    Lₖ: if(gₖ(j)) { Iₖ(j); }           Cₖ(tid);
}                                  }
```

Fig. 2. From a loop with a forward loop-carried dependency to an OpenCL kernel

---

[2] Note that the invariant properties are necessary to prove the iteration contract correct, but they are given as a global specification.

Consider the loop pattern for a loop with a forward loop-carried dependency on the left side of Fig. 2. Each statement S_k which is labeled by L_k consists of an atomic instruction I_k and its guard g_k. For simplicity, we assume that both the number of threads and the size of the work group is N. Naive compilation generates the annotated kernel on the right side of the figure, where:

- if $I_k(j)$ is a **send** annotation then it is ignored: $C_k(j) \equiv \{\ \}$
- if $I_k(j)$ is a **receive** statement with a matching **send** statement at L_i, then it is replaced by a barrier $C_k(j) \equiv$

  barrier(...) requires $g_i(j) \Rightarrow \phi_{send}(j)$; ensures $g_k(j) \Rightarrow \phi_{receive}(j)$;

  where the barrier contract specifies how the permissions are exchanged at the barrier.
- if $I_k(j)$ is any other statement then it is copied:

$$C_k(j) \equiv \texttt{if}\ (g_k(j))\ \{I_k(j);\}$$

Example 5. Applying this approach to the loop in Example 2 results in the following kernel.

```
/*@
    invariant a != NULL;
    invariant b != NULL;
    invariant c != NULL;
    requires Perm(a[get_global_id(0)], 1));
    requires Perm(c[get_global_id(0)], 1/2);
    requires Perm(b[get_global_id(0)], 1));
    ensures Perm(a[get_global_id(0)], 1));
    ensures Perm(c[get_global_id(0)], 1/2);
    ensures Perm(b[get_global_id(0)], 1/2));
    ensures get_global_id(0) > 0 ==> Perm(b[get_global_id(0) - 1], 1/2);
    ensures get_global_id(0) == N -1 ==> Perm(b[get_global_id(0)], 1/2);
@*/
__kernel void example2(int a[], int b[], int c[], int N) {
    int tid = get_global_id(0);
    b[tid] = c[tid] * 2;
    /*@
        requires Perm(a[tid], 1) ** Perm(b[tid], 1);
        requires Perm(c[tid], 1/2);
        ensures Perm(a[tid], 1) ** Perm(b[tid], 1/2);
        ensures Perm(c[tid], 1/2);
        ensures tid > 0 ==> Perm(b[tid - 1], 1/2);
        ensures tid == N - 1 ==> Perm(b[tid], 1);
    @*/
    barrier(CLK_GLOBAL_MEM_FENCE);
    if (tid > 0) {
        a[tid] = b[tid-1];
    }
}
```

```
// kernel code
/*@
requires Pre(tid, iter);
ensures Post(tid, iter);
@*/
__kernel K(int iter) {
    body (tid, iter);
}


// hostcode
//@ loop_invariant (\forall tid;
    Post(tid, i));
for (int i = 0; i < N; i++) {
    invoke kernel K(i);
}
```

```
// iterating kernel
/*@
requires Pre(tid, 0);
ensures Post(tid, N - 1);
@*/
__kernel K(int N) {
    body (tid, 0);
    //@ loop_invariant Post(tid, i -
        1);
    for (int i = 1; i < N; i ++) {
        // barrier_specification
        /*@
        requires Post(tid, i - 1)
        ensures Pre(tid, i);
        @*/
        barrier();
        body (tid, i);
    }
}
```

Fig. 3. Sketch of barrier introduction transformation

4   Correctness and Compiler Optimisations

The previous section discussed compilation from verified source programs to verified target programs. This has the advantage that the main verification effort can be invested into the high-level program, which in this concrete case is still a sequential program, and therefore its verification is still relatively easy to follow. By compiling the program and its specification, the result is a verifiable parallel OpenCL program.

However, as mentioned above, the compiler performs a very naive compilation, and the code will probably not be performing very well (of course, the concrete examples in the previous section are all very small, but imagine a similar approach is applied to larger and more realistic examples). Therefore, what typically happens in the design of an OpenCL kernel is that the kernel developer then starts to change and optimize the implementation, in order to improve the performance of the application. In the literature, a large collection of program transformations to improve performance of GPU applications is available, see e.g. [2,13,17,20]. We argue that such transformations should be specified formally, and whenever the transformation is applied to the code, the corresponding specifications also should be transformed, in such a way that the resulting program can be verified again (provided the original program could be verified). This enables a developer to apply various optimisations, trying to identify the best program performance, while making sure that the functionality of the application is not affected.

This section describes several commonly used program transformations that are used to make OpenCL programs more efficient. For each of these program transformations, we sketch the corresponding specification transformations. This description is still handwaving; it is future work to define the specification transformation precisely, and to implement it as part of the VerCors tool set. However, we believe that the sketches already show the feasibility of the approach. The other existing approach is to have a verified compiler to generate a verified low-level code. This method is very expensive and is not general enough in practice. We conjecture that an approach like the one advocated here is the only feasible way to make verification of high-performance, low-level concurrent software possible. Notice that, in our method, it is not necessary to have a meta-theorem that proves correctness of all individual transformations, it is sufficient to reverify the resulting annotated program.

Barrier Introductions. One common optimisation is to take an OpenCL kernel that implements a single iteration, and that is invoked repeatedly, and to transform this into an OpenCL kernel that repeatedly executes the same code. In order to do this safely, barriers need to be inserted to ensure all threads are working on the same iteration of the code.

Figure 3 sketches this transformation, both on the code and on the specifications. In the original program, we have host code that invokes a kernel K multiple times. The behaviour of each thread inside the kernel is specified by a thread specification, which depends on how many times the kernel has already been invoked (variable iter). In the transformed program, the new kernel K is invoked only once. It will first execute the original kernel body once, followed by N - 1 iterations, where each iteration first synchronises on a barrier and then executes the body another more. The new thread's precondition is the precondition of the very first iteration; the new thread's postcondition is the postcondition of the very last iteration. In order to make the code verifiable, a loop invariant and barrier specifications are added. The loop invariant states that the postcondition of the previous iteration holds. The barrier specification states that when the barrier is entered, the postcondition of the previous iteration holds, and that the precondition of the next iteration can be assumed. Since after the barrier, the body will be executed again, the loop invariant will be re-established. Thus, if the original program could be verified, the annotated program resulting from this transformation should also be verifiable.

Change of Data Locations. Another commonly used optimisation to improve the performance of an OpenCL kernel is to move the data from global to local memory (as the work groups have very fast access to local memory). For simplicity, Fig. 4 describes this transformation for the case of a single work group.

```
                                    /*@
                                    requires Pre();
                                    ensures Post();
                                    @*/
                                    __kernel K(args) {
                                        copy data from global to local memory
                                        // barrier_specification
/*@                                     /*@
requires Pre();                         requires Pre()
ensures Post();                         ensures Pre_local() // Pre[local/global]
@*/                                     @*/
__kernel K(args) {          ⇒          barrier();
    body (tid);                         body[local/global] (tid);
}                                       // barrier_specification
                                        /*@
                                        requires Post_local() // Post[local/global]
                                        ensures Post()
                                        @*/
                                        barrier();
                                        copy data from local to global memory
                                    }
```

Fig. 4. Sketch of change of data location transformation

Suppose that the behaviour of the original kernel was specified with precondition Pre() and postcondition Post(), capturing a property over the global memory. The new kernel first copies all global data to local memory, and then all threads synchronise with a barrier. The annotations show that at this point, the precondition still holds, except that all global memory locations are substituted by local memory locations. Next, the body of the kernel is executed, but again with all global memory locations substituted by the corresponding local memory locations. This should establish the kernel postcondition, modulo the local memory locations. This information is again made explicit as a barrier specification. After the second barrier, the local memory is copied back to global memory, and the kernel ends. Again, if the original program could be verified, the annotated program resulting from this transformation should also be verifiable.

Notice that if the work is distributed over multiple work groups, a similar approach can be used, but the transformation needs to be written down more precisely, to take the distribution of the data over the different work groups into account.

Data Redistribution. In a naive compilation from a sequential loop to an OpenCL kernel, one often ends up with each thread accessing a single entry of the data. This means that there are many threads, and the individual threads do not have that much work to do. An obvious optimisation is to increase the amount of work that each thread has to do by making it iterate over multiple entries of the data. This transformation is sketched in Fig. 5.

```
/*@                                      /*@
requires Pre(tid);                       requires (\forall int i; tid * N <= i && i < (tid + 1) * N;
ensures Post(tid);                                           Pre(i));
@*/                                      ensures (\forall int i; tid * N <= i && i < (tid + 1) * N;
  __kernel K(args) {                                          Post(i));
    body (tid);                          @*/
  }                                        __kernel K(args, N) {
                                             /*@
                                             loop_invariant tid * N <= j && j < (tid + 1) * N;
                                             loop_invariant (\forall int i; tid * N <= i && j < i;
                                                                 Post(i));
                                             @*/
                                             for (int j = tid * N, j < (tid + 1) * N, j++) {
                                                body(j);
                                             }
                                           }
```

Fig. 5. Sketch of data redistribution transformation

Where in the original kernel, each thread satisfied a pre-postcondition specification for a single item, now the properties become universally quantified. In the transformation as described here, thread `tid` now works on the data entries from `tid * N` to `(tid + 1)* N - 1`, where `N` is the factor that determines how the transformation redistributed the data. Therefore, the precondition now requires that the original precondition for all these entries is satisfied, and the kernel will establish the postcondition for all these entries. In order to prove this, we need some loop invariants that indicate that the postcondition is established for all data entries handled so far by the current thread. Again, if the original kernel program could be verified, also the transformed program can be verified.

Matrix Representations. In the case of 2-dimensional data, memory access patterns can have a great impact on the performance of the kernel: in certain cases column-major access patterns will perform better, in other cases row-major access patterns will be better (this can depend for example on the specific hardware on which the kernel is executed; notably there is a difference between CPU and GPU here [19]). Again, this can be described as a program transformation, where all `M * N` matrices are transformed into `N * M` matrices, and all matrix access operations `m[i,j]` are rewritten into `m[j,i]`. In that case, the same rewriting has to be applied on all specifications (taking care that all expression bounds are still correct) in order to make sure that the transformed program remains verifiable.

Loop Unrollings. Finally, the last program transformation that we consider is loop unrolling. This increases the code size, but can have a positive impact on program performance, for example because it simplifies control flow and can reduce branch penalty.

```
__kernel K(args) {
  /*@
  loop_invariant 0 <= i && i < N;
  loop_invariant Inv(i);
  @*/
  for (int i = 0; i < N; i++) {
    body (i);
  }
}
```

⇒

```
__kernel K(args) {
  body(0);
  /*@
  loop_invariant 1 <= i && i < N;
  loop_invariant Inv(i);
  @*/
  for (int i = 1; i < N; i++) {
    body (i);
  }
}
```

Fig. 6. Sketch of loop unrolling transformation

Figure 6 sketches a very basic loop unrolling example, where the first iteration of the loop is taken out of the loop body. Note that this transformation is only possible if we know that `N > 0`. The resulting kernel and its specification look almost the same, however the loop invariant that provides the bound on the loop variable has been adjusted. Again, if the original kernel could be verified, also the kernel resulting from the transformation can be verified.

5 Future Research Challenges

In this paper, we have argued that to develop provably correct low-level, high-performance code, verification should be part of the development chain. After proving an initial, unoptimised version of the program correct, both program and annotations should be gradually transformed in such a way that the program can be reverified after each transformation (where compilation from one language to another can also be considered as a form of program transformation). This paper considered some concrete cases, and showed how this could be achieved. However, the description is still very informal and hand-waiving.

In order to turn this approach into a full-fledged verification methodology, we still need to extend it much further. This section concludes the paper by outlining the open research challenges that need to be addressed.

- The compilation that we discussed in this paper was very limited. In practice, one would want to apply this on more complex examples, for example containing multiple parallelisable loops. In order to support this approach, the compilation step for program and annotations should be defined compositionally: for basic building blocks we define how they are compiled, and on top of that we define the compilation approach for more complex programs (and their annotations).
- The program transformations as they are defined here are all given in a hand-waving manner, and skip over many details. For a fully general approach, we would have to define this much more precisely, maybe with special instances in which the compilation can be simplified.
- The program transformations as they are discussed in this paper are given in ad hoc manner. For a more systematic approach, one would need to define a catalogue of known program transformations, with many variations (and possibly combine this with performance considerations, i.e., in which case would one expect a transformation to improve performance).
- The program transformations should be thoroughly tested, in particular to ensure that all auxiliary annotations that are necessary to reverify the program are indeed generated.

Acknowledgements. We are indebted to Jeroen Vonk, who started studying some of the annotation-aware program transformations as part of his Bachelor project. This work is supported by the ERC 258405 VerCors project (Huisman, Blom), the EU FP7 STREP 287767 CARP project (Huisman, Blom, Darabi), and the NWO VICI 639.023.710 Mercedes project (Huisman, Safari).

References

1. Amighi, A., Haack, C., Huisman, M., Hurlin, C.: Permission-based separation logic for multithreaded Java programs. LMCS **11**(1) (2015)
2. Amini, M.: Source-to-source automatic program transformations for GPU-like hardware accelerators. Master's thesis, Ecole Nationale Supérieure des Mines de Paris (2012)
3. Baghdadi, R., et al.: PENCIL: towards a platform-neutral compute intermediate language for DSLs. CoRR, abs/1302.5586 (2013)
4. Blom, S., Darabi, S., Huisman, M.: Verification of loop parallelisations. In: Egyed, A., Schaefer, I. (eds.) FASE 2015. LNCS, vol. 9033, pp. 202–217. Springer, Heidelberg (2015). https://doi.org/10.1007/978-3-662-46675-9_14
5. Blom, S., Darabi, S., Huisman, M., Oortwijn, W.: The VerCors tool set: verification of parallel and concurrent software. In: Polikarpova, N., Schneider, S. (eds.) IFM 2017. LNCS, vol. 10510, pp. 102–110. Springer, Cham (2017). https://doi.org/10.1007/978-3-319-66845-1_7
6. Blom, S., Huisman, M., Mihelčić, M.: Specification and verification of GPGPU programs. Sci. Comput. Program. **95**, 376–388 (2014)

7. Bornat, R., Calcagno, C., O'Hearn, P.W., Parkinson, M.J.: Permission accounting in separation logic. In: POPL, pp. 259–270 (2005)
8. Boyland, J.: Checking interference with fractional permissions. In: Cousot, R. (ed.) SAS 2003. LNCS, vol. 2694, pp. 55–72. Springer, Heidelberg (2003). https://doi.org/10.1007/3-540-44898-5_4
9. da Rocha Pinto, P., Dinsdale-Young, T., Gardner, P.: TaDA: a logic for time and data abstraction. In: Jones, R. (ed.) ECOOP 2014. LNCS, vol. 8586, pp. 207–231. Springer, Heidelberg (2014). https://doi.org/10.1007/978-3-662-44202-9_9
10. Darabi, S.: Verification of program parallelization. Ph.D. thesis, University of Twente (2018)
11. Darabi, S., Blom, S.C.C., Huisman, M.: A verification technique for deterministic parallel programs. In: Barrett, C., Davies, M., Kahsai, T. (eds.) NFM 2017. LNCS, vol. 10227, pp. 247–264. Springer, Cham (2017). https://doi.org/10.1007/978-3-319-57288-8_17
12. de Gouw, S., Rot, J., de Boer, F.S., Bubel, R., Hähnle, R.: OpenJDK's Java.utils.Collection.sort() is broken: the good, the bad and the worst case. In: Kroening, D., Păsăreanu, C.S. (eds.) CAV 2015. LNCS, vol. 9206, pp. 273–289. Springer, Cham (2015). https://doi.org/10.1007/978-3-319-21690-4_16
13. Huang, D., et al.: Automated transformation of GPU-specific OpenCL kernels targeting performance portability on multi-core/many-core CPUs. In: Silva, F., Dutra, I., Santos Costa, V. (eds.) Euro-Par 2014. LNCS, vol. 8632, pp. 210–221. Springer, Cham (2014). https://doi.org/10.1007/978-3-319-09873-9_18
14. Jung, R., et al.: Iris: monoids and invariants as an orthogonal basis for concurrent reasoning. In: POPL, pp. 637–650. ACM (2015)
15. Krebbers, R., Jung, R., Bizjak, A., Jourdan, J.-H., Dreyer, D., Birkedal, L.: The essence of higher-order concurrent separation logic. In: Yang, H. (ed.) ESOP 2017. LNCS, vol. 10201, pp. 696–723. Springer, Heidelberg (2017). https://doi.org/10.1007/978-3-662-54434-1_26
16. Leavens, G.T., et al.: JML Reference Manual. Department of Computer Science, Iowa State University, February 2007. http://www.jmlspecs.org
17. Nandakumar, D.: Automatic translation of CUDA to OpenCL and comparison of performance optimizations on GPUs. Master's thesis, University of Illinois at Urbana-Champaign (2011)
18. Sergey, I., Nanevski, A., Banerjee, A.: Specifying and verifying concurrent algorithms with histories and subjectivity. In: Vitek, J. (ed.) ESOP 2015. LNCS, vol. 9032, pp. 333–358. Springer, Heidelberg (2015). https://doi.org/10.1007/978-3-662-46669-8_14
19. Shen, J.: Efficient high performance computing on heterogeneous platforms. Ph.D. thesis, Technical University of Delft (2015)
20. Wu, B., Chen, G., Li, D., Shen, X., Vetter, J.: Enabling and exploiting flexible task assignment on GPU through SM-centric program transformations. In: ICS 2015 Proceedings of the 29th ACM on International Conference on Supercomputing, pp. 119–130. ACM (2015)

Design for 'X' Through Model Transformation

Michael Lybecait[(✉)], Dawid Kopetzki, and Bernhard Steffen

Chair for Programming Systems, TU Dortmund University, Dortmund, Germany
{michael.lybecait,dawid.kopetzki,steffen}@cs.tu-dortmund.de

Abstract. In this paper we sketch a transformation-oriented framework for establishing system characteristics like model-checkability, learnability, or performance. Backbone of our framework is CINCO, our meta tooling suite for generating DSL-specific development environments on the basis of specifications in terms of metamodels. CINCO is used here to specify the considered source and target languages, as well as the transformation language that allows one to transform source systems/models into semantically equivalent, X-conform target systems. In this paper, we focus on illustrating the power of domain-specific transformation languages by presenting a multi-level transformation pattern that allows one to elegantly capture refinement and aggregation aspects in a rule-based fashion. All this is explained along a number of examples.

Keywords: Transformation languages and patterns
Model transformation · 'X'-by-construction · Meta modeling
Domain-specific languages · Structured Operational Semantics
Active automata learning · Model checking

1 Introduction

Correctness by construction is a paradigm with a long tradition guided by the idea to stepwise transform specifications into implementations on the basis of transformation rules that are guaranteed to preserve the input/output-functional behaviour. It looks natural to generalize this idea to (partially) cover concerns, like security or dependability, as indicated by the topic of the X-by-construction track. A concrete example for this approach is the benchmark generation process [23,24] used to generate the benchmarks for the RERS competition [9,10], which employs property-preserving transformations to generate verification benchmarks with a clear *profile*: the generated C or Java programs are guaranteed to satisfy/violate temporal properties as required by the input specification (cf. Fig. 1). In this case the considered property profile is the 'X' of the employed X-by-construction process, which may also address different target formats: in its distributed systems variant, RERS also supports Promela and Petri-Nets, thus relaxing the considered notion of targeted code.

© Springer Nature Switzerland AG 2018
T. Margaria and B. Steffen (Eds.): ISoLA 2018, LNCS 11244, pp. 381–398, 2018.
https://doi.org/10.1007/978-3-030-03418-4_23

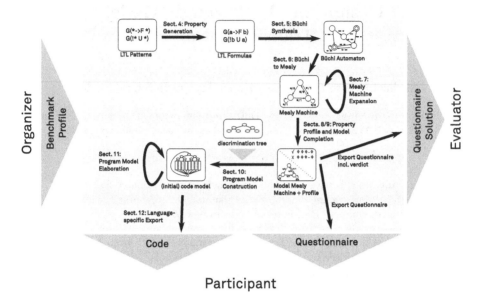

Fig. 1. Overview of RERS property-preserving transformations (reprinted from [24])

In this paper, we will illustrate our transformational approach to 'X' by construction by considering a conceptually quite different kind of 'X': performance, learnability/monitorability, and model checkability. Characteristic for our approach is its domain/purpose specificity: Based on the CINCO meta-tooling suite [18] we are able to provide dedicated graphical transformation languages whose transformational power is tailored to the task at hand. This may range from typical transformational patterns as known from aspect-oriented programming, and which suffice to capture the monitoring and learning aspect mentioned in this paper, to highly involved, quite generic graph transformation patterns as supported, e.g., by Groove [20].

In order to illustrate the power of domain-specific transformation languages, the paper introduces a multi-level transformation pattern and shows how it can be used to solve a concrete problem: how to enable involved graphical specifications (in this concrete case for specifying so-called WebStories, see Fig. 2) for model checking user-level properties. The point is here that the underlying specification language had been designed for educational purposes addressing students without any programming knowledge, and that the construction of corresponding models adequate for model checking (see, e.g., Fig. 6) requires the combination of some non-trivial semantic interpretation and the abstraction from computational detail. These two objectives can elegantly be solved by a transformation language supporting transformation rules reminiscent of Plotkin's structured operational semantics (SOS) [19]. The concrete realization for our scenario is a two-level transformation system comprising a small-step

(SOS-style) computational part whose computational details are aggregated in a big-step [13] fashion using more abstract behavioral rules.[1]

This two-level transformation is clearly beyond the capacity of state-of-the-art of aspect-oriented technology, and trying to express or just to understand the corresponding Groove transformation is anything but simple, even for experts. In contrast, our SOS-style specification is so natural and simple that even a corresponding correctness proof is straightforward. This motivates the introduction of a corresponding meta-level framework in the fashion sketched in Fig. 3, as, of course, other scenarios might profit from quite different transformation languages. E.g. the monitoring and learnability transformations can quite nicely be done in an aspect-oriented fashion using 'local' pre/post transformations, see e.g. Eq. 4, and also in our security by construction approach [2] encryption was enforced by similarly simple transformation.

The remainder of the paper is structured as follows. Section 2 sketches the CINCO Meta Tooling Suite, and Sect. 3 illustrates the power of a simple pre/-post transformation pattern, before Sect. 4 introduces the WebStory language, the application example for illustrating our multi-level transformation approach presented in Sect. 5. Subsequently, Sect. 6 shows the impact of the two-level transformation detailed in Sect. 5 as an enabler for model checking WebStories, and Sect. 7 provides our conclusions and direction to future work.

2   The CINCO Meta Tooling Suite

The CINCO Meta Tooling Suite [18] is a simplicity-driven meta tool allowing for full generation of domain-specific graphical modeling tools from high-level specifications. This specification are created using the Meta Graph Language (MGL) and the Meta Style Language (MSL) which describe the abstract and concrete syntax of the domain-specific language respectively. We won't discuss CINCO in detail here but provide the relevant information needed to understand our examples. An exhaustive description is provided in [18].

The core of CINCO is the MGL which allows for the definition of *node*, *container*, and *edge* types. These types may comprise attributes. Furthermore, node and container types specify structural graph constraints: node types define *incoming* and *outgoing* edge constraints whereas container types additionally specify constraints for *containable* elements. Minimum and maximum cardinalities may be added for elements or groups of elements referenced in such constraints. When no cardinalities are present arbitrary numbers of elements are allowed. The generated graphical modeling tool allows to create models conforming to this specification.

In the following, we illustrate the impact of using domain specific languages for transformation: Sect. 3 presents a particularly simple language capturing transformations of the form as they appear in the context of aspect-oriented

---

[1] This pattern is very similar to the semantics of so-called synchronous systems which distinguish between micro-steps (here the computational steps) and macro-steps (here the user interaction with the web story) [1].

programming, before we introduce our more elaborate but still very intuitive multi-level transformation approach in Sect. 5. The entire modeling environments for both transformation languages, which we illustrate with concrete application scenarios, have been generated using the CINCO Meta Tooling Suite [18].

3   A Simple Transformation Pattern

In this section we illustrate a simple transformation pattern that reminds of transformations well-known from aspect-oriented programming using two practical application scenarios: model transformation for optimized automata learning [16] and instrumentation of procedural programs to enable the learning of the underlying procedural system [6,7].

3.1   Performance by Construction

The first transformation turns Deterministic Finite Automata:

Definition 1 (Deterministic Finite Automata). *A Deterministic Finite Automaton (DFA) is a 4-tuple $DFA = (S, I, A, \rightarrow)$ with:*

- *S, a set of states,*
- *I, the input alphabet,*
- *$A \subseteq S$, a set of accepting states, and*
- *$\rightarrow \subseteq S \times I \times S$, the transition relation*
  (written $s \xrightarrow{i} s', s, s' \in S, i \in I$)

into semantically equivalent Mealy machines:

Definition 2 (Mealy machine). *A Mealy machine is a 4-tuple $M = (S_M, I_M, O_M, \Rightarrow)$ with:*

- *S_M, set of mealy states,*
- *I_M, the input alphabet,*
- *O_M, the output alphabet, and*
- *$\Rightarrow \subseteq S_M \times (I_M \times O_M) \times S_M$, the transition relation*
  (written $s \xRightarrow{i,o} s', s, s' \in S_M, i \in I_M, o \in O_M$)

This transformation guarantees performance by construction, as it allows one to switch from an DFA learner to a Mealy learner within the Learnlib [11], which leads to a significant performance gain [16].

Our pattern-based approach requires only two very simple and intuitive rules for transforming a $DFA = (S, I, A, \rightarrow)$ into a Mealy Machine $M = (S_M, I_M, O_M, \Rightarrow)$ with $S_M = S$, $I_M = I$, $O_M = \{tt, ff\}$, and $\Rightarrow$ defined by the following two rules:

Accepting Rule:

$$\frac{\begin{array}{c} s \quad\;\; \xrightarrow{\;\;\;i\;\;\;} \quad s' \end{array}}{\begin{array}{c} s \xrightarrow{\;\;i/tt\;\;} s' \end{array}} \quad s' \in A \tag{1}$$

and

Rejecting Rule:

$$\frac{\begin{array}{c} s \quad\;\; \xrightarrow{\;\;\;i\;\;\;} \quad s' \end{array}}{\begin{array}{c} s \xrightarrow{\;\;i/f\!f\;\;} s' \end{array}} \quad s' \notin A \tag{2}$$

3.2 Learnability by Construction

For the ease of exposition, we start our explanation at an already abstracted level, where procedural programs are modeled as procedural automata, which have been introduced as context-free processes [3,8].

Definition 3 (Procedural Automaton). *A Procedural Automaton is a 4-tuple $PA = (S, NA, A, \xrightarrow{a})$ with:*

- *S, a set of states,*
- *NA, a set of non-terminal symbols – the procedure calls,*
- *A, a set of terminal symbols, and*
- *$\xrightarrow{a} \subseteq S \times (A \cup NA) \times S, a \in (A \cup NA)$, the state transition function*

The point of our transformation is to make the internal structure defined by the non-terminals visible by adding corresponding terminal symbols as indicated by the definition of A_I in the following definition:

Definition 4 (Instrumented Procedural Automaton). *An Instrumented Procedural Automaton is a 4-tuple $IPA = (S_I, NA, A_I, \xrightarrow{x})$ with:*

- *S_I set of states,*
- *NA, a set of non-terminal symbols, the procedure calls,*
- *$A_I = A \cup \{r\} \cup \{x'|x \in NA\}$, set of terminal symbols, and*
- *$\xrightarrow{x} \subseteq S_I \times (A_I \cup NA) \times S, a \in (A_I \cup NA)$*

Transforming procedural automata into instrumented procedural automata is very similar to instrumentations as they are used for runtime verification [3,8].

In our case, it allows one to apply the algorithm for active automata learning of context-free systems presented in [6, 7].[2]

As in the previous subsection, our pattern-based approach requires only two very simple and intuitive rules for transforming a Procedural Automaton $PA = (S, NA, A, \xrightarrow{a})$ into an equivalent Instrumented Procedural Automaton $IPA = (S_I, NA, A_I, \xRightarrow{x})$, where S_I is the superset of S that also contains the 'artificial' states introduced in the non-terminal Rule below, A_I is constructed as indicated in Definition 4, and $\Rightarrow$ defined is by the following two rules:

Terminal Rule:

$$(3)$$

with $s, s' \in S, a \in A$.

Non-terminal Rule:

$$(4)$$

with $s, s' \in S, N \in NA, N', R \in A_I, k, k' \in K$.

The following two sections illustrate how the simple transformational pattern that was sufficient for the two application examples discussed above can be elegantly generalized to establish more ambitious 'X's, here model checkability for a heterogeneous graphical specification language: Sect. 4 sketches the WebStory language, an education-oriented, graphical modeling language, which we frequently use for undergraduate teaching and tutorials about what we call language-driven engineering [22], and Sect. 5 our multi-level transformation approach to generate corresponding model structures adequate to be fed to state-of-the-art model checkers.

4   The WebStory Language

The *WebStory* language is a CINCO based DSL for creating simple interactive story games similar to a point-and-click adventure.[3] It has been used in several

---

[2] There are a few subtleties, e.g. how to deal with non-determinism, which are beyond the scope of this paper.

[3] The full CINCO specification of the WebStory language is available as download at https://cinco.scce.info/examples/webstory/.

workshops and lectures as a hands-on example for the CINCO Meta Tooling Suite. The language has been designed with simplicity in mind to make it easy for the workshops' participants to expand the WebStory language in terms of functionality and to keep it easy for non-programmers to use the language.

A WebStory is modeled in a graphical DSL to describe the flow from one screen to the other with conditional paths depending on values of boolean variables. The modeled game can be generated to a website and can be executed in any web browser. The resulting story is played by clicking on clickable areas placed on screens with the aim to reach a predefined goal.

Main parts of a WebStory are the *Screen* elements. They correspond to the observable elements on the website the player can interact with. A special initial *Screen* has to be defined which specifies the starting point of the game. *Screen* elements contain a background image and can contain optional textual areas. To model player interaction *ClickableArea* elements are defined. These elements are placed on the *Screens* and must be connected to other elements through *Transition* edges. Possible targets for these edges are a *Screen*, a *ModifyVariable* element and a *Condition* element. The *ModifyVariable* element is used to set a boolean variable to a value. It is connected to the written variable through a *DataFlow* edge. It has a successor connected through a *Transition* edge. The *Condition* element checks a variable and chooses a successor based on the variable's value.

Figure 2 shows a model of a simple story where the player is challenged to get hold of a treasure which is hidden in a hut via finding the required key. This model uses all the model elements of the WebStory language. It consists of six *Screens* (1–6). Screen 2 on the upper-left side depicting a cabin for example contains two *ClickableAreas* (pink areas (A) and (B)). The pink *Transition* edges define the successor element of a clickable area. The area at the door is connected to a *Condition* (c). Depending on the value of the "key" variable (v), the successor of the *Condition* (c) is defined by the *true* edge (t) or the *false* edge (f). The variable is set by the *ModifyVariable* node (m1). The initial screen of the WebStory is defined by the successor of the *start marker* node (a).

Formal Definition of the WebStory. More formally a WebStory model (WS) is a ten tuple $WS = (S, Ca, V, M, C, \dashrightarrow, \rightarrowtail, \xrightarrow{tt}, \xrightarrow{ff}, s_0)$ with:

- S, a Set of *Screens*,
- Ca, a Set of *ClickableAreas*,
- V, a Set of *Variables*,
- M, a Set of *ModifyVariable* elements,
- C, a Set of *Conditions*,
- $\dashrightarrow \subseteq (M \times V) \cup (V \times C)$, *DataFlow* relation,
- $\rightarrow \subseteq ((Ca \cup M) \times (S \cup M \cup C))$, a *Transition* relation,
- $\xrightarrow{tt} \subseteq (C \times (S \cup M \cup C))$, *TrueTransition* relation,
- $\xrightarrow{ff} \subseteq (C \times (S \cup M \cup C))$, *FalseTransition* relation,
- s_0 with $s_0 \in S$, Screen marked with start marker, the initial Screen of the WebStory.

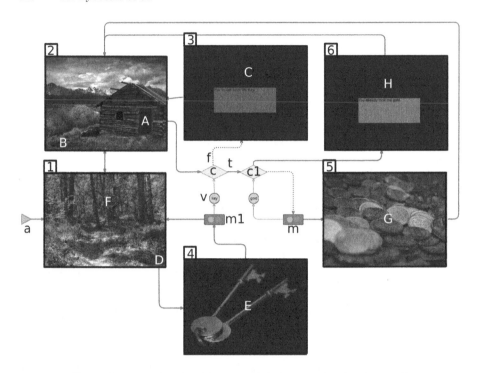

Fig. 2. An exemplary WebStory model (Images by: [5,14,21,26])

The goal of the next section is to transform WebStories into Kripke transition systems ($KTSs$), i.e., structures introduced in [17] for generalizing both labeled transition systems and Kripke structures. KTS are formally defined as 4-tuples $(S, Act, \rightarrow, I)$ where:

- S, a set of states,
- Act, a set of actions,
- $\rightarrow \,\subseteq S \times Act \times S$, a transition relation (written as $s \xrightarrow{a} s'$), and
- $I : S \rightarrow 2^{AP}$, a *valuation* function.

5   The Multi-level Transformation Pattern

In Sect. 3 we have seen, how to easily refine/instrument model structures in a simple fashion, which reminds of aspect-oriented programming. In this section we extend our language for specifying transformations by rules (cf. 10, 11, 12 and 13) that allow one to aggregate detail (computational steps) and thereby establishing a higher level of abstraction. Such transformation rules (perhaps in combination with some refining transformation rules like the one shown in Rule 4) are ideal to generate specific views that are guaranteed to support a certain 'X'. Key to achieve the aggregational power is the introduction of levels into our rule system in a way that establishes a multi-level transformation scheme which, in the case of two levels, structurally reminds of structural operational semantics (SOS) [19] for synchronous languages, where macro steps (the ones concerning the interaction with the environment) and micro steps (the ones concerning internal computation) are distinguished [1]. In this section we illustrate this idea for the case of two levels along a concrete application scenario: the transformation of graphical WebStory models (cf. Sect. 4) into model structures that can be directly handed over to a model checker. In other words, as also shown in Sect. 6, the transformation presented in Sect. 5.1 can be seen as a way to automatically achieve model checkability by construction.

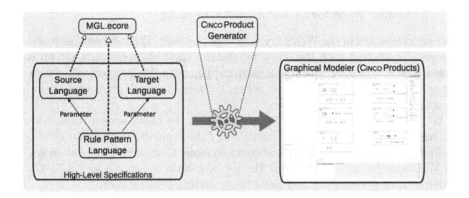

Fig. 3. Overview of model-transformation

Conceptual backbone for this transformation is our framework for creating domain-specific model-transformation languages, like the three languages used in this paper for illustration. Figure 3 presents the relevant artifacts used to generate a transformation language (left-hand side) and the generated modeling tool which is used to create specific transformations. Since we use CINCO as meta modeling tool the meta models of the source, target, and rule pattern language are described in MGL.

Transformations are defined in a highly modular way, focusing on three major topics:

1. The transformation itself (i.e. triggering the creation of elements of the target language).
2. Computational steps executed during the transformation.
3. Definition of the computational path.

For our two-level transformation language modularization is achieved by introducing two types of rules called MACRO and MICRO rules, resembling natural semantics (also called big step semantics) [13] and structural operational semantic (SOS) [19].

The transformation establishing the primary structure of the target model is modeled by MACRO rules which describe how artifacts of the target language are created when processing the source language. The concrete construction defined by a MACRO rule may depend on computational aspects which are handled by MICRO rules which very much resemble the structural operational semantics of a basic imperative language. Here an execution step typically consists of the execution of the current statement (assignment or conditional branching) together with the corresponding update of the program pointer in the source model.

In the following, we illustrate our approach along the definition of the transformation from WebStories to KTS as a prerequisite to a subsequent model checking.

5.1 Enabling WebStories for Model Checking

Web stories defined in the WebStory language (see Sect. 4) can be seen as reactive systems. Interacting with the story by clicking clickable areas on a screen will cause a sequence of small state changes to happen until the next screen is reached. The states can be distinguished by actual locations in the WebStory model and a configuration of model variables.

Locations are nodes that can be reached from the initial screen through control flow edges (*Transition, TrueTransition, FalseTransition*). Possible locations are *Screen, ModifyVariable* or *Condition* elements. Considering the definition of the WebStory in Sect. 4 we define the set of locations $Loc =_{df} S \cup M \cup C$. A state $\sigma \in \Sigma$ of a WebStory is defined by a variable configuration

$$\Sigma = V \times \{tt, ff\} \tag{5}$$

which maps each *Variable* $v \in V$ to a boolean value.

Our two-level transformations distinguish between locations observable by the player (i.e., *Screens*) and those hidden inside the game (*ModifyVariable, Condition*), in order to reveal the 'history-dependent' navigation potential between the *Screens*. Hence location transitions caused by user interactions must be reduced to one step per action, while in-between steps such as data modification or evaluation must be hidden.

The set of possible user interactions correspond to the clickable areas of each *Screen* location. We establish this by defining two separated transformations one covering the navigation between screens, the other taking care of necessary computations. This requires to partition the locations in the two classes $\mathcal{L} =_{df} S$ and $\ell =_{df} M \cup C$.

The MACRO rules map screens of a WebStory to states of a KTS which are essentially screens qualified with variable configurations σ, leading to the following definition:

$$ITS = (S \times \Sigma, Ca, \rightarrow) \tag{6}$$

where *ITS* stands for *interactive transition system*, and where

$$" \rightarrow " \subseteq (S \times \Sigma) \times Ca \times (S \times \Sigma)$$

is specified by rules 8 to 10 below.

MICRO rules traverse the model elements between two screens starting with a successor of a clickable area and a variable configuration σ, specifying a transition system

$$CTS = (Loc \times \Sigma, \dashrightarrow) \tag{7}$$

where CTS stands for *computational transition system*, and where

$$" \dashrightarrow " \subseteq (\ell \times \Sigma) \times Ca \times (Loc \times \Sigma)$$

is specified by rules 11 to 13 below.

The definition of the MACRO and MICRO rules requires the following notation:

$$L, L' \in \mathcal{L}, \; ca \in Ca,$$
$$Lc, T, F \in Loc,$$
$$l \in \ell, \; m \in M, \; c \in C, \; v \in V$$
$$\sigma, \sigma' \in \Sigma$$

The transformation from the WebStory language to ITS requires three MACRO rules distinguishing essential patterns over elements in $\mathcal{L}$.

The first rule serves for the initialization, i.e. it identifies the start state and the initial variable configuration:

$$\frac{L, \sigma \quad \rhd\!\!-\!\!\Box}{\langle L, \sigma \rangle} \tag{8}$$

The second rule describes the situation where the successor of a clickable area c of a screen L is a screen L' itself:

$$\frac{L, \sigma \quad L', \sigma \quad \boxed{c}\!\!-\!\!\Box}{\langle L, \sigma \rangle \xrightarrow{c} \langle L', \sigma \rangle} \tag{9}$$

If this pattern is matched in the input WebStory two states identified by (L, σ), $(L', \sigma) \in \mathcal{L} \times \Sigma$ are created and connected by a transition $(\xrightarrow{c})$.

The third rule describes a situation where computation is needed, i.e., the two screens L, L' are connected through elements $l \in \ell$:

$$\frac{L, \sigma \quad \boxed{c}\!\!-\!\!\blacksquare, \langle l, \sigma \rangle \dashrightarrow^* \langle L', \sigma' \rangle}{\langle L, \sigma \rangle \xrightarrow{c} \langle L', \sigma' \rangle} \tag{10}$$

Matching the pattern of the left hand side of the premise does not directly create elements of the ITS, but starts a computation, whose effect is obtained via the right hand side of the premise, and computed as a sequence of MICRO rule applications as indicated by the Kleene '*'. The required MICRO rules are defined as follows:

Assignment:

$$\frac{}{\langle m, \sigma \rangle \dashrightarrow \langle Lc, \sigma\{[\![m]\!]_{B_{exp}}(\sigma)/v\} \rangle} \tag{11}$$

Whenever the pattern for m is matched, the corresponding value of the Variable v in the configuration σ will be substituted by the value of m. The program pointer is set to the successor of m, namely the node matched by Lc.

The next two rules are used to compute the successor of a condition in the computational path of a WebStory depending on the value of a *Variable*.

ConditionTT:

$$\frac{}{\langle c, \sigma \rangle \dashrightarrow \langle T, \sigma \rangle} [\![v]\!]_{B_{exp}}(\sigma) = tt \tag{12}$$

ConditionFF:

$$\frac{}{\langle c, \sigma \rangle \dashrightarrow \langle F, \sigma \rangle} [\![v]\!]_{B_{exp}}(\sigma) = ff \tag{13}$$

Thus, whenever the pattern for *condition c* is matched the value of the connected *variable v* is evaluated with respect to the current state σ. If v evaluates to true (tt) the program pointer is set to the node matched by T. If v evaluates to false (ff) the program pointer is set to the node matched by F.

All these rules can conveniently be specified using our CINCO-generated graphical development environment. Figure 4 shows screenshots of the second *Macro* transformation rule (10), the *Assignment* (11) and the *ConditionTT* (12) rule.

5.2   A MACRO Rule Application

We describe the transformation process considering the rules defined in Sect. 5.1 and the WebStory depicted in Fig. 2. We will not show the whole transformation. Instead we focus on the *cabin screen* (Screen 2 in Fig. 2), the clickable area "A" and consider the variable configuration $\sigma_{t,f}$. The first and second index represent the value of the boolean variable *key* ($[\![key]\!](\sigma) = true$) and *gold*

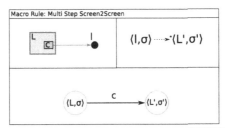

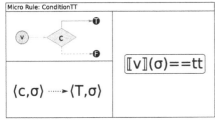 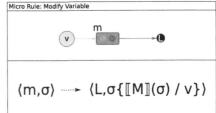

Fig. 4. Rules (10), (11), and (12) represented in concrete syntax of our pattern-based transformation language.

($[\![gold]\!](\sigma) = false$) respectively. The execution of the corresponding MACRO rule, including the MICRO step rules is shown in Fig. 5. Considering the above mentioned situation, rule (10) is matched which results in the rule instantiation shown in the bottom part of Fig. 5.

The successor of the clickable area "A" is the condition node (c.f. Fig. 2(c)) which is represented by the condition node identified by "c" in Fig. 5. The upper right part of the MACRO rule now defines the initial program pointer position for the execution of MICRO rules, namely condition "c". Consequently, the *ConditionTT* rule is applicable, with $v = key$, since the *key* variable evaluates to true in the current state $\sigma_{t,f}$.

Matching this rule to the current node defined by the program pointer results in the rule instance depicted by Micro$_1$ in Fig. 5. Here, the *true* successor of condition "c" is another condition node "c1" and the *false* successor is the *no key* screen (c.f. Fig. 2(3)). Thus, the program pointer is set to the *true* successor, namely condition "c1".

Condition "c1" checks the variable $v = gold$ which evaluates to *false* in the current state $\sigma_{t,f}$. This allows for the application of MICRO rule *ConditionFF* resulting in Micro$_2$ in Fig. 5 and updates the program pointer to the *Modify-Variable* node "m", matched by the false successor of condition "c1".

Now, the *Assignment* rule (11) is applied (Fig. 5 Micro$_3$), which updates the state by substituting the value of the *gold* variable "v" with the value of the *ModifyVariable* node "m". This results in $\sigma_{t,t}$ and updates the program pointer to the *gold* screen (Fig. 2(5)), which is terminal, as there are no Micro rules that start with a screen.

Applying the entire transformation system to the WebStory shown in Fig. 2 results in the interaction transformation system shown in Fig. 6.

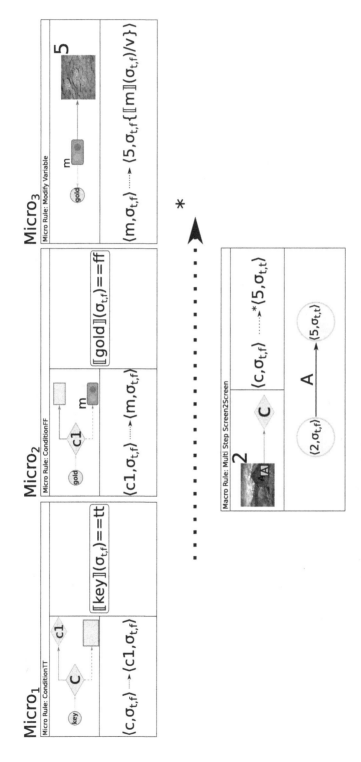

Fig. 5. An exemplary execution of the MACRO rule (10). The application of this rule on the *cabin screen* and the clickable area A leads to the rule instance depicted in M. MICRO rules M_1, M_2, and M_3 are instantiations resulting from the execution of M

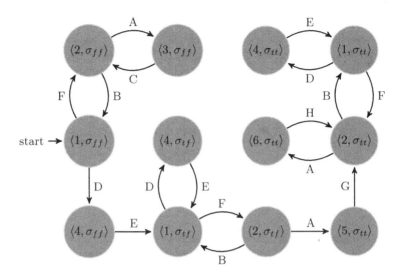

Fig. 6. Corresponding KTS to the WebStory shown in Fig. 2

6 Application: Model Checking by Construction

Model checking allows for formal verification of finite systems. Properties to verify are usually given in Linear Time Logic (LTL) or Computation Tree Logic (CTL) [4]. Given a model M of the system and a property φ specified in an appropriate logic a model checker checks if the model satisfies the property ($M \models \varphi$). As an example, one may want to verify for the Webstory in Fig. 2:

1. There is always a way to get hold of the key.
2. The gold is only accessible once.

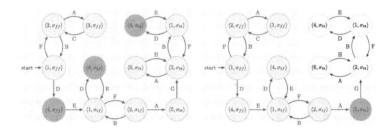

Fig. 7. Model checked KTS to WebStory in Fig. 2 (Color figure online)

In this section, we sketch how these properties can be verified using the transformation presented in Sect. 5. This requires the definition of a set of corresponding atomic propositions $AP = \{takeKey, takeGold\}$, together with an appropriate valuation for the KTS shown in Fig. 7. The result is shown in Fig. 7: The green states of Fig. 7(left-hand side) are the states that satisfy *takeKey* (they all correspond to *Screen*/node 4 of Fig. 2), and the green state of Fig. 7(right-hand side) is the only states that satisfy *takeGold* (it corresponds to *Screen*/node 5 of Fig. 2). Calling the KTS with this valuation $\mathcal{M}$, the corresponding model checking problems can be formulated as follows:

1. Always in the future a state can be reached where *takeKey* holds

$$\mathcal{M} \models AF(takeKey)$$

2. After a state is reached where *takeGold* holds, it will never hold again

$$\mathcal{M} \models \text{takeGold} \Rightarrow X(\neg EF(takeGold))$$

Figure 7 shows some feedback of the model checker for these two properties: The orange area indicates the states from which the green states can be reached. In particular, in Fig. 7(left-hand side) all states are in the orange area, meaning that from every state it is possible to reach a green state, whereas in Fig. 7(right-hand side) one can see that the only transition from the green state ends in the white area, meaning that the green state is no longer reachable.

Please note that, of course, all states of $\mathcal{M}$ satisfy both properties. However, in contrast to Fig. 7(left-hand side), which directly indicates all the states that satisfy the first property, Fig. 7(right-hand side) gives a refined picture serving as explanation of why the second property does indeed hold.

7   Conclusion and Future Work

We have illustrated our transformational approach to 'X' by construction by considering performance, learnability/monitorability, and model checkability as the property to be established. Backbone of our underlying framework is CINCO, our meta tooling suite for generating DSL-specific development environments on the basis of specifications in terms of metamodels. CINCO is used here to specify the considered source and target languages, as well as the transformation language that allows one to transform source systems/models into semantically equivalent, 'X'-conform target systems.

In this paper, we have focused on illustrating the power of domain-specific transformation languages by presenting a multi-level transformation pattern that allows one to elegantly capture refinement and aggregation aspects in a rule-based fashion. In particular, we have shown how to enable model checking for so-called WebStories that are specified in a graphical specification language addressing non-programmers. This requires the combination of some non-trivial semantic interpretation and the abstraction from computational detail which we achieve via a two-level transformation system reminiscent of the structural operational semantics for synchronous systems.

Currently, we are investigating other application scenarios, in particular to illustrate the power of moving beyond level two, to reveal the limitations of the multi-level pattern, to look for further patterns for extensions, and to compare our approach with more generic approaches to transformation like Groove [20], eMoflon [15], VIATRA [25] or even ATL [12].

References

1. Berry, G., Gonthier, G.: The Esterel synchronous programming language: design, semantics, implementation. Sci. Comput. Program. **19**(2), 87–152 (1992). http://www.sciencedirect.com/science/article/pii/016764239290005V
2. Boßelmann, S., Neubauer, J., Naujokat, S., Steffen, B.: Model-driven design of secure high assurance systems: an introduction to the open platform from the user perspective. In: Margaria, M.G., Solo, A. (eds.) The 2016 International Conference on Security and Management (SAM 2016), Special Track "End-to-end Security and Cybersecurity: from the Hardware to Application", pp. 145–151. CREA Press (2016)
3. Burkart, O., Steffen, B.: Model checking for context-free processes. In: Cleaveland, W.R. (ed.) CONCUR 1992. LNCS, vol. 630, pp. 123–137. Springer, Heidelberg (1992). https://doi.org/10.1007/BFb0084787
4. Clarke, E.M., Grumberg, O., Peled, D.A.: Model Checking. The MIT Press, Cambridge (1999)
5. Dachis, A.: Image (2014). https://www.flickr.com/photos/dachis/14569056769/
6. Frohme, M., Steffen, B.: Active Mining of Document Type Definitions (2018, under submission)
7. Frohme, M., Steffen, B.: Compositional Learning of Mutually Recursive Procedural Systems (2018, under submission)
8. Havelund, K., Reger, G., Rosu, G.: Runtime verification: Past experiences and future projections (2018)
9. Howar, F., Isberner, M., Merten, M., Steffen, B., Beyer, D.: The RERS greybox challenge 2012: analysis of event-condition-action systems. In: Margaria, T., Steffen, B. (eds.) ISoLA 2012. LNCS, vol. 7609, pp. 608–614. Springer, Heidelberg (2012). https://doi.org/10.1007/978-3-642-34026-0_45
10. Howar, F., Isberner, M., Merten, M., Steffen, B., Beyer, D., Pasareanu, C.S.: Rigorous examination of reactive systems. The RERS challenges 2012 and 2013. Softw. Tools Technol. Transf. **16**(5), 457–464 (2014)
11. Isberner, M., Howar, F., Steffen, B.: The open-source learnLib. In: Kroening, D., Păsăreanu, C.S. (eds.) CAV 2015. LNCS, vol. 9206, pp. 487–495. Springer, Cham (2015). https://doi.org/10.1007/978-3-319-21690-4_32
12. Jouault, F., Allilaire, F., Bézivin, J., Kurtev, I.: ATL: a model transformation tool. Sc. Comput. Program. **72**(1–2), 31–39 (2008)
13. Kahn, G.: Natural semantics. In: Brandenburg, F.J., Vidal-Naquet, G., Wirsing, M. (eds.) STACS 1987. LNCS, vol. 247, pp. 22–39. Springer, Heidelberg (1987). https://doi.org/10.1007/BFb0039592
14. Knowles, C.: Image (2010). https://www.flickr.com/photos/theknowlesgallery/4756008375/
15. Lauder, M., Anjorin, A., Varró, G., Schürr, A.: Bidirectional model transformation with precedence triple graph grammars. In: Vallecillo, A., Tolvanen, J.-P., Kindler, E., Störrle, H., Kolovos, D. (eds.) ECMFA 2012. LNCS, vol. 7349, pp. 287–302. Springer, Heidelberg (2012). https://doi.org/10.1007/978-3-642-31491-9_22

16. Margaria, T., Niese, O., Raffelt, H., Steffen, B.: Efficient test-based model generation for legacy reactive systems. In: Ninth IEEE International Proceedings of the High-Level Design Validation and Test Workshop, HLDVT 2004, pp. 95–100. IEEE Computer Society, Washington, DC (2004)
17. Müller-Olm, M., Schmidt, D., Steffen, B.: Model-checking. In: Cortesi, A., Filé, G. (eds.) SAS 1999. LNCS, vol. 1694, pp. 330–354. Springer, Heidelberg (1999). https://doi.org/10.1007/3-540-48294-6_22
18. Naujokat, S., Lybecait, M., Kopetzki, D., Steffen, B.: CINCO: a simplicity-driven approach to full generation of domain-specific graphical modeling tools. Softw. Tools Technol. Transf. **20**, 327–354 (2017)
19. Plotkin, G.D.: A Structural Approach to Operational Semantics. Technical report. University of Aarhus (1981). dAIMI FN-19
20. Rensink, A.: The GROOVE simulator: a tool for state space generation. In: Pfaltz, J.L., Nagl, M., Böhlen, B. (eds.) AGTIVE 2003. LNCS, vol. 3062, pp. 479–485. Springer, Heidelberg (2004). https://doi.org/10.1007/978-3-540-25959-6_40
21. Sierralupe, D.G.: Image (2016). https://www.flickr.com/photos/sierralupe/29262085202/
22. Steffen, B., Gossen, F., Naujokat, S., Margaria, T.: Language-driven engineering: from general-purpose to purpose-specific languages. In: Steffen, B., Woeginger, G. (eds.) Computing and Software Science: State of the Art and Perspectives. LNCS, vol. 10000. Springer (2018, to appear)
23. Steffen, B., Isberner, M., Naujokat, S., Margaria, T., Geske, M.: Property-driven benchmark generation. In: Bartocci, E., Ramakrishnan, C.R. (eds.) SPIN 2013. LNCS, vol. 7976, pp. 341–357. Springer, Heidelberg (2013). https://doi.org/10.1007/978-3-642-39176-7_21
24. Steffen, B., Isberner, M., Naujokat, S., Margaria, T., Geske, M.: Property-driven benchmark generation synthesizing programs of realistic structure. Softw. Tools Technol. Transf. **16**(5), 465–479 (2014)
25. Varró, D., Balogh, A.: The model transformation language of the VIATRA2 framework. Sci. Comput. Program. **68**(3), 214–234 (2007). http://www.sciencedirect.com/science/article/pii/S016764230700127X Special Issue on Model Transformation
26. Watson, I.: Image (2010). https://www.flickr.com/photos/dagoaty/4707352284/

Modelling by Patterns
for Correct-by-Construction Process

Dominique Méry[✉]

Université de Lorraine, LORIA UMR CNRS 7503, Campus Scientifique,
BP 239, 54506 Vandœuvre-lès-Nancy, France
dominique.mery@loria.fr

Abstract. Patterns have greatly improved the development of programs and software by identifying practices that could be replayed and reused in different software projects. Moreover, they help to communicate new and robust solutions for software development; it is clear that design patterns are a set of recipes that are improving the production of software. When developing models of systems, we are waiting for adequate patterns for building models and later for translating models into programs or even software. In this paper, we review several patterns that we have used and identified, when teaching and when developing case studies using the Event-B modelling language. The modelling process includes the use of formal techniques and the use of refinement, a key notion for managing abstractions and complexity of proofs. We have classified patterns in classes called paradigms and we illustrate three paradigms: the inductive paradigm, the call-as-event paradigm and the service-as-event paradigm. Several case studies are given for illustrating our methodology.

1 Introduction

Formal methods have been used successfully for developing software-based systems especially critical systems. The *correct by construct* approach has played an important role to develop and to verify systems progressively. The triptych [9–11] approach covers three main phases of the software development process: *domain description*, *requirements prescription* and *software design*. A formal notation, namely $\mathcal{D}, \mathcal{S} \longrightarrow \mathcal{R}$, relates three entities: $\mathcal{D}$ represents the domain concepts in form of properties, axioms, relations, functions and theories; $\mathcal{S}$ represents a system model; and $\mathcal{R}$ represents the intended system requirements. This notation states that the given domain description ($\mathcal{D}$) and the system model ($\mathcal{S}$) are correct with respect to the given requirements ($\mathcal{R}$) and it relates different elements involved, when developing a solution for a given problem. The triptych [9–11] $\mathcal{D}, \mathcal{S} \longrightarrow \mathcal{R}$ does not tell us how to build its three elements but it helps to *set the scene* and to express the *what should be defined*. The modelling process includes the use of formal techniques and the use of refinement, a key

---

This work was supported by grant ANR-13-INSE-0001 (The IMPEX Project http://impex.loria.fr) from the Agence Nationale de la Recherche (ANR).

© Springer Nature Switzerland AG 2018
T. Margaria and B. Steffen (Eds.): ISoLA 2018, LNCS 11244, pp. 399–423, 2018.
https://doi.org/10.1007/978-3-030-03418-4_24

notion for managing abstractions and complexity of proofs. In this paper, we propose patterns organized in classes called paradigms and we illustrate three paradigms: the inductive paradigm, the call-as-event paradigm and the service-as-event paradigm. Our aim is to help users, mainly students, to lean how to use the refinement relationship when developing software-based systems.

In a book entitled *How to Solve It*, Pólya [33] suggests the following steps, when solving a mathematical problem: First, understanding the problem (UP); second, making a plan (MP); third, carrying out the plan (CP); finally, looking back on the work by review and extend (RE).

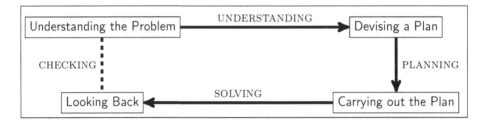

Understanding the problem (UP) is generally related to the formalisation of the domain of problem $\mathcal{D}$ and we are promoting the reuse of existing theories or libraries. The second step making a plan (MP) can be the search of a pattern; it may be also possible to sketch the system to build by a diagram. However, the question is to have a list of possible so called *patterns*, which can be applied and reused. Some advices of Pólya are very close to a creative point: *If you can't solve a problem, then there is an easier problem you can solve: find it.* or *If you cannot solve the proposed problem, try to solve first some related problem. Could you imagine a more accessible related problem?.* From Pólya and Gamma [21], *patterns* are a key concept for solving problems in a general settlement. Moreover, another key concept is the refinement of models handling the complex nature of such systems: the refinement is used for constructing models or patterns. Following Abrial et al. [22] and Cansell et al. [13], we revisit a list of patterns which can be used for developing programs or systems using the refinement and the proof as a mean to check the whole process and which can be a mean to reuse former proofs in new developments.

Patterns [21] have greatly improved the development of programs and software by identifying practices that could be replayed and reused in different software projects. Moreover, they help to communicate new and robust solutions for developing a software for instance; it is clear that design patterns are a set of recipes that are improving software production. When developing (formal) system models, we are waiting for adequate patterns for developing models and later for translating models into programs or even software. Abrial et al. [22] have already addressed the definition of patterns in the Event-B modelling language and have proposed a plugin which is implementing the instantiation of a pattern. Cansell et al. [13] propose a way to reuse and to instantiate patterns.

Moreover, patterns intends to make the refinement-based development simpler and the tool BART [17] provides commands for automatic refinement using the AtelierB toolbox [16]. The BART process is rule-based so that the user can *drive* refinement. We aim to develop patterns which are following Pólya's approach in a smooth application of Event-B models corresponding to classes of problems to solve as for instance an iterative algorithm, a recursive algorithm [27], a distributed algorithm ... Moreover, no plugin is necessary for applying our patterns.

We are organising patterns with respect to paradigms identified in our refinement-based development. A paradigm is a distinct set of patterns, including theories, research methods, postulates, and standards for what constitutes legitimate contributions to designing programs. A pattern for modelling in Event-B is a set (project) of contexts and machines that have parameters as sets, constants, variables ... The notion of pattern has been introduced progressively in the Event-B process for improving the derivation of formal models and for facilitating the task of the person who is developing a model. In our work, students are the main target for testing and using these patterns. Our definition is very general but we do not want a very precise definition since the notion of pattern should be as simple as possible and should be helpful. We review several patterns that we have used and identified, when teaching and when developing case studies using the Event-B modelling language. The modelling process includes the use of formal techniques and the use of refinement, a key notion for managing abstractions. Moreover, we have also identified some paradigms that can be used and can facilitate the design of formal models.

The structure of the article is as follows. In Sect. 2, we review preliminary material: the modelling framework. Section 3 presents the inductive paradigm, which is illustrated in Sect. 4. In Sect. 5, we consider the call-as-event paradigm and compare it with the inductive paradigm. A paradigm is gathering patterns and Sect. 7 proposes the service-as-event paradigm which is a generalization of the call-as-event paradigm. We illustrate patterns by developing a protocol namely the *Sliding Window Protocol*. Section 8 concludes the paper and discusses future works and perspectives.

2   The Modelling Framework: Event-B for Step-Wise Development

This section describes the essential components of the modelling framework. In particular, we will use the Event-B modelling language [1] for modelling systems in a progressive way. Event-B has two main components: *context* and *machine*. A *context* is a formal static structure that is composed of several other clauses, such as *carrier sets*, *constants*, *axioms* and *theorems*. A *machine* is a formal structure composed of *variables*, *invariants*, *theorems*, *variants* and *events*; it expresses state-related properties. A machine and a context can be connected with the *sees* relationship.

Events play an important role for modelling the functional behaviour of a system and are observed. An event is a state transition that contains two main

components: *guard* and *action*. A *guard* is a predicate based on the state variables
that defines a necessary condition for enabling the event. An *action* is also a
predicate that allows modifying the state variables when the given guard becomes
true. A set of invariants defines required safety properties that must be satisfied
by all the defined state variables. There are several proof obligations, such as
invariant preservation, non-deterministic action feasibility, guard strengthening
in refinements, simulation, variant, well-definiteness, that must be checked during
the modelling and verification process.

Event-B allows us modelling a complex system gradually using *refinement*.
The refinement enables us to introduce more detailed behaviour and the required
safety properties by transforming an abstract model into a concrete version. At
each refinement step, events can be refined by: (1) keeping the event as it is;
(2) splitting an event into several events; or (3) refining by introducing another
event to maintain state variables. Note that the refinement always preserves a
relation between an abstract model and its corresponding concrete model. The
newly generated proof obligations related to refinement ensures that the given
abstract model is correctly refined by its concrete version. Note that the refined
version of the model always reduces the degree of non-determinism by strengthening the guards and/or predicates. The modelling framework has a very good
tool support (RODIN) for project management, model development, conducting
proofs, model checking and animation, and automatic code generation. There
are numerous publications and books available for an introduction to Event-B
and related refinement strategies [1].

Since models may generate very *tough* proof obligations to automatically
discharge, the development of proved models can be improved by the refinement
process. The key idea is to combine models and elements of requirements using
the refinement. The refinement [7,8] of a machine allows us to enrich a model
in a *step-by-step* approach, and is the foundation of our *correct-by-construction*
approach. Refinement provides a way to strengthen the invariant and to add
details to a model. It is also used to transform an abstract model into a more
concrete version by modifying the state description. This is done by extending
the list of state variables, by refining each abstract event into a corresponding
concrete version, and by adding new events. The next diagram illustrates the
refinement-based relationship among events and models:

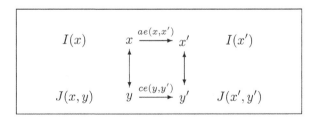

We suppose that an abstract model AM with variables x and invariant $I(x)$
is refined by a concrete model CM with variables y and gluing invariant $J(x,y)$.
The abstract state variables, x, and the concrete ones, y, are linked together by

means of the, so-called, *gluing invariant* $J(x, y)$. A number of proof obligations ensure that (1) each abstract event of AM is correctly refined by its corresponding concrete version of CM, (2) each new event of CM refines *skip*, which is intending to model *hidden* actions over variables appearing in the refinement model CM. More formally, if $BA(ae)(x, x')$ and $BA(ce)(y, y')$ are respectively the abstract and concrete before-after predicates of events, we say that *ce* in CM refines *ae* in AM or that *ce* simulates *ae*, if one proves the following statement corresponding to proof obligation: $I(x) \land J(x, y) \land BA(ce)(y, y') \Rightarrow \exists x' \cdot (BA(ae)(x, x') \land J(x', y'))$. To summarise, refinement guarantees that the set of traces of the abstract model AM contains (modulo stuttering) the traces of the concrete model CM.

The next diagram summarises links between contexts (CC extends AC); AC defines the set-theoretical logical and problem-based theory of level i called Th_i, which is extended by the set-theoretical logical and problem-based theory of level i called Th_{i+1}, which is defined by CC). Each machine (AM, CM) sees set-theoretical and logical objects defined from the problem statement and located in the CONTEXTS models (AC, CC). The abstract model AM of the level i is refined by CM; state variables of AM is x and satisfies the invariant $I(x)$. The refinement of AM by CM is checking the invariance of $J(x, y)$ and does need to prove the invariance of $I(x)$, since it is obtained freely from the checking of AM.

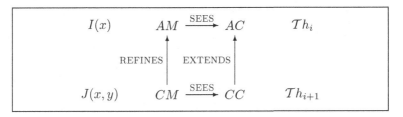

The management of proof obligations is a technical task supported by the RODIN tool [2], which provides an environment for developing correct-by-construction models for software-based systems according to the diagram. Moreover, the RODIN platform integrates ProB, a tool for animating EVENT-B models and for model-checking finite configurations of EVENT-B models at different steps of refinement. ProB is used for checking deadlock-freedom and for helping in the discovery of invariants.

3   The Inductive Paradigm

First at all, we analyse the inductive paradigm using the refinement and we develop specific patterns. A computation is often characterised by the effective computing of a value of a sequence of values. The problem is to define the sequence of values and then to find a process for computing the value of a member of the sequence. The methodology is based on the case studies developed in the last decade and is the result of observations when teaching students how to use Event-B and its refinement. Two questions are stated: how to model for getting an iterative algorithm computing a value defined by a given sequence at a given rank? and can we have a set of automatically discharged proof obligations as large as possible? The question is to define the sequence corresponding to the problem to solve and the sequence is giving the way for constructing the required value. The invariant is a very important part and is derived from analysis of the problem. The global pattern called the iterative pattern is sketched by the following diagram where machines and contexts are PREPOST, COMPUTING, PREALGO, ALGO, ALGOPC and C0. The context C0 contains the description of the problem which is the sequence (of values) defining the problem and the refinement is linking the machines. The last machine is ALGOPC which is translated into an algorithm *algorithm.*. The context C0 is enriched while the model is progressively refined.

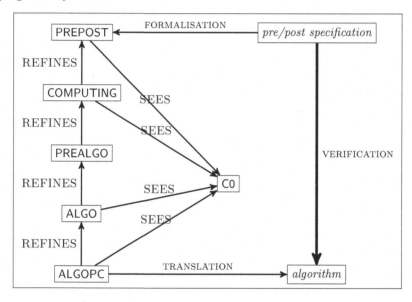

Fig. 1. The iterative pattern

CONTEXT $c0$
SETS
   U
CONSTANTS
   $x, v, d0, f, D$
AXIOMS
   $axm1 : x \in \mathbb{N}$
   $axm25 : D \subseteq U$
   $axm24 : f \in D \to D$
   $axm23 : d0 \in D$
   $axm2 : v \in \mathbb{N} \to D$
   $axm3 : v(0) = d0$
   $axm4 : \forall n \cdot n \in \mathbb{N} \Rightarrow v(n+1) = f(v(n))$
   $th1 : Q(d_0, d) \equiv (d = v(x))$

The context C0 is defining the sequence v which is used for expressing the post-condition $Q(d_0, d)$ with the precondition $P(d_0)$. The post-condition $Q(d_0, d)$ is equivalent to $d = v(x)$ where the sequence v is defined using d_0 as initial value of v. The theorem $th1$ should be proved in the context C0 and it states that the sequence v is soundly defining the problem. $th1$ expresses that the requested value d exists and the sequence provides an inductive process for computing it.

```
MACHINE PREPOST
SEES C0
VARIABLES
    r
INVARIANTS
    inv1 r ∈ D
EVENTS
INITIALISATION
    BEGIN
        act1 : r :∈ D
    END
EVENT computing
    BEGIN
        act1 : r := v(x)
    END
END
```

The theorem $th1$ is validating the definition of the result r to compute. The event computing is expressing the *contract* of the given problem. The step from the context to the machine PREPOST is redefining the contract in a machine. The domain D is any possible domain and not only $\mathbb{N}$ but it may be a complex domain with multiple dimensions. We will illustrate it by a very simple problem that is the computation of the function n^2 using the addition operator.

Following the refinement-based approach, we introduce a refinement which is expliciting the computation process using the sequence v as a guide for reasoning. The refinement is the introduction of a very expensive variable vv recording and storing successive and necessary values of the sequence v.

The variable vv is storing the value s of v and it may appear very inappropriate. However, the goal is to structure the proof process and to introduce *modelling* variables which will be *hidden* later in the final refinement. The invariant is simply expressing the relationship between *mathematical values* of v and *modelling variable* of vv. k defines the domain of vv which is evolving during the process. The properties of variables are derived from the relationship which exists by the definition of the computation process:

$$
\begin{aligned}
&(1)\ vv \in \mathbb{N} \nrightarrow D \\
&(2)\ k \in \mathbb{N} \\
&(3)\ \forall i \cdot i \in dom(vv) \Rightarrow vv(i) = v(i) \\
&(4)\ dom(vv) = 0 \mathrel{..} k \\
&(5)\ k \leq x
\end{aligned}
$$

Proofs obligations are discharged with a light interaction. The refinement is a progressive process and is progressing to a model close to an implementation. The refinement machine computing has a new event step updating the variable vv and the event computing is made more concrete by using the guard over the index k.

```
EVENT INITIALISATION
    BEGIN
        act1 : r :∈ D
        act3 : vv := {0 ↦ d0}
        act5 : k := 0
    END
```

```
EVENT computing
    REFINES computing,
    WHEN
        grd1 : x ∈ dom(vv)
    THEN
        act1 : r := vv(x)
    END
END
```

```
EVENT step
    WHEN
        grd1 : x ∉ dom(vv)
    THEN
        act2 : vv(k + 1) := f(vv(k))
        act4 : k := k + 1
    END
```

Now, we have to add a new refinement which is preparing the final transformation. The idea is to make the task of the proof assistant easier and to explain how the invariant is built in a progressive way. A new variable cv is used for storing the last computed value of the sequence v: $cv \in D$ and $cv = vv(k)$.

```
EVENT INITIALISATION
  BEGIN
    act1 : r :∈ D
    act3 : vv := {0 ↦ d0}
    act5 : k := 0
    act8 : cv := d0
  END
```

```
EVENT computing
  REFINES computing
  WHEN
    grd1 : k = x
  THEN
    act1 : r := cv
  END
```

```
EVENT step
  REFINES step
  WHEN
    grd1 : k < x
  THEN
    act2 : vv(k + 1) := f(vv(k))
    act4 : k := k + 1
    act5 : cv := f(cv)
  END
```

Proof obligations are discharged without toil, thanks to the incremental refinement. The statement $vv(k + 1) := f(vv(k))$ is *simulated* by the new statement $cv := f(cv)$. The new refinement is *hidden* the modelling variable vv. The variables r, cv and k are modelling the computation according to the safety properties: (1) $cv = v(k)$ (2) $k \leq x$ (3) $0 \leq k$. Events are modified by hiding the variable vv and correspond to the pattern.

```
EVENT INITIALISATION
  BEGIN
    act1 : r :∈ D
    act5 : k := 0
    act8 : cv := d0
  END
```

```
EVENT computing
  REFINES computing
  WHEN
    grd1 : k = x
  THEN
    act1 : r := cv
  END
```

```
EVENT step
  REFINES step
  WHEN
    grd1 : k < x
  THEN
    act4 : k := k + 1
    act6 : cv := f(cv)
  END
```

The final step is to derive an algorithm corresponding to the two events. A further refinement introduces the control variable called pc and we obtained the operational semantics based on relations between variables and primed variables.

Listing 1.1. Function derived from pattern for the sequence v

```
type (D)    f (int  x)
{int    r , k , cv , or , ok , ocv ;
   r =0; k=0; cv =0; or =0; ok=k ; ocv=cv ;
   while (k<x)
           {
              ok=k ; ocv=cv ;
              k=ok +1;
              cv=f ( ocv );
           }
   r=cv ;    return ( r );}
```

The produced algorithm can be now checked using another proof environment as for instance Frama-C [34]. The inductive property of the invariant is clearly verified and is easily derived from the Event-B machines. The verification is not required, since the system is correct by construction but it is a checking of the process itself. Abrial [1] has addressed the question of developing sequential algorithms and has proposed a list of transformations of Event-B models; our Event-B project (or pattern) based on Abrial's case studies has added intermediate refinements and has identified model variables from programming variables. We have developed the project called ITERATIVE-PATTERN; the project is the pattern itself and in the next section we apply it by specialising it for specific problems. The specialization leads to choose a sequence corresponding to the problem to solve and to complete the project ITERATIVE-PATTERN.

4 Applying the Iterative Pattern

The iterative pattern (see Fig. 1) can be applied by importing the previous project called ITERATIVE-PATTERN. We do not use the pattern plugin and the technique developed by Abrial and Hoang [22] and choose a solution which is simpler to apply with the RODIN platfom. The current project is then enriched by the definition of the sequence of the problem to solve. The user should find a way to express the problem by a sequence v over the domain D. The sequence v is a key point and it should be related to the required post-condition. A theorem should be derived in the context C0. We are considering two examples illustrating how the iterative pattern can be instantiated.

4.1 Example 1: x^2 and x^3 Without Toil

Computing the value x^2 for any natural number x without using the multiplication operator and using the addition operator, is a well known algorithm which is based on a simple observation. The value $(i + 1)^2$ is developed into $i^2 + 2 * i + 1$ and the sequence v is defined as follows from this equality: $v(i + 1) = v(i) + 2 * i + 1$ and then each term is defined as a term of another

$$\text{sequence} \begin{cases} v(i+1) = v(i) + w(i) + 1 \\ w(i+1) = w(i) + 2 \\ u(i+1) = u(i) + 1 \end{cases}$$

In fact, the sequence v is defined with the help of two auxiliary sequences namely w and u. We can apply the iterative pattern by rewriting the previous definitions of sequence as follows:

$$\begin{pmatrix} v(i+1) \\ w(i+1) \\ u(i+1) \end{pmatrix} = \begin{pmatrix} v(i) + w(i) + 1 \\ w(i) + 2 \\ u(i) + 1 \end{pmatrix} = \begin{pmatrix} 1 & 1 & 0 \\ 0 & 1 & 0 \\ 0 & 0 & 1 \end{pmatrix} \begin{pmatrix} v(i) \\ w(i) \\ u(i) \end{pmatrix} + \begin{pmatrix} 1 \\ 2 \\ 1 \end{pmatrix}$$

The domain D is $\mathbb{Z} \times \mathbb{Z} \times \mathbb{Z}$ and the sequence A is simply defined by:

$$\begin{cases} \forall i \in \mathbb{N} : A(i) = \begin{pmatrix} v(i) \\ w(i) \\ u(i) \end{pmatrix} \\ \forall i \in \mathbb{N} : A(i+1) = \begin{pmatrix} 1 & 1 & 0 \\ 0 & 1 & 0 \\ 0 & 0 & 1 \end{pmatrix} A(i) + \begin{pmatrix} 1 \\ 2 \\ 1 \end{pmatrix} \end{cases}$$

The sequence A is a vector of sequences satisfying properties related to the post-condition and these properties should be proved using the proof assistant: $\forall i \in \mathbb{N} : A(i)_1 = i * i$, $\forall i \in \mathbb{N} : A(i)_2 = 2 * i$ and $\forall i \in \mathbb{N} : A(i)_3 = i$. The notation $A(i)_j$ denotes the j-th component of the vector $A(i)$. Finally, we obtain the following function which is checked using Frama-C.

Listing 1.2. Function derived from pattern power2

```
#include <limits.h>
/*@   requires   0 <= x;
      requires  x*x <= INT_MAX ;
      ensures \result ==x*x;
*/
int power2(int x)
{int   r,k,cv,cw,or,ok,ocv,ocw;
   r=0;k=0;cv=0;cw=0;or=0;ok=k;ocv=cv;ocw=cw;
       /*@ loop invariant  cv == k*k;
        @ loop invariant  k  <= x;
        @ loop invariant  cw  == 2*k;
        @ loop assigns  k,cv,cw,or,ok,ocv,ocw; */
   while (k<x)
       {
           ok=k;ocv=cv;ocw=cw;
           k=ok+1;
           cv=ocv+ocw+1;
           cw=ocw+2;}
   r=cv;return(r);}
```

The same process can be applied for computing x^3 and we use the equality $(i+1)^3 = i^3 + 3i^2 + 3i + 1$. We introduce intermediate sequences and identify the following sequences:

- $z_0 = 0$ et $\forall n \in \mathbb{N} : z_{n+1} = z_n + v_n + w_n$
- $v_0 = 0$ et $\forall n \in \mathbb{N} : v_{n+1} = v_n + t_n$
- $t_0 = 3$ et $\forall n \in \mathbb{N} : t_{n+1} = t_n + 6$
- $w_0 = 1$ et $\forall n \in \mathbb{N} : w_{n+1} = w_n + 3$
- $u_0 = 0$ et $\forall n \in \mathbb{N} : u_{n+1} = u_n + 1$

$$
\begin{pmatrix} z(i+1) \\ v(i+1) \\ t(i+1) \\ w(i+1) \\ u(i+1) \end{pmatrix} = \begin{pmatrix} z_i + v_i + w_i \\ v(i) + t(i) \\ t(i) + 6 \\ w(i) + 3 \\ u(i) + 1 \end{pmatrix} = \begin{pmatrix} 1 & 1 & 01 & 0 \\ 0 & 1 & 1 & 0 & 0 \\ 0 & 0 & 1 & 0 & 0 \\ 0 & 0 & 0 & 1 & 0 \\ 0 & 0 & 0 & 0 & 1 \end{pmatrix} \begin{pmatrix} z(i) \\ v(i \\ t(i) \\ w(i) \\ u(i) \end{pmatrix} + \begin{pmatrix} 0 \\ 0 \\ 6 \\ 3 \\ 1 \end{pmatrix}
$$

The domain D is $\mathbb{Z} \times \mathbb{Z} \times \mathbb{Z} \times \mathbb{Z} \times \mathbb{Z}$ and the sequence B is simply defined by:

$$
\begin{cases} \forall i \in \mathbb{N} : B(i) = \begin{pmatrix} z(i) \\ v(i \\ t(i) \\ w(i) \\ u(i) \end{pmatrix} \\ \\ \forall i \in \mathbb{N} : B(i+1) = \begin{pmatrix} 1 & 1 & 01 & 0 \\ 0 & 1 & 1 & 0 & 0 \\ 0 & 0 & 1 & 0 & 0 \\ 0 & 0 & 0 & 1 & 0 \\ 0 & 0 & 0 & 0 & 1 \end{pmatrix} B(i) + \begin{pmatrix} 0 \\ 0 \\ 6 \\ 3 \\ 1 \end{pmatrix} \end{cases}
$$

The sequence B is a vector of sequences satisfying properties related to the postcondition and these properties should be proved using the proof assistant: $\forall i \in \mathbb{N} : B(i)_1 = i * i * i$. The notation $B(i)_j$ denotes the j-th component of the vector $B(i)$. Finally, we obtain the following function which is checked using Frama-C.

Listing 1.3. Function derived from pattern power3

```
#include <limits.h>
/*@   requires   0 <= x;
      requires  x*x*x <= INT_MAX ;
      ensures \result ==x*x*x;
*/
int power3(int x)
{int   r,ocz,cz,cv,cu,ocv,cw,ocw,ct,oct,ocu,k,ok;
   cz=0;cv=0;cw=1;ct=3;cu=0;  ocw=cw;ocz=cz;
   oct=ct;ocv=cv;ocu=cu;k=0;ok=k;
        /*@ loop invariant  cz  == k*k*k;
        @ loop invariant  cu   == k;
        @ loop invariant  cv+ct==3*(cu+1)*(cu+1);
        @ loop invariant  cz+cv+cw==3*(cu+1)*(cu+1)*(cu+1);
        @ loop invariant  cv== 3*cu*cu;
        @ loop invariant  cw == 3*cu+1;
        @ loop invariant  k  <= x;
        @ loop assigns  ct,oct,cu,ocu,cz,ocz,k,cv,cw,r,ok;
        @ loop assigns  ocv,ocw;*/
   while (k<x)
        {
          ocz=cz;ok=k;ocv=cv;ocw=cw;oct=ct;ocu=cu;
          cz=ocz+ocv+ocw;
          cv=ocv+oct;
          ct=oct+6;
          cw=ocw+3;
          cu=ocu+1;
          k=ok+1;}
   r=cz;return(r);}
```

In this case, the loop invariant is inductive but Frama-C does not prove it completely. This is not the case with the RODIN platform which is able to discharge the whole set of proof obligations. However, the Event-B model is using auxiliary knowledge over sequences used for defining the computing process. The most difficult theorem is to prove that $\forall n \in \mathbb{N} : z_n = n * n * n$. The second example is a new algorithm for computing n^3 with only addition operator and it is based on sequences which are defined from the equality simplifying $(i+1)^3$. The technique can be applied for the computation of i^k for any k.

4.2   Example 2: The Fibonacci Family

We consider a function $f \in \mathbb{Z} \times \mathbb{Z} \times \mathbb{Z} \to \mathbb{Z}$ defined the complete set of natural numbers and an infinite sequence of natural values defined using a inductive definition as follow:

- $u_0 \in \mathbb{N}$
- $u_1 \in \mathbb{N}$
- $\forall n \in \mathbb{N} : u_{n+2} = f(u_n, u_{n+1})$

The inductive definition is considering not only the last previous element of the sequence but two last previous terms. We use an expression for reformulating the problem to solve and introduce a sequence f defined as follows:

- $F_1 \in \mathbb{N} \times \mathbb{N}$ where $F_1 = (u_0, u_1)$
- $\forall n \in \mathbb{N} : n \neq 0 :$
$$\begin{pmatrix} F_{n+1} = g(F_n) \\ g(F_n) = (f((F_{n-1})_1, (F_{n-1})_2), f((F_n)_1, (F_n)_2)) = ((F_n)_2, f((F_n)_1, (F_n)_2)) \end{pmatrix}$$

The reformulation leads to the general format of the iterative pattern and it indicates also the necessity to have a specific variable for keeping the two previous values: cv is containing a pair.

Listing 1.4. Function derived from pattern fibo

```
type(D)    fibo(int x)
{int    r,k,cv,or,ok,ocv;
   k=0;cv=(u0,u1);ok=k;ocv=cv;
   while (k<x)
         {  ok=k;ocv=cv;
            k=ok+1;
            /* cv=g(ocv);
            cv= (ocv_2,f(ocv_1,ocv_2));}
   r=cv;    return(r); }
```

In the algorithm, the variable cv is a pair keeping the two last values and we denote ocv_i the i-th component of ocv.

4.3   On Proofs Summary

Applying the iterative pattern requires to replay the proofs by instantiating the constants of the problem. The new model is solving a specific problem and we should prove extra theorems to derive the final post-condition as for instance $\forall n \in \mathbb{N} : z_n = n * n * n$. The progressive design of models facilitates the proofs as we have noticed for the function **power3**: Frama-C was not able to discharge any proof of the loop invariant. In the case of Fibonacci, the development of the solution using Event-B and the refinement show that the resulting function is correct by construction and the use of Frama-C is not possible since we need to prove that r contains a value of the sequence: Frama-C necessitates the definition of a theory with definition of Fibonacci sequence.

5   The Call-as-Event Paradigm

The inductive paradigm and the iterative pattern are using a sequence of values in a domain $\mathcal{D}$ and the computation process is based on the recording of the values of the sequence. In the case of the call-as-event paradigm, the pattern is based on the link between the occurrence of an event and a call of a function or procedure or method satisfying the pre-condition and post-condition respectively at the call point and the return point. The context C0 defines the sequence of values and the definition of the sequence is used as a guide for the shape of events. The definitions of sequence are reformulated by a diagram which is simulating the different cases when the procedure under development is called namely $P(x,r)$.

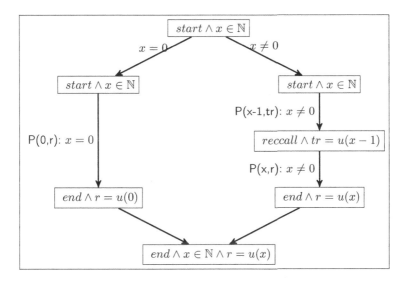

Fig. 2. Organisation of the computation in a recursive solution using assertion diagram

The diagram is derived from the Event-B model called ALGOREC and is a finite state diagram. It includes a liveness proof very close to the proof lattices of Owicki and Lamport [32]. We use special names for events in the diagram: P(0,r): $x = 0$ stands for the event observed when the procedure P(x,r) is called with x=0; P(x-1,tr): $x \neq 0$ models the observation of the recursive call of P; P(x,r): $x \neq 0$ stands for the event observed when the procedure P(x,r) is called with $x \neq 0$. P(0,r): $x = 0$ and P(x,r): $x \neq 0$ are refining the event computing which is observed when the procedure P is called.

MACHINE *ALGOREC*
REFINES *PREPOST*
SEES *C0*
VARIABLES
  r, pc, tr
INVARIANTS
  $art : pc \in L$
  $inv1 : tr \in D$
  $inv2 : pc = callrec \Rightarrow tr = v(x-1)$
  $inv3 : pc = end \Rightarrow r = v(x)$

The refinement is an organisation of the inductive definition using a control variable pc. The control variable pc is organising the different steps of the computations simulated by the events. The invariant is derived directly from the definitions of the intermediate values. Proof obligations are simple to prove. It remains to prove that the values of the sequence v correspond to the required value in the post-condition.

EVENT P(x,r):x=0
  REFINES computing
  WHEN
    $grd1 : x = 0$
    $grd2 : pc = start$
  THEN
    $act1 : r := d0$
    $act2 : pc := end$
  END

EVENT P(x-1,tr):x/=0
  WHEN
    $grd1 : pc = start$
    $grd2 : x \neq 0$
  THEN
    $act1 : tr := v(x-1)$
    $act2 : pc := callrec$
  END

EVENT P(x,r):x/=0
  REFINES computing
  WHEN
    $grd1 : pc = callrec$
  THEN
    $act1 : r := f(tr)$
    $act2 : pc := end$
  END

The machine is simulating the organisation of the computations following two cases according to the Fig. 2. The first case is the path on the left part of the diagram and is when x is 0 and the second case if when x is not 0.

The first path is a three steps path and is labelled by the condition $x = 0$ an d the event P(0,r):x=0. The event P(x,r):x=0 is assigning the value $d0$ to r according to the definition of $u(0)$. It refines the event computing in the abstraction. The third step is an implication leading to the postcondition.

The second path is a four steps path and is labelled by the condition $x \neq 0$, then the event P(x-1,r):$x \neq 0$ is modelling the recursive call of the same procedure. Finally the event P(,r):$x \neq 0$ is refining the event computing. The call as event paradigm is applied when one considers that one event is defining the specification of the recursive call and the user is giving the name of the call to indicate that the event should be translated into a call. The EB2RC plugin [15] generates automatically a C-like program.

The model **ALGOREC** is simple to checked. Proof obligations are simple, because the recursive call is hiding the previous values stored in the variable vv of the iterative paradigm. The prover is much more efficient.

The recursive pattern is linked to a diagram which is helping to structure the solution. We have labelled arrows by guards or by events. The diagram helps to structure the analysis based on the inductive definitions. Following this pattern, we have developed the ERB2RC plugin based on the identification of three possible events. When a pre/post specification is stated, the program to build can be expressed by a simple event expressing the relationship between input and output and it provides a way to express pre/post specification as events. The first model is a very abstract model containing the pre/post events.

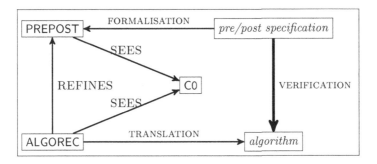

Fig. 3. The recursive pattern

Since the refinement-based process requires an idea for introducing more concrete events. A very simple and powerful way to refine is to introduce a more concrete model which is based on an inductive definition of outputs with respect to the input.

A first consequence is that the concrete model is containing events which are computing the same function but corresponding to a recursive call expressed as events (**EVENT** rec%PROC(h(x),y)%P(y)). The event **EVENT** rec%PROC(h(x),y)%P(y) is simply simulating the recursive call of the same function and this expression makes the proofs easier. The invariant is defined in a simpler way by analysing the inductive structure and a control variable is introduced for structuring the inductive computation. We have identified three possible events to use in the concrete model:

EVENT e **WHERE** $\ell = \ell_1$ $g_{\ell_1,\ell_2}(x)$ **THEN** $\ell := \ell_2$ $x := f_{\ell_1,\ell_2}(x)$ **END**	**EVENT** rec%PROC(h(x),y)%P(y) **ANY** y **WHERE** $\ell = \ell_1$ $g_{\ell_1,\ell_2}(x,y)$ **THEN** $\ell := \ell_2$ $x := f_{\ell_1,\ell_2}(x,y)$ **END**	**EVENT** call%APROC(h(x),y)%P(y) **ANY** y **WHERE** $\ell = \ell_1$ $g_{\ell_1,\ell_2}(x,y)$ **THEN** $\ell := \ell_2$ $x := f_{\ell_1,\ell_2}(x,y)$ **END**

6 Applying the Recursive Pattern

Applying the recursive pattern is made easier by the first steps of the iterative pattern. In fact, the context C0 and the machine PREPOST are the starting points of the iterative pattern as well as the recursive pattern. We use the computation of the function x^2 and we obtained the following refinement of PREPOST. Figure 2 is the diagram analysing the way to solve the computation of the value of $u(x)$ following the call-as-event paradigm.

```
MACHINE square
REFINES specquare
DoubSEES control0
VARIABLES
    r, c, tr
INVARIANTS
    inv1 : r ∈ ℕ
    inv2 : c = end ⇒ r = n * n
    inv3 : c = callrec ⇒ n ≠ 0
    inv4 : c = callrec ⇒ tr = (n − 1) * (n − 1)
    inv5 : c ∈ C
    inv6 : tr ∈ ℕ
    inv7 : c = end ⇒ r = n * n
    inv8 : c = end ∧ n ≠ 0
        ⇒ tr = (n − 1) * (n − 1) ∧ r = tr + 2 * (n − 1) + 1
    inv9 : c = callrec ⇒ n * n = tr + 2 * (n − 1) + 1
```

```
EVENT INITIALISATION
    BEGIN
        act1 : r := 0
        act2 : c := start
        act3 : tr :∈ ℕ
    END
EVENT square0
REFINES square(n;r)
    WHEN
        grd1 : c = start
        grd2 : n = 0
    THEN
        act1 : c := end
        act2 : r := 0
    END
```

```
EVENT squaren
REFINES square(n;r)
    WHEN
        grd1 : c = callrec
    THEN
        act1 : r := tr + 2 * (n − 1) + 1
        act2 : c := end
    END
EVENT rec%square(n-1;tr)
    WHEN
        grd1 : c = start
        grd2 : n ≠ 0
    THEN
        act1 : c := callrec
        act2 : tr := (n − 1) * (n − 1)
    END
```

The variable c is modelling the control in the diagram. We introduce control points corresponding to assertions in the labels of the diagram as $C = \{start, end, callrec\}$. Three events are defined and the invariant is written very easily and proofs are derived automatically. The event rec%square(n-1;tr) is the key event modelling the recursive call. In the current example, we have modified the machine by using directly the fact that $v(n) = n * n$ and normally we had to use the sequence following the recursive pattern and then we had to derive the theorem $v(n) = n * n$.

Proofs are simpler and invariants are easier to extract from the inductive definitions. The use of Frama-C shows that the proofs are also very simple in the case of a recursive algorithm. Missing expertise in using Frama-C leads to the introduction of auxiliary lemmas as $((x − 1) + 1)^2 = (x − 1)^2 + 2x + 1$. In this example, we do not use the event like call%APROC(h(x),y)%P(y) but the event is clearly a call for another procedure or function. For instance, when a sorting algorithm is developed, you may need an auxiliary operation for scanning a list of values to get the index of the minimum. It means that we have a way to define a library of models and to use correct-by-construction procedures or functions. In [15], we detail the tool and the way to define a library of *correct-by-construction programs*.

7   The Service-as-Event Paradigm

The next question is to handle concurrent and distributed algorithms corresponding to different programming paradigms as message-passing or shared-memory or coordination-based programming. Jones [23] develops the rely/guarantee concept for handling (possible and probably wanted) interferences among sequential programs. Rely/guarantee intends to make *implicit* [4, 12] interferences as well as cooperation proofs in a proof system. In other methods as Owicki and Gries [31], the management of non-interference proofs among annotated processes leads to a important amount of extra proof obligations: checking interference freeness is explicitly expressed in the inferences rules. When considering an event as modelling a call of function or a call of a procedure, we implicitly express a computation and a sequence of state. We [30] propose a temporal extension of Event-B to express liveness properties. The extension is a small bridge between Event-B and TLA/TLA$^+$ [24] with a refinement perspective. As C. Jones in rely/guarantee, we express implicit properties of the environment on the protocol under description by extending the call-as-event paradigm by a service-as-event paradigm. In [5,6], the service-as-event paradigm is explored on two different classes of distributed programs/algorithms/applications: the snapshot problem and the self-healing P2P by Marquezan et al. [26]. The self-healing problem is belonging to the larger class of self-$\star$ systems [18].

In previous patterns, we identify one event which *simulates* the execution of an algorithm either as an iterative version or as a recursive version. Figures 1 and 3 separate the problem to solve into three problem domains: the domain for expressing pre/post specifications, the domain of Event-B models and the domain of programs/algorithms. The translation function generates effective algorithms producing the same traces of states. We are now introducing patterns which are representatives of the service-as-event paradigm.

7.1   The PCAM Pattern

Coordination [14] is a paradigm that allows programmers to develop distributed systems; web services are using this paradigm for organising interactions among services and processes. In parallel programming, coordination plays also a central role and Foster [20] has proposed the PCAM methodology for designing concurrent programs from a problem statement: PCAM emphasizes a decomposition into four steps corresponding to analysis of the problem and leading to a machine-independant solution. Clearly, the goal of I. Foster is to make concurrent programming based on abstractions, which are progressively adding details leading to specific concurrent programming notation as, for instance MPI (http://www.open-mpi.org/). The PCAM methodology identifies four distinct stages corresponding to a Partition of identified tasks from the problem statement and which are concurrently executed. A problem is possibly an existing complex C or Fortran code for a computing process requiring processors and concurrent executions. Communication is introduced by an appropriate coordination among tasks and then two final steps, Agglomeration and Mapping complete the methodology steps. The PCAM methodology includes features related to the functional requirements in the two first stages and to the implementation in the two last stages. I. Foster has developed the PCAM methodology together with tools for supporting the implementation of programs on different architectures. The success of the design is mainly due to the coordination paradigm which allows us to freely organise the stages of the development.

The PCAM methodology includes features related to the functional requirements in the two first stages and to the implementation in the two last stages. The general approach is completely described in [28].

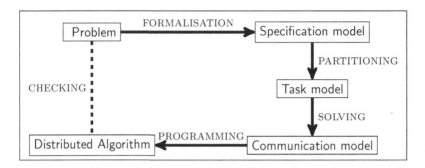

We consider the two first stages (Partitioning, Communication) for producing state-based models satisfying functional requirements and which will be a starting point for generating a concurrent program following the AM last suffix. We have described a general methodology for developing correct by construction concurrent algorithms and we have developed a solution specified by a unique event.

7.2   The Distributed Pattern

Section 5 introduces the call-as-event paradigm which is based on an implicit relationship between a procedure/function call and an event. The main idea is to analyse a problem as a pre/post specification which is then refined by a machine corresponding to the simulation of a recursive function or procedure. The class of algorithms is the class of sequential algorithms and there is no concurrent or distributed interpretation of an event. However, an event can be observed in a complex environment. The environment may be active and should be expressed by a set of events which are simulating the environment. Since the systems under consideration are reactive, it means that we should be able to model a service that a system should ensure. For instance, a communication protocol is a service which allows to transfer a file of a process A into a file of a process B.

Figure 4 sketches the distributed pattern. The machine SERVICE is modelling services of the protocol; the machine PROCESS is refining each service considered as an event and makes the (computing) process explicit. The machine COMMUNICATION is defining the communications among the different agents of the possible network. Finally the machine LOCALALGO is localizing events of the protocol. The distributed pattern is used for expressing *phases* of the target distributed algorithm (for instance, requesting mutual exclusion) and to have a separate refinement of each phase. We sketch the service-as-event paradigm as follows. We consider one service. The target algorithm $\mathcal{A}$ is first described by a machine M0 with variables x satisfying the invariant $I(x)$.

The first step is to list the services e $S \mathrel{\widehat{=}} \{s_0, s_1, \ldots, s_m\}$ provided by the algorithm $\mathcal{A}$ and to state for each service s_i a liveness property $P_i \leadsto Q_i$. We characterise by $\Phi_0 \mathrel{\widehat{=}} \{P_0 \leadsto Q_0, P_1 \leadsto Q_1, \ldots, P_m \leadsto Q_m\}$. We add a list of safety properties defined by $\Sigma_0 = \{Safety_0, Safety_1, \ldots, Safety_n\}$. An event is defined for each liveness property and standing for the eventuality of e by a

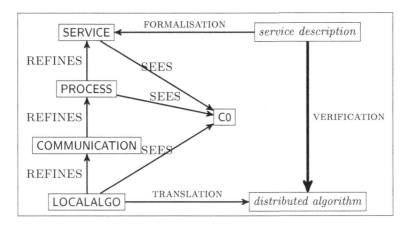

Fig. 4. The distributed pattern

fairness assumption which is supposed on e. Liveness properties can be visualised by assertions diagrams helping to understand the relationship among phases.

The second step is its refinement M1 with variables y glued properties in by $J(x, y)$ using the Event-B refinement and using the REF refinement which is defined using the temporal proof rules for expanding liveness properties. $P \rightsquigarrow Q$ in Φ_0 is proved from a list of Φ_1 using temporal rules. For instance, $P \rightsquigarrow Q$ in Φ_0 is then refined by $P \rightsquigarrow R, R \rightsquigarrow Q$, if $P \rightsquigarrow R, R \rightsquigarrow Q \vdash P \rightsquigarrow Q$. If we consider C as the context and M as the machine, C, M satisfies $P \rightsquigarrow Q$ and C, M satisfies $\Box Safety$. We use a temporal semantics relating contexts, machines and properties [30]. The link called LIVE expresses the satisfaction relationship. The next diagram is summarising the relationship among models.

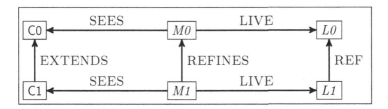

Liveness properties can be gathered in *assertions diagrams* which are already used for the recursive pattern in Fig. 2. For instance, $P \xrightarrow{e} Q$ means that

- $\forall x, x' \cdot P(x) \wedge I(x) \wedge BA(e)(x, x') \Rightarrow Q(x')$
- $\forall x \cdot P(x) \wedge I(x) \Rightarrow (\exists x' \cdot BA(e)(x, x'))$
- $\forall f \neq e \cdot \forall x, x' \cdot P(x) \wedge I(x) \wedge BA(f)(x, x') \Rightarrow (P(x') \vee Q(x'))$

$P \xrightarrow{e} Q$ expresses implicitly that tyhe event e is under weak fairness. Each liveness property $P_i \rightsquigarrow Q_i$ in Φ_0 is modelled by an event:

$$\textbf{EVENT } e_i \ \hat{=} \ \textbf{WHEN } P_i(x) \ \textbf{THEN } x : |Q_i(x') \ \textbf{END}$$

We can add some fairness assumption over the event:

- $P_i \xrightarrow{e_i} Q_i$ with weak fairness on e $(WF_x(e_i))$,
- $P_i \xRightarrow{e_i} Q_i$, with strong fairness on e $(SF_x(e_i))$.

If we consider the leader election protocol [3], we have the following elements:

- **Sets:** ND (set of nodes).
- **Constants:** g is acyclic and connected $(acyclic(g) \wedge connected(g))$.
- **Variables:** $x = (sp, rt)$ (sp is a spanning tree of g).
- **Precondition):**
  $P(x) \ \hat{=} \ sp = \varnothing \wedge rt \in ND$
- **Postcondition:** $Q(x) \ \hat{=} \ spanning(sp, rt, g)$

We can express the main liveness property: $(sp = \varnothing \wedge rt \in ND) \leadsto spanning(sp, rt, g)$ and we define the machine $\mathsf{Leader_0}$ satisfying the liveness property:

$$
\boxed{
\begin{array}{l}
\textbf{EVENT } \text{election}_0 \ \hat{=} \\
\quad \textbf{BEGIN} \\
\qquad sp, rt : |spanning(sp', rt', g) \\
\quad \textbf{END}
\end{array}
}
$$

$$\mathsf{C_0} \xleftarrow{\quad \text{SEES} \quad} \mathsf{Leader_0} \xrightarrow{\quad \text{LIVE} \quad} (WF_x(\text{election}_0), \{P \leadsto Q\})$$

We have introduced the service specification which should be refined separately from events of the machine $M0$. The next refinement should first introduce details of a computing process and then introduce communications in a very abstract way. The last refinement intends to localise the events. The model LOCALALGO is in fact an expression of a distributed algorithm. A current work explores the DistAlgo programming language as a possible solution for translating the local model into a distributed algorithm. Liu et al. [25] have proposed a language for distributed algorithms, DistAlgo, which is providing features for expressing distributed algorithms at an abstract level of abstractions. The DistAlgo approach includes an environment based on Python and managing links between the DistAlgo algorithmic expression and the target architecture. The language allows programmers to reason at an abstract level and frees her/him from architecture-based details. According to experiments of authors with students, DistAlgo improves the development of distributed applications. From our point of view, it is an application of the coordination paradigm based on a given level of abstraction separating the concerns.

7.3   Applying the Distributed Pattern

The distributed pattern (Fig. 4) is applied for the famous *sliding window protocol*. The *service description* is expressing that a process P is sending a file IN to a process Q and the received file is stored in a variable OUT. The service is simply expressed by the liveness property $(at(P, s) \wedge IN \in 0..n \rightarrow D) \rightsquigarrow (at(Q, r) \wedge OUT = IN)$ and the event **EVENT** communication $\hat{=}$ **WHEN** $at(P, s) \wedge IN \in 0..n \rightarrow D$ **THEN** $OUT := IN$ **END** is defining the service. $at(P, s)$ means that P is at the sending statement called s and $at(Q, r)$ means that Q is at the receiving statement r. The context C0 and the machine SERVICE are defined in Fig. 4. The next step is to decompose the liveness property using one of the possible inference rules of the temporal framework as transitivity, induction, confluence of the *leadsto* operatior. In this configuration, we have to introduce the computation process which is simulating the protocol. Obviously, we use and induction rule to express that te file *IN* is sent item per item and we introduce sending and receiving events and the sliding events. In the new machine PROTOCOL, variables are OUT, i, chan, ack, got and satisfied the following invariant:

INVARIANTS
$inv1 : OUT \in \mathbb{N} \nrightarrow D$
$inv2 : i \in 0 .. n + 1$
$inv3 : 0 .. i - 1 \subseteq dom(OUT) \wedge dom(OUT) \subseteq 0 .. n$
$inv7 : chan \in \mathbb{N} \nrightarrow D$
$inv8 : ack \subseteq \mathbb{N}$
$inv9 : got \subseteq i .. i + l \cap 0 .. n$
$inv10 : got \subseteq \mathbb{N}$
$inv12 : dom(chan) \subseteq 0 .. i + l \cap 0 .. n$
$inv13 : got \subseteq dom(OUT)$
$inv14 : ack \subseteq dom(OUT)$
$inv16 : 0 .. i - 1 \lhd OUT = 0 .. i - 1 \lhd IN$
$inv17 : chan \subseteq IN$
$inv18 : OUT \subseteq IN$
$inv19 : ack \subseteq 0 .. i + l \cap 0 .. n$

Name	Total	Auto	Inter
isola-swp	124	101	23
C0	1	1	0
SERVICE	4	2	20
PROCESS	63	51	12
WINDOW	19	13	6
BUFFER	21	18	3
LOCAL	16	16	0

The variable *got* is simulating a window identified by the values between i and i+l in the variables chan, got and ack. The sliding window is in fact defined by the variable i which is sliding or incrementing, when the value OUT(i) is received or equivalently when *iinack*. The events are send, receive, receiveack, sliding together with events which are modelling possible loss of messages. The machine PROCESS is simulating the basic mechanism of the sliding window protocol and is expressing the environment of the protocol. The next refinement WINDOW is introducing an explicit *window* variable satisfying the invariant $w \in \mathbb{N} \nrightarrow D \wedge w \subseteq chan \wedge dom(w) \subseteq i..i+l$. The events are enriched by guards and actions over the variable *window*. The *window* variable is still an abstract view of the window which is contained in a buffer b. The buffer b is introduced in the refinement called BUFFER. The new variable b is preparing the localisation and introduced the explicit communications: $b \in 0..l \nrightarrow D \wedge \forall k \cdot k \in dom(b) \Rightarrow i + k \in dom(w) \wedge b(k) = w(i + k) \wedge \forall h \cdot h \in dom(w) \Rightarrow h - i \in dom(b) \wedge w(h) = b(h - i)$. The visible variables of the machine are OUT, i, chan, ack, got, w and b and in the next refinement, we obtain a local modle called LOCAL with OUT, i, chan, ack, got and b: the window is not part of the implementation of the protocol. The events are localised by hiding the variable w and the final model can now be transformed into the Sliding Window Protocol. The proof obligations summary shows that proof obligations for the machine PROCESS correspond to the main effort of proof, when the induction is introduced. However, we have not checked the liveness properties using the temporal proof system namely TLA and it remains to be effectively supported by the toolbox for TLA/TLA$^+$. We use the temporal proof rules to as guidelines for decomposing liveness properties while we are refining events in Event-B. The technique has been already used for developing population protocols [30].

8   Conclusion and Perspectives

The refinement-based modelling technique combines modelling and proving through discharging proof obligations. Our contribution is to assist anyone who wants to obtain a completely checked Event-B project for a given problem with less toil. The toil is related to the use of the RODIN platform. The tool is a real and useful proof companion but it requires a specific skill in proof development.

Following the ideas of Pólya, we enrich the library of patterns for providing guidelines for defining fully proved Event-B models, when considering problems to solve defined by explicit inductive definitions. The iterative pattern (Fig. 1) is not defining the solution of the problem and it requires to prove that the computed term of the sequence is satisfying the postcondition. In our example, we have to prove the property $v(n) = n^2$ which is the key of the verification process with the definition of an invariant. The iterative pattern gives a very general invariant which should be improved for the specific problem. The summary of proof obligations shows that the refinement helps in the proof process. The proof of the property $v(n) = n^2$ is probably the most complicated task and the user is focusing on this main question. The invariants of the Event-B models can be reused in the verification using Frama-C, for instance, and the verification of the resulting algorithm is a confirmation of the translation.

The recursive pattern (Fig. 3) gives also a different way to discover the invariant and to discharge generated proof obligations. It improves the proof process as well as the definition of the invariant which is a reformulation of the inductive definition. The relationship between the iterative invariant and the recursive invariant is to explicit but a perspective is to have an effective process for deriving the iterative invariant from the recursive invariant. The motivation is to help in the definition of iterative solution. Another choice was to prove that the translation of a recursive solution into an iterative solution is correct and we used this argumentation in our paper in the call-as-event technique [29].

The call-as-event paradigm (Fig. 3) is generalised by the service-as-event paradigm which is based on a correspondence between temporal *leadsto* operator and events. The idea is to generalise the notion of call by the notion of service which is more appropriate for modelling distributed applications. The idea is based on the use of a graph of assertions (see Fig. 2 for the recursive pattern). Such a graph is close to the proof lattice of Owicki and Lamport [32] and we have developed self-⋆ systems using these diagrams and the service-as-event paradigm [5]. The Event-B models contain both events corresponding to the system under development. and the environment. When considering the service-as-event paradigm, liveness properties play the role of guidelines for refining machines.

Archives of Event-B projects are available at the following link http://eb2all.loria.fr and are used by students of the MsC programme at Université de Lorraine and Telecom Nancy. The mechanization of the liveness part should be done and is part of the perspectives. The distributed pattern can be adapted for given computation models as we have done for the local computation model [19]. Finally, the translation from Event-B models into a distributed algorithm should be improved and we plan to explore distributed programming languages with a high level of abstraction as for instance DistAlgo [25].

References

1. Abrial, J.-R.: Modeling in Event-B: System and Software Engineering. Cambridge University Press, Cambridge (2010)
2. Abrial, J.-R., Butler, M.J., Hallerstede, S., Hoang, T.S., Mehta, F., Voisin, L.: Rodin: an open toolset for modelling and reasoning in Event-B. STTT **12**(6), 447–466 (2010)
3. Abrial, J.-R., Cansell, D., Méry, D.: A mechanically proved and incremental development of IEEE 1394 tree identify protocol. Formal Asp. Comput. **14**(3), 215–227 (2003)
4. Ameur, Y.A., Méry, D.: Making explicit domain knowledge in formal system development. Sci. Comput. Program. **121**, 100–127 (2016)
5. Andriamiarina, M.B., Méry, D., Singh, N.K.: Analysis of self-* and P2P systems using refinement. In: Ait Ameur, Y., Schewe, K.D. (eds.) ABZ 2014. LNCS, vol. 8477, pp. 117–123. Springer, Heidelberg (2014). https://doi.org/10.1007/978-3-662-43652-3_9
6. Andriamiarina, M.B., Méry, D., Singh, N.K.: Revisiting snapshot algorithms by refinement-based techniques. Comput. Sci. Inf. Syst. **11**(1), 251–270 (2014)
7. Back, R.J.R.: On correct refinement of programs. J. Comput. Syst. Sci. **23**(1), 49–68 (1979)
8. Back, R.J.R.: A calculus of refinements for program derivations. Acta Inform. **25**, 539–624 (1988). https://doi.org/10.1007/BF00291051
9. Bjorner, D.: Software Engineering 1 Abstraction and Modelling; Software Engineering 2 Specification of Systems and Languages; Software Engineering 3 Domains, Requirements, and Software Design. Texts in Theoretical Computer Science. An EATCS Series. Springer, Heidelberg (2006). https://doi.org/10.1007/3-540-31288-9
10. Bjorner, D.: Software Engineering 2 Specification of Systems and Languages. Texts in Theoretical Computer Science. An EATCS Series. Springer, Heidelberg (2006). ISBN 978-3-540-21150-1
11. Bjorner, D.: Software Engineering 3 Domains, Requirements, and Software Design. Texts in Theoretical Computer Science. An EATCS Series. Springer, Heidelberg (2006). https://doi.org/10.1007/3-540-33653-2. ISBN 978-3-540-21151-8

12. Bjørner, D.: Domain analysis & description - the implicit and explicit semantics problem. In: Laleau, R., Méry, D., Nakajima, S., Troubitsyna, E. (eds.) Proceedings Joint Workshop on Handling IMPlicit and EXplicit Knowledge in Formal System Development (IMPEX) and Formal and Model-Driven Techniques for Developing Trustworthy Systems (FM&MDD). Electronic Proceedings in Theoretical Computer Science, Xi'an, China, 16 November 2017, vol. 271, pp. 1–23. Open Publishing Association (2018)

13. Cansell, D., Paul Gibson, J., Méry, D.: Formal verification of tamper-evident storage for e-voting. In: Fifth IEEE International Conference on Software Engineering and Formal Methods (SEFM 2007), 10–14 September 2007, London, England, UK, pp. 329–338. IEEE Computer Society (2007)

14. Carriero, N., Gelernter, D.: A computational model of everything. Commun. ACM **44**(11), 77–81 (2001)

15. Cheng, Z., Méry, D., Monahan, R.: On two friends for getting correct programs - automatically translating event B specifications to recursive algorithms in rodin. In: Margaria, T., Steffen, B. (eds.) ISoLA 2016, Part I. LNCS, vol. 9952, pp. 821–838. Springer, Cham (2016). https://doi.org/10.1007/978-3-319-47166-2_57

16. Clearsy System Engineering. Atelier B (2002). http://www.atelierb.eu/

17. Clearsy System Engineering. BART (2010). http://tools.clearsy.com/tools/bart/

18. Dolev, S.: Self-Stabilization. MIT Press, Cambridge (2000)

19. Fakhfakh, F., Tounsi, M., Mosbah, M., Méry, D., Kacem, A.H.: Proving distributed coloring of forests in dynamic networks. Comput. Sist. **21**(4), 863–881 (2017)

20. Foster, I.T.: Designing and Building Parallel Programs - Concepts and Tools for Parallel Software Engineering. Addison-Wesley, Reading (1995)

21. Gamma, E., Helm, R., Johnson, R., Vlissides, J.: Design Patterns - Elements of Reusable Object-Oriented Software. Addison-Wesley, Reading (1994)

22. Hoang, T.S., Fürst, A., Abrial, J.-R.: Event-B patterns and their tool support. Softw. Syst. Model. **12**(2), 229–244 (2013)

23. Jones, C.B.: Tentative steps toward a development method for interfering programs. ACM Trans. Program. Lang. Syst. **5**(4), 596–619 (1983)

24. Lamport, L.: The temporal logic of actions. ACM Trans. Program. Lang. Syst. **16**(3), 872–923 (1994)

25. Liu, Y.A., Stoller, S.D., Lin, B.: From clarity to efficiency for distributed algorithms. ACM Trans. Program. Lang. Syst. **39**(3), 12:1–12:41 (2017)

26. Marquezan, C.C., Granville, L.Z.: Self-* and P2P for Network Management - Design Principles and Case Studies. Springer Briefs in Computer Science. Springer, Heidelberg (2012). https://doi.org/10.1007/978-1-4471-4201-0

27. Méry, D.: Refinement-based guidelines for algorithmic systems. Int. J. Softw. Inform. **3**(2–3), 197–239 (2009)

28. Méry, D.: Playing with state-based models for designing better algorithms. Future Gener. Comp. Syst. **68**, 445–455 (2017)

29. Méry, D., Monahan, R.: Transforming event B models into verified c# implementations. In: Lisitsa, A., Nemytykh, A.P. (eds.) First International Workshop on Verification and Program Transformation, VPT 2013. EPiC Series in Computing, Saint Petersburg, Russia, 12–13 July 2013, vol. 16, pp. 57–73. EasyChair (2013)

30. Méry, D., Poppleton, M.: Towards an integrated formal method for verification of liveness properties in distributed systems: with application to population protocols. Softw. Syst. Model., 1–33 (2015)

31. Owicki, S., Gries, D.: An axiomatic proof technique for parallel programs I. Acta Inform. **6**, 319–340 (1976)

32. Owicki, S.S., Lamport, L.: Proving liveness properties of concurrent programs. ACM Trans. Program. Lang. Syst. **4**(3), 455–495 (1982)
33. Pólya, G.: How to Solve It. Doubleday, Garden City (1957)
34. The Frama-C Development Team. Frama-C. CEA. https://frama-c.com/

Modular, Correct Compilation
with Automatic Soundness Proofs

Dominic Steinhöfel$^{(\boxtimes)}$(iD) and Reiner Hähnle(iD)

Department of Computer Science, TU Darmstadt, Darmstadt, Germany
{steinhoefel,haehnle}@cs.tu-darmstadt.de

Abstract. Formal verification of compiler correctness requires substantial effort. A particular challenge is lack of modularity and automation. Any change or update to the compiler can render existing proofs obsolete and cause considerable manual proof effort. We propose a framework for automatically proving the correctness of compilation rules based on simultaneous symbolic execution for the source and target language. The correctness of the whole system follows from the correctness of each compilation rule. To support a new source or target language it is sufficient to formalize that language in terms of symbolic execution, while the corresponding formalization of its counterpart can be re-used. The correctness of translation rules can be checked automatically. Our approach is based on a reduction of correctness assertions to formulas in a program logic capable of symbolic execution of *abstract* programs. We instantiate the framework for compilation from Java to LLVM IR and provide a symbolic execution system for a subset of LLVM IR.

1 Introduction

Writing correct programs is hard. All the more painful it is, when a program with semantically correct source code does not execute as expected due to a compiler bug. Happily, this is not a common experience to programmers. Still, commonly used compilers, like any complex software product, *do* contain bugs [12]; and for safety-critical settings, one might just not want to take the chance. Testing compilers can only show the presence, but not the absence of bugs. A more ambitious undertaking is the construction of a *verified compiler*, as carried out in the CompCert project [13], Jinja [10] or the more recent CakeML [18]. In these approaches, the compiler is programmed in the executable language fragment of an interactive proof assistant and proven correct relative to a mechanized semantics of the source and target language. Such interactive approaches involve a significant amount of work for the construction of proof scripts alone (44% of all code in CompCert [13], for example). In addition, it is not easy to keep proofs modular in the sense that arguing the correctness of compilation of one language

This work was funded by the Hessian LOEWE initiative within the Software-Factory 4.0 project.

T. Margaria and B. Steffen (Eds.): ISoLA 2018, LNCS 11244, pp. 424–447, 2018.
https://doi.org/10.1007/978-3-030-03418-4_25

assgnPVTransl

$$\frac{(\mathcal{U} \circ (\texttt{x} := \texttt{y}), C, \pi\ \omega \dashv\!\vdash q^n)@(obs)}{(\mathcal{U}, C, \pi\ \texttt{x=y;}\ \omega \dashv\!\vdash \left(q \lhd_n \begin{pmatrix} \texttt{\%0 = load i32, i32* \%y} \\ \texttt{store i32 \%0, i32* \%x} \end{pmatrix}\right)^{(n)})@(obs)}$$

Fig. 1. Translation rule for a variable assignment

construct is not dependent on another. Here we lay down a theoretical framework of a *modular*, verified compilation approach that avoids these issues: (1) In compiler verification, local changes to syntax or semantics of source or target language as well as to compilation rules, are likely to affect the correctness proof globally. We avoid this by a rule-driven approach wherein local changes are confined to a single rule. (2) Proofs in assistants like Coq and Isabelle/HOL are mostly interactive. When adding support for new source elements or another front- or backend, new interactive proofs have to be constructed for the translation and existing ones might have to be adapted. In our rule-driven approach it is sufficient to *add* new rules whose correctness proofs, moreover, are automatic.

The paper is structured as follows. Next we give an informal overview of our approach. In Sect. 3, we introduce our logical foundation and Symbolic Execution semantics. Section 4 presents our formalization of a subset of LLVM IR. Central definitions and correctness properties of translation rules, as well as example rules for translation of Java to LLVM IR, are given in Sect. 5. In Sect. 6, we describe how to handle loops. Finally, we discuss related work in Sect. 7 and present a conclusion and outlook in Sect. 8.

2 Overview

Our approach is based on Symbolic Execution (SE) [5]. The compiler is defined by a set of translation rules, each of which realizes *simultaneous* SE of an aspect of the source and target language. An example of a rule assgnPVTransl for variable assignment is shown in Fig. 1. The rule expresses that the highlighted code fragments in Java and LLVM IR have the same *effect* (on a symbolic set of observable variables *obs*), namely setting the value of variable x to the value of y in an existing (symbolic) store $\mathcal{U}$. An alternative interpretation is that the Java fragment can be compiled in a behavior-preserving manner to the LLVM IR fragment. Compilation works in two phases: We symbolically execute the source program, then apply translation rules to the resulting Symbolic Execution Tree in a leaves-to-root manner to obtain the compiled program. Besides the high modularity of our system due to its rule-based nature, an important advantage is that we can prove the correctness of rules like assgnPVTransl *automatically*. Prerequisite is a formalization of the source *and* the target language in terms of SE rules.[1] The program fragments occurring in translation rules are typically *abstract*, because they contain placeholders for subprograms (e.g., the guard and

---

[1] Compiler verification with interactive proof assistants requires this as well, even separate formalizations for the target and source languages.

body of an `if` statement), as well as premises with assumptions about them. We obtain correctness results for translation rules by reflecting correctness assertions to a program logic capable of symbolically executing the *abstract* source and target programs of a rule. The resulting assertions can be proven by an automatic program verifier.

The logical basis of our approach is a new formalization of SE for abstract programs based on a notion of concretization and a definition of soundness of SE transition relations. We instantiate our framework for compilation from Java to LLVM IR. This choice is motivated by the following considerations: For Java, we can build on a mature SE system based on Java Dynamic Logic (JavaDL) [1] which suits our needs very well. LLVM IR [11] is the intermediate language of the state-of-the-art LLVM optimizing compilation framework, which is employed in a variety of commercial and open source products as well as academic research prototypes. The language comes with attractive properties: it is typed and uses an unbounded number of temporary registers instead of a stack. Finally, as far as we know, there is no compiler from Java to LLVM IR currently maintained.

Extending our compiler framework, for example, with a new target language, is achieved by providing that language's formalization in terms of SE rules (which, as a byproduct, can also be used for different purposes, such as program verification). The compilation rules defined below are proven without assistance. The compiler is, therefore, *correct-by-construction*. Our main contribution is a theoretical framework consisting of (1) a semantic foundation for SE of abstract programs, (2) a new, partial formalization of LLVM IR, and (3) theoretical results about proving the correctness of translation rules, illustrated by the compilation of Java to LLVM IR.

3   Program Logic and Symbolic Execution

Symbolic Execution [5] is a popular static program analysis technique that treats inputs to a program as abstract symbols. Whenever the execution depends on the concrete value of a symbolic variable, it performs a case distinction, following each possible branch individually. The outcome is a Symbolic Execution Tree (SET) whose root is labeled with the program under execution. Inner nodes are constructed by individual SE steps. The version of SE used in this paper consists of a static symbolic interpreter embedded in a logical framework—Dynamic Logic (DL): an extension of typed first-order logic for expressing assertions about program behavior, inspired by features of JavaDL [1, Chap. 3], a DL for Java.

The principles of our logic are general enough to be re-used for different languages, such as C# or Java bytecode. The translation rule in Fig. 1 highlights a central concept of our logic: The assignment of the variable y to x corresponds to a state *update* x := y. Updates describe state changes resulting from symbolic program execution. *Elementary* updates x := t syntactically represent the state changes where the variable x attains the value of the term t. Updates can be combined to *parallel* updates x := t_1 || y := t_2, and be *applied* to terms, formulas and other updates. We write $\{\mathcal{U}\}t$ for the application of $\mathcal{U}$ to term t.

Semantically, t is evaluated in the state represented by $\mathcal{U}$. The "empty update" is denoted by *Skip*. Our term language contains conditional terms; for instance, $(if\,(\mathtt{i} > \mathtt{j})\,then\,(\mathtt{i})\,else\,(\mathtt{j})) \geq 0$ means that the maximum of $\mathtt{i}$ and $\mathtt{j}$ is positive.

The semantics of our logic is based on a *valuation function* $val\,(K, \sigma|\cdot)$, where K is a structure and σ a concrete program state. The set of all concrete states σ assigning domain values to (program) variables is denoted by $\mathcal{S}_{concr}$. The valuation function assigns to *formulas* a truth value "true" or "false". We write $K, \sigma \models \varphi$ for $val\,(K, \sigma|\varphi) = \text{true}$ (similarly for $K, \sigma \not\models \varphi$). To *terms*, it assigns a value of the domain of the term, to *updates* a state transformer $\mathcal{S}_{concr} \rightarrow \mathcal{S}_{concr}$ and to *programs* a function $\mathcal{S}_{concr} \rightarrow 2^{\mathcal{S}_{concr}}$, where the output, for deterministic programs, is the empty set if the program does not terminate, or a singleton otherwise. A term domain we often use is that of booleans, which consists of the values TRUE and FALSE; we employ a function $for2bool(\varphi) := if\,(\varphi)\,then\,(\text{TRUE})\,else\,(\text{FALSE})$ to convert formulas to booleans. As an example for the valuation of an update, consider "$\mathtt{x} := \mathtt{y}$": The result of the valuation $val\,(K, \sigma|\mathtt{x} := \mathtt{y})\,(\sigma')(\mathtt{z})$ is either $\sigma(\mathtt{y})$, if $\mathtt{z} = \mathtt{x}$, or $\sigma'(\mathtt{z})$ otherwise.

For formulating assertions about program behavior, DL contains *modalities*: A formula $[p]\varphi$ expresses the partial correctness property that *if* p terminates, then the formula φ holds. Semantically, $val\,(K, \sigma|[p]\varphi)$ evaluates to true if for each $\sigma' \in val\,(K, \sigma|p)\,(\sigma)$, it holds that $val\,(K, \sigma'|\varphi) = \text{true}$. For full details on JavaDL for Java and complete definitions, we refer to [1]. Here we focus on the aspects of the logic that are specific to LLVM IR and SE: An LLVM IR program $q^{(n)}$ is an instruction list with an *instruction pointer* $n \in \mathbb{Z}$. If the pointer is omitted, we assume the default "0" pointing to the first instruction in the list. If n is negative or exceeds the number of instructions in q, the program has already been exited and its valuation is the identity function; this corresponds to an "empty" program for Java. We also write "$-$" in this case (for both languages).

The nodes of an SET are *symbolic execution states* $(\mathcal{U}, C, p)$ consisting of a *symbolic store* $\mathcal{U}$, a *path condition* C and a *program counter* p. In our framework, $\mathcal{U}$ is an update, C a set of quantifier-free formulas; p can either be a Java program $\pi\,stmt\,\omega$ or an LLVM IR program $q^{(n)}$ with instruction pointer as defined above. In case of Java, the *active statement* $stmt$ of a program is the next to be executed. The *prefix* π contains opening braces, labels etc., and ω the remaining program.

We use the associative operator $\mathcal{U}_1 \circ \mathcal{U}_2 := \mathcal{U}_1 \,||\, \{\mathcal{U}_1\}\mathcal{U}_2$ for combining sequential updates. SE aims to transform a program p into a set of states with empty program counters. The symbolic stores and path conditions of these states then together describe the effect of p. Consider the (Java) SE state $(\mathtt{y} := \mathtt{z}, \emptyset, \mathtt{x} = \mathtt{y};)$, which is in a single SE step transformed into $(\mathtt{y} := \mathtt{z} \circ \mathtt{x} := \mathtt{y}, \emptyset, -)$. By definition of $\circ$, this equals $(\mathtt{y} := \mathtt{z} \,||\, \{\mathtt{y} := \mathtt{z}\}(\mathtt{x} := \mathtt{y}), \emptyset, -)$, which can be simplified to $(\mathtt{y} := \mathtt{z} \,||\, \mathtt{x} := \mathtt{z}, \emptyset, -)$. With $\mathbb{S}_{SE}$ we denote the set of all SE states, Upd is the set of updates and Fml^{qf} the set of quantifier-free formulas. Semantically, an SE state represents (possibly infinitely many) concrete states. Given a concrete initial state, we can *concretize* a *symbolic* execution state to a *concrete* state.

The union of all those *concretizations* for all concrete initial states provides us with a complete description of the semantics of an SE state.

Definition 1 (Concretization Function). *The* concretization function *concr* : $\mathbb{S}_{SE} \times \mathcal{S}_{concr} \rightarrow 2^{\mathcal{S}_{concr}}$ *maps an SE state* $(\mathcal{U}, C, p) \in \mathbb{S}_{SE}$ *and a concrete state* $\sigma \in \mathcal{S}_{concr}$ *(1) to* $\emptyset$ *if* $K, \sigma \not\models C$, *and else (2) to the set* $val\,(K, val\,(K, \sigma|\mathcal{U})\,(\sigma)|p)\,(\sigma)$ *(which, as Java is deterministic, is either a singleton if* p *terminates, or empty).*

Example 1. The Java program in the SE state $s = (Skip, \emptyset, \texttt{if (x<0) x=-x;})$ computes the absolute value of variable x. The leaves of the corresponding SET are $(Skip, \{x \geq 0\}, \_)$ and $(x := -x, \{x < 0\}, \_)$. Intuitively, s represents all concrete states where x has a positive value. Given $\sigma \in \mathcal{S}_{concr}$ with $\sigma(x) = -17$, $concr(s, \sigma)$ is the singleton set of a state mapping x to 17 and all other variables to their values in σ. For each $\sigma' \in \bigcup_{\sigma \in \mathcal{S}_{concr}} concr(s, \sigma)$ it holds that $\sigma'(x) \geq 0$.

An *SE transition relation* $\delta \subseteq \mathbb{S}_{SE} \times \mathbb{S}_{SE}$, which defines how to obtain SETs of SE states, in our framework is composed of a set of *restricted* SE rules. The restriction is that each rule may only add to (and not remove or alter) the symbolic stores (by update concatenation) and path conditions (by set union). The resulting programs are not syntactically restricted.

A sound SE step has to transform programs into corresponding changes in the symbolic store, as in the Java part of the rule assgnPVTransl in Fig. 1: The assignment x=y is transformed into an update $x := y$ that leaves the concretizations of the state unchanged. Case distinctions have to be *exhaustive* and *disjoint*. A rule for an `if` statement creates two states. In the first, the guard is added to the path condition, and the program counter contains the *then* part; in the second, the path condition contains the *negation* of the guard, and the program counter the *else* part. A concrete state satisfying the path condition of the initial SE state will *either* satisfy the path condition of the first *or* the second successor, since it satisfies the guard or its negation, but not both. The following formal definition for the soundness of SE transition relations uses three projection functions, $\cdot_{store}$, $\cdot_{path}$ and $\cdot_{pc}$, to obtain the symbolic store, path condition and program counter of an SE state. Subsequently, we assume SE transition relations to be sound.

Definition 2 (Soundness of Symbolic Execution). *An SE transition relation* $\delta \subseteq \mathbb{S}_{SE} \times \mathbb{S}_{SE}$ *is called* sound *iff (1) for each input-output pair* $(i, o) \in \delta$ *and* $\sigma \in \mathcal{S}_{concr}$ *with* $K, \sigma \models o_{path}$, *it holds that* $concr(i, \sigma) = concr(o, \sigma)$, *and (2) for each* $i \in \mathbb{S}_{SE}$ *for which there is an outgoing transition in* δ, *and* $\sigma \in \mathcal{S}_{concr}$ *with* $K, \sigma \models i_{path}$, *there is* exactly one $o \in \mathbb{S}_{SE}$ *such that* $(i, o) \in \delta$ *and* $K, \sigma \models o_{path}$.

To handle placeholders in translation rules, we introduce *abstract programs*, which contain symbols $\widehat{P}$ from a set *AbsP* of abstract program symbols. Each $\widehat{P}$ represents an *equivalence class* of programs with the same effect. To formally define SE of abstract programs we use *abstract block contracts* that generalize the concept of *abstract operation contracts* [4,7]. A *block contract* for a code block bl is a pair $(\mathcal{U}_{bl}^a, C_{bl})$, where $\mathcal{U}_{bl}^a$ is an update representing the assignable clause of bl ($\mathcal{U}_{bl}^a$ assigns fresh constants to variables assigned in the block, and similarly anonymizes the heap), and C_{bl} is a set of formulas representing bl's postcondition. An SE application of the block contract rule transforms SE state $(\mathcal{U}, C, bl; \ p)$ to $(\mathcal{U} \circ \mathcal{U}_{bl}^a, C \cup \{\{\mathcal{U}_{bl}^a\}C_{bl}\}, p)$, which is sound provided that bl respects its contract. While in the block contract rule bl is a concrete program and $(\mathcal{U}_{bl}^a, C_{bl})$ a concrete contract, *abstract* contracts admit *placeholders* in post conditions and assignable clauses. We lift SE to *abstract execution*, because now, in addition, bl can be an abstract program symbol $\widehat{P}$:

Definition 3 (Abstract Execution). *Let $C_{\widehat{P}}, \mathcal{U}_{\widehat{P}}^a$ be fresh Skolem constants representing unknown postconditions and assignable clauses. Abstract execution transforms SE state of the form $(\mathcal{U}, C, \widehat{P}\ p)$ to $(\mathcal{U} \circ \mathcal{U}_{\widehat{P}}^a, C \cup \{\{\mathcal{U}_{\widehat{P}}^a\}C_{\widehat{P}}\}, p)$.*

```
1 %1 = load i32, i32* %x ; <label>:0
2 %2 = icmp slt i32 %1, 0
3 br i1 %2, label %3, label %6
4 %4 = load i32, i32* %x ; <label>:3
5 %5 = sub nsw i32 0, %4
6 store i32 %5, i32* %x
7 br label %6
8 ; ...                    ; <label>:6
```

Listing 1: Absolute of variable x

Observation 1. *Abstract execution of $\widehat{P}$ with the block contract rule is sound: any substitution of a concrete code block bl^c for bl, a concrete post condition C_{bl}^c for C_{bl}, and a concrete update $\mathcal{U}_{bl}^c$ for $\mathcal{U}_{bl}^a$, where bl^c respects C_{bl}^c and $\mathcal{U}_{bl}^c$, yields a sound concrete SE transition.*

Example 2. Consider the Java SE state $(i := 0, \emptyset, \widehat{P}\ i\text{=}17;)$ containing the abstract program $\widehat{P}$ as active statement. Abstract execution of $\widehat{P}$ results in $((i := 0) \circ \mathcal{U}_{\widehat{P}}^a, C_{\widehat{P}}, i\text{=}17;)$, which evaluates to $((i := 0) \circ \mathcal{U}_{\widehat{P}}^a \circ (i := 17), C_{\widehat{P}}, -)$. We can further simplify this state to $(\mathcal{U}_{\widehat{P}}^a \circ (i := 17), C_{\widehat{P}}, -)$ since i is overwritten in the last update. Based on the execution result, we can prove the assertion that i is 17 after each execution of the abstract program (we ignore the possibility of thrown exceptions for this example). This corresponds to showing the validity of the DL formula $\{i := 0\}[\widehat{P}\ i\text{=}17;]i \doteq 17$, which simplifies to $C_{\widehat{P}} \rightarrow \{\mathcal{U}_{\widehat{P}}^a \circ (i := 17)\}i \doteq 17$ after SE, and further to $C_{\widehat{P}} \rightarrow \{i := 17\}i \doteq 17$, which is true. A possible concrete substitution for the abstract elements is $\widehat{P} := (x\text{=}12; y\text{=}0;)$, $C_{\widehat{P}} := \{x \doteq 12\}$ and $\mathcal{U}_{\widehat{P}}^a := (x := c_x \,\|\, y := c_y)$ for fresh c_x, c_y.

4 Formalizing LLVM IR

LLVM IR [11] is a typed, low-level, SSA-based, RISC-like virtual instruction set. Unlike most RISC instruction sets, LLVM does not have a fixed set of named registers and a stack, but an *infinite set of temporaries* %0, %1, etc. which have to be assigned sequentially. Named registers %x, %y etc. can also be introduced. In our model, named registers represent program variables in the Java sense. LLVM IR code is structured into *basic blocks*, sequences of instructions ending in one terminator instruction (like a branch or return). If a basic block does not have an explicit label, it is assigned the next free temporary register as label. Labelling instructions *within* a basic block is not possible, only the start of a basic blocks can be a jump target. Listing 1 shows an LLVM IR program computing the absolute of a 32-bit integer variable (**i32**) x, whose address is contained in register %x. The first **load** instruction loads the value at address %x into register %1. The **icmp slt** ("signed less than") instruction compares the result with 0, setting %2 to 1 (i.e., TRUE) iff x is negative. Line 3 performs a case distinction via a labeled **br** instruction: If the bit (**i1**) in register %2 is 1 (the result of the comparison is that x is negative), the program continues with the code inverting x at label %3. Otherwise, we directly skip to the end of the program at label %6. In line 4, the program again loads the value of x, which is at line 5 subtracted (**sub**) from 0 (the **nsw** stands for "no signed wrap"). The **store** instruction at line 6 stores the result of that subtraction (the inverted, now positive variable x) at address %x; the unconditional **br** instruction at line 7 causes the start of a new basic block at line 8. Comments start with a semicolon. The comments in the listing indicate the implicit label registers: their type is a jump address.

We define a *statement injection function* $\triangleleft_n$: The result of $q \triangleleft_n q'$ is a program where at the n-th position of q, the program q' has been inserted, such that the first instruction of q' is the n-th in the result. The function updates temporary registers to maintain their sequential order. Figure 2 shows some SE rules for LLVM IR. They are read bottom-up like sequent calculus rules. The rules IlvmStoreInt and IlvmLoadBool illustrate the treatment of named vs. anonymous registers. For instance, a **store** instruction writing the value at register %i into *address* %x is executed by setting the *variable* x to the value %i in the symbolic store and incrementing the instruction pointer (the **load** of a boolean works similarly). Rule IlvmLtComp executes a less-than comparison of the contents of two registers %k and %l. The boolean expression $for2bool(\%k < \%l)$ evaluates to TRUE iff the formula $\%k < \%l$ evaluates to true. In those three rules, SE amounts to extending the update and increasing the instruction pointer by one. Rule IlvmCondBreakUnrestr is an example for a *branching* rule (we omit the—straightforward—unconditional variant). Since the value of %i is in general symbolic (and might be TRUE *or* FALSE), we perform a case distinction, following the possible branches independently. In the first case, we assume that %i is TRUE and continue at the position n_1 of the then-label %j, and analogously in the second case. For programs with backjumps, i.e. $n_i < n$, SE might not terminate, because of this rule. In Sect. 6 we introduce a method for handling loops which ensures termination.

$$\text{llvmStoreInt} \quad \frac{(\mathcal{U} \circ (\mathtt{x} := \%i), C, (q \lhd_n (\mathtt{store\ i32\ \%i,\ i32*\ \%x}))^{(n+1)})}{(\mathcal{U}, C, (q \lhd_n (\mathtt{store\ i32\ \%i,\ i32*\ \%x}))^{(n)})}$$

$$\text{llvmLoadBool} \quad \frac{(\mathcal{U} \circ (\%i := \mathtt{x}), C, (q \lhd_n (\%i\ \mathtt{=\ load\ i1,\ i1*\ \%x}))^{(n+1)})}{(\mathcal{U}, C, (q \lhd_n (\%i\ \mathtt{=\ load\ i1,\ i1*\ \%x}))^{(n)})}$$

llvmLtComp
$$\frac{(\mathcal{U} \circ (\%i := \mathit{for2bool}(\%k < \%l)), C, (q \lhd_n (\%i\ \mathtt{=\ icmp\ sle\ i32\ \%k,\ \%l}))^{(n+1)})}{(\mathcal{U}, C, (q \lhd_n (\%i\ \mathtt{=\ icmp\ sle\ i32\ \%k,\ \%l}))^{(n)})}$$

llvmCondBrUnrestr
$$\frac{\begin{array}{c}(\mathcal{U}, C \cup \{\%i \doteq \mathrm{TRUE}\}, (q \lhd_n (\mathtt{br\ i1\ \%i,\ label\ \%j,\ label\ \%k}))^{(n_1)}) \\ (\mathcal{U}, C \cup \{\%i \doteq \mathrm{FALSE}\}, (q \lhd_n (\mathtt{br\ i1\ \%i,\ label\ \%j,\ label\ \%k}))^{(n_2)})\end{array}}{(\mathcal{U}, C, (q \lhd_n (\mathtt{br\ i1\ \%i,\ label\ \%j,\ label\ \%k}))^{(n)})}$$

where n_1 and n_2 are the positions of the labels $\%j$ and $\%k$, respectively.

Fig. 2. Some LLVM IR SE rules

5   Program Translation

We follow the approach of *rule-based compilation* [2,3] and additionally base our system on *heavyweight symbolic execution* [17]. The advantages of rule-based over monolithic systems consist of a higher degree of abstraction and better modularity [3]. The latter not only increases reusability, but is also instrumental in defining the modular correctness notion of our framework. The basics of our compilation process were already sketched in earlier work [9]: First we symbolically execute the source program, and then apply to the resulting SET, starting from its leaves, a set of translation rules. The result is set consisting of *dual SE states*, each of which contains equivalent programs in the source and target language. The root of the tree contains the compiled program. Our rules are not mere transformation rules, but rules for *simultaneous symbolic execution*, where each element of the source language is associated with an SE rule. In the following we establish basic notions for simultaneous SE and state the main result for proving the correctness of translation rules. Then we exemplarily define some rules for the translation from Java to LLVM IR and illustrate our approach along the translation of an `if` statement.

Definition 4 (Dual SE States and Transition Relations). *Given an update* $\mathcal{U}$, *a path condition* C, *a Java program* p *and an LLVM IR program* $q^{(n)}$, *and a set of observable variables obs, we call the triple* $(\mathcal{U}, C, p \Vdash q^{(n)})@(obs)$ *a dual symbolic execution state. The set of all dual SE states is denoted by* $\mathbb{S}^{d}_{SE}$. *A Dual SE Transition Relation (DSETR) is a relation* $\delta^{d} \subseteq \mathbb{S}^{d}_{SE} \times \mathbb{S}^{d}_{SE}$.

We call a dual SE state *valid* if the source and target program have the same *observable semantics* in the states defined by the symbolic store and path condition, i.e. their concretizations coincide on the observable variables. Formally:

ruleName

$$(\mathcal{U} \circ \mathcal{U}_1, C \cup C_1, p_1 \dashv\!\!\vdash q^{(n_1)})@(obs_1)$$

$$\cdots$$

$$\frac{(\mathcal{U} \circ \mathcal{U}_m, C \cup C_m, p_m \dashv\!\!\vdash q^{(n_m)})@(obs_m)}{(\mathcal{U}, C, p \dashv\!\!\vdash q^{(n)})@(obs_1 \cup \cdots \cup obs_m)}$$

Fig. 3. Schematic translation rule

Definition 5 (Validity of Dual SE States). *A dual SE state* $(\mathcal{U}, C, p \dashv\!\!\vdash q^{(n)})@(obs)$ *is valid iff the concretizations of* $s_p = (\mathcal{U}, C, p)$ *and* $s_q = (\mathcal{U}, C, q^{(n)})$ *coincide on all* $pv \in obs$, *i.e.* p *and* $q^{(n)}$ *either both do not terminate, or they terminate and, where* $\sigma \in \mathcal{S}_{concr}$ *such that* $K, \sigma \models C$, *and* σ_p *and* σ_q *are the concrete states in the singleton sets* $concr(s_p, \sigma)$ *and* $concr(s_q, \sigma)$, $\sigma_p(pv) = \sigma_q(pv)$.

Definition 6 (Soundness of DSETRs). *A DSETR* δ^{d} *is sound iff the validity of each dual SE state* i *is implied by the validity of* all *of its output states, i.e. of all states in* $\{o : (i, o) \in \delta^{\mathrm{d}}\}$.

This definition of soundness of DSETRs is suitable to ensure that SE rules preserve validity (read "top-down"). Together, Definitions 5 and 6 imply: if, starting from a dual SE state $s = (\mathcal{U}, C, p \dashv\!\!\vdash q^{(n)})@(obs)$ and by applying a sound DSETR, we can derive a set of final states that all have the form $(\mathcal{U}', C', \_ \dashv\!\!\vdash\_)@(obs')$ for some $\mathcal{U}'$, C' and obs', then s is valid, which means that the programs p and $q^{(n)}$ have the same observable effects when started in a state satisfying $\mathcal{U}$ and C.

A DSETR can be defined in terms of rules for elements of the input programming languages. Hence, soundness of the resulting DSETR can be established by checking whether all *rules* meet the requirement of Definition 6. Figure 3 shows a schematic representation of such a rule. It can be viewed in two ways. First, as a rule for simultaneous symbolic execution, which is read "bottom-up": We transform the dual SE state in the conclusion to simpler states until the programs have been fully executed. Second, as a translation rule: Program p can be translated to program $q^{(n)}$ (relative to $\mathcal{U}, C$), where both programs may be abstract. The requirements on the placeholders and the corresponding symbolic stores $\mathcal{U}_i$ and path conditions C_i are defined in the premises. Figure 3 also illustrates the restrictions we impose on dual SE rules, which correspond to those of their non-dual counterparts: Symbolic stores and path conditions may only be *extended*, but not altered otherwise ($\mathcal{U}$ and C are still present in all premises).

According to Definition 6, a translation rule is proved sound by showing p and $q^{(n)}$ have the same observable semantics in the symbolic store $\mathcal{U}$ and path condition C, under the assumption that this holds for all p_i, $q^{(n_i)}$ in $\mathcal{U} \circ \mathcal{U}_i$, $C \cup C_i$. A trivial and useless way to prove soundness is by stipulating $obs_i := \emptyset$, however, in general we want to show program equivalence for non-trivial obs. A *semantic* soundness argument is either informal or else is very hard to automate (based on a formalization of the semantics of both input programming languages). We suggest a practical alternative, based on the assumption that we have sound SE systems for the source and target language at our disposal. The main idea is to

assgnPVTransl

$$\frac{(\mathcal{U} \circ (\text{x} := \text{y}), C, \pi\ \omega \Vdash q^n)@(obs)}{(\mathcal{U}, C, \pi\ \text{x=y; } \omega \Vdash \left(q \vartriangleleft_n \begin{pmatrix} \text{\%0 = load i32, i32* \%y} \\ \text{store i32 \%0, i32* \%x} \end{pmatrix}\right)^{(n)})@(obs)}$$

ItCompTransl

$$\frac{(\mathcal{U} \circ (\text{b} := \text{x} < \text{y}), C, \pi\ \omega \Vdash q^n)@(obs)}{(\mathcal{U}, C, \pi\ \text{b=x<y; } \omega \Vdash \left(q \vartriangleleft_n \begin{pmatrix} \text{\%0 = load i32, i32* \%x} \\ \text{\%1 = load i32, i32* \%y} \\ \text{\%2 = icmp sle i32 \%0, i32 \%1} \\ \text{store i1 \%2, i1* \%b} \end{pmatrix}\right)^{(n)})@(obs)}$$

ifElseTransl

$$\frac{\begin{array}{c}(\mathcal{U}, C \cup \{b \doteq \text{TRUE}\}, \pi\ \widehat{P_1}\ \omega \Vdash (q \vartriangleleft_n \widehat{P_2})^{(n)})@(obs_1) \\ (\mathcal{U}, C \cup \{b \doteq \text{FALSE}\}, \pi\ \widehat{P_1'}\ \omega \Vdash (q \vartriangleleft_n \widehat{P_2'})^{(n)})@(obs_2)\end{array}}{(\mathcal{U}, C, \pi\ \begin{array}{l}\text{if (b)} \\ \widehat{P_1} \\ \text{else} \\ \widehat{P_1'}\end{array}\ \omega \Vdash \left(q \vartriangleleft_n \left(\begin{pmatrix}\text{\%1 = load i1, i1* \%b} \\ \text{br i1 \%1, label \%2,} \\ \text{\qquad\qquad label \%3} \\ \text{br label \%4; <label>:\%2} \\ \text{br label \%4; <label>:\%3} \\ \text{; <label>:\%4}\end{pmatrix} \begin{array}{l}\vartriangleleft_3 \widehat{P_2'} \\ \vartriangleleft_2 \widehat{P_2}\end{array}\right)\right)^{(n)})@(obs_1 \cup obs_2)}$$

Fig. 4. Some example rules of the DSETR

reflect the validity requirement in Definition 5 into our program logic via *justifying formulas* for dual SE states. Thus, the semantic soundness notion is reduced to a DL *formula* which can be proven valid by automated deductive verification.

Definition 7 (Justifying Formula). *Let* $s = (\mathcal{U}, C, p \Vdash q^{(n)})@(obs)$ *be a dual SE state. For each variable* $\text{x} \in obs$, *let* $p_{\text{x}}^{\text{Sk}}(\text{x})$ *be a fresh unary Skolem predicate symbol uniquely associated with* x. *We define the* justifying formula $F(s)$ *of* s *as*

$$F(s) := \{\mathcal{U}\}\left(\bigwedge C\right) \rightarrow \left(\{\mathcal{U}\}[p](obs') \leftrightarrow \{\mathcal{U}\}[q]^{(n)}(obs')\right),$$

where $obs' := \bigwedge_{\text{x} \in obs}(p_{\text{x}}^{\text{Sk}}(\text{x}))$.

Proposition 1. *A dual state* $s \in \mathbb{S}_{SE}^{d}$ *is valid iff its justifying formula is valid.*

Figure 4 shows rules for variable assignment (the introductory example), less-than comparison, and if statement. Consider rule ifElseTransl. If we know how to translate $\widehat{P_1}$ given that the guard b is true, and likewise for $\widehat{P_1'}$, we can define the translation for an *arbitrary* if statement.

For practical application of Definition 7 in soundness proofs of a translation rule we have to decide how to handle the abstract parts of the rule that are only instantiated with concrete elements when translating a concrete program. The abstract parts are (1) the context information, i.e. the current symbolic store $\mathcal{U}$ and path condition C, as well as the program contexts $\pi\ \omega$ and q, (2) the sets of observable variables, and (3) abstract program placeholders.

Regarding (1), since $\mathcal{U}$ and C are present in both the conclusion *and* in the premisses of rules, because of the restrictions imposed on translation rules (cf. Fig. 3), we can simply omit them in justifying formulas. Java program contexts are treated as abstract program symbols. For LLVM IR, we introduce an additional simplification technique: Consider the modality $[q \lhd_n q']^{(n+n')}$, where n' is the number of instructions in q'. It can be simplified to $[q]^{(n)}$, since (i) the program q' has already been processed, and (ii) our approach to loop compilation ensures that back jumps exit the modality (see Sect. 6). After this simplification, q in $[q]^{(n)}$ can be handled as an abstract program symbol.

Regarding (2), we over-approximate observable variable sets by introducing fresh constant symbols $p_{obs_i}^{\text{Sk}}(\bar{x})$ for each symbolic set obs_i, which accept as arguments the program variables $\bar{x}$ occurring in any state involved in the rule (observable variable sets are generally assumed not to contain anonymous LLVM IR registers). A straightforward representation of a union $obs_1 \cup obs_2$ is the disjunction $p_{obs_1}^{\text{Sk}}(\bar{x}) \vee p_{obs_2}^{\text{Sk}}(\bar{x})$. We choose instead the more precise representation of *guarded conjunctions*: Each obs_i is associated to a dual SE state with branch condition C_i. Since our semantic framework for SE stipulates that branch conditions are exhaustive and mutually exclusive, there is always exactly one conjunct of the guarded conjunction $((\bigwedge C_1) \to p_{obs_1}^{\text{Sk}}(\bar{x})) \wedge ((\bigwedge C_2) \to p_{obs_2}^{\text{Sk}}(\bar{x}))$ that is valid in a concrete state. Finally, we assume that abstract block contracts are oblivious to anonymous LLVM IR registers, i.e. contract path conditions $C_{\widehat{p}}$ for abstract program symbols do not contain anonymous LLVM IR registers.

Remark 1. Programs p and $q^{(n)}$ might change program variables occurring in path conditions C_i, which is why guarded conjunctions as defined above do not work in general. This issue can be easily addressed by introducing fresh program variables that record the pre-state of all variables in the C_i. To keep the presentation readable, we avoid this technicality by assuming that program variables in path conditions are unchanged.

The subsequent theorem stipulates a generalized notion of justifying formulas instantiated for translation rules, taking into account the above considerations. Essentially, it is a syntactic representation of Definition 6 based on Proposition 1: A translation rule is sound if the conjunction of the generalized justifying formulas of the output states (the rule's premises) implies the formula for the input state (the conclusion). For brevity, we write C instead of $\bigwedge C$ for path conditions.

Theorem 1. *A translation rule with premises $pr_1, \ldots, pr_m$ and conclusion c is sound if the formula* $\left(\bigwedge_{i=1,\ldots,m} F'(pr_i) \right) \to F'(c)$ *is valid. We define F' as*

$$F'((\mathcal{U} \circ \mathcal{U}', C \cup C', \pi\, p\, \omega \dpl (q \lhd_n q')^{(n')})@(obs)) :=$$

$$\left(\{\mathcal{U}'\}C' \to \left(\{\mathcal{U}'\}[\pi\, p\, \omega](obs') \leftrightarrow \{\mathcal{U}'\}[q \lhd_n q']^{(n')}(obs') \right) \right),$$

where $obs' := p_{obs}^{\text{Sk}}(\bar{x})$ if obs is a single placeholder; and, if obs is a union of symbols obs_i arising from premises pr_i with path conditions C_i, $obs' := \bigwedge_i(C_i \to p_{obs_i}^{\text{Sk}}(\bar{x}))$. The predicates $p_{obs}^{\text{Sk}}(\bar{x})$ are fresh, uniquely associated with each obs, and $\bar{x}$ are all program variables occurring in $\mathcal{U}_i$, C_i of any pr_i.

Example 3 (Soundness of ifElseTransl*).* To prove rule ifElseTransl sound, by Theorem 1 it suffices to prove the following formula valid (we abbreviate the program in the LLVM IR part of the conclusion with dots):

$$(\mathtt{b} \doteq \mathrm{TRUE} \rightarrow ([\pi \, \widehat{P_1} \, \omega](p^{\mathrm{Sk}}_{obs_1}(\mathtt{b})) \leftrightarrow [q \lhd_n \widehat{P_2}]^{(n)}(p^{\mathrm{Sk}}_{obs_1}(\mathtt{b})))) \wedge \quad (1)$$

$$(\mathtt{b} \doteq \mathrm{FALSE} \rightarrow ([\pi \, \widehat{P_1'} \, \omega](p^{\mathrm{Sk}}_{obs_2}(\mathtt{b})) \leftrightarrow [q \lhd_n \widehat{P_2'}]^{(n)}(p^{\mathrm{Sk}}_{obs_2}(\mathtt{b})))) \quad (2)$$

$$\rightarrow \qquad (([\pi \, \mathtt{if} \, (\mathtt{b}) \, \widehat{P_1} \, \mathtt{else} \, \widehat{P_1'} \, \omega]) \qquad\qquad (3)$$

$$((\mathtt{b} \doteq \mathrm{TRUE} \rightarrow p^{\mathrm{Sk}}_{obs_1}(\mathtt{b})) \wedge (\mathtt{b} \doteq \mathrm{FALSE} \rightarrow p^{\mathrm{Sk}}_{obs_2}(\mathtt{b})))) \leftrightarrow$$

$$([q \lhd_n (((\cdots) \lhd_3 \widehat{P_2'}) \lhd_2 \widehat{P_2})]^{(n)} \qquad\qquad (4)$$

$$((\mathtt{b} \doteq \mathrm{TRUE} \rightarrow p^{\mathrm{Sk}}_{obs_1}(\mathtt{b})) \wedge (\mathtt{b} \doteq \mathrm{FALSE} \rightarrow p^{\mathrm{Sk}}_{obs_2}(\mathtt{b})))))$$

We first define some abbreviations. Let, for $k = 1, 2$,

$$pre_1^k := \quad C_{\widehat{P_1}} \wedge \{\mathcal{U}^a_{\widehat{P_1}}\} C_{\pi\omega} \rightarrow \quad \{\mathcal{U}^a_{\widehat{P_1}} \circ \mathcal{U}^a_{\pi\omega}\}(p^{\mathrm{Sk}}_{obs_k}(\mathtt{b}))$$

$$pre_2^k := \quad C_{\widehat{P_2}} \wedge \{\mathcal{U}^a_{\widehat{P_2}}\} C^a_q \rightarrow \quad \{\mathcal{U}^a_{\widehat{P_2}} \circ \mathcal{U}^a_q\}(p^{\mathrm{Sk}}_{obs_k}(\mathtt{b}))$$

and $\overline{pre}_i^k$ similarly for $\widehat{P_i'}$ instead of $\widehat{P_i}$. Treating $\pi\omega$ and q as abstract programs and simplifying $[q \lhd_n \widehat{P_2}]^{(n+1)}$ to $[q]^{(n)}$ as explained above, SE of the modalities in premise (1) by Definition 3 results in pre_i^1, and for (2) in $\overline{pre}_i^2$, $i = 1, 2$. We obtain

$$\mathtt{b} \doteq \mathrm{TRUE} \rightarrow (pre_1^1 \leftrightarrow pre_2^1) \quad (1\mathrm{se})$$

$$\mathtt{b} \doteq \mathrm{FALSE} \rightarrow (\overline{pre}_1^2 \leftrightarrow \overline{pre}_2^2) \quad (2\mathrm{se})$$

The if statement in formula (3) causes SE to split. The "then" branch, in which $\widehat{P_1}$ is executed, evaluates to

$$\mathtt{b} \doteq \mathrm{TRUE} \rightarrow \big(C_{\widehat{P_1}} \wedge \{\mathcal{U}^a_{\widehat{P_1}}\} C_{\pi\omega} \rightarrow$$

$$(\{\mathcal{U}^a_{\widehat{P_1}} \circ \mathcal{U}^a_{\pi\omega}\}((\mathtt{b} \doteq \mathrm{TRUE} \rightarrow p^{\mathrm{Sk}}_{obs_1}(\mathtt{b})) \wedge (\mathtt{b} \doteq \mathrm{FALSE} \rightarrow p^{\mathrm{Sk}}_{obs_2}(\mathtt{b})))))$$

Due to the premise $\mathtt{b} \doteq \mathrm{TRUE}$, the right conjunct of the guarded conjunction simplifies to true and can be removed, and similarly for the "else" branch of the if statement. Therefore, formula (3) simplifies to

$$\mathtt{b} \doteq \mathrm{TRUE} \rightarrow pre_1^1 \wedge \mathtt{b} \doteq \mathrm{FALSE} \rightarrow \overline{pre}_1^2 \quad (3\mathrm{se})$$

SE of (4) similarly splits and produces two conjuncts. Again, we focus on the "then" branch where the dots abbreviate the guarded conjunctions of $p^{\mathrm{Sk}}_{obs_i}(\mathtt{b})$:

$$(\{\%1 := \mathtt{b}\}(\%1 \doteq \mathrm{TRUE}) \rightarrow (\{\%1 := \mathtt{b}\} C_{\widehat{P_2}} \wedge$$

$$\{(\%1 := \mathtt{b}) \circ \mathcal{U}^a_{\widehat{P_2}}\} C^a_q \rightarrow \{(\%1 := \mathtt{b}) \circ \mathcal{U}^a_{\widehat{P_2}} \circ \mathcal{U}^a_q\}(\cdots)))$$

llvmLoopScopeEnter
$$\frac{(\mathcal{U} \circ \mathcal{U}_{havoc}, C, (q \lhd_n \circlearrowleft_x)^{(n+1)})}{(\mathcal{U}, C, (q \lhd_n \circlearrowleft_x)^{(n)})}$$

llvmLoopScopeExit
$$\frac{(\mathcal{U} \circ (x \doteq \mathrm{TRUE}), C, (q \lhd_{n\ x}\circlearrowleft)^{(n+1)})}{(\mathcal{U}, C, (q \lhd_{n\ x}\circlearrowleft)^{(n)})}$$

llvmLoopScopeCont
$$\frac{(\mathcal{U} \circ (x := \mathrm{FALSE}), C, \_\,)}{\left(\mathcal{U}, C, \left(q \lhd_n \left(\left(\begin{array}{c}\circlearrowleft_x \\ \texttt{br label } \%i \\ \texttt{br label } \%j \\ {}_x\circlearrowleft\end{array}; \texttt{label } \%i \begin{array}{c}\lhd_3\ q_2 \\ \lhd_2\ q_1\end{array}\right)\right)^{(n')}\right)\right)} \quad (*)$$

where $(*)$ n' points to the position of the second **br** statement, and $\%i$ is the label for the basic block indicated by the comment (starting after the first **br**).

Fig. 5. LLVM IR loop scope rules

The crucial difference to the Java part consists in the update $\%1 := \mathtt{b}$ resulting from loading the value of $\mathtt{b}$ into the anonymous register $\%1$. We have to perform a further simplification step. Generally, we can drop an update $\mathcal{U}_1$ in a formula $\{\mathcal{U}_1 \circ \mathcal{U}_2\}\varphi$ if φ does not contain any left-hand side of $\mathcal{U}_1$, and $\mathcal{U}_2$ does not contain as right-hand side any left-hand side of $\mathcal{U}_1$ [1, Chap. 3]. This simplification is applicable here, because we assumed abstract block contracts to be ignorant about anonymous LLVM IR registers: Formula $\{(\%1 := \mathtt{b}) \circ \mathcal{U}^a_{\widehat{P_2}}\}C^a_q$ is simplified to $\{\mathcal{U}^a_{\widehat{P_2}}\}C^a_q$, because $\%1$ does not appear in $C_{\widehat{P_2}}$ and not as a right-hand side in $\mathcal{U}^a_{\widehat{P_2}}$, which only assigns fresh constants (similarly for $\{\%1 := \mathtt{b}\}C_{\widehat{P_2}}$). Formula $\{(\%1 := \mathtt{b}) \circ \mathcal{U}^a_{\widehat{P_2}} \circ \mathcal{U}^a_q\}(\dots)$ is simplified to $\{\mathcal{U}^a_{\widehat{P_2}} \circ \mathcal{U}^a_q\}(\dots)$, because $\mathcal{U}^a_{\widehat{P_2}}, \mathcal{U}^a_q$ do not have $\%1$ as right-hand side. Finally, $\{\%1 := \mathtt{b}\}(\%1 \doteq \mathrm{TRUE})$ simplifies to $\mathtt{b} := \mathrm{TRUE}$. After simplification of the guarded predicates as before, we obtain

$$\mathtt{b} \doteq \mathrm{TRUE} \to pre^1_2 \ \wedge\ \mathtt{b} \doteq \mathrm{FALSE} \to \overline{pre}^2_2 \quad (4\mathrm{se})$$

In summary, we have reduced soundness of ifElseTransl to the following propositional formula, which is a tautology:

$$\begin{aligned}\left(\left(\mathtt{b} \doteq \mathrm{TRUE} \to (pre^1_1 \leftrightarrow pre^1_2)\right)\ \wedge & \quad (1\mathrm{se}) \\ \left(\mathtt{b} \doteq \mathrm{FALSE} \to (\overline{pre}^2_1 \leftrightarrow \overline{pre}^2_2))\right)\ \to & \quad (2\mathrm{se}) \\ \left(\left(\mathtt{b} \doteq \mathrm{TRUE} \to pre^1_1 \wedge \mathtt{b} \doteq \mathrm{FALSE} \to \overline{pre}^2_1\right)\ \leftrightarrow & \quad (3\mathrm{se}) \\ \left(\mathtt{b} \doteq \mathrm{TRUE} \to pre^1_2 \ \wedge \mathtt{b} \doteq \mathrm{FALSE} \to \overline{pre}^2_2\right)\right) & \quad (4\mathrm{se})\end{aligned}$$

□

The soundness proof just sketched is well in the realm of what is automatically provable with a deductive verification system such as KeY [1].

6   Handling of Loops

Symbolic execution of LLVM IR branch instructions and compilation of loops in a manner that ensures termination poses a challenge: Since LLVM IR programs may contain *back-* and forward jumps, SE of branching rules such as llvmCondBrUnrestr (Fig. 2) might diverge. The standard approach to ensure termination in *structured* programming languages uses *loop invariant* rules. Our solution for the unstructured case is based on the more general concept of *loop scopes*, introduced in [17] for Java. A (Java) loop scope statement $\circlearrowleft_x p_x \circlearrowright$ defines a scope for its body p; it has a boolean *index variable* x which is passed to the delimiters $\circlearrowleft_x$ and $_x\circlearrowright$ as a parameter. One can read $\circlearrowleft_x p_x \circlearrowright$ as "execute loop body p in its own scope with continuation information x". Loops are transformed into loop scope statements. Whenever a loop normally would execute a further iteration, SE of the loop scope terminates, and x is set to FALSE. When the loop would be exited, symbolic execution continues after the loop scope, and x is set to TRUE.

We implement this idea for LLVM IR: First, existing rules for jumps, such as llvmCondBreakUnrestr, are restricted to *forward* jumps. Second, we add new rules (Fig. 5) for loop scopes, including one for backward jumps. As there are no explicit loops in LLVM IR, we insert scope delimiters $\circlearrowleft_x, _x\circlearrowright$ at suitable positions. We assume LLVM IR programs correspond to well-formed Java loops.

Rule llvmLoopScopeEnter begins symbolic execution of a loop scope by setting all variables assigned in the scope to fresh constants via an update $\mathcal{U}_{havoc}$, because we cannot know their value during an arbitrary iteration. (In Java, this task is performed by the loop invariant rule.) Rule llvmLoopScopeExit signals that the loop scope has been exited by setting the index variable to TRUE. The only rule applicable to backward jumps is llvmLoopScopeCont. Using the loop scope concept constitutes a restriction of the LLVM IR fragment on which SE is complete; however, that fragment is sufficient for our compilation target.

Rule whileTransl in Fig. 6 is a translation rule for `while` loops based on loop scopes. In the LLVM IR code, "only" the instruction pointer is incremented, corresponding to an execution of the opening loop scope statement. Its structure corresponds closely to the Java part in the premise. It includes a `br` instruction (labelled %5) which is dead due to the translation of the `break` before. It is included to match the output of the rule ifElseTransl (Fig. 4—the removal of dead basic blocks is the task of subsequent simplification steps).

To execute a dual SE state with a loop, we apply whileTransl and ifElseTransl, execute both `if` branches, and finally apply continueLoopScopeTransl as well as breakLoopScopeTransl. We keep the LLVM IR loop scopes in the conclusion of whileTransl for handling the backward jump in the last `br` instruction. In a postprocessing step, loop scopes can safely be dropped: If a program is correct in the restricting presence of loop scopes, it is also sound without. An example for the translation of a factorial method, which contains a loop, is given in the appendix.

whileTransl

$$\dfrac{(\mathcal{U} \circ \mathcal{U}_{havoc}, C, \pi \begin{pmatrix} \circlearrowleft_x \texttt{if } (b) \; \{ \\ \widehat{P_1} \\ \texttt{continue;} \\ \texttt{\} else \{} \\ \texttt{break;} \\ \}_x \circlearrowleft \end{pmatrix} \omega \dashv\vdash \ldots^{(n+2)}) @(obs)}{(\mathcal{U}, C, \pi \;\overset{\texttt{while } (b)}{\underset{\widehat{P_1}}{\rule{0pt}{1.2em}}}\; \omega \dashv\vdash \left(q \lhd_n \left(\begin{pmatrix} \circlearrowleft_x \\ \texttt{br label \%1} \\ \qquad\qquad\texttt{; <label>:\%1} \\ \texttt{\%2 = load i1, i1* \%b} \\ \texttt{br i1 \%2, label \%3,} \\ \qquad\qquad\texttt{label \%4} \\ \texttt{br label \%6 ; <label>:\%3} \\ \texttt{br label \%7 ; <label>:\%4} \\ \texttt{br label \%6 ; <label>:\%5} \\ \texttt{br label \%1 ; <label>:\%6} \\ {}_x\circlearrowleft \qquad\quad\texttt{; <label>:\%7} \end{pmatrix} \lhd_4 \widehat{P_1} \right)^{(n)} \right))@(obs)}$$

where $\mathcal{U}_{havoc}$ is as above. The dots in the premise indicate that LLVM IR instructions there are the same as in the conclusion.

breakLoopScopeTransl

$$\dfrac{(\mathcal{U} \circ (\text{x} := \text{TRUE}), C, \pi \; \omega \dashv\vdash q^{(n)}) @(obs)}{(\mathcal{U}, C, \pi \; \circlearrowleft_x \texttt{break;} \; {}_x\circlearrowleft \; \omega \dashv\vdash \left(q \lhd_n \begin{pmatrix} \circlearrowleft_x \\ \texttt{br label \%1} \\ \texttt{br label \%3 ; <label>:\%1} \\ \texttt{br label \%1 ; <label>:\%2} \\ {}_x\circlearrowleft \qquad\quad \texttt{; <label>:\%3} \end{pmatrix}^{(n+2)} \right))@(obs)}$$

continueLoopScopeTransl

$$\dfrac{(\mathcal{U} \circ (\text{x} := \text{FALSE}), C, \_ \dashv\vdash \_) @(obs)}{(\mathcal{U}, C, \pi \; \circlearrowleft_x \texttt{continue;} \; {}_x\circlearrowleft \; \omega \dashv\vdash \left(q \lhd_n \begin{pmatrix} \circlearrowleft_x \\ \texttt{br label \%1} \\ \texttt{br label \%1 ; <label>:\%1} \\ {}_x\circlearrowleft \end{pmatrix}^{(n+2)} \right))@(obs)}$$

Fig. 6. Translation rules for loops

7   Related Work

Our work takes up the concept of "dual" SE states and SE-based compilation introduced in [8] (see also [9]), where compilation from Java to Bytecode was studied as an application of a program transformation framework. The system proposed there is not based on a formalization of the target language, therefore, the employed correctness notions remain underspecified. We define correctness differently, based on a new semantics for symbolic execution (not depending on a validity calculus) and focus on how to show the correctness of translation rules automatically. For the execution of abstract programs, we generalize abstract operation contracts [4,7] to abstract block contracts. In contrast to the former, where contracts are abstract, but programs are concrete, our blocks may consist of abstract program symbols. This gives rise to the concept of *abstract execution* that permits to reduce a limited second-order inference (no induction, no higher-order quantification) about programs to first-order dynamic logic. The resulting formulas can be proven automatically by a program verifier.

The two most relevant research areas to compare with are: (1) program logics, formal models, and symbolic execution for low-level languages, in particular LLVM IR, and (2) rule-based or certified correct compilation and program transformation. Vellvm [19], implemented in Coq, provides an operational semantics of LLVM IR based on a formalized memory model. The authors name as long-term goal to provide a semantic basis for a fully verified LLVM IR compiler. Our scope is verification of correctness and behavioral equivalence, i.e. of functional and relational properties, which is reflected in our more high-level formalization. In future work, it would be interesting to investigate whether it can be proved with Vellvm that our SE rules faithfully model their LLVM IR semantics. The only (implemented) SE system for LLVM IR we know of is KLEE [6], an automatic tool, mainly aiming at creating high-coverage test suites and unveiling generic errors, such as memory faults. Various program logics for low-level, unstructured programs have been suggested in the literature, for example, in [15]. This results in theoretically complete proof systems, however, it is difficult to come up with suitable intermediate assertions during verification. Since we target *compilation* and not functional verification, it suffices to use schematic intermediate assertions that are built into our rules. We envision an implementation of our SE framework for LLVM IR in a logic-based system like KeY [1], facilitating semi-interactive proofs of complex functional properties of LLVM IR code.

Regarding area (2), Rotan [3] is a rule-based compiler for parallel programs. It features a specialized rule language and puts focus on modularity. We currently only consider sequential programs, but achieve fully automated correctness proofs of our rules. Of great interest is the work on verified compilers. A prominent example is the CompCert project [13], a verified compiler from C to PowerPC assemblies (mostly) written in Coq. CompCert covers all compilation phases including optimization. Its correctness notion, "forward simulation for safe programs", is more flexible than, e.g., bisimulation. Our approach only takes the *outcome* of source and target programs (its big-step semantics) into account, and not *how* it is computed (its small-step semantics). Therefore, our justifying formulas permit more far-reaching optimizations, abstracting away from concrete control flow. To some degree, CompCert follows different goals than our approach. Its extensive formalizations permit meta proofs about programs (e.g., taking into account a realistic memory model), while we only formalize operational semantics and relate source and target. A strength of our approach is its modularity, entailed by its rule-based nature; furthermore, Coq proofs are interactive, whereas our goal is to automate the proofs of the translation rules. A related and noteworthy system which shares our source language Java is Jinja [10], a formalization in Isabelle/HOL of semantics, virtual machine and compiler of a Java-like language including a mechanized proof that the compiler preserves the semantics. This system is also based on an interactive proof assistant and requires manual proof effort. CakeML [18] is a more recent verified compiler for a functional programming language developed in Isabelle/HOL which invests a lot of effort in modularity; still, the backend does not provide automated support for correctness proofs of individual source elements.

For parts of the compilation process, automated solutions exist: One example is Alive [14], a verification/code generation framework for peephole optimizations in LLVM. Within Alive, it is possible to formalize local algebraic simplifications and code optimizations in a restricted DSL, which are then transformed to first-order logic assertions that are passed to an SMT solver. While being automatic, the addressed problem is relatively simple compared to full-fledged compilation.

8   Conclusion and Future Work

We presented a theoretical framework for correct-by-construction, modular rule-based compilation from Java to LLVM IR. The framework is based on a new semantics of Symbolic Execution (SE) and a formalization of the source and target languages in terms of SE rules, which constitutes the trust anchor. For the Java part, we build on Java DL, the mature logical basis of the KeY system [1]. Our new (partial) SE system for LLVM IR is designed to integrate smoothly with it. Translation rules are proven correct automatically by reducing correctness assertions about abstract programs to first-order dynamic logic formulas, which can be fed to an automatic program verifier.

There are several interesting directions for future work which we plan to pursue: We aim to extend an existing formalization of our SE semantics in Coq to our compilation framework, instantiated to a structured, imperative and a simple unstructured language. Our current main focus is the integration of the SE system for at least a subset of LLVM IR into the Java verifier KeY. Based on this, we will construct a compiler for sequential Java realizing the theoretical framework outlined in this paper. Since an SE engine that simplifies away all complex Java constructs and that produces SSA is available in KeY already [1, Chap. 3], this is likely to succeed quickly. KeY's program logic can also deal with complex Java constructs such as method calls, for example, using method frames and non-schematic program transformation rules. Again, these techniques are transferable to LLVM IR compilation. We intend to add a rule-based modular optimization phase, allowing for high-level optimizations exploiting the global knowledge gained by Symbolic Execution. Our correctness notion, which is more general than (bi-)simulation used elsewhere, because it takes the context into account and permits abstract programs, should be adequate for this purpose. Finally, it would be natural to attach our framework as a backend to a refinement-based correct-by-construction tool. This opens the possibility of an "end-to-end" correctness-by-construction approach—from declarative specifications to executable machine code.

Appendix

This appendix provides additional material for the reader, including a sketch of the integration of state merging techniques into our approach, an extended compilation example, and a proof of Theorem 1.

A State Merging

Our SE transition relation defined in Sect. 3 outputs tree structures: all states, but the root, have exactly one predecessor. *State Merging* [16] has originally been invented to mitigate the state explosion problem of SE. It permits to merge symbolic states with identical program counter as arising, for example, after the execution of the then and else branch of an if statement, thus reducing the state space. Definition 2 can be extended to transition relations with state merging by applying the same conditions reversely for "merging" transitions:

$$\text{mergeTransl} \quad \frac{(\mathcal{U}_{merge}, \bigwedge C_1 \vee \bigwedge C_2, p \dashv\vdash q^{(n)})@(obs_1 \cup obs_2)}{\begin{array}{c}(\mathcal{U}_1, C_1, p \dashv\vdash q^{(n)})@(obs_1)\\(\mathcal{U}_2, C_2, p \dashv\vdash q^{(n)})@(obs_2)\end{array}}$$

where $\mathcal{U}_{merge}$ is a merging update.

Fig. 7. State merging translation rule

Definition 8 (Soundness of SE with State Merging). *Let δ_m be an SE transition relation with state merging (some states have more than one predecessor). We call δ_m sound iff the transition relation*

$$\delta' := \{(i,o) \in \delta_m : \neg \exists i' \neq i, (i',o) \in \delta_m\} \cup$$
$$\{(o,i) : (i,o) \in \delta_m \wedge \exists i' \neq i, (i',o) \in \delta_m\}$$

is sound in the sense of Definition 2.

Translation rule mergeTransl (Fig. 7) merges two branches with identical program counters. Without it, compiling programs with branching statements leads to duplicated code, for example, in rule ifElseTransl. The double horizontal line below the rule's premise indicates its special status: it is the only rule with more than one conclusion. For constructing the merged symbolic store, there is more than one option [16]. In the simplest case, we create a fully precise value summary by means of an if-then-else term.

B   Factorial Example

The program in Fig. 8 (p. x) computes the factorial of variable x, contained in variable res after termination. Figure 12 shows the SET of the dual SE states corresponding to the translation of the Java to LLVM IR code. Constructing the tree works by first symbolically executing the Java program. The Java SET has the same structure, without the LLVM IR parts and observable variables sets.

In the second phase, we apply translation rules from the leaves to the root, obtaining the dual SE states. The root of the tree contains the compiled LLVM IR program q_{result} depicted in Fig. 9 (with dropped loop scopes). The tree is slightly simplified: we sometimes abbreviate programs with "..." and combine several translation rules into one, for example, in the translation of Java's i++, which in the course of SE would be simplified to SSA form first. Two subtrees have been factored out for better readability (Figures 10 and 11).

The example also shows an artifact occurring due to our rule-based compilation: The basic block with label %13 is never reached since it is not targeted by jumps, and the block before jumps outside the loop (this is the translation of the break instruction). The instruction has been added because of the general definition of the if translation rule; if the else block did not jump out of the

```int i=1;```	```%i = alloca i32``` ```store i32 1, i32* %i```
```while (```	```br label %1```

``` i < x```	```%b = alloca i1 ; <label>:%1```
	```%2 = load i32, i32* %i```
	```%3 = load i32, i32* %x```
	```%4 = icmp sle i32 %2, %3```
	```store i1 %4, i1* %b```
	```%5 = load i1, i1* %b```
	```br i1 %5, label %6, label %12```

```) {```	``` ; <label>:%6```

```res = res*i;```	```%7 = load i32, i32* %res```
	```%8 = load i32, i32* %i```
	```%9 = mul i32 %7, %8```
	```store i32 %9, i32* %res```

```i++;```	```%10 = load i32, i32* %i```
	```%11 = add i32 %11, 1```
	```store i32 %11, i32* %i```
	```br label %14```
	```br label %15 ; <label>:%12```
	```br label %14 ; <label>:%13```
	```br label %1 ; <label>:%14```

```}```	``` ; <label>:%15```

Fig. 8. Factorial program in Java   **Fig. 9.** Factorial program in LLVM IR

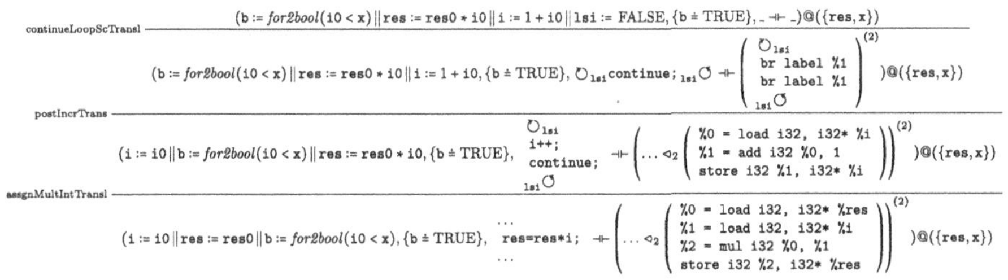

$$\text{continueLoopScTransl} \;\frac{(\texttt{b} := \mathit{for2bool}(\texttt{i0} < \texttt{x}) \,\|\, \texttt{res} := \texttt{res0} * \texttt{i0} \,\|\, \texttt{i} := 1 + \texttt{i0} \,\|\, \texttt{1si} := \texttt{FALSE}, \{\texttt{b} \doteq \texttt{TRUE}\}, \_ \dashv\!\!+ \_)@(\{\texttt{res}, \texttt{x}\})}{(\texttt{b} := \mathit{for2bool}(\texttt{i0} < \texttt{x}) \,\|\, \texttt{res} := \texttt{res0} * \texttt{i0} \,\|\, \texttt{i} := 1 + \texttt{i0}, \{\texttt{b} \doteq \texttt{TRUE}\}, \circlearrowleft_{\texttt{1si}} \texttt{continue};\,_{\texttt{1si}}\circlearrowleft \dashv\!\!+ \left(\begin{array}{l} \circlearrowleft_{\texttt{1si}} \\ \texttt{br label \%1} \\ \texttt{br label \%1} \\ _{\texttt{1si}}\circlearrowleft \end{array} \right)^{(2)})@(\{\texttt{res}, \texttt{x}\})}$$

$$\text{postIncrTrans} \;\frac{(\texttt{i} := \texttt{i0} \,\|\, \texttt{b} := \mathit{for2bool}(\texttt{i0} < \texttt{x}) \,\|\, \texttt{res} := \texttt{res0} * \texttt{i0}, \{\texttt{b} \doteq \texttt{TRUE}\}, \begin{array}{c}\circlearrowleft_{\texttt{1si}} \\ \texttt{i++;} \\ \texttt{continue;} \\ _{\texttt{1si}}\circlearrowleft\end{array} \dashv\!\!+ \dots \vartriangleleft_2 \left(\begin{array}{l} \texttt{\%0 = load 132, 132* \%i} \\ \texttt{\%1 = add 132 \%0, 1} \\ \texttt{store 132 \%1, 132* \%i} \end{array} \right)^{(2)})@(\{\texttt{res}, \texttt{x}\})}{}$$

$$\text{assgnMultIntTransl} \;\frac{}{(\texttt{i} := \texttt{i0} \,\|\, \texttt{res} := \texttt{res0} \,\|\, \texttt{b} := \mathit{for2bool}(\texttt{i0} < \texttt{x}), \{\texttt{b} \doteq \texttt{TRUE}\}, \begin{array}{c}\dots \\ \texttt{res=res*i;} \\ \dots\end{array} \dashv\!\!+ \dots \vartriangleleft_2 \left(\begin{array}{l} \texttt{\%0 = load 132, 132* \%res} \\ \texttt{\%1 = load 132, 132* \%i} \\ \texttt{\%2 = mul 132 \%0, \%1} \\ \texttt{store 132 \%2, 132* \%res} \end{array} \right)^{(2)})@(\{\texttt{res}, \texttt{x}\})}$$

Fig. 10. Subtree "then" for the example tree in Fig. 12

$$\text{breakLoopScopeTransl} \;\frac{(\texttt{i} := \texttt{i0} \,\|\, \texttt{res} := \texttt{res0} \,\|\, \texttt{b} := \mathit{for2bool}(\texttt{i0} < \texttt{x}) \,\|\, \texttt{1si} := \texttt{TRUE}, \{\texttt{b} \doteq \texttt{FALSE}\}, \_ \dashv\!\!+ \_)@(\{\texttt{res}, \texttt{x}\})}{(\texttt{i} := \texttt{i0} \,\|\, \texttt{res} := \texttt{res0} \,\|\, \texttt{b} := \mathit{for2bool}(\texttt{i0} < \texttt{x}), \{\texttt{b} \doteq \texttt{FALSE}\}, \circlearrowleft_{\texttt{1si}} \texttt{break};\,_{\texttt{1si}}\circlearrowleft \dashv\!\!+ \left(\begin{array}{l} \circlearrowleft_{\texttt{1si}} \\ \texttt{br label \%1} \\ \texttt{br label \%3} \\ \texttt{br label \%1} \\ \texttt{; <label>:\%3} \\ _{\texttt{1si}}\circlearrowleft \end{array} \right)^{(2)})@(\{\texttt{res}, \texttt{x}\})}$$

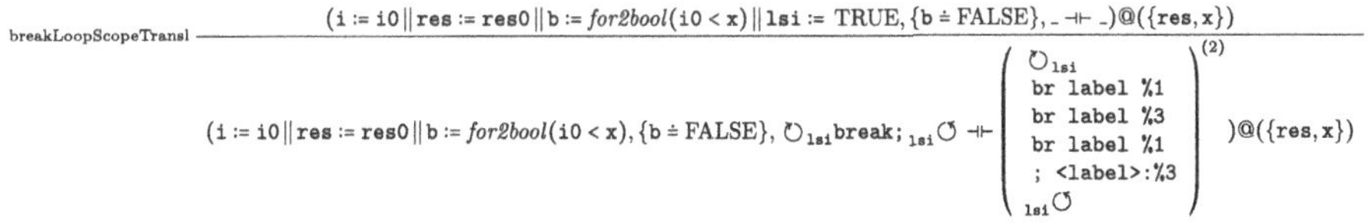

Fig. 11. Subtree "else" for the example tree in Fig. 12

loop, it would also make sense. Removal of such dead code, as well as other optimizations, are subject to subsequent post-processing steps and not within the scope of this paper.

C Proofs

Proof (Theorem 1). We must prove that a translation rule is sound (Definition 6) if $\mathcal{F} = \left(\bigwedge_{i=1,\dots,m} F'(pr_i) \right) \to F'(c)$ is valid. By Proposition 1, a dual SE state is valid iff its justifying formula is valid, and the shape of $\mathcal{F}$ directly encodes Definition 6. Hence, it suffices to show that the validity of justifying formulas $F'(s')$ for *abstract* states s' implies the validity of $F(s)$ for all *concrete instantiations* s of s'. Let $s' = (\mathcal{U}^a \circ \mathcal{U}, C^a \cup C, p_j^{abs} \dashv\!\!+ p_{IR}^{abs})@(obs^a)$ be an abstract SE state where $\mathcal{U}^a$, C^a and obs^a are symbolic and p_j^{abs}, p_{IR}^{abs} contain abstract placeholder symbols. An instantiation s has the shape $(\mathcal{U}' \circ \mathcal{U}, C' \cup C, p_j \dashv\!\!+ p_{IR})@(obs)$, where p_j and p_{IR} result from p_j^{abs} and p_{IR}^{abs} by replacing placeholders with concrete programs. We have to show the following implication:

$$\models (\{\mathcal{U}\}C \to (\{\mathcal{U}\}[p_j^{abs}]obs'_{F'} \leftrightarrow \{\mathcal{U}\}[p_{IR}^{abs}]obs'_{F'})) \qquad \Longrightarrow$$
$$\models (\{\mathcal{U}' \circ \mathcal{U}\}(C' \cup C) \to (\{\mathcal{U}' \circ \mathcal{U}\}[p_j]obs'_F \leftrightarrow \{\mathcal{U}' \circ \mathcal{U}\}[p_{IR}]obs'_F))$$

Since the validity of $\{\mathcal{U}' \circ \mathcal{U}\}(C' \cup C)$ implies the validity of $\{\mathcal{U}\}C$, it suffices to show the following, stronger property:

$$\models ((\{\mathcal{U}\}[p_j^{abs}]obs'_{F'} \leftrightarrow \{\mathcal{U}\}[p_{IR}^{abs}]obs'_{F'})) \Longrightarrow$$
$$\models ((\{\mathcal{U}' \circ \mathcal{U}\}[p_j]obs'_F \leftrightarrow \{\mathcal{U}' \circ \mathcal{U}\}[p_{IR}]obs'_F)) \qquad (*)$$

Since abstract execution is sound (Observation 1), the premise of $(*)$ holds for all concrete contracts substituted for the abstract ones induced by the placeholders in the programs; this means that in particular, we can substitute p_j/p_{IR} for

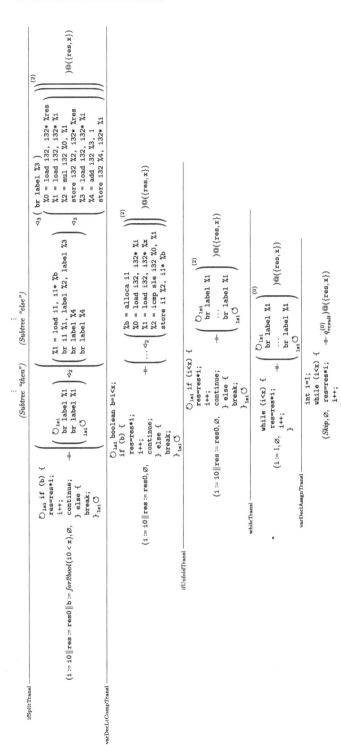

Fig. 12. An example compilation tree (slightly simplified)

p_j^{abs}/p_{IR}^{abs}. Let $\mathcal{U}_{Java}$, $\mathcal{U}_{IR}$ be the updates resulting from SE of the concrete programs (if SE splits, we can obtain summaries by state merging, see Appendix A).

Now there are two possibilities: Either, $obs'_{F'}$ is an atom, or it is a guarded conjunction (and s constitutes the conclusion of a dual SE rule application). We focus on the more complicated second case. Let obs be the (concrete) set of observable variables of s, C_i the path conditions of the premisses of the rule that has s in its conclusion, and $\bar{\mathbf{x}}$ the variables occurring in any symbolic store or path condition of those premisses. Then, after instantiation, (*) expands to:

$$\models (\{\mathcal{U} \circ \mathcal{U}_{Java}\}(\bigwedge_i (C_i \to p_{obs_i}^{Sk}(\bar{\mathbf{x}}))) \leftrightarrow \{\mathcal{U} \circ \mathcal{U}_{IR}\}(\bigwedge_i (C_i \to p_{obs_i}^{Sk}(\bar{\mathbf{x}})))) \implies$$

$$\models (\{\mathcal{U}' \circ \mathcal{U} \circ \mathcal{U}_{Java}\}(\bigwedge_{\mathbf{x} \in obs} p_{\mathbf{x}}^{Sk}(\mathbf{x})) \leftrightarrow \{\mathcal{U}' \circ \mathcal{U} \circ \mathcal{U}_{IR}\}(\bigwedge_{\mathbf{x} \in obs} p_{\mathbf{x}}^{Sk}(\mathbf{x})))$$

Generally, $\bar{\mathbf{x}}$ can contain variables not occurring in obs, due to over-approximation. On the other hand, if obs contains variables not in $\bar{\mathbf{x}}$, those are not in the scope of the currently investigated rule, and are therefore taken out of consideration here.[2] Additionally, we perform a strengthening by dropping the updates $\mathcal{U}'$ in the conclusion (this can be regarded as an abstraction step, since we discharge information). W.l.o.g., consider two different variables $\mathbf{x}$, $\mathbf{y}$ and $obs = \{\mathbf{x}\}$; their right-hand sides in the updates $\mathcal{U} \circ \mathcal{U}_{Java}$ and $\mathcal{U} \circ \mathcal{U}_{IR}$ are $t_{Java}^{\mathbf{x}}$, $t_{IR}^{\mathbf{x}}$, etc. Under the assumption that $\mathbf{x}$ and $\mathbf{y}$ do not occur in the C_i (see Remark 1), the problem simplifies to:

$$\models (\bigwedge_i (C_i \to p_{obs_i}^{Sk}(t_{Java}^{\mathbf{x}}, t_{Java}^{\mathbf{y}})) \leftrightarrow \bigwedge_i (C_i \to p_{obs_i}^{Sk}(t_{IR}^{\mathbf{x}}, t_{IR}^{\mathbf{y}}))) \implies \qquad (\dagger)$$

$$\models (p_{\mathbf{x}}^{Sk}(t_{Java}^{\mathbf{x}}) \leftrightarrow p_{\mathbf{x}}^{Sk}(t_{IR}^{\mathbf{x}})) \qquad (\triangle)$$

For simplicity, we assume that the terms do not contain program variables. The equivalence in $(\triangle)$ is valid iff for all interpretations $\mathcal{I}$, it holds that

$$\mathcal{I}(t_{Java}^{\mathbf{x}}) \in \mathcal{I}(p_{\mathbf{x}}^{Sk}) \iff \mathcal{I}(t_{IR}^{\mathbf{x}}) \in \mathcal{I}(p_{\mathbf{x}}^{Sk}) \qquad (\triangle^{sem})$$

Let $\mathcal{I}_0$ be an arbitrary interpretation; we show that $(\triangle^{sem})$ holds for $\mathcal{I}_0$. All C_i are mutually exclusive due to the restriction built into our semantics (Definition 2), i.e. $C_i \leftrightarrow \bigwedge_{k \neq i} \neg C_k$ for all $i = 1, \ldots, n$. Since $(\dagger)$ is valid, for *any* interpretation $\mathcal{I}$ there is *exactly one* i such that

$$(\mathcal{I}(t_{Java}^{\mathbf{x}}), \mathcal{I}(t_{Java}^{\mathbf{y}})) \in \mathcal{I}(p_{obs_i}^{Sk}) \iff (\mathcal{I}(t_{IR}^{\mathbf{x}}), \mathcal{I}(t_{IR}^{\mathbf{y}})) \in \mathcal{I}(p_{obs_i}^{Sk}) \qquad \dagger^{sem}$$

We choose an interpretation $\mathcal{I}_1$ that (i) interprets $t_{Java}^{\mathbf{x}}$, $t_{IR}^{\mathbf{x}}$ in the same way as $\mathcal{I}_0$, (ii) satisfies $\mathcal{I}_1(p_{obs_i}^{Sk}) = \{(d_1, d_2) : d_1 \in \mathcal{I}_0(p_{\mathbf{x}}^{Sk})\}$ and, at the same time, (iii) satisfies $(\dagger^{sem})$ for some i. By definition of $\mathcal{I}_1$ we have that $(\mathcal{I}_1(t_{Java}^{\mathbf{x}}), \mathcal{I}_1(t_{Java}^{\mathbf{y}})) \in \mathcal{I}_1(p_{obs_i}^{Sk})$ implies $\mathcal{I}_0(t_{Java}^{\mathbf{x}}) \in \mathcal{I}_0(p_{\mathbf{x}}^{Sk})$, and, similarly, for $t_{IR}^{\mathbf{x}}$, $t_{IR}^{\mathbf{y}}$. Hence, $(\triangle^{sem})$ holds in $\mathcal{I}_0$. $\square$

---

[2] When using Theorem 1 to automatically prove the soundness of translation rules with a deductive verification system such as KeY, this aspect can and must be precisely modeled. This can be done by tracking for each abstract program an (abstract) set of variables it depends on.

References

1. Ahrendt, W., Beckert, B., Bubel, R., Hähnle, R., Schmitt, P.H., Ulbrich, M.: Deductive Software Verification - The KeY Book. LNCS, vol. 10001. Springer, Cham (2016). https://doi.org/10.1007/978-3-319-49812-6
2. Augustsson, L.: A compiler for lazy ML. In: Proceedings of LFP 1984. ACM (1984)
3. Breebaart, L.: Rule-based compilation of data parallel programs. Ph.D. thesis, Delft University of Technology (2003)
4. Bubel, R., Hähnle, R., Pelevina, M.: Fully abstract operation contracts. In: Margaria, T., Steffen, B. (eds.) ISoLA 2014. LNCS, vol. 8803, pp. 120–134. Springer, Heidelberg (2014). https://doi.org/10.1007/978-3-662-45231-8_9
5. Burstall, R.M.: Program proving as hand simulation with a little induction. In: Information Processing, pp. 308–312. Elsevier (1974)
6. Cadar, C., Dunbar, D., et al.: KLEE: unassisted and automatic generation of high-coverage tests for complex systems programs. In: 8th USENIX Conference on OSDI, pp. 209–224. USENIX Association, Berkeley (2008)
7. Hähnle, R., Schaefer, I., Bubel, R.: Reuse in software verification by abstract method calls. In: Bonacina, M.P. (ed.) CADE 2013. LNCS (LNAI), vol. 7898, pp. 300–314. Springer, Heidelberg (2013). https://doi.org/10.1007/978-3-642-38574-2_21
8. Ji, R.: Sound program transformation based on symbolic execution and deduction. Ph.D. thesis, Technische Universität Darmstadt (2014)
9. Ji, R., Bubel, R.: Program transformation and compilation. In: Ahrendt, W., Beckert, B., Bubel, R., Hähnle, R., Schmitt, P.H., Ulbrich, M. (eds.) Deductive Software Verification – The KeY Book. LNCS, vol. 10001, pp. 473–492. Springer, Cham (2016). https://doi.org/10.1007/978-3-319-49812-6_14
10. Klein, G., Nipkow, T.: A machine-checked model for a Java-like language, virtual machine, and compiler. ACM Trans. PLS **28**(4), 619–695 (2006)
11. Lattner, C., Adve, V.: LLVM: a compilation framework for lifelong program analysis & transformation. In: Proceedings of CGO 2004, p. 75. IEEE Computer Society (2004)
12. Le, V., Afshari, M., et al.: Compiler validation via equivalence modulo inputs. In: Proceedings of 35th ACM SIGPLAN Conference on PLDI, pp. 216–226. ACM (2014)
13. Leroy, X.: Formal verification of a realistic compiler. Commun. ACM **52**(7), 107–115 (2009)
14. Menendez, D., Nagarakatte, S., Gupta, A.: Alive-FP: automated verification of floating point based peephole optimizations in LLVM. In: Rival, X. (ed.) SAS 2016. LNCS, vol. 9837, pp. 317–337. Springer, Heidelberg (2016). https://doi.org/10.1007/978-3-662-53413-7_16
15. Saabas, A., Uustalu, T.: A compositional natural semantics and Hoare logic for low-level languages. Theor. Comput. Sci. **373**(3), 273–302 (2007)
16. Scheurer, D., Hähnle, R., Bubel, R.: A general lattice model for merging symbolic execution branches. In: Ogata, K., Lawford, M., Liu, S. (eds.) ICFEM 2016. LNCS, vol. 10009, pp. 57–73. Springer, Cham (2016). https://doi.org/10.1007/978-3-319-47846-3_5
17. Steinhöfel, D., Wasser, N.: A new invariant rule for the analysis of loops with nonstandard control flows. In: Polikarpova, N., Schneider, S. (eds.) IFM 2017. LNCS, vol. 10510, pp. 279–294. Springer, Cham (2017). https://doi.org/10.1007/978-3-319-66845-1_18

18. Tan, Y.K., Myreen, M.O., et al.: A new verified compiler backend for CakeML. In: Proceedings of 21st International Conference on Functional Programming, pp. 60–73. ACM (2016)

19. Zhao, J., Nagarakatte, S., et al.: Formalizing the LLVM intermediate representation for verified program transformations. In: Proceedings of 39th ACM SIGPLAN-SIGACT Symposium on POPL, pp. 427–440. ACM (2012)

Deployment by Construction
for Multicore Architectures

Shiji Bijo[1], Einar Broch Johnsen[1(✉)], Ka I Pun[1,2], Christoph Seidl[3],
and Silvia Lizeth Tapia Tarifa[1]

[1] Department of Informatics, University of Oslo, Oslo, Norway
{shijib,einarj,violet,sltarifa}@ifi.uio.no
[2] Western Norway University of Applied Sciences, Bergen, Norway
[3] Technical University of Braunschweig, Braunschweig, Germany
c.seidl@tu-bs.de

Abstract. In stepwise program development, abstract specifications can be transformed into (parallel) programs which preserve functional correctness. Although tackling bad performance after a program's deployment may require a costly redesign, deployment decisions are usually made very late in program development. This paper argues for the introduction of deployment decisions as an integrated part of a development-by-construction process: Deployment decisions should be expressed as part of a program's high-level model and evaluated by how they affect program performance, using metrics at an appropriate level of abstraction. To illustrate such a deployment-by-construction process, we sketch how deployment decisions may be modelled and evaluated, concerning data layout in shared memory for parallel programs targeting shared-memory multicore architectures with caches. For simplicity, we use an abstract metric of data access penalties and simulate data accesses on a memory system which internally ensures data coherency between cores.

1 Introduction

Software development following the correctness-by-construction approach introduces transformation steps to gradually turn abstract, declarative specifications into concrete constructive programs, such that each transformation step preserves the functional correctness of the original specification [23]. This line of work has deep roots in computer science, going back to Dijkstra's Guarded Command language, programming from specifications [1, 26], as well as to work on refinement [6, 25]. While transformations originally focused on strategies such as *divide and conquer*, to introduce *branching* and *recursion*, other transformation steps were developed to introduce *concurrency*, e.g., in the context of Action systems [4, 5] and Unity [13, 14].

A computer system includes not only its (functionally correct) program code but also the *deployment* of this code on, e.g., multicore or distributed hardware.

Supported by *SIRIUS – Centre for Scalable Data Access* (www.sirius-labs.no).

ⓒ Springer Nature Switzerland AG 2018
T. Margaria and B. Steffen (Eds.): ISoLA 2018, LNCS 11244, pp. 448–465, 2018.
https://doi.org/10.1007/978-3-030-03418-4_26

Although the careful planning of deployment is critical, deployment decisions are generally made after design, implementation, and validation (e.g., [20,30]). Deployment decisions affect both data-driven applications and service-oriented scenarios with traffic fluctuations and peaks, typical for parallel software running on distributed cloud or multicore HPC architectures. While "bad deployment" need not affect the functional correctness of software, it may be crucial for its perceived quality, for example in terms of increased runtimes. Tackling performance problems may require considerable changes in design and even impact the requirements level [7]. For example, a program may be tweaked to run more efficiently on parallel on distributed machines by replacing synchronized code with carefully hand-crafted lock-free procedures, just to see its runtime severely increased by unfortunate cache misses. These could be avoided by a different data layout in memory or by reintroducing locks to protect regions of memory.

In this paper, we approach this problem in the context of parallel architectures with shared memory and caches, by providing a formalism to abstractly represent and analyze a program's memory accesses with regard to their impact on runtime behavior, given a set of deployment decisions. We further provide a model-based proof of concept implementation that allows to specify programs in a high-level programming language as well as custom memory layouts for deployment, which are compiled to our formalism. With these contributions, it is possible to model, simulate, analyze and optimize potential interactions of a program and the memory of a chosen deployment architecture *before* deploying (and possibly even writing) the program, which makes the procedure part of the software construction process. Hence, in this paper, we coin the term *Deployment-by-Construction (D-b-C)*.

In summary, the contributions of the paper are as follows:

- We motivate and discuss deployment decisions in the context of D-b-C;
- we illustrate how deploying a parallel program on a shared memory multicore machine with caches could work, seeing the operational model of this machine as a black box from the developer's perspective;
- we extend our framework for data accesses with locks to control exclusive access to data, preserving atomic regions from the source program, and show the correctness for the operational model inside the black box; and
- we provide a proof of concept implementation that allows reducing artifacts of a high-level programming language and a resource model describing memory layouts to our formalization for analysis, simulation and optimization.

2   Deployment-by-Construction: An Overview

This section outlines our D-b-C approach. Consider a toolbox that receives inputs from a software developer (including a high-level *program* describing the functional behavior of the targeted system, a *resource model* specifying the deployment configuration on which the program executes) and returns a performance indicator for the program in terms of *data access penalties*, i.e., a metric to compare the quality of different deployment configurations for a particular program. Figure 1 depicts the abstract model of the D-b-C approach.

To focus on the data access aspect of a given program, we abstract from other aspects of its behavior. In a first phase, each program written in a high-level language, provided by the programmer, is automatically translated into a low-level program, which, together with the deployment configuration of a multicore architecture generated from the provided resource model, serve as inputs to the toolbox. Note that the developer can also provide a low-level program as an input to the toolbox. The developer need not worry about formalizing aspects of deployment which are provided in the actual architecture. In particular, the toolbox handles the communications between different cores and caches in the multicore architecture specified in the generated deployment configuration to ensure consistency of the concurrently existing data. In a second phase, the low-level program is executed and the toolbox returns the corresponding penalties with respect to data access. In the following, we briefly present each component in our D-b-C approach.[1]

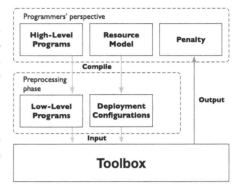

Fig. 1. The components of the deployment-by-construction approach.

High-Level Programming Language (HLP) is a Turing-complete synthetic programming language featuring constructs for variables, assignments, expressions, control flow branching, loops and synchronized execution of parallel calculations. Its purpose is to illustrate basic features of a high-level programming language, which are compiled to LLP (see below) to simulate the effects of program deployment. Details regarding its syntax and semantics are given in Sect. 3.1. In a real-world scenario, languages such as Java or C# could be substituted for HLP without the need to change any of the other components.

Low-Level Programming Language (LLP) is an abstraction from concrete programming instructions to only represent memory accesses. It serves as basis for simulation and analysis but does not have to be written by software developers directly. Details regarding its syntax and semantics are given in Sect. 3.2. Artifacts of LLP are compiled to the toolbox (see below).

Resource Model (RM) is an input format, enabling developers to provide information regarding the number and type of cores in the multicore architecture along with their respective memory layouts. The information contained in RM artifacts is used when compiling to the toolbox (see below) as values for configuration parameters. Details regarding RM are given in Sect. 3.3.

---

[1] The full approach with the different components can be download from: https://github.com/ShijiBijo84/DbC.

```
1  HLP ::= "Program" <String> ["Variables" VariableDeclaration
2    {"," VariableDeclaration} "."] {Task} [Schedule] "End" ".";
3  Schedule ::= "Schedule" "(" <String> {"," <String>} ")" ".";
4  Task ::= "Task" <String> "Variables" VariableDeclaration
5    {"," VariableDeclaration} ".")? Block "End" ".";
6  VariableDeclaration ::= Variable [":=" Value];
7  Variable ::= <String>
8  Block ::= {Statement};
9
10 Statement ::= Assignment | If | For | Synchronized | ExpressionStatement;
11 Assignment ::= Variable ":=" Expression ".";
12 If ::= "If" "(" Condition ")" "Then" Block ["Else" Block] "End" ".";
13 Condition ::= Expression ("=" | "!=" | "<" | "<=" | ">=" | ">") Expression;
14 For ::= "For" Variable ":=" Value ("To" | "Down To") Value "Do" Block "End" ".";
15 Synchronized ::= "Synchronized" "(" Variable {"," Variable} ")" Block "End" ".";
16
17 Expression ::= UnaryExpression | BinaryExpression | ParenthesisExpression;
18 UnaryExpression ::= "-" Expression;
19 BinaryExpression ::= Expression ("+" | "-" | "*" | "/") Expression;
20 ParenthesisExpression ::= "(" Expression ")";
21
22 Value ::= <Integer>;
```

Listing 1.1. Syntax of the High-Level Programming Language (HLP).

Toolbox contains a formalism and operational semantics of LLP that respect the memory configuration provided in the resource model. With the toolbox, it is possible to simulate and compare different deployments of a program or different variations of a program with similar/different deployment decisions to choose the more beneficial configuration. An inside view of the toolbox is provided in Sect. 4.

3   Using the Toolbox: A Practical Modeling Environment for Deployment-by-Construction

A user of our toolbox need not know the details of its construction. To demonstrate this transparency, we now focus on the artifacts relevant for applying D-b-C. (The construction of the toolbox is detailed in Sect. 4.)

3.1   HLP: An Example Programming Language with Parallelism

A plethora of languages may be used to implement functionality for a parallelizable application, also within the C-b-C framework. The artifacts of these languages may be subject to the effects of bad deployment with respect to non-functional properties and negatively impact the execution times as we investigate with our toolbox. We deliberately decided to not limit our approach to a particular programming language, but instead make it suitable for a variety of languages. To demonstrate the use of our toolbox, we have devised a synthetic programming language simply called *High-Level Programming Language (HLP)*, which serves as placeholder for other languages, e.g., Java or C#.

Listing 1.1 provides an overview of the language concepts of HLP in terms of syntax in Extended Backus-Naur Form (EBNF). A high-level program **HLP** has a name, may declare variables and consists of a sequence of tasks and a **Schedule** instruction that may be used to instantiate those tasks. A **Task** is an individual unit, which may be run in parallel to other tasks. It has a name, may declare local variables and provides an implementation consisting of a sequence of program statements. Note that, depending on where they are declared, variables may be either local to a task or global to the program, i.e., available for all tasks and, thus, subject to potential *concurrent accesses*.

HLP provides fairly standard program statements: An **Assignment** associates a variable with a (calculated) value. An **If** statement performs conditional control flow branching with an optional else block. A **For** loop increments/decrements a loop variable to repeat a specific number of times. To deal with concurrency (as in multicore or distributed systems), apart from tasks, HLP offers a **Synchronized** statement similar to that of Java, which allows *intrinsic locking* over a set of variables for a particular block of statements to prohibit concurrent access to these variables. To perform calculations, HLP contains **Expressions**, e.g., for arithmetic operations. For simplicity, all variables in HLP are implicitly of type integer and, thus, **Value** literals may only consist of integers.

Listing 1.2 contains a code snippet covering most aspects of the HLP language. The code consists of three tasks which access shared variables, protected by the **Synchronized** statement. From the functional point of view, there is no race conditions in this example. However, as we will see in Sect. 3.3, an inopportune memory layout may cause race conditions due to the *false sharing* phenomenon [18], in which various variables are allocated in the same memory block as commonly done when allocating arrays.

In a practical application of the toolbox, HLP should be replaced by the respective programming language(s) used to implement functionality (e.g., Java or C#). Due to the structuring of our toolbox, the concepts of the respective programming language just have to be abstracted to data access patterns when compiling to LLP to use the full capabilities of the toolbox.

3.2   LLP: An Abstraction Model for Data Accesses

To get an insight into the impact of deployment decisions for a particular program, it is of utmost importance to analyze the interaction of the program logic with the existing memory structures. To abstract from unnecessary details and specifics of programming languages such as Java or C#, we introduce *Low-Level Programming Language (LLP)* to focus on *data access patterns* of programs in terms of their possible read and write accesses to memory rather than their computation. LLP is generally the target of compilation from HLP (or any other suitable design or programming language) and serves as input for our further analyses and simulation.

Listing 1.3 presents the syntax of LLP in EBNF. A low-level program **LLP** consists of a set of tasks and a main **Block**. Each **Task** has a name and a **Block** with a sequence of data access patterns. A data access pattern **DAP** may take

```
 1  Program Example
 2    Variables x1, x2, x3, y1, y2, y3, z1, z2, z3.
 3
 4    Task T1 Variables i1.
 5      For i1 := 1 To 20 Do
 6        Synchronized(x3) x1 := x3 + 1. End.
 7        Synchronized(y1) y1 := 6. End.
 8        Synchronized(z1, z3) z1 := z3 + 4. End.
 9      End.
10    End.
11
12    Task T2 Variables i2.
13      For i2 := 1 To 30 Do
14        Synchronized(x3) x2 := x3 + 2. End.
15        Synchronized(y1) y2 := y1. End.
16        x2 := 7.
17      End.
18    End.
19
20    Task T3 Variables i3.
21      For i3 := 1 To 50 Do
22        Synchronized(x3) x3 := 5. End.
23        y3 := 1.
24        Synchronized(z1, z3) z3 := z1 + 1. End.
25      End.
26    End.
27
28    Schedule(T1, T2, T3).
29  End.
```

Listing 1.2. Running example: Code snippet in the High-Level Programming Language (HLP).

multiple forms: For input/output operations, it is possible to **Read** and **Write** a memory reference. Memory allocation for local variables is done using **Malloc**. For cached access, **Commit** flushes the contents of the cache line with the given reference, or the entire cache if no reference is given, to main memory. For mutual exclusion, **Lock** and **Unlock** take and release a lock[2], respectively. For control flow, there are instructions for **ControlFlowBranching** (perceived as non-deterministic choice at the abstraction level of LLP), a **Repetition** with a specified number of loops and a standard **Skip** instruction. Finally, there is the option for nesting with **Parentheses** and dynamic task creation with **Spawn**, which instantiates and executes a specified task. A **Reference** to memory is given via a descriptive name similar to a variable name.

Listing 1.4 shows the LLP representation of the HLP program in Listing 1.2, obtained via an automatic translation of the HLP language concepts to the respective LLP concepts by considering the operational semantics of HLP. For example, a variable in HLP is automatically initialized when declared, which means that there is a write access for every variable declaration. Of particular note for the example is the translation of the **For** statement of HLP: While the

---

[2] Note that a special memory block is reserved for each lock reference, whose value is either 0 or 1, indicating whether a lock is taken.

```
 1  LLP ::= {Task} "main" "{" Block "}";
 2
 3  Task ::= "task" <String> "{" Block "}";
 4  Block ::= [DAP {";" DAP}];
 5
 6  DAP ::= Read | Write | Malloc | Commit | Lock | Unlock | ControlFlowBranching |
 7          Repetition | Skip | Parentheses | Spawn;
 8
 9  Read ::= "read" "(" Reference ")";
10  Write ::= "write" "(" Reference ")";
11  Malloc ::= "malloc" "(" Reference {"," Reference } ")";
12  Commit ::= "commit" ["(" Reference ")"];
13  Lock ::= "lock" "(" Reference ")";
14  Unlock ::= "unlock" "(" Reference ")";
15  ControlFlowBranching ::= "(" Block ")" "||" "(" Block ")";
16  Repetition ::= "(" Block ")" "*" <Integer>;
17  Skip ::= "skip";
18  Parentheses ::= "(" Block ")";
19  Spawn ::= "spawn" "(" <String> ")";
20
21  Reference ::= <String>;
```

Listing 1.3. Syntax of the Low-Level Programming Language (LLP).

body of the for-loop is repeated the specified number of times via an LLP repetition, there are also additional memory accesses to consider. Before entering the LLP repetition, the HLP loop variable is initialized with the lower bound of the HLP **For** statement resulting in a write access. At the beginning of each repetition, the HLP loop variable is checked for whether it has reached the upper bound resulting in a read access. Finally, at the end of each LLP repetition, the loop variable is incremented resulting in a read and a write access. During the translation procedure, a HLP assignment, e.g., **x1:=x3+1** (Listing 1.2, l. 6) will be translated to read accesses to variables in the right hand side, e.g., **x3**, followed by a write access to the variable in the left hand side, e.g., **x1** (Listing 1.4, l. 4). Also, the HLP **Synchronized** statements over variables are translated to LLP **lock ... unlock** sequences where each unique constellation of HLP variables is translated to a specific LLP lock variable, e.g., the HLP **Synchronized** statement over variables **z1** and **z3** (Listing 1.2, l. 23) is translated to a lock variable **13** (Listing 1.4, l. 24).

By focusing on memory accesses in LLP and abstracting from unnecessary details of more high-level programming languages, it is possible to analyze the interaction of deployment decisions and program execution. While LLP artifacts are usually generated as part of compilation so that they do not have to be written manually, LLP code may also be written manually to give very fine-grained control over memory accesses to analyze the resulting impact on execution. LLP programs are used as input to the toolbox to perform simulation and analysis.

```
1  task T1 {malloc(i1);
2    write(i1); write(i1);                //Initialize variables and loop variable.
3    (read(i1);                           //Check loop condition.
4    lock(11); read(x3); write(x1); unlock(11);
5    lock(12); write(y1); unlock(12);
6    lock(13); read(z3); write(z1); unlock(13);
7    read(i1); write(i1)) * 20            //Increment loop variable and repeat.
8  }
9
10 task T2 {malloc(i2);
11   write(i2); write(i2);                //Initialize variables and loop variable.
12   (read(i2);                           //Check loop condition.
13   lock(11); read(x3); write(x2); unlock(11);
14   lock(12); read(y1); write(y2); unlock(12);
15   write(x2);
16   read(i2); write(i2)) * 30            //Increment loop variable and repeat.
17 }
18
19 task T3 {malloc(i3);
20   write(i3); write(i3);                //Initialize variables and loop variable.
21   (read(i3);                           //Check loop condition.
22   lock(11); write(x3); unlock(11);
23   write(y3);
24   lock(13); read(z1); write(z3); unlock(13);
25   read(i3); write(i3)) * 50            //Increment loop variable and repeat.
26 }
27
28 main {
29   write(x1); write(x2); write(x3); write(y1); write(y2); write(y3);
30   write(z1); write(z2); write(z3);     //Initialize variables.
31   spawn(T1); spawn(T2); spawn(T3)      //Spawning tasks.
32 }
```

Listing 1.4. Running example: Automatically generated code in the Low-Level Programming Language (LLP).

3.3 RM: A Modeling Notation for Deployment Configurations

Potential deployment configurations may differ in memory availability, distribution, sharing and layout. We propose the *Resource Model (RM)* to specify the deployment configuration relevant for a particular deployment setup.

```
1  RM ::= Memory Device+;
2  Memory ::= "memory" "{" "size" ":" <Integer> ";"
3    ["references" "{" { <String> ":" <Integer> ";"} "}" ] "}";
4  Device ::= "device" "{" "cacheSize" ":" <Integer> ";"
5    [ "localMemory" ":" <Integer> "-" <Integer> ";"] "}";
```

Listing 1.5. Syntax of the Resource Model (RM).

A resource model **RM** consists of a shared **Memory** and possibly multiple **Devices** operating on that memory. The size of the **Memory** may be configured and an initial layout may be defined via references associating variable names with memory locations. Each **Device** conceptually consists of a *core*, doing calculations, with an associated *cache* of configurable size that can buffer data from the *shared memory* to improve access times. Additionally, each device may declare a range of blocks from the shared memory as being local, which automatically makes the remaining memory remote. Thus, the model supports architectures with non-uniform memory access; remote memory has a more severe penalty for access. The RM artifact is used as input for the compilation process to the toolbox to perform simulation and analysis, where it is reflected by specific configuration values.

```
1  memory {
2    size: 20;
3
4    references {
5      x1 :  1; x2 :  1; x3 :  1; 11 :  3;
6      y1 :  7; y2 :  7; y3 :  7; 12 :  9;
7      z1 : 13; z2 : 13; z3 : 13; 13 : 15; 14 : 18;
8    }
9  }
10
11 device {
12   cacheSize: 5;
13   localMemory: 0 - 5;
14 }
15
16 device {
17   cacheSize: 5;
18   localMemory: 6 - 11;
19 }
20
21 device {
22   cacheSize: 5;
23   localMemory: 12 - 17;
24 }
```

Listing 1.6. Resource model of the running example.

Listing 1.6 shows a possible resource model for the running example, in which variables **x1,x2,x3** have been allocated in the same memory block, which is local to the first device. Similarly, **y1,y2,y3** and **z1,z2,z3** have been allocated local to the second and third device, respectively. In addition, the local variables have been allocated in different memory blocks. In particular, we assume that lock variables are always taking one memory block, which is justified by the common practice of padding blocks to isolate certain data. We add an extra lock **14**, which will be used later to avoid the race conditions introduced by this particular memory layout, see Sect. 3.4 for further details.

3.4 Running the Example in the Toolbox

Recall from Fig. 1 that the toolbox takes as input the LLP program from Listing 1.2 and the compiled version of the resource model from Listing 1.6. We can now simulate the example. The toolbox takes care of coherent accesses to caches and shared memory while running the simulations. To measure the quality of the simulation, the tool introduces penalties for accesses to the memory system as a metric. Inspired by a real NUMA system [27], we let accesses to the local cache, local shared memory and remote shared memory differ by an order of magnitude and have penalties of 10, 100 and 1,000, respectively. Out of 1000 simulations, 175 are inconclusive after a timeout of six seconds. (Observe that inconclusive simulations within the time bound may be explained by ping pong effects betweens cores repeatedly requesting exclusive access to a memory block and invalidating each other without making progress.) We observed that the minimum, maximum and average penalty for the given inputs are 208 205, 479 605 and 351 705 respectively.

For comparison, we run a variant of the example that contains an extra lock surrounding the previous contents of the block of each task as shown in Listing 1.7. This lock aims to remove the race conditions introduced by the allocator in the memory layout and to reduce the overall penalty. For these inputs, all 1000 simulations terminate, and we observed obviously better results with the minimum, maximum and average penalty of 108 311, 265 311 and 202 606, respectively.

```
1  task T1 {
2     lock(14); /* Previous T1 */ unlock(14);
3  }
4
5  task T2 {
6     lock(14); /* Previous T2 */ unlock(14);
7  }
8
9  task T3 {
10    lock(14); /* Previous T3 */ unlock(14);
11 }
12
13 main {
14    //Previous main
15 }
```

Listing 1.7. Running example with additional locks in LLP, aiming to reduce race conditions due to the false sharing in the memory layout.

4   A Peek Inside the Toolbox: A Formal Model of Distributed Computations and Data Accesses

This section details the construction of the toolbox, realized as a proof-of concept implementation of a formal model in the rewriting logic system Maude [17]. The formal model captures a multicore architecture consisting of cores with a private cache and main memory with a NUMA design, as shown in Fig. 2.

Tasks, expressed in terms of data accesses, are scheduled for execution on available cores from a shared pool. Task execution in a core requires memory blocks to be transferred from main memory to the corresponding cache. The main memory where the needed blocks are residing, can be either local to the core or remote. Each cache has a queue of fetch/flush instructions to move memory blocks between cache and main memory. To ensure consistency between concurrently existing copies of data in caches and main memory, the model implements the MSI cache coherence protocol (e.g., [28]), a standard protocol from in the literature. In MSI, a cache line can be in one of the three states: modified, shared or invalid. A *modified* state indicates that the block in that cache line has the most recent value and that all other copies are *invalid* (including the copy in main memory), while a *shared* state indicates that all copies of the block have consistent data (including the copy in main memory). This protocol broadcasts messages between the cores. We abstract from the specific shape of this broadcast (e.g., a mesh or a ring) in terms of a communication medium. Following standard nomenclature, *Rd* messages request read access to a memory block and *RdX* messages request exclusive read access to a memory block (for writing purposes), thereby invalidating other copies of the same block.

To read data from block n, the core first looks for n in its local cache. If n is not in the cache, then a read request $!Rd(n)$ is instantaneously broadcast to other caches and main memory. The cache *fetches* the block when it is available in main memory. Eviction is required if the cache is full. Writing to block n requires that n is in either shared or modified state in the local cache, an *invalidation request*

$!RdX(n)$ is then instantaneously broadcast to obtain exclusive access. We use $?Rd(n)$ and $?RdX(n)$ to denote the reception of read and invalidation requests, respectively. If a cache receives a read request $?Rd(n)$ and it has the block in modified state, the cache *flushes* the block to main memory; if the cache receives an invalidation request $?RdX(n)$ and it has the block in shared state, the cache line will be *invalidated*; the requests are discarded otherwise. A full formal description of this model can be found in [8].

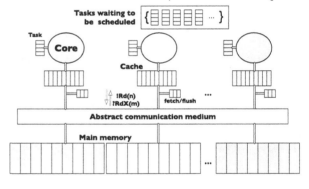

Fig. 2. A distributed layer of computations with coherent data accesses.

As a technical contribution of this paper, we have extended the model to support tasks with atomic sections implemented by *binary locks*. We model lock manipulations according to *test and test-and-set* instruction [3]: to take a lock located in block n, the core first checks the block locally in the cache. If the lock value is 0 (lock is free), it sends an invalidation message $!RdX(n)$ to the other components in the architecture and takes the lock; if the value is 1 (lock is taken), it waits until its local copy is invalidated to fetch the lock from main memory and repeats the process until it succeeds.

For simplicity, this model abstracts the actual data in memory blocks to symbolic values, except for the binary value of the locks. We assume that locks must be released before they are taken again. We also assume that a cache line has the same size as a memory block, and that blocks are transferred between cores via this main memory. Read and invalidation requests in the communication medium are broadcast instantaneously in our model, which captures *true concurrency* for an arbitrary number of cores in the proposed semantics.

4.1 Operational Semantics for Tasks with Binary Locks and Coherent Data Accesses

We extend previous work [8,9] with binary locks. While the previous work describes a memory system with multilevel caches, this paper only considers single-level caches. This simplification is orthogonal to the extension.

Runtime syntax. A configuration *Config* consists of main memory M, shared among cores $\overline{CR}$ with their own caches $\overline{Ca}$, and a set of tasks $\overline{T}$ to be executed. A core $(Cid \bullet rst)$ has identifier Cid and executes runtime statements rst. A cache $(Cid \bullet M \bullet dst)$ consists of a core identifier to which it belongs, a local memory M and a sequence of data instructions dst with $\mathbf{fetch}(n)$ and $\mathbf{flush}(n)$ instructions to be performed. A memory $M : n \rightharpoonup \langle val, st \rangle$ maps address n to a pair of a stored value val and a status st. The status tags mo, sh, and inv refer to the three states of the MSI protocol. Blocks in main memory are in sh or inv state.

The task table $Tb : T \rightharpoonup dap$ associates task identifiers T to *data access patterns* dap, which are sequences of the basic operations described in Sect. 3. To ensure data consistency, a statement $\mathbf{commit}$ is added at the end of each task to flush the entire cache after execution. We assume that the task table is statically given and is always available. Cores execute *runtime statements* rst, which extend dap with additional statements $\mathbf{readBl}(r)$, $\mathbf{writeBl}(r)$, $\mathbf{lockBl}(r)$ and $\mathbf{unlockBl}(r)$ to indicate that the core is blocked, waiting for data to be fetched.

Semantics. The semantics is divided into local and global levels. The local semantics captures the execution of statements in each core and local state changes in each cache line according to the finite state controller enforcing the MSI protocol during execution. The global semantics captures the synchronization and coordination between the different components in a configuration. In an *initial* configuration *Config*, all blocks in main memory M have a default initial value with status sh, all locks are free, all cores are idle, all caches are empty, and the task pool in $\overline{T}$ has a single task representing the main block of a program. Let *Config* $\xrightarrow{*}$ *Config'* denote an execution starting from *Config* and reaching *Config'* by recursively applying global transition rules, which in turn apply local transition rules for each component. To give a feel for the operational semantics within the available space, we focus on the subset of local rules extending previous work; the full semantics can be found in an accompanying technical report [10].

$$\frac{n = addr(r)}{(c \bullet \boxed{M[n \mapsto \langle k, 0, mo \rangle]} \bullet dst) \circ (c \bullet \boxed{\textbf{lock}(r); rst})} \quad (\text{Lock}_1)$$
$$\rightarrow (c \bullet \boxed{M[n \mapsto \langle k, 1, mo \rangle]} \bullet dst) \circ (c \bullet \boxed{rst})$$

$$\frac{n = addr(r)}{(c \bullet \boxed{M[n \mapsto \langle k, 0, sh \rangle]} \bullet dst) \circ (c \bullet \boxed{\textbf{lock}(r); rst})} \quad (\text{Lock}_2)$$
$$\xrightarrow{!RdX(n)} (c \bullet \boxed{M[n \mapsto \langle k, 1, mo \rangle]} \bullet dst) \circ (c \bullet \boxed{rst})$$

$$\frac{n = addr(r) \quad status(M, n) = inv \vee n \notin dom(M)}{(c \bullet \boxed{M \bullet dst}) \circ (c \bullet \boxed{\textbf{lock}(r); rst})} \quad (\text{LockBlock}_1)$$
$$\xrightarrow{!Rd(n)} (c \bullet \boxed{M \setminus n \bullet dst; \textbf{fetch}(n)}) \circ (c \bullet \boxed{\textbf{lockBl}(r); rst})$$

$$\frac{n = addr(r)}{(c \bullet \boxed{M[n \mapsto \langle k, 0, sh \rangle]} \bullet dst) \circ (c \bullet \boxed{\textbf{lockBl}(r); rst})} \quad (\text{LockBlock}_2)$$
$$\xrightarrow{!RdX(n)} (c \bullet \boxed{M[n \mapsto \langle k, 1, mo \rangle]} \bullet dst) \circ (c \bullet \boxed{rst})$$

$$\frac{n = addr(r) \qquad status(M, n) = inv}{(c \bullet \boxed{M \bullet dst}) \circ (c \bullet \boxed{\textbf{lockBl}(r); rst})} \quad (\text{LockBlock}_3)$$
$$\xrightarrow{!Rd(n)} (c \bullet \boxed{M \setminus n \bullet dst; \textbf{fetch}(n)}) \circ (c \bullet \boxed{\textbf{lockBl}(r); rst})$$

$$\frac{n = addr(r)}{(c \bullet \boxed{M[n \mapsto \langle k, 1, mo \rangle]} \bullet dst) \circ (c \bullet \boxed{\textbf{unlock}(r); rst})} \quad (\text{Unlock}_1)$$
$$\rightarrow (c \bullet \boxed{M[n \mapsto \langle k, 0, mo \rangle]} \bullet dst) \circ (c \bullet \boxed{rst})$$

$$\frac{n = addr(r)}{(c \bullet \boxed{M[n \mapsto \langle k, 1, sh \rangle]} \bullet dst) \circ (c \bullet \boxed{\textbf{unlock}(r); rst})} \quad (\text{Unlock}_2)$$
$$\xrightarrow{!RdX(n)} (c \bullet \boxed{M[n \mapsto \langle k, 0, mo \rangle]} \bullet dst) \circ (c \bullet \boxed{rst})$$

$$\frac{n = addr(r) \quad status(M, n) = inv \vee n \notin dom(M)}{(c \bullet \boxed{M \bullet dst}) \circ (c \bullet \boxed{\textbf{unlock}(r); rst})} \quad (\text{UnLockBlock}_1)$$
$$\xrightarrow{!Rd(n)} (c \bullet \boxed{M \setminus n \bullet dst; \textbf{fetch}(n)}) \circ (c \bullet \boxed{\textbf{unlockBl}(r); rst})$$

$$\frac{n = addr(r)}{(c \bullet \boxed{M[n \mapsto \langle k, 1, sh \rangle]} \bullet dst) \circ (c \bullet \boxed{\textbf{unlockBl}(r); rst})} \quad (\text{UnLockBlock}_2)$$
$$\xrightarrow{!RdX(n)} (c \bullet \boxed{M[n \mapsto \langle k, 0, mo \rangle]} \bullet dst) \circ (c \bullet \boxed{rst})$$

Fig. 3. Local semantics for taking and releasing locks in cache coherent multicore architectures.

The local transition rules for lock manipulations are given in Fig. 3, where the function $addr(r)$ returns the address n of the block containing reference r and $status(M, n)$ the status of n in memory M. A task running in a core can take a lock with reference r when its value in the local cache is 0 (i.e., free) and the status of block n, where $n = addr(r)$, is either sh or mo, see rules Lock_1 and

Lock$_2$. After a lock is taken, the value and status of block n in the local cache are updated to 1 (taken) and mo (modified), respectively. Taking or releasing a lock implies writing to a reference and getting exclusive access to the block. If the status in the local cache is shared, the core broadcasts message $!RdX(n)$ to get exclusive access to n, see Lock$_2$. If the requested lock is not available in the cache, the core first broadcasts a $!Rd(n)$ message and appends a **fetch** instruction to fetch the block in LockBlock$_1$. The execution is then blocked by the statement **lockBl**(r) until the lock is available in the local cache, see LockBlock$_2$. A new read request message $!Rd(n)$ occurs if the lock has been invalidated after it has been fetched while the core was blocked, see LockBlock$_3$. Releasing a lock is similar to locking, except that a core can only release a lock r that it owns (i.e., val equals 1 in the local cache), see Unlock$_1$ and Unlock$_2$. Observe that only the core that owns the lock can release it. During execution, a block n may be evicted from the cache to give space to another block, and may therefore need to be fetched again. This is handled by UnLockBlock$_1$ and UnLockBlock$_2$.

4.2   Correctness of the Model

We evaluated the correctness of the model with respect to standard correctness properties for data consistency and cache coherence [18,29] including: (1) the result of any execution of the global system is equivalent to interleaving the results of the data access from each core in some serial order, (2) task execution preserves program order, and (3) for all memory blocks and for any synchronous or asynchronous parallel global step, cores cannot access stale data. The formal formulation and full proof of these properties can be found in the accompanying technical report [10]. These properties show that the formal model correctly captures a coherent multicore memory system and are following the same idea of the proofs shown in previous work by the authors [8,9].

To ensure mutually exclusive access to read/write operations protected by a lock, we first provide the definition of a lock being taken by a core.

Definition 1 (Taken lock). *Let $M \circ \overline{T} \circ \overline{Ca} \circ \overline{CR}$ be a global configuration, $CR_i \in \overline{CR}$, $Ca_i \in \overline{Ca}$ a cache such that $Ca_i = (c_i \bullet M_i \bullet dst_i)$ and belongs(Ca_i, CR_i). Then, a lock with address n is considered to be taken by a core if and only if either*

(a) value(M,n) = 1 and status(M,n) = sh; or
(b) $\exists Ca_i \in \overline{Ca}$ such that value(M_i,n) = 1 and
    (i) status(M_i,n) = sh; or (ii) status(M_i,n) = mo.

The following lemma shows that once a lock is taken, no other locking step for the same lock is allowed until it has been unlocked.

Lemma 1 (Mutual exclusion). *Let a configuration $M \circ T \circ \overline{Ca} \circ \overline{CR}$ be reachable from an initial configuration. For $CR_i \in \overline{CR}$, let $CR_i = (c_i \bullet rst_i)$ and for $Ca_i \in \overline{Ca}$, $Ca_i = (c_i \bullet M_i \bullet dst_i)$. Consider a lock reference r with addr(r)=n.*
    *If $(c_i \bullet M_i \bullet dst_i) \circ (c_i \bullet rst_i) \rightarrow (c_i \bullet M_i' \bullet dst_i') \circ (c_i \bullet rst_i')$ such that $rst_i \neq$ **unlock**(r); rst_i'' or $rst_i \neq$ **unlockBl**(r); rst_i'' for any rst_i'', then (a) $n \notin dom(M_i)$ or (b) value(M_i,n) = value(M_i',n).*

Proof (Sketch). We show that the property holds for initial configurations and proceed by induction on the transition rules, see [10]. □

5   Related Work

Taylor et al. [30] point out that the deployment view of a software system's architecture can be critical in assessing whether the system will be able to satisfy its requirements. In order to model deployment decisions, we need modelling abstractions that capture relevant aspects of the system structure. Programming languages like ArchJava [2] and Koala [31] take steps in this direction by integrating architectural concepts such as components and connectors into the design, allowing high-level logical structure to be expressed inside programs. To support deployment decisions, similar concepts are needed to express properties of physical or virtual devices.

For cloud-deployed software, the modelling of resource management strategies can be done in terms of *deployment components* with associated resources [22], which are first-class modelling concepts in ABS [21]. For cyber-physical systems there is a similarly recognized need capture that computation and communication take time, which can be addressed by platform models to support design space exploration [19]. Our work in this paper is motivated by this need to express deployment decisions early in program construction. Rather than directly addressing the timing aspects of communication, we have opted for a more abstract approach, using a metric of penalties for data access patterns reflecting the program deployed with a given data layout on *shared memory multiprocessor architectures*.

Methods for model-based performance prediction which build custom performance models can generally be classified as being based on queuing networks, process algebra, Petri nets, simulations or stochastic models [7]. For multicore systems, simulation based approaches are most common. For example, a recent model-driven engineering methodology for deployment optimisation of task allocations for multicore embedded systems at design time [15,16] is based on the UML MARTE profile for Modeling and Analysis of Real-Time and Embedded systems. This methodology uses model transformation techniques to optimise task allocation by refining the model of task allocations according to the simulation results. This work is complementary to our work by their focus on optimizing task allocation, which is non-deterministic in our model. Furthermore, in contrast to our work they do not focus on data access or caches.

Many simulation tools have been developed to analyse the performance of parallel programs running on multicore architectures. For instance gem5 [11] performs evaluations of, e.g., the cache hit/miss ratio and response time by running benchmark programs written as low-level read and write instructions to memory. Tools such as Graphite [24] and Sniper [12] run programs on distributed clusters to simulate executions on multicore architectures with thousands of cores. Compared to our work, these simulation tools take as their starting point the finished program and do not expose how data accesses affect the performance of a parallel program for a particular choice of data layout.

6   Conclusion and Future Work

This paper argues that deployment decisions should be modelled and analyzed as part of by-construction program development. Although common practice tackles deployment after validation, resulting performance problems may in the worst case require considerable changes in design and even impact the requirements level. To move deployment decisions earlier, models need to express platform artefacts and how the logical structure of the program maps to these artefacts.

To illustrate deployment modelling and decisions, this paper presents a toolbox for simulation, comparison and analysis of the effects of deployment decision for a particular parallel program when interacting with existing memory structures. We make this toolbox available to users by providing two programming languages at different levels of abstraction as well as a notation for resource models to specify memory availability, distribution, sharing and layout. Although the content of the toolbox can be ignored from the developer's perspective, it can be formalizes as an operational semantics for data access patterns executing in parallel on different cores and moving data between shared memory and local caches, and embodies a cache coherence protocol for data consistency. We show that the model guarantees correctness properties concerning data consistency and protected access to atomic sections.

As a next step, we plan to enrich the data access patterns and data layout to support more complex data structures and their dynamic allocation in memory (e.g., object creation). This opens for extracting data access patterns from richer high-level languages such as parallel object-oriented languages. Another interesting direction is to extend the architecture to support shared caches. It is also interesting to relate our high-level language (HLP) to existing correctness by construction formalisms such as Unity [13,14]. Finally, models, as developed in this paper, could serve as a foundation to study the effects of program specific optimizations of data layout and scheduling.

References

1. Abrial, J.-R.: The B-Book: Assigning Programs to Meanings. Cambridge University Press, Cambridge (1996)
2. Aldrich, J., Chambers, C., Notkin, D.: ArchJava: connecting software architecture to implementation. In: Tracz, W., Young, M., Magee, J. (eds.), Proceedings of the 24th International Conference on Software Engineering (ICSE 2002), pp. 187–197. ACM (2002)
3. Andrews, G.R.: Foundations of Multithreaded, Parallel, and Distributed Programming. Addison Wesley, Reading (2000)
4. Bac, R., Kurki-Suonio, R.: Decentralization of process nets with centralized control. In: Probert, R.L., Lynch, N.A., Santoro, N. (eds.), Proceedings of the Second Annual ACM SIGACT-SIGOPS Symposium on Principles of Distributed Computing, pp. 131–142. ACM (1983)
5. Back, R., Sere, K.: Stepwise refinement of parallel algorithms. Sci. Comput. Program. **13**(1), 133–180 (1989)

6. Back, R.-J.J., Wright, J.V.: Refinement Calculus: A Systematic Introduction, 1st edn. Springer, New York (1998). https://doi.org/10.1007/978-1-4612-1674-2
7. Balsamo, S., Marco, A.D., Inverardi, P., Simeoni, M.: Model-based performance prediction in software development: a survey. IEEE Trans. Softw. Eng. **30**(5), 295–310 (2004)
8. Bijo, S., Johnsen, E.B., Pun, K.I., Tapia Tarifa, S.L.: A formal model of parallel execution in multicore architectures with multilevel caches (long version). Research report, Department of Informatics, University of Oslo (2017). http://violet.at.ifi.uio.no/papers/mc-rr.pdf
9. Bijo, S., Johnsen, E.B., Pun, K.I., Tapia Tarifa, S.L.: A formal model of parallel execution on multicore architectures with multilevel caches. In: Proença, J., Lumpe, M. (eds.) FACS 2017. LNCS, vol. 10487, pp. 58–77. Springer, Cham (2017). https://doi.org/10.1007/978-3-319-68034-7_4
10. Bijo, S., Pun, K.I., Tapia Tarifa, S.L.: Modelling data access patterns with atomic sections for multicore architectures (long version). Research report, Department of Informatics, University of Oslo (2017). http://violet.at.ifi.uio.no/papers/mc-lock-rr.pdf
11. Binkert, N., et al.: The gem5 simulator. SIGARCH Comput. Arch. News **39**(2), 1–7 (2011)
12. Carlson, T.E., Heirman, W., Eeckhout, L.: Sniper: exploring the level of abstraction for scalable and accurate parallel multi-core simulation. In: Proceedings of International Conference for High Performance Computing, Networking, Storage and Analysis (SC), pp. 52:1–52:12. ACM (2011)
13. Chandy, K.M., Misra, J.: Parallel Program Design: A Foundation. Addison-Wesley, Reading (1988)
14. Chandy, K.M., Taylor, S.: An Introduction to Parallel Programming. Jones and Bartlett, Austin (1991)
15. Ciccozzi, F., Corcoran, D., Seceleanu, T., Scholle, D.: Smartcore: boosting model-driven engineering of embedded systems for multicore. In: Proceedings of the 12th International Conference on Information Technology - New Generations, pp. 89–94. IEEE Computer Society (2015)
16. Ciccozzi, F., Feljan, J., Carlson, J., Crnković, I.: Architecture optimization: speed or accuracy? both! Softw. Qual. J., November 2016
17. Clavel, M., et al.: All About Maude - A High-Performance Logical Framework. LNCS, vol. 4350. Springer, Heidelberg (2007). https://doi.org/10.1007/978-3-540-71999-1
18. Culler, D.E., Gupta, A., Singh, J.P.: Parallel Computer Architecture: A Hardware/Software Approach, 1st edn. Morgan Kaufmann Publishers Inc., San Francisco (1997)
19. Derler, P., Lee, E.A., Sangiovanni-Vincentelli, A.L.: Modeling cyber-physical systems. Proc. IEEE **100**(1), 13–28 (2012)
20. Hähnle, R., Johnsen, E.B.: Designing resource-aware cloud applications. IEEE Comput. **48**(6), 72–75 (2015)
21. Johnsen, E.B., Hähnle, R., Schäfer, J., Schlatte, R., Steffen, M.: ABS: a core language for abstract behavioral specification. In: Aichernig, B.K., de Boer, F.S., Bonsangue, M.M. (eds.) FMCO 2010. LNCS, vol. 6957, pp. 142–164. Springer, Heidelberg (2011). https://doi.org/10.1007/978-3-642-25271-6_8
22. Johnsen, E.B., Schlatte, R., Tarifa, S.L.T.: Integrating deployment architectures and resource consumption in timed object-oriented models. J. Log. Algebr. Meth. Program. **84**(1), 67–91 (2015)

23. Kourie, D.G., Watson, B.W.: The Correctness-by-Construction Approach to Programming. Springer, Heidelberg (2012). https://doi.org/10.1007/978-3-642-27919-5
24. Miller, J.E., et al.: Graphite: a distributed parallel simulator for multicores. In: Proceedings of the 16th International Symposium on High-Performance Computer Architecture (HPCA), pp. 1–12. IEEE Computer Society (2010)
25. Morgan, C.: Programming from Specifications. Prentice Hall International Series in Computer Science, 2nd edn. Prentice Hall, Upper Saddle River (1994)
26. Morgan, C.: Programming from Specifications. Prentice-Hall International, Upper Saddle River (1998)
27. Schmidl, D., Vesterkjær, A., Müller, M.S.: Evaluating OpenMP performance on thousands of cores on the Numascale architecture. In: PARCO, vol. 27 of Advances in Parallel Computing, pp. 83–92. IOS Press (2015)
28. Solihin, Y.: Fundamentals of Parallel Multicore Architecture, 1st edn. Chapman & Hall/CRC, Boca Raton (2015)
29. Sorin, D.J., Hill, M.D., Wood, D.A.: A Primer on Memory Consistency and Cache Coherence, 1st edn. Morgan & Claypool Publishers, San Francisco (2011)
30. Taylor, R.N., Medvidovic, N., Dashofy, E.M.: Software Architecture: Foundations, Theory, and Practice. Wiley Publishing, Hardcover (2009)
31. van Ommering, R.C., van der Linden, F., Kramer, J., Magee, J.: The Koala component model for consumer electronics software. IEEE Comput. **33**(3), 78–85 (2000)

Towards Software Performance
by Construction

Mirco Tribastone$^{(\boxtimes)}$

IMT School for Advanced Studies, Lucca, Italy
mirco.tribastone@imtlucca.it

Extended Abstract

Performance is an important *extra-functional* factor that directly impacts on the quality of a software system as perceived by its users. It indicates *how well* the software behaves, thus complementing *functional* properties that concern *what* the software does. Its ever-increasing relevance cannot be underestimated. To mention but a few notable cases, Google Search is ranking faster mobile pages higher as of July 2018 [3]; a survey among IT administrators revealed that software performance is considered to be one of most pressing concerns [23]. Indeed, business performance is directly affected by software performance: US retail giant Walmart reported incremental revenues by up to 1% for every 100 ms of page load improvement in their web site [1].

It is clear that performance analysis cannot be left to the latest stages of the software development process, for instance when the system is ready to be deployed—in this case, serious flaws discovered at that time would be too expensive to fix [2]. In addition, if the analysis is only conducted through testing or runtime profiling, several issues arise about the cost, the predictive power, and the degree of coverage of the experiments. The latter is particularly problematic in more stringent, safety-critical domains.

Performance-by-construction would hold the promise of generating executable code from a specification such that the software provably meets a desired performance target. In order to be able to predict performance, the specification could be best represented by an appropriate quantitative *model* of the software, for instance a Markov chain or a higher-level representation such as a stochastic Petri net [4] or a stochastic process algebra [11]. However, the amount of knowledge required in both the problem domain and the modeling techniques hinders the widespread use of model-based analysis in the practice of software engineering [29].

Model-driven development techniques can offer a mitigation to this issue by putting forward the generation of software artifacts directly from models [20]. Such an approach can be suitably adapted to take quantitative information into account. For instance, considerable work has focussed on the use of UML diagrams extended with performance-related annotations [7,26,27]. However, since the generated code is typically subjected to manual intervention by the developer, the hard problem of keeping the model synchronized with the code is

© Springer Nature Switzerland AG 2018
T. Margaria and B. Steffen (Eds.): ISoLA 2018, LNCS 11244, pp. 466–470, 2018.
https://doi.org/10.1007/978-3-030-03418-4_27

introduced (e.g., [13]). Indeed, lack of consistency jeopardizes the validity of the model with respect to the actual program behavior, and has been recognized as another major factor in limiting the adoption of quantitative models of software in practice [29].

Here we propose the idea of achieving performance-by-construction by looking at the code itself as the model of the software system, rather than resorting to other artifacts. Thus, we imagine a software development process where a quantitative model, derived from the actual version of the code, is used to evaluate if the given performance target is reached, suggesting possible performance fixes otherwise. There are two orthogonal issues to tackle in this framework:

- which quantitative models to use;
- how to derive models from code.

The quantitative model should be expressive enough to cover the essential features of realistic programs, i.e., loops/recursion, contention for shared resources, inter-thread communication. Stochastic models appear particularly helpful in reasoning about performance because of their strong tradition in this area [22] and because interesting requirements, e.g., percentiles of response times, are probabilistic in nature. A relevant model for this purpose may be that of layered queuing networks, since it incorporates most of the aforementioned features as first-class citizens of the formalism [12,25]. Because of such richness, one can envisage algorithms to translate program constructs into components of a layered queuing network.

We now briefly identify two possible avenues of future research to contribute to achieving software performance by construction.

One crucial aspect is that of model validation, i.e., ensuring that the model predictions accurately match the observed behavior of the system. A critical step regards model parameterization, i.e., choosing the values of parameters such as routing probabilities, service demands, and concurrency levels that directly affect the model's dynamics. Typically, parameterization would be conducted by executing sample runs of the program and collecting measurements. Since we are assuming an iterative process which requires parameterization at every update of the code base, we need efficient techniques that can provide frequent up-to-date estimates.

We can identify two main challenges.

(i) It may not be appropriate to assume the steady-state regime, in particular when it is subjected to hopefully simple test runs that are only assumed to exercise the software system. The steady-state assumption is important because it allows the use of many well-known relationships and/or analytical results for queuing network (see e.g., [8]). Crucially, a recent survey on service demand estimation does not report of any technique that does not use such assumption [21].

(ii) It is not possible to employ techniques that require major intrusions into the running system such as, for instance, the injection of measurement traffic to exercise the system under different utilization levels (e.g., [6]). Approaches that involve different quantities (e.g., throughput and utilization) may introduce instrumentation overheads and may cause estimation bias [16].

Some recent work has aimed at tackling these two challenges, developing a low-overhead estimation technique for models in the transient regime [14]. However, it is applicable to a specific kind of queuing networks, namely single-class networks with exponentially distributed service demands, which is quite restrictive with respect to the ambition of modeling general-purpose software. Further investigation is required to suitably adapt these ideas to more general classes of stochastic models.

Other open questions arise from issues related to the *portability* of the predictions, hence to the validity of the performance guarantees. Indeed, the performance of a system depends not only on the software, but also on the hardware on which it is executed. A performance target that is satisfied on a test deployment may no longer hold on the final, target deployment. This mismatch can be due to (at least) two causes. The first is the difference in the hardware features (e.g., CPU clock speeds, disk speed, cache sizes). The second cause is the difference in the execution environment (e.g., operating system) which may affect the runtime behavior in ways that are very difficult to predict.

In this context, a possible way of capturing this heterogeneity is to reason about quantitative models where *uncertainty* is a first-class citizen. One would then account for differences by treating the relevant parameters of the model as uncertain/imprecise, for instance by assigning a range of values within which the true behavior may be found, instead of assigning a fixed, certain parameter.

Uncertainty may be interpreted in different ways, with different implications on the underlying techniques for the model analysis. One interpretation might consist in representing a *family* of software performance models, where each member is characterized by precise parameter values drawn from the given uncertainty ranges [15,17,18]. This formalization is convenient if one is able to effectively perform a so-called *family-based analysis* [24], consisting of a single evaluation of a super-model that accounts for such parametric differences. The state of the art in family-based analysis of software performance models covers only a fragment of layered queuing networks [17,18], hence more research effort is required in extending the solution techniques.

Another interpretation of uncertainty is to give *robustness bounds*, i.e., distributions of the estimated performance targets as a function of assumptions on a probability distribution of the uncertainty (see, e.g., [5]). In this respect, an interesting avenue for future research is to relax the probabilistic assumption of the input in favor of a more general nondeterministic setting. Here the aim is to model the parameter values as a choice made by an adversary, finding performance bounds that represent the best and the worst dynamical behavior of the model under such adversarial choices. If one was able to represent the behavior of a program as a stochastic process such as a Markov chain, such nondeterminism could be encoded as Markov Decision Process and analyzed directly with state-of-the-art tools such as Prism [19]. We envisage that the complexity of realistic programs calls for the development of analysis techniques that trade off precision with scalability, for instance by using statistical methods [10] or by working with approximations of stochastic processes [9,28].

Acknowledgement. This work is partially supported by a DFG Mercator Fellowship, project DAPS2 under the Special Priority Programme (SPP) 1593 "Design for Future — Managed Software Evolution".

References

1. 4 awesome slides showing how page speed correlates to business metrics at walmart.com. http://www.webperformancetoday.com/2012/02/28/4-awesome-slides-showing-how-page-speed-correlates-to-business-metrics-at-walmart-com/. Accessed 12 Jan 2018
2. NASA delays satellite launch after finding bugs in software program. https://fcw.com/Articles/1998/04/19/NASA-delays-satellite-launch-after-finding-bugs-in-software-program.aspx. Accessed 4 Feb 2018
3. Using page speed in mobile search ranking. https://webmasters.googleblog.com/2018/01/using-page-speed-in-mobile-search.html. Accessed 18 Jan 2018
4. Marsan, M.A., Conte, G., Balbo, G.: A class of generalized stochastic Petri nets for the performance evaluation of multiprocessor systems. ACM Trans. Comput. Syst. **2**(2), 93–122 (1984)
5. Aleti, A., Trubiani, C., van Hoorn, A., Jamshidi, P.: An efficient method for uncertainty propagation in robust software performance estimation. J. Syst. Softw. **138**, 222–235 (2018)
6. Awad, M., Menasce, D.A.: Deriving parameters for open and closed QN models of operational systems through black box optimization. In: Proceedings of the International Conference on Performance Engineering (ICPE) (2017)
7. Balsamo, S., Di Marco, A., Inverardi, P., Simeoni, M.: Model-based performance prediction in software development: a survey. IEEE Trans. Softw. Eng. **30**(5), 295–310 (2004)
8. Bolch, G., Greiner, S., de Meer, H., Trivedi, K.: Queueing Networks and Markov Chains: Modeling and Performance Evaluation with Computer Science Applications. Wiley, Hoboken (2005)
9. Bortolussi, L., Gast, N.: Mean field approximation of uncertain stochastic models. In: 46th Annual IEEE/IFIP International Conference on Dependable Systems and Networks (DSN) (2016)
10. Bortolussi, L., Milios, D., Sanguinetti, G.: Smoothed model checking for uncertain continuous-time Markov chains. Inf. Comput. **247**, 235–253 (2016)
11. Clark, A., Gilmore, S., Hillston, J., Tribastone, M.: Stochastic process algebras. In: Bernardo, M., Hillston, J. (eds.) SFM 2007. LNCS, vol. 4486, pp. 132–179. Springer, Heidelberg (2007). https://doi.org/10.1007/978-3-540-72522-0_4
12. Franks, G., Al-Omari, T., Woodside, M., Das, O., Derisavi, S.: Enhanced modeling and solution of layered queueing networks. IEEE Trans. Softw. Eng. **35**(2), 148–161 (2009)
13. Garcia, J., Krka, I., Mattmann, C., Medvidovic, N.: Obtaining ground-truth software architectures. In: Proceedings of the 35th International Conference on Software Engineering (ICSE), pp. 901–910 (2013)

14. Incerto, E., Napolitano, A., Tribastone, M.: Moving horizon estimation of service demands in queuing networks. In: 26th IEEE International Symposium on the Modeling, Analysis, and Simulation of Computer and Telecommunication Systems (MASCOTS) (2018, to appear)

15. Incerto, E., Tribastone, M., Trubiani, C.: Symbolic performance adaptation. In: Proceedings of the 11th International Symposium on Software Engineering for Adaptive and Self-managing Systems (SEAMS) (2016)

16. Kalbasi, A., Krishnamurthy, D., Rolia, J., Richter, M.: MODE: mix driven online resource demand estimation. In: 7th International Conference on Network and Service Management (2011)

17. Kowal, M., Schaefer, I., Tribastone, M.: Family-based performance analysis of variant-rich software systems. In: Gnesi, S., Rensink, A. (eds.) FASE 2014. LNCS, vol. 8411, pp. 94–108. Springer, Heidelberg (2014). https://doi.org/10.1007/978-3-642-54804-8_7

18. Kowal, M., Tschaikowski, M., Tribastone, M., Schaefer, I.: Scaling size and parameter spaces in variability-aware software performance models. In: 30th IEEE/ACM International Conference on Automated Software Engineering (ASE), pp. 407–417 (2015)

19. Kwiatkowska, M., Norman, G., Parker, D.: PRISM 4.0: verification of probabilistic real-time systems. In: Gopalakrishnan, G., Qadeer, S. (eds.) CAV 2011. LNCS, vol. 6806, pp. 585–591. Springer, Heidelberg (2011). https://doi.org/10.1007/978-3-642-22110-1_47

20. Sendall, S., Kozaczynski, W.: Model transformation: the heart and soul of model-driven software development. IEEE Softw. **20**(5), 42–45 (2003)

21. Spinner, S., Casale, G., Brosig, F., Kounev, S.: Evaluating approaches to resource demand estimation. Perform. Eval. **92**, 51–71 (2015)

22. Stewart, W.J.: Probability, Markov Chains, Queues, and Simulation. Princeton University Press, Princeton (2009)

23. Thereska, E., Doebel, B., Zheng, A.X., Nobel, P.: Practical performance models for complex, popular applications. In: ACM SIGMETRICS International Conference on Measurement and Modeling of Computer Systems, pp. 1–12 (2010)

24. Thüm, T., Apel, S., Kästner, C., Schaefer, I., Saake, G.: A classification and survey of analysis strategies for software product lines. ACM Comput. Surv. **47**(1), 6:1–6:45 (2014)

25. Tribastone, M.: A fluid model for layered queueing networks. IEEE Trans. Softw. Eng. **39**(6), 744–756 (2013)

26. Tribastone, M., Gilmore, S.: Automatic extraction of PEPA performance models from UML activity diagrams annotated with the MARTE profile. In: Proceedings of the Seventh International Workshop on Software and Performance (WOSP) (2008)

27. Tribastone, M., Gilmore, S.: Automatic translation of UML sequence diagrams into PEPA models. In: Fifth International Conference on the Quantitative Evaluaiton of Systems (QEST), pp. 205–214 (2008)

28. Tschaikowski, M., Tribastone, M.: Approximate reduction of heterogeneous nonlinear models with differential hulls. IEEE Trans. Autom. Control **61**(4), 1099–1104 (2016)

29. Woodside, M., Franks, G., Petriu, D.C.: The future of software performance engineering. In: Proceedings of the Future of Software Engineering (FOSE), pp. 171–187 (2007)

Is Privacy by Construction Possible?

Gerardo Schneider[✉]

Department of Computer Science and Engineering, University of Gothenburg,
Gothenburg, Sweden
gerardo@cse.gu.se

Abstract. Finding suitable ways to handle personal data in conformance with the law is challenging. The European General Data Protection Regulation (GDPR), enforced since May 2018, makes it mandatory
to citizens and companies to comply with the privacy requirements set
in the regulation. For existing systems the challenge is to be able to show
evidence that they are already complying with the GDPR, or otherwise
to work towards compliance by modifying their systems and procedures,
or alternatively reprogramming their systems in order to pass the eventual controls. For those starting new projects the advice is to take privacy
into consideration since the very beginning, already at design time. This
has been known as *Privacy by Design* (*PbD*). The main question is how
much privacy can you effectively achieve by using PbD, and in particular
whether it is possible to achieve *Privacy by Construction*. In this paper
I give my personal opinion on issues related to the ambition of achieving
Privacy by Construction.

1 Introduction

Handling *personal data* adequately and in conformance with common sense,
standards and regulations is a big challenging task. The already approved European General Data Protection Regulation (GDPR) [20], put into force this year,
attempts to protect individuals by putting stringent constraints on how personal
data should be collected, stored and treated. Companies and individuals must
comply or pay huge fines.

The obvious approach for those developing new software is to consider this
important non-functional requirement as part of its design and development.
Privacy by Design [13] is based on the idea that any personal data processing
environment should be designed so that privacy is taken into account as early as
the requirement elicitation phase and when designing the software architecture.
Given that not all software development is done following a rigorous methodology
(i.e., quite often one does not make an explicit design but just write the code
having the design "in mind"), the idea would be that privacy should then be
taken into account at least when programming. That is, the overall suggestion
is that privacy should be as important as the functional aspect of your design
and programming task.

© Springer Nature Switzerland AG 2018
T. Margaria and B. Steffen (Eds.): ISoLA 2018, LNCS 11244, pp. 471–485, 2018.
https://doi.org/10.1007/978-3-030-03418-4_28

This is easier to say than to do. In practice there is a big gap between the technical concepts handled by software architects and the prescriptions stated by laws and regulations. From the design point of view, software architects usually use different kinds of diagrams at different levels of abstractions in order to make conceptual models and more detailed architectures describing how the software system is to be structured. Many levels of abstraction may be present in such design (if any) including the modeling of basic units, their integration into bigger components and modules, their interconnection, and communication protocols among such elements.

From the programming point of view, programmers mostly focus in the functionality of the software (*what* the software is supposed to do) and eventually on very specific non-functional requirements like performance (execution and data retrieval speed, response time, etc.). That said, most of our software engineers and programmers are not trained in security and privacy, and thus they might not have the necessary background to handle such non-functional requirements. Even if they are aware and knowledgeable in those areas, there is a general lack of tools and methodologies to design and program having privacy in mind. They are not to blame though. Security and privacy threats have been around for a while but only recently became an imperative, not only because of the external (legal) pressure (e.g., GDPR) but also because the number of vulnerabilities, and misuse cases, has been made more apparent due to increased media coverage (e.g., recent scandal with Facebook [5,10], and the Google case [7]). Complying with new privacy requirements it is not easy though (see for instance an analysis of how Facebook tries to address GDPR issues [17]).

Though each user has an own understanding on what is personal and sensitive data, it is in general not always clear what defines the privacy frontiers. Independently of the individuals' perspective on their own data[1] we are here concerned with privacy from the legal point of view. That is, what is required by standards and regulations like the already mentioned GDPR. The law is generally written in a normative way stating the rights and obligations of citizens and corporations in different circumstances. The GDPR defines what personal data is and establishes constraints in the way data may be collected, used and stored. Such regulations and principles, written in natural language, need to be interpreted and implemented by software engineers into technical designs and concrete software that are required to be compliant with the privacy legislation. One way to do this would be to follow the PbD philosophy, and in particular we could aim at a systematic and (semi-)automatic way of achieving that, i.e. achieving privacy *by construction*.

X-by-Construction approaches may be defined as *"a step-wise refinement process from specification to code that automatically generates software (system) implementations that by construction satisfy specific non-functional properties [...]"*.[2] In this paper we assume the premise that it could be desirable to achieve

---

[1] Technically, the individual or companies we are taken data from/about are called *data subjects*, and those handling the data are the *data controllers*.

[2] http://fmt.isti.cnr.it/~mtbeek/ISoLA18.html.

Privacy by Construction, that is the possibility to automatically refine (formal) specifications so the generated code satisfies the privacy properties under consideration.

Privacy cannot be enforced uniquely by technical means and requires to be seen from a multidisciplinary perspective, including computer science, computer security and cryptography, law, social sciences and economics [18]. In this paper we focus only on privacy from a computer science perspective, starting in particular from Privacy by Design (PbD)[3], and we discuss about the feasibility of achieving *Privacy by Construction*.

The paper is organized as follows. In next section we give a very brief overview of some key privacy concepts from the GDPR. Section 3 recalls the main ideas behind PbD and gives an incomplete account of the state of the art in the area, and provides some examples for achieving privacy *a posteriori*. Section 4 presents a personal point of view on what may be achieved with PbD, and list some limitations and challenges for specific privacy issues concerning PbD and Privacy by Construction. Finally, we conclude in the last section with a general discussion.

2   GDPR

The European *General Data Protection Regulation* (GDPR) [21] is a document containing around 90 articles whose aim is to regulate *personal data* processing. The text replaces, among others, the Directive 95/46/EC of the European Parliament, and improves over the original proposal given in 2012 [20]. As any text of this kind, the regulation is complex and full of definitions.

For the purpose of this paper we are only interested in naming that the regulation talks about seven *personal data processing principles*, namely (i) Lawfulness, fairness and transparency; (ii) Purpose limitation; (iii) Data minimization; (iv) Accuracy; (v) Storage limitation; (vi) Integrity and confidentiality; (vii) Accountability. Besides the above, the GDPR stipulates that data subjects have several *rights* including (i) Right to information, access and rectification of personal information; (ii) Right to object to personal data processing; (iii) Right not to be subject to automated individual decisions; (iv) Right to be forgotten (concerning data erasure); (v) Right to data portability. Moreover, Article 6 of the regulation stipulates six *lawful grounds* for data processing operations, namely: (i) Consent; (ii) Performance of a contract; (iii) Compliance with a legal obligation; (iv) Protection of vital interests; (v) Public interest; (vi) Overriding interest of the controller.

Besides the original document, it is worth reading the critical review of the regulation (and on the comparison with previous versions) done by de Hert and Papakonstantinou [25].

---

[3] In the rest of the paper we will use the acronyms PbD for Privacy by Design.

3   Privacy by Design

In this section we briefly give an overview of PbD, we discuss some issues concerning the achievement of PbD, and we provide some examples following the approach. We finish with some examples of *a posteriori* techniques for very specific aspects of privacy.

3.1   What Is PbD?

In a nutshell and informally, *Privacy by Design* (PbD) is an approach for ICT project development that promotes taking privacy and data protection compliance from the very beginning. The concept was introduced by Ann Cavoukian[4] in the 90's and further developed over the following years. In [12] Cavoukian describes the following seven foundational principles for PbD: (i) Proactive not reactive, preventative not remedial; (ii) Privacy as the default setting; (iii) Privacy embedded into design; (iv) Full functionality: positive-sum, not zero-sum; (v) End-to-End Security: full lifecycle protection; (vi) Visibility and transparency: keep it open; (vii) Respect for user privacy: keep it user-centric. (See [12] for more details).

The concept was taken by several researchers in the last ten years or so mostly due to the increasing problem associated with Big Data, and more recently due to the GDPR and other strong regulations.

In December 2014 Danezis et al. [18] wrote a report for the European Union Agency for Network and Information Security (ENISA) in order to *"promote the discussion on how PbD can be implemented with the help of engineering methods"* and to *"[...] provide a basis for better understanding of the current state of the art concerning privacy by design with a focus on the technological side"*.

A more telling explanation of the scope of PbD is given in such report: *"[...] privacy by design is neither a collection of mere general principles nor can it be reduced to the implementation of PETs.[5] In fact, it is a process involving various technological and organisational components, which implement privacy and data protection principles. These principles and requirements are often derived from law, even though they are often underspecified in the legal sources."*

The report is very clear on that PbD is still in infancy[6] and makes concrete recommendations for taking the next step in engineering PbD (cf. [18, Sect. 5.2]). See also [23,24,37] concerning the engineering of privacy.

3.2   How to Achieve PbD?

From the design point of view, it could be great if software engineers do not need to worry too much about privacy and may only concentrate on the functional

---

[4] Former Information & Privacy Commissioner of Ontario (Canada).

[5] PET: Privacy-Enhancing Technologies.

[6] The report is from 2014, but to the best of our knowledge the advances in the area have not yet produced mature tools as to be used by industry.

aspect, while tool-assisted design methodologies automatically add the needed privacy checks to the design. This is an ideal situation and some privacy aspects might be handled in this way. Ideally, software engineers will design their software with the tools they are already familiar with and after pressing a "convert" button they would get an enhanced model containing specific privacy checks in some parts and proposals or warning for others. Those models/diagrams would be then edited by a privacy engineer who would validate or modify such checks and add meta-annotations on the model so programmers get more precise hints on how to implement those checks.

That would of course be the first step. A design needs to be synthesized (materialized) into programming code that effectively implements the (privacy-compliant) design. How to ensure such transformation is *sound* (correct) and *complete* (it does address all the privacy principles under consideration)? Formal methods would help to prove soundness. Completeness is more difficult but it could be achieved with respect to a small set of predefined privacy concepts.

A complementary (ideal) solution, from the programming point of view, would be to have specialized libraries offering an API for handling personal data. These libraries would not only ensure that data have been collected with the consent of the user, that it has a time-stamp on when it was collected and eventually a timeout (for retention time). The data would carry the history (its *provenance* as well as information on where it was sent and stored). Ideally, each operation on the data would be checked against the consented purpose, only if the retention time has not expired.

3.3   Some Proposals Following PbD

PbD has been applied to specific real(istic) cases, including electronic traffic pricing (ETP), smart metering, and location based services (see [29] and references therein). In [29] Le Métayer proposed a framework to express different parameters to take into account for making a choice when defining software architectures, and applied the framework to an ETP.

According to [1] previous work has "focused on technologies rather than methodologies and on components rather than architectures". In that paper, Antignac and Le Métayer moves forward towards an application of PbD to the "architectural level and be associated with suitable methodologies", proposing a more formal approach. In particular they use a *privacy epistemic logic* as a way to specify and prove privacy properties about software architectures.

In [3,4] Antignac et al. propose an approach based on model transformations, which guarantees that an architectural design, originally focused on functional data requirements, is enhanced with certain privacy principles. In particular, the proposal is to automatically transform data flow diagrams (DFDs) into so-called *privacy-aware data flow diagrams* (or PA-DFDs for short). PA-DFDs are DFDs enhanced with a log system (for accountability), and suitable checks concerning retention time and purpose for each operation on sensitive data (storage, forwarding, and processing of data). The software architect then focuses only on defining the function part as DFDs, and then check and eventually extend the obtained PA-DFD. The ultimate goal would be to automatically get a program template from the PA-DFD, helping the programmer to identify in which points to perform suitable privacy checks. The approach has not been implemented so it remains to check whether it is feasible, it captures relevant privacy checks, and it scales.

More recently Basin et al. [6] proposed a methodology for auditing GDPR compliance by using *business process models*. One of the key insights of the paper is to identify "purpose" with a "process". Besides, it shows how to automatically generate privacy policies from the model and detect violations of data minimization, and gives arguments on why GDPR compliance cannot be entirely automated.[7]

A different, and complementary, way of viewing PbD is to consider privacy even at a higher level of abstraction, not from the architectural point of view but rather from the meta-level. This is the line of work proposed by Hoepman on the definition of privacy *design strategies* [26]. These strategies are to be taken into account during the analysis and requirements engineering phase, before designing the software architecture. Colesky et al. [16] suggest an additional level of abstraction between privacy design strategies and privacy patterns by considering *tactics*. Notario et al. [30] present a methodology for engineering privacy based on existing state-of-the-art approaches like PIA (Privacy Impact Assessment) and risk management, among others. These approaches, though valuable in the context of PbD, are even further from the implementation and they "suffer" from the same issues as for PbD in what concerns its relatedness to the implementation.

Finally, it is worth mentioning the work by Schaefer et al. [35], presented in this very same track of ISoLA'18, on the definition of rules for achieving *Confidentiality-by-Construction*. The approach is based on replacing functional pre-/postcondition specifications (Hoare triples, as traditionally used for classical functional correctness) with confidentiality specifications listing which variables contain secrets. The approach is promising. That said, this is an ongoing work so it remains to see whether it is feasible in practice.

3.4   A Posteriori Techniques for Privacy

Though not the main objective of this paper, we mention here a few attempts to ensure compliance to some of the privacy principles, not by following PbD but rather by do *a posteriori* analysis (once the software has already been developed, both before and after deployment).

In [22] Ferrara and Spoto suggest the use of tainting and other static analysis techniques to detect the potential leak of private sensitive information, combined with abstraction techniques so the results are shown differentially to the players interested in privacy. Despite the generality of the title, the ideas of the paper

---

[7] Some of the arguments of our paper are very much along the same line as the ones presented in [6]. In particular, the identification of the difficulty to represent purpose at the programming language level.

are applicable to compliance w.r.t. very specific privacy aspects. Note that the static analysis of such properties is undecidable in general.

In [2] Antignac et al. provide a characterization of the data minimization principle in a restricted setting: deterministic (functional) programs and for a notion of minimization based only on the *collection* of data (not on data *processing*). The paper contains results for both the *monolithic* case (when the input comes from only one source) and for the *distributed* case (when the input is collected from multiple independent sources). A technique based on symbolic execution and SAT solvers is presented for computer a *minimizer*, that is a pre-processor that filters the input so data minimization is guaranteed. The main limitations are that computing the minimizer is undecidable in general, that the source code is required (it is white box) and that it only considers a very restrictive version of data collection (the technique only works for the case when minimization is achieved when restricting the input domain, and it should be generalized for more complex notions).

A black box approach for monitoring whether a give program satisfies (strong) data minimization has been proposed in [33,34] (under the same definition given in [2]). Giving a final verdict (at runtime) that a given program minimizes data is in general not possible, but if the program is non-minimal then the runtime monitor might be able to detect that (no completeness results are given, but if the current, or any past, execution of the program violates data minimization, the monitor would detect it). Under very strict conditions (finiteness of the input domain), it is possible to effectively determine using off-line monitoring if the program satisfies data minimization or not, and in the latter it is possible to extract a minimizer (always using a black box technique). Monitoring a more general (weaker) version of data minimization is not possible in general as it is a more complex hyperproperty, lying in a fragment of HyperLTL known not to be monitorable (it is a "$\forall\forall\exists\exists$" property). This is also the case for a negation of the property. That said, recent ideas on combining static and runtime verification might be useful to help getting a monitor for the negation of the property [8].

4   Is Privacy by Construction Possible?

In the previous section we discussed, at a high level, how PbD may be used at design time, hinted on the possibility of integrating privacy at the programming level, gave some links to the literature on the use of PbD in concrete scenarios as well as some examples of achieving privacy *a posteriori*. The question is still how much privacy may be achieved in practice by PbD. In other words, if you follow a PbD approach how much privacy is really "propagated" into the running software so it could be considered privacy compliant (with for example the GDPR)? Is that possible at all? For which principles? Can we effectively characterize what is achievable by PbD and what is not? Even more, how much of that maybe done *automatically*, achieving then Privacy by Construction?

In this paper we will not be able to answer all the above questions but will rather focus on some aspects. In particular, in this section we list some general limitations of PbD, and we present challenges concerning few specific privacy issues. Note that the challenges we mention are not necessarily in correspondence with the listed limitations.

4.1   Some Limitations

Section 5.1 of the ENISA report [18] lists a number of limitations of PbD. We will not enumerate them all here but will just mention few keys points (see details and examples in the report).[8]

- One important issue is the lack of *compositionality*: a system satisfying a given privacy property is not guaranteed to do so when composed with another one. So, even when we might achieve privacy by using PbD on given components, it is not clear that this could propagated to the whole system.
- There currently is no way to measure how private a system is, nor to compare whether a system is more private than another one: there is lack of suitable privacy *metrics*. So, it is not easy to make a good privacy risk assessment or to assign any kind of economic value to (lack of) privacy.
- There is a trade-off between privacy and utility, so the designer needs to take this into account when taking a PbD approach. The risk is that if privacy takes too much importance at design time, it might jeopardize the utility of the developed software.
- There is a lack of design methodologies and tools, integrated in the software development cycle, facilitating a practical use of PbD.

The above thus gives already a good hint that PbD, by itself, cannot in general guarantee Privacy by Construction; we elaborate on some of the above and other difficulties to achieve it.

Our first (obvious) observation is that by following PbD we run, at least, into the very same problems as when you develop software from (in)formal functional requirements and specifications. Unless you automatically (and with a proof of correctness) translate (*synthesize*) your program, you can only assert with a limited degree of confidence that your software is correct *by construction*. This is because most of the time your design (model or specification) is a different creature from the implemented software, and in most cases the step from your design (model or specification) into the software that will effectively be running in your computer is manual. This step may introduce bugs, or your model (or specification) might be partial, incomplete, or too abstract.

So following PbD will not, by itself and in general, guarantee a private by construction software as new techniques for (automatic) refinement should be developed, and this might be more difficult for privacy as it is for functional properties. That said, for very specific privacy aspects it might be possible to achieve the intended goal. For instance, we could envisage similar techniques as

---

[8] The report stresses a few times the privacy is much wider than technology (social, legal, political, etc.) but the focus on the discussion here is on the (software-based) technological side only.

the one proposed in [35] for confidentiality. The full feasibility and applicability of this approach is still to be assessed though.

That said, in our opinion it is strongly recommended to use PbD given that you may at least ensure that you have taken (certain) privacy aspects into consideration when you design your software, expecting that in the development phase such considerations are followed and applied so they are reflected in the final product.

4.2   Some Challenges

We summarize in what follows some of the key challenges in achieving Privacy by Construction, and we list possible ways to handle some of those. Obviously technology cannot help solve all the problems, but even if we were to limit our analysis only to those aspects related to the technical, we would not be able to cover all of them in this paper. Instead of focusing on how to deal with specific privacy principles or properties, we take our discussion based on some of the key concepts in the GDPR. In particular, we consider one principle (*purpose*), one right (the *right to be forgotten*), and two lawful grounds (*consent* and *compliance*).[9]

Purpose. Today's programming languages do not give good support to represent purpose as required by the GDPR, maybe with the exception of having an enumerative type with the different purposes the service might use the data. This, on the other hand, would not ensure by itself that the data will be indeed used only for the intended purpose. For that there might be a need to define specialized libraries, with carefully defined abstract data type *purpose* (or defined special programming language primitives), guaranteeing that only certain operations may be applied to the data according to the consented purpose. That said, it will not be easy to take care of this if one allows for the data to navigate to non-controlled parts of the program, or if it is processed in a way that the sensitive (*high*) data is propagated through explicit and implicit flows to public (*low*) data. So, it will be difficult to give strong guarantees as it may be difficult to ensure the programmer uses such library operations or built-in constructs. In order to handle this and do something "by construction" one possibility would be to define new data types where each piece of data comes with its purpose (and other relevant privacy information). Very much like "sticky policies" [31], that are conditions and constraints (*policies*) attached to data that describe how it should be treated. These policies would travel with the data so they (ideally) are enforced whenever the data is to be used.

If one follows a PbD approach, it might be possible to include purpose at the design level, but it is not clear how this could be translated into the real implementation. For instance, some of the approaches mentioned in Sect. 3.3 envisage the declaration of the purpose in different ways. Basin et al. [6] proposes that business processes explicitly represent one or more purposes, by associating a

---

[9] The reader may want to see [36,40] for a different perspective on challenges in PbD.

"process" with a "purpose". They propose a methodology for auditing GDPR based on proving a correspondence between GDPR, the business process representation and the implementation. It is not clear, however, how this could be done automatically. In particular, the relation between the business process and the implementation is very much the same that exists today between any (functional) formal specification and an implementation. Similarly Antignac et al. [3, 4] propose to have purposes just as a meta-data associated with the data, and then getting a PA-DFD that would add a check before using the data on whether the intended use is for the consented purpose. Though not presented in the papers, the idea would be that the programmer gets a skeleton of a program (automatically synthesized from the PA-DFD) manually adding the concrete privacy checking during implementation (at design time, the purpose is just a string with no concrete meaning except its belonging to an enumerative set).

Finally, a last example on how to deal with purpose is the one discussed in [2] in the context of data minimization. In such papers the "purpose" is defined by the program itself. This, however, is a quite simplistic way of handling purpose and would only work for limited number of applications handling data for very specific purposes.

As a final comment, the issue of purpose is very much related to the general problem of data *usage*, so it could be interesting to investigate whether techniques from *usage control* could be used in this context (see for instance [28] and references therein). Another interesting line of work, and probably more relevant than usage control, in relation to purpose is that of *purpose-based access control* [9], and other similar work, whose aim is to design access control mechanisms based on purpose. See the related work section in [6] for an overview of these and other access control variants aiming at capturing the notion of purpose.

Right to be forgotten and retention time. In order to enforce data deletion whenever the data subject requires it, or whenever there is a timeout, seems very difficult. This would require to keep very advanced techniques to track data provenance [14]. One way to approach this issue could be to follow a technique based on information-flow security, in particular the one developed for *information erasure* [15]. In [39] Del Tedesco et al. use dynamic taint analysis to track how sensitive data propagate through a program and erase them on demand. The method is implemented as a library for Python. The approach is further developed in [38] Hunt el al. were it is presented a framework to express a rich class of erasure policies. Similar approaches could be used for the GDPR rights, but the main issue still remains: the above would only work if the date remains inside one specific software program. As soon as the data is forwarded somewhere else (or saved on an external device) it should be thus tracked and we do not know today how to solve this.

Another idea would be to use *stick policies* [31] (cf. purpose above). As today, this is a nice theoretical concept but it lacks practical implementations. As for the erasure papers mentioned above, implementing sticky policies for one specific software might be feasible, but still the challenge is to make it work across different applications and platforms.

Consent. The problem of consent seems to be a bit easier to handle if the focus is only on asking permission from the data subject to collect certain data for a given purpose: it only suffices to always add a standard question whenever the data controller collects data and only do so if the data subject agrees. So, consent might be easy to implement whenever there is an explicit collection of data where the data subject is directly asked before the collection of data. This, however, it is an oversimplification.

First, we know that if consent is asked for every explicit collection of data and for approval of specific policies (e.g. *terms of service*) the user will simply agree without really knowing what is she giving consent to.[10]

Second, sometimes data is collected in a continuous manner in ways that makes it extremely difficult to ask for consent. Think about street cameras and broadcasting of wi-fi devices, just to mention a couple of ways of getting personal data without explicit consent. An example of this is the data collection performed by Google Street View cars: "*It is now clear that we have been mistakenly collecting samples of payload data from open wifi networks, even though we never used that data in any Google products*" [27]. The software should be selective on which wi-fi data to collect, but is this possible? A possible solution would be to develop a specialized software that runs in a protected environment (enclave) where the collected data is stored and analyzed in a "smart" way so only what is relevant is forwarded outside the enclave for further processing. How to implement this "smart" solution?

The position paper [11] discusses an approach based on the use of registries to deal with consent in the context of the Internet of Things. It could be interesting to see how this solution could be generalized.

Compliance. The notion of compliance is very much related to purpose [6], and as we have discussed above including the notion of purpose as a first class citizen in programming languages is still a challenge. So, giving a technical means to have privacy compliance "by construction" will only be possible whenever all the other issues are solved, and even then it might be very difficult if not impossible. This is the case since in order to be able to enforce compliance might require to have solutions that are enforced by the runtime execution environment in many different platforms.

Think of a photo that is collected for the purpose of helping researchers in image processing. Let us assume that the photo comes with a sticky policy explicitly specifying that the purpose is "research", that it should not be forwarded to any other data controller, and that the retention time (the photo should be erased from any storage device) is two weeks. In order to enforce this, in a relatively easy way, the photo should be received via an application (via suitable APIs) and only handled by that application. If so, we could save the photo and make all needed manipulations in a safe enclave (very much like a sandbox) where only the so-called research engine would be running. If we cannot

---

[10] The GDPR [21] is very explicit on that consent should be given *freely*, in an *informed and unambiguous* way, and that it should *cover all processing activities carried out for the same purpose*. A separate consent should be given for each separate purpose.

guarantee that every single device and platform contains the needed enforcement mechanism, we cannot make any strong claim. The photo might be uploaded to a different application, or stored in a disk and then forwarded to somewhere else (there is no way to enforce the sticky policy unless the software associated with handling the photo has the mechanisms to do so).[11]

Some researchers believe that we should not worry very much about trying to enforce compliance "by construction" but rather leave the burden to data controllers: it is on their own interest to be able to give evidence that they do comply with the law whenever they are challenged to do so. This, however, might seem an attempt to solve the problem by avoiding it, or even by assuming it is not a problem. Not quite. The idea is to provide as much support as possible to data controllers (e.g., in the form of guidelines, and programming libraries as discussed earlier) to handle data according to the law. If they do not do that (e.g., do not use the specialized libraries) and misuse the data (e.g., use them for a different purpose than the one consented by the data subject) it is their problem as they will have to prove that they are not guilty.

5   Final Discussion

Achieving privacy compliance is not easy. Many solutions should be addressed at the level of organizational procedures and practices, and others by technical means (software-based solutions). Guaranteeing most privacy principles in already existing systems is in most cases impossible, and if possible then extremely difficult and costly. When building new systems, following a PbD approach is definitively a step forward but not a panacea. More research is needed in order to be able to advance the state-of-practice in this domain. Achieving perfect Privacy by Construction is, in my opinion, impossible in general and extremely expensive in the best case. That said, the fines for non-compliance are extremely high[12] so investment in privacy solutions is a must.

Another way to think about privacy compliance is to provide the technical means to enhance data with *sticky* privacy policies containing retention time, purpose, etc. and ask the data controller to respect and enforce the data subject's policy. That is, it is up to the data controller to prove that its handling of data complies with the data subject's policy and the law. In this approach, the controlling agencies do not try to ask for proofs of absence of privacy breaches

---

[11] An example of such a (limited) mechanism is given in [32] for photo sharing in social networks by using a combination of sticky policies with attribute-based encryption. The mechanism works by encrypting parts of the picture so only allowed users can see what they are supposed to, but if somebody has permission to download the picture to the local disk, there is no way to enforce the sticky policy after that. Since the enforcement mechanism (encryption/decryption, permission checking, etc.) is only done in a particular application platform (Diaspora [19]), the user could forward the decrypted picture to anyone else if she has permission to download it.

[12] It is stipulated that non-compliance might imply fines up to €20 million or 4% of the annual turnover of the company.

a priori, but if there is any privacy leak then it should be detected *a posteriori* by suitable audits. The burden is thus upon the data controller on choosing the best solution to avoid paying for non-compliance.

A notion left out in this paper has been the notion of *adversary* (or *attacker model*). This has been intentional as the objective of this paper is not to give an exhaustive overview of the field nor to propose solutions but rather to give a personal point of view on the issue of Privacy by Construction. That said, any feasible solution should provide a proper attacker model as well as proofs (or at least convincing evidence) that the proposed approach preserves privacy with respect to those attackers. If possible, it should also make explicit what are the assumptions in order to make it easier to detect potential vulnerabilities (claims in only one direction usually hide some unwanted side effects that could compromise privacy). Besides, we have not been able to cover many other interesting and very relevant aspects of privacy, including anonymization, accountability, unlinkability, transparency, intervenability, and many other concepts present in the GDPR.

All the statements and claims done in this paper reflects a personal point of view, not based on experimental nor on theoretical (im)possibility results. I would like to be proved wrong on my pessimistic views and right on those more optimistic opinions. Hope for new advancements in privacy research so we can all achieve a good trade-off between privacy and utility+transparency.

Acknowledgements. I would like to thank Daniel Le Métayer for his valuable comments on an early draft of this paper, and Thibaud Antignac for all the fruitful discussions we have had on privacy by design. This research has been partially supported by the Swedish Research Council (*Vetenskapsrådet*) under grant Nr. 2015-04154 (*PolUser: Rich User-Controlled Privacy Policies*).

References

1. Antignac, T., Le Métayer, D.: Privacy by design: from technologies to architectures. In: Preneel, B., Ikonomou, D. (eds.) APF 2014. LNCS, vol. 8450, pp. 1–17. Springer, Cham (2014). https://doi.org/10.1007/978-3-319-06749-0_1
2. Antignac, T., Sands, D., Schneider, G.: Data minimisation: a language-based approach. In: De Capitani di Vimercati, S., Martinelli, F. (eds.) SEC 2017. IAICT, vol. 502, pp. 442–456. Springer, Cham (2017). https://doi.org/10.1007/978-3-319-58469-0_30
3. Antignac, T., Scandariato, R., Schneider, G.: A privacy-aware conceptual model for handling personal data. In: Margaria, T., Steffen, B. (eds.) ISoLA 2016. LNCS, vol. 9952, pp. 942–957. Springer, Cham (2016). https://doi.org/10.1007/978-3-319-47166-2_65
4. Antignac, T., Scandariato, R., Schneider, G.: Privacy compliance via model transformations. In: International Workshop on Privacy Engineering (IWPE 2018), IEEE EuroS&P Workshops, pp. 120–126. IEEE (2018)
5. Aziza, B.: Facebook privacy scandal hearings: What you missed. Appeared at Forbes online, April 2018. https://www.forbes.com/sites/ciocentral/2018/04/16/facebook-privacy-scandal-hearings-what-you-missed/#9a41af57ab9c. Accessed 16 May 2018

6. Basin, D., Debois, S., Hildebrandt, T.: On purpose and by necessity: compliance under the GDPR. In: Twenty-Second International Conference on Financial Cryptography and Data Security (2018, to appear)
7. BBC News: Google loses 'right to be forgotten' case, April 2018. http://www.bbc.com/news/technology-43752344?SThisFB. Accessed 14 Apr 2018
8. Bonakdarpour, B., Sanchez, C., Schneider, G.: Monitoring Hyperproperties by combining static analysis and runtime verification. In: Margaria, T., Steffen, B. (eds.) ISoLA 2018. LNCS, vol. 11244, pp. 8–27. Springer, Cham (2018)
9. Byun, J., Bertino, E., Li, N.: Purpose based access control of complex data for privacy protection. In: 10th ACM Symposium on Access Control Models and Technologies (SACMAT 2005), pp. 102–110. ACM (2005). https://doi.org/10.1145/1063979
10. Cadwalladr, C., Graham-Harrison, E.: Revealed: 50 million facebook profiles harvested for cambridge analytica in major data breach. Appeared at The Guardian, March 2018. https://www.theguardian.com/news/2018/mar/17/cambridge-analytica-facebook-influence-us-election. Accessed 16 May 2018
11. Castelluccia, C., Cunche, M., Le Métayer, D., Morel, V.: Enhancing transparency and consent in the IoT. In: EuroS&P Workshops 2018, pp. 116–119 (2018)
12. Cavoukian, A.: Privacy by design: The 7 foundational principles (2009)
13. Cavoukian, A.: Privacy by design: Origins, meaning, and prospects. Privacy Protection Measures and Technologies in Bus. Org.: Aspects and Standards 170 (2011)
14. Cheney, J., Chiticariu, L., Tan, W.C.: Provenance in databases: why, how, and where. Found. Trends Databases $1(4)$, 379–474 (2009)
15. Chong, S., Myers, A.C.: Language-based information erasure. In: Proceedings of the 18th IEEE Workshop on Computer Security Foundations, CSFW 2005, pp. 241–254. IEEE Computer Society (2005)
16. Colesky, M., Hoepman, J., Hillen, C.: A critical analysis of privacy design strategies. In: IEEE Security and Privacy Workshops, pp. 33–40. IEEE Computer Society (2016). http://ieeexplore.ieee.org/xpl/mostRecentIssue.jsp?punumber=7517741
17. Constine, J.: A flaw-by-flaw guide to facebook's new GDPR privacy changes, April 2018. https://techcrunch.com/2018/04/17/facebook-gdpr-changes
18. Danezis, G., et al.: Privacy and data protection by design. ENISA Report, January 2015
19. Diaspora: Diaspora (2016). https://joindiaspora.com
20. European Commission: Proposal for a General Data Protection Regulation. Codecision legislative procedure for a regulation 2012/0011 (COD), European Commission, Brussels, Belgium, January 2012
21. European Commission: General Data Protection Regulation (GDPR). Regulation 2016/679, European Commission, Brussels, Belgium, April 2016
22. Ferrara, P., Spoto, F.: Static analysis for GDPR compliance. In: ITASEC 2018, CEUR Workshop Proceedings, vol. 2058. CEUR-WS.org (2018)
23. Gürses, S., Troncoso, C., Diaz, C.: Engineering privacy by design (2011)
24. Gürses, S., Troncoso, C., Diaz, C.: Engineering privacy by design reloaded (2015)
25. Hert, P.D., Papakonstantinou, V.: The new general data protection regulation: still a sound system for the protection of individuals? Comput. Law Secur. Rev. $32(2)$, 179–194 (2016)
26. Hoepman, J.-H.: Privacy design strategies. In: Cuppens-Boulahia, N., Cuppens, F., Jajodia, S., Abou El Kalam, A., Sans, T. (eds.) SEC 2014. IAICT, vol. 428, pp. 446–459. Springer, Heidelberg (2014). https://doi.org/10.1007/978-3-642-55415-5_38

27. Kiss, J.: Google admits collecting wi-fi data through street view cars. The Guardian, May 2010. https://www.theguardian.com/technology/2010/may/15/google-admits-storing-private-data
28. Lazouski, A., Martinelli, F., Mori, P.: Usage control in computer security: a survey. Comput. Sci. Rev. **4**(2), 81–99 (2010)
29. Le Métayer, D.: Privacy by design: a formal framework for the analysis of architectural choices. In: CODASPY 2013, pp. 95–104. ACM (2013)
30. Notario, N., et al.: PRIPARE: a new vision on engineering privacy and security by design. In: Cleary, F., Felici, M. (eds.) CSP 2014. CCIS, vol. 470, pp. 65–76. Springer, Cham (2014). https://doi.org/10.1007/978-3-319-12574-9_6
31. Pearson, S., Mont, M.C.: Sticky policies: an approach for managing privacy across multiple parties. IEEE Comput. **44**(9), 60–68 (2011)
32. Picazo-Sanchez, P., Pardo, R., Schneider, G.: Secure photo sharing in social networks. In: De Capitani di Vimercati, S., Martinelli, F. (eds.) SEC 2017. IAICT, vol. 502, pp. 79–92. Springer, Cham (2017). https://doi.org/10.1007/978-3-319-58469-0_6
33. Pinisetty, S., Antignac, T., Sands, D., Schneider, G.: Monitoring data minimisation. Technical report (2018). http://arxiv.org/abs/1801.02484
34. Pinisetty, S., Sands, D., Schneider, G.: Runtime verification of hyperproperties for deterministic programs. In: 6th Conference on Formal Methods in Software Engineering (FormaliSE@ICSE 2018), pp. 20–29. ACM (2018)
35. Schaefer, I., Runge, T., Knüppel, A., Cleophas, L., Kourie, D., Watson, B.W.: Towards confidentiality-by-construction. In: Margaria, T., Steffen, B. (eds.) ISoLA 2018. LNCS, vol. 11244, pp. 502–515. Springer, Cham (2018)
36. Spiekermann, S.: The challenges of privacy by design. Commun. ACM **55**(7), 38–40 (2012). https://doi.org/10.1145/2209249.2209263
37. Spiekermann, S., Cranor, L.F.: Engineering privacy. IEEE Trans. Softw. Eng. **35**(1), 67–82 (2009)
38. Del Tedesco, F., Hunt, S., Sands, D.: A semantic hierarchy for erasure policies. In: Jajodia, S., Mazumdar, C. (eds.) ICISS 2011. LNCS, vol. 7093, pp. 352–369. Springer, Heidelberg (2011). https://doi.org/10.1007/978-3-642-25560-1_24
39. Del Tedesco, F., Russo, A., Sands, D.: Implementing erasure policies using taint analysis. In: Aura, T., Järvinen, K., Nyberg, K. (eds.) NordSec 2010. LNCS, vol. 7127, pp. 193–209. Springer, Heidelberg (2012). https://doi.org/10.1007/978-3-642-27937-9_14
40. Tsormpatzoudi, P., Berendt, B., Coudert, F.: Privacy by design: from research and policy to practice – the challenge of multi-disciplinarity. In: Berendt, B., Engel, T., Ikonomou, D., Le Métayer, D., Schiffner, S. (eds.) APF 2015. LNCS, vol. 9484, pp. 199–212. Springer, Cham (2016). https://doi.org/10.1007/978-3-319-31456-3_12

X-by-C: Non-functional Security Challenges

Thomas Given-Wilson$^{(\boxtimes)}$ and Axel Legay

Inria, Rennes, France
`thomas.given-wilson@inria.fr`

Abstract. Correctness-by-Construction (C-by-C) approaches software development as formal engineering and builds correct code by iterating from a correct specification. However, C-by-C is focused on functional properties of the system. X-by-Construction (X-by-C) extends C-by-C to also consider non-function properties concerning aspects such as security, dependability, reliability or energy consumption. In this work we consider the challenges of applying X-by-C to non-functional security properties such as side-channel attacks. We demonstrate how such non-functional security can be captured and reasoned about in an X-by-C manner, yielding the benefit of C-by-C for non-functional properties and security challenges.

1 Introduction

Correctness-by-Construction (C-by-C) approaches software development as formal engineering [1,10,16]. The core methodology is to formally specify requirements of software being developed, and then to iterate the requirements and software development together such that iterations are always correct and converge on a correct and final implementation. In practice this has led to significant improvements in the correctness (measured by lack of errors) of software developed using C-by-C [16,33].

The underlying requirements to utilise C-by-C are as follows. It is necessary to be able to specify requirements in a formal manner, such that properties about them can be proved (or disproved). The language of development must have a semantics that can support formal statements about requirements, in particular be free from ambiguities. Further, the lack of ambiguity must also follow through from the specifications and programming language, through the entire tool chain to the final instructions in the compiled software.

For a simple example, consider the problem of checking a user password from an input buffer. The following code may be used to check that the input buffer is equal to the password before granting access.

```
if (strcmp(password, buffer) == 0) {
  access = granted;
} else {
  access = denied;  }
```

© Springer Nature Switzerland AG 2018
T. Margaria and B. Steffen (Eds.): ISoLA 2018, LNCS 11244, pp. 486–501, 2018.
https://doi.org/10.1007/978-3-030-03418-4_29

This code is correct if the `strcmp` function returns 0 iff `password` and `buffer` are equal. Thus, in turn requires considering the implementation of the standard `strcmp` function[1]

```
int strcmp (const char * s1, const char * s2) {
  for(; *s1 == *s2; ++s1, ++s2) {
    if(*s1 == 0) {
      return 0; } }
  return *(unsigned char *)s1 < *(unsigned char *)s2;
}
```

which can be verified to conform to the above requirement. In practice this could be achieved by defining a property such as

$$\forall \tau. F(equal(\texttt{password}, \texttt{buffer}) \iff \texttt{access} = \texttt{granted})$$

that checks that for all traces of execution τ, eventually (F) the property that the `password` and `buffer` are *equal* holds iff `access` equals `granted`. Naturally some care is required in the specification of some of the details, however such a property can be verified by (for example) model checking a model of the program.

C-by-C has proven successful in improving the development of critical software [33]. However, C-by-C is focused only on functional properties of the system being developed. There are many other properties about system that raise new challenges to address in software development.

Recall from the example above that the result relies upon the implementation of the `strcmp` function to determine whether the password is correct or not. Observe that the result of `strcmp` is returned as soon as any character differs. Thus, a timing sensitive attacker would be able to detect how quickly access was denied and thus determine how many leading characters of the password were correct. This shows that despite being correct, the code can still have vulnerabilities. Indeed these kinds of side-channel attacks can be exploited in real systems [6,26,32]. Thus, mere correctness of the code is no longer sufficient to ensure the code is not vulnerable. Fortunately it is possible to specify many non-functional properties that consider such security challenges.

For example, a naïve first attempt to repair the above code may be to ensure that all paths of execution have the same execution time, regardless of the contents of `buffer` or `password`. This could be resolved by checking the entire length of the password (plus one character) regardless of inequality along the way. For example, using the alternative `strcmp2` function below.

```
int strcmp2(const char *s1, const char *s2) {
  int ret = *(unsigned char *) s1 - *(unsigned char *) s2;
  while (!(*s1)) {
    ++s1, ++s2;
```

---

[1] Available from https://en.wikibooks.org/wiki/C_Programming/string.h/strcmp and here adapted by allowing return values to be any positive or negative, not just -1, 0 or 1.

```
    if (!ret) {
        ret = *(unsigned char *) s1 - *(unsigned char *) s2;  }  }
    return ret;  }
```

This solution requires a little care in declaring the original `password` and `buffer` to be suitably large enough not to cause a buffer overflow, and also safety in reading the input. However, this does resolve the initial timing concern of exiting early and leaking information to a potential attacker. Indeed, consider the property

$$\forall \tau_1, \tau_2.(time(\tau_1) = time(\tau_2))$$

that for every pair of traces τ_1 and τ_2 their execution *times* (e.g. measured in clock cycles) are equal. This can again be verified by (for example) model checking pairs of traces.

This example motivates the development of non-functional properties of systems to also be considered, or the X in X-by-Construction (X-by-C) that extends C-by-C to consider other properties beyond mere functional requirements.

The rest of this paper considers how to reason about security challenges in an X-by-C manner by adapting them into non-functional properties. The focus here is to illustrate how an X-by-C approach *can* effectively be used to address security challenges. This is achieved by demonstrating how to address known security challenges by defining non-functional properties that can capture the core security vulnerability. These properties are then refined in conjunction with development of some illustrative examples. The working through this refinement of non-functional properties along with the code development reinforces the C-by-C and X-by-C approach, while also highlighting new challenges of X-by-C. In particular, the trade-offs that can arise when trying to address multiple properties, and the subtle understanding of correctly addressing the desired behaviour.

A broader reading of this paper is intended to motivate non-functional properties in other areas such as power consumption, execution time, resource usage, etc., although deeper discussion of them is omitted for brevity and clarity. Further, challenges with respect to the definition and verification of non-functional properties as used in X-by-C are presented, as well as consideration of the evolution of traditional approaches such as model checking and statistical model checking to address these new kinds of non-functional properties.

The rest of the paper is structured as follows. Section 2 recalls C-by-C and its components. Section 3 introduces a simple logic to define properties for use in this work. Section 4 develops the motivating examples of this work more thoroughly. Section 5 considers how to define and reason about non-functional properties. Section 6 works through the properties and examples to demonstrate X-by-C. Section 7 discusses the broader context of X-by-C. Section 8 concludes.

2   Background

This sections recalls the key aspects of the C-by-C approach to software development. This is a high level overview of the core concepts and requirements to be able to achieve C-by-C in practice. Greater detail on C-by-C can be found in the references here.

The foundation of C-by-C is to develop software in a manner that combines specification of the software, formal methods for verifying or checking the source code matches the specification, and a compilation tool chain that is guaranteed to preserve the behaviour of the source code [1,5,9,10,16,19,30,31,33].

One early focus of C-by-C was in the improvement of tools that could check specifications and that interfaced with the development environment to provide immediate feedback to developers [1,27,28]. These relied upon assurances of the programming language and compiler that the source code was then correctly compiled and without errors [1,4].

More recent works have considered a broader array of approaches to the specification and verification used in C-by-C development [5,9,10,19,30,31,33]. As modern software becomes more complex, tools become more effective, and formal methods are improved, a larger set of programs can be developed using C-by-C approaches. This is illustrated by the recent focus on more advanced aspects of the formalism [3,5,24,30,31] and more advanced case studies [33].

As a parallel, the tool chains and supporting software has also been advancing, with language enhancements and verified compilation [2,22,23].

3   Specification

There are a variety of formal (and semi-formal) approaches that can be used to support the C-by-C approach to software development [1,4,5,8,10,14,19,28,30, 31]. The focus in this paper will be on strictly formal approaches that can be checked or verified to hold for a given program [2,4,8,9,14,19].

Typically such formal approaches require specifying the behaviour and/or properties of the program using a formalism that can be verified or checked. Here the details of the verification or checking shall be elided, although many possible techniques can be used, e.g. model checking [8,11,14], statistical model checking [20,21], or others [2,3,9].

To enable validation and checking there must be a way to define properties that can be applied to the program in question. Various methods can be used to define properties, usually a combination of logical and behaviour components. Here the choice is to have an abstract notion of properties that can be defined over program execution traces.

For the purpose of this paper the focus will be upon the program execution trace. This is similar in concept to properties that are checked over program execution such as model checking and statistical model checking. However, for some of the properties here it is desirable to reason over multiple traces.

Although basic functional and non-functional properties could be defined over a single trace, there are some more subtle properties that may wish to relate multiple program execution traces.

For example, consider determining if two execution traces of a program have the same execution time. Given the traces τ_1 and τ_2 we could define a function $t(\cdot)$

that given a trace τ determines the number n of clock cycles taken for that trace, i.e. $t(\tau) = n$. We could then consider the property $\mathcal{P}(\tau_1, \tau_2) \stackrel{\text{def}}{=} t(\tau_1) = t(\tau_2)$.

We now define an abstract property language as follows:

$$\phi = \alpha \mid \phi \vee \phi \mid \phi \wedge \phi \mid \neg\phi \mid \mathrm{F}(\phi) \mid \forall\tau.\phi \mid \mathcal{P}(\tau_1, \tau_2).$$

The α denotes an atomic property that is *true* or *false*. The $\phi \vee \phi$ denotes the logical *or* operator, and similarly $\phi \wedge \phi$ denotes *and*, and $\neg\phi$ denotes negation. The $\mathrm{F}(\phi)$ is the *eventually* operator of temporal logics that states that ϕ must eventually hold. The $\forall\tau.\phi$ is the standard *forall* operator, here binding traces τ in the property ϕ. Lastly, the $\mathcal{P}(\tau_1, \tau_2)$ denotes a functional or non-functional property of the pair of traces τ_1 and τ_2.

Note that the definition above allows the definition of further traditional logical operators, such as *implication* $\Rightarrow$ and *iff* $\Leftrightarrow$, *existence* $\exists\tau.\phi$, etc. Also, the choice to have $\mathcal{P}(\tau_1, \tau_2)$ over a pair of traces is to reason about properties that must be verified by considering more than one trace, here two traces is sufficient, and this can be generalised to any number of traces as required.

Aside: Observe that many of these logical operators could be incorporated into properties $\mathcal{P}(\cdot, \cdot)$. The goal here is to illustrate how to construct X-by-C processes around a logical framework. Thus, the abstract property language is designed for illustration and *not* for elegance or simplicity. That said, the properties expressed later in the paper should be definable in hyperLTL or similar logics [12].

The verification of the properties here can be done using techniques such as model checking [13,17,34] or statistical model checking [21]. (Model checking of even large and complex C code bases has been demonstrated before and so the creation of such models and checking properties is merely engineering effort [8,14,15].) For the property language primitives, all except for $\mathcal{P}(\tau_1, \tau_2)$ are a subset of existing languages such as bounded linear temporal logic (LTL) that are commonly used in model checking and statistical model checking. The $\mathcal{P}(\tau_1, \tau_2)$ functional or non-functional property can be easily verified using model checking or statistical model checking by comparing the two traces τ_1 and τ_2 (that are traces of the model). Of course depending on external qualifiers this may be relatively expensive to compute. In particular, a forall of a pair of traces $\forall\tau_1, \tau_2.\mathcal{P}(\tau_1, \tau_2)$ would require every pair of traces be tested together, but this is analogous to the state space explosion problem of model checking [13,17] that can in practice be addressed with statistical model checking [21]. Another possibility is to lift to hyperproperties that operate directly on traces and the related hyper variations of the appropriate properties and specifications (such as using hyperLTL) [12].

4   Motivating Examples

This section presents two examples that are used to motivate X-by-C and non-functional properties of systems. The examples focus on security, but exhibit classes of non-functional properties that are also important in other domains.

Note that typically in C-by-C related papers the choice of language is significant to the correctness and a high level of abstraction is usually desired. Often Ada or some other language with strong linguistic properties is chosen, where the programmer cannot bend or break linguistic rules easily [1,4,19,29,33]. Instead here the choice is to use a comparatively low level and weak language (C) for several reasons. A low level language allows reasoning about low level concepts in practice such as timing and cache usage. The libraries for many high level languages are written in low level languages to exploit performance optimisations (that are significant to the non functional properties considered in this work). The weakness of C is not significant here, and indeed the examples do not require any permissiveness of the compiler, or exploitation of linguistic weakness. Lastly, correctness of compilation of C can be achieved [22,23] so this is not an inherent barrier to the use of C for examples here.

4.1   Password Example

The first example to consider here is checking the input from a user is the correct password (as in Sect. 1). The example here is explored in low level C/C++ style source code to clearly illustrate the subtleties that may occur, and also since the underlying libraries of many other languages (such as those used in C-by-C [4,19,29]) exploit C/C++ libraries themselves.

The concept is to check whether the password is equal to the input buffer of user input before deciding whether or not to grant access based on their equality.

```
if (strcmp(password, buffer) == 0) {
  access = granted;
} else {
  access = denied;  }
```

As is best practice, library code is used to compare the two buffers using strcmp. The source code for strcmp is as below.

```
int strcmp (const char * s1, const char * s2) {
  for(; *s1 == *s2; ++s1, ++s2) {
    if(*s1 == 0) {
      return 0; } }
  return *(unsigned char *)s1 < *(unsigned char *)s2;
}
```

Observe that there is nothing particularly complex here, and it is straightforward (to apply C-by-C) to validate that access is only granted when the password and buffer are equal.

4.2   Encryption

The second example is a fragment of the PRESENT encryption algorithm [7,18]. PRESENT is a lightweight block cipher designed for use on low power and

CPU constrained devices. The PRESENT algorithm consists of 31 rounds of a Substitution-Permutation Network (SPN) with block size of 64 bits. The canonical implementation[2] supports key lengths of 80 or 128 bits. The core encryption algorithm is the same for both 80 and 128 bit keys. The fragment of PRESENT here is from the canonical version in C for 32 bit architectures (size optimised, 80 bit key). The choice of PRESENT is illustrative of block cipher encryption algorithms such as AES [25].

Significant to block ciphers is the use of SBox values used in the encryption. In PRESENT this SBox (sBox4) is used in the following code fragment

```
do {
  i--;
  state[i] = sBox4[state[i]>>4]<<4 | sBox4[state[i] & 0xF];  }
while(i>0);
```

where i is initially 8 (from previous operations). Here state is used to in-place store and update the ciphertext as it is generated.

Several kinds of side channel attacks can gain information by exploiting the access of the SBox [6,26,32]. In general such an approach works by determining which elements of the SBox (or which SBoxes when many are used) have been accessed by the encryption. Combined with timing information that can be used to infer values for the plaintext and/or key used by the encryption algorithm.

The general weakness that can be exploited here for an attacker is that the SBox is accessed inconsistently depending upon the plaintext and key values. This exactly corresponds to known cache attacks [6,26,32].

Indeed, even with incomplete information from such side-channel attacks, vulnerabilities are known to exist in PRESENT [35].

Observe that checking the mathematical correctness of the implementation is straightforward, albeit requiring significant time and/or engineering investment to achieve. Thus, applying C-by-C to validate the implementation is correct can ensure that the encryption does not produce incorrect results, although this does not mitigate other attacks, including those cited above.

5   Non-functional Properties

This section considers various properties that are desirable in systems from a security perspective. In particular the focus is on non-functional properties, in that they do not define or rely upon the functional correctness of the code and would be difficult or impossible to easily account for using traditional C-by-C approaches. The non-functional properties (2–4) here are chosen to illustrate potential security vulnerabilities that are not detected by functional correctness.

Property 1: Correctness. The first property to consider is a simple functional property defined for each example. In each case, this property is that the

---

[2] Available at http://www.lightweightcrypto.org/implementations.php.

output of the function is correct. Here this property is included as a link back to ensure that iterations and improvements of doing X-by-C do not alter the C-by-C properties of the examples (from Sect. 4).

For the password example (Sect. 4.1) functional correctness is defined by:

$$\forall \tau.F(eq2null(\texttt{password}, \texttt{buffer}) \Leftrightarrow \texttt{access} = \texttt{granted}) \tag{1}$$

where the $eq2null$ function determines equality of characters in both arguments in order until both arguments have the null character. Overall this property defines that over all traces τ eventually: the password and buffer are equal up to termination by the null character iff access is granted. This captures the correct functional behaviour of the password example.

For the PRESENT example (Sect. 4.2) functional correctness is more complex and so will be abstractly represented by

$$\forall \tau.F(\texttt{state} = enc(init(\texttt{state}), \texttt{key})) \tag{2}$$

where $enc(p, k)$ is the encryption (using the PRESENT algorithm) of the plaintext p with key k, and where $init(\cdot)$ is the initial value of its argument, here state. Abstracting away the details here is for simplicity, when in practice such a complex algorithm would instead be dealt with by ensuring smaller components achieved smaller properties that can be composed to achieve the overall result. (Also the property here is for the whole function, not just the code fragment considered here.) Overall this property defines that over all traces τ eventually the values in state are the correct result of encrypting the initial values of state with the key (using the PRESENT algorithm). Again this captures the correct functional behaviour of the encryption example.

Property 2: Equal Time. The first attempt to define a non-functional property is to prevent the leakage of timing information. The goal here is to ensure that the time taken for the function to produce a result is not impacted by the inputs, since different timings could leak information about the input values.

For the password example (Sect. 4.1) differences in timing between different traces/executions of the function can yield information about the (relative) correctness of the input given by the user. For example, if the first character of the password is incorrect, this yields a different timing than if the n characters of the input are correct. A (possible) solution to this is to have a property that checks that execution time is the same for all inputs. This can be formalised by:

$$\forall \tau_1, \tau_2.(time(\tau_1) = time(\tau_2)) \tag{3}$$

where $time(\tau)$ is a function that returns the execution time in clock cycles of the trace τ. Again the $time$ of a trace would not be considered a monolithic function, but instead be defined by composition component functions that could sum the time of various instructions. Note that the inputs do not need to be explicitly denoted here, since this is accounted for by the quantification over all possible pairs of traces.

Observe that for the PRESENT example (Sect. 4.2) the same property is desirable. A violation of this property would imply that for some value of the key or plaintext, the timing is different. This would allow a timing sensitive attacker to distinguish some inputs (keys and plaintexts) from others, and so potential gain useful information.

Property 3: Constant Time. A more rigid non-functional property related to timing information could be to ensure that execution time is constant. This ensures that the function takes a fixed constant amount of time to compute regardless of the inputs. Such a property is stronger than the Equal Time property above and in practice prevents other kinds of information leakage. However, this requires a potentially less efficient implementation and places a heavier burden on the program.

For both examples a constant time property can be formalised by:

$$\exists n.\forall \tau.(time(\tau) \;=\; n). \tag{4}$$

This property specifies that there exists a constant n such that all traces τ have the same execution time of n cycles as calculated by the $time$ function.

Again observe that this property can easily be applied to both the password and encryption examples.

Property 4: Consistent Access. Another kind of property that is more specific to examples such as PRESENT (Sect. 4.2) would be to ensure that the same blocks of code are accessed during all executions. This prevents cache based attacks where the attacker exploits the architecture of the system cache, e.g. to detect which code blocks (SBox sections) were used in the computation of the encryption, and in turn yield information about the encryption key [6, 26, 32].

Defining a property that accounts for the usage of particular code or memory fragments is a little more complex (particularly since many approaches rely on execution trace rather than data access [1, 5, 8, 14, 19, 30, 31]). However, with some care such a property that captures the required detail can be defined.

Consider the following property defined by:

$$\forall \tau_1, \tau_2. \left(\forall i. \left(\begin{array}{c} i \leq length(\tau_1) \;\wedge\; length(\tau_1) = length(\tau_2) \\ \wedge\; read(instr(i, \tau)) \;=\; read(instr(i, \tau)) \end{array} \right) \right) \tag{5}$$

where the $length(\tau)$ function returns the length of the trace τ, and the $instr(i, \tau)$ function returns the instruction at position i in the trace τ, and the $read(\cdot)$ function returns the memory location(s) read by an instruction (if any). Overall this property is very strict, but captures the ideal that every trace must read the same memory locations in the same sequence and at the same time.

Observe that this property can be applied to both the password and the encryption examples. Note that this does *not* ensure any form of correctness of the code behaviour or that all the memory locations are read from, only that the pattern of reading from memory is identical across all possible traces.

Finally, observe that these various properties are designed to be combined to evaluate the functional and non-functional properties of a program. Thus, although each may not ensure that all the required functional and non-functional behaviours are achieved, satisfying all the properties should yield a correct and secure implementation. This is demonstrated in the next section.

6   Worked X-by-C Examples

This section explores some of the delicacy and subtely of non-functional properties in security. The focus here is on evolving the examples and properties together to yield a good solution. Observe that this is illustrated to guide correct development of non-functional properties and highlight potential mistakes.

6.1   Methodology

Before going into the detail of the worked examples, a brief overview of the methodology used in C-by-C and X-by-C as exploited here. The principle of C-by-C and X-by-C is to develop the source code and the properties together, with the properties being checked (and refined) in parallel with the development. Typically most properties are known a priori and refined only in the face of changing requirements or new understanding, although later properties can be added as the project evolves. For clarity all the properties were defined a priori here, but shall be considered incrementally along with refinement and development of the source code.

In practice the approach implemented here is to develop a model from the source code that allows the construction of traces. These traces are then used for the checking of the abstract property language (Sect. 3). The checking here can be done with either model checking or statistical model checking (with preference given depending the optimisation for total coverage with model checking, or efficient computation with statistical model checking). Thus, at each stage below, the source code is used to build a model, and the properties are checked upon the model. Here each property is defined independently for clarity, but in practice the functional and non-functional properties can easily be combined into a single property (with conjunction $\wedge$) if this is preferable for a single pass/fail result.

6.2   Worked Password Example

This section considers the password example (Sect. 4.1) and the properties from Sect. 5. Observe that the initial version of the code meets the functional property of Correctness, but does not meet any non-functional properties of Eqs. 3, 4, or 5.

The first violation of the non-functional properties is that the time taken to calculate the `strcmp` function depends upon the values of `password` and `buffer`.

The naïve first attempt (as in Sect. 1) shown below attempts to resolve the Equal Time property by using a new `strcmp2` function.

```
int strcmp2(const char *s1, const char *s2) {
  int ret = *(unsigned char *) s1 - *(unsigned char *) s2;
```

```
while (!(*s1)) {
  ++s1, ++s2;
  if (!ret) {
    ret = *(unsigned char *) s1 - *(unsigned char *) s2;  }  }
return ret;  }
```

This solution requires a little care in declaring the original **password** and **buffer** to be suitably large enough not to cause a buffer overflow, and also safety in reading the input. This resolves the Equal Time non-functional timing property (Eq. 3) that all execution paths are equal in length (and also the functional Correctness property of Eq. 1).

Unfortunately this solution still yields information about the length of the **password**. Observe that the code confirms equality of the input with the password. However, changes to the length of the password yield information to a timing sensitive attacker. Thus, the definition of the Constant Time property in Eq. 4 that ensures the execution time is constant.

An improved **strcmp3** function is shown below that addresses the Constant Time property to yield constant execution time.

```
int strcmp3(const char *s1, const char *s2) {
  int ret = *(unsigned char *) s1 - *(unsigned char *) s2;
  int ex;
  int i = 0;
  while (i < 1024) {
    ++s1, ++s2, ++i;
    if (!ret) {
      ret = *(unsigned char *) s1 - *(unsigned char *) s2;
    } else {
      ex = *(unsigned char *) s1 - *(unsigned char *) s2;  }  }
  return ret;  }
```

Here the **password** and **buffer** arrays are both defined to be of length 1024. The additional int **ex** is used to store unused comparison between the arrays and so ensures that regardless of the return state **ret**, the comparison is still computed. (This is used to ensure that not performing the comparison would not reduce the execution time.) Observe that some care must be taken to ensure that **ex** is not dropped by compiler optimisation, since this would then reduce the execution time and re-introduce information leakage to a timing sensitive attacker.

In all cases now the execution time is equal and so this can be validated to hold for the functional Correctness property (Eq. 1) and non-functional timing properties of both Equal Time (Eq. 3) and Constant Time (Eq. 4).

Finally, observe that the above code also ensures the same reading of memory locations in all cases. The only places that the code differs in where the writing is done inside the conditional, and so the Consistent Access property of Eq. 5 also holds.

Combining all of these properties together and ensuring that they all hold in the final version of the code has allowed us to develop a correct and secure implementation using X-by-C approaches. The variety of different properties here do not conflict with each other and can easily be checked independently. The only redundancy is between the Equal Time and Constant Time properties, where the latter generalises the former.

6.3   Worked Encryption Example

This section considers the encryption example of Sect. 4.2 with various properties from Sect. 5. Observe that, again, the original code meets the functional correctness property (Eq. 2). Further, here the properties of Equal Time and Constant Time are also both achieved with the initial source code.

The vulnerability here is in the Consistent Access property, since in the code

```
do {
  i--;
  state[i] = sBox4[state[i]>>4]<<4 | sBox4[state[i] & 0xF];  }
while(i>0);
```

accessed sBox4 only at state[i]>>4 and state[i]. To illustrate the weakness, consider that when state is entirely populated by zeros then both state[i]>>4 and state[i] will always by zero, and only a single value in sBox4 will be accessed.

To resolve this requires accessing all possible elements of sBox4 (here 16 possible single byte elements). Consider the modified fragment of the PRESENT code below.

```
do {
  i--;
  uint8_t ignore;
  uint8_t p1 = sBox4[i]<<4;
  for (uint8_t j = 0; j < 16; j++) {
    uint8_t p2 = sBox4[j];
    if ((state[i] & 0xF) == j) {
      state[i] = p1 | p2;
    } else {
      ignore = p1 | p2;  }  }  }
```

Again, a spurious variable (here ignore) is included to ensure the access is identical across all traces. (Again care must be taken to ensure ignore is not removed by compiler optimisations.) Observe that this code is not the most efficient approach, but does ensure that every value of sBox4 is accessed (indeed for each iteration of the do-while loop). Thus, the above code fragment ensures constant access of the sBox4 and so mitigates access based attacks. (This is a known counter-measure against such attacks [32].) Further, by ensuring that the entire loop is iterated for all executions, this maintains the Constant Time property of Eq. 4.

Observe that the checking of properties on components or code fragments and then combining them to achieve an overall property is an efficient approach used in C-by-C and X-by-C. The same solutions for Constant Access would need to be applied over other fragments of the PRESENT code to achieve the property for the whole algorithm.

Note that the above solution has been written to clearly illustrate how to ensure the entire sBox4 is accessed. Optimisations can reduce this to require the access of all the values of sBox4 to occur only once. However, these have been omitted here since this has a larger impact on the control flow and clarity, and the focus here is illustration rather than optimisation.

7   Discussion

This section discusses the implications of the worked X-by-C examples here, and this relation to broader application of X-by-C.

The examples here illustrate that X-by-C and non-functional properties can be combined in a manner that can address known security concerns that cannot be captured easily within tradition C-by-C approaches. The limitations of traditional C-by-C here relate to the focus on correctness, but not upon other properties that may or may not hold while achieving correctness. The focus here has been on security challenges, since these are well documented and well understood, albeit not easy to address in practice.

The ability to represent and reason about non-functional security properties allows X-by-C to incorporate them into the development process. This should allow such non-functional security properties to then be caught early in the development process, and reduce their incidence in practice.

The choice of non-functional properties to address security challenges must also be made with some care. The first attempt to address the security challenge of timing attacks by using the Equal Time property appears to yield X-by-C, but still has a timing vulnerability. This reinforces the approach of C-by-C and X-by-C in iterating and improving both the source code and the properties together. Of course good practice and experience can reduce such accidents in the definition of non-functional properties (and indeed these were put in here precisely to demonstrate potential accidents).

One potential drawback of accounting for additional (here non-functional) properties is that they may impact the performance. Clearly the initial code for both the password and PRESENT examples (Sect. 4) are more efficient. In practice it is not unsurprising that code that meets more stringent functional and non-functional properties may be less efficient (and indeed is a known cost of more secure code [32]). However, by being able to reason about and formalise when the properties are met, allows optimisations to be developed that maintain the desired (functional and non-functional) properties.

This potential drawback in optimisation is also an example of a larger potential conflict when many (functional and non-functional) properties come into play. The focus here is on non-functional security challenges that tend to reduce performance (but do not harm correctness). If other non-functional challenges such as power usage are considered then there is potential for greater conflicts.

Observe that the less optimal (but here non-functionally secure) implementation will tend to also be more costly in power usage due to increases instructions and data access. If a non-functional challenge is to try and minimise power usage, or keep power usage under a certain bound, then this will potentially be in conflict with non-functional security challenges.

As many more non-functional properties are considered as part of X-by-C approaches, it is expected that there may be conflicts or trade-offs to be resolved. It may be straightforward to try and define properties that can be satisfied by both, e.g. require Constant Time for execution, and also under a fixed bound for energy usage. However, in practice many non-functional aspects of software are not so easily captured by strict formal properties. An obvious example is the minimisation of: run-time, energy usage, memory usage, etc. This in turn implies that there may be some interest in non-functional properties that are *not* simply answered by a boolean (verified/failed), but instead by some metric.

Lastly, the non-functional properties presented here are properties that can be ensured to be met by a compiler. The time based non-functional properties are a little subtle to handle precisely since they can rely upon the time taken for specific instructions that could vary slightly between branches (and of course out-of-order execution in modern processors). However, information on the chosen architecture and machine instructions is sufficient to allow reasonable confidence in the execution. The Consistent Access property is much easier to ensure, and straightforward to observe through the compilation into machine instructions.

8   Conclusions

The C-by-C approach to software development has yielded significant improvements in correctness and software quality by considering functional properties during development. The C-by-C approach can be extended to the X-by-C approach, where non-functional properties are also considered during development. Non-functional security properties are straightforward to define that can mitigate several known security vulnerabilities.

The worked examples here demonstrate that non-functional security properties can be defined and incorporated into an X-by-C development process. The detail of these worked examples highlights how to achieve this with X-by-C, and how to refine and iterate on both the non-functional properties and the development to address serious security challenges.

However, this paper also illustrates new challenges related to X-by-C and non-functional properties. Although some approaches to their development and verification are highlighted here, open questions in this area will require addressing if such X-by-C is to be achieved in larger examples and projects.

More broadly this paper highlights how to address many different non-functional challenges in an X-by-C development process. Examples of such non-functional challenge domains include: security, power usage, execution time, resource usage, and others. Naturally increasing the scope of the functional and non-functional properties considered to address different challenges during X-by-C development can also result in conflicts and trade-offs.

References

1. Amey, P.: Correctness by construction: better can also be cheaper. CrossTalk: J. Def. Softw. Eng. **2**, 24–28 (2002)
2. Appel, A.W.: Program Logics for Certified Compilers. Cambridge University Press, Cambridge (2014)
3. Attie, P., Baranov, E., Bliudze, S., Jaber, M., Sifakis, J.: A general framework for architecture composability. Form. Asp. Comput. **28**(2), 207–231 (2016)
4. Barnes, J.G.P.: High Integrity Ada: The SPARK Approach, vol. 189. Addison-Wesley, Reading (1997)
5. ter Beek, M., Carmona Vargas, J., Kleijn, J.: Communication and compatibility in systems of systems: correctness-by-construction. ERCIM News **2015**(102), 21–22 (2015)
6. Bernstein, D.J.: Cache-timing attacks on AES (2005)
7. Bogdanov, A., et al.: PRESENT: an ultra-lightweight block cipher. In: Paillier, P., Verbauwhede, I. (eds.) CHES 2007. LNCS, vol. 4727, pp. 450–466. Springer, Heidelberg (2007). https://doi.org/10.1007/978-3-540-74735-2_31
8. Bradley, M., Cassez, F., Fehnker, A., Given-Wilson, T., Huuck, R.: High performance static analysis for industry. Electron. Notes Theor. Comput. Sci. **289**, 3–14 (2012)
9. Brady, E., Hammond, K.: Correct-by-construction concurrency: using dependent types to verify implementations of effectful resource usage protocols. Fundam. Inform. **102**(2), 145–176 (2010)
10. Chapman, R.: Correctness by construction: a manifesto for high integrity software. In: Proceedings of the 10th Australian Workshop on Safety Critical Systems and Software, vol. 55, pp. 43–46. Australian Computer Society Inc. (2006)
11. Clarke, E.M., Grumberg, O., Peled, D.: Model Checking. MIT Press, Cambridge (1999)
12. Clarkson, M.R., Finkbeiner, B., Koleini, M., Micinski, K.K., Rabe, M.N., Sánchez, C.: Temporal logics for hyperproperties. In: Abadi, M., Kremer, S. (eds.) POST 2014. LNCS, vol. 8414, pp. 265–284. Springer, Heidelberg (2014). https://doi.org/10.1007/978-3-642-54792-8_15
13. Emerson, E.A.: The beginning of model checking: a personal perspective. In: Grumberg, O., Veith, H. (eds.) 25 Years of Model Checking. LNCS, vol. 5000, pp. 27–45. Springer, Heidelberg (2008). https://doi.org/10.1007/978-3-540-69850-0_2
14. Fehnker, A., Huuck, R.: Model checking driven static analysis for the real world: designing and tuning large scale bug detection. Innov. Syst. Softw. Eng. **9**(1), 45–56 (2013)
15. Fehnker, A., Huuck, R., Jayet, P., Lussenburg, M., Rauch, F.: Goanna—a static model checker. In: Brim, L., Haverkort, B., Leucker, M., van de Pol, J. (eds.) FMICS 2006. LNCS, vol. 4346, pp. 297–300. Springer, Heidelberg (2007). https://doi.org/10.1007/978-3-540-70952-7_20
16. Hall, A., Chapman, R.: Correctness by construction: developing a commercial secure system. IEEE Softw. **19**(1), 18–25 (2002)
17. Kinder, J., Katzenbeisser, S., Schallhart, C., Veith, H.: Proactive detection of computer worms using model checking. IEEE Trans. Dependable Secur. Comput. **7**(4), 424–438 (2010)
18. Knudsen, L.R., Leander, G.: PRESENT-block cipher. In: van Tilborg, H.C.A., Jajodia, S. (eds.)Encyclopedia of Cryptography and Security, pp. 953–955. Springer, Boston (2011). https://doi.org/10.1007/978-1-4419-5906-5

19. Kourie, D.G., Watson, B.W.: The Correctness-by-Construction Approach to Programming. Springer Science & Business Media, Berlin (2012)
20. Kwiatkowska, M., Norman, G., Parker, D.: PRISM 4.0: verification of probabilistic real-time systems. In: Gopalakrishnan, G., Qadeer, S. (eds.) CAV 2011. LNCS, vol. 6806, pp. 585–591. Springer, Heidelberg (2011). https://doi.org/10.1007/978-3-642-22110-1_47
21. Legay, A., Delahaye, B., Bensalem, S.: Statistical model checking: an overview. In: Barringer, H., et al. (eds.) RV 2010. LNCS, vol. 6418, pp. 122–135. Springer, Heidelberg (2010). https://doi.org/10.1007/978-3-642-16612-9_11
22. Leroy, X.: Formal certification of a compiler back-end or: programming a compiler with a proof assistant. In: ACM SIGPLAN Notices, vol. 41, pp. 42–54. ACM (2006)
23. Leroy, X.: A formally verified compiler back-end. J. Autom. Reason. **43**(4), 363 (2009)
24. Mavridou, A., Baranov, E., Bliudze, S., Sifakis, J.: Configuration logics: modeling architecture styles. J. Log. Algebr. Methods Program. **86**(1), 2–29 (2017)
25. National Institute of Standards and Technology. Advanced Encryption Standard. Federal Information Processing Standards Publication, 197 (2001)
26. Osvik, D.A., Shamir, A., Tromer, E.: Cache attacks and countermeasures: the case of AES. In: Pointcheval, D. (ed.) CT-RSA 2006. LNCS, vol. 3860, pp. 1–20. Springer, Heidelberg (2006). https://doi.org/10.1007/11605805_1
27. Sutton, J., Carré, B.: Ada: the cheapest way to build a line of business. In: Proceedings of the Conference on TRI-Ada 1995: Ada's Role in Global Markets: Solutions for a Changing Complex World, pp. 320–330. ACM (1995)
28. Sutton, J., Carré, B.: Achieving high integrity at low cost: a constructive approach. Microprocess. Microsyst. **20**(8), 455–461 (1997)
29. Taft, S., Duff, R., Brukardt, R., Ploedereder, E., Leroy, P., Ada 2012 reference manual. Language and Standard Libraries-International Standard ISO/IEC 8652 (2012)
30. ter Beek, M.H., Carmona, J., Hennicker, R., Kleijn, J.: Communication requirements for team automata. In: Jacquet, J.-M., Massink, M. (eds.) COORDINATION 2017. LNCS, vol. 10319, pp. 256–277. Springer, Cham (2017). https://doi.org/10.1007/978-3-319-59746-1_14
31. ter Beek, M.H., Carmona, J., Kleijn, J.: Conditions for compatibility of components. In: Margaria, T., Steffen, B. (eds.) ISoLA 2016, Part I. LNCS, vol. 9952, pp. 784–805. Springer, Cham (2016). https://doi.org/10.1007/978-3-319-47166-2_55
32. Tromer, E., Osvik, D.A., Shamir, A.: Efficient cache attacks on AES, and countermeasures. J. Cryptol. **23**(1), 37–71 (2010)
33. Watson, B.W., Kourie, D.G., Cleophas, L.: Experience with correctness-by-construction. Sci. Comput. Program. **97**, 55–58 (2015)
34. Yamane, S., Konoshita, R., Kato, T.: Model checking of embedded assembly program based on simulation. IEICE Trans. Inf. Syst. **100**(8), 1819–1826 (2017)
35. Yang, L., Wang, M., Qiao, S.: Side channel cube attack on PRESENT. In: Garay, J.A., Miyaji, A., Otsuka, A. (eds.) CANS 2009. LNCS, vol. 5888, pp. 379–391. Springer, Heidelberg (2009). https://doi.org/10.1007/978-3-642-10433-6_25

Towards Confidentiality-by-Construction

Ina Schaefer[1]([✉]), Tobias Runge[1], Alexander Knüppel[1], Loek Cleophas[2,3], Derrick Kourie[3,4], and Bruce W. Watson[3,4]

[1] Software Engineering, TU Braunschweig, Braunschweig, Germany
{i.schaefer,tobias.runge,a.knueppel}@tu-bs.de
[2] Software Engineering Technology Group,
TU Eindhoven, Eindhoven, The Netherlands
[3] Department of Information Science,
Stellenbosch University, Stellenbosch, South Africa
{loek,derrick,bruce}@fastar.org
[4] Centre for Artificial Intelligence Research, Stellenbosch, South Africa

Abstract. Guaranteeing that information processed in computing systems remains confidential is vital for many software applications. To this end, language-based security mechanisms enforce fine-grained access control policies for program variables to prevent secret information from leaking through unauthorized access. However, approaches for language-based security by information flow control mostly work *post-hoc*, classifying programs into whether they comply with information flow policies or not after the program has been constructed. Means for constructing programs that satisfy given information flow control policies are still missing. Following the correctness-by-construction approach, we propose a development method for specifying information flow policies first and constructing programs satisfying these policies subsequently. We replace functional pre- and postcondition specifications with confidentiality properties and define rules to derive new confidentiality specifications for each refining program construct. We discuss possible extensions including initial ideas for tool support. Applying correctness-by-construction techniques to confidentiality properties constitutes a first step towards security-by-construction.

1 Introduction

Modern software applications often process confidential information, such as personal information, credit card numbers, health records etc. It is important to enforce that this confidential information is not leaked to unauthorised access. Language-based security mechanisms [19] allow fine-grained control over the confidential information and its influence on program execution in order to prevent such unwanted leakage. Information flow control approaches [19,20] model confidentiality by defining *security policies* which determine how secret information in a program may be used for computation and influence program execution. In a very simple security policy, the set of program variables is classified into *high* and *low variables.* Information may flow within the classes and from low to

© Springer Nature Switzerland AG 2018
T. Margaria and B. Steffen (Eds.): ISoLA 2018, LNCS 11244, pp. 502–515, 2018.
https://doi.org/10.1007/978-3-030-03418-4_30

high variables, but not from high to low variables. This captures the intuition that high information, i.e., confidential information, may not influence low, i.e., public information, or that it may not be observable or deducible from public information. However, approaches for language-based security by information flow control mostly work *post-hoc*. They classify programs into the ones which comply to information flow policies and the ones that do not, but do not provide means to construct programs that satisfy given information flow control policies.

Correctness-by-construction (CbC) [14] in contrast aims at developing programs in a way such that they satisfy their correctness specification by their design and development methodology. Classical CbC as proposed by Dijkstra [10] and others [11,16] aims at developing functional programs that are correct-by-construction. For this purpose, a number of refinement rules are proposed that allow refining an abstract specification into a concrete program that satisfies the given specification. CbC programs are guaranteed to be correct in the same sense as a proof of a mathematical theorem is guaranteed to be correct. CbC-based development tends to minimise post-hoc quality assurance costs and thereby reduce time to market [21].

In this paper, we propose to apply correctness-by-construction techniques to guarantee confidentiality properties that are expressed by information flow policies over programs leading to an approach for *confidentiality-by-construction (C14bC)*[1] as a first step towards *security-by-construction (SbC)*. We replace functional pre-/postcondition specifications—as traditionally used for classical functional correctness—with confidentiality specifications, expressing which variables contain secrets. Then we provide rules for each possible program construct to refine a program by introducing such a construct, and we derive a new information flow specification for the program statement, in the spirit of classical CbC. In order to allow assigning secret values to public variables, we incorporate means to explicitly declassify information [17,22]. Furthermore, we discuss extensions of C14bC as well as potential for tool support.

The remainder of this paper is structured as follows: In Sect. 2, we provide the background on classical CbC and language-based information-flow control. In Sect. 3, we describe our approach to confidentiality-by-construction. In Sect. 4, we present initial ideas for tool support. Section 5 provides an overview of related work, and Sect. 6 concludes the paper with a discussion of extensions of the presented approach.

2   Background

In this section, we provide the necessary background on classical CbC and information flow control policies as a basis for the approach proposed in this paper. In order to simplify the discussion and focus on the main ideas of C14bC, we restrict programs to procedural programs that can be expressed in the guarded command language [10].

---

[1] The numeronym C14bC abbreviates confidentiality as C14, as there are 14 letters after the first C.

2.1 Classical Functional CbC

CbC [14] is a formal approach which is used to develop code incrementally. CbC starts with an abstract program and its specification which is a Hoare triple consisting of a precondition, an abstract statement, and a postcondition. The program between the pre- and postconditions is specified in the *Guarded Command Language* (GCL) as proposed by Dijkstra [10]. The Hoare triple T should be read as a total correctness assertion, i.e., an assertion that if T's precondition holds and its abstract statement executes, then the execution will terminate and its postcondition will hold. The triple can be stepwise evolved to a concrete program by using refinement rules. The rules each replace an abstract statement by more concrete ones, cf. Fig. 1. By only using correctness-preserving refinement steps that are accurately applied, we know that the concrete program obtained by refinement is correct by construction.

To refine the program, GCL uses five different rules—one for each of its statements—as shown in Fig. 1. The skip statement (1) does not alter the program. The assignment statement (2) refines an abstract statement S to an assignment $x := E$. This refinement can only be used if the precondition P implies the postcondition Q where x is replaced by E. A composition statement (3) splits an abstract statement S into two statements S1 and S2 with an intermediate condition M between both statements. In the selection statement (4), for simplicity and similarity to, e.g., Java, we use an if-else-construct while the classical formulation of GCL uses a more complex switch-like statement. If the guard is evaluated to true, the first statement is executed, else the second one is. The repetition statement (5) is similar. As long as the guard is evaluated to true, the statement is executed repeatedly. The repetition statement requires an *invariant* and a *variant*. The invariant specifies the effect of the loop and is true before and after every loop iteration. The variant shows the termination of the loop. It is a term which decreases monotonically and is bounded from below; here we choose zero without loss of generality. In this discussion, we omit the refinement rules that allow strengthening of postconditions and weakening of preconditions.

{P} S {Q}	*can be refined to*	
Skip :	{P} *skip* {Q} *iff* P *implies* Q	(1)
Assignment :	{P} $x := E$ {Q} *iff* P *implies* Q[$x := E$]	(2)
Composition :	{P} S1 ; S2 {Q} *iff there is* M *s.t.* {P} S1 {M} *and* {M} S2 {Q}	(3)
Selection :	{P} **if** G **then** S1 **else** S2 **fi** {Q} *iff*	(4)
	{P ∧ G} S1 {Q} *and* {P ∧ ¬G} S2 {Q}	
Repetition :	{P} **do** G → S **od** {Q} *iff there is invariant* I *and variant* V *s.t.*	(5)
	(P *implies* I) *and* (I ∧ ¬G *implies* Q) *and* {I ∧ G} S {I}	
	and {I ∧ G ∧ V = V_0} S {I ∧ 0 ≤ V < V_0}	

Fig. 1. Refinement Rules in CbC [14]

To give an example of how CbC-refinements work, we consider the abstract triple $\{x > 0\}$ S $\{x > 1\}$. An assignment refinement rule associated with line (2) of Fig. 1 indicates how this triple can be refined to $\{x > 0\}$ x := x + 1 $\{x > 1\}$, delivering a program that ensures the postcondition if the precondition holds.

2.2 Information Flow Control

Information flow control [19,20] can be used to establish confidentiality of program data. A security policy defines security domains for data and determines how information may flow between those domains. In this paper, we restrict ourselves to a simple security policy by only considering two security domains, secret and public, where information may flow from public to secret, but not the other way around. The program variables are subdivided into high (secret) and low (public) variables. The high variables contain information which must not flow to low variables. Information in a program can flow in two ways: first, there can be direct information flow in an assignment, e.g., $l = h$ assigns the confidential value of h to a low variable l; second, there can be indirect information flow through conditional statements where secret information is used in the guard of the statement. For example, the statement $if\ h == 0 \rightarrow l := 0\ else\ l := 1$ reveals information about the variable h. If l is zero, we know that h is also zero.

To discard programs which violate confidentiality as expressed by a security policy, a security type system can be introduced (cf. Fig. 2) according to [19]. The type system assigns every variable and expression a security type. $E : t$ means that expression E has security type t; in our case t can be either *high* or *low*. The type system uses a security context which is an environment variable tracking the current status of the program (high or low) to control implicit information flow. In a high context, no assignments to low variables may occur. The typing rules are depicted in Fig. 2. The rules define that an expression exp can always have a high type (1), but can only have a low type if no high variables occur in the expression (2). A skip is always typeable (3), and every expression can be assigned to a high variable (4). If we want to assign an expression to a low variable, the expression must be low (5). A composition of two statements keeps the same context (6). Rules (7) and (8) are used to ensure that if the guard has a high context, the statements are typable in a high context.

$$\vdash \text{exp} : \text{high} \qquad \frac{h \notin \text{Vars}(\text{exp})}{\vdash \text{exp} : \text{low}} \qquad [\text{ct}] \vdash \text{skip} \qquad [\text{ct}] \vdash h = \text{exp} \qquad (1\text{–}4)$$

$$\frac{\text{exp} : \text{low}}{[\text{low}] \vdash l = \text{exp}} \qquad \frac{[\text{ct}] \vdash S_1 \quad [\text{ct}] \vdash S_2}{[\text{ct}] \vdash S_1; S_2} \qquad \frac{\vdash \text{exp} : \text{ct} \quad [\text{ct}] \vdash S}{[\text{ct}] \vdash \text{while exp do S}} \qquad (5\text{–}7)$$

$$\frac{\vdash \text{exp} : \text{ct} \quad [\text{ct}] \vdash S_1 \quad [\text{ct}] \vdash S_2}{[\text{ct}] \vdash \text{if exp then } S_1 \text{ else } S_2} \qquad (8)$$

Fig. 2. Security Type System [19]

3   Confidentiality-by-Construction

In this section, we present the confidentiality-by-construction (C14bC) approach by providing a specification framework and refinement rules for the basic high-low security policy as described in Sect. 2.2. Essentially, the C14bC approach re-casts the typing rules of the security type system (cf. Fig. 2 in [19]) in a constructive fashion, thereby enabling the construction of programs that preserve the desired security policy *ab initio* rather than rejecting a program as non-compliant *ex post facto*.

3.1   C14bC Refinement Rules

In the following, we present refinement rules for all five statement types of the GCL to enforce the basic high-low information flow policy. In Fig. 3, we define the basic notation we use for defining the refinement rules.

A triple $\{\mathcal{H}^{pre}\}S\{\mathcal{H}^{post}\}[\eta]$ in C14bC defines the following: The set of high variables before execution of the statement S is captured in $\mathcal{H}^{pre}$, the set of high variables after execution of statement S is $\mathcal{H}^{post}$, the confidentiality level η classifies the confidentiality context for the execution of the statement S, which in our case can be either *high* or *low*. So a triple $\{\mathcal{H}^{pre}\}S\{\mathcal{H}^{post}\}[\eta]$ can be read as: if a program S is executed in a program state that satisfies $\mathcal{H}^{pre}$, i.e. where the variables in $\mathcal{H}^{pre}$ are classified as high, then the program will finish in a program state that satisfies $\mathcal{H}^{post}$, i.e., the high variables are contained in $\mathcal{H}^{post}$, while in confidentiality level η. Note that we are not concerned with termination here, so the triple can either refer to partial or total correctness.

The confidentiality level η is necessary to reason about implicit information flow in selection and repetition statements. If the if-condition or loop-guard contains high variables, the following program block is executed in a high-context, as its execution depends on the high variables contained in the if-condition or the loop-guard. Thus, at confidentiality level *high*, assignments to variables classified as *low* are forbidden, as this would implicitly reveal confidential information. For the considered high-low security policy, we additionally enforce the invariant $\mathcal{H}^{pre} \subseteq \mathcal{H}^{post}$ (i.e., variables can not be degraded to a lower confidentiality level). As the assignment statement creates explicit information flow, the assignment statement is the only statement where the set of high variables in the post-condition can be extended. We also assume the implicit frame condition that all program variables in *Vars* that are not classified as high are classified as low variables.

We now proceed by defining the C14bC refinement rules for the five possible GCL statements. Refining a triple in C14bC means that we refine an abstract statement S in a triple $\{\mathcal{H}^{pre}\}S\{\mathcal{H}^{post}\}[\eta]$ into a more concrete statement such that the more concrete statement satisfies the same specification w.r.t. the confidential variables in $\mathcal{H}^{pre}$ and $\mathcal{H}^{post}$. However, if the refinement is by a repetition or selection statement, the confidentiality level may change to reflect indirect information flow introduced. In our approach, once the confidentiality level has switched to high it will stay high for all subsequent refinements. The refinement

Vars	Set of program variables
$\mathcal{H}^{pre}, \mathcal{H}^{post} \subseteq Vars$	Sets of variables classified as *high*
S	Statement (from the GCL)
$x \in Vars$	Program variable
E, G	Expressions over the program variables in *Vars*
$Vars(E) \subseteq Vars$	Set of variables occurring in expression E
$\eta \in \{high, low\}$	Confidentiality level
$\{\mathcal{H}^{pre}\}S\{\mathcal{H}^{post}\}[\eta]$	C14bC triple

Fig. 3. Basic notions for C14bC

rules presented below are formulated in a way that the refinement property holds if the side conditions of the rules are satisfied.

The statement `skip` applies the identity function to the current state in a program. In compliance with our information flow policy, any statement regardless of the current confidentiality level can be refined to statement `skip` without changing the set of high variables.

Rule 1 (Skip)
$\{\mathcal{H}^{pre}\}$ S $\{\mathcal{H}^{post}\}[\eta]$ *is refinable to* $\{\mathcal{H}^{pre}\}$ `skip` $\{\mathcal{H}^{post}\}[\eta]$.

Assignments represent typical direct information flow where information flows directly from one location to another. Refining a statement S to the assignment `x := E` is possible in the following cases: (a) if the confidentiality level is *high* or the expression E comprises high variables, then the assigned variable x has to be a high variable after the execution of the assignment, i.e., $x \in \mathcal{H}^{post}$; or (b) if the confidentiality level is *low* or the expression E comprises only low variables, then the set of high variables remains unchanged. For instance, {h} 1 := h * 2 {h} does not comply with our policy, since variable 1 must be *high* after the assignment (i.e., {h} 1 := h * 2 {h, 1}).

Rule 2 (Assignment)
$\{\mathcal{H}^{pre}\}$ S $\{\mathcal{H}^{post}\}[\eta]$ *is refinable to* $\{\mathcal{H}^{pre}\}$ x := E $\{\mathcal{H}^{post}\}[\eta]$ *iff*
$(\eta = high$ *or* $Vars(E) \cap \mathcal{H}^{pre} \neq \emptyset)$ *implies* $\mathcal{H}^{post} = \mathcal{H}^{pre} \cup \{x\}$.

In a composition statement, the two single statements are executed sequentially. Therefore, there has to be an intermediate condition denoting the high variables and the confidentiality level after the execution of the first statement which then serves as precondition specification for the second statement. The composition statement S1;S2 itself does not change the current confidentiality level for its composed statements S1 and S2.

Rule 3 (Composition)
$\{\mathcal{H}^{pre}\}$ S $\{\mathcal{H}^{pre}\}[\eta]$ *is refinable to* $\{\mathcal{H}^{pre}\}$ S1; S2 $\{\mathcal{H}^{post}\}[\eta]$
if there exists $\mathcal{H}' \subseteq Vars$ *such that*
$\{\mathcal{H}^{pre}\}$ S1 $\{\mathcal{H}'\}[\eta]$ *and* $\{\mathcal{H}'\}$ S2 $\{\mathcal{H}^{post}\}[\eta]$ *and* $\mathcal{H}^{pre} \subseteq \mathcal{H}' \subseteq \mathcal{H}^{post}$

The selection statement may give rise to implicit information flow if the if-guard contains high variables such that the confidentiality level has to be adapted to prevent insecure implicit information flow. Hence, the selection statement determines the confidentiality level of its sub-statements S1 and S2. We distinguish two cases. If the confidentiality level of the statement to be refined is *high* or the guard of the selection statement contains high variables, we have to set the confidentiality level of the sub-statements to *high*. In the other case, the confidentiality level of the sub-statements is *low*. To give an example, the selection statement $\{h\}$ **if** $h == 1 \rightarrow l := 1$ **else skip fi** $\{h\}$ does not comply with our security policy because the guard comprises a high variable, and therefore the confidentiality level set to high for the sub-statement, such that the assignment to a low variable is forbidden or the variable l has to become high as well.

Rule 4 (Selection)
$\{\mathcal{H}^{pre}\} \, S \, \{\mathcal{H}^{pre}\}[\eta]$ *is refinable to* $\{\mathcal{H}^{\texttt{pre}}\}$ **if** $G \rightarrow$ S1 **else** S2 **fi** $\{\mathcal{H}^{\texttt{post}}\}[\eta]$ *if*

(i) $(\eta = \texttt{high} \ or \ Vars(G) \cap \mathcal{H}^{pre} \neq \emptyset)$
   implies $\{\mathcal{H}^{\texttt{pre}}\} \, S1 \, \{\mathcal{H}^{\texttt{post}}\}[high] \wedge \{\mathcal{H}^{\texttt{pre}}\} \, S2 \, \{\mathcal{H}^{\texttt{post}}\}[high]$
(ii) $(\eta = \texttt{low} \ and \ Vars(G) \cap \mathcal{H}^{pre} = \emptyset)$
   implies $\{\mathcal{H}^{\texttt{pre}}\} \, S1 \, \{\mathcal{H}^{\texttt{post}}\}[low] \wedge \{\mathcal{H}^{\texttt{pre}}\} \, S2 \, \{\mathcal{H}^{\texttt{post}}\}[low]$

The considerations for the confidentiality level of the repetition statement are similar as for the selection statement. If the confidentiality level of the statement to be refined is *high* or the loop-guard comprises high variables, the confidentiality level of the loop body is set to *high*. If the confidentiality level of the refined statement is *low* and the guard excludes high variables, the confidentiality level of the loop body is set to *low*. In this way, we can prevent insecure implicit information flow for loops (the same as for selection statements). As an example, consider the following repetition statement: $\{h\}$ **do** $h > 0 \rightarrow l := l + 1; h := h - 1$ **od** $\{h\}$. From the value of the low variable l, an attacker can infer the value of the high variable h, therefore the confidentiality level is *high* and the assignment $l := l + 1$ is either forbidden or the variable l has to be included in the high variables.

Rule 5 (Repetition)
$\{\mathcal{H}^{pre}\} \, S \, \{\mathcal{H}^{pre}\}[\eta]$ *is refinable to* $\{\mathcal{H}^{\texttt{pre}}\}$ **do** $G \rightarrow$ S1 **od** $\{\mathcal{H}^{\texttt{post}}\}[\eta]$ *if*

(i) $(\eta = high \ or \ Vars(G) \cap \mathcal{H}^{pre} \neq \emptyset)$ *implies* $\{\mathcal{H}^{\texttt{pre}}\} \, S1 \, \{\mathcal{H}^{\texttt{post}}\}[high]$.
(ii) $(\eta = low \ and \ Vars(G) \cap \mathcal{H}^{pre} = \emptyset)$ *implies* $\{\mathcal{H}^{\texttt{pre}}\} \, S1 \, \{\mathcal{H}^{\texttt{post}}\}[low]$.

3.2   Declassification

According to the high-low security policy considered in this paper, we are not allowed to assign an expression comprising high variables to a low variable. However, in order to develop meaningful applications, it may sometimes be necessary to allow some information flow from high values to low values. This, however, needs to be made explicit and might need some kind of declassification [17,22] such that the initial secret is not directly deducible. In order to allow declassification in the above sense, we extend our refinement rules with a specific rule for declassification. We introduce a function to declassify a high expression, so that the assignment of the declassified expression to a low variable is valid. The declassification function on an expression should be used with care and not lead to a leak in confidentiality. The concrete declassification operation performed depends on the application context. In general, it is assumed that declassification removes some secret information such that the secret is not (easily) deducible from the declassified data. For example, if a password is encrypted (and thus declassified), the encrypted value can be assigned to a low variable. By application of a declassification operator to the expression used in an if-condition or a loop-guard before executing the selection or repetition statement, respectively, also implicit information flow can be avoided.

The declassification operation modifies the assignment rule of the C14bC framework. In the case of an assignment, if the assigned expression comprises high variables or the confidentiality level of the specification is high, the assigned variable has to be contained in the set of high variables of the post-condition $((\eta = high$ or $\mathtt{vars}(E) \cap \mathcal{H}^{pre} \neq \emptyset)$ implies $x \in \mathcal{H}^{post})$. With declassification, we alter the condition to $(\eta = high$ or $(\neg\mathtt{isDecl}(E)$ and $Vars(E) \cap \mathcal{H}^{pre} \neq \emptyset))$ implies $x \in \mathcal{H}^{post}$. The predicate $\mathtt{isDecl}(E)$ checks if the expression is declassified. Only if we do not declassify the expression and the expression comprises high variables, the assigned variable x has to be a high variable in the post-condition as well. These considerations give rise to a modified assignment rule for declassification. This refinement rule only makes sense if it is applied at a low confidentiality level, if the assigned variable is a low variable and if the declassified expression indeed contains high variables.

Rule 6 (Declassification Assignment)
$\{\mathcal{H}^{pre}\}$ S $\{\mathcal{H}^{post}\}[\mathtt{low}]$ *is refinable to* $\{\mathcal{H}^{pre}\}$ x = $\mathtt{declassify}(E)$ $\{\mathcal{H}^{post}\}[\mathtt{low}]$ *iff* $x \notin \mathcal{H}^{pre}$ *and* $Vars(E) \cap \mathcal{H}^{pre} \neq \emptyset)$.

3.3 Example

In Listing 1, we show an example for C14bC. The program checks if the user wants to pay, and if this is the case, a valid credit card number is required. In the end, the masked credit card number is passed to an output variable.

To construct the program, we start with an abstract program $\{\mathcal{H}^{pre}\}$ S $\{\mathcal{H}^{post}\}[low]$ where both sets $(\mathcal{H}^{pre}, \mathcal{H}^{post})$ are empty. The refinement steps are shown in Fig. 4. Note that we only add program variables to the set of high variables in the postcondition if that is required by the refinement rules in order to keep track of where information flow actually occurs. In this sense, we are treating the refinement rules rather like transformation rules. Of course, the variables added to the set of high variables in the postcondition need to be added to the postconditions up the refinement hierarchy as well in order to establish a proper refinement relationship. A way to allow expressing information flow policies without having to refer to concrete variables in the program during refinement would be to introduce ghost variables [2] for the set of high variables in the pre- and postcondition whose value is an symbolic expression that can be dynamically updated. We leave this to future work.

```
 1  boolean low paymentAction := true;
 2  if (paymentAction) {
 3    int high creditCard := getNumber();
 4    while (!valid(creditCard)) {
 5      creditCard = getNumber();
 6    }
 7    String low output := declassify(mask(creditCard);
 8  } else {
 9    skip
10  }
```

Listing 1. C14bC example for credit card payment

The first statement, on line 1 of the listing, is an assignment. The assignment is introduced by using the composition and the assignment rule (ref. 1 and 2). The composition splits the program into the first statement and the rest. In line 1, a constant is assigned to a low variable which stays low. This is possible without problems at any confidentiality level. By introducing the selection statement of lines 2–10 (ref. 3), the confidentiality level stays low because the guard does not comprise a high variable and the level was low before. The skip statement of the else branch in line 9 is introduced by refinement 4. The sets of variables and the confidentiality level are unaffected. The assignment in line 3 is introduced by refinement 5 and 6. A composition statement is needed to split the program. In line 3, we assign a value to a variable `creditCard`. We assume that `getNumber` is a high expression. We have to ensure that `creditCard` is in the post set of high variables. This propagates up to the composition statement. The variable `creditCard` (cC in the high variable sets in Listing 1) is added: $\{\}$ TS1 $\{cC\}[low] \land \{cC\}$ TS2 $\{cC\}[low]$. The repetition statement of lines 4–6 is introduced by using refinement 7 and 8. A composition statement is needed, so the assignment in line 7 can be created. The repetition statement changes the confidentiality level. We have a guard which comprises a high variable, so the level is raised to high for all sub-statements. For the assignment in line 5 (ref. 9), the variable `creditCard` has to be in $\mathcal{H}^{post}$ which is the case. The assignment in line 7 (ref. 10) is inside the scope of the selection statement, but outside the scope of the repetition statement. It has the low confidentiality level of the selection statement and the intermediate composition statements. Here, we assign a high to a low variable. This violates our assignment Rule 2. With declassification in Rule 6, we allow this assignment since the credit card number is masked.

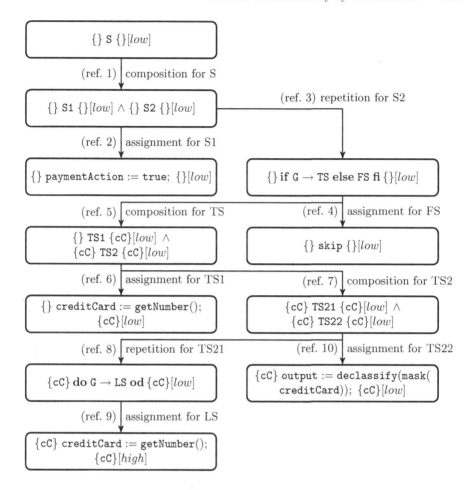

Fig. 4. Refinement steps for the credit card payment example

4   Tool Support

In order to make C14bC applicable to larger programs, we need to provide tool support. Currently, we are developing tool support for classical functional CbC by providing an IDE-like development environment for deriving programs in a CbC-based fashion in a textual and graphical manner[2].

This tool support can be easily extended with the above ideas to cover C14bC. From an analysis and verification point of view, C14bC specifications are easier to check and analyse than functional CbC specifications. For functional CbC specifications, we need a way to verify functional Hoare triples over assignments and establish variants and invariants over repetition statements. For this task, we can use a program verification tool, such as the KeY prover [2]. For C14bC

---

[2] https://github.com/TUBS-ISF/CorC.

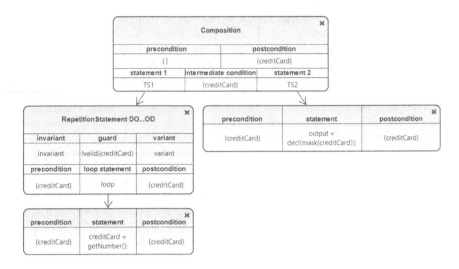

Fig. 5. Graphical representation in the C14bC editor

specifications, as presented in this paper, it is sufficient to be able to statically analyse the variables contained in expressions and to reason about their usage in the program while maintaining their classification as high and low program variables. Of course, if we apply a richer programming language with side effects, we need more sophisticated static program analysis techniques to reason about the respective information flow.

In Fig. 5, we show what the editor could look like. The lines 4–7 from the example in Listing 1 are shown. We have a composition statement at the top, containing the high variable `creditCard` in the intermediate- and postcondition. The statement `TS1` is refined to a repetition statement, and the other statement is refined to an assignment. The assignment contains the assignment `output := decl(mask(creditCard))`. In the repetition statement, invariant, guard and variant (needed for functional CbC) can be specified. The pre- and postcondition contain again the high variable `creditCard`. The inner loop statement is refined to an assignment.

5   Related Work

The CbC approach to software construction was pioneered by Dijkstra, Hoare and others and based on weakest precondition semantics [10,11,16]. Kourie and Watson [14] propose a light-weight version of this approach. In [21], we have proposed a combination of CbC and post-hoc verification in order to obtain the best of both worlds. The approach should not be confused with other concepts that carry the same name, such as the correctness-by-construction (CbyC) promoted by Hall and Chapman [13]. Their CbyC is a software development process where formal modeling techniques and analyses are used for different development phases, in order to detect and remove any defects that do occur as early as possible after introduction [8]. Another approach to correctness-by-construction is the Event-B framework [1] where automata-based system specifications are refined by provably correct transformation steps until an implementable program is obtained [15].

Language-based information flow security is a broad field in the literature; for a survey or earlier work consult [19]. The main approaches essentially rely on static or dynamic program analysis [18], such as taint analysis [7], or security type systems [20] etc. Some approaches combine information flow control with logic-based or Hoare-style program logics. An early effort was made by Andrews and Reitman [6], who proposed a compile-time certification technique for information policies with multiple security levels based on a Hoare-style semantics. Their work also covers programs beyond the sequential ones we cover, i.e., involving parallelism and semaphores. However, their approach is a post-hoc one, unlike our by-construction approach. Amtoft and Banerjee [4] formulated compositional intraprocedural analyses of conditional information flow, which served as the basis for a formulation of Hoare-style contracts for conditional information flow for SPARK Ada [5].

The first paper to reformulated information flow properties as a deductive verification problem in a program logic was [9]. Hähnle et al. [12] show how a type system ensuring confidentiality can be embedded into a form of dynamic logic. The setting is once again one focused on post-hoc verification, with an eye to using the KeY theorem prover. This paper, to the best of our knowledge, is the first to propose constructive CbC style reasoning for information flow properties by means of a refinement-based approach such that by a sequence of small, incremental refinement steps, a program is obtained that preserves security policies by construction.

6 Conclusion and Future Work

The presented approach on C14bC can be seen as a first step in the direction of security-by-construction. In this paper, we only focus on confidentiality and base our considerations on a simple programming language. There are several directions to extend this work:

- Besides evaluation of the practical applicability and scalability on larger scale case examples, we also have to formally verify the correctness and completeness of our C14bC construction approach. This includes formulating the ideas in a formal refinement framework and proving the soundness against the corresponding type system-based approaches. Furthermore, we should investigate the benefits of C14bC when combined with post-hoc verification and analysis approaches, similar to the work presented in [21].
- We can extend the programming language constructs that are considered for deriving a program. In order to achieve modularity of our approach, we can integrate a refinement rule that introduces a method call and thus allow modular refinement of the program into several methods. However, in that, we

have to be careful about side effects and appropriate frame conditions. Furthermore, we can lift the presented approach to object-oriented programs, following information flow control approaches for object-oriented languages [3].

- By considering security policies in information flow as specifications for integrity (rather than confidentiality), we can also provide an approach for integrity- or trust-by-construction. To this end, we label program variables as trusted and untrusted (in contrast to high and low) and only allow information to flow from trusted to untrusted, but not vice versa, as this would allow untrusted information to influence trusted information. In essence, this is the same set-up as the high-/low security policy considered in this paper, i.e., the presented framework directly lends itself to trust-by-construction.
- Additionally, we can make the presented C14bC approach generic with respect to the information flow policy. In the paper, we have only focused on a very simply high/low security policy with the possibility to declassify data. However, for practical applications, it might be necessary to introduce several security layers and more fine-grained security policies. To this end, the refinement rules presented in this work need to be generalised with respect to the security policies they can operate on.
- In this paper, C14bC is considered in isolation. We focused on confidentiality specifications only, for ease of presentation. However, we can of course combine functional CbC with C14bC in order to derive a functionally correct program that also complies to the desired security policy. Technically, this is a combination of the classical functional pre-/post-conditions and refinement rules with the C14bC pre/post-conditions and refinement rules laid out in this paper.

Acknowledgements. The authors would like to thank the anonymous reviewers for valuable comments and suggestions for improvements and future work.

References

1. Abrial, J.: Modeling in Event-B - System and Software Engineering. Cambridge University Press, New York (2010)
2. Ahrendt, W., Beckert, B., Hähnle, R., Schmitt, P.H., Ulbric, M. (eds.): Deductive Software Verification The KeY Book From Theory to Practice. LNCS, vol. 10001. Springer, Heidelberg (2016). https://doi.org/10.1007/978-3-319-49812-6
3. Amtoft, T., Bandhakavi, S., Banerjee, A.: A logic for information flow in object-oriented programs. In: POPL, pp. 91–102 (2006)
4. Amtoft, T., Banerjee, A.: Information flow analysis in logical form. In: SAS, pp. 100–115 (2004)
5. Amtoft, T., Hatcliff, J., Rodríguez, E., Robby, Hoag, J., Greve, D.A.: Specification and checking of software contracts for conditional information flow. In: Cuellar, J., Maibaum, T. (eds.): FM 2008. LNCS, vol. 5014, pp. 229–245. Springer, Boston (2008)
6. Andrews, G.R., Reitman, R.P.: An axiomatic approach to information flow in programs. ACM Trans. Program. Lang. Syst. **2**(1), 56–76 (1980)

7. Arzt, S., et al.: Flowdroid: precise context, flow, field, object-sensitive and lifecycle-aware taint analysis for android apps. In: PLDI, pp. 259–269 (2014)

8. Chapman, R.: Correctness by construction: a manifesto for high integrity software. In: Proceedings of the 10th Australian Workshop on Safety Critical Systems and Software, SCS 2005, vol. 55, pp. 43–46 (2006)

9. Darvas, Á., Hähnle, R., Sands, D.: A theorem proving approach to analysis of secure information flow. In: Hutter, D., Ullmann, M. (eds.) SPC 2005. LNCS, vol. 3450, pp. 193–209. Springer, Heidelberg (2005). https://doi.org/10.1007/978-3-540-32004-3_20

10. Dijkstra, E.W.: A Discipline of Programming. Prentice Hall, Englewood Cliffs (1976)

11. Gries, D.: The Science of Programming. Springer, New York (1987). https://doi.org/10.1007/978-1-4612-5983-1

12. Hähnle, R., Pan, J., Rümmer, P., Walter, D.: Integration of a security type system into a program logic. Theor. Comput. Sci. 402(2–3), 172–189 (2008)

13. Hall, A., Chapman, R.: Correctness by construction: developing a commercial secure system. IEEE Softw. 19(1), 18–25 (2002)

14. Kourie, D.G., Watson, B.W.: The Correctness-By-Construction Approach to Programming. Springer, Heidelberg (2012). https://doi.org/10.1007/978-3-642-27919-5

15. Méry, D., Monahan, R.: Transforming event B models into verified C# implementations. In: First International Workshop on Verification and Program Transformation, VPT 2013, Saint Petersburg, Russia, pp. 57–73, 12–13 July 2013 (2013)

16. Morgan, C.: Programming from Specifications, 2nd edn. Prentice Hall, New York (1994)

17. Myers, A.C., Liskov, B.: Protecting privacy using the decentralized label model. ACM Trans. Softw. Eng. Methodol. 9(4), 410–442 (2000)

18. Nielson, F., Nielson, H.R., Hankin, C.: Principles of Program Analysis. Springer, Heidelberg (1999). https://doi.org/10.1007/978-3-662-03811-6

19. Sabelfeld, A., Myers, A.C.: Language-based information-flow security. IEEE J. Sel. Areas Commun. 21(1), 5–19 (2003)

20. Volpano, D.M., Irvine, C.E., Smith, G.: A sound type system for secure flow analysis. J. Comput. Secur. 4(2/3), 167–188 (1996)

21. Watson, B.W., Kourie, D.G., Schaefer, I., Cleophas, L.: Correctness-by-construction and post-hoc verification: a marriage of convenience? In: Margaria, T., Steffen, B. (eds.) ISoLA 2016. LNCS, vol. 9952, pp. 730–748. Springer, Cham (2016). https://doi.org/10.1007/978-3-319-47166-2_52

22. Zdancewic, S., Myers, A.C.: Robust declassification. In: 14th IEEE Computer Security Foundations Workshop (CSFW-14 2001), 11–13 June 2001, pp. 15–23, Cape Breton, Nova Scotia, Canada (2001)

STRESS 2018

A Tutorial Introduction to Graphical Modeling and Metamodeling with CINCO

Michael Lybecait, Dawid Kopetzki, Philip Zweihoff, Annika Fuhge,
Stefan Naujokat$^{(\boxtimes)}$, and Bernhard Steffen

Chair for Programming Systems, TU Dortmund University, Dortmund, Germany
{michael.lybecait,dawid.kopetzki,philip.zweihoff,annika.fuhge,
stefan.naujokat,bernhard.steffen}@tu-dortmund.de

Abstract. We present a tutorial introduction to the usage of CINCO, our framework for the generation of graphical development environments, highlighting two recent additions: the possibility to bringing any CINCO-based graphical modeling language into the web, and a graphical editor for meta modeling. All the discussed features are illustrated step by step along the development and evolution of the WebStory, a simple education-oriented modeling language for adventure games.

Keywords: Abstract tool specification · Domain-specific languages
Metamodeling · Simplicity · Graphical modeling · Bootstrapping
Web-based modeling environment · Language-driven engineering

1 Introduction

The use of modeling languages gains more and more attention in software engineering research and practice, resulting in various forms of *Model-Driven Development* [7], *Language-Oriented Programming* [10,34] and *Language-Driven Engineering* [15,32]. In contrast to general-purpose modeling languages, *Domain-Specific Languages (DSLs)* usually require so-called *Language Workbenches* [11] for the development of the according editor and tooling. Many prominent frameworks (like Xtext [3] or JetBrains MPS [18]) focus on textual DSLs with support for graphical DSLs usually being less sophisticated. The CINCO SCCE Meta Tooling Suite [29] aims at closing this gap by providing a simplicity-oriented [25] solution for the development of graphical modeling languages[1], which itself realizes a domain-specific model-driven approach for the domain 'graphical modeling tools' [28]. Key concept of CINCO is the full generation of such tools from meta-level specifications and models.

In this paper, we present a tutorial introduction to the usage of CINCO along an ongoing simple example: The *WebStory* language allows for the easy

---

[1] Examples for other frameworks focusing on the development of graphical editors are Marama [17], GME [21,22], or MetaEdit [19]. See [29] for a comparison on their degree of usage simplicity.

T. Margaria and B. Steffen (Eds.): ISoLA 2018, LNCS 11244, pp. 519–538, 2018.
https://doi.org/10.1007/978-3-030-03418-4_31

visually driven creation of browser-based Point&Click adventure games following a 'storyboard' model. The presentation focuses on two recent additions to
CINCO:

Pyro. While CINCO originally generated modeling tools based on the Eclipse
framework [16, 27], Pyro [36] enhances the CINCO ecosystem by fully generating any CINCO-based graphical modeling language into a web application
accessible via browser.

GCS. Due to limited existing support for graphical languages prior to CIN-
CO, CINCO's specification languages are themselves developed textually using
Xtext. Now that CINCO exists, the Graphical CINCO Specification (GCS) [13]
introduces graphical editors to the meta level in a bootstrapping fashion.

The paper is structured as follows. Section 2 introduces the running *WebStory*
example by presenting a simple story and (informally) introducing the central
language elements for modeling. Section 3 then first introduces the Pyro modeling platform (Sect. 3.1) before guiding the reader through the necessary steps
of modeling a *WebStory* from scratch (Sect. 3.2). Finally, we discuss in Sect. 4
how to extend the *WebStory* language. After a short introduction on CINCO
and the graphical metamodeling language GCS in Sect. 4.1, the full *WebStory*
language definition is presented in Sect. 4.2. In Sect. 4.3, we elaborate on the
required steps to extend the existing language with new features. The paper
closes in Sect. 5 with a brief summary, hints to advanced topics, and indications
for future development.

2   The *WebStory*

The *WebStory* modeling tool allows for easy visually driven creation of simple
browser-based Point&Click adventure games following a 'storyboard'. A *Web-
Story* consists of several screens, which primarily show a picture in the background. During the game, one screen is visible at a time. Furthermore, a player
may click on dedicated areas of a screen to either trigger an event (i.e., change
the 'game state') or directly move to another screen. Some screens or events
might not be reachable/enabled until certain events occurred, meaning that the
game has to be in a designated state to allow for this action.

Figure 1 shows a simple example story. It models the search for a treasure
which can only succeed if the player finds the required key. This story consists
of five *screens* (1-5), one (boolean) *variable* 'v', one *condition* 'c', one *variable
modifier* 'm', and a *start marker* 's'. Also, screens contain so-called *click areas*
(A-G), which connect to other screens, variable modifiers, or conditions with
directed control flow edges (purple edges). Variable modifiers and conditions are
connected through data edges (grey edges) to variables, whose values define the
current game state. In this example, the 'key' variable holds the information
whether or not the player found the key yet. The value of a variable can be
set by variable modifiers and evaluated by conditions. Thus, conditions have

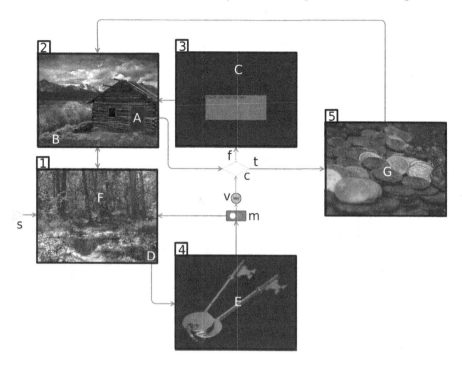

Fig. 1. An exemplary *WebStory* model (Images by: [9,20,31,35])

two outgoing control flow edges: a *true* edge 't' (solid line) and a *false* edge 'f' (dashed line).

Considering a game state in which the player did not find the key yet (variable 'key' evaluates to false), clicking the click area 'A' in screen '2' will show screen '3', because the evaluation of condition 'c' results in the next step in the control flow being the target of the condition's *false* edge ('f'). If the control flow of a *WebStory* reaches a variable modifier, the value of the connected variable is set to the value represented by the modifier. Thus, clicking the (fullscreen) click area 'E' in screen '4' sets the value of the 'key' variable to **true**, since the modifier 'm' represents the constant value **true** (indicated by the green circle).

3   Modeling a *WebStory*

In this section we present Pyro, a web-based platform, which is used for modeling with domain-specific graphical languages like the *WebStory* language introduced in Sect. 2. We first describe the environment of Pyro, before giving a detailed instruction for the creation of a first adventure.

3.1   Pyro

Pyro [36] is a web-based modeling tool for DSLs built with CINCO [29]. It enables a simplified distribution of newly created DSLs and directly allows for advanced

Fig. 2. User interface of Pyro web modeling environment with views: (1) *menu bar* (2) *explorer* (3) *canvas* (4) *palette* (5) *miniature map* (6) *properties view* (Images by: [9,20,31,35])

features like simultaneous collaborative editing. The Pyro web modeling environment utilizes the *DyWA* [30] (Dynamic Web Application) for data modeling, empowering prototype-driven application development. Pyro follows the *OTA* (One Thing Approach) [24] and *XMDD* (Extreme Model-Driven Design) [26] to provide a DSL developer with an automated distribution of their language in the web, accessible by everyone with a browser. Basing on graphical DSL definitions in Cinco, Pyro's central goal is a one-click-generation to a running web modeling environment.[2]

The Pyro modeling platform has been specifically tailored towards simplification of recurrent modeling steps, i.e., to provide guidance for the user by means of quick access to available model entities and relevant properties. This section provides a short overview of the Pyro user interface as well as more details on features supporting the user during modeling.

Pyro is based on the Cinco SCCE Meta Tooling Suite and developed with *JointJS* [8], *Angular* [5] and *Java EE* [14]. In general, Pyro is divided into a public area, including user registration and login, and a secured area for logged-in users consisting of a project management and the editor. The editor is shown in Fig. 2. As a *rich internet application* [12], Pyro provides the look and feel of a desktop application, supporting effective model editing and specific *views* on

---

[2] In this regard, the Pyro concept differs from, e.g., WebGME [1], which mixes meta level and modeling level into one web application.

models in the current project. They follow simple and standard principles of user interface design, such as drag&drop functionality.

Menu Bar (1). The *menu bar* is placed at the top of the editor and offers drop-down menus. The *Project* entry provides standard functions for the current project, as well as the *Sharing* control, which can be used to add other users to the project and start collaborative modeling. The other entries depend on the currently opened graph model, like *Redo* and *Undo* buttons. For enhanced layout, Pyro utilizes different routing algorithms which automatically align all present edges.

Explorer (2). The *explorer* is a standard user interface component established by common IDEs and lists all files and folders contained in the currently active project. It mostly serves the purpose to navigate through folders for opening models and other files.

Canvas (3). The *canvas* is situated in the middle of the Pyro web modeling interface showing the graphical models. New nodes can be created via drag&drop of an entry in the palette to the canvas. Hovering with the mouse over a node overlays a menu with actions like 'delete node' and 'create edge'. Two nodes can be connected via an edge by drag&drop of the corresponding action onto the target node. Connection constraints defined by the language devoloper determine whether an edge may connect one node to another. If multiple edge types are allowed, a context menu for selection appears after the aforementioned drag&drop. The route of an edge can be modified via *bending points* and the routing algorithms. It is possible to have multiple models opened at the same time. They are arranged in tabs, but only one model can be active at a time and is shown in the canvas.

Palette (4). The *palette* lists all available types of nodes and containers for creation that are applied to the active model in the canvas. The node types are ordered in collapsible groups and previewed by icons.

Miniature View (5). The *miniature view* displays a small scale overview of the currently visible graph model for easy navigation in larger models. It is continuously synchronized with the canvas, so that editing, like the movement of a node, is displayed at once.

Properties View (6). The *properties view* shows attributes as well as their actual values for the currently selected component in the active model. In particular, the contents of this view are updated, when the selected element changes.

The properties view allows for a comfortable way of editing via its form-based layout as well as its structuring into *property groups*. Thus, most model

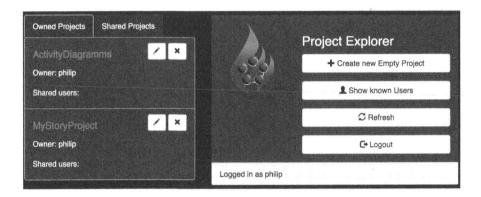

Fig. 3. Project management area

elements have only a single property group. Otherwise, the groups are ordered thematically in a tree view on the left and determine the shown properties on the right.

3.2 The First Adventure

The following instructions to create a *WebStory* can be reproduced online in the *Pyro Playground*.[3]

Register and Login. The first examination of the Pyro modeling environment begins with the registration of a new user. This requires the submission of personal information, like an email address and a password for authentication. Fill the entire form and press the *submit* button to create a new user account. After an email verification process is completed, the user is enabled to login and enter the project management area (cf. Fig. 3).

Create a Project. Projects are considered as root folders associated with an owner who created the project and multiple other invited users. As a result of this differentiation between ownership and participation, the management area shows two separate lists of projects. The owned projects can be extended, edited and deleted by the current user, whereas the shared ones can only be entered.

Create a project by clicking the *Create new Empty Project* button on the right (cf. Fig. 3). In the upcoming dialog select a name for your project and click the create button. The newly created project is opened and the editor view appears.

Create a *WebStory*. The next step demands the creation of a new model as instance of the *WebStory* (see Sect. 2). In the explorer on the left, the project is

---

[3] https://pyro.scce.info/playground/webstory.

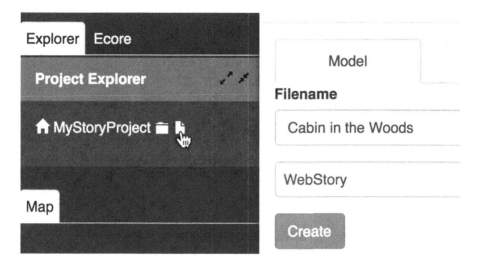

Fig. 4. File creation dialog

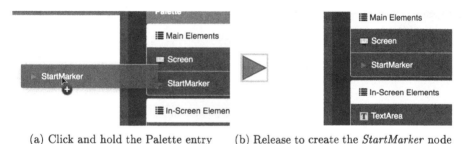

(a) Click and hold the Palette entry   (b) Release to create the *StartMarker* node

Fig. 5. Create a *StartMarker* node by dragging it to the canvas

presented as the root folder, followed by two buttons to create a sub folder or file.

To create a new *WebStory*, click on the file icon besides the project entry in the explorer (cf. Fig. 4, left). The upcoming modal dialog (cf. Fig. 4, right) presents the different kinds of files supported by Pyro at the top. The *model* file type lists available DSLs, including the *WebStory*. Click the model file type tab and choose the *WebStory* in the appearing form. Enter a *Filename* for the model in the other field and click the create button. The newly created *WebStory* appears in the explorer underneath the root folder.

Start Modeling. Click the created file in the explorer to open it in a tab in the middle of the editor. The *WebStory*, as a model file type, is presented on the canvas for graphical DSLs. In addition to this, the other editor parts, like the miniature view, palette and properties view are shown. To build a new *WebStory*,

(a) Click and hold the Palette entry   (b) Release above a *Screen* to create the *RectangleClickArea*

Fig. 6. Create a *RectangleClickArea* node by dragging it to the canvas

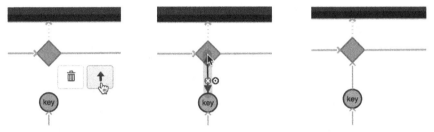

(a) Hover over the node   (b) Click and hold the edge button   (c) Drop the edge on the target

Fig. 7. Create an *DataFlow* edge on the canvas

a *StartMarker* node is required to initiate the control flow, by dragging it from the palette (cf. Fig. 5a) to the canvas (cf. Fig. 5b).

Add Screens. In a similar way, multiple *Screen* containers can be placed on the canvas (cf. Fig. 5). Selecting one of them refreshes the properties view underneath the canvas and presents the *backgroundImage* attribute. An image uploaded by this form is instantaneously displayed as the shape of the *Screen*. Repeat this step to add multiple screens to the story and upload different images for each *Screen* in the properties view.

Define Click Areas. The *ClickArea* nodes can be placed on the *Screen* containers to show which spot continues the story, when the user clicks on it (cf. Fig. 6). There are two different shapes to define an elliptic and a rectangular click-area. Drag&drop at least one *EllipseClickArea* or *RectangleClickArea* node from the palette (cf. Fig. 6a) to each *Screen* (cf. Fig. 6b). Move the areas to a part of the pictures which should continue the story. *ClickArea* nodes can be resized on their borders to fit the right spot.

Link the Control Flow. At this point the *Transition* edges can be used to connected the *ClickArea* nodes with a successive *Screen* to define an image sequence. A Transition can be created by click and holding the edge button (cf. Fig. 7a), visible in the node hover-menu and dragging the appearing line to the target (cf. Fig. 7b). After releasing, the edge will be created (cf. Fig. 7c). Connect each *ClickArea* with a *Screen* and the *StartMarker* node with the initial *Screen*. The edge layout algorithms can be utilized from the menu bar at the top to automatically arrange all *Transition* edges of the *WebStory*.

Generate and Play the Story. To play the game, executable code is required, which can be created by the registered code generator. The generator has been created by the DSL developer and is included in Pyro. It reads the present graph model to generate JavaScript and HTML files, realizing an executable point&click adventure for the browser. This process can be started by the *G* button on the menu bar. The generated files appear in the explorer underneath the *generated-html* folder. Clicking the created *index.html* file, opens the generated *WebStory* and shows the first screen in the middle of the Pyro interface. Feel free to extend the story with additional *Screens*. After a re-generation, by clicking the *G* button again, the modified story can immediately be played.

4 *WebStory* Language Development

In this section, we first briefly introduce CINCO, our Meta Tooling Suite used to develop domain-specific graph-based modeling tools like the *WebStory* modeler presented in Sect. 3. We align the description using simplified elements of the *WebStory* language. Afterwards, we present the full *WebStory* language and show how it can be extended by an additional condition node type.

4.1 CINCO Meta Tooling Suite

The CINCO Meta Tooling Suite [29] is a simplicity-driven meta modeling tool allowing for full generation of domain-specific graphical modeling tools from high-level specifications. We call these generated tools CINCO *Products* (CP).[4] The specifications are either created with dedicated textual DSLs (MGL: meta graph language; MSL: meta style language) or with the combined Graphical CINCO Specification (GCS) [13]. GCS describes the abstract and concrete syntax of the domain-specific language in a WYSIWYG style.[5] CINCO is discussed in great detail in [29], so we here focus on information needed to understand our examples.

---

[4] The *Pyro* approach presented in Sect. 3 is a consequent refinement of the CINCO realization of its CINCO PRODUCTS and offers an alternative web-based solution, instead of a local desktop tool based on the Eclipse platform.

[5] See https://cinco.scce.info/applications/gcs to download the enhanced CINCO version with included GCS.

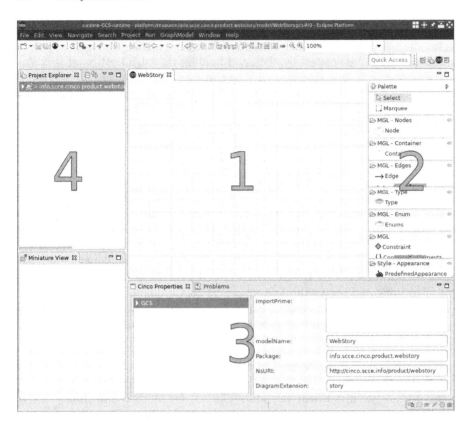

Fig. 8. GCS modeling tool used to create CINCO Product definitions

To develop a domain-specific graph-based language with CINCO, the developer has to define its abstract syntax – i.e, which types of elements exists – and its concrete syntax – i.e., how these elements should be displayed. The abstract syntax mainly defines node types, container types, and edge types, which all may hold attributes. Node types define constraints on incoming and outgoing edge types. Container types, which are special node types that include other nodes, can furthermore have constraints on these included types of nodes. The concrete syntax, on the other hand, defines how the nodes and edges are displayed in the editor by means of various (potentially nested) shapes (like ellipse, rectangle, polygon, etc.) and their appearance in terms of colors, line style and width, etc.

Figure 8 shows CINCO with the GCS modeling canvas (1). Here, the CP developer may create for instance new node types by dragging and dropping the *Node* type from the palette (2) onto the canvas. The property view (3) is used to set attributes of the selected elements, such as the node type's name. The project structure is shown on the left-hand side (4). In the following, we exemplarily show how to model a simplified *Screen* and *ClickArea* types from the *WebStory* language. First, create a new project for the language definition:

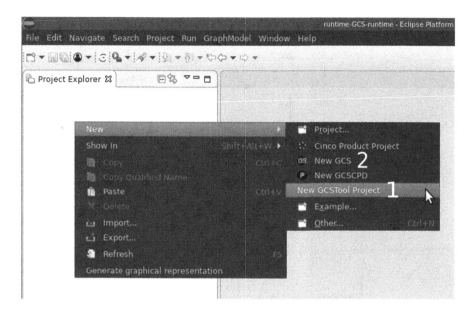

Fig. 9. Creating a new language specification

– Right-click in the *Project Explorer* view and select *New GCSTool Project* (cf.
  Fig. 9 (1))
– Select the newly created project and repeat the step, now choosing *New GCS*
  (cf. Fig. 9 (2)).
– Name the GCS file 'WebStory' and click *Finish*.

Now, the modeling canvas should be visible and we can start to specify the metamodel of the *WebStory* language. As introduced in Sect. 2, *Screen*s may contain
*ClickArea*s. Modeling this structure is part of the abstract syntax, as introduced
above. Figure 10 shows the definition of a container type *Screen*, a node type
ClickArea and a *ContainEdge* specifying the constraint of the containable elements of the *Screen*. This can be done by following these steps:

– Add a new container type and a new node type by dragging and dropping a
  Node and *Container* from the palette on the canvas (cf. Fig. 10 (drag&drop))
  and name the container type *Screen* and the node type *ClickArea* using the
  property view (cf. Fig. 8 (3)).
– Connect the *Screen* with the *ClickArea* through a *ContainEdge*, starting the
  edge creation at the *Screen*. Therefore, hover over the *Screen* node click and
  hold the arrow that appears in the upper right corner. Release the mouse over
  the *ClickArea* and select *ContainEdge* from the upcoming context menu.
– Specify lower and upper bounds of this containment using the property view,
  where '*' is used to define an arbitrary upper bound of the contained element.

Defining constraints on incoming and outgoing edge of *Node*s and *Container*s is
done in a similar way using *MultiplicityEdge*s. After creation, the types *Screen*

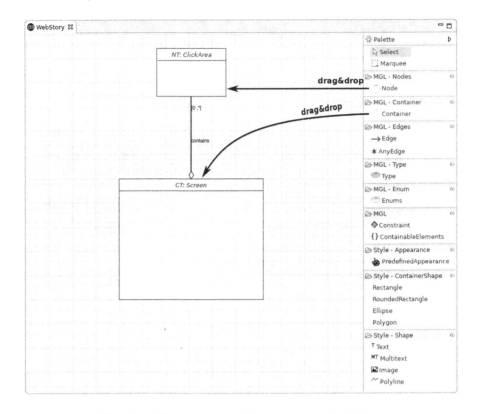

Fig. 10. GCS screenshot of the *Screen* type definition

and *ClickArea* do not look like the types in the resulting *WebStory* modeling
tool (cf. Fig. 1). We can change this, adding the concrete syntax of a type (cf.
Fig. 11):

- Drag&drop an *Ellipse* from the palette on the *ClickArea* node.
- Right click the *Ellipse* entry in the property view and create an *Appearance*
- Choose a `background`
- Activate the `lineInvisible` flag
- Set the `transparency` to 0.7

    For the graphical representation of the *Screen* node

- Create a *Rectangle* in the Screen node.
- Create an *Appearance* for the Rectangle and set the `lineWidth` to 3. Choose
  a `foreground` color.
- Create an *Image* inside the newly created *Rectangle*.
- Select an image using the property view. This image will be shown in the
  modeling tool after a *Screen* is created.

This model can already be generated to a fully functional modeling tool, which
just would allow for the creation of *Screens* and *ClickAreas* contained in *Screens*.

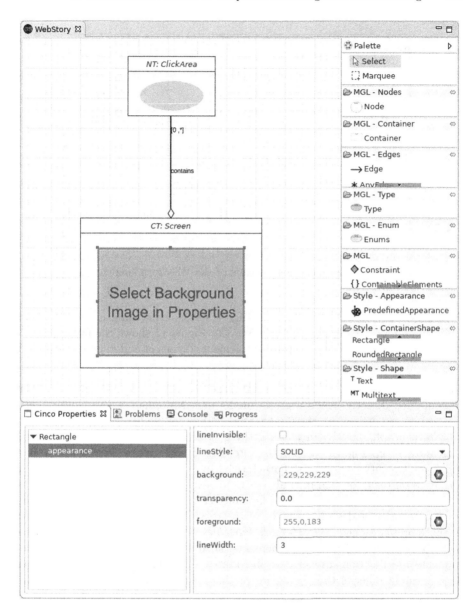

Fig. 11. Property view showing the `appearance` attribute of a (container) shape

4.2 The *WebStory* Language

In the following we describe the *WebStory* language specification which was used to model the example in Sect. 2. It can be obtained in the examples category of

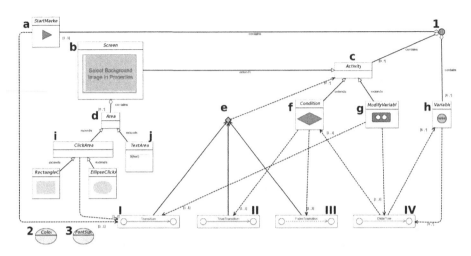

Fig. 12. Graphical specification of the *WebStory* language

the CINCO project website.[6] This package contians everything needed to build
a fully functional *WebStory* tool with CINCO. Figure 12 shows the full graphical
language specification, i.e., the possible elements (types of nodes, containers, and
edges) and the relationships between them.

Node Types of the *WebStory* Language. Nodes and containers can either
be contained directly inside a graph model or a container. These containment
constraints are defined by the `ContainableElements` node (cf. Fig. 12 *(1)*) The
WebStory graph model can contain three node types: *Activity*, *Variable* and
StartMarker (cf. Fig. 12 *(a, c, h)*). Note that `containableElements` can also
define multiplicity constraints characterized by a lower and an upper bound. A
correct *WebStory*, for example, always needs exactly one *StartMarker* element.

The node types of the *WebStory* language can roughly be divided into two different categories: nodes which can be placed directly in the *WebStory* model, such
as the aforementioned *StartMarker*, *Variables*, or *Activities*, and nodes which
need to be contained in *Screen* elements, such as *ClickArea* or *TextArea*. The
language specification furthermore introduces an abstract node *Activity*. Each
Activity node inherits the properties of this abstract node represented by the
edges labeled `extends`. For example, all activities have in common that they
can be the target of an arbitrary number of *Transition*, *TrueTransition* and
FalseTransition edges (cf. Fig. 12 *(I - III)*). This is shown by the dashed arrows
connected from the edge definitions to the *Constraint* node (cf. Fig. 12 *(e)*) which
is connected to the *Activity* node type. There are three different types of *Activity*
nodes (*ModifyVariable*, *Condition* and *Screen* cf. Fig. 12 *(b, f, g)*).

ModifyVariable elements describe assignments to *Variables*. They set a *Variable* connected through a *DataFlow* edge (cf. Fig. 12 *(IV)*) to a constant value

---

[6] https://cinco.scce.info/examples/webstory.

which can be adjusted with the CINCO *Properties View*. The *Variable* nodes describe a boolean variable declaration in the story with a given name. Variables in a story have a start value of *false*. *Condition* nodes check the value of a connected *Variable*. *Screen* nodes depict the observable elements of a *Web-Story*. They have a path to a `backgroundImage` which is shown in the generated story as well as the model editor. *Screens* can contain several *Area* nodes (cf. Fig. 12 *(d, i, j)*). A special start *Screen* needs to be assigned. This is done with the *StartMarker*. It is connected with a *Transition* edge to the designated *Screen*. The *TextArea* nodes are used to display text on a *Screen*. Besides the *text* attribute *TextAreas* have a `fontSize` and a `color` attribute. Color and font size are presented by the enumeration types *Color* and *FontSize* (cf. Fig. 12 *(2, 3)*). *ClickAreas* are the interactive elements of a *WebStory*. These nodes exist in rectangle and ellipse shape. They are placed on a *Screen* at the position of an interactive spot in the resulting story.

Modelling the Language's Control Flow Aspect. The *ClickAreas* together with *Activities* are the main parts of the control flow of a story. A flow is modelled starting with a *ClickArea* inside a *Screen*. This area is connected through a *Transition* edge to suitable targets which can be any type of *Activity*. While *Screen* nodes form the end of a control flow 'step' (determined by a single click), *Condition* and *ModifyVariable* nodes always need to be inside such a step. *ModifyVariable* needs to have exactly one successor connected through a *Transition* edge. *Condition* has exactly two possible successors: one connected through a *TrueTransition* the other connected through a *FalseTransition*.

4.3   Extending the *WebStory* Language

Now, consider the following extension to the story we presented in Sect. 2: we want to add a second hidden key that also enables opening the door keeping the player from reaching the treasure. In the *WebStory* shown in Fig. 13 we added a second variable named 'key2' which represents the possession of that second key. We also have to check if the player found one of the keys by cascading two condition nodes: if the first evaluates to false (and thus follows the dotted edge), the second is evaluated. Only if both evaluate to false, the screen with the 'no key' message is shown. At this point, it is obvious that we are just emulating logical connectors by cascading multiple conditions. In the following, we will thus enhance the *WebStory* language by adding a dedicated 'or condition' node for such tasks (cf. Fig. 14).

Adding a New Type of Condition. As seen in Fig. 13, decisions based on multiple boolean variables may cause (potentially very big) cascades of *Condition* nodes. We will show, how to easily customize the *WebStory* language by introducing an *OrCondition* node type that allows disjunction of several *Variables* (cf. Fig. 14). To introduce a new type of node, we have to do the following steps:

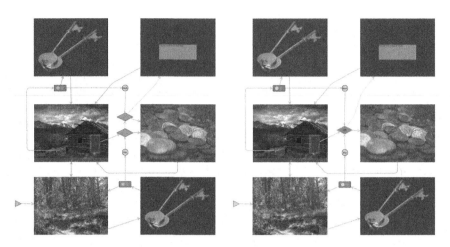

Fig. 13. Enhanced *WebStory*: Added a second key in the story (Images by: [9,20,31,35])

Fig. 14. Enhanced *WebStory* language with *OrCondition* node (Images by: [9, 20,31,35])

- Add a new node type to the GCS specification
- Modify the *WebStory* code generator to acknowledge the new node type.

Adding the New Node Type. Figure 15 shows the updated part of the *WebStory* language definition after adding the new node type *OrCondition*. The node type is modeled after the *Condition* node. Like this node the *OrCondition* type inherits the properties of the abstract *Activity* type. Main syntactic differences are the option to connect multiple variables through *DataFlow* edges, a different color, and a label 'Or'. Generating the CINCO product will create the *WebStory* tool with the newly added node type.

Modifying the Code Generator. The code generator for the *WebStory* language is small and easy to understand. The code generator can be found in the package `info.scce.cinco.product.webstory.generator`. Based on a *WebStory* model it generates a configuration for a pre-designed web framework. The configuration files are written in *JSON* [4]. Generally, the generator iterates over all *Activities* and generates configurations based on the specific *Activity* type using an automatically generated type-switch. Configurations are generated using the *Template Expression* feature of the programming language *Xtend* [2]. Since the new *OrCondition* type inherits from *Activity* it is only needed to add a new case for this type to the type-switch. To modify the code generator a simple method `caseOrCondition` has to be added to the class `ActivityGenerator` in the before mentioned package. Listing 1.1 shows the *Template Expression* `caseOrCondition` for the *OrCondition* type. It is in fact very similar to the `caseCondition` method already included in the code generator. The only difference is the evaluation (cf. line 5): here, all names of predecessor variables (which by the metamodel's constraints always happens through data edges) are joined into one expression with separating || characters.

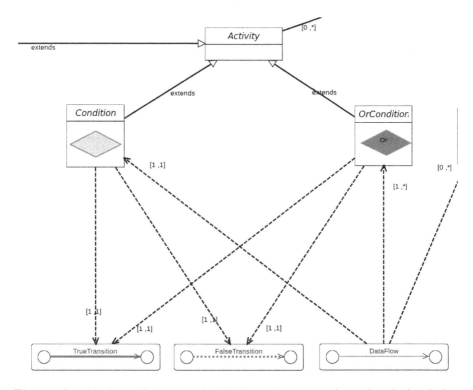

Fig. 15. Graphical specification of the *WebStory* language enhanced with the *OrCondition* type

Adding Further Types of Nodes. Of course adding the *OrCondition* node is just an easy example on how to enhance the *WebStory* language. Several different enhancements can be thought of. For example it might be utile to reduce the number of conditions even further or removing them all together. This could be done by adding a new edge type *ConditionalTransition* that can be labeled with boolean expressions. This edge type would allow more complex conditions without overloading the model with *Condition* nodes. Though introducing this edge type could be done easily, it would also call for modifications on other node types, the code generator and even the aforementioned framework, which would be clearly off scope for this tutorial. Furthermore, this kind of changes are not as trivial as adding new types to the language. Regarding already existent *WebStorys*, these changes would require a migration step for models not conforming to the new *WebStory* language. We tackle this problem in [23] through generation of a tailored migration language. This language is used to describe migration steps that can not by automatically computed.

Further enhancements might include the introduction of optional images for the *ClickAreas* to allow visible objects, conditional *TextAreas* or even some form of hierarchy for the *WebStory* models.

```
1  override caseOrCondition(OrCondition it) '''
2  {
3    type: "condition",
4    activity: «activityNumber»,
5    condition: "«variablePredecessors.map[name].join("||")»",
6    trueSuccessor: «outgoing(TrueTransition).head.targetElement.activityNumber»,
7    falseSuccessor: «outgoing(FalseTransition).head.targetElement.activityNumber»
8  }
9  '''
```

Listing 1.1. caseOrCondition method for the *WebStory* generator

5   Conclusion

We have presented a tutorial introduction to the usage of CINCO along the ongoing example of the *WebStory* language with the focus on two recent additions. On the one hand, Pyro enhances the CINCO ecosystem by bringing any CINCO-based graphical modeling language into the web. On the other hand, GCS introduced graphical editors to the meta level in a bootstrapping fashion.

The huge gain of Pyro's web modeling [36] over Eclipse-based desktop modeling is the immediate availability to everybody. Providing an easily accessible graphical modeling tool for one's domain is not only a big enabling factor for teaching and research, but also for production from early prototypes to collaborative model-based projects. We will channel all available modeling tools in the Pyro playground[7] and the CINCO examples section on the website.[8]

One of the original motivations developing CINCO was the lack of simple means for developing graphical modeling editors [29]. That is why the meta-level DSLs included in CINCO were originally developed textually using the Xtext [3] framework. Now that CINCO is there, we were able to enhance it in a bootstrapping fashion with the CINCO-developed GCS language [13].

Another bootstrapping possibility opens up when combining Pyro and GCS: Pyro is able to bring any CINCO-based modeling editor into the web. This naturally also comprises the GCS language, as it is developed with CINCO. Thus, bootstrapping CINCO with Pyro can even bring language development itself into the web, which will radically reduce the entry hurdle to graphical domain-specific modeling.

Finally, fully exploiting the power of LDE [15,32] and DSLs as a new kind of Archimedean points [33] that 'freeze' taken design decisions for future development and evolution [6] introduces a novel cooperative development paradigm that is tailored to specifically address all stakeholders.

---

[7] https://pyro.scce.info/playground/webstory.
[8] https://cinco.scce.info/examples/webstory.

References

1. WebGME. https://webgme.org/. Accessed 10 Apr 2018
2. Xtend - Modernized Java. http://xtend-lang.org. Accessed 23 Sep 2018
3. Xtext - Language Engineering Made Easy! http://www.eclipse.org/Xtext/. Accessed 10 Apr 2018
4. Standard ECMA-404. The JSON Data Interchange Format. http://www.ecma-international.org/publications/standards/Ecma-404.htm, October 2013
5. Angular Dart (2018). https://webdev.dartlang.org/angular. Accessed 29 Sep 2018
6. Boßelmann, S., Naujokat, S., Steffen, B.: On the difficulty of drawing the line. In: Margaria, T., Steffen, B. (eds.) ISoLA 2018. LNCS, vol. 11244, pp. 340–356. Springer, AG (2018)
7. Brambilla, M., Cabot, J., Wimmer, M.: Model-Driven Software Engineering in Practice. Morgan & Claypool, San Rafael (2012)
8. Client.IO: Jointjs api (2015). http://www.jointjs.com/api. Accessed 29 Sep 2018
9. Dachis, A.: (2014). https://www.flickr.com/photos/dachis/14569056769/, image
10. Dmitriev, S.: Language Oriented Programming: The Next Programming Paradigm. JetBrains onBoard Online Magazine 1 (2004). http://www.onboard.jetbrains.com/is1/articles/04/10/lop/
11. Fowler, M.: Language Workbenches: The Killer-App for Domain Specific Languages? June 2005. http://martinfowler.com/articles/languageWorkbench.html. Accessed 10 Apr 2018
12. Fraternali, P., Rossi, G., Sánchez-Figueroa, F.: Rich internet applications. IEEE Internet Comput. **14**(3), 9–12 (2010)
13. Fuhge, A.: Graphische Modellierung von Cinco Produktspezifikationen. BSc thesis, TU Dortmund (2018)
14. Gorman, B.: Learning Java EE 7. InfiniteSkills (2014)
15. Gossen, F., Margaria, T., Murtovi, A., Naujokat, S., Steffen, B.: DSLs for decision services: a tutorial introduction to language-driven engineering. In: Margaria, T., Steffen, B. (eds.) ISoLA 2018. LNCS, vol. 11244, pp. 546–564. Springer, AG (2018)
16. Gronback, R.C.: Eclipse Modeling Project: A Domain-Specific Language (DSL) Toolkit. Addison-Wesley, Boston (2008)
17. Grundy, J., Hosking, J., Li, K.N., Ali, N.M., Huh, J., Li, R.L.: Generating domain-specific visual language tools from abstract visual specifications. IEEE Trans. Softw. Eng. **39**(4), 487–515 (2013)
18. JetBrains: Meta Programming System. https://www.jetbrains.com/mps/. Accessed 10 Apr 2018
19. Kelly, S., Lyytinen, K., Rossi, M.: MetaEdit+: a fully configurable multi-user and multi-tool CASE and CAME environment. In: Constantopoulos, P., Mylopoulos, J., Vassiliou, Y. (eds.) CAiSE 1996. LNCS, vol. 1080, pp. 1–21. Springer, Heidelberg (1996). https://doi.org/10.1007/3-540-61292-0_1
20. Knowles, C. (2010). https://www.flickr.com/photos/theknowlesgallery/4756008375/, image
21. Lédeczi, A., Maróti, M., Völgyesi, P.: The generic modeling environment. Technical report, Institute for Software Integrated Systems, Vanderbilt University, Nashville, TN, 37221, USA (2003). http://www.isis.vanderbilt.edu/sites/default/files/GMEReport.pdf
22. Ledeczi, A., et al.: The generic modeling environment. In: Workshop on Intelligent Signal Processing (WISP 2001) (2001)

23. Lybecait, M., Kopetzki, D., Naujokat, S., Steffen, B.: Towards Language-to-Language Transformation (2018, to appear)
24. Margaria, T., Steffen, B.: Business process modelling in the jABC: the one-thing-approach. In: Cardoso, J., van der Aalst, W. (eds.) Handbook of Research on Business Process Modeling. IGI Global (2009)
25. Margaria, T., Steffen, B.: Simplicity as a driver for agile innovation. Computer **43**(6), 90–92 (2010)
26. Margaria, T., Steffen, B.: Service-orientation: conquering complexity with XMDD. In: Hinchey, M., Coyle, L. (eds.) Conquering Complexity, pp. 217–236. Springer, London (2012). https://doi.org/10.1007/978-1-4471-2297-5_10
27. McAffer, J., Lemieux, J.M., Aniszczyk, C.: Eclipse Rich Client Platform, 2nd edn. Addison-Wesley Professional, Reading (2010)
28. Naujokat, S.: Heavy Meta. Model-Driven Domain-Specific Generation of Generative Domain-Specific Modeling Tools. Dissertation, TU Dortmund, Dortmund, Germany, August 2017. http://hdl.handle.net/2003/36060
29. Naujokat, S., Lybecait, M., Kopetzki, D., Steffen, B.: CINCO: a simplicity-driven approach to full generation of domain-specific graphical modeling tools. Softw. Tools Technol. Transfer **20**(3), 327–354 (2017)
30. Neubauer, J., Frohme, M., Steffen, B., Margaria, T.: Prototype-driven development of web applications with DyWA. In: Margaria, T., Steffen, B. (eds.) ISoLA 2014, Part I. LNCS, vol. 8802, pp. 56–72. Springer, Heidelberg (2014). https://doi.org/10.1007/978-3-662-45234-9_5
31. Sierralupe, D.G. (2016). https://www.flickr.com/photos/sierralupe/29262085202/, image
32. Steffen, B., Gossen, F., Naujokat, S., Margaria, T.: Language-driven engineering: from general-purpose to purpose-specific languages. In: Steffen, B., Woeginger, G. (eds.) Computing and Software Science: State of the Art and Perspectives. LNCS, vol. 10000. Springer (2018, to appear)
33. Steffen, B., Naujokat, S.: Archimedean points: the essence for mastering change. Trans. Found. Mastering Change (FoMaC) **1**(1), 22–46 (2016)
34. Ward, M.P.: Language oriented programming. Softw. Concepts Tools **15**(4), 147–161 (1994)
35. Watson, I. (2010). https://www.flickr.com/photos/dagoaty/4707352284/, image
36. Zweihoff, P.: Cinco Products for the Web. Master thesis, TU Dortmund, November 2015

Model-Based Development
for High-Assurance Embedded Systems

Robby$^{(\boxtimes)}$, John Hatcliff, and Jason Belt

Kansas State University, Manhattan, USA
{robby,hatcliff,belt}@ksu.edu

Abstract. Low cost embedded cyber-physical systems and ubiquitous networking have opened up a new world of connected devices in our homes and workplaces, and in safety critical contexts such as automobiles, medical care, and drone-based air vehicles. There are many different approaches to developing and assuring these systems, but not all take a rigorous approach and even fewer offer integrated assurance frameworks.

In this STRESS 2018 tutorial, we introduce students to an integrated modeling and verification environment for high-assurance embedded systems based on the Sireum translation, analysis, and verification platform from Kansas State University. Sireum includes a programming language called Slang for developing high-assurance embedded applications and a verification framework called Logika that uses symbolic execution technology to provide highly automated and easy-to-use software contract checking capabilities. Slang and Logika align with the Architecture and Analysis Definition Language (AADL) for architecture modeling and component interface declarations, analysis of AADL models, and configuration of execution platforms using standard AADL properties. AADL component behavioral properties can be specified and verified using, for example, the Behavioral Language for Embedded Systems with Software (BLESS).

1 Overview

Figure 1 shows our approach to critical system development and assurance that emphasizes the use of formally specified architectures as the "scaffolding" through which many different activities are organized and synchronized. A key theme of our approach is the deep integration of architectural models and programming leading to the following features:

This work is sponsored in part by US National Science Foundation Food and Drug Administration Scholar-in-Residence program (CNS 1238431,1355778,1446544, 1565544), the Department of Homeland Security (DHS) Science and Technology Directorate, Homeland Security Advanced Research Projects Agency (HSARPA), Cyber Security Division (DHS S&T/HSARPA/CDS) BAA HSHQDC- 14-R-B0005, the Government of Israel and the National Cyber Bureau in the Government of Israel via contract number D16PC00057.

© Springer Nature Switzerland AG 2018
T. Margaria and B. Steffen (Eds.): ISoLA 2018, LNCS 11244, pp. 539–545, 2018.
https://doi.org/10.1007/978-3-030-03418-4_32

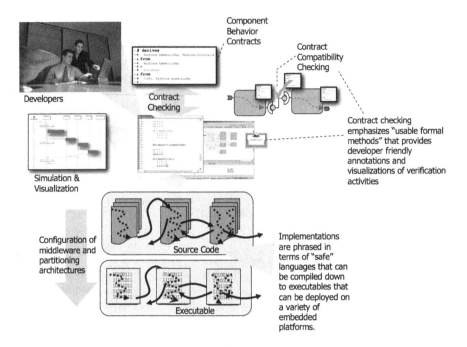

Fig. 1. Approach overview

– component code skeletons and realization of communication between components are automatically generated from architectural models, leading to
  strong traceability between models and deployed executables,
– configuration of underlying platform aspects including real-time threading
  policies and communication quality-of-service policies that are often specified
  at the programming language level are instead specified at the modeling level,
– analyses shift freely between the different abstraction levels provided by models and conventional programming languages.

The modeling approach is based on the SAE standard Architecture Analysis
and Definition Language (AADL) [10]. AADL supports our vision of: (a) providing a computational model for real-time embedded systems, and (b) enabling
strong traceability between models and deployed systems.

AADL was created in response to the high cost associated with (far too frequent) failed subsystem integration attempts due to ambiguous or incompletely
documented component interfaces. AADL is now used in several industrial development settings. For example, on the System Architecture Virtual Integration
(SAVI) effort [3], aircraft manufacturers together with subcontractors use AADL
to define a precise system architecture using an "integrate then build" design
approach. In this approach, important interactions are specified, interfaces are
designed, and integration is verified before the internals of components are built.
Once correct integration is established, contractors provide implementations that

are compliant with the architecture. The virtual integration approach is an example of how a tightly integrated modeling and programming paradigm enables a shifting of development focus between different levels of abstraction to better suit development needs; integration activities are: (a) emphasized at the modeling level instead of the source code level, and (b) shifted earlier in the development process due to the ability to leverage models.

The AADL modeling elements include software components, execution platform components, and general components. The categories of software components are data, subprogram, subprogram group, thread, thread group, and process. Execution platform component categories that represent computing hardware are processor, virtual processor, memory, bus, virtual bus, and device (which is used to model sensors, actuators, or custom hardware).

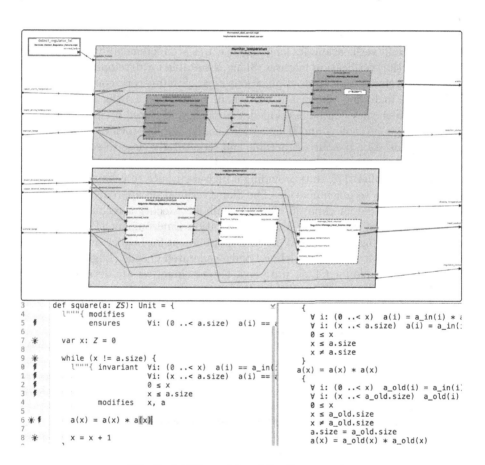

Fig. 2. AADL model and Logika examples

2   Development and Assurance

In this tutorial, we provide a brief overview of modeling in AADL using several examples, including the simple building temperature controller example shown in the top of Fig. 2. AADL systems are built from components integrated by connections between component ports. Components may be nested, as illustrated in the example where the top component represents a temperature monitoring subsystem, while the bottom component represents a temperature regulation subsystem. The business logic of the components is realized by Slang with interface specifications phrased in Sireum Logika.

The bottom of Fig. 2 shows a screen shot of the user interface of Sireum Logika, which is both a highly-automated program verifier and a manual (natural deduction) proof checker for propositional, predicate, and programming logics, where manual proof steps can be used to help automation. The Slang programming language that Logika targets is a subset of Scala that is designed for analysis and verification; its language features are incrementally added along with supporting verification features. Slang is suitable for developing both small embedded systems and large applications (e.g., Sireum core components and frameworks, including Slang, are written in Slang). As Logika programs are Scala programs, they can be developed, compiled, and tested by using the regular Scala language tooling and IDEs. Additionally, Logika provides an automatic program translation to source-traceable and structurally-close-to-source C code, whose results can be compiled using clang and gcc, as well as using the CompCert Verified C Compiler [17], thus providing a high-assurance toolchain for program correctness down to machine code. The Slang verification approach builds off of our previous model checking [5,19] and symbolic execution technologies [2,6]. The IntelliJ-based Sireum Integrated Verification Environment (IVE) provides an all-in-one coding, testing, and proving environment for Logika, and CLion can be used to integrate, test, and debug Logika generated C code (Logika generates CMake files suitable for CLion projects). For teaching, we are developing a set of course materials described in the next section.

A high-level view of the Sireum workflow is as follows:

- architecture is defined using AADL,
- AADL component interface contracts are specified using BLESS [13], a behavioral interface specification language [8],
- Slang and Logika code generation automatically generates infrastructure code, component skeletons, and component contracts in Slang (alternatively, component contracts can be specified directly in Slang),
- component implementations are developed in Slang (alternatively, component behaviors can be specified in BLESS at the AADL level and compiled to Slang),
- Slang component implementations are verified against Slang contracts using the Logika framework (alternatively, BLESS behaviors can be verified against BLESS contracts using the BLESS proof engine [15]),
- Slang implementations can be simulated and tested using the Slang simulation environment,

– Slang implementations can be translated to deployable implementations on specific embedded run-time environments (e.g., Slang can be translated to C to execute within the context of a particular separation kernel for a particular processor platform).

3   Application Domains and Resources

Slang and the Logika framework are being applied in several different safety critical domains including medical devices, secure building control systems, and avionics systems. We are particularly interested in addressing challenges in the development of *certified* safety-/security-critical systems [9,16]. In this tutorial, we provide an overview of these applications, and then illustrate end-to-end development in the framework using a simple yet realistic building control system.

Open PCA Pump – The Open Patient Controlled Analgesic (PCA) Pump project is a joint research effort between Kansas State University researchers, US Food and Drug Administration (FDA) engineers, and industry experts [7]. The project aims to provide open source design artifacts for a realistic medical device – a PCA Pump – along with an integrated collection of development artifacts that illustrate advanced development and assurance technologies in the context of realistic development processes and work products used to support safety and security reviews [14]. AADL is used to specify the architecture of the Open PCA Pump and BLESS, Slang, and Logika are used to provide behavioral specifications and implementations of the PCA Pump. The Open PCA Pump artifacts also include error modeling to support model-based hazard analysis and medical device risk management activities [12,18] as well as assurance cases arguing for the safety of the device and its interoperability features [11,21].

The Open PCA Pump artifacts are being used by the Intrinsically Secure, Open, and Safe Cyber-physically Enabled, Life-critical Essential Services (ISOSCELES) project sponsored by the US Department of Homeland Security Cyber-Physical System Security (CPSSec) research program led by Adventium Labs [1,4]. The DHS CPSSec project supports research to improve the security of critical infrastructure technologies. The ISOSCELES project is developing an open-source software platform, running on generic hardware, to provide both safety and security features for networked, interoperable medical devices to be used by (small) manufacturers more knowledgeable about medical functions than computer security.

The Open PCA Pump web site [20] includes open source artifacts including concept of operations documents (including detailed use cases), system requirements, AADL architectural models, simulatable implementations in Slang, and assurance cases. A variety of lecture materials are also available to support the use of this material in a classroom setting.

Logika Website – http://logika.sireum.org, includes instructions to install and use Logika using its Command-Line Interface (CLI) and through the Sireum

Integrated Verification Environment (IVE) on popular operating systems such as macOS, Linux, and Windows. In addition, it details the logical inference rules that Logika uses for its reasoning.

Lecture Materials and Online Textbook – using Logika as a tool for teaching propositional/predicate logic and contract-based verification. The online textbook is available at the Logika website, and lecture materials (e.g., slides, examples, etc.) can be found at http://proglogics.sireum.org (instructor-only materials such as homework and exam problems and their solution are available upon request).

4   Tutorial Outline

This tutorial is organized into four sessions as follows. Participants are first introduced to the Slang language, the Logika verifier, and Sireum IVE through some examples to see how Logika can check system contracts. Second, participants have a hands-on experience on specifying contracts, programming system implementations, and verifying that the implementations satisfy the contracts. In the third session, participants are introduced to AADL and its development environment through a simple, yet realistic system architecture that can be used to generate implementation building blocks for the architecture components whose behaviors are then implemented in Slang. Lastly, similar to the second session, participants have a hands-on exercise to adapt the architecture and its implementation, for example, to add more features to the system.

References

1. Carpenter, T., Hatcliff, J., Vasserman, E.Y.: A reference separation architecture for mixed-criticality medical and IoT devices. In: Proceedings of the 1st ACM Workshop on the Internet of Safe Things, SafeThings 2017, New York, pp. 14–19. ACM (2017)
2. Deng, X., Robby, Hatcliff, J.: Kiasan/KUnit: automatic test case generation and analysis feedback for open object-oriented systems. In: Testing: Academic and Industrial Conference Practice and Research Techniques - MUTATION (TAICPART-MUTATION 2007), pp. 3–12, September 2007
3. Feiler, P.H., Hansson, J., de Niz, D., Wrage, L.: System architecture virtual integration: an industrial case study. Technical report CMU/SEI-2009-TR-017, CMU (2009)
4. Harp, S., Carpenter, T., Hatcliff, J.: A reference architecture for secure medical devices. Biomed. Instrum. Technol. **52**(5), 357–365 (2018). Association for the Advancement of Medical Instrumentation (AAMI)
5. Hatcliff, J., Dwyer, M.B., Robby: Bogor: a flexible framework for creating software model checkers. In: Testing: Academic Industrial Conference - Practice And Research Techniques (TAIC PART 2006), pp. 3–22, August 2006
6. Hatcliff, J., Robby, Chalin, P., Belt, J.: Explicating symbolic execution (xSymExe): an evidence-based verification framework. In: 35th International Conference on Software Engineering (ICSE), pp. 222–231, May 2013

7. Hatcliff, J., Larson, B., Carpenter, T., Jones, P., Zhang, Y., Jorgens, J.: The Open PCA pump project: an exemplar open source medical device as a community resource. In: Proceedings of the 2018 Medical Cyber-Physical Systems (MedCPS) Workshop (2018)
8. Hatcliff, J., Leavens, G.T., Leino, K.R.M., Müller, P., Parkinson, M.: Behavioral interface specification languages. ACM Comput. Surv. **44**(3), 16:1–16:58 (2012)
9. Hatcliff, J., Wassyng, A., Kelly, T., Comar, C., Jones, P.L.: Certifiably safe software-dependent systems: challenges and directions. In: Proceedings of the on Future of Software Engineering (ICSE FOSE), pp. 182–200 (2014)
10. SAE International: SAE AS5506 Rev. C Architecture Analysis and Design Language (AADL). SAE International (2017). http://www.sae.org
11. King, A.L., et al.: Towards assurance for plug & play medical systems. In: Koornneef, F., van Gulijk, C. (eds.) SAFECOMP 2014. LNCS, vol. 9337, pp. 228–242. Springer, Cham (2015). https://doi.org/10.1007/978-3-319-24255-2_17
12. Larson, B., Hatcliff, J., Fowler, K., Delange, J.: Illustrating the AADL error modeling annex (v.2) using a simple safety-critical medical device. In: Proceedings of the 2013 ACM SIGAda Annual Conference on High Integrity Language Technology, HILT 2013, New York, pp. 65–84. ACM (2013)
13. Larson, B.R., Chalin, P., Hatcliff, J.: BLESS: formal specification and verification of behaviors for embedded systems with software. In: Brat, G., Rungta, N., Venet, A. (eds.) NFM 2013. LNCS, vol. 7871, pp. 276–290. Springer, Heidelberg (2013). https://doi.org/10.1007/978-3-642-38088-4_19
14. Larson, B.R., Hatcliff, J., Chalin, P.: Open source patient-controlled analgesic pump requirements documentation. In: Proceedings of the 5th International Workshop on Software Engineering in Health Care, Piscataway, pp. 28–34. IEEE (2013)
15. Larson, B.R., Zhang, Y., Barrett, S.C., Hatcliff, J., Jones, P.L.: Enabling safe interoperation by medical device virtual integration. IEEE Des. Test **32**, 74–88 (2015)
16. Lee, I., et al.: Challenges and research directions in medical cyber-physical systems. Proc. IEEE **100**(1), 75–90 (2012)
17. Leroy, X., Blazy, S., Kästner, D., Schommer, B., Pister, M., Ferdinand, C.: CompCert - a formally verified optimizing compiler. In: ERTS 2016: Embedded Real Time Software and Systems. SEE (2016)
18. Procter, S., Hatcliff, J.: An architecturally-integrated, systems-based hazard analysis for medical applications. In: Twelfth ACM/IEEE International Conference on Formal Methods and Models for Codesign (MEMOCODE), pp. 124–133. IEEE (2014)
19. Robby, Dwyer, M.B., Hatcliff, J.: Bogor: an extensible and highly-modular software model checking framework. In: Proceedings of the 9th European Software Engineering Conference Held Jointly with 11th ACM SIGSOFT International Symposium on Foundations of Software Engineering, ESEC/FSE-2011, pp. 267–276 (2003)
20. Kansas State University: Open PCA pump project (2018). http://openpcapump.santoslab.org
21. Zhang, Y., Larson, B., Hatcliff, J.: Assurance case considerations for interoperable medical systems. In: Gallina, B., Skavhaug, A., Schoitsch, E., Bitsch, F. (eds.) SAFECOMP 2018. LNCS, vol. 11094, pp. 42–48. Springer, Cham (2018). https://doi.org/10.1007/978-3-319-99229-7_5

DSLs for Decision Services: A Tutorial Introduction to Language-Driven Engineering

Frederik Gossen[1,2], Tiziana Margaria[2], Alnis Murtovi[1], Stefan Naujokat[1(✉)],
and Bernhard Steffen[1]

[1] Chair for Programming Systems, TU Dortmund University, Dortmund, Germany
{frederik.gossen,alnis.murtovi,stefan.naujokat,
bernhard.steffen}@tu-dortmund.de
[2] CSIS, University of Limerick, Limerick, Ireland
{frederik.gossen,tiziana.margaria}@ul.ie

Abstract. Language-Driven Engineering (LDE) is a new paradigm that aims at involving stakeholders, including the application experts, in the system development and evolution process using dedicated domains-specific languages (DSLs) tailored to match the stakeholders' mindsets. The interplay between the involved DSLs is realized in a service-oriented fashion, with corresponding Mindset-Supporting Integrated Development Environments (mIDEs). This organization eases product line and system evolution, because one can introduce and exchange entire DSLs as if they were services. Using as example a smart email classification system that highlights important emails in the inbox, we model its decision procedure in a tailored graphical domain-specific language based on Binary Decision Diagrams. BDDs are a compact form of the popular decision trees and thus a mindset natural to many application experts. We then evolve this language and its mIDE to meet the new users' wish to model some uncertainty in the classification. To evolve the language, we first manually adapt its metamodel and code generator. Subsequently we show, how this step can be automated by refining the BDD DSL with a dedicated DSL for defining algebraic structures. As this exchange happens in a service-oriented fashion, it does not impair the optimization potential and nicely follows the successive refinement of the users' mindset.

Keywords: Domain-specific languages
Language-Driven Engineering · Language evolution · Code generation
Abstract tool specification · Binary Decision Diagrams
Algebraic Decision Diagrams

1 Introduction

The *Language-Driven Engineering* (LDE) [17] paradigm aims at bridging the semantic gap [15] between the various stakeholders of a software project by means

© Springer Nature Switzerland AG 2018
T. Margaria and B. Steffen (Eds.): ISoLA 2018, LNCS 11244, pp. 546–564, 2018.
https://doi.org/10.1007/978-3-030-03418-4_33

of tailored *Domain-Specific Languages* (DSLs) [6,11] that capture each stake-holder's preferred mindset. These languages are provided via language-specific *Mindset-Supporting Integrated Development Environments* (mIDEs). mIDEs are comfortable state-of-the-art development environments that allow stakeholders to think in their chosen mindset. Once various DSLs are available, a new class of stakeholders provides, maintains, and evolves the needed mIDEs.

In this paper, we introduce the LDE paradigm using as example a smart email selection/classification system that highlights important emails in the inbox. We apply the LDE paradigm to the decision services that classify, categorize, and label the incoming emails as they are received. Initially, the application classifies email in two categories (urgent, not urgent). After a refinement, it also ranks them according to their importance, and in a further refinement the emails are assigned colours.

Each evolution step improves the user's overview of the inbox, making the e-mails organisation system smarter. The interesting evolution, however, concerns the underlying domain-specific languages and their mIDEs, which allow application experts to model the appropriate decision service in their chosen mindset – in this case, the initial mindset of decision diagrams. We show how easily the language is then adapted to new users' needs, introducing a means to rank emails instead of classifying them into just two categories. We illustrate that the evolution of domain-specific languages and mIDEs can be fast enough to be applied iteratively, in a successive refinement fashion during system development and evolution. The possibility to refine DSLs in a service-oriented fashion, here by introducing a dedicated DSL for the specification of algebraic structures, support the LDE vision.

In a user-friendly world, we wish the user to concentrate on the own needs, and enabled to express those needs in a possibly easy and natural way, for example, in terms of predicates as in this paper, or predicates and then rules for a rule-based approach like miAamics [7]. We wish then the technical environment to be able to ingest that description and deliver a most efficient and runtime optimal decision structure, that is computed, maintained and executed outside of the care by the user. The reuse and the meta-level reuse advocated in [14] and demonstrated in [3] come here into play.

In Sect. 2, we consider the binary classification case, where we classify emails along urgency in two categories and introduce domain-specific languages for predicate abstraction (in Sect. 2.1), decision diagrams (in Sect. 2.2), and their composition (in Sect. 2.3). In Sect. 3, we demonstrate how the language evolves along changing user needs. We first move from binary decision to fuzzy min-max logics. Subsequently, we show how easily the LDE approach allows the replacement of the underlying algebraic structure. Section 4 concludes this paper.

2   Email Classification with Binary Decision Diagrams

Organizing the stream of incoming emails in the inbox can be very challenging: choosing what emails to read first and what are not worth reading at all takes time and individual evaluation. The automation of this classification is common practice in mail management tools. For example, spam filters are typically configured with a set of rules. A rule-based mindset yields great potential for optimization of decision functions [7], but it is only one of many possible mindsets. A binary classification can be easily generalized to a classification into many categories, or to ranking emails along some adequate criteria. Email classification is a prime example of a decision service and serves as an ongoing example in this paper.

We consider the simple case of a binary email classification like spam detection or the selection of particularly important emails. The yes/no outcome makes it a Boolean decision for each individual email. The criteria for the decision can be fairly complex, and so is the Boolean predicate that encapsulates the entire decision process for the yes/no evaluation. We focus instead on a set of simple predicates that express individual relevant traits of the email under consideration, and that together characterize the email in its entirety for the purpose of this classification. We call this set of predicates an *email profile*. This abstraction from the concrete email to its profile allows to focus on the important characteristics and discarding irrelevant information early in the process.

Using rules to define a decision service, as many spam filters do, is only one of the many mindsets that foot on this abstraction. We focus here instead on decision trees, a popular tool for representing decision making knowledge that is a familiar mindset to many users, and represent the decision trees in a canonic minimal form as *Binary Decision Diagrams* (BDDs) [4,5]. The intuitive graphical representation of the BDDs links well with the predicates of the email profile. At the same time their minimality and optimality is operationally fully hidden from the users, who do not need to think about how to compose and minimize the decision diagram when they specify the criteria for the profile of their decision service. This property nicely separates an easy specification (the WHAT-level) by the user, from an optimal implementation (the HOW-level) as advocated in [17] and initially in [10].

2.1   The WHAT Level: Defining Email Profiles

The DSL for email profiles is a domain-specific modelling language for binary decision services consisting of a finite set of predicates that characterize properties of the emails. Given an email, the Boolean decision service computes the predicates and takes a decision. They can be regarded either as a set of individual functions with Boolean co-domain, or collectively as a single function that characterizes the input by a Boolean vector. Each predicate is defined by a name and the implementation of its characteristic function. Already a symbolic representation of predicates is sufficient to use the full power of our modelling language, because both the optimization and the code generation work with predicate symbols, independently of their concrete implementation. For this reason, predicates are a key element of the decision models, but their implementation is not needed until the generated decision service is executed.

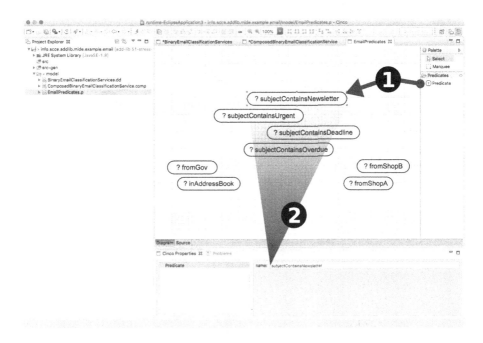

Fig. 1. Screenshot of a predicates model in its dedicated mIDE for the email domain.

Among the many ways to specify a set of predicate symbols, e.g., by a list of their names, we represent predicate models in a graphical form (cf. Fig. 1). For the user, it has the advantage that predicates can be arranged and organized on a two-dimensional canvas – an interface preferred by many non-programmer users – rather than in a linear textual format. From the technical support point of view, it has the decisive advantage that we can use meta tooling frameworks, like CINCO [13], providing full mIDE support for the graphical representation without additional effort. Another advantage is that this specific DSL is also seamlessly integrable into other graphical languages that build up on it.

In this paper, we regard the predicates as mutually independent, a criterion for the optimality of the corresponding BDD optimization. In future evolutions of the predicate DSL, however, we aim at covering also implications between predicates or even predicate groups. With our graphical DSL for predicates this extension is easy: just add a new type of edge to represent implication. This extension would not impact validity: as this extension only adds model elements, previous predicate models are guaranteed to remain valid.

In our email example, predicates convey one bit of information about the email. Information expressed through predicates can be, for example, whether or not an email was sent from a contact in the address book, or presence/absence of keywords in the email's subject or in its content. The set of predicates collectively characterizes essential traits of the email and discards unnecessary information, namely the exact textual content of the email. The complete characterization is

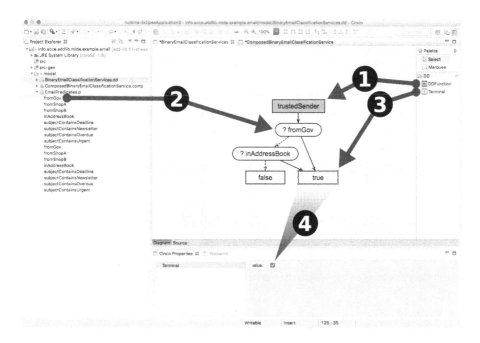

Fig. 2. Screenshot of a decision diagram model in its dedicated mIDE. The model specifies a strategy to identify trustworthy senders.

captured in a Boolean vector (the email profile) where each component represents the evaluation of one individual predicate.

Figure 1 shows the small exemplary set of predicates we use for the email DSL. They are arranged in the two-dimensional canvas and grouped by similarity. This set is relatively small, yet it characterizes some key characteristics of emails with regard to their urgency. Because this predicate language is realized with an mIDE, users can drag and drop new predicate nodes from the tool's palette onto the canvas (cf. 1 in Fig. 1), whose only attribute is the name of a predicate that can be edited through the properties menu (cf. 2 in Fig. 1).

While some predicates may be cheap to compute, e.g., checking for a word in the subject, others can be very expensive, e.g., requiring full text search. The email profile is therefore not computed in its entirety, but predicates are evaluated only when actually needed.

2.2   Binary Decision Diagrams

Binary Decision Diagrams (BDDs) are widely popular in computer science. In fact, the paper introducing their ordered variant (OBDDs) [4] was for a long time one of the most cited papers in computer science. Even outside of computer science, decision diagrams are a popular representation of decision processes. Their popularity indicates that describing decision procedures this way is a pretty natural mindset for large and diverse user groups: one simply visually follows the path from a starting point through the various decision points in the diagram down to the (here binary) result. The exemplary diagram in Fig. 2 determines whether an email was sent from a trustworthy person or not. Given an e-mail, simple yes or no questions are answered by evaluating the corresponding predicates until either *true* is reached, indicating that the email was sent from a trustworthy source, or *false* otherwise.

Formally, Binary Decision Diagrams are a rooted, directed and acyclic graph structure. The graph's internal nodes are associated with a predicate, and the terminals are associated with the Boolean values *true* and *false*. Every internal node has exactly two successors, one then-successor and one else-successor, while terminals, as their name suggests, have no successor. The diagram's evaluation starts at its root. For every internal node the evaluation of the associated predicate determines which successor to choose. The evaluation's result in the given situation is the Boolean value of the reached terminal.

As for the predicates model, we provide full mIDE support for Binary Decision Diagrams, too. Elements of the model can be created per drag and drop from the tool's node palette, allowing users to rapidly create and modify decision diagrams and to experiment with variations. The modelling language for BDDs comprises three node types: predicate and terminal nodes correspond to the standard node types of decision diagrams, function nodes are new and serve to select and label root nodes.

Function nodes are introduced in our modelling language to assign a name to a BDD: their only successor is the initial node of the decision diagram. This way, users identify decision services by name and set the entry point to the body of the decision diagram, which is either a predicate node or a terminal node. Function nodes are created by drag and drop from a palette in the mIDE (cf. 1 in Fig. 2) and are labelled in the tool's properties menu.

Predicate nodes correspond to the internal nodes of BDDs, which are usually associated with a variable. Here, they are associated to previously defined predicates of the predicate model: The available predicate symbols are shown in the mIDE's project explorer, and users build the decision structure by drag and drop of the predicate symbols onto the canvas, where they become predicate nodes (cf. 2 in Fig. 2). For each predicate node, one solid then-edge and one dashed else-edge is drawn to the desired successor nodes, which are themselves either another predicate node or a terminal node.

Terminal nodes hold the (here Boolean) result of the decision process. Terminal nodes have no successor, are taken directly from the mIDE's palette (cf. 3 in Fig. 2), and their value is edited through the mIDE's properties menu (cf. 4 in Fig. 2).

Figure 2 shows a screenshot of a decision service modelled in the mIDE for Binary Decision Diagrams. Based on the predicate abstraction of emails, this service determines whether or not the email was sent from a trustworthy source, whereby here trustworthiness is based on a governmental address or an entry in the receiver's address book. Together with the decision diagrams shown in Fig. 3, this decision service forms the rule base for the case study presented in [17].

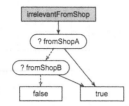

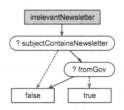

(a) Identifies as unimportant emails from one of two online shops.

(b) Identifies as irrelevant newsletters those that were not sent from a government email address.

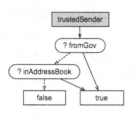

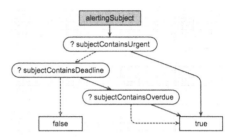

(c) Indicates emails from known contacts and trusted senders.

(d) Indicates emails with alerting subjects based on the occurrence of certain keywords.

Fig. 3. Four exemplary decision diagram models as realized in our DSL for decision diagrams (Examples reused from [17]).

2.3 Composition of Binary Decision Diagrams

Decision diagrams are great to model small decision services, like those in the previous examples. As soon as the decision services becomes more complex and concern a variety of different aspects, like those displayed in Fig. 3, scalability becomes an issue. Modularity can help: As individually modeled decision services simply represent Boolean functions, they can be combined using logical operators $\wedge$, $\vee$ $\neg$. Our corresponding graphical mIDE resembles typical abstract syntax trees, as shown in Fig. 4. Yet, this user-centric modelling does not impair the performance of later realizations, as we see next.

2.4 Fully Automatic Optimization and Code Generation

In mIDE-based development, efficient realization is a clearly separate issue from modelling, and it is delegated to the code generator. Typically, this domain-specific code generator has a much bigger optimization potential than compilers for general-purpose programming languages, because it takes advantage of the knowledge about the specific domain. This effect is particularly striking for

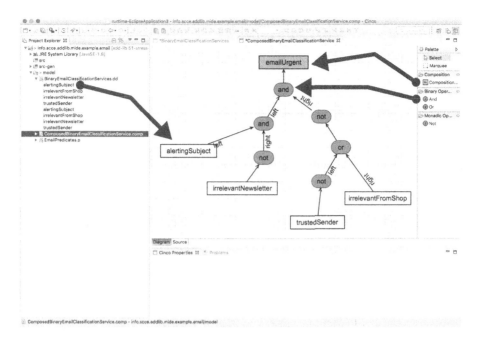

Fig. 4. Screenshot of a composition model in its dedicated mIDE. The model composes the four decision diagrams shown in Fig. 3 respectively in Fig. 6.

the logical combinations of BDDs, and actually far beyond what could ever be achieved in a general purpose setting.

For a fixed order of the involved predicates, Boolean functions have a canonical BDD representation. If a number of BDDs share the same predicate ordering, the logical combinations of their individual canonical BDD representations can be efficiently evaluated to obtain a corresponding resulting canonical BDD, which is computationally optimal [4]. This evaluation uses standard powerful tools and frameworks [1, 16].

Figure 5 visualizes the overall decision structure resulting from the generation process for the five decision services of the email example: the four predicate-level evaluations of the profile in Fig. 3 and the composition model of Fig. 4. If an email's subject contains neither **urgent** nor **deadline**, the overall result is clear and none of the remaining predicates is evaluated. This illustrates the inherent optimality aspect of canonical BDDs: only the required predicates are considered, in this case two of four.

The optimized Binary Decision Diagram in Fig. 5 is good for visualization, but not executable, so it must be translated into code. The current mIDE comes with a code generator for Java that provides the executable version with ease, without need to program. The mIDE also allows users to view the canonical diagram with one click, and to transform any of the models to a canonical version of a decision diagram model. These features support users not only to

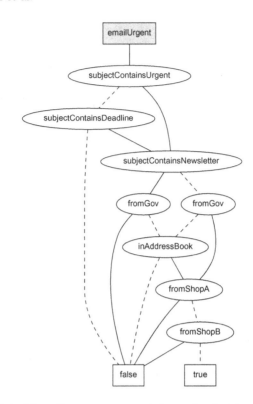

Fig. 5. Canonical decision diagram generated from the decision service models (cf. Figs. 3 and 4) to detect urgent emails.

model decision services and integrate them into their applications, but provide a quick and direct way to experiment with Binary Decision Diagrams, in a rapid prototyping fashion. For the moment, the mIDE supports Java, but it could be extended to support other target languages with relatively little effort.

3   Evolving the Modelling Language and Its mIDE

Detecting urgent emails in a realistic stream of incoming emails is not an obvious task. A Boolean classifier may be too coarse: for some emails, the result may be ambiguous, others may not conform to the modeller's expectations, so that a too blunt decision model treats them differently than the modeller intended. A decision service that provides a *degree of certainty* about how urgent an email is could be more useful than a yes or no answer.

Generalizations capable to deal with degrees of certainty exist for both Boolean logic and Binary Decision Diagrams. Various fuzzy logics [8,9] operate on the complete interval [0, 1] rather than on just two values. The corresponding algebraic structures require a generalization of the BDDs to *Algebraic Decision*

Diagrams (ADDs) [2], which incorporate the underlying algebraic structure into the decision diagrams.

The new algebraic structure can be incorporated in our modelling languages and their corresponding mIDEs, too. Fuzzy logics have the same set of operations as standard Boolean logic, so previously modeled services can be easily adapted to the newly introduced concept of certainty: the only difference is that decision diagrams must now deliver a real value within the interval $[0, 1]$ instead of the previous Boolean values. In fact, the fuzzy logics used in the remainder of this paper generalize standard Boolean logic, in the sense that a Boolean model is an instance of fuzzy model where all the Boolean models' semantics remains untouched and 1 is used instead of *true* and 0 instead of *false*.

3.1   Language-Driven Engineering

Applying the fuzzy generalization to our domain-specific modelling languages requires adapting both the languages and the mIDEs. In this case, we incorporate the concept of degree of certainty into the modelling language for decision diagrams, and change the mIDEs accordingly. This is the key characteristic of Language-Driven Engineering [17]: developing domain-specific languages with mIDE support becomes part of the application development itself [3]. The change needed to accomplish this is small and close to the users' mindset, rather than forcing a new one on them. The powerful optimization of the language is maintained. As stated before, the development of domain-specific languages has become cheap, and this applies to their evolution as well.

In the following, we present two variants of fuzzy logic, *fuzzy min-max logic* and *fuzzy probabilistic logic*. We realize them in different ways, in order to showcase two different ways of coping with evolution. In the fuzzy mindset, a value of 0 resp. 1 indicates maximum certainty that the truth value is *true* resp. *false*.

3.2   Fuzzy Min-Max Logic

A particularly simple variant of fuzzy logics is min-max logic. Its carrier set is the interval $[0, 1]$ and it defines conjunction, disjunction, and negation as follows:

$$MinMaxLogic := ([0, 1], \{\wedge_m, \vee_m\}, \{\neg_m\}) \text{ with}$$
$$a \wedge_m b := min(a, b)$$
$$a \vee_m b := max(a, b)$$
$$\neg_m a := 1 - a.$$

Adapting the modelling language: Because all operation symbols remain the same as in the Boolean case, the only change is the carrier set, namely the type of the values in the decision diagrams' terminal nodes. Adapting the modelling language means incorporating the new value type in the language's metamodels and the semantic change of the operations, which requires the implementation of the new operations' definitions, $\wedge_m$, $\vee_m$, and $\neg_m$. These are only minor changes to the code generator.

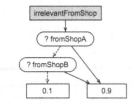

(a) Indicates degrees of unimportance of emails from one of two online shops on a scale from 0 to 1.

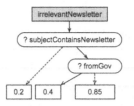

(b) Indicates degreed of irrelevance of newsletters on a scale from 0 to 1.

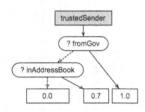

(c) Indicates degrees of trustworthiness of emails from known contacts and trusted senders on a scale from 0 to 1.

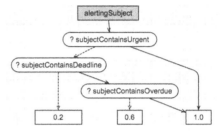

(d) Indicates the degree of conspicuity based on the occurrence of certain keywords in an emails subject on a scale from 0 to 1.

Fig. 6. Fuzzy variants of the BDDs displayed in Fig. 3 [17].

Adapting the mIDE: Everything else, namely the entire tool support, can be regenerated by the metamodelling framework, making the evolution of our language easy and cheap.

Also, the already modelled decision diagrams can easily be adapted to conform to the new language. Figure 6 shows the fuzzy adaptations of the BDD models of Fig. 3. Now these predicates take into account the different accuracy of the rules, improving the overall model accuracy. The composition model remains untouched and with the same operation symbols as before. However, their semantics has changed in the code generator, allowing for an adapted form of reuse, even in an evolved domain-specific language. The resulting canonical decision diagram in Fig. 7 is obviously different from the previously seen case in Fig. 5. As was to be expected, it distinguishes more than the Boolean decision service, and the new classifier has six different categories, with certainty degrees ranging from 0.0 to 0.8.

We showed how to manually evolve from BDDs to fuzzy min-max logic. However, in LDE, there is another, more elaborate, option, which we will discuss in the upcoming sections.

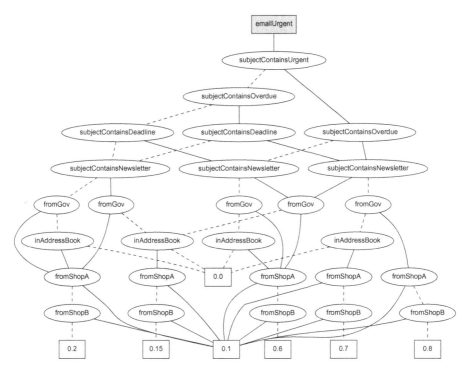

Fig. 7. Canonical fuzzy decision diagram generated from fuzzy decision service models (cf. Figs. 6 and 4) to detect urgent emails. In this case the underlying code generator implemented a fuzzy min-max logic.

3.3 Another Level of Language Refinement

Min-max logic is just one realization of fuzzy logics. Many alternatives to it have all their strengths and weaknesses, and correspond to different languages in Language-Driven Engineering. As the LDE paradigm is all about the evolution of domain-specific languages, our modelling languages can be adapted to other fuzzy logic variants within the paradigm. The wealth of domain-specific languages in this development paradigm introduces a new stakeholder type, responsible for the maintenance and evolution of the DSLs and their associated mIDE.

Instead of evolving the DSL through manual adaptation of its metamodels and code generators as just showed, we can embrace the LDE paradigm and add another refinement level: we introduce a new domain-specific language for the *evolution of the decision service modelling languages*.[1]

---

[1] See [3] for a discussion on completely loosening the meta-level classification of languages.

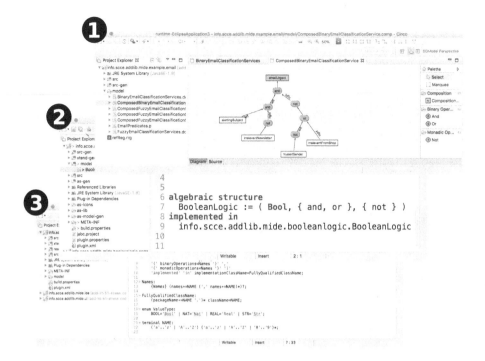

Fig. 8. Three meta levels of the domain-specific language for decision diagrams: (1) the concrete language for decision diagrams with an arbitrary algebraic structure, (2) the meta-level domain-specific language for the definition of algebraic structures, and (3) the implementation of the meta-level domain-specific language.

We demonstrate the power of this approach by introducing, now in the new way, probabilistic logic as a second variant of fuzzy logics[2], leading altogether to a third step of our language evolution. The language element subject to change is again the underlying algebraic structure: initially standard Boolean algebra, it then evolved to min-max fuzzy logic, and it changes again.

The three meta levels we use now are illustrated in Fig. 8. The *modelling language designer* works with an own mIDE for language definition at the middle level (2): this designer defines the algebraic structure to be used by the end user, so that end users can use the concrete modelling tool shown in the top-most mIDE (1), which is the concrete modelling tool for the end user. To implement the defined language primitives, the modelling language designer works at the bottom level (3) where he or she now implements the just defined domain-specific language for algebraic structures. This idea was sketched as $meta_n modeling$ in [12]. Following that nomenclature, here the algebra definition is the $meta_3$model of the decision and composition models.

---

[2] We are not claiming this logic to be more or less appropriate to the email case study. Rather, we want to put the users in the focus and give them the choice of mindset among many.

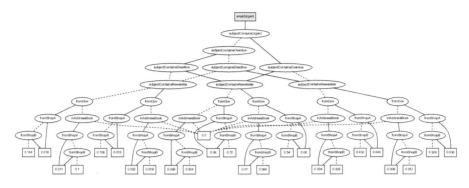

Fig. 9. Canonical fuzzy decision diagram generated from fuzzy decision service models (cf. Figs. 6 and 4) to detect urgent emails. In this case the underlying code generator implemented a fuzzy probabilistic logic.

3.4 Fuzzy Probabilistic Logic

Probabilistic logic is a variant of fuzzy logics that resembles probabilities, with the implicit assumption that variables are independent. Its operations are defined as follows:

$$ProbabilisticLogic := ([0,1], \{\wedge_p, \vee_p\}, \{\neg_p\}) \text{ with}$$
$$a \wedge_p b := a * b$$
$$a \vee_p b := 1 - ((1 - a) * (1 - b))$$
$$\neg_p a := 1 - a.$$

The assumption of independent variables has remarkable consequences, e.g., the conjunction of a variable and its negation is no longer guaranteed to have probability 0. However, while probabilistic logic may not conform to all the properties one naturally expects from a logic, it is nevertheless a useful mindset for specific tasks. Here, we will use it primarily to show the adaptability of our modelling languages with the LDE approach of adding a level of meta languages.

From the point of view of adaptation needs, the operation symbols are the same as in fuzzy min-max logics. Consequently, the exact same models from our previous examples remain valid, and the newly introduced semantics only plays a role in the code generator. The resulting canonical decision diagram is shown in Fig. 9.

In the following, we show how to achieve this within our Language-Driven Engineering approach by adding a new domain-specific language for the definition of algebraic structures.

3.5 Domain-Specific Language for Algebraic Structures

Applying the necessary changes appears a minor task at first glance, and in fact most of the implementation remains untouched and becomes an Archimedean

Fig. 10. Canonical decision diagram to colourize important emails. The decision structure was generated from colour decision service models structurally similar to those in Figs. 6 and 4).

point of the evolution step [18]. However, the few changes that are required spread across the entire project. In this section, we show how the service-oriented refinement of the BDD DSL and mIDE tackle this problem: instead of doing manual changes all the time, all the required changes can be elegantly captured using a specific DSL for defining algebraic structures equipped with a syntax close to the well-established mathematical notation. Once this is available, the use of probabilistic logic becomes very simple:

```
algebraic structure
  ProbabilisticLogic := (Real, {and, or}, {not})
implemented in
  info.scce.addlib.mide.ProbabilisticLogic
```

Essentially, the new DSL allows one to define the signature of the considered algebra and to link it to an implementation of the operators' semantics, here $\wedge_p, \vee_p$, and $\neg_p$, in a service-oriented fashion. Based on this description, the graphical language's metamodel, the code generator, as well as features to transform decision models to canonical decision diagrams are fully automatically generated.

Service-oriented language refinement makes the evolution of modelling languages fast, cheap and compliant with the LDE paradigm. In summary, the language refinement can happen at two levels, as sketched in Fig. 8:

– directly at the language level, as in the evolution of the decision service modelling language from Boolean logic to fuzzy min-max logic, or
– at the meta-level, as in the just described DSL refinement, that eases the definition of algebraic structures in general.

The flexibility achieved by defining the algebraic structures this way is significant: models developed in the concrete mIDE can be reused, even when the language they were modeled in changes. As long as the carrier set type remains stable and operation symbols are only added, models remain completely valid, and only their semantics shift. Even when the type of the carrier set changes, models may still be adaptable, as seen in the first step of evolution from standard Boolean logics to min-max logics.

3.6   Colours as Algebraic Domain

The evolution of the language for decision services is by no means limited to logics. Graphical properties can be used to support the visualization, like the use of colours to highlight the email classification with colour codes. We consider now the algebraic treatment of colours according to the following signature:

$$ColourAlg := ([0..255]^3, \{+, avg\}, \{inv\}) \text{ with}$$
$$a + b := (min(a_0 + b_0, 255), \ min(a_1 + b_1, 255), \ min(a_2 + b_2, 255))$$
$$avg(a, b) := (\frac{a_0 + b_0}{2}, \ \frac{a_1 + b_1}{2}, \ \frac{a_2 + b_2}{2})$$
$$inv(a) := (255 - a_0, \ 255 - a_1, \ 255 - a_2).$$

This algebraic structure interprets colour in the commonly used 'RGB' representation, i.e., as a combination of its red, green, and blue component. Binary operations are additive colour mixing ($+$) and mean colour mixing (avg), while inversion (inv) is the only unary operation. Like these, many more operations on colours can be lifted to decision diagrams as well as to their composition.

Exploiting LDE for algebraic structures, the following specification, together with the implementation of the operators' semantics, is sufficient for the required service-oriented language refinement:

```
algebraic structure
  ColourAlg := (Nat*Nat*Nat, {add, avg}, {inv})
implemented in
  info.scce.addlib.mide.ColourAlg
```

The corresponding decision diagram language and mIDE can now be generated in the exact same way as seen in previous examples, except that terminals are now labeled with RGB triples representing the resulting colours. The languages for the corresponding decision diagrams, for their composition, and also their optimization remain essentially unchanged. To evolve our ongoing email example to the colour domain, we used red as an indicator for the most urgent emails and cyan for unimportant emails. All emails were assigned a colour in this spectrum according to their importance. The generated decision structure is visualized in Fig. 10.

The advantage of using the colour domain is that it can provide a comprehensive multi-dimensional overview. With a slightly elaborated set of models the following exemplary decision structure can be generated that highlights (cf. Fig. 11)

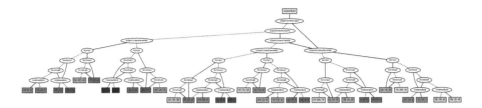

Fig. 11. Canonical decision diagram to colourize emails: Red for newsletters, Green for alerting email subjects, lighter colours for trusted senders, and darker colours for suspicious senders.

- newsletters in red,
- alerting emails in green,
- trusted senders with lighter colours, and
- suspicious senders with darker colours.

4   Conclusion

We showcased the flexibility of the Language-Driven Engineering paradigm on an increasingly smarter email selection/classification system. The power of the approach resides in the ability to define according languages and meta languages, and to evolve and refine over time both

- the specific Domain-Specific Languages used at the application level, in this case the decision structures that classify the mails and thus make the mailbox organisation system smart, but also
- the meta level in order to feed new, more powerful entities into the DSL level world and correspondingly also its mIDEs.

In the specific example, one can go from a binary classifier to a fuzzy min-max logic classifier by manually modifying the metamodel of the DSL for binary classifiers. Meta-level language refinement has then been illustrated by providing a dedicated mIDE for defining the algebra underlying the terminal nodes of the decision diagrams. With this refinement, changing from min-max logic to probabilistic logic is just a matter of a few lines: the algebra specification and a slight modification of the code generator. Considering a colour and application for mixing application illustrates the generality of this approach.

Evolution is typically done by substitution or refinement, and follows the changing needs of the user's mindset, in this case, the wish of increasing precision in the classification and of increased user support, e.g., with colour coding for provenance or urgency level. Contrary to the general perception, a language-driven approach can accomplish two things at the same time:

- capture its users' mindset and provide descriptive means for specification (at the WHAT-level), and
- provide powerful domain-specific optimization and code generation hidden from its users (at the HOW-level).

The interplay of DSLs growth over time – due to, e.g., the addition of predicates, and inherent sophistication of the analysis, due to, e.g., the addition of uncertainties and then of richer algebraic structures – supports an evolution-friendly and manageable style of application design for knowledge-intense domains.

This flexibility goes far beyond state of the art development scenarios, where application experts are often unable (or not allowed by the used IT systems) to change and evolve the design or configuration environment they use. With LDE, language primitives and the entire support mechanisms (editor, composition mechanisms, code generators) evolve along the needs and gracefully accompany the increasing sophistication of the entire environment.

References

1. ADD-Lib. http://add-lib.scce.info
2. Bahar, R., et al.: Algebraic decision diagrams and their applications. Form. Methods Syst. Des. **10**(2), 171–206 (1997)
3. Boßelmann, S., Naujokat, S., Steffen, B.: On the difficulty of drawing the line. In: Margaria, T., Steffen, B. (eds.) ISoLA 2018. LNCS, vol. 11244, pp. 340–356. Springer, Heidelberg (2018)
4. Bryant, R.E.: Graph-based algorithms for Boolean function manipulation. IEEE Trans. Comput. **35**(8), 677–691 (1986)
5. Drechsler, R., Sieling, D.: Binary decision diagrams in theory and practice. Softw. Tools Technol. Transf. (STTT) **3**(2), 112–136 (2001)
6. Fowler, M., Parsons, R.: Domain-Specific Languages. Addison-Wesley/ACM Press (2011)
7. Gossen, F., Margaria, T.: Generating optimal decision functions from rule specifications. In: Electronic Communications of the EASST, vol. 74 (2017)
8. Klir, G.J., Yuan, B.: Fuzzy Sets and Fuzzy Logic: Theory and Applications. Prentice-Hall Inc., Upper Saddle River (1995)
9. Kosko, B., Isaka, S.: Fuzzy logic. Sci. Am. **269**, 76–81 (1993)
10. Margaria, T., Steffen, B.: From the how to the what. In: Meyer, B., Woodcock, J. (eds.) VSTTE 2005. LNCS, vol. 4171, pp. 448–459. Springer, Heidelberg (2008). https://doi.org/10.1007/978-3-540-69149-5_48
11. Mernik, M., Heering, J., Sloane, A.M.: When and how to develop domain-specific languages. ACM Comput. Surv. **37**(4), 316–344 (2005)
12. Naujokat, S.: Heavy Meta. Model-Driven Domain-Specific Generation of Generative Domain-Specific Modeling Tools. Dissertation, TU Dortmund, Dortmund, August 2017. http://hdl.handle.net/2003/36060
13. Naujokat, S., Lybecait, M., Kopetzki, D., Steffen, B.: CINCO: a simplicity-driven approach to full generation of domain-specific graphical modeling tools. Softw. Tools Technol. Transf. **20**(3), 327–354 (2017)
14. Naujokat, S., Neubauer, J., Margaria, T., Steffen, B.: Meta-level reuse for mastering domain specialization. In: Margaria, T., Steffen, B. (eds.) ISoLA 2016, Part II. LNCS, vol. 9953, pp. 218–237. Springer, Cham (2016). https://doi.org/10.1007/978-3-319-47169-3_16
15. Naur, P., Randell, B. (eds.): Software Engineering: Report of a Conference Sponsored by the NATO Science Committee, Garmisch, 7–11 October 1968. Scientific Affairs Division, NATO, Brussels 39 Belgium (1969)

16. Somenzi, F.: Efficient manipulation of decision diagrams. Int. J. Softw. Tools Technol. Transf. **3**(2), 171–181 (2001)
17. Steffen, B., Gossen, F., Naujokat, S., Margaria, T.: Language-driven engineering: from general-purpose to purpose-specific languages. In: Steffen, B., Woeginger, G. (eds.) Computing and Software Science: State of the Art and Perspectives. LNCS, vol. 10000. Springer (2018, to appear)
18. Steffen, B., Naujokat, S.: Archimedean points: the essence for mastering change. In: Steffen, B. (ed.) FoMaC 2016. LNCS, vol. 9960, pp. 22–46. Springer, Cham (2016). https://doi.org/10.1007/978-3-319-46508-1_3

Tutorial: An Overview of Malware Detection and Evasion Techniques

Fabrizio Biondi[1]([✉]), Thomas Given-Wilson[2], Axel Legay[2], Cassius Puodzius[2], and Jean Quilbeuf[2]

[1] CentraleSupélec/IRISA, Rennes, France
fabrizio.biondi@inria.fr
[2] Inria, Rocquencourt, France
{thomas.given-wilson,axel.legay,
cassius.puodzius,jean.auilbeuf}@inria.fr

Abstract. This tutorial presents and motivates various malware detection tools and illustrates their usage on a clear example. We demonstrate how *statically-extracted syntactic signatures* can be used for quickly detecting simple variants of malware. Since such signatures can easily be obfuscated, we also present *dynamically-extracted behavioral signatures* which are obtained by running the malware in an isolated environment known as a *sandbox*. However, some malware can use sandbox detection to detect that they run in such an environment and so avoid exhibiting their malicious behavior. To counteract sandbox detection, we present *concolic execution* that can explore several paths of a binary. We conclude by showing how *opaque predicates* and *JIT* can be used to hinder concolic execution.

1 Introduction

Context. Malicious software known as *malware* is a growing threat to the security of systems and users. The volume of malware is dramatically increasing every year, with the 2018 Cisco report estimating a 12 times increase in malware volume from 2015 to 2017 [5]. For this reason, effective and automated malware detection is an important requirement to guarantee system safety and user protection.

Malware signatures. *Signature-based malware detection* refers to the use of distinctive information known as *signatures* to detect malware. An extraction procedure is performed on an unclassified binary file to extract its signature, this signature is then compared against similar signatures of malware to determine whether the unclassified binary's signature indicates malicious behavior. The simplest kind of signatures are *syntactic signatures* [28,30] that detect malware based on syntactic properties of the malware binaries (like their length, entropy, number of sections, or presence of certain strings). Alternatively, *behavioral signatures* [28,30] can be based on behavioral properties of malware (like their interaction with the system and its network communications).

© Springer Nature Switzerland AG 2018
T. Margaria and B. Steffen (Eds.): ISoLA 2018, LNCS 11244, pp. 565–586, 2018.
https://doi.org/10.1007/978-3-030-03418-4_34

Static analysis. Syntactic signatures can be easily extracted from binaries using *static analysis* [28], i.e. analyzing the binary without having to execute it e.g. by disassembling the binary or by scanning it for specific strings. Importantly, malware detection based on statically-extracted syntactic properties is in practice the only technique fast enough to be used for on-access malware detection, which is why antivirus software are typically based on this type of analysis. However, obfuscation techniques [16] exist that modify the binary code to change its syntactic properties and make it harder to analyze by static analysis while keeping the same behavior. We present static malware detection based on syntactic signatures in Sect. 2.

Dynamic analysis. Due to the weaknesses of static signatures, behavioral signatures are used to counter obfuscation techniques that change the malware's syntactic properties but not its behavior. A common technique to analyze a binary's behavior is *dynamic analysis* [28] consisting of executing the malware and observing its effects on the system. To avoid infecting the analyst's system and to prevent the malware from spreading, the malware is commonly executed in a *sandbox*, i.e. a protected and isolated environment that has been instrumented to be easy to analyze and restore after infection. However, malware can implement sandbox detection techniques to determine whether they are being executed in a sandbox, in which case the malware avoids exhibiting its malicious behavior and often delete itself. We present dynamic malware detection based on behavioral signatures in Sect. 3.

Concolic analysis. The main limitation of dynamic analysis is that it extracts and analyzes only one of the possible execution paths of the analyzed binary, e.g. the one that avoids exhibiting malicious behavior. To address this limitation, *concolic analysis* (a portmanteau of CONCrete symbOLIC) [9,25] has been developed to extract a binary file's behavior while covering as many of the binary's possible execution paths as possible. Concolic analysis maintains a symbolic representation of the constraints found during its analysis, and relies on an external SMT solver to simplify such constraints and determine whether the possible paths can actually be executed or correspond to dead code. However, malicious techniques can be used to highly complicate the conditional constraints of the code, exponentially increasing the size of the symbolic representation and hindering concolic analysis. We present concolic malware detection based on behavioral signatures in Sect. 4.

For the sake of clarity and safety we will not work on a real malware. We provide in Fig. 1 a very simple C program that prints "I am evil!!!" to standard output, and we will treat this as malicious behavior. This simplification allows us to showcase various detection and obfuscation techniques in the rest of the paper. Unless otherwise stated, all examples are compiled using gcc with default settings, on an AMD64 GNU/Linux machine.

```
1  #include<stdio.h>
2
3  int malicious_behaviour(){
4    printf("I am evil!!!\n");
5  }
6
7  int main(int argc, char **argv){
8    malicious_behaviour();
9  }
```

Fig. 1. The running example of fake malware written in C that will be used throughout the paper.

2   Static Analysis: Syntactic Pattern Matching

Syntactic signatures are used to classify binaries by looking at particular patterns in their code. Due to the simplicity of syntactic pattern matching, these techniques tend to be very fast in practice. In this section, we present the principles of syntactic pattern matching, then illustrate the approach with three different tools. We then explain how binaries can be obfuscated against such detection techniques and show a very simple case of obfuscation for our running example.

2.1   Principle

Signatures are defined by attributes and properties which describe some object of analysis. In the context of binary analysis, syntactic signatures refer to sequences of bytes that describe proprieties such as file checksum [1], type, API calls [11], etc.

For instance, once it is verified that a given binary follows the format of a Portable Executable (PE) file [21], other properties such as imported and exported functions, base addresses of the section headers, debug information, presence & features of standard binary sections, and physical & virtual addresses can be easily extracted due to the way the PE header format is defined.

This information can provide a rich understanding of how the binary is expected to run on the system as well as contextual information, such as the date on which the binary was (supposedly) compiled. However, as easily as this information can be extracted, it is also easy to modify or corrupt this information in order to mislead analysis [18].

To hinder syntactical analysis, an adversary can employ obfuscation techniques to conceal the syntactical properties of the original malware sample. Such techniques comprise simple ones such as *packing*, a technique to to compress the executable code as plain data and uncompress it only at runtime, or more advanced ones such as polymorphism and virtualization [26].

Despite their limitations [22], static syntactic signatures are largely employed in malware analysis. For example, ClamAV [6] allows the usage of syntactic signature in the YARA [23] format for protection against malicious files, and VirusTotal [32] provides an interface that takes YARA signatures to lookup matching files throughout its whole database.

Some of the biggest advantages of static signatures are the fact that they are very lightweight, cheap, and capable to capture architecture-dependent binary file attributes like binary section names and sizes. However, it is non-trivial to create and maintain syntactic signatures that: are specific enough to match only to the intended malware family; but not so specific that minor variants of the malware are not detected.

We now present some of the most popular tools for syntactic pattern matching including their signature formats, and discuss in more details their limitations.

2.2   Example Tool: PEiD

PEiD[1] is a tool for the detection of PE malware, packers, and compilers. Despite being already discontinued, PEiD is still largely used and sometimes updated by the users community.

PEiD defines an underlying grammar that allows the creation of new matching rules. This way, the inclusion of new rules to address a new malware, packer, or compiler does not depend on updating the tool and permits researchers to conveniently create and share rules.

As a first example, rules for .NET objects are displayed below.

```
 1  [.NET DLL -> Microsoft]
 2  signature = 00 00 00 00 00 00 00 00 5F 43 6F 72 44 6C 6C
 3  4D 61 69 6E 00 6D 73 63 6F 72 65 65 2E 64 6C 6C 00 00 ??
 4  00 00 FF 25
 5  ep_only = false
 6
 7  [.NET executable -> Microsoft]
 8  signature = 00 00 00 00 00 00 00 00 5F 43 6F 72 45 78 65
 9  4D 61 69 6E 00 6D 73 63 6F 72 65 65 2E 64 6C 6C 00 00 00
10  00 00 FF 25
11  ep_only = false
12
13  [.NET executable]
14  signature = FF 25 00 20 40 00 00 00 00 00 00 00 00 00 00
15  00 00 00 00 00 00 00 00 00 00 00 00 00 00 00 00 00 00 00
16  00 00 00 00 00 00 00 00 00 00 00 00 00 00
17  ep_only = true
```

Each rule starts with a string identifier between square brackets, which is displayed to the user whenever the rule is matched. The `signature` line contains the signature definition as a byte array that is expected to match with the file content, where `??` is used to match any byte. Finally, the `ep_only` line indicates whether the rule is expected to match only the bytes at the binary's entry point or anywhere in the file.

The following PEiD rule detects our running example from Fig. 1.

```
 1  [2018-ISOLA-Tutorial -> PEiD]
 2  signature = 49 20 61 6d 20 65 76 69 6c 21 21 21
 3  ep_only = false
```

---

[1] https://www.aldeid.com/wiki/PEiD.

The signature matches the byte array that corresponds to the string "I am evil!!!", not limiting the match to the entry point (since `ep_only = false`). The command below shows that the string is present in the compiled binary for the malware.

```
1   $ hexdump -C malware_version1 | grep evil
2   000005e0   01 00 02 00 49 20 61 6d 20 65 76 69 6c 21 21 21   |....I am evil!!!|
```

```
1   #include<stdio.h>
2   #include<wchar.h>
3
4   int malicious_behaviour(){
5     wprintf(L"I am evil!!!\n");
6   }
7
8   int main(int argc, char **argv){
9     malicious_behaviour();
10  }
```

Fig. 2. Our fake malware example, using wide characters to avoid simple string detection.

To easily bypass this detection the malware author can slightly change the malware to store the string using wide characters instead of ASCII characters (which does not change the malware's behavior). This modification is depicted in Fig. 2. In this case, looking for string "I am evil!!!" in the usual format will not work anymore. The command below shows that the string is detected only if specifically looking for wide characters.

```
1   $ hexdump -C malware_version2 | grep evil
2   $ strings -e L malware_version2 | grep evil
3   I am evil!!!
```

A new rule could be created to match wide-chars, however requiring a whole new rule for this illustrates one of the biggest limitations of PEiD rules: the lack of flexibility in the rule grammar. For instance, the most recent PEiD database[2] uses 829 rules (out of 3714) just to define version 1.25 of the VMProtect[3] packer.

2.3   Example Tool: DIE

Another tool to match pattern in files is DIE[4], which stands for "Detect It Easy". DIE supports a JavaScript-like scripting language for signatures. DIE allows the creation of flexible rules by using matching conditions, despite being limited by the lack of a well-defined code pattern for rule creation.

An example of a DIE rule is shown below.

---

[2] https://handlers.sans.org/jclausing/userdb.txt.
[3] http://vmpsoft.com/.
[4] https://github.com/horsicq/Detect-It-Easy.

```
1   // DIE's signature file
2
3   init("protector","PE␣Intro");
4
5   function detect(bShowType,bShowVersion,bShowOptions)
6   {
7        if(PE.compareEP("8B04249C60E8........5D81ED........
8   ␣␣␣␣␣␣␣␣␣␣␣␣␣␣␣␣␣␣␣80BD..........0F8548"))
9        {
10            sVersion="1.0";
11            bDetected=1;
12        }
13
14        return result(bShowType,bShowVersion,bShowOptions);
15  }
```

The rule matches files protected with PE Intro, which is detected by an expected sequence of bytes at the entry point. The rule starts by declaring a new signature at "init" and then by proving a description of the rule in the "detect" function.

Like PEiD, DIE has a simple flag (PE.compareEP) determining whether to look for byte arrays at the entry point. DIE uses "." as wildcards to match any byte. Rule matching is indicated by the variable bDetected, which is set to 1.

DIE also support more sophisticated rules that depends on multiple conditions and code reuse as in the rule below.

```
1   // DIE's signature file
2
3   includeScript("rar");
4
5   function detect(bShowType,bShowVersion,bShowOptions)
6   {
7        detect_RAR(1,bShowOptions);
8        return result(bShowType,bShowVersion,bShowOptions);
9   }
```

Among the main drawbacks of DIE are: its rule syntax, which is very verbose and requires an ad-hoc script for each rule, and also DIE's lack of documentation. Furthermore, DIE lacks features like annotations and well-defined modular interfaces.

2.4   Example Tool: YARA

A more modern tool and the current de facto standard is YARA [23]. YARA rules are defined using a JSON-like format and are meant to provide greater flexibility than PEiD and DIE rules. A YARA rule consist of strings (possibly including binary strings) and conditions that determine whether to trigger the rule. Furthermore, YARA rules provide annotations that simplify rule description, enable referencing between rules, and use modules that describe high-level file properties.

In our running example, both versions of the code in Fig. 1 and in Fig. 2 can be matched using a single YARA rule.

```
1  rule 2018ISOLATutorialYara {
2    meta:
3      description = "Example␣of␣YARA␣rule␣for␣ISOLA␣2018"
4    strings:
5      $ascii_string = "I␣am␣evil!!!"
6      $wide_string  = "I␣am␣evil!!!" wide
7    condition:
8      $ascii_string or $wide_string
9  }
```

This example shows that the YARA rule format is more readable than PEiD's or DIE's and also that it can cover both wide and ASCII characters with a single rule. Still, the YARA grammar allows for even more straightforward description of the rule using multiple annotations for a single string.

```
1  rule 2018ISOLATutorialYaraSimpler {
2    meta:
3      description = "Simpler␣YARA␣rule␣for␣ISOLA␣2018"
4    strings:
5      $evil_string = "I␣am␣evil!!!" wide ascii
6    condition:
7      $evil_string
8  }
```

YARA provides many high-level modules allowing to include higher level properties in rules, like file size or entropy[5].

However, with small modifications to the code an adversary can bypass detection without changing any malicious behavior. One way to achieve this result is depicted in Fig. 3. In this version, the targeted string will not be contiguously placed in memory, therefore all the YARA rules above for the running example will fail to match.

```
1   #include<stdio.h>
2
3   int malicious_behaviour(){
4     printf("I␣am");
5     printf("␣evil!!!\n");
6   }
7
8   int main(int argc, char **argv){
9     malicious_behaviour();
10  }
```

Fig. 3. Our fake malware sample, with broken strings to avoid string-based detection.

These simple obfuscation techniques illustrate the limitations of syntactic signatures, showing a toy example of how malware can be modified to avoid syntactic pattern matching. It is easy for malware creators to create new versions of their malware that avoid syntactic pattern matching [20].

---

[5] http://yara.readthedocs.io/en/v3.5.0/modules.html.

2.5   Limitations: Obfuscating Against Syntactic Pattern Matching

In order to avoid pattern matching, it is common to use generic techniques like obfuscation in which important strings, parts of the code or even the whole code are transformed into some obfuscated representation. Generally, malware authors use obfuscation to hide information like the address of their Command & Control (C&C) server, targeted business, eventual credentials hardcoded into the sample, etc.

Figure 4 shows how our running example from Fig. 1 can be modified to remove any plain representation of the string targeted in our previous example. The commands below show that the string "I am evil!!!" is not contained in the file in either its ASCII or wide format.

```
1  $ strings malware_version4 | grep evil
2  $ strings -e L malware_version4 | grep evil
```

In this example, the string "I am evil!!!" is XORed with the keystream "ISOLA-TUTORIAL-2018" resulting in the following byte array "0x00 0x73 0x2e 0x21 0x61 0x48 0x22 0x3c 0x38 0x6e 0x73 0x68 0x4b". The byte array is hardcoded along with the keystream so as to recover the original string whenever needed. Despite being an insecure practice to store the ciphertext along

```
1   #include<stdio.h>
2   #include<string.h>
3   #include<stdlib.h>
4
5   char *keystream = "ISOLA-TUTORIAL-2018";
6   char *obf = "\x00\x73\x2e\x21\x61\x48\x22\x3c\x38\x6e\x73\x68\x4b";
7
8   char *xor(char *str){
9     int i;
10    char *cipherstr;
11    int len = strlen(keystream);
12    cipherstr = malloc(len * sizeof(char));
13    for(i = 0; i < len; i++) {
14      cipherstr[i] = str[i] ^ keystream[i];
15        if(cipherstr[i] == '\n') {
16              cipherstr[i + 1] = '\0';
17              break;
18        }
19    }
20    return cipherstr;
21  }
22
23  int malicious_behaviour(){
24    int i;
25    //char *str = "I am evil!!!\n";
26    char *str = xor(obf);
27    printf("%s", str);
28  }
29
30  int main(int argc, char **argv){
31    malicious_behaviour();
32  }
```

Fig. 4. Our fake malware sample, with XOR-obfuscated strings to avoid string-based detection.

with the key, the main intention of malware creators is to remain undetected until infection, rather than long term security.

The same idea can be achieved with other encryption methods. Nevertheless, one strategy employed to detect such cases is to pattern match constants defined in their algorithms, as shown below for a constant used by AES.

```
1  rule RijnDael_AES
2  { meta:
3      author = "_pusher_"
4      description = "RijnDael AES"
5      date = "2016-06"
6    strings:
7      $c0 = { A5 63 63 C6 84 7C 7C F8 }
8    condition:
9      $c0
10 }
```

Another possibility is to completely obfuscate the code by changing the syntactic structure of the binary. The commands below show how to compile the binary statically and how to pack it with UPX, and how this changes the syntactic properties of the binary without modifying its behavior.

```
1  $ gcc -static -o malware_version4 malware_version4.c
2  $ upx-3.94-amd64_linux/upx -f malware_version4 \
3  -omalware_version4_upx
4  $ readelf -h malware_version4 | tail -n 2
5    Number of section headers:         33
6    Section header string table index: 30
7  $ readelf -h malware_version4_upx | tail -n 2
8    Number of section headers:         0
9    Section header string table index: 0
10 $ ./malware_version4
11 I am evil!!!
12 $ ./malware_version4_upx
13 I am evil!!!
```

As we have seen, syntactic properties are easy to extract, however, since they are easily modifiable without changing the malicious behavior of the binary, they are also easy to bypass. This has a major impact on the effectiveness of syntactic signatures.

Hence, behavioral signatures have to be used to detect malware based on their behavior, since behavior is harder to automatically obfuscate. The next section explains how to extract behavioral signatures dynamically by executing the malware samples in a sandbox.

3 Dynamic Analysis: Sandbox Execution

Dynamic analysis refers to techniques that rely on executing a sample to analyze it. Sandbox execution lets the malware execute in an isolated environment, while tracking the malwares' behavior. Contrarily to the syntactic pattern matching methods presented in the previous section, this section builds a signature based on malware behavior which is resistant to syntactic obfuscation.

3.1   Principle

In order to provide an isolated environment, sandboxes typically rely on virtual machines (VMs) [10]. VMs exploit the fact that a processor can theoretically be simulated by a program. The Operating System (OS) running on a virtual machine is usually called the *Guest* while the OS running on the real hardware is usually called the *Host*.

In the context of malware detection, a sandbox isolates the effects of an untrusted binary to a VM, i.e. to the Guest OS without affecting the Host OS. In practice, some vulnerabilities in VMs [24] or in processors [33] may compromise such isolation. A snapshot of the state of the Guest is taken before each malware analysis, and the Guest is restored to this snapshot after the analysis.

The analysis of a binary in a sandbox relies on observations at various levels. Based on these observations, the binary is labeled or given a score which indicates whether it is likely to be malware. Typically, a sandbox observes the memory, interactions with the Guest OS, and network activity of the executed binary.

The memory is analyzed by dumping it to a file. This dump can be obtained by taking a snapshot of the VM during execution, which by design stores the full VM memory for resuming it. Tools such as Memoryze[6] and dumpit[7] are able to capture and save the full memory image of a physical machine or VM. The memory dump can then be analyzed a posteriori with dedicated tools such as Volatility [8,17]. Such analysis tools list the processes running, the opened ports, and the state of the windows registry at the time the memory was dumped. In particular, it is possible to retrieve artifacts such as uncompressed or unencrypted binaries that are temporary stored in the memory and can be analyzed further.

In order to observe the processes running in the sandbox, the binary can be launched with a debugger to observe all the steps done in the execution of the binary. Another option is to observe the execution by recording the system and library calls, along with their argument values. These calls track what the binary is actually doing in the system, since any action on the system (e.g. writing to a file, changing a registry key, sending a network packet, etc.) has to be done via such a call. Some techniques define various patterns of calls [2,4] (see [3] for a comparison of different kind of patterns) or rely on system call dependency graphs [14] to represent and recognize (malicious) behaviors. Such approaches often involve machine learning to classify the calls of an unknown binary based on patterns learned on known malware and cleanware. The software in charge of observing the processes (debugger and/or process monitor) needs to be running in the sandbox as well.

Finally, the network behavior of the malware can be observed from outside the sandbox, by looking at the traffic on the virtual network card of the sandbox. Also, the monitoring process in the sandbox can save the keys used for TLS traffic, in order to decrypt HTTPS packets. Depending on the context, the

---

[6] https://www.fireeye.com/services/freeware/memoryze.html.

[7] https://my.comae.io/login.

analyst can fake the Internet (i.e. reply with standard packets for each protocol) or monitor and block the traffic while allowing access to the real Internet. The latter approach is potentially more dangerous (i.e. a malware could potentially infect another system) but may enable some particular behavior that are not observable otherwise.

3.2 Example Tool: Cuckoo

Cuckoo[8] is an open-source sandbox written mainly in Python. In the sandbox, the Cuckoo agent handles the communication with the Host. The agent receives the binary to analyze as well as the analysis module, written in Python. The analysis module is in charge of performing the required observation from within the sandbox. Since the analysis module is uploaded to the sandbox along with the sample to execute, the agent can handle several types of analysis.

The default analysis module monitors and registers the system calls made by the binary to analyze and all its children processes. This information is then used to produce a score indicating whether the binary is malicious.

While analysis commands can be submitted from the command line, Cuckoo also features a web interface allowing the user to submit files to analyze and to receive the results of the analysis. We focus here on behavioral analysis since it is complementary to the syntactic analysis techniques presented in the previous section. Cuckoo includes YARA, which can also be used on the binary or its memory during the execution of the binary.

Time & API	Arguments	Status	Return	Repeated
brk July 3, 2018, 4:53 a.m.	p0: 0x0		9397874 8002304	0
brk July 3, 2018, 4:53 a.m.	p0: 0x557921e63000		9397874 8137472	0
write July 3, 2018, 4:53 a.m.	p2: 13 p0: 1 p1: I am evil!!!		13	0
exit_group July 3, 2018, 4:53 a.m.	p0: 0			0

Fig. 5. End of the behavioral analysis report from Cuckoo for our malware sample in Fig. 3

Figure 5 shows the end of the call trace for the example from Fig. 3. In the trace, we can see that the argument passed to "write", which is the lower level call used for implementing "printf", is the string "I am evil !!!". This is sufficient to recognize the malicious behavior, even if syntactic signatures were unable to detect it. Of course, our malicious behavior is oversimplified here and is kind of trivial to recognize.

---

[8] https://cuckoosandbox.org/.

3.3   Limitations: Anti-Sandboxing Techniques

Some malicious binaries may try to attack the sandbox. A common approach is to try to detect that they are being run in a sandbox, and hide their malicious behavior in that case. If a sandbox is detected, the malware can try to crash it, like AntiCuckoo[9] does, or even try to infect it [33].

Most malware won't try to attack the Host of a sandbox because their goal is to remain hidden. A sample that would crash or take over the Host of a sandbox would indeed be immediately classified as highly suspicious. In fact, malware samples commonly delete themselves if they detect a sandbox. Therefore, we will focus here on detecting that the current execution is within a sandbox.

There are various techniques to detect that the current environment is a virtual environment. For instance, the default name of hardware devices in VirtualBox contains the string "VirtualBox", which can be easily detected. In a similar way, interrogating the features of the CPU via the x86 instruction cpuid can provide evidence of a virtual environment. Additionally, some malicious binaries analyze the documents and the activity of the user and don't execute if the number of documents is abnormally low. See [13] for more examples of sandbox detection and [31] for the sandbox detection techniques used by the recent Rakhni malware.

```
1   #include <stdio.h>
2
3   int hv_bit(){
4     int cpu_feats=0;
5     __asm__ volatile("cpuid"
6            : "=c"(cpu_feats) //output: ecx or rcx -> cpu_feats
7            : "a"(1));        //input: 1 -> eax or rax
8     return (cpu_feats >> 31) & 1;
9   }
10
11  void malicious_behaviour(){
12    printf("I am");
13    printf(" evil!!!\n");
14  }
15
16  void benign_behaviour(){
17    printf("I am nice.\n");
18  }
19
20  int main(){
21    int i,a;
22    a=hv_bit();
23    if ( a > 0) {
24      benign_behaviour();
25    } else {
26      malicious_behaviour();
27    }
28    return 0;
29  }
```

Fig. 6. Our fake malware sample, including sandbox detection.

---

[9] https://github.com/David-Reguera-Garcia-Dreg/anticuckoo.

For our running example, we provide in Fig. 6 a C program that relies on a low-level instruction to discriminate between a virtual environment and a non-virtual one. The cpuid argument provide an assembly-level way to interrogate the processor about its features, in order, for instance, to use optimized instructions if available. In particular, when the register eax is set to one before cpuid is called, it returns various information about the processor. Notably, the highest bit of the register ecx is set to 1 if the current execution is controlled by an hypervisor (i.e. a virtual machine). See [12] for the specification of the cpuid instruction.

The function hv_bit leverages this behavior to output that particular bit. The cryptic inline assembly code is specified using the GNU syntax: __asm__ volatile (<code> : <outputs> : <inputs>). The code is simply the cpuid instruction (line 6), the output specifies that the register c (here ecx or rcx) should be put in the variable named cpu_feats (line 7) and finally the input specifies that the register a (here eax or rax) is set to 1 (line 8). The returned value is the bit 31 of the cpu_feats variable (the binary and zeroes the bits that were originally at position 32–64 in the rcx register, if any). Finally, the main function executes the malicious behavior only if the hv_bit function returns 0 (we're not in a hypervisor).

Time & API	Arguments	Status	Return	Repeated
brk July 3, 2018, 5:59 a.m.	p0: 0x0		9401092 4871680	0
brk July 3, 2018, 5:59 a.m.	p0: 0x55809fca4000		9401092 5006848	0
write July 3, 2018, 5:59 a.m.	p2: 11 p0: 1 p1: I am nice.		11	0
exit_group July 3, 2018, 5:59 a.m.	p0: 0			0

Fig. 7. End of the behavioral analysis report from Cuckoo for our malware sample in Fig. 6

Figure 7 shows the output of Cuckoo when analyzing a binary obtained from the code in Fig. 6. As expected, the hypervisor bit is set to one and the output in this version is "I am nice." which corresponds to the benign behavior. However, running the same program on a non-virtual machine will print "I am evil !!!" showing that the malicious behavior executes in that case.

An expensive way to detect whether a sample is trying to evade a sandbox is to compare its behavior in different contexts [15], such as in a VM, in a hypervisor, on a bare metal machine (i.e. an isolated machine) and on an emulation platform. However, the various tests performed by modern malware such as Rakhni [31] would hide the malicious behavior in most of these contexts, based on the environment. For instance, Rakhni has a list of more that 150 names of tools used for process monitoring and analysis; if one of the running processes is in that list, Rakhni will hide its malicious behavior.

Note that these sandbox detection techniques succeed because dynamic analysis by sandboxing aims at executing only a single execution path of the malware binary analyzed. Hence, by prefixing the malicious behavior with multiple checks on the execution environments, malware creators can guarantee that the malicious behavior will be executed only if the system is not a sandbox, is used by a real user, does not have an antivirus software installed, and so on. To circumvent this protection, we need to follow these environment checks in the execution of the binary and ask, what does the malware do when the check succeeds and what does it do when the check fails? Only by exploring both possible execution paths we can arrive at analyzing the malicious behavior. This is the basic idea behind concolic analysis, described in the next section.

4   Concolic Analysis: Symbolic Execution

Concolic analysis does not execute the binary but rather simulates it, with the aim of covering as many of the execution paths as possible of the binary. This increases the probability of detecting malicious behavior that would not be executed in a sandbox due to sandbox detection techniques.

In concrete execution, variables are assigned with *concrete* values that are re-evaluated whenever some assignment statement is reached during the execution. In symbolic execution, variables are *symbolic*, i.e. are assigned with a set of constraints representing a set of possible concrete values.

In practice, as the execution of the program proceeds, symbolic variables accumulate constraints on the possible values of the concrete variables, whereas concrete variables keep only the last actual assigned value. Therefore, symbolic execution does not scale as well as symbolic execution.

In symbolic execution, conditional statements are evaluated not just as True or False as with concrete execution, but as *satisfiable* or *unsatisfiable* instead. This means that, for a given symbolic variable on a given conditional statement, if it is possible to satisfy both the conditional statement and its negation, the execution will take both paths, whereas in concrete execution only one of them would be taken.

As a result, while concrete execution is able to traverse only one trace of execution at a time, symbolic execution can traverse multiple traces of execution simultaneously. Thus, concolic execution aims to combine the efficiency and scalability of concrete execution with high code coverage of symbolic execution.

4.1   Principle

To illustrate the difference between concrete and symbolic execution, we will use the following toy example.

In this example, x is taken as a user input and then it is tested on being non-negative and a root for $x^2 - 3x - 4$. If x satisfies both conditions, then the

```
 1    #include<stdio.h>
 2
 3    /*
 4            Trial and error to find a solution for x^2 - 3x - 4 = 0 for x >= 0
 5    */
 6    int main() {
 7            int x;
 8            printf("Let's␣try␣to␣solve␣x^2␣-␣3x␣-␣4␣=␣0␣for␣x␣>␣0.\n");
 9            printf("Enter␣a␣value␣for␣x:␣");
10            scanf("%5d", &x);
11            if(x * x - 3 * x - 4 == 0) {
12                    if(x >= 0)
13                            printf("%d␣is␣a␣positive␣root.\n", x);
14                    else
15                            printf("x␣has␣to␣be␣positive.\n");
16            }
17            else
18                    printf("%d␣is␣not␣a␣root.\n", x);
19    }
```

Fig. 8. Sample code for a trial and error root solution.

`printf` at line 12 is reached and we say that the execution *succeeded*, otherwise the execution *failed*.

This example's concrete execution is straightforward: a value is assigned to x, then it is checked for being a root and non-negative. It is very efficient to test whether the input satisfies both conditions or not, however it is not equally easy to find one value for x in which the execution succeeds.

Using concrete execution it is possible to find an x for which the execution succeeds randomly taking values for x and executing the program. However, this approach might succeed with a very low probability, and when there is no root for the equation, this approach will run end forever. Two traces of execution (for x = −1 and x = 0) are displayed in Fig. 9.

In contrast, it is possible to use symbolic execution to explore traces of execution in a more structured way. Using symbolic execution, x is assigned to a symbolic variable which will accumulate constraints along different execution paths. The equality for $x^2 - 3x - 4 = 0$ is met when x = −1 or x = 4, therefore it follows:

– Line 11 will be reached only if x is constrained to one of the root values (i.e. −1 or 4). For any other case, the execution will reach line 17.
– Line 12 is reached only if x is constrained to root values (line 10) and if it is positive (line 11), otherwise line 14 is reached.

Hence the execution *succeeds* and line 12 is reached only if x = 4. Figure 10 depicts how symbolic execution proceeds with the constraints of each path and is able to build a tree of execution traces, extending the single execution trace explored by concrete execution.

4.2   Example Tool: angr

angr [27] is a tool enabling concolic execution of binaries, written in Python and composed of different modules.

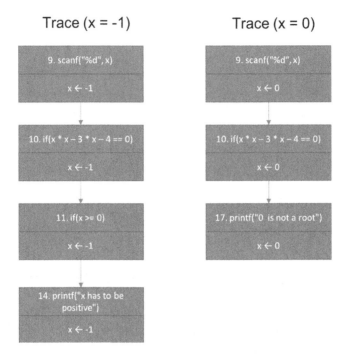

Fig. 9. Example of concrete traces of trial and error root solution.

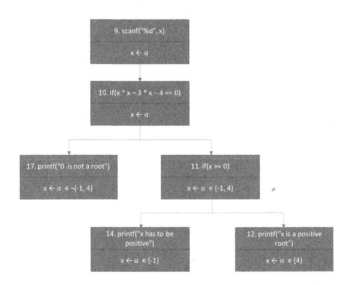

Fig. 10. Example of symbolic tracing of trial and error root solution.

- CLE: stands for "CLE Loads Everything" and is responsible for loading binaries and libraries.
- Archinfo: contains architecture-specific information.
- PyVEX: Python module to handle VEX, which is an intermediate representation that enables angr to work on different architectures.
- Claripy: module that interfaces with a constraint solver.

The execution starts by loading the binary, using the CLE module. To do so, CLE needs information about the architecture the program is target for, which is provided by Archinfo.

Once the binary is loaded, the angr symbolic execution engine coordinates the symbolic execution. The analysis unit of angr's analysis is the *basic block*, defined as a continuous sequence of code that has no branching (such as jumps or calls), and for each basic block angr creates a new state. A state contains the program's memory, registers, file system, and any other so-called "live data".

angr's execution evolves in steps. Each step transforms the current active states into their successor states. Constraints accumulated from past basic blocks/states are *solved* whenever some instruction depends on a symbolic variable (e.g. memory address). If the current state ends up in a conditional jump, angr evaluates the condition against the current constraints and proceed as follows.

- If both the conditional and its negation are satisfiable, angr creates two new successors states, one for each of the two possible states.
- If only one of the conditional and its negation is satisfiable, angr creates only one new successor state.
- If neither the conditional nor its negation are satisfiable, angr marks the state as deadended and terminates its execution.

Constraints are solved by SMT solvers interfaced by Claripy. Currently, the default SMT solver used is Microsoft's Z3, however others can be plugged into angr by writing an appropriate Claripy backend.

The procedure above is able to emulate a bare metal environment, including abstractions provided by the underlying operating system, such as files, network, processes and others. In order to fulfill these abstractions, angr includes a module called SimOS, which provides all the required OS objects during the analysis.

Finally, to allow angr to work with multiple architectures, instead of running concolic analysis on instructions charged by CLE, these instructions are first lifted to the VEX intermediary representation before the analysis is done. Multiple architectures can be lifted to VEX without any loss in the overall analysis.

Figure 11 from [29] depicts the relationship between the different modules.

To illustrate the benefits of concolic analysis, we use the code example in Fig. 8. Running a full automated analysis with angr, it is possible to verify that angr reaches 3 final states (i.e. deadended states), corresponding to the leaves of the execution tree presented in Fig. 10.

Figure 12 shows the commands required to perform the analysis. It is possible to check that for each one of the three deadended states, the analysis reached a different line of the original code (corresponding to a different printed message).

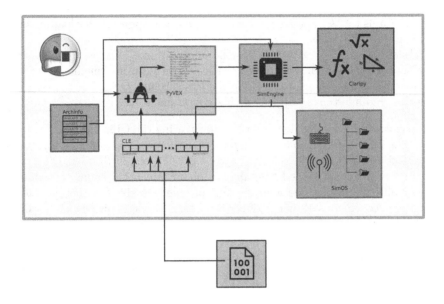

Fig. 11. Relationship between angr modules.

```
In [1]: import angr
WARNING | 2018-07-04 16:19:17,147 | angr.analyses.disassembly_utils | Your verison of capstone does not support MIPS instruction groups

In [2]: p = angr.Project("root")

In [3]: state = p.factory.entry_state()

In [4]: sm = p.factory.simgr(state)

In [5]: sm.run()
WARNING | 2018-07-04 16:20:04,490 | angr.manager | No completion state defined for SimulationManager; stepping until all states deadend
WARNING | 2018-07-04 16:20:05,052 | angr.state_plugins.symbolic_memory | Concretizing symbolic length. Much sad; think about implementing.
Out[5]: <SimulationManager with 3 deadended>

In [6]: s0 = sm.deadended[0]

In [7]: s1 = sm.deadended[1]

In [8]: s2 = sm.deadended[2]

In [9]: s0.posix.dumps(0)
Out[9]: '42222'

In [10]: s0.posix.dumps(1)
Out[10]: "Let's try to solve x^2 - 3x - 4 = 0 for x > 0.\nEnter a value for x: 42222 is not a root.\n"

In [11]: s1.posix.dumps(0)
Out[11]: '-0001'

In [12]: s1.posix.dumps(1)
Out[12]: "Let's try to solve x^2 - 3x - 4 = 0 for x > 0.\nEnter a value for x: x has to be positive.\n"

In [13]: s2.posix.dumps(0)
Out[13]: '00004'

In [14]: s2.posix.dumps(1)
Out[14]: "Let's try to solve x^2 - 3x - 4 = 0 for x > 0.\nEnter a value for x: 4 is a positive root.\n"
```

Fig. 12. Example of angr analysis on trial and error root solution.

For a given state, stdin can be accessed through *posix.dump(0)* while stdout can be accessed by *posix.dump(1)*. Hence it is straightforward to verify that the execution succeeds if $x = 4$.

4.3   Limitations: Symbolic Explosion

The ability to explore all the possible traces of a given binary is one of the core advantages of concolic execution. However, this can be exploited by malware authors to generáte a binary for which concolic execution has a huge number of possible paths. For instance, starting the binary by a sequence of n conditional jumps depending on a value that is not treated as concrete by the symbolic execution will possibly create 2^n traces. The malware author can use this technique to try to fill the memory of the machine running the symbolic execution. A way to mitigate that technique is not to a breadth-first search (BFS) for ordering the exploration of the reachable states.

Another weakness of symbolic execution is the constraint solver. Indeed, some malware include *opaque predicates* that are commonly used to hinder static analysis [19]. A simple example is to write a complicated conditional jump whose condition always evaluates to true, so that at runtime only one branch of the conditional jump is taken, but static analysis requires a lot of effort to conclude that the predicate is always true. In the context of symbolic execution, such predicates might become very complex expressions involving several symbolic variables. These predicates will be analyzed by the constraint solver, forcing the solver to use a large amount of resources (time and memory) to try to solve the constraint. If the constraint solver runs out of resources the concolic execution has to analyze both paths, and complex dead code (possibly including more opaque predicates) can be inserted in the path that is never selected at runtime to hinder the analysis.

Finally, symbolic execution also struggles with just-in-time (JIT) code, i.e. code that writes the next instructions to execute in the memory just before executing them. If some of the written instructions are symbolic at the time of writing, the execution now faces the problem of having a symbolic instruction to execute. One expensive solution would be to list all instructions that meet the constraint of the symbolic instruction and try each of them. Otherwise the symbolic execution can be stopped at this point or miss some branches [34]. A similar problem is encountered whenever the address of a jump is symbolic.

For our running example, we use Tigress [7] to produce an obfuscated version of the code from Fig. 6. The commands presented in Fig. 13 yields a *a.out* executable that is obfuscated against symbolic execution. When trying to analyzing the executable with angr, the tool will execute without terminating.

```
1   echo "#include_\"$TIGRESS_HOME/jitter-amd64.c\"" > tmp.c
2   cat malware_version5.c >> tmp.c
3   tigress --out=malware_version5.c \
4     --Environment=x86_64:Linux:Gcc:4.6 \
5     --Transform=Jit --Functions=main tmp.c
```

Fig. 13. Command using Tigress to builds a version of the code of Fig. 6 using JIT compilation to obfuscate the code, to prevent angr from analyzing it.

5   Conclusion

This paper presents different techniques to perform malware detection based on different kinds of signatures: syntactic signatures by static analysis; and behavioral signatures by dynamic and concolic analysis. Each technique is presented with a simple example, and with an example of how to counter it based on its limitations.

The techniques are presented in increasing order of complexity, and justified by the fact that each one is effective against the techniques hindering the previous one.

- Syntactic pattern matching is hindered by packing and obfuscation.
- Packed and obfuscated malware can be analyzed by dynamic execution in a sandbox.
- Sandboxes can be prevented from observing malicious behavior by sandbox detection.
- Sandbox detection can be countered by concolic execution.
- Concolic execution can be prevented from finding interesting execution branches by opaque predicates and JIT compilation.

However, in practice the different costs of these techniques mean that even simple ones like string-based static detection should not be discarded. YARA is widely used by security researchers, and in fact it is common to complement reports on new malware with YARA rules able to detect such malware, exactly because YARA is an efficient and optimized tool for pattern matching whose cost is negligible compared to the cost of starting a sandbox or a concolic binary execution engine.

Hence, all of the tools and techniques presented are useful to security analysts in different scenarios. Binaries that are detected as suspicious but not definitively malicious by static analysis, for instance because they employ packing and other obfuscation techniques, can be analyzed in a sandbox to characterize their behavior. Were the sandbox to fail due to sandbox evasion, the analyst can employ concolic analysis, and so on. Advanced malware can require multiple tools and significant analysis time by an expert before it is thoroughly dissected and understood, but this can lead to the creation of syntactic and behavioral rules to automatically detect new samples of the malware in the future without having to repeat the analysis.

References

1. Agrawal, H., Bahler, L., Micallef, J., Snyder, S., Virodov, A.: Detection of global, metamorphic malware variants using control and data flow analysis. In: 31st IEEE Military Communications Conference, MILCOM 2012, Orlando, October 29 – November 1, 2012, pp. 1–6 (2012). https://doi.org/10.1109/MILCOM.2012.6415581
2. Alazab, M., Venkatraman, S., Watters, P., Alazab, M.: Zero-day malware detection based on supervised learning algorithms of API call signatures. In: Proceedings of the Ninth Australasian Data Mining Conference, vol. 121, pp. 171–182. AusDM 2011, Australian Computer Society Inc., Darlinghurst (2011). http://dl.acm.org/citation.cfm?id=2483628.2483648

3. Canali, D., Lanzi, A., Balzarotti, D., Kruegel, C., Christodorescu, M., Kirda, E.: A quantitative study of accuracy in system call-based malware detection. In: Proceedings of the 2012 International Symposium on Software Testing and Analysis, pp. 122–132. ISSTA 2012. ACM, New York (2012). https://doi.org/10.1145/2338965.2336768

4. Christodorescu, M., Jha, S., Seshia, S.A., Song, D., Bryant, R.E.: Semantics-aware malware detection. In: 2005 IEEE Symposium on Security and Privacy (SP 2005), pp. 32–46, May 2005. https://doi.org/10.1109/SP.2005.20

5. Cisco: Annual Cybersecurity Report (2018). https://www.cisco.com/c/m/en_au/products/security/offers/cybersecurity-reports.html

6. ClamAV: Clamav 0.99b meets yara! ClamAV blog. https://blog.clamav.net/2015/06/clamav-099b-meets-yara.html

7. Collberg, C., Martin, S., Myers, J., Nagra, J.: Distributed application tamper detection via continuous software updates. In: Proceedings of the 28th Annual Computer Security Applications Conference. ACSAC 2012, pp. 319–328. ACM, New York (2012). https://doi.org/10.1145/2420950.2420997

8. Ehsan, F.: Detecting unknown malware: security analytics & memory forensics. Presentation at RSA 2015 Conference (2015). https://www.rsaconference.com/events/us15/agenda/sessions/1517/detecting-unknown-malware-security-analytics-memory

9. Godefroid, P., Klarlund, N., Sen, K.: Dart: Directed automated random testing. In: Proceedings of the 2005 ACM SIGPLAN Conference on Programming Language Design and Implementation, pp. 213–223. PLDI 2005, ACM, New York (2005). https://doi.org/10.1145/1065010.1065036

10. Goldberg, R.P.: Survey of virtual machine research. Computer **7**(6), 34–45 (1974)

11. Idika, N.C., Mathur, A.P.: A survey of malware detection techniques (2007)

12. Intel: Intel® 64 and ia-32 architectures software developer's manual combined volumes 2a, 2b, 2c, and 2d: Instruction set reference, a-z. Technical report, May 2018. https://software.intel.com/sites/default/files/managed/a4/60/325383-sdm-vol-2abcd.pdf, order Number: 325383–067US

13. Jung, P.: Bypassing sanboxes for fun! Presentation at hack.lu (2014). http://archive.hack.lu/2014/Bypasss_sandboxes_for_fun.pdf

14. Karbalaie, F., Sami, A., Ahmadi, M.: Semantic malware detection by deploying graph mining. Int. J. Comput. Sci. Issues (IJCSI) **9**(1), 373 (2012)

15. Kirat, D., Vigna, G., Kruegel, C.: Barecloud: bare-metal analysis-based evasive malware detection. In: USENIX Security Symposium, pp. 287–301 (2014)

16. Kuzurin, N., Shokurov, A., Varnovsky, N., Zakharov, V.: On the concept of software obfuscation in computer security. In: Garay, J.A., Lenstra, A.K., Mambo, M., Peralta, R. (eds.) ISC 2007. LNCS, vol. 4779, pp. 281–298. Springer, Heidelberg (2007). https://doi.org/10.1007/978-3-540-75496-1_19

17. Ligh, M.H., Case, A., Levy, J., Walters, A.: The Art of Memory Forensics: Detecting Malware and Threats in Windows, Linux, and Mac Memory. Wiley, Indianapolis (2014)

18. MissMalware: Tdsanomalpe - identifying compile time manipulation in pe headers. Miss Malware blog. http://missmalware.com/2017/02/tdsanomalpe-identifying-compile-time-manipulation-in-pe-headers/

19. Moser, A., Kruegel, C., Kirda, E.: Limits of static analysis for malware detection. In: Twenty-Third Annual Computer Security Applications Conference (ACSAC 2007), pp. 421–430, December 2007. https://doi.org/10.1109/ACSAC.2007.21

20. Moser, A., Kruegel, C., Kirda, E.: Limits of static analysis for malware detection. In: ACSAC, pp. 421–430. IEEE Computer Society (2007). http://dblp.uni-trier.de/db/conf/acsac/acsac2007.html#MoserKK07

21. Pietrek, M.: Peering inside the PE: A tour of the win32 portable executable file format. Microsoft Developer Network blog (1994). https://msdn.microsoft.com/en-us/library/ms809762.aspx

22. Preda, M.D., Christodorescu, M., Jha, S., Debray, S.: A semantics-based approach to malware detection. SIGPLAN Not **42**(1), 377–388 (2007). https://doi.org/10.1145/1190215.1190270, https://doi.org/10.1145/1190215.1190270

23. Project, Y.: Yara documentation. https://yara.readthedocs.io/

24. Schwartz, M.: Oracle virtualbox multiple guest to host escape vulnerabilities. SecuriTeam Secure Disclosure blog (2018). https://blogs.securiteam.com/index.php/archives/3649

25. Sen, K., Marinov, D., Agha, G.: Cute: a concolic unit testing engine for c. In: Proceedings of the 10th European Software Engineering Conference Held Jointly with 13th ACM SIGSOFT International Symposium on Foundations of Software Engineering, pp. 263–272. ESEC/FSE-13, ACM, New York, (2005). https://doi.org/10.1145/1081706.1081750

26. Sharma, A., Sahay, S.K.: Evolution and detection of polymorphic and metamorphic malwares: a survey. Int. J. Comput. Appl. **90**(2), 7–11 (2014)

27. Shoshitaishvili, Y., et al.: SoK: (state of) the art of war: offensive techniques in binary analysis. In: IEEE Symposium on Security and Privacy (2016)

28. Sikorski, M., Honig, A.: Practical Malware Analysis: The Hands-On Guide to Dissecting Malicious Software, 1st edn. No Starch Press, San Francisco (2012)

29. Subwire, l.: throwing a tantrum, part 1: angr internals. Angr blog. http://angr.io/blog/throwing_a_tantrum_part_1

30. Szor, P.: The Art of Computer Virus Research and Defense. Addison-Wesley Professional, Boston (2005)

31. Vasilenko, E., Mamedov, O.: To crypt, or to mine - that is the question. post on Securelist - Kaspersky Lab's cyberthreat research and reports (2018). https://securelist.com/to-crypt-or-to-mine-that-is-the-question/86307/

32. VirusTotal: Malware hunting. https://www.virustotal.com/#/hunting-overview

33. Wojtczuk, R., Rutkowska, J.: Following the White Rabbit: Software attacks against Intel (R) VT-d technology (2011). http://www.invisiblethingslab.com/resources/2011/Software%20Attacks%20on%20Intel%20VT-d.pdf

34. Yadegari, B., Debray, S.: Symbolic execution of obfuscated code. In: Proceedings of the 22nd ACM SIGSAC Conference on Computer and Communications Security, pp. 732–744. ACM (2015)

Author Index

Printed in the United States
By Bookmasters